NATURE'S GOVERNM

CW01669164

NATURE'S GOVERNMENT

Science, Imperial Britain, and the 'Improvement' of the World

RICHARD DRAYTON

with an Introduction by
MAHESH RANGARAJAN

Orient Longman

For Harry and Kathleen
George
Margaret
Lucie
and those who meet me on the other side of the world

NATURE'S GOVERNMENT
Science, Imperial Britain, and the 'Improvement' of the World

ORIENT LONGMAN PRIVATE LIMITED

Registered Office
3-6-752 Himayatnagar, Hyderabad 500 029 (A.P.), INDIA
e-mail : hyd2_orlongco@sancharnet.in

Other Offices
Bangalore, Bhopal, Bhubaneshwar, Chennai, Ernakulam, Guwahati, Hyderabad, Jaipur, Kolkata, Lucknow, Mumbai, New Delhi, Patna

Published by arrangement with Yale University Press

© Richard Harry Drayton, 2000
Introduction by Mahesh Rangarajan © Orient Longman, 2005

First published 2000 by Yale University Press

First published in India by
Orient Longman Private Limited, 2005

ISBN 81 250 2277 5

Printed in India at
Chaman Enterprises
New Delhi

Published by
Orient Longman Private Limited
1/24 Asaf Ali Road
New Delhi 110 002
e-mail : olldel@del6.vsnl.net.in

For sale in India, Bangladesh, Bhutan, Nepal, Maldives and Sri Lanka only. Not for export to other countries.

[We shall] reclaim them from their barbarous manners ... populate plant and make civil all the provinces of that kingdom ... as we are persuaded that it is one of the chief causes for the which God hath brought us to the imperial crown of these Kingdoms
Francis Bacon on the Irish (1603)

They inclose noe Land, neither have any setled habytation, nor any tame Cattle to improve the Land by, and soe have noe other but a Naturall Right to those Countries
John Winthrop on the Natives of New England (c. 1660)

The latest Posterity ... will wonder how their ancesters were able to exist without them & revere the names of their British conquerors to whom they will be indebted for the Abolition of Famine
Sir Joseph Banks on the Bengalis (1787)

Our own interests are so manifestly connected with the advancement and improvement of the native states, that it is obvious we can have no views which are not equally to their advantage
Sir Stamford Raffles on the East Indies (1819)

If Quashee will not honestly aid in bringing out those sugars, cinnamons, and nobler products of the West Indian Islands, for the benefit of all mankind, then I say neither will the Powers permit Quashee to continue growing pumpkins there for his own lazy benefit
Thomas Carlyle on 'The Nigger Question' (1849)

The last thing our civilisation is willing to permanently tolerate is the wasting of the resources of the richest regions of the earth through the lack of the elementary qualities of social efficiency in the races possessing them
Benjamin Kidd on Tropical peoples (1898)

The trouble with the Engenglish is that their hiss history happened overseas, so they dodo don't know what it means
Mr 'Whisky' Sisodia on the English, in Salman Rushdie's The Satanic Verses *(1988)*

Contents

Illustrations

Plates

Illustrations in the text

Preface

Nature's Government is an experiment at writing a history which does justice to both the 'big' and the 'small'. It is, on the one hand, a 'world history': it seeks to explain the origins of how we live and think today in terms of processes which operated over several centuries, and through all the continents of human experience. But it also 'zooms' in, describing and explaining the particular circumstances of Europe, Britain, and ultimately it focusses on a small cast of scientific and political actors. You may feel at times like Alice in Wonderland, as its lens asks you to grow, shrink, and grow again. But as Ranke suggested, it is in this movement between the texture of the local and specific, and the larger human story, that we might discover the secrets of universal history. Let us start with the 'big'.

If we examine the pattern of modern history from 1500 to the present, we may notice that the world's population has vastly increased, and with it the scope of the earth's surface put to human use. With this increase in the scale of existence came the replacement of local structures of life by a new cosmopolitan dependency. In terms of units of identity, production, exchange, language, politics, and values, we share a world wholly different from that lived, imagined, or imaginable in 1500. Our difference lies, in part, in our insight into the place of our species in nature: our knowledge that we are all, under the skin, the same, is a crucial basis of the new order. For this we may thank the natural sciences. A third aspect of our era has been the elaboration of symbols and laws which make sense of the processes which govern the experience of all matter. The knowledge of nature has transformed the boundaries of human power, and with it our attitudes to the universe and to ourselves. The progress of human settlement, interdependency, and the sciences, all depended, this book argues, on what historians have called 'The Expansion of Europe'. Empires which found their centres in European nations were the principal instruments through which ideas, knowledge, styles of economy and politics, plants and people, once specific to particular places, were given international reach. They set the boundaries of nations, and the terms on which the rich now encounter the poor. Empires, the children of the medieval world, were the midwives of the modern.

This book is an attempt to make sense of the origins of the modern world. It explores the interactions of science and imperial expansion. The drama under our lens is woven from the histories of the knowledge and use of plants, and of Britain and its empire. Its protagonist, whose origins and achievements we shall pursue, is the Royal Botanic Gardens at Kew. Through the story of a garden we may explore the history of the world. To understand why, let us begin at the beginning.

*

On his third voyage, Columbus reached a country at the mouth of a great river which the people who discovered him called Paria. He named it 'the Gardens ... for the place and the people correspond with that appellation ... there are great indicators of this being the terrestrial paradise'. I was born in this corner of South America at the fall of the British Empire. British Guiana was small, relative that is to its neighbours, Brazil and Venezuela—at 83,000 square miles it might happily have engulfed England. The territory of my country had been part of the English imagination since Walter Ralegh had first sought 'the large, rich, and bewtiful empyre of Guiana'. Ralegh promised a cargo of strange 'beasts, birds, fishes, fruites, flowers, gummes, sweet woods ... divers berries, that die most perfect crimson and carnation'. He hoped to give his Protestant monarch that 'Indian Golde' which in Spanish hands 'indaungereth and disturbeth all the nations of Europe'. But the gold was scattered in a thousand creeks, and Ralegh never found the mine which might either have saved his neck, or tempted James I to found a new colony. It was instead the wealth from plants—cotton and sugar-cane—which two centuries later led the British to seize Guyana from the Dutch during the 1790s. Anderson, the botanist–spy who then surveyed its rivers in the 1790s, agreed with Ralegh: 'For the naturalist and speculative observer there is not perhaps a finer country in the world.' That El Dorado of tropical nature remained to my time.

I journeyed as a child through the botanic gardens of the city, never thinking of the king after which it was named. After Georgetown's wooden cathedral, high gates opened on a road which led to a pool crowned with vast saucers of water lilies. These were *Victoria regia*—the lilies which came in the 1840s from the Guyanese jungles to inspire Joseph Paxton's plan for a Crystal Palace. Everything green wore a mysterious Latin name. Dark paths led to Macaw palms which tempted you with poisonous red berries and kept you away with their spiny trunks. There were serpents too in this garden, oily coils of watersnakes in the drainage trenches. The smell of rot was everywhere, a background rankness from surrounding clumps of vegetation, and occasional gusts of animal stink from the zoo in the corner of the gardens. Somewhat older, I found the place strangely ennobled by the fact that, like the British Governors before him, our erudite tyrant of a Prime Minister lived here. I was more surprised to learn that the Victorian proconsul who founded the gardens had given part of them to agricultural experiments.

This mixture of meditative retreat, scientific collection, menagerie, public playground, palace, and experimental station, was more common that I realized. In Trinidad, to the north, the ornamental pattern of the botanic garden merely extended that of the Governor's grounds, which they surrounded. In the island of St. Vincent, a few hundred miles to the north-east, the Governor in 1765 had turned a portion of his palace grounds into a garden for useful and ornamental plants. Around the same time in London, George III began to patronize a collection formed by his parents at Kew. Science and nature worship, the theatrical projection of authority and civility had long before found common expression in the pleasure grounds of European princes.

By the 1780s, Sir Joseph Banks began to turn Kew into 'a great botanical exchange house for the empire', as the centre for the movement of economic plants between the Eastern and Western hemispheres, and of ornamental plants between the North and the South. Kew became connected to the St. Vincent Botanic Garden, and to newer establishments in Calcutta, St. Helena, and elsewhere. In 1840, after a period of royal neglect, Kew came into public control. While becoming a pleasure ground for all the people of London, under its directors—William Hooker, Joseph Hooker, and William Thiselton-Dyer—it became a central institution of both Victorian science and the British Empire. It helped entrepreneurs to plant empires of sugarcane, cocoa, tea, coffee, palm oil, and rubber on which the sun has still not set. By the beginning of the twentieth century it stood at the centre of a global network of botanic gardens and agricultural stations—including that of Georgetown. It is likely that few promenaders in any botanic garden recognize the many faces of what they simply see as a beautiful space. Nor indeed, perhaps, in general, do those who live in the ruins of empire yet understand what this means.

*

It is only now, a generation after Decolonization, that we are beginning to put back together the histories of Britain and its empire. By the 'Imperial Britain' of the title, I seek to extend that removal of the frontier between the domestic and external histories of Britain now visible in the work of C.A. Bayly, Linda Colley, P.J. Cain, A.G. Hopkins, David Hancock, John MacKenzie, P.J. Marshall, Kathleen Wilson, and others.[1] We are beginning, just barely, to recognize modern Britain to be as much a product of processes of empire as modern India, Nigeria, New Zealand, Barbados, or Guyana. In the era in which you read this, such a proposition may appear to you to be ordinary common sense. But even at the end of the twentieth century, another perspective on Britain and its empire predominated. From it one saw, with Sir John Seeley in 1883, an England which 'expanded' to reach its Victorian stature, or with Anthony Low in 1983, one which 'contracted' in the second Elizabethan age to become again a minor power on the flank of Europe.[2] Popular sentiment and historical scholarship clung to an idea of a Celtic–Roman–German–Norse–Norman people winning then losing the world. The British Empire, as a consequence, was cordoned off into, at best, a chapter of modern British history, to be jumped over, perhaps, where it contradicted the preferred narratives of the rise of liberty, politeness, or class consciousness. Many even chose to ignore it all altogether, so relieving themselves of the tiresome business of learning strange names, places, or languages. The idea that Britain sprang directly from its medieval insular or European cultural roots supported an intellectual tradition of many political persuasions which—from Clarendon to Hume to Macaulay to Alan Taylor to Edward Thompson—helped an emerging nation make sense of itself. Historians of the empire once knew their place and kept to it, confining their comments on modern Britain to Indian or African history.[3] Even the *Oxford History of the British Empire* of the 1990s, which so boldly presented the whole span of modern history, rarely dared examine how Britain was formed by its empire over its five volumes.

On a world map no longer pink, we began to discover some islands at the fringes of a small continent, which had been tugged out of local structures of production, consumption, government, and feeling, into new global arrangements. At a time when Britain appeared on the verge of disintegrating as a nation–state, historians came to realize that the process we inexactly call the 'expansion' of Europe, but by which we mean the contraction of the world, had consumed the separate histories of England and Scotland, as it had those of Bengal, Benin, and Peru. Empires, from this perspective, are engines which bring human communities, once separated by distance and culture, into systems of exchange and interdependence. These systems have cores which are forged by these processes of expansion: Rome, as much as Gaul, was formed by the empire. It is in extension of this emerging tradition that this study seeks to situate modern Britain in the histories of Europe and the wider world.

But by Europe I may mean more than many readers expect. For while the study of the modern histories of Latin America, Asia, Africa proceeds from the assumption that exogenous factors mattered, it has long been the magnificent conceit of Europeans that their history springs from dark autochthonous forces, species of technical and social magic rooted in the specific environment of Europe. In the many glosses on 'the rise of the West', this parthenogenetic fantasy persists. Long after the theory of spontaneous generation had been extinguished in biology, it continued to condition research into the history of Europe. By its lights the extra-European history of Europe had impact, for good or ill, purely on extra-European terrain. This book explores how, on the contrary, imperial expansion both before and during the modern era shaped culture and society at its centre.

Its focus is on the impact of 'expansion' on science of plants.[4] It suggests that what we may call the sciences of collection and comparison—among which we may include botany, zoology, anthropology, and geology—depended on Europeans becoming exposed to the planet's physical and organic diversity, and often to the scientific traditions of non-European people. These disciplines needed the world as a whole to make sense. What I try to do, throughout, is to treat the intellectual history of botany, and its professional and public life, with equal care.[5] For both the 'internal' and 'external' histories of the sciences responded to the opportunities of European power. I hope, through this attempt at keeping metropolis and periphery, ideas and institutions, in the same tableau, to go beyond earlier histories of Kew and colonial botanic gardens.[6]

It is equally my hypothesis that the sciences shaped the pattern of imperial expansion. The research of local plants and their uses was part of reconnaissance and conquest from the sixteenth century. New economies then arose on the basis of the discovery of the raw materials for food, medicines, dyes, and perfumes. Others depended on the importation and cultivation of favoured species. New cultures of ornament and order were equally consequences of new learning. Beyond this practical impact, the sciences, with their promise of insight into, and control over, nature, lent potent ideological help.

It is this last theme which is at the centre of this essay. I seek to trace the history of the idea that the knowledge of nature would allow the best possible use of resources, to which I give the name 'Nature's Government'. This argument was first made by those medieval English who wished to justify the enclosure of common land. It was exported to Ireland, and then to the Americas, where it supported the extension of English plantations, and Irish and Amerindian dispossession. It depended on a mixture of Christian and classical ideas about Man's place in nature.[7] But the natural sciences, even in the seventeenth century, became implicated in its defence. Political economy, later, provided new ways of asserting that the command of exotic territory might tend to the good of colonized as well as colonizers. By the late eighteenth century we see the rise of an imperialism of 'improvement' which promised that people and things might be administered, in the cosmopolitan interest, by those who understood nature's laws. European power, joined to the scientific mastery of nature, would necessarily confer the greatest good on the greatest number. This was a hypothesis as useful to proconsuls, who sought to justify their dominion, as it was to those men of science who premised their appeals for public support and patronage on their utility. In the story of Kew, tugged in one direction by the history of science, and in the other by the needs of the state, we may observe the terms on which the interests of naturalists and administrators came into convergence. In this convergence, we may discover new ways of understanding imperialism, and the 'international society' left in its wake. For the enterprise of 'Development' launched during the contraction of the world became the idol of economists and politicians of all races and nations. Under its spell great rivers are dammed, forests condemned to flood or fire, and oceans of concrete poured. The nature of government, both at home and in the (former) colonies, was shaped by these assumptions about how nature might be governed.[8]

*

While my argument reaches backwards to Classical civilization and examines, from several perspectives, the Renaissance, the heft of this book addresses the eighteenth and nineteenth centuries. For it is my hypothesis that it was over the long eighteenth century that the natural sciences and political economy became inflected, by reforming monarchs and by both loyal and querulous subjects, into an idea of government in the public and cosmopolitan interest; while it was over the long nineteenth that this ideology came to guide the practice of administration, at home and abroad. This is the basis of the division of this book into two parts. Put together, this book might be read as an essay on the origins and consequences of the Enlightenment in the context of Britain and its empire. But I do not see that European movement, as my teacher Peter Gay did in the 1960s, as the rupture which separated a rational secular democratic world from the medieval shadows. What interests me about the 'science of freedom' is the way it gave modern inflection to older political and economic assumptions, projects, and superstitions, and lent help, with an even hand, to despotism as well as democracy. It is in particular my concern to trace the recurrent influence on both science and government of those ideas about man's place in nature woven into the Judaeo-Christian myth of the Garden of Eden.

Part I, 'Adam out of Eden' includes three chapters which connect the histories of science of plants, of gardens, Britain and the British Empire. Chapter 1, 'The World in a Garden', follows the history of botany, as a field of knowledge, from Athens, to Alexandria, to the Arab World, through Renaissance Europe and the Scientific Revolution to the Enlightenment. It suggests, in particular, how imperial expansion shaped ideas of classification and the keeping of botanic gardens. Chapter 2, 'Plants and Power', considers the political uses of knowledge and plants, particularly in the British Isles, from the sixteenth century to the eighteenth. My concern is to examine how monarchy, nobility, and ordinary people came to patronize botany and gardening. I trace, at the end of this, the Hanoverian origins of the Royal gardens at Kew. Chapter 3, 'The Useful Garden', explores the history of the idea that the efficient use of resources justified their command. It examines how the natural sciences became included in that ideology of 'Improvement' which ordered enclosure at home and expansion abroad. Indeed it pursues the history of the making of the First British Empire in terms of these economic doctrines. It suggests that the British Crown responded to those European monarchies which made the patronage of science into the work of government.

Part II, 'Nature and Empire', follows a narrative course from 1783 to 1903, via four chapters, each of which addresses about thirty years in the life of my story's protagonist. Chapter 4, ' "Improving" the British Empire' examines how, in the age of Sir Joseph Banks, Kew emerged as an imperial and scientific institution. Chapter 5, 'From Royal to Public', explains how an emerging group of professional scientists, in alliance with patrician politicians, undertook the 'reform' of Kew in the 1830s. It was only in 1840 that the gardens became part of government, rather than merely an appendage of the Crown. The man appointed to direct the gardens was Sir William Hooker, and on his death in 1865, he was succeeded by his son Joseph Hooker. Chapter 6, 'The Professionals and the Empire', looks at how the Hookers shaped the work of the gardens in response to personal and intellectual objectives, and contemporary pressures and opportunities. I argue here that it was in imperial work that these men of science found the most effective way to secure their private and public ends. At the same time, the entrepreneurs and administrators catapulted, in this age of the Pax Britannica, to unexpected challenges, were hungry for the practical help and ideological consolation of the sciences. The professionals of Science and Imperialism found common advantage in the idea that knowledge might guide the best management of nature. Chapter 7, 'The Government of Nature', examines the evolution of this relationship of mutual advantage in the age of 'High Imperialism'. The presiding figure at Kew in this period was William Thiselton-Dyer, who formed an important working relationship with both businessmen and the Colonial Office, while presiding over a revolution in the science of botany. The new laboratory and evolutionary science he supported had more to give and gain from colonial work than its taxonomical predecessors. The worlds of science and expansion converged on new terms at Kew. But as faithfully as we tell the story of the heroic century of the Royal Gardens, our concern is not Kew in and for itself. What matters is Kew as an agent and product of modern history, as a space in which ideas about nature, economy, and legitimate authority interacted with concrete policies over Imperial Britain's nineteenth century. These chapters equally examine the evolution of British government and empire in the ages, respectively of Pitt and Dundas, Russell and Melbourne, Palmerston and Cobden, and Disraeli and Chamberlain.

In moving from 'big' to 'small', my intention is not to lose in the close detail the major reinterpretations which underpin this study:

(i) Christian assumptions about man's place in nature played a central role in the making of Imperial Britain well into the nineteenth century. Ideas of Providence, and of Adamic responsibilities and prerogatives, were the ideological taproot of the First British Empire and, translated into political economy, they underpinned the Second, and the nation–states which were its successors.

(ii) Agriculture, as a way of using nature sanctified by the religious and economic assumptions of the West, was equally crucial to the culture of British expansion, again from the Tudor plantations to the ages of Pitt, and even Chamberlain. A possible subtitle for this book might have been 'The agrarian origins of the British Empire'.

(iii) The ultimate victory of 'Free Trade' as a modern idol has obscured the power and persistence of *dirigiste* strains of political economy in the eighteenth and nineteenth centuries. Cameralist and Physiocratic doctrines, imported to Britain from the European continent, shaped domestic and imperial policy in numerous ways. We might recognize Liverpool's 1815 Corn Law and Peel's 1846 repeal as part of the same initiative: *laissez-faire* in the end was only another way of governing the economy. The roots of the interventionist public policy of the Edwardian era, and ultimately the welfare capitalism and developmental imperialism of the mid twentieth century, lie in older visions of the Crown becoming useful to its subjects.

(iv) In the last chapters, I frame a Weberian interpretation of British imperialism in the later nineteenth century. Whatever strategic or local explanations we may find for the spread of 'Formal' empire in Asia or Africa, colonial administrations need to be fitted into the larger history of Bureaucracy. The British Empire, its Whig historians once thought, disseminated liberty. We may instead recognize its most enduring legacy, on every continent, as bureaucratic government. The willingness of Salisbury and his contemporaries to assume responsibility for vast new territories depended on their confidence in the capacity of administration. The story which follows of scientists and proconsuls, the professionals of nature and empire, helps to explain where this came from. The idea of efficient government lent its charisma to a range of domestic and imperial experiments and institutions.

(v) Over all, we should begin to conceive of European 'expansion' as the colonization of Europe by extra-European interests. The same process was at work at the imperial centre as at the frontier: particular individuals and groups found private interest in 'collaborating' with a distant outside.[9] In Europe, as in Asia, Africa, and the Pacific, the same actors were at work untangling the indigenous and committing the local to the global: merchants, bankers, rulers, grandees, scheming bureaucrats, savants, ambitious soldiers, large landowners, restless peasants, townsmen, missionaries, and warlords. The history of this 'collaboration' at the centre remains a fruitful field for historical enquiry. We may eventually discover that the modern world was produced through the collaboration of the labour, wit, and learning of all of the world. Neither the Scientific nor the Industrial Revolutions, no merchant bank or university would have arisen in the West had they depended on the material or cultural resources of the people who lived closest to their headquarters. How we will share the world we have made remains to be decided.

*

In the journey towards this book I have accumulated many kinds of debts.

The government and people of Barbados honoured me with the Barbados Scholarship which made possible my undergraduate study at Harvard University. The Center for European Studies at Harvard provided a grant in 1985 which permitted research in British archives of which this is only the most recent outcome. Yale University provided a University Fellowship (1986–8), and later an Andrew Mellon Dissertation Fellowship (1991–2). I began research for my doctoral dissertation in January 1989, as the Rhodes Scholar for the Commonwealth Caribbean at the University of Oxford. A grant from Balliol College in 1990 allowed me to visit European botanic gardens, and another in 1992 from the American Philosophical Society supported work in its collections. The thesis was completed and the book began at the University of Cambridge, where the Master and Fellows of St. Catharine's College elected me Town and City Properties Research Fellow in Modern History in 1992. In 1994, I returned to Oxford as a Darby Fellow and Tutor in Modern History at Lincoln College. I am grateful to the Rector and Fellows of Lincoln for a term of sabbatical leave from teaching in 1997. Since September 1998, I have had the stimulating company of the Corcoran Department of History of the University of Virginia; I wish to thank, in particular, Michael Holt, Peter Onuf, and the Committee on Small Grants. Besides institutions, family, and friends including Alison Drayton and Edmund Falzon, Terry and Carol Connolly, Adrian Lunn, Mark Harding, Maureen Heron, Peggy and Jean-Louis Rigaud, Vikki Jackson, Corinne Locke and Nigel Rogers, shared their salt and shelter with me during important periods of research and writing.

The Library and Archives of the Royal Botanic Gardens Kew are the rock on which this work rests. I am always grateful for the help of Sylvia FitzGerald and John Flanagan (Chief Librarians), Marilyn Ward (Curator of Visual Materials), Cheryl Piggott and Leonore Thompson (Archivists), and other members of staff. Whenever I walk through the graceful red wrought-iron of the Herbarium towards the Library I have the strangest sense of going home. Extracts from material in the Archives at the Royal Botanic Gardens, Kew, are reproduced with permission and are the copyright of the Trustees of the Royal Botanic Gardens, Kew. Gina Douglas at the Linnean Society, Beth Carroll-Horrocks and Roy Goodman of the American Philosophical Society, also made a significant personal difference to my work. I wish to offer more general thanks to the staff of many libraries including Widener, Houghton, and Gray Herbarium at Harvard; Sterling and Beinecke at Yale; the New York Public Library; the British and India Office Libraries, the British Museum, the Public Record Office, the Society of Arts, the Royal Society, the Royal Geographic Society, the Tate Gallery and the Natural History Museum in London; the Bodleian, Indian Institute, Rhodes House, Balliol and Lincoln College, and Plant Sciences libraries at Oxford; the Archives Nationales, Bibliothèque Nationale de France, and Bibliothèque Centrale du Muséum d'Histoire Naturelle in Paris; the Archives d'Outre Mer in Aix; and in particular the Cambridge University Library.

I have benefited equally from a remarkable range of teachers. I wish to record my debt to those who handled this difficult boy so gently at Harrison College in Barbados, in particular O.A. Wiltshire, who turned Latin classes into discussions about the state of the world, and my history teachers, Ralph Jemmott, and the late Isaac Carmichael, Maurice Hutt, and Joan Reid. I hope that my science and mathematics teachers, in particular Oudit Persaud, will forgive my desertion of the true path. At Harvard, John Clive, Pietro Corsi, Deborah Fitzgerald, Everett Mendelsohn, Margaret Rossiter, Simon Schama, Peter Stevens, Leroy Vail, Jeff Weintraub, and, in particular, Donald Fleming and John Womack were responsible for my wanting to take up this craft. At Yale, Ivo Banac, Linda Colley, Emilia da Costa, William Cronon, Peter Gay, John Merriman, John Reeve, Paul Kennedy, and Frank Turner showed me the scope of problems historians might address, and the textures their writing could seek to achieve. Kennedy and Turner guided me through the writing of the doctoral dissertation, and their influence on this book will be clear to those who know their work. It was Frank who made me understand Victorian Britain, and helped me recognize the persistent importance of religion, and the difficult path through which the sciences became professional. He later made valuable comments on the manuscript. Paul introduced me to the historiography of imperialism, and I doubt I would have dared to wrestle with problems on this scale without the encouragement of his benevolent gaze, and of his own experiments at comparative history. During and after the brief period when this was an Oxford dissertation, John Prest, Judith Brown, and in particular John Darwin, gave important advice.

I received many useful comments from lecture and seminar audiences in Berlin, Cambridge, Cape Town, Cave Hill, Charlottesville, Grahamstown, London, Manchester, Montpellier, Oxford, Paris, Princeton, St. Augustine, Sussex and elsewhere, in particular from participants in the seminar on 'Collection and Comparison in the Sciences' which I ran with Jim Bennett at Oxford between 1995 and 1998. I benefited too from conversations with many friends and colleagues over the years, including Eric Anderson, Michael Anderson, Peter Anderson, David Armitage, Jim Basker, Susan Bayly, Jim Bennett, Elleke Boehmer, Christophe Bonneuil, Michael Bravo, Susan Brigden, Angela Briggs, Graham Burnett, Peter Cain, Peter Carey, Jim Caudle, Harriet Deacon, Helen Denham, Robert Fox, Richard Grove, Jerry Handler, Richard Hart, Tony Hopkins, Colin Hudson, Giles Hudson, Ronald Hyam, John Illiffe, Joanna Innes, Steve Innes, Fiona Jenkins, Anthony Kenny, Gill Lewis, John MacKenzie, Peter Marshall, Colin Matthew, Helène Mialet, Erik Midelfort, Staffan Mueller-Wille, Patrick O'Brien, Judith Olsowy, Peter Onuf, Jeremy Osborn, Duane Osheim, Andrew Porter, Ravi Rajan, Mahesh Rangarajan, Edward Sawyer, Simon Schaffer, Nathan Schlanger, Ann Secord, Jim Secord, Ajay Skaria, Humphry Smith, Nancy Leys Stepan, Peter Stevens, Barry Supple, John Thompson, Stanley Trapido, Megan Vaughan, David Washbrook, Glyn Williams, Maxine Williams, Michael Wintroub, Nuala Zahediah, and Olivier Zunz. Paul Langford gave particular encouragement during my Lincoln years.

It was at Cambridge that the idea for this book came together, and its realization, in the years after 1994, depended on two St. Catharine's colleagues, Chris Bayly and Chris Clark. Bayly's journey through the imperial looking-glass to knowing India in its own terms has been an inspiration for my own passage into British history. His *Imperial Meridian* stands at the foundation of several of the hypotheses I explore here. Clark was, however, the midwife of this book. His Australian wit and his broad historical intelligence were winds pushing me out of Oxford doldrums from which I feared I would never escape. Without his friendship, the path from thesis to manuscript would have been much longer and more painful. I am grateful too to Robert Baldock, my editor at Yale University Press, who gave me room to take risks, and was willing to wait to see the outcome. He, and Anna Hodson, Yale University Press's learned copyeditor, have saved me from many errors and indelicacies.

But everything I owe to my parents, Harry and Kathleen. They made a home in which History was a matter which embraced present and future, and through which interesting people were always passing. The copy of *Black Jacobins* on the shelf bore C.L.R. James's inscription, and one could come home from school to find Walter Rodney laughing at the dinner table, and conversation on the politics, learning, and literature of every human tribe. Through them, I met George Lamming, with whose *Season of Adventure*, *Pleasures of Exile*, and *Natives of My Person* this essay is in dialogue. You gave me a Caribbean which stood at the centre of the world.

This book is dedicated to you, and to Margaret, who for almost ten years has offered me lessons on the uses of light. Her intellect and aesthetic sense, patience and impatience, and stubborn love were always around me. Everything that has ripened is hers. And for Lucie, who teaches me without words how to separate the shades. 'What we call wings the birds can give no name.'

Richard Drayton

Paynes Bay, Barbados
1 January 1999

Introduction

It is a pleasure to introduce to the South Asian reader a book that has left a mark on the wider world of scholarship. However, I would like to begin by presenting the author, as history makes little sense without a sense of the historian. Most scholars of South Asia have less than a nodding acquaintance with the Caribbean. It rarely extends beyond C.L.R. James and perhaps Eric Williams's pioneering works on the history of slavery. But the linkages of these with the wider critiques of empire, hegemony and domination are never quite so far away. As he tells us in his preface, the author grew up in a house where the copy of *Black Jacobins* was one inscribed by C.L.R. James himself. The Caribbean stood at the centre of his world, says Richard Drayton. And, in a sense, it has not slipped away from the midpoint of his intellectual and philosophical sphere. Let me also declare an interest of a more personal nature. Richard Drayton is a former fellow student and was part of a small band that gathered together to discuss how to transform ambitious though often not-entirely-clear ideas into a thesis.

Many of the arguments in these pages began to take shape in the early 1990s. By then, the older story of the expansion of Europe in the modern world and its domination of other continents and peoples had undergone many changes. Empire was falling out of fashion except as an entity that was pulled 'outwards'. As a challenge there were deeply thoughtful and evocative studies of the cultures of conquest, the idiom and grammar of control. On another level, the study of dominated and subordinated peoples, their consciousness and struggles were commanding more attention than ever before. The long-term impact of a host of initiatives across continents and countries that linked issues of ecology to those of justice were also making their impact on the world of academia.

It is against this wider backdrop that historians studied the connections between colonial empires and ecology. This involved the understanding of broader changes in the land- and waterscape, and in techniques of command and control of plants and animals as much as people. In the process, however, several older divisions reappeared. South Asia, southern Africa, the Americas and Europe were often studied in isolation from each other. This was not quite so unexpected, given the internal heterogeneity of each theatre and the way in which archival sources were and are organized. Anyone located in the former colonial world faces huge disparities of access to both primary and secondary materials from other regions. One major consequence was a tendency for the history of the nations at the heart of the empires to be written in a way that did not look at the interconnections between events in Europe and the world beyond. To go beyond one region and look at the larger whole is easier said than done. This is the gap that the publication of this special South Asian edition will help fill.

Other recent works have tried to address this vacuum. Most notable among these are Richard Grove's pioneering work, *Green Imperialism*, published a decade ago, and the shorter *Environmentalism: A Global History* by Ramachandra Guha. The former set the stage for this work, for it argued powerfully that the colonies of the Indian Ocean region and elsewhere were the first sites of modern conservation. Rather than being imported from the metropolis, the techniques and tactics of land and water control to avert resource abuse originated in the rim of empire. Grove's work is too vast in its scope to be dealt with justly in such a pithy manner and Drayton does dispute some of its key conclusions. In particular, he sees exploitation and conservation as two sides of the same coin, rather than as inherently conflicting ideological stances. The idea of saving nature via science was allied to the marginalization of diverse claimants to land, from Xhosa pastoralists to New South Wales Aborigines. In turn, the ideas of conservation had older roots in royal claims over naval timber. The darker shades and sides of green catch the eye of this author who will make the reader think afresh about a phenomenon many of us tend to see as an unmixed blessing.

Drayton also helps place botany as a science in the context of a British empire that was not only expanding but also evolving anew. Kew Gardens, earlier a royal retreat and a place of recreation for the upper classes, underwent a series of profound changes in the mid-nineteenth century. These changes and the men who powered and shaped them are the substance of *Nature's Government*. The propagation, reproduction and use of plants was integral to the networks of imperial power, patronage and knowledge. It was a signifier and instrument of 'improvement', a simple word bolstered by a deeper view that the betterment of the human condition was often coterminus with science as an instrument of empire.

Drayton is not the first or the only one to trace the role of plants in the context of imperial rivalry and expansion. Authors such as Warren Dean, Nick Noltie, Kavita Philip, John Prest and S. Ravi Rajan have done so as well. But Richard goes further than many others in making us rethink broader notions and concepts. He treats Kew as a setting, and only a setting, for men like the Hookers who saw and asserted the coherence of the empire with science as the medium. The financial wherewithal of empire helped underwrite the expansion of the Gardens. British domination of the world between the end of the Napoleonic Wars in 1815 and the coming of the Great War in 1914 has had many a chronicler. But few have traced the wider role and impact of the botanical sciences in the process with such skill, verve and finesse. Gutta-percha was vital for undersea cables, while the breeding of new strains of tea and coffee helped add value to possessions as far-flung as Assam and Kenya. But the reordering of nature relied on the 'shantytowns of labour'. The botanical gardens advanced the knowledge of nature's working but they did so in specific ways at specific times.

Does the history of Pax Britannica really matter and to whom? After all, by the middle of the twentieth century the United States displaced Europe as a powerhouse of biological knowledge, and former colonies now have to work out their equations with the new colossus. The past still matters, and anyone who reads this work will find new ways in which the ecology of the modern world owes much to the ways it was organized and recast by imperial rulers of yesteryear. Just as those who challenged empires had to ask which aspects of science they would retain and which they would transcend, the present too requires a similar process of critical reflection. Doing so in a rooted sense is vital, for history is about specific and particular contexts.

Drayton's work is critical in another context. With growing concern about the environment being such a common feature of our times, cutting across cultures and the boundaries of nation states, it is essential to ask how we got to where we are at the moment. Over the last decade, pioneering work by scholars such as Richard H. Grove and Ramachandra Guha, J.F. Richards and Richard Tucker has served to remind us of the inter-connectedness of ecological and scientific changes that affect more than one country or even continent. Grove was among the first to point to the tendency to see most world developments through the prism of the American experience. The renewed emphasis on the period when Pax Britannica prevailed over much of Asia and Africa, not to mention smaller possessions across the oceans is retained in *Nature's Government*. Where it does matter, and it gains fresh significance given the great disparities of scientific power and knowledge in the world of the twenty-first century, is in tracing the links between imperial power, botanical knowledge and ecological outcome. These were never simple cut and dried affairs either then or now. Yet a reminder of these linkages will help. The environment even the living parts of it, are too important a matter to be left only to technical experts or to economists. And living in a world where there is enormous power and wealth not only in material terms but also in terms of scientific and technological capability, this book will have a salutary role to play.

The French historian Fernand Braudel wanted scholars to choose between being a truffle hunter and an eagle. The former has the micro picture, the latter the broad sweep. *Nature's Government* is a rare book that combines both these sterling qualities.

MAHESH RANGARAJAN
January 2005

PART I
Adam out of Eden

CHAPTER 1

The World in a Garden

And God said, Behold, I have given you every herb bearing seed, which is upon the face of the earth, and every tree, in the which is the fruit of a tree yielding seed ...

And the Lord God took the man and put him into the garden of Eden to dress and to keep it ... and whatsoever Adam called every living creature, that was the name thereof.

Genesis, 1:29 and 2:15–19.

The Garden of Eden in *Genesis* does not mark the absolute origin, for Creation had preceded God's planting of a garden. Eden instead explains men and women's place in nature, both the potential scope of human power, and our actual predicament. God invested Man with perfect insight into, and dominion over, all living things. When Adam and Eve trafficked with the Serpent, they were expelled from Eden into all the sufferings of mortality, and particularly into a struggle for survival against nature. Secular history—and the possibility of both sin and religion—began when Adam met Good and Evil, and his once absolute knowledge and power became partial.

The loss of Eden however contained within it the promise of future redemption. All religious hope was rooted in the possibility that God might forgive a pious humanity and welcome its contrite members back into the original communion. Isaiah (*51:3*) prophesied such redemption,

For the lord shall comfort Zion: he will comfort all her waste places; and he will make her wilderness like Eden and her desert like the garden of the Lord; joy and gladness shall be found therein ...

But if history ended in Paradise, the gate to that second garden lay in the four corners of the mortal world outside of Eden, throughout which were scattered the descendants of Adam, Eve, and the plants and the animals they had once commanded. Theology was deeply divided about the degree of perfection which the devout might achieve in the profane world. But it appeared, with the spread of religion and the growth of technology, that human institutions might assist in the work of redemption—liberating souls from sin, and bodies from hunger and disease. Had Ezekiel (47:13) not foretold the planting of a new garden on the banks of the river, where 'the fruit thereof shall be for meat, and the leaf thereof for medicine'? Perhaps Man, in his journey towards salvation, might even recover some of his original wisdom and power, and turn the wilderness into a province of order and abundance. This was a task in which devout princes, the inheritors of Adam's authority, might take a rightful part.

Those terrestrial gardens through which people farmed food, medicine, and delight, stood therefore as a middle term between Eden and Paradise. The human garden was a fallen garden: living things were out of balance, as the failure of crops, regular famines and plagues testified. But all the elements of perfection were contained in its imperfect order, if only the devout lent themselves to the study and service of God's created truth. For the herbs which once made Adam and Eve immortal and content were still in the world. There was therefore, for those influenced by Christian eschatology, great hope implicit in the idea of a garden which would collect in one place all the plants of the world. The botanic garden emerged in fifteenth- and sixteenth-century Europe as part of an attempt to realize this dream, to 'recreate the antediluvian and prelapsarian past' by gathering together all the creations scattered at the fall of Man.[1] Pagan philosophy, infidel science, and the discovery of a New World, would spark the translation of *Genesis* into the scientific garden of the Renaissance.

The Gathering in of Creation

All human communities have turned to plants for food and medicine, naming them and plotting their affinities. The science of botany has its beginnings in the collection and organization of such insight in the Lyceum of fourth-century Athens. Aristotle followed Plato in urging that there were Universals immanent in nature. Through knowing Universals, men might turn nature or society to the highest human purposes.[2] But Aristotle, unlike his master, placed particular importance on the study of living things, which unlike the stars could be lifted up to the human eye.[3] His Lyceum therefore made biology a priority, and while Aristotle enquired into animals, his pupil and successor Theophrastus pursued the philosophical study of plants. Theophrastus indeed formed a garden in which he collected all manner of herbs, both those local to Athens and others returned by the soldiers of Alexander the Great from distant Asian outposts.[4] While Hippocratic doctrine had long urged Greek physicians to study the plants which surrounded them, a new rigour in method stems from the Lyceum.[5] The Museum of Alexandria continued the Aristotelian experiment, and joined philosophical gardens to its zoo, astronomical observatory, and dissecting rooms. Half a millennium of research, and the herbal knowledge of many eastern

Mediterranean peoples, found their culmination in the work of Dioscorides of Anazarba (50 AD).

But like much of Greek science, the Hellenic botanical tradition survived in Western Christendom only through the quotations of Pliny's *Historia Naturalis.* While small gardens of fragrant and medicinal herbs adorned the monasteries and castles of medieval Europe, none of the scientific works of Aristotle or Theophrastus was in Latin before the end of the tenth century. It was instead through contact with Arab civilization, which had preserved and extended the scientific learning of Athens and Alexandria, that Christendom felt the influence of the Lyceum. The scholars of Paris and Oxford met the *Analytics* and the *Physics*, the Hippocratic corpus, Euclid and Ptolemy through contact, particularly in the twelfth and thirteenth centuries, with the flourishing communities of Arab scholars in Spain and the southern fringes of the Italian peninsula. This was as crucial for botany as for geometry: the study of plants had achieved an unequalled sophistication in the work of Arab herbalists such as Abu Mansur, Avicenna, and Ibn al Baitar, and in the medical and ornamental gardens of Spain, Turkey, and the Levant.[6] Through translators, such as Gerard of Cremona, Christian Europe began to benefit from almost a thousand years of commentary on Dioscorides and Galen (see plates 1 and 2).

Under the influence of new and purified classical texts and of Arab example, Christian Europe turned in its second millennium towards the rational study of nature. Aristotle, Plato, Muslim medicine and alchemy, offered motives and methods for the research of all living and dead things. In Naples and Palermo, under the protection of Emperor Ferdinand II, Michael Scot (d. 1235) translated Aristotle's biological works while serving as Court apothecary, astrologer, and alchemist. Albertus Magnus (1206–80) turned study of the 'virtues' of herbs, stones, and beasts into a means of Catholic devotion.[7] Roger Bacon (1214–94) similarly argued that knowledge of alchemy, 'medicaments', optics, everything above or below the heavens which made up the Book of Nature, was a necessary supplement to the reading of scripture. This Naturalistic mysticism, which sought religious insight in the study of creation, was joined to a mystical Naturalism, which sought to uncover magical means of working with nature. Bacon indeed believed that unlocking the secrets of stars, stones, and herbs would allow men to conquer disease and death.[8] The transmutation of base metals into gold was only one of the aims of medieval alchemy, its other goal was the prolongation of life, the discovery of an elixir which would perhaps even make the Magus immortal. Folk medicine, often with a strong magical and superstitious character, supported such 'rational' enthusiasms, for which herbs and plants—pure, mixed, or distilled—were vital sources.[9]

The humanists of fourteenth- and fifteenth-century Italy combined such higher interests with the pursuit of agricultural plenty and ornamental luxury. While the broader fields of the Tuscan villa answered material needs, its *giardino segreto*, like the Roman peristyle or Persian paradise, was intended to offer both intellectual and aesthetic delight. Nicholas V at the Vatican, Lorenzo de' Medici at the Villa Careggi, and Alfonso II in Naples created gardens aimed particularly at accumulating large numbers of different plants. The reasons for this are clear at Careggi. Gemisthus Plethon, from the ruins of Byzantium, had brought the gospel according to Plato to the court of the Medici. Lorenzo and Cosimo de' Medici attempted to recreate the Academy of Plato at their villa, with the help of the Magi, Marsilio Ficino and Pico della Mirandola.[10] The collection of universal nature into one synoptic *hortus conclusus* was a high religious and philosophical labour for Neoplatonists—for would this not mean a reassembling of God's original creative intentions, the reconciliation of all the fragments of the original *eidos*? The Christian enclosed garden, symbol both of Eden and Paradise, thus became decisively entangled with pagan idealism. The resurrection of the lost earthly Paradise became a task connected with the scientific ideal of comprehending universal nature.

These princely collections were the direct precursors of the botanic garden. Christian Neoplatonists considered that research into the superficial qualities of plants would lead to insights into their *proprietates occultae,* their hidden powers to modify the properties of other things, including human health.[11] For Ficino, for example, the wise herbalist could unlock supernatural means of promoting longevity. Neoplatonic medicine prized living collections of plants, for esoteric insight into the therapeutic efficiency of a plant depended on discernment of its 'signature' through its external physical form.[12] Christian Neoplatonism thus directly underlies the early modern ideal of the botanic garden as both a resource for healing and a philosophical theatre in which God's truth might be discovered in the diversity of his creations.

The invention of printing helped to propagate both botanical insight and the new philosophical enthusiasms. The publication in Venice of the complete *De Materia Medica,* first in Latin in 1478 and finally in the original Greek in 1499, and new editions of Theophrastus and Galen, provided the Renaissance with both a key to the uses of plants, and a chart with which scholars might explore the half-perfected, half-fallen world. But there were other reasons why medical botany would attract great attention in this era. Syphilis and other diseases spread widely across Italy at the end of the fifteenth century in the wake of French and Spanish troops, while bubonic plague also flourished in the disorder.[13] Venice became a centre for the production of compound drugs for all of Europe—in his *Book of Triacles* of 1568, William Turner recommended that medicines came from its apothecaries, 'as faithfully compounded at this time as any Triacles have been made there this forty years'. Its physicians and apothecaries became systematic collectors of plants from around the eastern Mediterranean. At Paris, as Erasmus joked, the medical faculty could scarcely identify parsley, but their peers at Padua, Pisa, and Salerno began to keep sophisticated gardens of simples and to assemble a critical knowledge of natural history.[14]

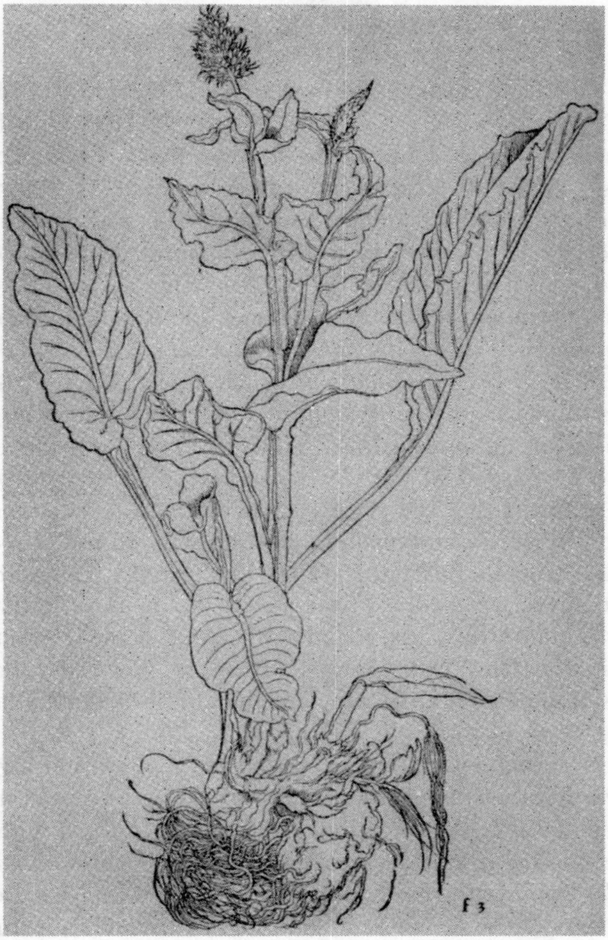

1. An illustration by Hans Weiditz, a student of Dürer, from Brunfels, Herbarium vivae icones *(1530). Brunfels, a Lutheran, promised, in this revolutionary book, that his illustrations were exact drawings of living plants (see p. 8).*

The Reformation also made its own contribution to the progress of the science of botany. This was in part because the polarization of European cultural life promoted, perversely, a kind of cosmopolitan intellectual exchange. This is clear in the case of early sixteenth-century England where it was as refugees that its two leading botanists travelled to the most advanced centres of their science. John Clement, a Catholic, thus knew Dodoens and the gardens of Flanders and France during the reigns of Edward VI and Elizabeth, while William Turner met Ghini, Gesner, and Fuchs during the 1540s and the Marian terror.[15] But Protestants also held natural knowledge in particular esteem: they argued that the dogma of the Church, which was as polluted with barbarisms as the early medieval store of classical literature, should be replaced by the study of Scripture and the Book of Nature.[16] The scrutiny of herbs might lead as clearly towards salvation as the searching of

Habakkuk. This view is suggested in the title of Konrad von Megenberg's *Hye Nach Volget das Puch der Natur* (1475), literally 'Here Now Follows the Book of Nature'—which contains the first printed collection of botanical illustrations.[17] Many Protestant reformers, such as Otto Brunfels and Leonard Fuchs, who were lieutenants of Luther, became profound students of botany, declaring plants a means of meditating on and glorifying the works of God.[18] William Turner, 'the father of English botany', was himself a student and friend of the martyred Latimer and Ridley. The author of the great national herbals began his career with a fiery translation of Rhegius's *Novae Doctrinae ad Veterem Collatio* in which he denounced 'the false doctrines and ordinances of the Byshop of Rome' and continued to publish such polemics throughout his life.[19] Much as Protestants argued that the *Bible* had to be purged of the *Apocrypha* or the *Vulgate*, they made the humanist argument that the science of plants had to be saved from the errors of ancient, Arab, and medieval descriptions. In the *Herbarium vivae icones* (1530), Brunfels boasted the first illustrations made directly from living plants rather than copied from a copy of a manuscript (see illustration 1). Protestants thus asserted for doctrinal reasons what the most advanced apothecaries had practical cause to advocate: the study of Dioscorides or Galen had to be supplemented by the examination of living gardens.

The sixteenth century appeared to be a particularly promising season for the gathering in of all the plants of the world. The European discovery of America, and the opening of a trade route to the East brought about an unparalleled flood of strange new plants. From de Oviedo's *Historia general y natural de las Indias* of 1535, travellers' reports introduced the abundant natural wonders of the Americas.[20] The English title of the natural history of Nicholas Monardes announced the *Joyfull Newes out of the newe founde worlde*, a gospel of 'the rare and singular vertues of diverse and sundrie hearbes, trees, oyles, plants, and stones'.[21] Hippocratic doctrine suggested that American diseases, which it was thought included syphilis, could only be cured by American remedies. Plants such as tobacco, called a panacea, and guaiacum, a *Wunderbaum*, thus became prized specifics.[22] For the more chiliastic of Protestants, the discovery of a New World in the era of the Church's reformation suggested that God had saved these lost realms for this new age. If God had endowed man with a cure for every ill, then perhaps the remedies to the diseases which had plagued Europeans for centuries lay in the new continents? Even those healers who did not imbibe full-strength versions of this utopian enthusiasm believed that all plants contained medicinal virtues. Thus an accumulation of the flora of all continents promised spectacular therapeutic resources. It is this hope which underlay Gerard's promise to Burghley that if he founded a physic garden at Cambridge it would contribute to making the 'noble science of physicke ... absolute'.[23] From the collection of all of the world's plants in a garden, Adam's progeny might establish dominion over their bodies.

The Physic Garden in the Renaissance

It was in Italy that the first botanic gardens emerged from a merging of the traditions of the Prince and the apothecary. The politicians of the peninsula lent their patronage to the much older work of assembling a philosophical pharmacopoeia. In May 1545 the Senate of the Republic of Venice founded by decree an *orto botanico* at Padua.[24] In the same year Cosimo de' Medici directed the creation of such a garden in Pisa, and invited Luca Ghini to become its Professor and Director.[25] Within the next decade the medical schools of Florence and Ferrara formed their own collections, with Bologna in 1568 electing Ulisse Aldrovandi, the pupil of Ghini at Pisa, to form a botanic garden at its medical school.[26] Across Europe the Italian example was followed in the *horti botanici* of Vienna (1573), Göttingen (1576), Leipzig (1580), Leyden (1587), Basel (1588), Fronecker (1589), and Montpellier (1593). In July 1621, a procession lead by the Vice-Chancellor, both Proctors, several heads of houses and scholars went solemnly from St. Mary's Church to consecrate the first English physic garden at Oxford.[27] Within a decade Paris also enjoyed a *hortus medicus*.[28]

The structure of these collections expressed the hubristic ambition of their planters that they should contain the world in a garden. The catalogue of the Oxford Botanic Garden (1658) declared: 'as all creatures were gathered into the Ark, comprehended as in an epitome, so you have the plants of this world in microcosm in our garden.'[29] At Padua this ark took the form of a perfect circle, elsewhere a square (see illustration 2). All the gardens then were divided into four parts, each intended to contain all the plants of one continent. Each continent was itself subdivided into four again, with each subdivision also partitioned, to provide several hundred beds which each would contain one kind of plant. This careful distribution of plants had to do with the garden's principal function as a place for medical instruction. The serried ranks of plants represented a philosophical or mnemonic theatre through which a student might learn his *materia medica*.[30] The ranging of diversity in such gardens became itself a useful Renaissance trope.[31] It was intended that doctors would study the beds of the garden side-by-side with the pages of Theophrastus or Dioscorides, fitting plants into the inherited categories.

But these gardens were also intended to provide powerful new medicines. We are here at that peculiar Renaissance conjunction of the worlds of religion, philosophy, magic, and experimental science.[32] Plants were supposed to reveal their medical powers, to astute eyes, in their outer form—as Robert Turner advised in 1664, 'God hath imprinted upon the plants, herbs, and flowers as it were in Hieroglyphics the very signature of their Virtues'—thus growing them for inspection might lead to the discovery of new cures.[33] The work of finding a botanical 'philosopher's stone' with which to transmute disease to health was also assisted by chemical techniques which might unlock hidden virtues: as a testimonial bound with

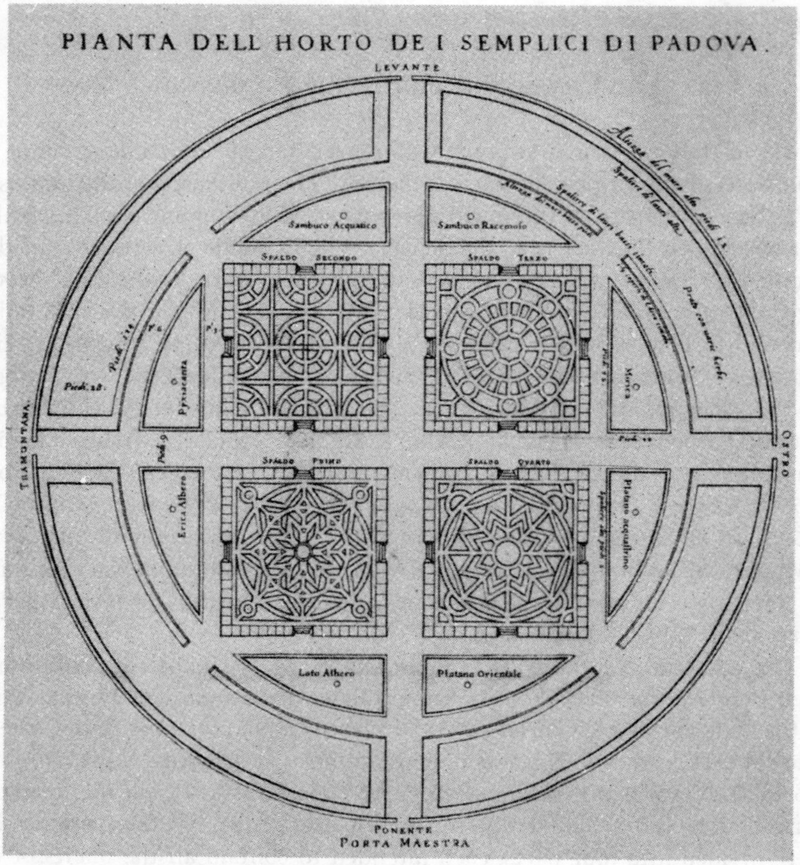

2. Plan of the botanic garden in Padua which divided the world into four quarters, from G. Porro, Horto de i semplici di Padova *(1590).* Bodleian Library, Oxford.

Gerard's *Herbal* urged, 'the laboratorie of an industrious chemist, [should be erected] by the sweete garden of flourishing simples'. *The Newe Jewell of Health* (1576) proclaimed that 'Alchyma' (illustration 3) would help 'the weake to become strong, and the old crooked age become yong and lustye'.[34] As the master had instructed in his *Herbarius,* Paracelsian medicine aimed at distilling magical quintessences from herbs and ores.[35] With the recuperation of Adamic knowledge, as easily as stones could be turned into metals, poisonous plants might be rendered into medicine. Samuel Hartlib predicted in his *Chymical Addresses* (1655) that with the perfected alchemical powers of the new Adam, 'another Garden will be found, whence shall be had herbs, that shall preserve men not only from sickness, but from death itself'.[36] Others, like Nicholas Culpeper, turned to astrological contemplation for help in using plants for healing.[37]

But the botanical garden could serve esoteric, as well as efficient, ends. As Guillaume du Bartas exulted, God might be sought in and under the fabric of the world:

Plate 1. A ninth-century AD *manuscript of Dioscorides,* De Materia Medica, *from southern Italy. Note the Arabic annotations juxtaposed to the Greek text, which reminds us that it was mainly through Islamic scholars that Christendom encountered Hellenic science (see p. 5).* Bibliothèque Nationale de France.

Plate 2. 'Quince', from a manuscript attributed to Ibn al Baitar. The twist of the branches, crowned with golden fruit, is in dialogue with the rhythms of his calligraphy below. Healing and beauty, for Islamic scholars, both stemmed from a sacred knowledge of nature (see p. 5). Bibliothèque Nationale de France.

Plate 3. Mango (Mangifera indica) *from the* Hortus Malabaricus *(1683). Each plate of this remarkable book shows how extra-European knowledge came to be included into European science. Note that the plant is named in five languages at the same time, including Arabic and Malayalam, as well as in Latin (see p. 16).* Wellcome Institute Library.

Plate 4. The cocoa pod is painted in vivid reds in this watercolour by Charles Plumier (1646-1704), the French Minim priest whom Louis XIV sent to survey the natural riches of the West Indies in the late seventeenth century (see p. 17). Bibliothèque Nationale de France.

Plate 1. A ninth-century AD *manuscript of Dioscorides,* De Materia Medica, *from southern Italy. Note the Arabic annotations juxtaposed to the Greek text, which reminds us that it was mainly through Islamic scholars that Christendom encountered Hellenic science (see p. 5).* Bibliothèque Nationale de France.

Plate 2. 'Quince', from a manuscript attributed to Ibn al Baitar. The twist of the branches, crowned with golden fruit, is in dialogue with the rhythms of his calligraphy below. Healing and beauty, for Islamic scholars, both stemmed from a sacred knowledge of nature (see p. 5). Bibliothèque Nationale de France.

Plate 3. Mango (Mangifera indica) *from the* Hortus Malabaricus *(1683). Each plate of this remarkable book shows how extra-European knowledge came to be included into European science. Note that the plant is named in five languages at the same time, including Arabic and Malayalam, as well as in Latin (see p. 16).* Wellcome Institute Library.

Plate 4. The cocoa pod is painted in vivid reds in this watercolour by Charles Plumier (1646-1704), the French Minim priest whom Louis XIV sent to survey the natural riches of the West Indies in the late seventeenth century (see p. 17). Bibliothèque Nationale de France.

Plate 5. The cover page of John Dee's General and Rare Memorials *(1577). Dee, a mathematician and mystic, argues in this essay that naval and commercial expansion would guarantee England's safety and happiness. The sun of divine knowledge illuminates Elizabeth I, who holds the rudder of the ship of state (see p. 29).* Trinity College, Cambridge.

Plate 6. Helleborine americana, *a plate from John Martyn's* Historia Plantarum Rariorum *(1728), one of the most sumptuously illustrated scientific books of the eighteenth century. It bears a dedication to Peter Collison, a merchant whose North American connections made him a particularly important source of colonial plants (see p. 37).* Cambridge University Library.

Plate 7. Strelitzia augusta, *the bird of paradise flower collected at the Cape by Francis Masson whom George III sent to South Africa in the 1770s. Its generic and specific names honour, respectively, the King's wife and his mother (see p. 47).* Marianne North Gallery, Royal Botanic Gardens, Kew.

Plate 8. 'Le Café', a 1735 French gouache and watercolour. Coffee, which the French had introduced into the New World two decades earlier, was the success story which inspired later schemes for moving spices and breadfruit from the East to the West Indies (see p. 74). Bibliothèque Nationale de France.

Il me plaist de voir Dieu, mais comme revestu
Du manteau de ce Tout, tesmoin de sa Virtue.[38]

The reconciliation of families of plants from all four corners of the world had special poignancy for those influenced by Neoplatonic or Protestant mysticism. Each such family united the imperfect variations on one original creative thought of God. The botanic garden was thus more than a magazine of cures or a medical encyclopaedia: by bringing all the tributaries of Creation to a synoptic climax it represented religious opportunity. This mystical endeavour found full expression in the botanic garden of Leyden where the plants were generically arranged in parallel beds called *pulvilli* (see illustration 4).[39] Since each genus represented a pure *eidos*, then a walk through Leyden was a journey through the mind of God. As Ralph Austen, the Puritan divine, advised in *The Spirituall Use of an Orchard*:

3. Alchyma, *a sixteenth-century image of the implements with which an alchemist might distil 'quintessences' from plants. Title page of George Baker's* Newe Jewell of Health *(1576).*

> the world is a great library, and Fruit trees are some of his Bookes wherein we may read & see plainly the Attributes of God his Power, Wisdom, Goodness etc. ... the Lord Bacon says, God hath two great Books which we ought to study, his Word, and his Workes: the one Discovers his Will, the Other his Power ... Naturall, and visible things are shadowes to us of the Spiritual, and the Spirit of God from things Sensible & visible, raiseth our minds to things spiritual and invisible.[40]

The botanic garden was a means through which the power of God might both be understood and mustered to human purposes, an Eden in the fallen world which might guide Christians towards the Paradise to come.

But botany would contribute to medicine and the life of the spirit only if the true nature of each plant was known. The botanic garden thus became a centre for the study of plants for their own sake. It was true that neither criticism nor emendation of Theophrastus or Dioscorides ever depended on such collections.[41] But the new philosophical gardens increased the scope of such revisions, partly because they provided the means of comparing classical descriptions and actual plants, and also because they inspired new techniques. The community around the botanic garden at Padua, for example, generated, and attracted to the printers of Venice, many path-breaking studies.[42] Luca Ghini, Prefect of the living botanic garden at Pisa, taught his students how to dry plants and store them on paper in an *hortus siccus* (literally a 'garden of dried plants'). *Herbaria*, which needed neither earth nor seasons, provided an entirely new resource for the comparative work of botanists. It could no longer be enough to squeeze strange herbs into the 500 plants known to Theophrastus or the 600 of Dioscorides. Hellenic texts which had once given that stimulus to the study of plants which the Greek New Testament had added to late medieval religion now wholly restrained the progress of the science.[43] As observational astronomy led to the ruin of the Ptolemaic system, empirical research helped botanists to break through the yoke of the ancients.

The initial focus of such research was the flora of individual European countries. There was a practical motive for this: Hippocrates, Christian Providentialism, and the popular tradition of healing all urged, as Hartlib declared, 'Where any Endemicall or Natural disease reigneth, there God hath also planted a specifique for it.'[44] By around 1550, for example, the physicians of Montpellier and Basel regularly searched for herbs in the hills that surrounded their cities. But for Protestants the pragmatic pursuit of local herbs had both religious and political resonance. For William Coles, for example, plants were

> Trumpets of God's Glory, setting forth itself so wonderfully in these vegetables, they are also by some called the Handes of God, because they are his instruments to [apply] those things unto Mankind, that he has Created for their preservation.[45]

It was thus a Christian labour to study nearby plants and spread knowledge of them. Just as Lutherans urged the translation of the Bible and Church liturgy into the common tongue, so they sought accurate local herbals in the vernacular. For through such herbals the *regnum*—that community which God had charged to seek its salvation under a particular ruler—might discover those plants which both solved human pain and testified to God's excellence and mercy. Thus William Turner in his *Names of Herbs* (1548) promised to 'declare to the great honour of our contre what numbre of souvereign & strange herbs were in England that were not in other nations', and further offered in his *Herball* (1551, 1562, 1568), 'to the proper profit of [my] naturall countre ... unto the English, my countrymen, an English herbal'.[46] The Protestant botanists of Holland and the Empire, such as Rembert Dodoens and Charles de L'Écluse (Clusius), with similar motives, produced studies local in their canvass and often vernacular in address.[47] While they helped, in Turner's phrase, 'the olde wyves, that gather herbes', they also greatly added to the store of botanical knowledge.

But it is unlikely that European plants would alone have caused the rupture which took place in late sixteenth-century botanical thought. More crucial was the impact of imperial expansion, which had brought home to Europe, in sudden stages, the immense diversity of the world's plants. At the beginning of the Age of Discovery, there was no idea of a New World: Columbus, of course, imagined himself sailing to Asia, and indeed equipped himself with a sailor fluent in Hebrew and Aramaic. Similarly, botanists had attempted to accommodate all plants to Old World categories: William Turner, for example, reported maize, an American plant, as 'Turkische corn' or 'Wheate of Turkey', while John Gerard, called it 'Corne of Asia'.[48] By the 1560s this came to be decisively challenged. Nicolas Monardes, for example, presented the rich diversity of new plants which came only from 'neustras Indias Occidentales'.[49] Garcia da Orta and Christopher Acosta, at the same time, reported a vast range of Asian plants which neither Greek nor Arab botany comprehended.[50] Orta presented his discoveries in 1563 as a dialogue between himself and the learned Dr. Ruano from Salamanca, to whom he responds,

> Do not try to frighten me with Dioscorides or Galen, because I merely speak the truth and say what I know ... the Greeks [were] the inventors of good letters, but they were also inventors of many lies.[51]

If the astronomers found reasons in the sky to break free of ancient cosmology, it was the experience of empire, and the local knowledge of East and West Indians, which helped botanists to shake the influence of the schools.

Clusius, who directed the Imperial Garden at Vienna (1573–89) and who later created the new garden at Leyden (1593–1609), was the Copernicus who shattered the Hellenocentrism of Renaissance botany.[52] Annotations in Clusius's copy of da Orta's *Coloquios dos simples* in Cambridge University

Library show that Clusius had acquired it just months after it was published.[53] By 1567 he had translated it into Latin, and it was through his editions and commentaries that the implications of da Orta, Monardes, and Acosta became widely realized.[54] The world beyond Europe appeared newly important: this was the context for the proposal by Aldrovandi to the Grand Duke of Tuscany in 1568 that an expedition be sent to search for plants in America.[55] It was Clusius, also, who commented on the plants found in the New World for De Bry's *America* including a description of 'Mayz' among his record of its novelties.[56] His *Rariorum Plantarum Historia* of 1601 represented the first full attempt to arrive at the idea of a world flora through integrating European plants with those of the New World and Asia. As the testimonial of Petrus Tornacensis which prefaced this last work boasted, Clusius had become the eye of the world, comprehending the plants of Europe, America, Africa, and Asia. After Clusius, the botanist was no longer a mere commentator on the ancients, he now had the daunting Adamic responsibility of naming every new herb. By the same token, Europeans now needed to know exotic lands and peoples to understand their own corner of Providence.

Discovering the Order of Providence

The botanists who surrounded the new philosophical gardens were forced to consider new ways of understanding the diversity of vegetable creation. Most herbals simply listed them alphabetically. Others took inspiration from the Greeks who had made Man the measure of plants: Theophrastus using size to distinguish between trees, shrubs, and herbs, and Dioscorides dividing the fragrant from the culinary and the medicinal on the basis of their utility. Such anthropocentric criteria long influenced students of plants. William Coles, for example, used the human body to order plants according to their effects on it: guided by the doctrine of signatures, he began with that category of plants manifestly suited for 'the Crown of the Head', such as walnuts with their cerebral shape, and running down to broad-leafed herbs clearly meet for 'the soal of the foot'.[57] Even where some attempted to divide plants into their own kinds, their human uses remained significant, as in the system of seventeen baroque categories, borrowed from de L'Obel, with which Parkinson divided green nature in his *Theatrum Botanicum* (1640):

Sweet smelling plants
Purging plants
Venomous, Sleepy and Hurtfull Plants, and their Counterpoysons
Saxifrages or Breakstone plants
Vulnerary or Wound herbs
Cooling or succary type Herbs
Hot and Sharp Biting Plants

Umbilliferous Plants
Thistles and Thorny Plants
Fearnes and Capillary Plants
Pulses
Cornes
Grasses, Rushes & Reeds
Marsh, Water & Sea Plants and Mushrooms
The Unordered Tribe
Trees and Shrubs
Strange and Outlandish Plants

Such residual categories as the 'Unordered' and the 'Strange and Outlandish' did not however satisfy all scholars.

As botanists tried to think more rigorously about the unity in diversity, they received valuable, if somewhat contradictory, advice from classical philosophy. For Plato in the *Timaeus*, the completeness of the one creative principle required, paradoxically, its infinite differentiation, so that 'the Whole may be really All'.[58] The pure Platonic botanist, had she or he existed, might thus journey from God into Nature then back to God: the soul would guide the intelligence to the research of those creations which themselves testified to the origin of that soul. Aristotle preferred his Prime Mover to be already complete, with no need to become the organisms which were its own effects: the One was constant in its Oneness, even as it penetrated the turbulent All. The 'All', for Aristotle, were distributed continuously on a *scala naturae*, a Great Chain of Being, which ran up from inanimate matter through plants, then animals, to Man and thus to the First and Final Cause.[59] Imperfect human reason thus might survey Nature upwards towards Universals which might later instruct its activity in the world. But since stable Truth resided only in Universals, Aristotle himself gave a mixed message about this scanning of Nature. On the one hand he urged that each group of organisms might be distinguished as a rung on the *scala naturae.* But Aristotle the student of Plato questioned whether such groups ultimately existed except as emanations of the Prime Mover, and implicitly suggested that the natural philosopher should pursue the tendency towards perfection expressed in the Chain of Being as a whole. Both perspectives would shape the new botanical philosophy of the late sixteenth century.

Andrea Cesalpino (1515–1603), Prefect of the Pisa garden, formed the first classificatory system on the skeleton of the Great Chain of Being.[60] He pursued the Aristotelian contention that plants expressed different degrees of 'privation' of the Vegetative Soul.[61] What this meant in practice was that plants reached up from minerals towards animals in terms of how sophisticated were their structures of nutrition and reproduction. Cæsalpinus thus used the flowers, fruit, and roots, and later Fabio Collona (1567–1650), director of the Padua *orto botanico*, used seed, to order plants on a hierarchy of development. This was a convenient approach, since with only two criteria it allowed relatively easy marking of any plant on a single scale from the fruitless mushroom upwards to the most complex flowering epiphyte. But this convenience depended clearly on 'artificial' assumptions which found no intrinsic justification in the plant kingdom. Protestant natural historians came to argue, as Brunfels and Fuchs had in the 1530s, that botanists should study actual plants before they confected botanical ideas. For Clusius, Lobelius, and other Neoplatonic Protestants, God had differentiated his glory into all of his creations, and his herbalists thus should study the relations which connected each plant to its family and then to all others. Through slow and painful study of all the characteristics of every plant, rather than simply its fruit or roots, a scholar might arrive at the hidden *Bauplan* of Creation. Gaspard Bauhin (1560–1634), the Huguenot who presided over the botanic garden of Basel, bravely assumed the challenge, in the wake of Alechamps and Clusius, of forming a universal history of plants according to their family relationships.[62] It was Bauhin who first classified binomially, naming plants both under their genera and species. His *Pinax* (1623), the culmination of more than forty years in pursuit of a 'natural' system of classification, encompassed descriptions of some 6,000 species of plants over twelve volumes.[63]

Bauhin and Cæsalpinus may be said to have set the philosophical parameters for all subsequent botanical classification. But as universal systems, both were rapidly outflanked by the flood of new plants which arrived from distant lands in the first half of the seventeenth century. 'Infinite are the plants which we have, and they knew not', Hartlib noted in 1651, 'as well apparent by their small and our large Herballs, and dayly new Plants are discovered.'[64] *Conquistadores*, merchants, missionaries, and chartered companies had transformed Europe's knowledge of the world's plants and animals. Spanish and French churchmen and adventurers revealed the variety of New World nature.[65] But it was the Dutch East and West India Companies, searching both for cures for tropical diseases and new commodities to monopolize, which set the standard. The Dutch set up botanic gardens in the Cape, Malabar, Java, Ceylon, and Brazil which exchanged plants with Amsterdam and Leyden.[66] The servants of the companies also committed themselves to careful study of the plants of their Asian and American dominions. From these initiatives resulted Bont's *Historia Naturalis Indiae Orientalis* and *De Medicina Indiorum* of 1643 and 1658, Piso and Marcgrave's *De medicina brasiliense* and *Historia rerum naturalium Brasiliae* of 1648, van Rheede tot Drakenstein's *Hortus Indicus Malabaricus* and Rumpf's *Herbarium Amboinense.*[67] These studies not only described many new plants, but their descriptions also carried interwoven with them the botanical and medical knowledge of Brazilians and South Asians.[68] Every plate of the *Hortus Malabaricus*, for example, attempted to bring European and Asian botanical knowledge into convergence (plate 3). Much as the herbal expertise of many *xenoi* and *barbaroi* came into the hands of Theophrastus or Dioscorides,

European botany now benefited from the wealth of scientific insight accumulated over centuries by many extra-European communities.

After 1650, botanists had to wrestle with an even greater tide of novelty. As France and Britain after 1648 imitated Holland in forming overseas trading empires, so they took inspiration from Dutch colonial natural history. Louis XIV and Colbert sponsored the development of the Jardin du Roi and launched scientific missions of exploration, sending La Salle to Canada (1670), Jesuits to China (1685), Plumier to the French West Indies (1689), Tournefort to the Levant (1700), and Lippi to Abyssinia (1704) (plate 4).[69] French colonists, such as Flacourt in Madagascar, told of the treasuries of bizarre plants they uncovered.[70] In Britain, within a few years of the passage of the Navigation Acts, the new Royal Society harnessed national commerce to the chariot of natural history. Robert Boyle in the first volume of the *Transactions of the Royal Society* (1666) gave detailed instructions on the collection of specimens 'for the use of travellers and navigators', which would be issued again in 1692, and echoed by John Woodward in his *Brief Instructions for Making Observations in All Parts of the World* of 1696.[71] The archives of the Royal Society record the results of such encouragement with reports coming from Winthrop on the plants of Massachusetts (1662), Tyler on Virginian flowers (1664), Governor Sir Thomas Lynch of Jamaica on cocoa (1671), and Hans Sloane on the pimento and wild cinnamon tree of Jamaica (1690).[72] Missions against the Barbary pirates led to catalogues of plants from the fortifications of Tangier.[73] 'Ye coasts of Guinea', while feeding the New World with slaves, supplied London with 'divers [strange] animals, shells, insects, [and] plants'.[74] A number of new books appeared reporting on the extraordinary flora and fauna of British colonies.[75] Below the surface of these publications were new links between natural history amateurs at home and in the colonies. Henry Compton, Bishop of London, for example, maintained an active correspondence about the plants of Virginia with Rev. John Banister.[76] A botany club which met at the Temple Coffee House joined gentlemen like Sloane with enthusiasts such as James Petiver, a London apothecary, who was praised by John Ray as 'the best skilled in Oriental & indeed all exotick plants of any man I knew ... and a man of the greatest correspondence of any in England as to these matters.'[77] James Sutherland, who directed the Physic Garden founded at Edinburgh in 1670, forwarded to the London amateurs, through Petiver, dried specimens of plants sent to him by Archibald Stewart 'from the Scotch plantation in Darien in the West Indies'.[78] Sutherland also explained how he benefited from a larger informal network of overseas correspondents since the apothecaries he trained in his garden usually took up posts 'as surgeons in ships to the East and West Indies, or any other place that offers'.[79] It is not surprising that Sloane could write to Ray in 1684 describing the 'vast number of East and West India seeds come over this year'.[80]

The systems of Joseph Pitton de Tournefort and John Ray continued the endeavour launched by the Bauhins.[81] Ray, for example, took pains in 1674 to criticize the 'artificial' methods which led herbalists to mistake 'accidents for notes of specific distinction'.[82] They disagreed only over whether the species or the family should be the 'natural' category of classification: Ray preferred the species, while Tournefort used the genus as the basis for unifying families and ultimately twenty-two classes of plants. But the breakthrough in botanical classification at the end of the seventeenth century depended as much on the bounty of imperial exotica as on revision of inherited ideas.[83] Ray himself acknowledged the importance of the many new plants which had been discovered at the periphery of European power in the preface of his *Historia Plantarum Generalis* (1686–1704). He recorded his debt, in particular, to Piso and Marcgrave, Bont, Hernandez, Alpinus, Rochefort, Rheede, and Banister.[84] They described a world which wholly surprised European systems. In volume two, Ray marvelled at the immense diversity which Dutch imperial science had uncovered in the tropics: 'Who could believe that in the one province of Malabar, hardly a vast place, that there would be three hundred unique indigenous species of trees and fruit?'[85] Ray looked towards the New World for yet more novelty: 'there being in the vast continent of America as great a variety of species as with us, and yet but few common to Europe, or perhaps Africk and Asia.'[86] The implication of this influx, as Ray explained, was that while Bauhin's *Pinax* had contained 6,000 plants in 1623, already twelve times the number known to Theophrastus, more than double that number again had been discovered half a century later, allowing for the more than 17,000 species he described in the *Historia Plantarum*.

Carl von Linné (1707–78) owed a similar debt to both his botanical predecessors and the fruits of empire. Linnaeus integrated Ray's careful delineation of species with Tournefort's generic insights. His synthesis of the two depended on the discovery made by Camerarius in the 1690s, on a suggestion of Nehemiah Grew, that plants reproduced sexually through female pistils and male stamens.[87] This discovery appeared to give a natural basis for the 'artificial' system of Cæsalpinus, with its emphasis on flowers. Linnaeus opted for the convenience and speed of a method based on a single criterion. He used the numbers of male and female sex organs to constitute twenty-four classes of plants which were subdivided into orders, families, and finally into the genera and species of Bauhin's binomial nomenclature. Linnaeus thus brought to a climax two centuries of botanical thinking. At the same time he may be seen as the culmination of three centuries of European reconnaissance of a wider world. It is striking that it was in Holland, in proximity to botanic gardens and Rijksherbaria of Leyden and Amsterdam, rather than in Sweden, that his systematic ideas came to full flower. The Dutch held the finest collections of living and dried exotic plants of any European nation.[88] Between 1735 and 1738, Linnaeus lived and studied in Holland, and published his most important theoretical works including the *Systema Naturae* (Leyden, 1735), *Genera Plantarum* (Leyden, 1737), *Hortus Cliffortianus* (Amsterdam, 1737), and the *Classes Plantarum* (Leyden, 1738). It was in this period also that he consulted the gardens and herbaria of London and Paris. As Linnaeus admitted in the *Species*

Plantarum (1753), his work once he returned to Sweden continued to depend on the collections of Hermann, Rheede, Ray, Tournefort, and Plumier formed at the centres of the Dutch, English, and French seaborne empires. The scientific activity of the servants of the *VOC* clearly also inspired his request that the Swedish East and West India Companies supply his botanic garden at Uppsala.

It was perhaps appropriate that the philosophical critique of Linnaean botany began in Africa, at the fringe of another empire. Michel Adanson in 1749 confronted the plants and animals of Senegal and decided that they simply did not fit the categories framed by any natural historian, including the Swede.[89] Tropical nature had again overthrown a system too provincial in its dependence on Europe, as Adanson concluded, not unlike da Orta at Goa in 1563, 'la Botanique semble changer entièrement sa face, dès qu'on quitte nos pays tempérés pour entrer dans la zone torride'.[90] Adanson criticized Linnaeus along lines similar to those with which Bauhin questioned Cæsalpinus: artificial 'Classes', 'Genera' and 'Species' were mere juggling with names. He urged the pursuit of a 'natural method' which would elucidate families through the study of all of the characteristics of living plants.[91] Bernard de Jussieu in 1759 set about organizing the Jardin Royal at the Trianon to explore such 'natural' relationships.[92] From Adanson, through Jussieu *oncle*, to the research of Antoine-Laurent de Jussieu at the botanic garden in Paris runs the root of the modern 'natural system' of botanical classification.[93] The facts of the world had again surprised the paradise of philosophy.

The Climax of Botany, or the Second Loss of Eden

From Cæsalpinus to Jussieu, botanic gardens had provided a laboratory for the research of natural relationships. But while the success of this comparative work added to their cultural prestige, it also undermined the utopian optimisms which had once supported the Renaissance ideal of the *hortus conclusus*. For taxonomical endeavour and imperial expansion had revealed the plant kingdom to be vastly larger and more complex than any had imagined. To know all the kinds of plants, let alone to collect them all in one place, no longer seemed in 1700 to be a realizable project. Ray admitted as much where he speculated as to how many thousand unknown species remained in America, Africa, or Asia. Botanists, in any event, found in the emerging scientific world view reason to discard their Promethean ambitions that a world in a microcosm might liberate supernatural powers. Natural philosophy and the immense variety of verdant nature forced a second loss of Eden.

The central place of the garden in botany was itself under attack. As the testimonial of J. Harmarus to Parkinson's *Theatrum Botanicum* noted, one printed book could contain far more plants than the great botanic gardens of Leyden, Padua, Oxford, or Montpellier:

Here's more than grows in Batavian ground
And more than in Patavian Garden's found
Or Vernant Oxford's Plat neere River's side
By which brave Maudles Cherwell still shall Glide
Montpelliers flow'ry meadows yield to thee
More in thy leaves, then on their beds we see.

But the pages of the *hortus siccus,* even more than those of the herbal, began to displace the garden as the principal instrument of botanical research. Herbaria could easily contain many thousand plants, and could quickly be formed by those who travelled in distant lands. At the same time, those without land or talent for the cultivation of exotics might hoard them in their cabinets of curiosities. Like the *pulvilli* of the botanic garden, the drawers of the *hortus siccus* offered a space for philosophical accumulation. Museums, such as those formed by the Tradescants, Elias Ashmole, Nehemiah Grew, or Sloane, became increasingly important.[94] This was the brunt of the somewhat unfair complaint of Robert Morison, curator of the Oxford Botanic Garden, that John Ray, his rival, 'studied Plants in his Closet rather than in Gardens and Fields'. From Ray and Tournefort onwards, the book and the herbarium had become more important for botany than the garden.

The gradual fading, after 1650, of the hope that all Eden's herbs might return to one chamber was only one symptom of a larger retreat. The mystical naturalism implicit in the doctrine of signatures was also in decline. It was true that even in 1719 the Royal Society received a paper on how the virtue of plants might be discerned from their external structure.[95] But for perhaps fifty years few botanists of the calibre of Ray or Tournefort had entertained such fantasy.[96] More typical of its age was a submission to the society of 1668 which framed a programme of research which directly questioned the intellectual foundations of Renaissance botany.[97] It urged that it be settled, once and for all, 'Whither plants are more medicinal in Substance, Essence, or Separated into their immediate properties', 'Whether Every Country affords Plants for the Cure of its Vernacular diseases', 'Whither Plants afford a Universal Medicine', and concluded with an appeal for the discovery of 'a mechanicall account of ye various operations of medicines in the body of man'. The successes of mathematics, astronomy, and the physical sciences in the hands of Galileo, Descartes, Huygens, Hooke, Boyle, and Newton had encouraged the search for a 'mechanicall account' of all natural processes. Like their chemical colleagues, late seventeenth-century botanists pursued rational processes rather than occult powers.[98] As Harvey had demonstrated the rôle of the heart in the motion of the blood, so Ray, Francis Willoughby, and Nehemiah Grew sought the basis for plant growth in the movement of sap, and for reproduction in flowers.[99]

A change in how botanists viewed their work as students of nature came with the new science. What room was there for the Neoplatonic Magus, the new Adam who would recover esoteric knowledge, in a world of mechanism which opened its secrets to all comers? The decline of magic, as Keith Thomas noted, went along with a new ideal of God and Nature:

> When the devil was banished to Hell, God himself was confined to working through natural causes. 'Special providences' and private revelations gave way to the notion of a Providence which itself obeyed natural laws accessible to human study.[100]

For political as well as broader intellectual and cultural reasons, hermetic quests and sectarian enthusiasm yielded to the 'public' experimental science of the Royal Society and the rational religion of the Anglican Church.[101] The new alliance might well be symbolized by the intimate relations formed between John Ray and Henry Compton, who kept at Fulham Palace perhaps the largest collection of exotic plants in all of England.[102] In the research of nature, the erstwhile Puritan found common ground with the Bishop who had opposed the repeal of the Test Act in 1685, and who crowned William and Mary in 1689. It was Ray who gave perhaps the most influential exposition of the new 'natural theology' in *The Wisdom of God Manifested in the Works of the Creation* (1691).[103] Ray there charged the naturalist to search for the efficiency and 'plenitude' of God's love in the search for process and pattern in nature. What this meant for eighteenth-century botany was that Ray had consecrated two main lines of research, premised respectively on the fitness and fullness of Creation. The first, through experimentation, searched for mechanisms, since as Stephen Hales later argued in *Vegetable Staticks* (1727):

> the divine Architect ... has made all things to concur with wonderful conformity, in carrying on, by various and innumerable combinations of matter, such a circulation of causes, and effects, as was necessary to the great ends of nature.[104]

The second urged study of the variety of nature *as a whole*, since the vast number of creations revealed 'how great nay immense must needs be the Power and Wisdom of him who form'd them all!'.[105] *The Wisdom*, reprinted a dozen times in a century, 'more than any other single book', Raven argued, 'initiated the true adventure of modern science'.[106] The plant physiology and classification of the eighteenth and early nineteenth centuries, and ultimately Darwin's 'natural selection' (which explained the process *in* diversity), were its direct descendants.

The new 'Natural Theology' did not offer the botanic garden the privileged place it had enjoyed in Christian Neoplatonism. For while the garden might reveal the mechanisms or diversity in Nature, it now only supplemented the 'closet' of the philosopher or the survey of Creation beyond its walls. Here for botany, as perhaps for all comparative disciplines, one may

4. *John Parkinson,* Theatrum Botanicum *(1640).*

5. *Jan Commelin,* Horti Medici Amstelodamensis *(1697).*

6. *Christian Mentzel*, Index Nominum Plantarum *(1696)*.

7. *C. Linnaeus*, Hortus Cliffortianus *(1737)*.

perceive the impact of imperial expansion on the passage from the Renaissance to the Enlightenment. Empire brought home to Europe the shock of the world's diversity. The new things arrived in waves, with increasing speed, from the middle of the sixteenth century. In a hundred years there was no way back home to Eden, no means of reinaugurating a Golden Age. The 'joyful news out of the newe-found world' forced Europe to grasp the challenge of the modern. We may see this shift expressed in the territory of the *hortus medicus* of Leyden: in 1601 it was a perfect square divided into quarters for the four continents, but by 1720 however it was a rambling system of beds, clearly struggling to contain the novelties rushing in. What the flood of new plants showed was that the only garden which could contain the world was the garden of philosophy or the world itself. Clusius and Porro had hoped that the botanic garden might contain all of God's differentiated glory, for Linnaeus it was the world as a whole which stood as the 'theatre of the Almighty'.[107] The botanic gardens of the Enlightenment, under the influence of the new taxonomy, sought to *represent* rather than encompass the plants of the world. Thus Linnaeus suggested to the King and Queen of Sweden that their gardens assembled '*deputies* of the whole wide world'.[108] When Jussieu reordered the Jardin du Roi he intended to comprehend all 'the families of plants', not every species: the ideal of the microcosm had yielded to that of a map.

This map, however, found its centre within Europe. In this lay an entirely new identity for the botanic garden, for eighteenth-century Europe, through its commercial and naval power, had placed itself at the centre of the world. The iconography which represented the botanical enterprise came to express its engagement with European power. In the sixteenth-century gardens of Padua or Leyden, Europe had merely occupied one of four quarters of the world. Thus in Parkinson's herbal of 1640, America on a llama, Africa on a zebra, Asia on a rhinoceros, and Europe borne by two white horses, equally delivered their tribute to the *Theatrum Botanicum* (illustration 4). By the end of the century, however, Europe had clearly become *primus inter pares.* In Jan Commelin's *Horti Medici Amstelodamensis* (1697), for example, it is crowned Europe who presides over the Goddess Flora's meeting with the other continents (illustration 5). Christian Mentzel, more starkly, did not even invite Flora to adorn the frontispiece of his *Index Nominum Plantarum* (1696). Instead Europe, poised on her throne, raises her sceptre over voluptuous Africa, and tobacco- and tea-bearing America and Asia (illustration 6). By 1737, the frontispiece of Linnaeus's *Hortus Cliffortianus* presented Europe with the key of knowledge in her right hand and attended on by Night and Day, while Asia (bearing coffee), Africa, and America wait to deliver their gifts (illustration 7).

It was not the first time that the plant kingdom had provided a theatre for the representation of the imperial theme. Pliny, in the last botanical book of the *Natural History*, had exulted that the plants brought 'from all quarters throughout the whole world for the welfare of mankind' revealed

> the boundless grandeur of the Roman Peace, which displays in turn not only men with their different lands and tribes, but also mountains ... their offspring and also their plants ... Thus truly do [the Gods] seem to have given the Romans to the human race as a second sun.[109]

While Pliny celebrated the Roman Empire through medical herbs, the engravers of Linnaeus and Mentzel's books had chosen tea, tobacco, and coffee. Botanical knowledge, linked to the global transit of exotic commodities, had come to symbolize an *imperium* both rational and divine. As Milton counselled Puritan Adam and Eve after the fall of the English Republic, the consolation for the loss of Eden was the conquest of the world.

CHAPTER 2
Plants and Power

Gardens played many roles in the culture of early modern Europe. They were, first, sources of vegetables, fruit, flowers, perfumes, and drugs. At the same time, they offered space for rest, and sensuous or spiritual pleasure. Both function and delight were connected to intellectual satisfactions, as the mind searched Creation for its order and laws. Gardens and *Wunderkammers* came, in turn, to symbolize the wealth and cultivation of their owners. In the age of Erasmus, Popes and Holy Roman Emperors were pre-eminent collectors, their pre-eminence usurped by merchant princes like Johann Volckamer in Nuremberg or George Clifford in Holland in that of Linnaeus.[1] These collections were not merely status symbols. They helped to identify secular authority and wealth with a Providential or natural right. The dream of possessing all nature in microcosm, and understanding its order, was comforting to those seeking earthly power. From a world in a garden, men might organize the government of the world.

In this chapter I explore the complicated relations of the science of plants to power, tracing the history of botany in England from around 1550 to the mid eighteenth century. In particular, I am concerned to explain how botany found patronage. Earlier, I discussed how religion, medicine, and scientific curiosity influenced the rise of botany in Renaissance Europe. Here I address how the garden, as it ministered to the needs of body and soul, acquired a political significance. Herbal craft was linked in antiquity, and in the Judaeo-Christian tradition, with the *arcana imperii*, that knowledge of nature which was the key to wise government. English botanists made recurrent appeals to this concept of the sacred and politic character of their science. For different reasons, from the Tudor age onwards, spectacular gardens became associated with the display of royal and aristocratic grandeur: power was to be beautiful as well as natural and necessary. Those who wished to ornament their authority proved good patrons of the emerging science of plants. Other help came from a new urban middle class, which turned with passion to gardening and the study of nature. By the age of Linnaeus and Buffon, however, the intellectual prestige of botany made it fashionable among European princes. All these influences shaped the rise of an English royal garden at Kew.

Imperial Magic

Both the sacred and secular literature of the West had suggested that the love of the study of plants was a token of wise government. William Turner, 'the father of English botany', made many appeals to his craft's association with the prudence of Solomon and the virtue of Rome. In his dedication of *A New Herball* (1551) to the Lord Protector Somerset, his first patron, he argued that the only science or art 'openly commended by the verdict of any holy writer in the Bible, is y knowledge of plantes, herbes, and trees, and of Physick'. To Elizabeth I, in the 1568 edition of the *Herball*, he proposed that Virgil's 'sylvas sunt consule dignae' should be revised as 'plantas sunt principe dignae': plants were part of the dignity of a prince. The knowledge of herbs, trees, and shrubs, was

> not only very delectable for a Prince's minde but Profitable for all the bodies of the Prince's hole Realme both to preserve men from sickness, sorrow and payne that commeth thereby and also from poison and death.

The science was useful to the commonwealth, a means for the recovery of Adam's lost resources of food and medicine.

Turner's heirs enlarged this theme that botany was kingly knowledge, deserving of patronage. Henry Lyte's *Niewe Herbal* (1578), dedicated to our 'most High, Noble, and Renowned Princesse, our most dread redoubted Souveraigne Lady Elizabeth', urged the examples of Solomon, Lysimachus, Mithradates, Gentius, and Artemesia, 'such noble and mighty princes ... by their diligent *inquisitio* they wittily found our the use of [herbs]'. John Gerard, dedicating his *Herball* (1597) to Burghley, his patron, similarly praised 'nobel princes that haue ioyned this studie with their most important matters of state', and celebrated his science for providing 'meates to maintain life, and for medicine to recover health'. Solomon, Gerard suggested, loved plants 'for the honour of his Creator, whose gifts and blessings these are; secondly for the good of his subjects'. The testimonial of St. Bredwell Phisition, which prefaced Gerard's catalogue, offered more contemporary examples, praising 'Ferdinand the Emperor, and Cosimus Medices Prince of Tuscane [as] herein registerd for furthering this science of plants'. Thomas Johnson's 1633 edition of Gerard's *Herball* lauded the recent support given by Charles IX to Pierre Pena, the Emperors Maximilian II and Rudolph II to Charles IX, and William of Orange (1581–4) to Rembert Dodoens and Charles de L'Écluse (Clusius). Those who helped the science were demonstrating the virtue of their rule.

The medical and economic importance of plants might alone have supported such an assertion. But other, more esoteric, arguments joined the study of nature's mysteries to a Providential authority. As a way in to these, we may examine the title page of Clusius's *Rariorum Plantarum Historia*

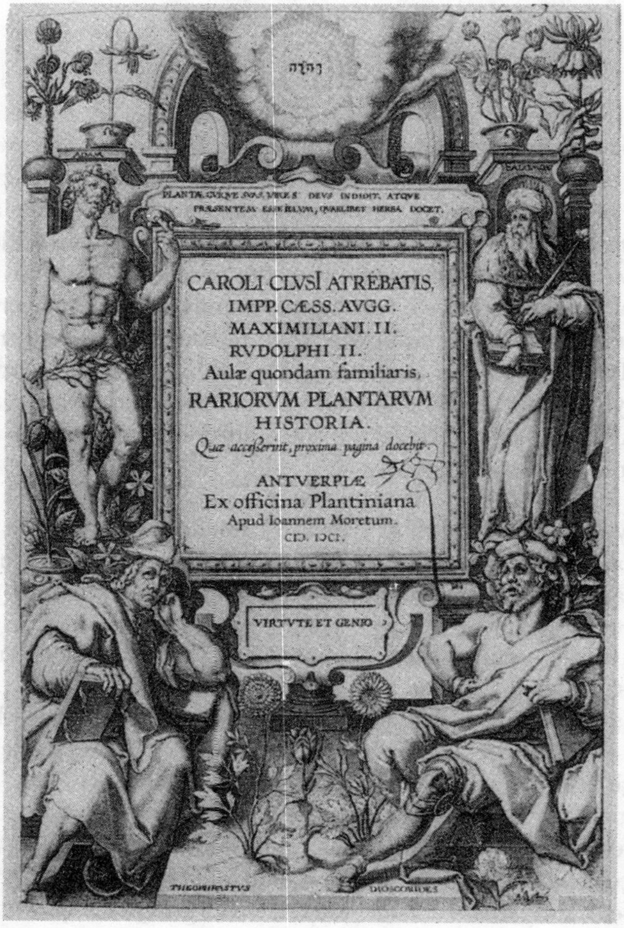

8. Charles L'Écluse (Clusius), Rariorum Plantarum Historia *(1601).*
Cambridge University Library.

(1601) (see illustration 8), which presents Adam and Solomon, on the left and right of a slab bearing the names of Maximilian II and Rudolf II, which is crowned by a cloud of light containing the tetragrammaton (the mystical 'unpronouncable' Hebrew word for God). We may interpret this to suggest that the Emperors Maximilian and Rudolph, wise Solomons, through their patronage of Clusius, were allowing that recovery of that Adamic knowledge which lay at the reconciliation of secular and sacred law.

This representation reminds us that the knowledge of plants had always been linked in mystical ways with kingly power. The Hebrew word *mashiach*, after all, meant literally 'the anointed': the Davidic king baptized in magical essences. The coronation of Christian princes from Charlemagne onwards thus involved the application of botanical oils, such as those supplied by the Royal Apothecary Daniel Malthus (the grandfather of Thomas

Malthus) to 'his sacred majesty' George I in 1715.[2] This ideal of sacred monarchy, symbolized by David or Solomon, linking a benevolent universal knowledge with legitimate political authority, was central to late medieval imperial theory. Within that tradition, the Imperial Prince, heir ultimately of Adam, the original monarch, and more proximately of Constantine, was presumed equal in God's eyes to the Pope, and was charged with the defence of peace and religion, and the institution of order, justice, and public abundance. Imperial theory, once the property of the Holy Roman Empire, came to support the sovereignty of a variety of early modern princes. Thus Henry VIII in the Act of 1533 proclaimed 'This realme of England is an empire.' John Dee, in *The General and Rare Memorials,* similarly urged Elizabeth I to occupy 'the Helm of the Imperiall Monarchy, or rather at the helm of the Imperiall Ship, of the most parte of Christendome', a hope expressed on his title page where Elizabeth holds the rudder of the ship 'Europa', while her soldiers and sailors guard Britain from the horrors of war engulfing the Continent (see plate 5).[3] Appointed by God to inherit Adam's role as governor of the fallen world, the Imperial Prince might, like Solomon, find the keys to wise government in universal nature. Indeed, the prince or princess might show their fitness for power through encouraging learning. John Speed, who described James I, in a broadside of 1603, as a 'most princely Imperiall Seede', presented him in *The Theatre of the Empire of Great Britaine* (1611) as Solomonic *Defensor Pacis et Religionis* and advancer of learning and national power:

> The most high and Potent Monarch James ... the Most Constant and Most Learned Defender of the Faith; Inlarger and Uniter of the British Empire; ... Establisher of Perpetual Peace ... President of All Princely Virtues and Noble Arts.[4]

Through patronage of learning and the arts the Imperial Prince would benefit his or her *regnum* and Christendom as a whole. Where Turner urged that botany was 'Profitable for all the bodies of the Prince's hole Realme', it is likely that he was appealing as much to the Commonwealth tradition, the Tudor idiom of the imperial tradition, as to Elizabeth's desire to rule a healthy kingdom.[5] Imperial theory was thus useful to botanists, for it identified them as important agents of the Commonwealth, as Adams which deserved the patronage of Solomons. John Parkinson in his *Theatrum Botanicum* (1640) referred to 'the compact between Adam and Solomon', while praising his own Solomon—Charles I—as 'the chief of your people under God', blessing them with Religion, Law, and now through a physic garden, Health.

We may usefully pursue this dialogue between botany (among other kinds of scientific knowledge) and political thought in the English Renaissance. Henry Lyte, author of *A Niewe Herball* (1577), also wrote *The Light of Britayne* (1588), a political pamphlet which, in presenting the Tudor imperial myth of the origins of the English monarchy in 'Brute of Albania', wrapped Elizabeth I in mysterious authority derived from Classical and British antiquity, Christian Neoplatonism, and Christian (that is, Protestant) prerogative.[6] If botanists such as Turner or Lyte made political allusions, others, framing political themes, made appeal to the knowledge of nature. The young Francis Bacon, in his script for the *Gesta Grayorum* (1594), has an actor advise that the best policy for a Prince would be 'the conquest of the works of nature' by forming, as well as 'a most perfect and general library' and a cabinet of machines and inventions,

> a spacious, wonderful garden, wherein whatsoever plant the sun of divers climates, out of the earth of divers moulds, either wild or by the culture of man brought forth, may be ... set and cherished: This garden to be built about with rooms to stable in all rare beasts and to cage in all rare birds; with two lakes adjoining,... for like variety of fishes. And so you may have a model of universal nature made private.... [Finally] a still house, so furnished with mills, instruments, furnaces, and vessels, as may be a palace fit for a philosopher's stone.[7]

For Bacon, a recreated Eden was an essential resource for the Prince. The rational study of nature led directly to miraculous political gifts. The Prince through his learning and patronage would become a 'Trismegistus', the only miracle left in a world where all wonders could be naturally explained, 'the Eye of the World, that both carrieth and useth light'. Botany, in this scheme, might be included in the *arcana imperii,* the secret sources of knowledge on which a ruler might depend:

> Antiquity ... informeth us that the kingdomes have always had an affinity with the secrets and mysteries of learning. Amongst the Persians the kings were attended on by Magi. The Gymnosophists had all the government under the princes of Asia ... and Saloman was a man so seen in the universality of nature that he wrote a herbal of all that was green upon the earth.[8]

In his *Brief Discourse Touching the Happy Union of the Kingdoms of England and Scotland* (1603), Bacon enlarged on this argument that knowledge was useful for politics, arguing, indeed, that insight into the laws which governed nature was vital to the most prudent government of men, for

> There is a great affinity and consent between the rules of nature, and the rules of policy: the one being nothing else but an order in the government of the world and the other an order in the government of an estate... The Persian magic, which was the secret literature of their Kings, was an observation of the contemplations of nature and an application thereof to a sense politic... making the government of the world a mirror for the government of the state.[9]

As Julian Martin and Brian Wormald have argued, Bacon believed that the monarchical state might harness knowledge to augment its power.[10] Walter Ralegh, similarly, precedes his discussion of magic—'the wisdom of nature'—in his *History of the World* (1614), with an exploration of the responsibilities of Princes, and of the beginnings and ends of government.[11] Ralegh believed that Noah left to his son the knowledge of 'Horoscopes or Nativities ... the nature of hearbs, stars, and minerals, ... their sympathetical and antipathetical workings'.[12] Because all earthly power derived from the prerogatives passed through Adam, Noah, David, and Solomon, the monarch or gentleman with scientific interests was engaged in the reconciliation of the natural and social providence. It is this millenarian hope, linking universal knowledge with imperial right, which is expressed in the iconography, discussed above, of Clusius's *Rariorum Plantarum Historia*, and in the declaration of Bacon, in the preface to the *Instauratio Magna*, that he wished to restore 'that commerce between the mind of man and the nature of things to its perfect and original position'.

We should not overestimate the direct impact of esoteric doctrines. The elder Francis Bacon kept a prudent distance from the magical and hermetic traditions in order, perhaps, 'to protect his programme from witch-hunters, [and] from the cry of sorcery'.[13] But they represent, in perhaps an extreme form, more pervasive assumptions about the relationship of the laws which regulated nature to those which ordered government, and of the powerful to the learned. The Tudor and Stuart *noblesse de la robe*, of which Francis Bacon was only the most intellectually distinguished representative, shared a faith that the statesman was responsible for the enlargement of the civil happiness of a people. They recognized that the patronage of learning was both a means towards, and a symbol of, this duty. The Lord Protector Somerset thus patronized Turner, while William Cecil, who began his own rise to power as Secretary to Somerset, had, from 1577, cultivated his own botanist, Gerard.[14] Burghley, who as Pliny, and Erasmus's Eusebius, had advised, always kept a copy of Cicero's *De officiis* in his pocket, assisted a number of other intellectuals, including the mathematician Thomas Diggs and the magus John Dee.[15] Sir Nicholas Bacon, the father of Francis, also lent help to Leonard Digges, the mathematician. Digges in exchange dedicated *A Geometrical Practise, named Pantometria* (1571) to Bacon, offering, much as Turner promised Somerset he would provide to the English an English herbal, that he would store 'our native tongue with mathematicall demonstrations'.[16] Ralegh, to whom Gerard dedicated the *Catalogus Arborum* (1599), also lent practical encouragement to Dee, Hakluyt, Hooker the antiquary, Jacques Morgues the painter, and Thomas Hariot the mathematician.[17] Lord Zouche, contemporaneously, helped Mathias de L'Obel, bringing him to the attention of James I and thus to his appointment as Botanicus Regius in 1607.[18] Salisbury and Buckingham, in the same way, through cultivating John Tradescant and John Parkinson, led to Charles I recruiting them as 'the King's First Herbarist' and 'Apothecary to London and the King's Herbarist'.

It is as much within this national context of gentlemanly patronage, as through the influence of European medicine, that we may understand the decision of the Earl of Danby to pay for the walling, gating, levelling, and planting of the 'Physick Garden' at Oxford, the first botanic garden in this country.[19]

The Ornaments of Solomon

Yet in the patronage of gardens and botany we may also observe a less lofty set of influences at work. For new courtly tastes arrived along with political and philosophical doctrines from the European continent. From Popes and the Medici, to the lesser proprietors of the villas of Tuscany and Rome, to Holland, France, and England, gardens had become theatres for the demonstration of wealth and civility by the sixteenth and seventeenth centuries.[20] If the architectural stamp of medieval authority had been the battlements and earthworks of the castle, Renaissance power found expression in the luxury of the palace with its pleasure grounds. While Henry VII had been content to make his progresses from monastery to monastery, Henry VIII instead constructed a series of grandiose palaces: Hampton Court and Westminister, extorted from Wolsey, absorbed over £62,000 and £43,000 respectively, while Nonesuch, Henry's answer to Francois I's Chambord, took another £25,000.[21] His political servants followed his example in the vast estates which they secured out of lands confiscated from the Church.

The efficiency with which policy was policed in Tudor England allowed a transformation in the style of aristocratic and royal homes. *Holinshed's Chronicle* alluded to 'the forme of building used in our daies which is more for pleasure than profit or safeguard'.[22] Courtiers and statesmen such as Somerset, the Cecils, the Bacons, Raleghs, and Brookes, built sumptuous retreats rather than the fortified strongholds of a hundred years before. Such palaces required gardens. Without them, as Francis Bacon later warned, 'buildings and Pallaces are but Grosse Handy-works'.[23] As at the Vatican Belvedere and the Villa d'Este, England's gardeners sought after strange new plants which might give distinction to ornamental collections. William Harrison wrote in 1577 that

> strange herbs, plants and ... fruits, are daily brought unto us from the Indies, Americans, Taprobone [Java], Canarie Islands, and all parts of the World ... There is not almost one noble man, gentleman, or merchant, that hath not great store of these flowers.[24]

Rare and unusual plants were prized for collections, or as courtly gifts, such as the tobacco seeds returned by Jean Nicot to Catherine de' Medici. While busy on his military campaign in the Netherlands, the Earl of Leicester found time to correspond on horticulture with Jean Hotman, while the Earl of

Cumberland brought to Elizabeth I a *Mimosa* species, 'the herb of love', from the sack of Puerto Rico.[25]

It is as much through service to horticulture, as for their medical or scientific expertise, that botanists found the friendship of the powerful. At Syon House, the Lord Protector Somerset, remaking the former nunnery given him by Edward VI in 1547, spent more than £5,000 between 1548 and 1551 on works.[26] Somerset accumulated a remarkable collection of plants. All of William Turner's botanical works, from *The Names of Herbs* (1548) onwards, contain references to rare plants 'in my Lord's gardine in Syon'. Sir William Cecil who spent almost as much on the grounds and gardens of Theobalds as he did on buildings, sent to Paris for pomegranate and lemon trees, and recruited Gerard as his steward.[27] Gerard, like Turner, made many references to his patron's collection, praising 'gardens, especially such as your Honor hath, furnished with many rare simples' in the preface of the 1597 *Herball.* These great private gardens, it is likely, could have rivalled, in the extent of their collections, many of the smaller physic gardens of continental universities. They had no public equivalent in England.

It may be, as Roy Strong and Francis Yates suggested, that even this gardening was under the influence of those Hermetic or other magical ideas which allied Clusius and the Holy Roman Emperors, or Solomon de Caus and the Elector Palatine.[28] Sir Christopher Hatton's garden at Holdenby was, for example, equipped with its own 'Destilling House' where alchemists might extract quintessences from herbs or flowers.[29] The ideal of forming in a garden what Bacon called a 'model of universal nature made private' could never be free of its Neoplatonic pedigree. But we must acknowledge, distinct from philosophical or religious motive, the power of fashion and the concrete attractions of form, colour, and perfume. By the seventeenth century, a sophisticated international market in exotic plants was already emerging. Emanuel Sweert's sumptuous *Florilegium* (1612) was essentially a catalogue of the bulbs and flowers which he was selling at the Frankfurt Fair. The example of Sweert, a former gardener to Rudolf II, reminds us that Clusius was as favoured by the Holy Roman Emperors for his skill in propagating exotics, such as the 'Crown Imperial', received by Maximilian II's court from their Ambassador in Constantinople, as for his taxonomical prowess. By the 1600s, Clusius had arranged, through the directors of the Dutch East India Company, for sea captains to collect bulbs and succulents in the East Indies and at the Cape.[30] The Dutch tulip craze of 1634 showed how far beyond the circle of Emperors and Popes the passion for showy novelties had spread. In England, similarly, those with botanical skill prospered more perhaps as suppliers of decorative exotics than as the allies of physicians.

As an example of the power of these new fashions, we might note that while Somerset and Burghley had supported Turner and Gerard, Salisbury cultivated John Tradescant. As Mea Allen noted, the Tradescants had scarcely any interest in the medicinal value of plants: they sought size, colour, and strangeness of flowers, and succulence of fruit.[31] The younger

Cecil sent him to the Netherlands in 1610 to buy novelties for Hatfield. In Harlem and Delft, Tradescant purchased cherry, quince, apple, apricot, peach, and mulberry trees, seeds and bulbs for rare anemones, tulips, lilies, and irises. The account books of Hatfield in 1612 show that Tradescant received about £48 per annum, twice what was paid to the 'French gardeners', who themselves earned more than Salisbury's falconer, coachman, armourer, and bargeman. Cecil, and Tradescant's later patron, Buckingham, arranged for him to accompany diplomatic and military missions abroad. In 1620, for example, when a fleet was sent to punish the pirates of Algiers, he collected new apricot varieties from the Barbary Coast.[32] In 1625, Tradescant wrote Edward Nicholas, Secretary of the Admiralty, requesting him, in Buckingham's name, to arrange that British merchants should 'procure all manner of curiosities from abroad':

> I have Bin Commanded By My Lord to Let Yr Worshipe Understand that It is H[is] Grace's Plesure that you should In His Name Deall withe All Marchants from All Places But Espetially the Virgine & Bermewde & Newfownd Land Men that when they [go] Into those Parts that they will take Care to furnish His Grace Withe All manner of Beasts & fowells ... slipes or seeds Plants trees or shrubs Also from Gine or Binne or Senego Turkye Espetially to Sir Thomas Rowe Also to Captain North.[33]

This remarkable letter shows how early Britain's naval and commercial power was applied to natural history collecting, and how important were the concerns of princely horticulture in organizing this activity. For the interest which Buckingham, and later Charles I, showed in exotic plants was not nourished by reading Gesner or Clusius, it was instead a symptom of courtly fashion, an analogue of their art-collecting passions.[34] For Charles I, Tradescant was merely someone who would collaborate with de Caus or Guy Mollet where they attempted to form English equivalents to Fontainebleau or Honselaarsdijk.[35]

Without deprecating the considerable talents of the Tradescants or John Parkinson, one may note how much botanical curiosity was constrained in seventeenth-century England by the aristocratic and princely enthusiasms which sustained it. We may take Parkinson's *Paradisi in Sole* (1629) as evidence of this ensnaring of botany by courtly horticulture. It did not share Turner's concern with equipping 'the olde wyves' with a key in English to the medicinal plants of their country, instead its subject was flowers and the planting of orchards, while its own title was a pun, 'park-in-sun', framed for the delight of those with Latin. His *Theatrum Botanicum* (1640) also appears preoccupied by the more luxurious aspect of the science. It was not then inappropriate that the 1648 catalogue of the Oxford Physic Garden began with an image of a crown hidden within a cluster of flowers and vines: botany, at the Stuart court, was principally an adornment to royal power.[36] The vegetable kingdom was to crown earthly monarchy, as John Rose, on his knees, in the portrait at Ham House, presented the thorny coronet of a pineapple to Charles II.

In this respect, we may observe again the impact of Continental courtly fashion on England, in particular the influence of the Bourbons. Henri IV had founded the physic garden at Montpellier, the first in France, as Louis XIII and XIV later supported Brosse, Robin, and Fagon at the Jardin du Roi in Paris.[37] As patrons of these collections, they were, in part, attracted to the glory of supporting the progress of learning and healing.[38] But they were also, perhaps increasingly, preoccupied by their possible contribution to the grandeur of royal palace gardens. The botanic garden at Blois, for example, which Gaston d'Orleans entrusted to Robert Morison, fits into this model.[39] On his restoration, Charles II recruited Morison from Blois to be 'king's botanist', installing him as the first Professor of Botany at Oxford in 1669, naming him King's Physician, and awarding him a salary of £200 per annum, with a further £216 for the publication of his book.[40] Morison, in turn, cultivated the Stuarts, dedicating his *Hallucinationes Caspari Bauhini* (1669), for example, to James, Duke of York. But we may guess, from Charles II's decision in 1660 to make him master of St. James's Park and Hampton Court, that the King was more concerned with Morison's past success as keeper of the gardens of the Duke of Blois, than with his taxonomical prowess. (By 1682, parenthetically, Morison complained to the Archbishop of Canterbury that his salary was then many years in arrears.)[41] Charles II sought ornamental gardens which might equal those Le Nôtre had created for the Sun King at Versailles. In fact, Charles II wished Le Nôtre to design the royal garden at Greenwich, and took plans from him for St. James's Park.[42] But the Stuarts were too poor to afford their own Versailles.[43] It was in part because Britain lacked a great *jardin du roi*, that visiting foreign dignitaries, such as Charles, Elector Palatine (in 1680) and Hamet ben Hamet ben Haddu Ottar, Ambassador of the Emperor of Morocco (in 1682) went instead to the Oxford botanic garden.[44]

The revocation of the Edict of Nantes sent Hugenot refugees, like Daniel Marot, carrying French style to William of Orange's gardens of Het Loo, Clingendaal, and Huis ten Bosch in the 1680s. The Glorious Revolution thus did not mean a diminution of the influence of the Le Nôtre clan, and grand systems of avenues and parterres were brought to the landscape of England at Hampton Court, Windsor, and Kensington.[45] William and Mary spent vast sums on parks and gardens: some £87,714 between 1689 and 1702 went on the landscaping of Marot at Hampton Court, and on *jets d'eau*, with £2,160 going solely for the ornamental iron gates and railings designed by Jean Tijon.[46] The Earl of Portland even succeeded in having Le Nôtre produce a design in 1698 for gardens at Windsor.[47]

By the early eighteenth century, the demand for exotic plants reached new heights within Britain. As Henry Wise and George London, whose Brompton nurseries catered to grand gardeners, wrote in *The Retir'd Gard'ner* (1706): 'A Florist's Curiosity is not to be confined to his own

Country, nor to such flowers as he might find there.'[48] William and Mary brought from Holland their own botanical and gardening interests, and by 1690 Hampton Court had a sizeable collection of plants from the East and West Indies, while by 1695 Holyrood Castle had its own small physic garden.[49] Their courtiers were even more assiduous, with the Duke and Duchess of Beaufort at Badminton and Bishop Henry Compton at Fulham acquiring perhaps the finest contemporary English collections of exotics.[50]

But by the late seventeenth century figures such as Compton were also responding to a very different set of indigenous influences.[51] Élite botany and horticulture had always drawn sustenance from the larger world of apothecaries, farmers, and gardeners, much as practical mathematics, and the skills of artisans and instrument makers, had sustained the development of natural philosophy and the experimental tradition.[52] Turner recognized his debt, and offered his book to the improvement of this popular herbal tradition. By 1617, the Society of Apothecaries had secured its charter in London and in 1618 published its first *Pharmacopoeia Londiniensis.* Francis Bacon, and those who found inspiration in his call for the empirical renovation of learning, looked with respect at the practical learning of herbalists.[53] It was not merely by coincidence that the meetings in London organized by William Petty which culminated in the Royal Society were held in an apothecary's house.[54] Both Puritan radicals such as Worsely and Culpeper, and such Restoration gentlemen as Robert Boyle, sought a natural philosophy founded on direct encounter with nature, and involved with the facts of everyday life. Thus Thomas Sprat, in his *History of the Royal Society* (1667), praised the knowledge of 'artisans, countrymen, and merchants' above the mannered learning of 'scholars'.[55] If once the gentleman had kept his distance from a practical knowledge of nature, the Restoration ideal of the 'virtuoso' honoured instead the man of property who cultivated a curiosity about all civil and natural history. Natural knowledge, also, was now as devout as it was polite. Sprat and Boyle, with the later help of Newton, the devout botanist John Ray and the pious astronomer William Derham had brought science into the heart of the Anglican Church.[56] By the late seventeenth century, natural history had become a respectable enterprise joining together those of the stature of Bishop Compton and Ray, with apothecaries like Petiver, American settlers, East India merchants, and sea captains on every ocean.[57] Setting the seal on this alliance of 'high' and 'low' botany was the Chelsea Physic Garden, founded by the Society of Apothecaries in 1673, which in leasing the land from Sir Hans Sloane committed itself to sending a tribute of fifty new plants each year to the Royal Society.[58]

Sloane (1660–1753), physician to Queen Anne and George II, and President of the Royal Society (1727–53) symbolized the new cultural prestige of natural history in the early eighteenth century.[59] After a two-year spell in Jamaica, he returned with what Evelyn called 'an universal collection of the natural productions' of that island.[60] This became the core of a museum of natural and artificial curiosities, on which Sloane spent over

£50,000, which had no rival in Augustan England. At the same time he stood at the centre of an informal empire of gentlemanly knowledge, maintaining a correspondence which embraced the world. The plants of John Martyn's *Historia Plantarum Rariorum* (1728), published under Sloane's patronage—*Niruri barbadense, Aster virginianus, Cassia marilandica, Corono solis caroliniana*, and *Helleborine americana*—tell us much about the Royal Society under his presidency. Each lavish plate was dedicated to a Fellow of the Royal Society, *Helleborine americana*, for example, to Peter Collinson, the North American merchant and naturalist, and bore tribute equally to an outpost of overseas influence (plate 6). They remind us that private initiative would probably have founded a great botanic garden in England at the middle of the century, if the Crown had not done so. Natural history, joined to commerce and religion, had captured the attention of the upper and middle classes of imperial Britain. If the Hanoverians came to respond to foreign princely example, they also had the prodding of their own subjects' enthusiasm.

A Royal Garden at Richmond

The origins of the royal garden at Kew fall easily into the story of English botany and gardening.

English kings had held land in the manor of Sheen since Saxon times. One royal house had lasted until Richard II demolished it in 1394, and its replacement, built by Henry V around 1420, survived until gutted by fire in 1497. Henry VII decided in 1499 to plant a monument to the grandeur of his reign, spending more than £20,000 by 1501 to construct a Gothic castle surrounded by a vast enclosed garden.[61] This palace, christened Richmond, became a 'Tudor dynastic symbol', named in allegorical tributes to Henry Richmond and his Rich Mount of England.[62] Under Elizabeth I, the sculpted figures of those dead and mythic English kings most important to the identity of the Tudor dynasty—Brute the Trojan, Arthur, Edward the Confessor, William the Conqueror, Richard I, and Henry VII—decorated its Hall and Privy Gardens.[63] When James I named his son Henry as Prince of Wales, a further £5,000 went on works done under the guidance of de Caus.[64] More extensive renovations were planned but never executed, including schemes for grottoes, grand galleries, waterworks. Devastated during the Civil War, the property passed to James, Duke of York, who sought to construct a 'Chateau de Richemont', and took plans for it from France in 1664.[65] Nothing was done with the site, however, although William III allocated £3,500 for renovations, of which £120 went to George London for 'making and levelling the great walke leading from the House to the Thames, planting it with trees and other services'.[66] Under Anne, the estate was leased to the Duke of Ormonde, Lord-Lieutenant of Ireland, and an intimate of the late king. Ormonde, who had been educated in France, continued the Le Nôtrean style, and by 1714, his estate was described as 'A perfect Trianon, everything in it and about it answerable to the grandeur and magnificence of its great master.'[67] But in 1715 Ormonde threw in his lot with the Jacobites, and the Crown annexed his improvements. In 1718, the Prince and Princess of Wales, fleeing the anger of George I, set up house at Richmond.

In *A Tour Through the Whole Island of Great Britain* (1724), Defoe reported how Caroline and George Augustus created a princely *salon* on the upper Thames:

> From hence we come to Richmond, the delightful retreat of their royal highnesses, the Prince and Princess of Wales, ... The Prince's Court being so near must need have fill'd Richmond ... with a great deal of the best company in England.[68]

They reached out to the brightest lights of their age, many of whom had also settled west of London. In 1725, for example, the Prince and Princess lent a company of their workmen to landscape the gardens of Alexander Pope.[69] Caroline was a clever and ambitious woman, a product of the cultivated Brandenburg court in Berlin, where she had won the friendship of Leibniz.[70] When at the accession of George II in 1727, she received Richmond Lodge, with an income of £100,000 per annum, she set about to remake it in her own manner. The German princes had followed the models set by Le Nôtre, Le Vau, and Mansart. Queen Caroline, similarly, sought to use gardens and architecture, as Louis XIV had used the Fountains of Apollo and Latona, and the Grotto of Thetis at Versailles, to offer a message.

William Kent and Charles Bridgeman raised a political allegory in the grounds of Richmond.[71] Two bizzare structures, 'Merlin's Cave' and the 'Hermitage' (otherwise known as the 'Grotto'), argued for the legitimacy of the Hanoverian accession to the English throne (see illustration 9). Merlin's Cave contained life-sized wax figures of Merlin, said to have prophesied the Hanoverian dynasty, seated in a central shrine, surrounded by magical instruments and an armillary sphere, facing his secretary who, quill in hand, was poised to record his master's vision. With them were Elizabeth of York (the wife of Henry VII, who had created Richmond), Elizabeth I (the female culmination of the Tudor dynasty, and the last monarch to maintain a palace at Richmond), with Britomart, a Queen of the Amazons, and a nurse or prophetess, together with what a contemporary account described as a library of 'modern authors bound in vellum'.[72] We may fairly speculate, from 'The Hermitage', that natural philosophy and Anglican theology filled the shelves. For that structure housed, besides a hermit and his wife, five busts: Newton and 'Lock' stood to the right and Rev. Wollaston and Rev. Dr. Clarke to the left, with Robert Boyle, above it all, in an alcove. From Merlin's Cave we might infer that the Hanoverians, who like Arthur and the Tudors had come from obscurity to the English throne, now justly continued the Providential line of English monarchy, with Caroline as their warrior priestess. The 'modern authors' in the Hermitage, among them the nation's two greatest students of nature, lent philosophical and theological support to the 1688 Revolution, the 1701 Act of Settlement, and the 1714 accession of George I.[73]

The many opponents of Sir Robert Walpole made fun of Caroline's follies and dissented from these political implications. In the eyes of *The Craftsman*, the opposition's journal, Caroline was

> a most illustrious example of a Queen, who not only relieves her Husband from the Fatigues of Government at Home, but hath put all the powers of Europe in a Ferment, for several years past. Indeed, she has always done this, in Concert with a favourite Minister, whom she adopted, as it were, into a Partnership of her Throne, like some of the ancient Roman Emperors, and divided the Sovereignty with Him.[74]

In the year after the completion of Merlin's Cave, it reflected on this alliance of Caroline and Walpole: 'We have some great Men amongst us, who have justly acquir'd the reputation of being Wizards, or Conjurers.'[75] Cobham at Stowe constructed 'Monuments of BritishWorthies' which embodied a quite different vision of the place of monarchy in the English constitution. Besides King Alfred, Edward the Black Prince, Queen Elizabeth I, William III, and such cultural monuments as Shakespeare and Inigo Jones, he chose to honour those, such as Ralegh, John Hampden, and Milton, who were the victims and opponents of unjust kings.[76] While Caroline provided a Providential theory of monarchy, Cobham, the 'Country Party' Tories and 'Patriot' Whigs argued that kings ruled in partnership with the liberty and pleasure of their subjects. As Gilbert West, in an epic poem on Stowe, interpreted the message of William III's bust:

> O that like Thee, Succeeding Kings had Strove
> To build their Empire on their people's love!
> That taught by Example they had known
> That only Justice can support a Throne.[77]

Caroline's allegory was, in some ways, out of season. While she conjured with Whig ideology, including Locke in her Hermitage, she failed wholly to understand its implications. The opposition, including Tories, appealed however to its presumption that kings and queens should be seen as servants of their subjects, rather than as the inheritors of mystical authority. In *The Idea of A Patriot King*, Bolingbroke argued that monarchical power should be founded on consent and the claims of reason, kingship 'ought to have been, whenever it began, according to the rule of reason, founded in the common rights, and interests, of mankind'.[78] Appealing both to the dignity of kingship and the rights of subjects, Bolingbroke provided a cunning Enlightenment negotiation of the 'Divine Right of Kings':

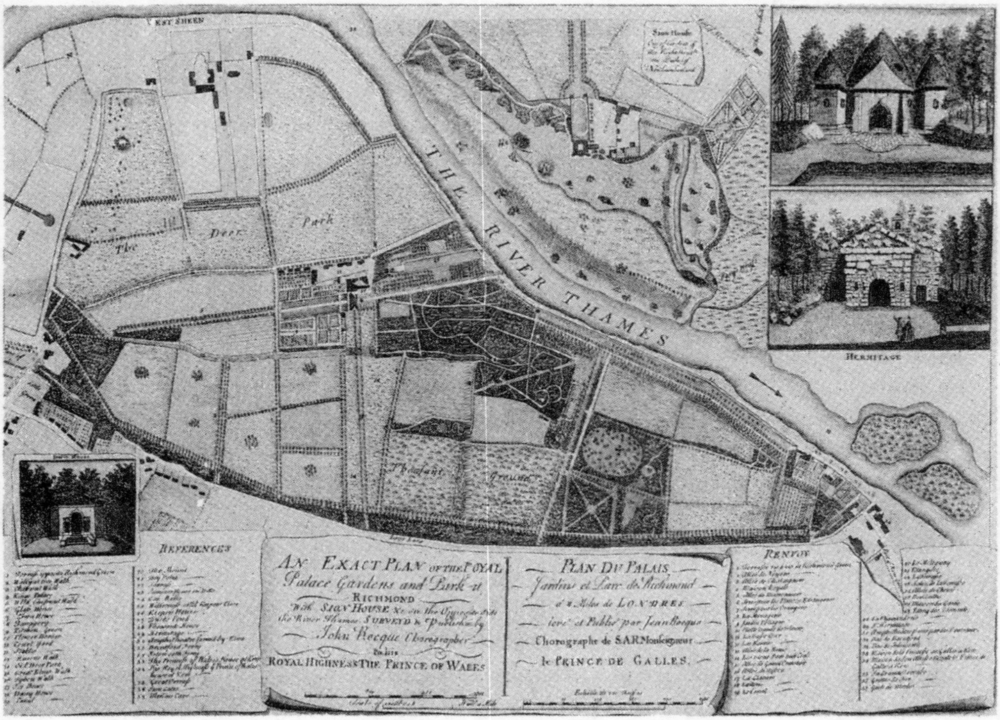

9. John Rocque's plan of the Royal Gardens at Richmond (1735), with drawings of Merlin's Cave and the Hermitage, Queen Caroline's follies, flanking the map. Royal Botanic Gardens, Kew.

> we are subject . . . to two laws. One given immediately to all men by God . . . . The other given by man to man. . . . By the first I mean the universal law of reason; and by the second the particular law, or constitution of laws, by which every distinct community has chosen to be governed. . . . A divine right in kings is to be deduced evidently from [these principles]. A divine right to govern *well*, and conformable to the constitution at the head of which they are placed. A divine right to govern *ill*, is an absurdity: to assert it, is blasphemy . . . good government alone can be in the divine intention.[79]

Princes were charged with empire by God in order that they might defend peace and liberty, and extend the prosperity and civility of their subjects.

It was in alliance with this Augustan vision of monarchy that Frederick Louis, Prince of Wales, his wife Augusta, and their son, George III, came to plant a botanic garden at Kew in opposition to Caroline's Richmond. The Prince, hating his parents, flirted with their political opponents. Frederick leased the White House at Kew, with its fine collection of exotic plants, from the Capel family—a convenient act of identification with a great aristocratic political family which had stood loyal to Charles I, while having opposed, at great cost, James II.[80] More explicitly, Frederick Louis in 1735 accepted Cobham's allegorical invitation and placed in his gardens in Pall Mall statues of King Alfred and the Black Prince, with Latin inscriptions on the former declaring that 'This Prince Was the Founder of the Liberties and Commonwealth of England', and on the later pronouncing his intention of 'making that AMIABLE PRINCE the Pattern of his own CONDUCT'.[81] Frederick put much effort into charming his own supporters, playing cricket, and using his gardens, as he did his art collection, to demonstrate that he was in step with the Augustan ideal of a cultivated and civilizing Prince. In the 1740s, for example, he planned (although never began) a scheme to dig a canal and with the earth removed to create a Mount Parnassus on which busts of Western philosophers might sit opposite to a House of Confucius.[82] In 1748 he called Sloane's museum an 'ornament to the nation', and suggested 'how much it must conduce to the benefit of learning, and how great an honour would redound to *Britain*, to have it established for publick use to the latest posterity'.[83] It is likely that he understood also how the patronage of learning might also conduce and redound to the prestige of princes.

When Frederick Louis in the 1740s projected his garden of exotics, he was responding equally to a new current of Continental cultural influence. Botanic gardens had from the Renaissance been supported by monarchs as collections of the strange and unusual, part of the panoply of ornamental display, and as places where gifted individuals mustered plants to cure disease or to glorify the nation. But with the Enlightenment the humble knowledge of apothecaries became the pastime of the powerful. This depended in part on the power of new systems of classification, and in particular the prestige of Linnaeus. The Swede's importance did not lie in his conversion of all Europe to his methods: many in England stuck to Ray until well into the century, while the French remained faithful to Tournefort, Adanson, Buffon, and Jussieu for all of it. Linnaeus's real contribution was in appearing to make the heights of natural philosophy accessible to those unequipped by extensive training. His aim was that any individual who knew his system would be able to achieve an act of discovery—either placing the plant in its correct class or order or claiming it as rare and unique.[84] Far more than Ray or Tournefort, let alone Newton, Linnaeus brought the frontier of knowledge within reach of amateurs: princes might praise the achievement of the *Principia* to the skies, the *Systema Naturae* instead invited their participation. His system represented a game which allowed its initiates to name and reorder the variety of creation, and helped to make natural history, and botany in particular, more popular in the eighteenth and early nineteenth centuries than any other science then or since.

John Seeley, in a long-forgotten article in the first volume of the *English Historical Review*, described how the cultural power of France from Louis XIV on, and the interlocking ties between the Mediterranean and Central European royal families, produced the 'Bourbonization' of the courts of eighteenth-century Europe.[85] Much of the style of the Absolutist monarchy diffused through Europe—including Britain, although Seeley did not recognize this—imitated in rituals of power and patronage. Even William and Mary, mortal enemies of the Bourbons, turned directly to the Sun King for the model on which they constructed Het Loo and Hampton Court. In much the same way, in the 1720s, 1740s, and 1760s, three generations of Hanoverians formed rival political gardens at Kew under the influence of the Trianon and Rambouillet. Frederick, Augusta, and ultimately George III, borrowed directly from the cultural repertoire of the Rococo princes. Peter the Great in the 1720s, for example, had made a botanic garden the centre of his Imperial Academy of Sciences.[86] The Swedes, a generation later, built their own Royal Academy under the leadership of Linnaeus. Frederick the Great in 1746 similary honoured botany in his reform of his father's Academy of Sciences.[87] In France, as Michel Adanson wrote Bernard de Jussieu in 1751, natural history, and especially botany, had become popular with those at court. Louis XV, already preening under the name *roi–géographe*, started botany lessons, with Madame de Pompadour's encouragement, under Lemonnier, and created new royal botanic gardens at Trianon, Auteuil, and Marly.[88] Francis I by 1753 had begun the great Habsburg collection at Schönbrunn.[89] In many ways this patronage of science represented a reinterpretation of kingship. Louis XIV and Colbert, Charles II, William of Orange, and many others had certainly sponsored science, arts, and letters, with ostentatious generosity. But with the Enlightenment we see an idea of virtuous kingship emerging of the monarch not just as the sponsor of the progress of the nation, but as a participant. For Louis XV, and later for Louis XVI in France and George III in Britain, the botanic garden would provide a conspicuous means of demonstrating such participation.

The creation of a formal botanic garden at Kew resulted from the effort of Augusta, after the death of Frederick Louis in 1751. She had the support of the Earl of Bute. Bute was a true son of the Scottish Enlightenment, with wide interests and expertise in agriculture, architecture, and natural philosophy—he had even travelled to Leiden to study botany with Linnaeus.[90] Peter Collinson, in writing to Linnaeus in 1755, rated Bute as the finest botanist in England.[91] John Hill, one of Bute's circle, in 1758 proposed, doubtless with his patron's encouragement, that Britain should have a botanic garden in Britain which could be compared to the Jardin du Roi.[92] From 1759, the 'Physick Garden' at Kew was planted. With the accession of George III, and the arrival of Bute to the Secretary of Stateship in 1761, the resources available for its development increased immensely.

George III unified the former demesnes of his parents and grandparents. Lancelot 'Capability' Brown remade the gardens, for which Sir William Chambers, former drawing tutor of Prince George and another protégé of Bute, designed a variety of imposing structures. The intergenerational feud between George II and the late Frederick Louis was settled decisively by the Dowager Princess and her son: Carthage, rather than simply being razed, was turned into landscape. George III obliterated the architectural traces of his grandparents and planted instead structures like the Observatory and the Pagoda which glorified the view from the river and from his mother's palace at Kew. A satirical poet mourned the loss:

> To Richmond come, for see, untutor'd Brown
> Destroys those wonders which were once thy own
> Lo, from his melon-ground the peasant slave
> Has rudely rush'd, and levell's Merlin's Cave.[93]

Chambers's constructions may be divided into two categories.[94] The first, including some of the most popular and enduring symbols of Kew, were exotic follies, typical playthings of a royal pleasure ground in the age of Enlightenment—a Mosque, an Alhambra, a House of Confucius, and a Pagoda (illustration 10).[95] But several structures were direct allegorical references to the advance of British power internationally under the Hanoverian dynasty: temples to Arethusa (1758), Victory (commemorating the Battle of Minden, 1761), and the Peace (1763). Kew became fully a theatre in which George III attempted to project the glory of his reign.

Botany was at the centre of this endeavour. In 1763 Chambers wrote:

> The physic or Exotic garden was not begun before the year 1760, so that it cannot possibly be in perfection; but from the great botanical learning of him who is the principal manager, and the assiduity with which all curious productions are collected from every part of the globe, without any regard to expense, it may be concluded that in a few years, this will be the amplest and best collection, in Europe.[96]

Collinson, Bartram, and John Ellis had returned the plant riches of the North American colonies. In 1763, for example, Ellis, appointed as Provincial Agent for the new colony of West Florida, asked the President of the Board of Trade and Plantations to arrange that all his pay should be 'in rare plants and seeds for the Royal Garden at Kew'.[97] William Aiton, a former student of Chelsea Physic Garden, became the keeper of the plants. Bute himself in 1767 claimed sanguinely that 'the Exotick Garden at Kew is by far the richest in Europe ... getting plants and seeds from every Corner of the Habitable world.' Kew, both with ornamental buildings such as its Temple of Victory and its collections of rare plants, came to symbolize the grandeur and civility of Britain after the Seven Years' War.

At Kew we may thus see, in part, how the Hanoverian monarchy shared the style of Continental princes. But we must not assume, *pace* Jonathan Clark, that Britain's *ancien régime* was static, monolithic, or backward looking. If it was devout, its religion sought its certainty in scientific knowledge and in confronting exotic lands and unbelievers. If it was aristocratic or monarchical, its lords and princes had to negotiate with the conflicting interests of the political nation. By the eighteenth century, power was no

10. A view of the oriental follies erected at Kew in the 1760s, from Sir William Chamber's Plans . . . of the Gardens and Buildings at Kew in Surrey *(1763).*

longer principally responsible to itself, with its prerogatives founded securely on divine or oligarchical election. Its legitimacy depended increasingly on the service it rendered to those over whom it presided. Once, God had ordained the compact between king and subject, now many considered that God had merely ordered Nature's efficiency, within which men could choose to submit to good kings. Pope in his *Epistle to Burlington* thus framed government's responsibility to create ports, build roads, encourage religion, dig canals, and, in general, to reorder land and water in the public interest:

Bid harbors open, public Ways extend,
Bid Temples, worthier of the God, ascend
. . .
Back to his bounds their subject Sea command,
and roll obedient Rivers thro' the Land;
These Honours, Peace to happy Britain brings,
these are Imperial Works, and worthy things. (ll. 191–204)

Nature was the theatre in which power might prove its virtue. The future of Kew in the age of Sir Joseph Banks would depend on this faith that kings or empires might purchase their right to rule with plants and gardens.

We should briefly gather the threads of the argument which have so far been laid. In chapter I, we examined how the expansion of European trade and settlement into the wider world shaped the science of botany. Empire transformed the scope and character of European knowledge, as it brought apothecaries and philosophers into contact with both strange plants and with the science and pharmacy of non-European peoples. We may discover this effect more generally, I would suggest, in all of those modes of scientific knowledge which depend on collection and comparison: including astronomy and geophysics, as much as zoology, mineralogy, or anthropology.[98] Botany, like these disciplines, needed the world as a whole to make sense. Empire, as it brought exotic nature and knowledge into the fabric of European learning, changed the environment within which the botanist operated. It might even be argued that Europe's experience of power gave its intellectuals, scientists as much as divines, a confidence in their systems. The Edenic miraculous view of Europe's place as a corner of Creation, as it was represented in the Renaissance *hortus conclusus*, gave way to the ideal of a Nature governed by rational mechanism, with Europe as the mistress of its laws. The success of mathematics and natural philosophy in the age of Newton was, reciprocally, as comforting as the Gospel to those who found themselves at the limits of distant plantations or trading factories. Systems of classification, as much as sextants and chronometers, allowed Europeans to perceive themselves as the magistrates of Providence, equipped by their knowledge of its laws with responsibilities over all of Creation.

In this chapter, we have connected the idea of 'empire', that is of sanctified power, with the history of botany and gardening in England. The knowledge of nature had a central place in one Judaeo-Christian myth of the origins of human sovereignty, within which power over and within nature was a right which had been passed from God to Adam to Solomon, David, and thus through Constantine and Charlemagne to the Christian princes and lords of modern Europe. Science, in the inclusive sense of all learning, was presumed to be practically and politically useful, and thus deserving of patronage.

One aspect of the political value of plants lay in their contribution to the aestheticization of power. Ornamental gardens became part of the mask worn by European princes and potentates, a living equivalent to royal art collections. Exotic plants, by their sheer strangeness and beauty, provided a kind of dignity behind which arbitrary power could hide. Botanical classification, moreover, brought to a culmination in Linnaeus and Jussieu, embroidered these objects of wonder into the fabric of universal truth. By the mid-eighteenth century, at Richmond, as across Europe, botanic gardens, associated at the same time with learning and spectacle, were standard parts of the life of European courts.

Kew, throughout the reign of George III, was a royal pleasure ground. As a botanic garden, its chief purpose was the cultivation and care of spectacular ornamental exotics. The needs of the court excited new British efforts for the collection of exotic plants. Rare plants and animals, for example, became part of the currency of *ancien régime* diplomatic relations. In 1788, for example, France sent seeds and bulbs of European flowers and fruit trees from the Jardin du Roi, together with gardeners, engineers, a physician, a surgeon, and a clock maker, to the court of the Sultan of Mysore.[99] Sir Joseph Banks, who oversaw Kew from 1772 until his death in 1820, similarly selected collections which sweetened Britain's relations with the Princess of Württemburg and Grand Duchess Catherine of Russia.[100] To remain a source of such gifts worthy of a king, the collection at Kew had to be exclusive to the sovereign. Banks was thus furious when he heard that the commercial nursery of Kennedy and Lee had received seeds collected specially for Kew.[101] Banks and William Aiton (its superintendent) refused even to share its riches with the Marquis of Blandford.[102]

Banks, like Bute before him, could depend on amateurs at the fringes of British power to supply the King's Garden with novelties. Merchants stationed in Africa, Asia, or the New World, soldiers and naval officers on foreign campaigns, and planters in British colonies, returned seeds of strange plants.[103] William A'Court, Secretary of the British Legation at Naples, sent papyrus plants.[104] Governors and other senior colonial officials corresponded with special energy, either as private enthusiasts like Raffles, or as actual or prospective beneficiaries of Banks's patronage such as Philip King (Governor of Norfolk Island) or Henry de Ponthieu (keeper of the jail in Antigua).[105]

But this informal system of collectors was supplemented from the 1770s by gardeners sent out to hunt for Kew at Royal expense. In 1772 Francis Masson left to forage in South Africa. Masson's travels represented a turn away from Britain's traditional dependence on the American colonies for new flowers and trees.[106] A unique hoard of specimens from the rich Cape flora fell into the hands of Banks and Aiton. Later horticultural collectors, including James Smith and George Austin in New South Wales in 1789, George Caley in New South Wales in 1798, William Kerr in China in 1803, and Allen Cunningham and James Bowie in Brazil and at the Cape in 1816, extended this southern initiative at the expense of the Crown.[107]

The cost of collecting novelties for Kew was justified by Banks in several ways. Kew Gardens, Banks wrote the Treasury, 'does honour to the science of the country, promotes in some degree its commerce, aids its population, and enables the Sovereign and his Ministers to make acceptable presents to crowned heads'.[108] Banks offered the King a flattering judgement that Masson's collections had contributed to the grandeur of his court by allowing Kew Gardens to attain to 'that acknowledged superiority' it now enjoyed over the Trianon, Paris, Uppsala, and 'every similar establishment in Europe'. The Southern Hemisphere, he suggested in 1815, would supply other plants which could could be kept without the expense of hothouses.[109] These plants, as well as contributing to the dignity of the Crown and benefiting Britain's diplomatic relations, would eventually enrich its horticultural merchants.

With his encouragement, moreover, George III and Charlotte themselves acquired botanical interests. In 1773, one genus of spectacular ornamental plants from among Masson's spoils came to carry the name *Strelitzia*, after Mecklenberg-Strelitz, from which the Queen had come (see Plate 7 of *Strelitzia augusta*, named after both the King's mother and his wife). This was an established way of securing assistance from the King who, in any event, was attracted to the sciences.[110] In 1781, for example, Banks communicated to George III that William Herschel had given the name Georgium Sidus to a new planet (now called Uranus). By 1785, Herschel thanked Banks for thus introducing him to that 'Royal Protection and Patronage', which had enabled Herschel to devote all his time to astronomy.[111] In 1785, similarly, Charlotte required William Aiton, His Majesty's Gardener at Kew, to tutor her in botany.[112] The royal family came to take a personal interest in the botanical collection, with immediate consequences. By 1796 Aiton remarked that the patronage of the Queen was a continual cause of gifts being made to the garden:

> No events, however, have so materially tended to the increase of the Royal Collection, as that decided preference which our most gracious Queen has of late condescended to bestow on the science of Botany, and the rapid progress her Majesty and the Princesses, her daughters, have made in the most difficult parts of that most pleasing study.[113]

Erasmus Darwin in his long poem *The Botanic Garden* used the botanizing of the royal couple at Kew as an emblem for the growth and prosperity of England under George and Charlotte:

> So Sits enthron'd in vegetable pride
> Imperial Kew by Thames's Glittering Side ...
> Sometimes retiring from the public weal
> one tranquil hour the Royal Partners steal;
> Through glades exotic pass with step sublime,
> or mark the growth of England's happier clime;
> With beauty blossom'd, and with virtue blaz'd
> *Mark the fair Scions, they themselves have rais'd*;
> Sweet blooms the Rose, the towering oak expands,
> The Grace and Guard of Britain's golden lands.[114]

Royal horticulture at Kew, in Darwin's hands, symbolized the Hanoverians' patriotic participation in the life of the nation. Why had botany become such a fitting object of royal attention and assistance?

We may note that George III was not the only monarch drawn to botany. Kew was in competition with European royal gardens. In 1815, Banks

11. Detail from bottom of title page of John Gerard's Herbal *(1596)*
Cambridge University Library.

advised Cunningham, the Kew collector who accompanied the H.M.S. *Mermaid* to Northern Australia, that he was privileged to enrich the collections of his royal patron 'with Plants which otherwise will have been added to the Royal Gardens at Paris & have tended to make their collection superior to ours'.[115] Indeed it was in imitation of the French and Spanish, among others, that Banks arranged for the Crown to dispatch collectors on behalf of Kew. As Fagon had sent out collectors to add to the glory of Louis XIV, so Buffon and the Thouins, with the encouragement of Louis XV and Louis XVI, dispatched collectors to all corners of the Earth.[116] Arthur Young commented, after visiting the garden of the Petit Trianon: 'The World has been successfully rifled to decorate it.'[117] The Spanish Bourbons, certainly in imitation of Louis XV's patronage of science, created the Royal Botanic Gardens of Madrid in 1755 and the Royal Natural History Museum in 1776, and in 1777 dispatched an expedition to their New World colonies in order, as Carlos III framed it: 'to foster nature, describing and making drawings of the plants found in these, my fertile dominions, in order to enrich my Museum of Natural History and the Botanical Garden of the Court'.[118] In Portugal the Academy of Sciences of Lisbon in 1781, on the model of Boyle's *Brief Instructions* of a century before, requested Portuguese abroad and in particular every Royal Governor in the colonies to forward specimens, and with the collaboration of the Minister of the Marine dispatched collectors to Brazil, Angola, Mozambique, and São Tomé.[119]

But neither in Britain nor France, Spain, or Portugal was this collecting driven merely by the desire to collect flowers for the King. By the late eighteenth century it was no longer enough for monarchy to suggest its divine origin with plumage stolen from nature. Princes such as Louis XV in France, Frederick the Great in Prussia, and Frederick Louis and George III in Britain sought to show that their power was as useful as it was beautiful.

An image on the title page of John Gerard's *Herbal* (1596) (illustration 11), both recapitulates the journey we have taken, and suggests where the future of the garden lay. The ordered beds of rare herbs, in its foreground, showed the garden as a space of learning. A gentleman and lady in conversation—perhaps Burghley, Gerard's patron, accompanying Elizabeth—presents the place of the ornamental garden within a certain courtly style. In the background, however, there is a third avatar of botany: the field of wheat. In the eighteenth century, this association of the scientific garden with agriculture became particularly important. It was as an economic instrument that the botanic garden, and Gerard's heirs, then found patronage from princes and statesmen who sought to identify their power with that of civil society. The muddy acres of corn provided monarchy with a new kind of dignity.

CHAPTER 3

The Useful Garden: Agriculture and the Science of Government

Royal botanic gardens, in the second half of the eighteenth century, became instruments through which kings (or, more proximately, their ministers) sought to show the virtue of their authority. The key was agriculture, which Banks and his contemporaries expected could, with the help of science, make estates, nations, or colonies self-sufficient or wealthy. This was an age in which Louis XVI chose to wear a *boutonnière* made from potato flowers presented him by Parmentier. The relationship of the science of plants to the management of land and people, and thus to political and economic ideas, is the subject of this chapter. It was through its connection to agriculture that botany at the King's Garden played its role in the making of the Second British Empire.

That agriculture might yield a politic plenty, encouraged by royal power and assisted by science, was by no means new, however, in the age of George III. Many medieval English kings had sought to enrich their state through the enclosure and manuring of Crown lands.[1] Closer to hand, James I had in 1620 proposed the enclosure of 12,000 acres, the drainage of 4,000, and the plantation of mulberry for silkworms.[2] It was below, however, among their subjects, that agricultural improvement became an almost sacred cause. The history of the royal garden at Kew after 1780, and indeed the career of Sir Joseph Banks, is in part the story of how Enlightened monarchy sought to attach itself to these rural virtues. Let us trace the origins of these agrarian enthusiasms, and assess their place in the politics and culture of Imperial Britain in the eighteenth century.

The Enclosure of Eden

Adam, in the book of *Genesis*, had two identities. If Adam the Sovereign, on the one hand, presided over nature, Adam the Toiler, on the other, was charged with perfecting the fallen world with his skill and labour. Agriculture was an art which led men back to their original communion with God. Gervase Markham thus advised that manuring was 'the reducing of the earth to his first goodnesse'.[3] Henry Plat in *The New and Admirable Art of Setting Corne* (1600) alluded also to the original garden, adorning his title page with a drawing of a spade wrapped in a banner with the legend: 'Adams Toole Revived'.[4] Adolphus Speed's account of husbandry, similarly, appeared under the millenarian title: *Adam out of Eden* (1659). The improvement of agriculture had a moral character, preventing famine, creating employment, and transforming land left idle or inefficiently used into sustenance for human bodies and souls.[5] This had obvious importance in early modern Britain, which in the 1590s and 1620s had felt the edge of famine.[6] Gabriel Plattes, in his *A Discovery of Infinite Treasure* (1639), thus claimed that the only approved medicine for 'an Overcrowded Common-wealth [could be] good improvements of the earth'. Agriculture, as the basis of a peaceful and prosperous kingdom, was patriotic labour. In the *Boke of Husbandry* (1534), Fitzherbert offers his agricultural knowledge 'to the weale of this mooste noble realme', while his publisher deemed *Xenephons Treatise of Household* (1534), 'for the welthe of this realme ... very profitable to be red'. Farming and grazing also had other positive consequences. Burghley believed, for example, that agriculture made the lower order more governable than textile manufacture.[7] Bacon, similarly, in his essay 'Of the True Greatness of Kingdoms and Estates', urged that agriculture would toughen yeomen into material fit for an army.[8]

The improvement of agriculture depended, for contemporaries, on private property. Indeed the verb 'to improve', which we use in the sense of 'to ameliorate' or 'to perfect', originally meant to put to a profit, and in particular to enclose 'waste' or common land.[9] Not everyone agreed that 'improvement', and the expansion of the frontier of private farming and grazing, had necessarily such positive consequences. Its critics, including the magus John Dee, argued that enclosure led to the replacement of people with sheep, and thus unemployment and homelessness.[10] Dee also drew attention to the 'Incredible spoyle of Woods and Forests', for which he particularly blamed the smelters of iron. Those who privatized land, or planted foundries, argued however that their prosperity was in everyone's interest. The wealth of the realm was to arise from the private profit of farmers—some of whom might become rich while others stayed poor, since, as Fitzherbert noted in *The Boke of Surveying and Improvements* ([1523] 1560), God had 'ordeyned dyvers estates and degrees in hys people and creatures'.

Seventeenth- and eighteenth-century versions of the debate would merely recapitulate the case put in a dialogue of 1581: to the complaint of the Husbandman that 'by these Inclosures many doe lack lyvinges and be ydle', the Knight replied:

> Experience should seeme to prove playnely that Inclosure should be profitable and not hurtful to the Commonweale: for we see y countres wheremost Inclosures be, are the most wealthy: as Essex, Kent, Northamptonshire etc. ... Tenaunts in common bee not so good Husbands as when every Man has his part in Severalty.[11]

Private profit led necessarily to the best use of resources. As an English Republican argued in 1654:

> the greatest advantage to the Commonwealth ... [is] when [land] is imployed unto that use ... for which it is fittest, and in such a manner, that the greatest proportion of profit may be raised.[12]

Enclosure was also later defended on Republican grounds. Lee in 1654 described common fields as 'the Conqueror's curse', arguing that the Normans arranged things so that their subjects would be too busy squabbling among each other over the use of common resources to combine against despotic monarchs.[13] Through enclosure a landowning class could arise with the means to defend the nation's liberty.

The cult of 'improvement' turned as much on the faith that reason might enable men to use resources more efficiently. Within England, between 1560 and 1673, contemporaries could see how canal drainage, floating meadows, burnbaking, liming, marling, and the planting of turnips, sainfoin, and clover had added to the prosperity of farmers.[14] The disciples of Bacon believed that the fertility of land might be multiplied as much as tenfold through the application of these techniques, and others which would be revealed through natural philosophy.[15] They fitted 'improvement' through knowledge of plants, soils, and chemicals into an eschatology which was as much scientific and patriotic as it was Christian. Husbandry, Hartlib advised, was 'the Mother of all other Trades and Scientificall Industries', and compared its improvement to the work of reforming and diffusing religion.[16] Cressy Dymock exulted that through the propagation of agricultural knowledge the English might 'make our valleys stand so thicke with corn that they shall laugh and sing'.[17] 'God', Walter Blith began *The English Improover* (1649), 'was the original and first Husbandman', and the farmer could, through fencing and drainage, reclaim his corner of Creation.[18] The title page of his second edition—*The English Improver Improved* (1652), which he dedicated to Cromwell and the Council of State—was crowned with the emblem 'Vive la Republick', with the swords of the New Model Army being turned into the ploughshares of Providential abundance, and the English Republican, in the detail at the bottom, turned into the surveyor (and improver) of the world (illustration 12). Science joined to private property would make the Earth again abundant: England, he argued, might become the 'the paradise of the World, if we can but bring ingenuity into fashion'. As Adam's heirs recovered his insight into Nature, they would reclaim Eden's plenty.

The Royal Society, from its foundation in 1660, made agriculture and forestry one of its central concerns.[19] The chemistry and physics of plant growth, as I discussed in chapter 1, became a focus of earnest discussion, with Robert Sharrock publishing a *History of the Propagation and Improvement of Vegetables* (1660). The brightest lights of the Society, including Boyle and Newton, turned attention to the problem of vegetative growth. A Georgical

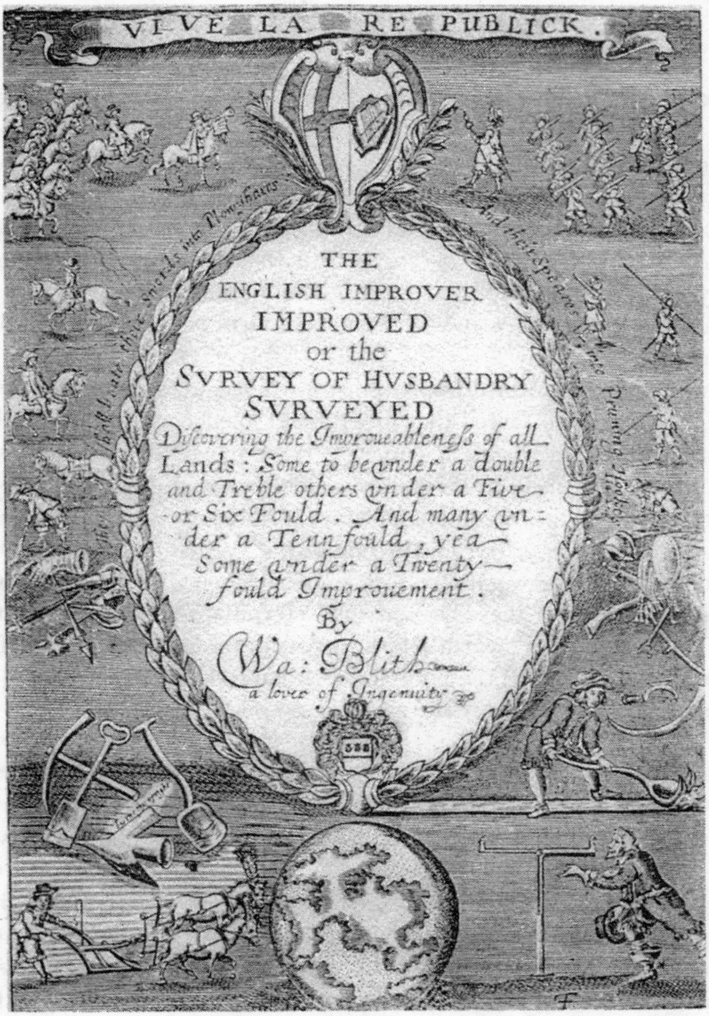

12. Title page of Blith's The English Improver Improved *(1652), showing the swords of the New Model Army turned into the ploughshares and pruning hooks of Providential abundance.*

Committee investigated how 'waste lands, healthy grounds and boggs may be well employed and improuved', for agricultural plenty was understood to be the basis of social peace.[20] The Royal Society was equally concerned about the danger that English forests could no longer meet the timber needs of the Royal Navy.[21] John Evelyn, its Secretary, for example, formed a patriotic and scientific argument for the planting of trees and the better tending of the earth in *Sylva* (1664). Evelyn argued that as 'philosophers' equipped with learning, landlords would be better equipped to manage their estates. From this early period, a faith in science penetrating the mysteries of the world, with natural knowledge assumed to have a divine origin, lent support to the idea of agricultural improvement through private property. Just as Hartlib and Blith had justified enclosure in terms of the techniques which the Adamic volunteer brought with him, so Evelyn and his contemporaries saw the philosophical landlord as a Providential agent. Matthew Hale in his *The Primitive Origination of Mankind* (1677) indeed provided a theory of God as a landlord who had appointed man his 'steward' or 'bayliff', and who collected in exchange the rent of prayer and thanksgiving. John Houghton, similarly, in his pamphlets on the improvement of husbandry and trade juxtaposed quotations from *Genesis* with reports of farm prices and discussions of experimental philosophy.[22]

The work of agricultural improvement, guided by science and revealed religion, was a task so sacred that it justified violence and coercion. Hartlib argued that governments should in fact be equipped with powers to force farmers to improve their land: 'it were a noble piece of policy and justice if authority should oblige or compel men into it'.[23] He advised the appointment of 'Publique Stewards or Surveyors, one of the Husbandry, the other of the Woods of this Commonwealth'.[24] Blith similarly argued for the need for laws against idleness so that 'these Drones and Caterpillars the bane of a Christian State . . . would not so swarm among us', while Moore in 1653 defended enclosure as encouraging the poor to work hard at making the land rich.[25] Plattes similarly contended that

> It is the Interest of the Commonwealth, that every subject should make a right use of his own Estate ... [thus] a Guardian should be set over the person and Estate, not only of Madmen, but of all prodigal Persons.[26]

The enclosure of common land and the raising of rent were moral and patriotic responsibilities. The prodigal would be forced to be fruitful. Andrew Yarranton in *England's Improvement by Land and Sea* (1673) urged that poor children whom the land could not support should be confined in 'Schools', where, sitting on benches, they would labour under the gaze of a pulpit and the discipline of the rod. While the girls weaved lace, the boys would make toys, in what we would call an assembly line, some forming heads, others bodies, a few painting the finished objects.[27] The discipline of the improving landlord could be applied far from the happy corn.

It may indeed be argued that this Christian agrarian tradition is a strand of English social and political thought which has not so far received adequate historical attention. It contains within it embryonic reflections on unemployment, the role of private initiative and state action in economic growth, the relationship of wealth to poverty, the equilibrium of population and food supply, and the place of science in managing resources. Agriculture, as it embraced the government of land and people, provided a language through which Classical concerns about the nature of the state found new inflection. Mandeville, Adam Smith, Malthus, the Utilitarians and the Keynesians, are all, in varying ways, in dialogue with it. The economics of Eden could embrace society and state, trade, colonies, and the world.

Corn and Periphery

The ideology of agrarian improvement, as it arose in early modern England, joined Christian Providentialism, patriotism, and the ambitions of natural philosophy to the cupidity of landlords. This potent mixture quickly found application beyond the soil of England.

In Ireland, the claim of territory by the ancient right of the English Crown was supplemented by the doctrine that its lands were either unoccupied or not efficiently used.[28] The English and Scots undertook to reclaim the Irish wastes, and in the process to redeem the barbarous Irish themselves. Edmund Spenser in *A View of the Present State of Ireland* (1596) urged that husbandry, 'the nurse of thrift and the daughter of industry', would lead the Irish away from 'barbarism and savage life' turning them from thieves and rebels into contented farmers with a stake in the peace. *A Direction for the Plantation in Ulster* (1610) argued that unless towns were planted and land ploughed, castles and forts could never secure Ireland. For Francis Bacon in 1603, agriculture was central to England and Scotland's civilizing mission in Ireland. We shall, he wrote,

> reclaim them from their barbarous manners ... [and] populate plant and make civil all the provinces of that kingdom ... as we are persuaded that it is one of the chief causes for the which God hath brought us to the imperial crown of these Kingdoms.[29]

Overseas, as at home, agriculture justified taking land without others' consent. In the aftermath of Cromwell's bloody campaign, Gerard Boate in *Ireland's Naturall History* (1652) argued that the conquerors were making Ireland fruitful through manuring and drainage.[30] The Irish, on the other hand, he suggested, had caused the decline of their country into bog and marshland: 'daily [they] let more & more of their good land grow boggy through their carelessness, whereby also most of the Bogs at first were caused'.[31] The English would not only save Ireland from the Irish, but make it rich since 'all the [iron, lead, and silver] Mines in Ireland [were] discovered by the New-English.'[32] William Petty and other of the Commonwealth's philosophers promised that through surveying, canal drainage, new roads, and harbours, the western kingdom would be civilized.[33] The Act of 1662 which encouraged 'Protestant-Strangers and others, to Inhabit and Plant in the Kingdom of Ireland' similarly presented agriculture as both the purpose and best means of colonization.

In Virginia and Massachusetts, agriculture had a similar importance, as conquest there was also justified by use and Adamic right.[34] *Nova Britannia*, which urged the extension of the Virginia plantation, charged that such territories could not remain in the hands of 'savage people ...who have no Christian or civil use of any thing'.[35] Indians, it argued, had 'no law but nature'. Robert Cushman, in a later tract on *The Lawfulness of Removing out of England into the Parts of America*, argued similarly that Indians were not industrious, 'neither having art, science, skill or faculty to use either the land or the commodities of it; but all spoils, rots, and is marred for want of manuring, gathering, ordering, etc. ... [Indians] do but run over the grass, as do also the foxes and wild beasts', thus their land was 'spacious and void' free for English taking.[36] John Winthrop similarly distinguished between settler's 'civil right' to the soil against the Indians mere 'natural right': 'As for the Natives of New England ... they inclose noe Land, neither have they any setled habytation, nor any tame Cattle to improve the Land', the country was thus 'open to any that could and would improve it.' The minister John Cotton concurred: 'In a vacant soyle ... hee that taketh possession of it, and bestoweth culture and husbandry upon it, his Right it is.' The American Indians were vagrants who had wasted nature's wealth and thus forfeited their claim to their lands. But they might still benefit as the New English covered 'their naked miserre, with civil use of foode, and clothing', sharing the blessings of Christ and sedentary agriculture. The cause of agrarian improvement was exported wholesale, and the Virginian settlers who sailed on the *Supply* in 1620 left equipped with a library of agricultural works including Heresbach's treatises on *Landwirtshaft*.[37] As in the English fens, the improving farmer predicted that in America 'our intrusion ... shall tend to their great good'.[38] The author of *Nova Britannia* assured prospective settlers that the barbarian children of Virginia would come 'to bless the day when first their father saw your faces'. The landlord appointed by Providence became the heroic colonist.

Agrarian thinkers never separated agriculture from commerce. John Worlidge in the *Systema Agriculturae*, for example, always reminded his readers of 'the great advantages that Husbandry bringeth to Trade, and the dependencies the latter hath on the former'.[39] Lewis Roberts, after asserting that the earth was 'the fountaine and mother of all riches and abundance of the world', proposed in *The Merchant's Map of Commerce* (1638) that Britain might make London the centre of the world's trade.[40] Agriculture was the foundation of trade, and the basis of wool, leather, and other industries, and the source of foodstuffs and luxuries through which England might preserve its independence, and possibly become rich.

Colonial agriculture was central to this project. In 'A Discourse of Western Planting', Hakluyt argued that new colonies would provide a means for the export of surplus population, and for the vast expansion of opportunities for employment of all kinds.[41] A pamphleteer of 1620 urged that Britain might secure from Virginia all the raw materials and luxuries it now imported from outsiders: colonial agriculture and hunting would save the bullion now squandered on Russian furs, Scandinavian and Baltic masts, planks, pitch, tar, hemp, and flax, Spanish sugar, wine, and fruit, and Persian silks.[42] In his essay 'Of Plantations', Bacon, who was himself involved in the Virginia and East India Companies, added to the list tobacco, timber, drugs, and perfumes.[43] It was not coincidental that the age of Hartlib and Evelyn also saw the passage of the Navigation Acts (1651, 1660, 1662) and wars with the Protestant Dutch (1652–4, 1665–7, 1672–4) which were driven, in part, by commercial ambition.[44] Agrarian improvement, and the imperialism of settlement it sustained, were from the the seventeenth century in partnership with naval and mercantile expansion.[45]

We may understand 'mercantilism' to mean the attempt to unify and integrate economic activity, by state action, and in order to add to the power of the state, over the space of a nation and its colonies.[46] Trade, the business of 'selling more to strangers yearly than we consume of theirs in value' was only partly the end of the Navigation Acts.[47] Profit, the building of ships, and the toughening of seamen, were also means through which a nation might preserve its liberties. Indeed through wealth, one power might impose its religion on others. Benjamin Worsley, Secretary of Cromwell's 'Office of Husbandry and Traffic', Surgeon-General and Apothecary to the Army in Ireland, and one of the principal figures behind the 1651 Navigation Act, suggested that commercial empire might allow Britain to become *defensor pacis* within Europe, and implicitly a Protestant superpower. England, he urged, restating the medieval imperial idea in its pristine form, might 'sitt as judge and Umpire of al Christian differences, and may draw and ingross the blessings and promises to ourselves that are made Peace makers'.[48] Even those who were less optimistic about Britain's ability to impose its religious will on Spain or France agreed with Henry Robinson in *England's Safety in Trade's Increase* (1641) that if Britain did not expand its plantations and commercial reach into Africa, the East and West Indies, it would become the footstool of the Iberian powers or the United Provinces.[49] The nation's sovereignty depended on its economic health which in turn rested on the share it secured of the world's trade.

Agriculture occupied centre stage in many contemporary schemes for reforming the British economy. In Gabriel Plattes's utopian *Description of the Famous Kingdome of Macaria* (1641), the state guided the growth of husbandry, fishing, and trade by land and sea through distinct agencies.[50] The 'Councell of Husbandry', first of these, was charged with applying the proceeds from 5% death duties to improving land, highways, and bridges, so that 'the whole Kingdome is like to fruitfull Garden'.[51] William Goffe, the future regicide, similarly projected in 1641 a government of improvement which would awaken agriculture and iron smelting as it nurtured a fleet of fishermen and merchants.[52] Robinson, in 1652, translated Plattes's vision into an economic programme which joined agricultural reform to the expansion of trade, the widening of rivers, and the building of roads and bridges.[53] Yarranton in 1673 projected that an entirely new financial system might be founded on land and agriculture. A 'Publick Bank' based on a national register of property, would map credit for foreign trade onto the national territory, so that 'every acre of land ... [would] trade all the world over'.[54] A 'Publique Granary' would similarly allow merchants to store corn for later sale, and to trade or borrow on its potential value, since their deposits were registered at the Guild Hall in the City of London. His 'Publique-bank-Granaries', which we would now call a Commodity Futures Exchange, would attract speculation on the price of corn, thus 'fetch[ing] out all moneys now Unimploy'd' and providing capital for trade.[55] The ideal of agricultural improvement had thus come to inform projects for turning nature into capital that embraced every kind of economic activity.

As in the case of domestic 'improvement', the enclosure of agrarian colonies and of their trade also took encouragement from the sciences, as much as from religion and patriotism.[56] Colonies were involved, in part, in a Providential natural philosophy. Samuel Hartlib, dedicating Gerard Boate's *Ireland's Naturall History* (1652) to Cromwell, promised that this was the age in which Man would regain those powers which Adam lost when an angry Creator had closed 'the conduit pipes of Natural Knowledge', soon the 'Intellectual Cabinets of Nature [would be] opened ... [and] Spiritual and Natural Sanctified Knowledge' liberated.[57] Ireland, under English care, he and Boate argued, was to be the immediate beneficiary of this scientific revelation. Natural philosophy, if it did not foreshadow the millennium, might still help to develop new sources of riches. Puritans like John Winthrop, Jr. and Robert Child carried equivalent scientific concerns to New England.[58] Winthrop, for example, sought through alchemical skill to discover metal ores and improve agriculture, and with Child encouraged the rise of iron foundries at Saugus and Lynn in Massachusetts.[59] Worsley promised that by applying its philosophy to Caribbean plantations, Britain might, *inter alia*, supply itself and all Europe with the sugar then bought from the Dutch, and employ all its citizens.[60]

As they guided surveying and exploitation, the sciences encouraged settlers to think they would use resources more efficiently than locals. William Petty, a founder of the Royal Society, argued in his *Political Anatomy of Ireland* (1691), that the subjugation of the Irish was justified, in part, by their lack of 'Geometry, Astronomy, Anatomy, Architecture, Engineering ...'.[61] Colonial annexation meant, implicitly, the inclusion of barbarians within a space sanctified by learning as much as by religion or law. Indeed, Petty, borrowing from the vocabulary of the contemporary sciences, described colonial rule as political alchemy, the work of '*transmuting* one people into another'.[62] He priced the base metal of the Irish at the going rates for African slaves, £25 for men, £15 for women, and £5 for children, and suggested that England would make its inhabitants worth £70, the golden value of Englishmen. People might be 'improved' as easily as land, if submitted to the discipline of those gifted by their knowledge for government.

The Scientific Revolution, equally, lent support to the mercantilist vision of commercial empire. It provided a vision of Nature ordered by laws, and subject in turn to those who discovered these rules. The simple formulae with which Robert Hooke and Robert Boyle were able to link force and extension, pressure and volume, and the laws with which Newton explained the movement of cannon balls on earth and the most distant stars, suggested that Britain had particular access to Providential truth. The tools of measurement, calculation, and comparison used for the natural world now constructed human society as governed equally by process and mechanism.[63] William Petty, Charles Davenant, and Gregory King proceeded, in the late seventeenth century, to survey the human and material wealth of the kingdom, confident that they might elucidate the principles which regulated its development.[64] The apparently irresistible logic of statistics affected domestic debates about expansion. For 'political arithmetic' encouraged Britain to take the Dutch Republic as its model, to continue its reach for Atlantic and Asian trade, and to reorganize taxation around this international exchange. Science, inherently expansive in its universal appetites, thus helped to commit Britain to this 'Blue Water' destiny: expansion and empire were made into the facts of a rational Providence.

The agrarian tradition, it is true, produced its own critics. Petty attacked the emphasis of Hartlib and his circle on the English farmer. While agreeing that the Husbandman was 'the pillar of any Commonwealth', he argued in *Political Arithmetick* that a seaman was worth three farmers.[65] Pointing to the Dutch, he argued that more was to be gained from manufacture than from husbandry, and more from trade than manufacture. The wealth of a nation was determined by its share of the world's trade. But Petty, while warning against punishing trade on behalf of agriculture, still affirmed that corn, wool, meat, sugar, tobacco, indigo, spices, and drugs were the basis of commerce. Like the Victorian enemies of the Navigation Acts a few generations after, Petty and others who prized trade as the basis of national prosperity and security were not agriculture's enemies. They merely urged the nation to enclose and improve the world as a whole, and not just its original territory.

Out of the economics of Eden had come an ideology of development which was fundamental to the making of the British Empire. The haphazard system of sugar islands, African and Indian trading outposts, Newfoundland fisheries, American bread and tobacco colonies was held together by an alliance of the farmer, the colonist, the merchant, religion, and science. God had given the world to any who was willing to apply labour and knowledge to making it 'like to fruitfull Garden'. As John Locke argued in his *Second Treatise of Government*, while God had given the world to men in common, 'it cannot be supposed that he meant it should always remain common and uncultivated. He gave it for the use of the Industrious and Rational.'[66]

Improving Gentlemen and the First British Empire

An 'Industrious and Rational' landlord, John Smith, made an appeal in *England's Improvement Reviv'd* (1673) for the alliance of commerce and agriculture. Venice, Genoa, the Hanse towns, and Holland, he argued, showed that trade was the principal source of national wealth and power. But the basis of such trade was agriculture. Thus he argued: 'Let no man spare charges according to his abilities in improving his land ... every foot of land in England should be improved that is capable of improvement.'[67] But at the end of his book Smith added an aesthetic and scientific excursion to his politico-economic discourse. He offered detailed instructions for planting 200 acres for pleasure as well as profit, recommending open grass, a maze folded around a marble fountain, a bowling green, plum trees cut into topiary, rows of quince trees, beds of roses and exotic flowers, with plots of licorice, asparagus, and tobacco, and with a 'Physick Garden ... with Roots, Herbs, and Seed to preserve your health'. He concluded with a list of herbs recommended with their medicinal properties.[68]

This mixture of an economic essay with a gentleman's manual of horticulture and medicine had many precedents. Evelyn's *Sylva* included his 'kalendarium hortense', a gardener's guide, together with discussion of botany and of the need for a national forest policy. Gervase Markham, a generation before, had joined agricultural advice and patriotic appeals for improvement to advice on 'recreations meete for a gentleman'.[69] He advised them on *Excellent and New Invented Knots and Mazes* (1623), hunting, horsemanship, hawking, shooting, and angling, while sharing a juicy tale about 'The Famous Whore'.[70] John Smith in *Pleasure and Profit United* (1684), an 'exact treatise' on husbandry—the first chapter of which advised 'How to Know If Your Cow is Desirous of the Bull'—also offered his recommendations on 'The Art of Angling, Hunting, Hawking, and the Noble Recreation of Ringing and making Fireworks'. These authors remind us that the hero of the drama of agrarian improvement was the private landlord, who was driven by private delight as much as by the urge to make his country (or himself) rich and secure. His prudence, industry, and patriotism would be visible in the beauty of his estate, the range of his amusements, and, sometimes, his learning. We should not be surprised that the Royal Society, until the middle of the nineteenth century, was dominated by aristocrats and rich farmers. The 'virtuoso tradition' which linked Evelyn to Sir Hans Sloane in the 1740s or Sir Joseph Banks in the 1780s, has its roots in the cultural appetites of English landowners.[71] As Locke argued in his *First Treatise*, God's command to Man to 'be fruitful' included 'the improvement too of Arts and Sciences, and the Conveniences of Life'.[72] The virtuous landlord could preside over the perfection of learning and landscape as well as manuring and drainage.

The political settlement of 1688 rested in theory and practice on the power and virtue of the landowning classes. The 'Ancient Constitution' had depended on the mythic engagement of Saxon farmers with the English soil.[73] John Locke in his *Two Treatises of Government* thus made the *zoon oekonomikon*, an Adamic volunteer who mixed his labour with nature, into the basis of political society. The agrarian theory of liberty supported the new constitutional arrangements which subjected all central power to the control of a parliament based essentially on landed wealth. The landlord, Augustan authors asserted, had a permanent interest in the nation, and the independent means to defend its liberties.[74] Agriculture remained central to the identity of Britain's political classes, throughout the eighteenth century, even after East India and slave merchants and absentee West Indian planters entered their ranks. The new money usually sought to cleanse itself by buying into land.

Government and Opposition, Whig and Tory, came to appeal to the Roman ideal of the farmer–statesman. George II thus invited Jethro Tull to explain his system, Queen Caroline subscribed to *Horse-hoeing Husbandry*, and Robert Walpole boasted that he opened the letters of his farm steward before he broke the seal on state papers.[75] Walpole enclosed and drained new Norfolk acres, and planted them with root crops, as 'Turnip Townshend', his brother-in-law and political ally, had recommended. Bolingbroke, in turn, adorned Dawley Farm with images of ricks, spades, and prongs, winning Whig jeers that 'Dawley has become famous for a Great Cry and little Wool. Tup Harry become Mutton master.'[76] Whig opponents of Robert Walpole and his 'Robinocracy', such as Cobham, similarly represented themselves as patriots rooted in the soil of England standing against a system of patronage, coercion, and ever-increasing public debt which found its centre in the Court and the City of London. The land sanctified many kinds of political initiative.

What is sometimes forgotten, however, is that neither government nor opposition, whatever their hesitations about the domestic consequences of overseas expansion, ever proposed that Britain should surrender its ultramarine interests.[77] The supporters of the 1688 settlement and of the Hanoverians recognized that overseas trade and colonies allowed Britain to wage expensive wars, and thus to secure its independence. The growth of the Royal Navy, expeditions to the Low Countries, and subsidies to allies depended on a tariff regime which in 1784, for example, placed a duty of 24 shillings on a hundredweight of sugar of 26 shillings value.[78] Commerce with the West and East Indies, Africa, and America, and the re-exports it provided, allowed land taxes to remain relatively low, while fattening the banks and fundholders of the City of London, and filling the purses of placemen. West Indian sugar, Virginian tobacco, Carolinian rice, and Georgian cotton were, in any event, considered as British as Suffolk wheat. Pitt the Elder characteristically affirmed that 'the sugar islands [are part of] the landed interest of this kingdom and it was barbarism to consider it otherwise'.[79] East Indian and West Indian wealth, of course, had allowed the Pitt and Beckford families to enter politics, as much as they contributed powerfully, as Burke suggested, to national prosperity.[80] It was not surprising that the 'Country' opposition joined agrarian themes to complaints that Walpole had neglected Britain's Atlantic interests.[81] Those who knew Rome's history did fear that territorial empire could endanger liberty by creating a standing army which a Caesar or Cromwell might command against the people. But they had no quarrel with navies and trade, which were seen to complement the landed interest. Bolingbroke in the closing lines of *The Idea of a Patriot King* made such a claim explicit, dreaming of a future in which Britons would be

> busy to improve their private property and the public stock; fleets covering the ocean, bringing home wealth by the returns of industry, carrying assistance and terror abroad by the direction of wisdom, and asserting triumphantly the right and honour of Great Britain, as far as waters roll and winds can waft them.[82]

As Kramnick comments, *Patriot King* of 1739 and 'Rule Britannia' of 1740 represent a 'unique marriage of the gentry and the trader'.[83] This alliance of agrarianism and mercantilism was at the basis of Hanoverian politics and, perhaps, of an emerging British national identity.[84]

Agriculture retained a political and cultural primacy, even as commerce, to which it was allied, began to eclipse its economic significance. For Atlantic trade, dominated by sugar and slaves, was the most dynamic sphere of Britain's eighteenth-century economy.[85] It was vital to the growth of London, Bristol, Glasgow, and Liverpool, to cotton and iron working, shipping, insurance, banking, and to over three million new non-agricultural jobs between 1700 and 1801.[86] The importance of India, the United States, and the home market in the nineteenth and twentieth centuries has, to a considerable extent, distorted our approach to Britain's eighteenth-century empire. Atlantic trade, by which we mean principally slaves, the goods which purchased slaves, the foods slaves ate, and the commodities wrested from nature by slaves, was overwhelmingly larger than trade with Asia:[87]

Atlantic vs. East Indian Trade

	1761–1765		1781–1785		1786–1790	
(£ millions)	Exports	Imports	Exports	Imports	Exports	Imports
Atlantic	3.583	3.71	4.053	3.537	5.103	4.671
East India	0.976	1.102	0.93	2.03	1.914	3.31

The East was of merely supplementary interest. It is worth noticing also the relative importance of the West Indies to North America. In 1697, for example, British imports from Barbados were five times in value those from the bread colonies, while imports from Jamaica in 1773 were in a similar proportion to imports from the mainland. Montserrat (24 square miles) produced three times the value of British imports than Pennsylvania between 1714 and 1773, Nevis (around 60 square miles) generated about three times as much imports as New York during the same half-century, and Antigua (about 100 square miles) three times those of New England. One-third of all British exports were tropical re-exports, while the luxuries of Calcutta and Canton had to be bought with either the silver of New Granada or African and Brazilian gold, and while much of the East India Company's cloth revenue could only be recouped as specie through exchange in Africa for slaves to be sold in the Iberian New World.[88] Domestic textile and metal industries found relief from stagnant European markets in Atlantic trade, which in 1772 took 72% of Yorkshire's woollens and 90% of broadcloth, and about 40% of its copper and brass.[89] At the same time, new tastes for tea, coffee, tobacco, sugar, chocolate, generated new patterns of consumption and sociability.[90] Notwithstanding some twentieth-century economic historians of Britain, the British Empire under the 'Old Colonial System' was as Postlethwayt put it: 'a magnificent superstructure of American commerce and naval power on an African foundation'.[91] If the Hanoverian British were indeed Blackstone's 'polite and commercial people', their commerce was driven by international exchange, and their politeness was consummated over sweetened tea.

This system of overseas agricultural and commercial interests shaped the course of British experience in the eighteenth century. Its expansion and defence were central priorities prosecuted on every known continent and ocean in the Wars of the Spanish Succession (1701–13) and Austrian Succession (1739–48), the Seven Years' War (1756–63), and the War of the American Revolution (1776–83). New imperial opportunities, and the taxes needed to pay for these wars, carried social upheaval in their wake. Many controversies which historians have tended to treat as if they were part of a purely domestic history—such as the South Sea Bubble (1720), the Excise Crisis (1733), or the larger Augustan debate about public debt and commercial society—were ultimately consequences of Britain's imperial history, and reflected, in particular, the importance of Atlantic trade in the economy and politics of the nation. The 'Financial Revolution', from which these crises flowed, depended, after all, on long-distance trade and the domestic employment and consumption it engendered. The colonial farmers who rebelled in North America in the 1760s and 1770s rose initially to revise their place in these arrangements, before they found reasons to oppose the Crown. It was, after all, the enforcement of the Molasses Act (1733) and the Sugar Act (1764) during and after the Seven Years' War which first prompted 'No Taxation without Representation', and turned Samuel Adams into a patriot.

The pleasure and splendour of Hanoverian England rested, equally, on slave agriculture and the imperial economy which surrounded it. West and East Indian fortunes supported the building of country houses such as Fonthill in Wiltshire, of libraries such as the Codrington in Oxford, and of careers, such as Sir Hans Sloane's. Colonial gentlemen also graced the Royal Society, returning specimens and observations, as well as sugar and tobacco.[92] We have much still to learn about how books, religious and scientific controversy, taste and fashion moved between the centres and peripheries of the British Empire in the eighteenth century.[93]

What should be recognized however is that Agriculture was the cause which tended to precede other kinds of cultural initiative. The improvement of agriculture was the most important stimulus for the empire's gentlemen when they came to constitute such learned societies as the Dublin Society for Improving Husbandry, Manufactures, and other Useful Arts (1734), the Society for Improvers in the Knowledge of Agriculture of Scotland (1734), the Society for the Encouragement of Arts, Manufactures, and Commerce of England (1754), the Society for Promoting Arts, Agriculture, and Oeconomy of New York (1764), the Society for the Encouragement of Natural History and Useful Arts of Barbados (1784), and the Physico-Medical Society of Grenada (1791).[94] The Society of Arts in England, for example, the most important of these, made domestic and colonial agriculture the centre of an enterprise which encompassed metallurgy, machines, trade, and natural history, as well as the 'polite arts' of painting.[95] The 'virtuoso' was, as we noted earlier, usually first a farmer.

In these new associations we may observe, in part, the continuation of older patterns. These gentlemen's societies were the culmination of the patriotic agrarianism of the previous century, which new authors and editions had introduced to a Hanoverian readership.[96] The Society of Arts clearly saw itself as taking the baton from Bacon and Evelyn, most obviously in its proposal in 1755 for 'the planting of timber trees in the commons and waste ground all over the kingdom, for the supply of the Navy, the employment and advantage of the poor, as well as the ornamenting of the nation'.[97] The Society's programme for the reform of colonial agriculture and trade also had clear Restoration precedents. Thomas Sprat in 1667 had urged, on behalf of the Royal Society, that gentlemen should 'experiment' with 'transplanting the Eastern spices and other useful Vegetables, into our Western Plantations', and with raising hemp and silkworms in Ireland and Virginia. It cannot be wholly coincidental that the first colonial 'premium' issued by the Society of Arts in 1755 was for the cultivation of silk in America. Over the next decade it issued a number of premiums for the introduction to Britain's New World colonies of Asian and African plants, including indigo, coffee, cotton, cloves, vanilla, opium, nutmeg, mace, camphor, pepper, tea, breadfruit, mangoes, and cinnamon.[98] In March 1759, for example, it issued a Gold Medal to reward the first person 'to preserve the seeds of spice trees' in transit from the East Indies, and in 1767 for the introduction into America of Senegambian cotton.[99]

Scientific agriculture was to serve Britain's mercantile interests, as Sprat had projected a century before, planting in its possessions those commodities which it traditionally purchased from the Dutch, French, or Spanish, or Asian and African princelings. To this end, the Society of Arts, during the Seven Years' War, came to encourage the creation of colonial botanic gardens to facilitate this plant exchange. Its Committee on Colonies and Trade in 1759 proposed the planting of 'Provincial Gardens' in American colonies where 'experiments' in introducing new plants might be conducted and, from 1762 onwards, it announced prizes for anyone who would cultivate a spot in the West Indies 'in which plants, useful in medicine, and profitable as articles of commerce, might be propagated, and where nurseries of the valuable productions of Asia and other distant parts, might be formed for the benefit of his Majesty's colonies'.[100]

Yet these initiatives, and the societies which propelled them, were clearly more than the realization of an agenda set a century before. They were quickened, obviously, as Colley has suggested, by new kinds of patriotism. But civic enthusiasm, under the pressure of wars with France and Spain, had begun to take unusual forms.

In 1765 a new botanical ground on the island of St. Vincent began to test Asian and American plants in the West Indian climate.[101] It was not the first of its kind: John Bartram in 1728 had planted an experimental garden near Philadelphia. But it was, for two reasons, a new kind of initiative. The grounds in the hills above Kingstown, to begin with, contained an unusual collection of instruments: a 16-foot refractory telescope, a thermometer, a barometer, microscopes, a concave mirror, a hydrostatic balance, an air pump, and an 'electrick machine'.[102] The St. Vincent botanic garden was much more than the Society of Arts had intended: it was a laboratory equipped to conduct the most modern kinds of scientific research. The second curiosity was that no cultivated gentleman, on the model of Bartram or Thomas Jefferson, had privately responded to the Society of Arts's appeal. It was Melville, the Governor of St. Vincent, who had set aside twelve acres beside his house. The Crown had undertaken to answer to the gentlemen's appeal.

The British agrarian tradition had once prized private initiative in husbandry as in the sciences. But in the aftermath of the Seven Years' War, patriotic gentlemen appeared increasingly to include government in their economic or cultural projects, while the British government responded to the challenge in novel ways. St. Vincent, for example, was only the first of many overseas scientific gardens which would be planted and run by colonial governors. At home, Lord Kames in his *Gentleman Farmer* (1776) proposed that the state should apply 'rational principles' to the improvement of agriculture, organizing a body which would study farming across the country.[103] By 1793, Sir John Sinclair, with Pitt's support, had realized this project in the Board of Agriculture. How had the gentlemen come to turn to the state, and how, in turn, had the British government become interested in patronizing science and agriculture?

It is possible to find domestic British precedents for the idea of the state as improver. As we observed earlier, the Tudor and Stuart monarchs had intervened in agriculture, not least through redistributing land. Elizabeth I's imposition of 'fish days' to encourage the development of shipping and maritime trades, restrictions on the export of raw materials, and ultimately the Navigation Acts of 1651 onwards, clearly represented attempts by the state to shape the economy. During the Interregnum there were many ambitious projects for governing the economy. Hartlib, for example, had urged that an 'Office of Address' survey all the territory, people, flora, fauna, and resources of the nation, and plan for their best use.[104] The Royal Society, at its foundation, aimed, in part, at realizing similar ends through private voluntary activity. More immediately, Kames in 1776 was only urging the institutionalization of an informal alliance of Whig landowners, naturalists, chemists, and the government which had pitted its forces, from 1715 onwards, against the 'idleness' of the (usually Jacobite) Highland peasantry.[105]

But the English agrarian and mercantilist traditions cannot explain, in themselves, the later eighteenth-century pattern. To this extent, Gascoigne's sketching of an English virtuoso tradition which unites Hans Sloane and Joseph Banks requires significant qualification. In the aftermath of the Seven Years' War, science began to work in alliance with government in new ways. Information and expertise had an importance in the late Georgian empire which they had lacked in the Britain of Queen Anne.

The political crises of the long seventeenth century had made a parliament and judiciary of landowners into the masters of the state. The Hudson Bay and East India Companies exerted the Crown's powers in North America and Asia, while colonial legislatures, as in Barbados (from 1639), ruled in the Sugar Islands and North America. Particular lobbies were certainly able to persuade the Board of Trade and Plantations or the House of Commons to give them advantages. Scientific and cultural life, like trade and justice, were constituted chiefly through voluntary initiative. There were however two crucial spheres in which the Crown assumed control, in partnership with its masters: war and finance.[106] In the second half of the eighteenth century, new state intervention in science, colonies, and the economy as a whole, emerged out of the areas which had been fully surrendered to the executive. Out of the Army and the Royal Navy, and the financial predicament which resulted from military expenditure, the Crown began to expand its efficiency. St. Vincent, for example, was a colony without a planting community, since its difficult terrain allowed its Carib population to wage a permanent campaign against European settlement, even after the Union Jack rose in 1762.[107] It was the War Office and the governors it named, which created its scientific garden.

Riding this new tide, an unlikely expedition left Plymouth harbour in August 1768 bound for the South Seas. The vessel, a converted collier, christened the *Endeavour*, was under the command of James Cook. Cook, in part, was merely following in the wake of Dampier, Anson, and Byron. He carried secret instructions to find the rumoured southern continent, which Alexander Dalrymple hoped might 'maintain the power, dominion, and sovereignty of BRITAIN by employing all its manufactures and ships'. But while this thirst for commercial advantage was not new, it was joined now to new kinds of cultural appetites. The Admiralty had agreed to convey the Royal Society to Tahiti, where observation of the transit of Venus would allow a calculation of the distance of the earth from the sun. Cook, to this end, carried with him some unusual passengers: the 25-year-old Joseph Banks, a Lincolnshire magnate, who had contributed around £10,000 to the expedition, occupied a cabin next to his own, while under that naturalist were Daniel Solander and Herman Spöring (two students of Linnaeus), Alexander Buchan and Sydney Parkinson (painters, respectively, of landscape and natural history), and four servants, including Richmond and Dalton, soon to be the first black circumnavigators. Never before had a Royal Navy expedition carried such a scientific party: one civilian supernumerary for every nine seamen.[108] Curiosity about strange plants and animals animated the expedition. As an officer of the French Ministry of the Marine noted,

> Le premier soin de ce grand navigateur en touchant aux îles qu'il decouvrait était d'y chercher des plantes avec le même soin que d'autres y eussent cherché de l'or et des marchandises précieuses.[109]

They stocked their vessel with this new kind of treasure.

Reaching Dover in May 1771, the naturalists unpacked more than a thousand new species of plants, five hundred fishes, another five hundred bird skins, innumerable insects, thirteen hundred drawings and paintings, and the clothes, weapons, tools, musical instruments, and elements of ritual and language of dozens of hitherto unknown peoples. Presiding over this bounty was Joseph Banks, the broad-acred *philosophe*, who in a few years became the confidante of George III and President of the Royal Society. The *Endeavour* expedition marked in this way the opening of a new kind of alliance between agrarian wealth and the natural sciences, private initiative and Crown patronage. Its consequences would extend to the stelled ark of the Royal Gardens at Richmond which George III entrusted to Banks in 1772.

The Science of the Monarchical State

The British Crown, of course, was not alone in its desire to identify itself with exploration and the natural sciences. As Cuvier noted in his *Éloge Historique* after Banks's death, the Transit of Venus expeditions marked a watershed in the patronage of natural history by governments. As well as the *Endeavour,* Pallas travelled in Siberia on the orders of the Empress Catherine II of Russia, while Bougainville, by order of Louis XV, circumnavigated the globe, taking with him Commerson, the royal botanist.[110] The alliance of George III and Banks needs to be put into this wider European context.

In part these missions were merely expressions of the old idea that princes would win glory as they sponsored learning. As de Brosses had urged Europe's princes in 1756, in his treatise on the search for the southern continent, the discovery of new lands, or even new plants or types of human beings was 'L'Enterprise la plus grande, la plus noble, et la plus utile peut-être que puisse faire un souvérain, la plus capable d'illustrer à jamais son nom'.[111] But the mid eighteenth-century engagement of monarchy with the natural sciences expressed also more contemporary doctrines that science could be useful for royal power. It is the history of this engagement of science and monarchy which we now examine, particularly as it embraced agriculture and botany. A king, a statesman, or a colonial governor could also come to be construed as a divinely appointed gardener.

Francis Bacon had projected that a reformed natural philosophy would enhance the powers of the state. But it was on the European continent, rather than in Britain, that his programme for a formal alliance of monarchy and science was realized.[112] Colbert incorporated the Paris Academy of Sciences into Louis XIV's political system: natural knowledge was from the outset in France part of the enterprise of mercantilism.[113] In the Holy Roman Empire, after the Thirty Years' War, Seckendorff, Becher, Hörnigk, and Schröder envisioned princes making their realms rich and happy (and thus secure) through applying scientific principles to statecraft, industry, and agriculture.[114] Leibniz, first in the service of the Hanoverian court and then for the Hohenzollerns in Berlin, similarly projected that the natural sciences would both reveal the place of the Prince at the climax of this best of all possible worlds and practically assist his work. His Berlin scientific society became the nucleus of Frederick I's Academy of Sciences. A generation later, Christian von Wolff, under the influence of Leibniz, argued that science and religion, as they revealed the divine order of nature, were essential to good government.[115] For both Colbertian mercantilism and German Cameralism, knowledge of Nature's laws would guide the regulation of society. The lucidity and power of Newtonian thought, its capacity to predict the motion of cannon balls and stars, and the shape of the earth, encouraged these enthusiasms.

During the reign of George III, these Baconian enthusiasms were repatriated. In ways which we have only begun to assess, the European Enlightenment came to include Britain in its *imperium.* The scope and pattern of this influence remain largely uncharted, principally because the paradigms through which the discipline of British history is still studied were constituted in the era after the French Revolution, an era in which Europe appeared turbulent and backward, more than a channel away. The task of reconciling Britain to the larger European picture is likely to be a central preoccupation of the next generation of its historians. Eventually it will not surprise us that British princes and statesmen learnt from Europe as much as they taught it, and came to imitate the styles of government, copy the institutions, or respond to the ideologies of their contemporaries. Where James I, for example, as I discussed earlier, enclosed acres and encouraged silkworms, he clearly responded to the example of Henri IV. Caroline administrators—such as William Blathwayt at the Board of Plantations and Samuel Pepys at the Navy—borrowed similarly, if quietly, from Colbert.[116] As Europe's principal power, and its most sophisticated and glittering court in the eighteenth century, France attracted attention around Europe. The Hanoverians were no more immune to its seductions than other German princelings.

The Hanoverians and their ministers, and Continental equivalents, faced similar problems. Long and increasingly expensive wars had put states under great fiscal pressures. Earlier, the Thirty Years' War, which left central Europe battered and impoverished, had stimulated the first wave of Cameralist thinkers. Their principal concern was the improvement of the 'camera', the royal treasury. The even more costly eighteenth-century conflicts, in particular the War of the Austrian Succession and the Seven Years' War, forced statesmen to apply yet more ingenuity to raising revenue. Even Britain, with its sophisticated apparatus of public debt, vast overseas trade, and effective excise taxes, felt squeezed. France, with its inefficient and unpopular fiscal structure, faced more serious financial crises, aggravated by the progressive decline in the proceeds of its land taxes from the 1730s on. The problem was worse for the German states, which lacked colonies and significant commerce. Its princes concentrated their efforts on enlarging the tax base, through encouraging agriculture and manufacture.[117] Like Machiavelli and Sully, many considered that agrarian plenty was the basis of a large population which in turn would allow a powerful army. Food shortages, on the other hand, as Austria discovered during the Seven Years' War, eroded military efficiency, while on the home front, riots and social protest came in the wake of famine and unemployment.[118] Agriculture, as much an internal security question as the foundation of a strong foreign policy, thus attracted practical and theoretical attention.[119] By the 1740s in central and northern Europe, in the 1750s and '60s in France, and in Spain, Portugal, and the Italian peninsula afterwards, reform programmes made agriculture and science central to the renovation of the state. From the 1760s, and with particular force from the 1780s, these experiments, and the ideologies at their heart, would influence policy in Britain and its empire.[120]

These initiatives began in central Europe. The medieval imperial tradition, which I alluded to in chapter 2, clearly influenced the Cameralist ideal of the Prince founding his power on the happiness, peace, and wealth of his subjects. The Holy Roman Emperors had, in particular, sought to make science part of statecraft, and just as Rudolf II had patronized Kepler, Dee, or Clusius, so Emperor Leopold I made Becher his advisor on alchemy and economics. The success of seventeenth-century natural philosophy and mathematics provided another kind of impetus. Alchemy only represented the most extreme expression of the faith that science might help fill a Prince's coffers. (Newton, it is worth remembering, while Master of the Mint, spent years attempting to transmute base metals into bullion.) The less occult arts of measurement and natural history had as obvious an economic and political importance. The German-speaking philosophers argued that counting, surveying, describing, and tabulating should be made the tools of monarchical government. They projected a *Polizeiwissenschaft*, a science through which a government might promote security, welfare, and happiness in a Commonwealth.[121]

The German theorists of rational statecraft, moved, in a sense, from an ideal of Adam as Sovereign: if the English agrarian improvers had implicitly appealed to the economics of *Genesis*, they asserted, via Aristotelian theory, the primacy of its politics.[122] The Prince, for the Cameralists, was the patriarch who presided over the large family which was political society, the farm which was its economy, and the crop which was his tax revenue. Schröder argued in the 1680s:

> A ruler is in fact the same as a *Hausvater*, and his subjects are, in respect of their having to be ruled his children. . . . Now a Hausvater has to plough and manure a field if he wishes to reap a harvest. . . . Thus a ruler has to assist his subjects in obtaining a sufficient livelihood if he wishes to take something from them.[123]

The state was the royal estate. Its 'plouging and manuring', the work of governing the economy, depended on the research of its nature. Seckendorff urged careful survey and mapping of the kingdom's territory, the study of its soils, plants, and animals, the discovery of minerals, and the counting of its people and their skills. Schröder called this information '*Staatsbrille*': the lens through which the state could see, and thus manage, the territory it controlled.[124] By the early eighteenth century the science of 'Cameralism' began to have genuine political influence, visible, for example, in the decision of Frederick William I of Prussia in 1727 to establish a chair in 'Oeconomie, Policey und Cammersachen' at Halle and in 'Kameral-Ökonomie und Polizeiwissenschaft' at Frankfurt an der Oder. Over the next decades, 'Ritterakademien' and 'Realschulen', scientific academies which combined the natural and political sciences, were founded by the Margrave of Hessen-Kassel in 1730, by the Hanoverians at Göttingen in 1737, and in 1747 the Habsburgs formed the Theresanium in Vienna. The prestige of Cameralism grew rapidly, particularly after the application of its methods in the Haugwitz reforms which followed the War of the Austrian Succession. The 'Theresian Cadastres' (1748–56), and the reform of the land tax, resulted in an estimated 50% increase in royal revenues.[125]

Cameralism merely asserted the usefulness of science for government. In the 1750s in France, however, a school of political thinkers emerged, which came to be called the Physiocrats, which made natural knowledge central to a programme of monarchical reform.[126] The *économistes* read Newton and Montesquieu, and came to the conclusion that the (divine) laws which governed nature, might be discovered, and human society brought into harmony with them. *Physiocratie*, the name of the 1767 collection of essays, and ultimately of the movement, meant Nature's government. Its central figure was Quesnay, physician to Madame de Pompadour, of whom Buffon wrote: 'Il a fait autrefois de la médecine pour l'individu; ceci est de la médicine du gouvernment, c'est à dire de l'espèce entière.'[127] This political medicine would be administered by the monarch, guided by his 'physicians'.

The Physiocrats provided a powerful argument for the augmentation of royal power, taking the line framed by Machiavelli in the *Discorsi*, that only a single individual (naturally, in consultation with his ministers) could rapidly implement urgent reforms. The first maxim, offered by Quesnay, for the 'economic government of an agricultural kingdom' was that 'l'autorité souveraine soit unique, et supérieure à tous les individus de la société'.[128] Le Mercier de la Rivière in *L'Ordre Naturel et Essential des Sociétés Politiques* (1767), thus argued for a 'despot patrimonial et légal' who would govern society according to the laws of Nature.

Agriculture was central to the reform programme offered by the Physiocrats. This was because land was the original and recurrent 'natural' source of all riches. Agriculture, Herbert wrote in 1755, was the real source of the wealth of nations. Quesnay in his article on 'Grains' in the *Encyclopédie,* and in the *Tableau Économique,* argued that agriculture was the essential support for commerce, manufacture, ultimately a nation's tax base and power. The land provided food for everyone and raw materials for industry, while generating rent which allowed landlords to support manufacture and urban employment through the consumption of luxuries. They urged the removal of mercantilist restrictions, where 'Laissez-faire, laisser-passer', in Mirabeau's phrase, would allow the growth of the agricultural sector. This preference for agriculture, and Quesnay's description of the urban economy as 'sterile', has often been misunderstood to mean that the Physiocrats considered commerce and industry to be nugatory. What they were asserting instead was, as de la Rivière explained while a colonial governor, 'Il n'existe point de commerce que sous les matériels que fournait l'Agriculture': commerce depended ultimately on the products of the land.[129] They wished merely to complete the attack on Colbert's favouring of industry over agriculture which Boisguilbert had offered in his *Detail de la France* (1695) and *Traité des Grains* (1707). This intellectual climate helps explain the desire of the Dauphin, the future Louis XVI, to be seen ploughing at the Trianon in the 1770s, while his mother teased milk from the teats of prize cattle at Rambouillet.

Recognition of the political value of the science of plants had never, of course, depended on Cameralist or Physiocratic thought. Sully, for example, had urged, in chapter CXCI of the *Oeconomies Royales,* that a monarch might justly seek to form botanic gardens 'pour élever et entretenir toutes sortes de plantes, arbustes, herbes, et autres simples, avec les hommes, et choses nécessaires pour y faire toute sorte d'épreuves et d'expériences de médicine et d'agriculture'. There were, moreover, many obvious examples of botany's contributions to the wealth of kingdoms. Vast fortunes had grown out of the craft of introducing plants, such as sugar-cane, to European colonies, and from the discovery of the uses and culture of new foods, dyestuffs, and drugs overseas.[130] Reports on tobacco or sassafras in medical texts, or in the volumes of De Bry's *America,* had thus at the same time scientific and commercial importance. The scientific study of plants indigenous to colonies was a standard component of Dutch colonial government by the middle of the seventeenth century. Bont's *Historia Naturalis Indiae Orientalis* and *De Medicina Indiorum* of 1643 and 1658, Piso and Marcgrave's *De medicina brasiliense* and

Historia rerum naturalium Brasiliae of 1648, van Rheede tot Drakenstein's *Hortus Indicus Malabaricus,* Rumpf's *Herbarium Amboinense,* and Commelin's *Flora Malabarica* (1696) were attempts to advertise the political value of the Dutch West and East Indian Companies' dominions in Brazil, South India, and Ceylon. The Dutch formed botanic gardens in their colonies which profitably exchanged flowers and economic plants with Leiden, Amsterdam, and each other. The French came to imitate the Dutch. Sébastien Vaillant, on the example of Leiden, constructed two hothouses in Jardin du Roi for the acclimatization of tropical plants in 1714 and 1716. Through these the French succeeded in 1715 in introducing coffee, via Paris, to the French West Indies. This was, arguably, the botanical coup of the eighteenth century, and it was the model for many later dreams of making territory rich through introducing plants. But it was only in the 1730s that botany came to be considered a branch of economics and an instrument of government.

The idea of making academic gardens assist the work of economic renovation began in the German states, but reached its maturity in Sweden.[131] Linnaeus, more than any other single figure, turned botany into an economic science.[132] He wrote, of course, against the background of Dutch and French practical achievement in making wealth from the science of plants, and it is clear that his residence in Holland in the 1730s was formative.[133] He was a product of a Sweden which had been battered by long wars with Russia, and which was already under the influence of Pietist and Cameralist reform ideologies which had permeated northwards. Linnaeus believed that God had granted nature, through the sciences, for the use of men in general, and the Swedish nation in particular. He helped to found the Swedish Economic Academy of Sciences in 1739, and collaborated with the 'Hats' in the organizing of a national statistical bureau and census of the population in 1749.[134] He happily co-operated with restoration of monarchical power in 1772, and was involved in the Royal Patriotic Society (1775), Sweden's first physiocratic club. Under his influence, professors of 'Practical Economics' came to instruct in natural history combined with mining, economics, agriculture, and manufacture in Åbo, Turku, Uppsala, and Lund.[135] The chair of Peter Kalm, the naturalist student of Linnaeus, for example, concerned what the Cameralists called 'Haushaltungskunst', the arts of managing the 'household' of the nation.

Linnaeus gave botany two principal economic responsibilities. The first of these was the survey of new resources. In lectures and essays which were translated around Europe, he identified the discovery of the profitable uses of plants with Man's work of redeeming Creation.[136] This task began at home, as he explained in his dissertation 'On the Importance of Travelling in One's Own Country', which disseminated the idea of the natural historian as a patriotic actor. As we have seen with Ray and Hartlib, the idea of the survey of local flora and fauna was not new, and Linnaeus was clearly responding in part to the Hippocratic idea, still influential, that the remedies for diseases would be found in the territory in which they were endemic.[137] He was, after all, Professor of Medicine. But Linnaeus particularly urged travellers both to make economical plants their priority, and to collect, from the people whose lands they surveyed, agricultural and industrial techniques. His own great mission to Lapland in 1741, had, as its principal concern, the search for 'dyestuffs and other useful plants, and ... [whatever] in the animal, vegetable, or mineral kingdom might be useful to the Kingdom'.[138] Linnaeus popularized within Europe the ideal of the 'philosophical' traveller, who would observe, record, and sample every aspect of the natural world, and the culture and antiquities of the territories through which he passed. His students comprehensively searched Sweden's provinces, and travelled, often at the expense of other European powers, on missions to every corner of the world: Peter Kalm travelled to Russia (1744–5) and to Britain's North American colonies (1748–51), Peter Löfling to New Granada at the expense of the Spanish Crown (1751–6), Carl Peter Thunberg as a Dutch East India Company surgeon to the Cape, Java, Ceylon, and Japan (1770–9), and, most illustriously, Daniel Solander and Hermann Spöring sailed with James Cook and Joseph Banks on the *Endeavour*.[139] It is worth noting that Linnaeus insisted that only native Swedes should survey Sweden.

Linnaeus, secondly, made the botanist responsible for the acclimatization of plants which might add to his nation's wealth and power. This aspect of his programme was, in practice, a failure, at least in Sweden, where opium, tea, and pineapples refused to be persuaded that they should flourish in the open air.[140] But his faith that the skilful botanist might transform national agriculture spread across Europe. Frederick V, under Swedish influence, founded a Royal Botanical Institution in Denmark in 1752, which trained students to survey the kingdom's limits, involved clergymen and gentlemen in reporting plants for the *Flora Danica*, dispatched natural historians to the tropics, most celebratedly, Johan Kønig, to India, all with the aim of renovating the national economy through the introduction of valuable plants.[141] Benjamin Stillingfleet's 1759 translation of selections from Linnaeus's *Amoenitates Academicae*, one must conjecture, equally influenced the Society of Arts's appeal, in the same year, for botanic gardens to acclimatize exotic crops in Britain's American colonies.[142] In Austria, the Habsburg state intervened with the same agenda: from 1764, Kaunitz founded agricultural societies in every province of the kingdom, and required them to experiment with, and popularize, non-indigenous crops.[143] Economists and botanists advised politicians that 'economical gardens' were vital to the renovation of agriculture.[144] Their influence extended to the Italian peninsula, where the *scienzi camerali* had already led in 1754 to a chair in economics at Naples.[145] Domingo Vandelli, a botanist trained at Padua, carried the enthusiasm to Portugal, where he published in an influential memoir on the usefulness of botanic gardens for agriculture.[146] With the support of Pombal, Vandelli founded *jardim botanicos* at Coimbra and Lisbon, and while serving on the Royal Council of Commerce, Agriculture, Manufacture, and Navigation, advised on reforming the economy of Portugal and its colonies.[147]

Linnaeus received equal attention within France. But there the alliance of botany and monarchy did not depend on a diffused Cameralism. Among the legacies of Colbert were the assumption that science would serve the state and a number of practical experiments in the survey of the resources of colonies, and of the acclimatization of new economic plants. Dominican priests, such as Charles Plumier, and gentlemen in the employ of the Crown, in particular surgeons, had supplied Fagon and his successors at the Jardin du Roi with exotic plants.[148] A gift of a 'pied de café' to Louis XIV by the Dutch led, for example, to the spectacular introduction of coffee to the French West Indies (plate 8). The Dutch example of planting scientific gardens in colonies was copied, and by 1732 in the Guianas a large 'Jardin du Roi' was part of the town of St. Michel de Cayenne.[149] The success of coffee prompted the expectation, as early as 1730s, that through such experimental grounds other valuable crops, in particular spices, could be brought within the French economy. Desportes, 'médecin du roi' at le Cap in St. Domingue, referring to the success of coffee, urged that such gardens might allow the introduction of nutmegs, pepper, ginger, and cinnamon:

> il est necessaire d'avoir un jardin où on puisse cultiver toutes les plantes qui peuvent être transportée ... On pourrait dans la suite procurer des pieds de mouscadier, de poivrier, et de clous de giroffle. Le succès de caffé dans les îles semble repondre de celui de ces arbrisseaux ...[150]

Yet before circa 1740, there was no clear identification of botany with the business of economic government.

Two naturalists were responsible for a new seriousness of purpose in the era of the War of the Austrian Succession: Duhamel de Monceau and Buffon. They, together with political patrons, such as Maurepas, sought to put botany, agriculture, forestry, and every kind of practical science at the service of the French Crown. Duhamel, like Buffon, greatly admired English natural philosophy and agronomy. In the 1730s Duhamel began to advise the Ministry of the Marine on naval timber, and conducted experiments, with Buffon, on timber's resistance as a material.[151] Buffon, who had begun his career with translations of Newton's *Method of Fluxions*, Hales's *Vegetable Staticks*, and Tull's *Horse-hoeing Husbandry*, offered memoirs to the Academy of Sciences on the conservation and husbandry of forests, clearly under Evelyn's influence. In 1739, Duhamel was appointed Inspector General of the Ministry of the Marine, while Buffon became Director of the Jardin du Roi. Duhamel proceded to organize and foster schools of nautical science and of naval architecture in Paris, Brest, Rochefort, and Toulon.[152] In all three of the latter port cities, he arranged for the Ministry of the Marine to nurture botanic gardens to assist the movement of new plants both into France and outwards to its colonies.[153] He was convinced that the rational use of the soil would produce agricultural abundance, and his writings on husbandry, in particular his *Traité de la Culture des Terres* (1750) and *Éléments de L'Agriculture* (1760), were widely influential. Buffon, along with Daubenton, Thouin, and the Jussieus, equally made his domain, the Jardin du Roi, into the focus of researches on the culture and economic exploitation of plants and animals.[154]

Buffon wished to form the most complete possible collection of specimens and living objects in the Cabinet d'Histoire Naturelle and the Jardin du Roi. Clearly, his private scientific passions were central to this desire. But he also believed, on grounds which a Cameralist or a Physiocratic might have conceded, that only through such a universal collection could the sciences make their contribution to France's prosperity and power. The Maison du Roi allowed Buffon to spend considerable sums on the acquisition of natural history specimens. A pension of 3000 livres, for example, went to Duhameau, in exchange for several cases of Caribbean shells and marine plants he sent from Le Cap to the Cabinet.[155] But Buffon's real success was his recruitment of gifts, and his cultivation, throughout the limits of French power, of a concern with botanical experimentation. With the collaboration of the French Ministry of the Marine and Colonies, particularly under Maurepas, Choiseul, and Choiseul-Praslin, Buffon succeeded in turning many naval officers and officials in the French colonies into the suppliers of specimens and observations.

From the 1740s, the agents of the Ministry of the Marine and Colonies and the Compagnie des Indes began, in turn, to give serious attention to economic botany. In the Indian Ocean, de la Bourdonnais and the Compagnie des Indes fostered experimental gardens in Pondicherry in India, Mauritius, and Réunion, for the acclimatization of spices, dyes, and drugs within the orbit of French mercantilism. In 1748, Pierre Poivre, the naturalist and adventurer, proposed to obtain nutmeg and clove plants, as part of his secret mission to open a French *comptoir* in Cochin China.[156] In 1750, Dupleix offered twenty thousand pieces of silver to whoever brought twenty-five nutmeg plants to Pondicherry.[157] By 1752, the Commander of Karikal, south of Pondicherry, brought cinnamon to Mauritius, other species arriving from Cochin China in 1759, along with pepper from Malabar, and vetiver from the Coromandel Coast. They were joined in that island by the ultimate prize: the seeds and roots of spice trees which Cossigny smuggled out of Java in 1761–2.[158] The long projected end to the Dutch control of the spice trade was suddenly at hand.

This botanical coup came at a peculiar time. The 1760s were most unfortunate years for French imperialism. The humiliations of the Seven Years' War, which led to almost complete retreat from India and Canada, were followed by the disastrous adventures in Guyane and Madagascar. Yet strategic setbacks and financial crises provided the ideal climate for projects of reform. In Choiseul, the Duc de Praslin, Bertin, Turgot, and later Castries and La Luzerne, France enjoyed a tradition of reforming statesmen. Their hand was strengthened after the accession of Louis XVI in 1774. It is in this context of crisis that the Physiocratic programme for the reform of the monarchy acquired real influence. The application of science to the improvement of the Navy and of domestic and colonial agriculture, already in train, found new theoretical justification. Maurepas, encouraged by *économistes* such as de la Rivière, created Committees on Agriculture and Commerce within the colonies which discussed crops, animals, implements, and technique. The year 1766 saw the birth of the École Vétérinaire and the Société Royale d'Agriculture, which its founders urged should be placed 'à la tête des autres académies'. Agricultural societies emerged around the country. The Jardin du Roi entered into increasingly close collaboration with departments of state. Daubenton, Buffon's lieutenant, began his experiments on the improvement of sheep, using the royal flock, for which the Crown had acquired the precious Spanish merino sheep. His work, encouraged by Turgot and others, led to trials conducted throughout France which were published in the two volumes of the *Traité des Bêtes à Laine* (1771). 'Following the experiments of M. Daubenton,' wrote the Comte d'Angevillier in 1777, we can turn the grossest fleece into superfine wool in two or three generations.[159] It was with equal optimism that the Ministry of the Marine and Colonies looked after 1763 to economic botany to help reverse France's overseas misfortunes.[160]

Between 1763 and the Revolution, botanists and officers of the French Navy and colonial administration collaborated formally in ways which had no precedents in the history of European imperialism. Buffon and the Ministers of the Marine dispatched several able botanists and apothecaries to search for food plants, drugs, and dyestuffs. In the name of the King, but on Buffon's recommendation, Jean-Baptiste Le Blond left for the Antilles in 1766, then to French Guiana in 1770, where he was joined by the botanist Nectoux.[161] Their special target was 'Jesuits' bark' (cinchona), the only known remedy for malaria. That disease was, of course, one of the principal impediments to France's tropical imperial ambitions, not least in Guyane itself. But cinchona was also a valuable commodity, over which Spain enjoyed a complete monopoly. Le Blond and Nectoux failed, and quinine, as we shall see in later chapters, remained the holy grail of economic botany for another century. But there were many other successes. Spices were acclimatized in Mauritius, Réunion, and Madagascar, and this inspired attempts to introduce them, along with other Asian plants, to France's New World empire.[162] In 1773, Buffon and the Ministry of the Marine sent cloves from Madagascar and mangoes from India to the French Antilles, receiving in exchange Caribbean plants.[163] In September 1776, vessels of the Marine took a further Asian cargo of sandalwood, mangoes, and mangosteen to Martinique, Guadeloupe, and St. Domingue. By 1777 a Guadeloupe official projected that Asian plants would transform Antillean agriculture, while providing new sustenance to national commerce and industry.[164] In that year, Thierry de Menonville, with the covert support of the Ministry of the Marine, attempted to break another Spanish commercial monopoly: he took cochineal insects (the source of a valuable red dye) and their nopal cactus host from Mexico.[165] Louis Claude Richard and Le Blond also travelled, following the instructions of Necker and Castries, to search for dyes in Cayenne in 1781.[166] It was not surprising that La Luzerne, Louis XVI's last minister, described the Jardin du Roi as the natural mediator of 'une communication réciproque entre nos colonies'.[167]

Physiocracy provided a new scientific vocabulary for Colbertian initiatives. Louis XIV's forest laws, for example, had protected timber in the name of preserving the king's exclusive privileges; many imposed at the end of Louis XV's reign instead 'conserved' timber in the name of Nature and 'la Fécondité des Terres'.[168] The use of the earth's riches, and in particular the 'mise en valeur' of France and its dependencies, was similarly made a 'natural' responsibility of the Bourbon Crown. 'Development' was now not just politically prudent, it was a sacred responsibility imposed on those to whom the sciences had revealed the fabric of the universe. By the same token, the success of princely (or imperial) government now depended on mastery of what Mirabeau in the *Philosophie Rurale* (1763) called the 'immutable order of physical and moral law which assured the prosperity of empires'.[169] If, as Dupont de Nemours similarly asserted, the political efficiency of a Prince depended on his understanding of the 'Natural Order' given by God to the universe, then his patronage of the natural sciences was central to the legitimacy of his authority.[170] This had clear implications for the resources which Enlightened monarchies chose to apply to natural history.[171] Buffon and his successors thus found it easy to secure support for their scientific work.

Buffon's reign (1740–88) saw the dramatic expansion in the physical size of the Jardin du Roi, and in the extent of the collections of the plants, animals, and minerals. By 1770, the Cabinet du Roi had become so large that Buffon had to move out of his house in the garden to give it room. The Maison du Roi allowed Buffon adjacent plots of land, and a regular annual vote from which he was able to pay for gardeners, assistants in the laboratory, and to purchase collections.[172] Royal patronage significantly increased the number of opportunities available for paid employment as a man of science. At home there were such savant dynasties as the Jussieus, the Richards, or the Thouins, while scientific travel abroad became worth a gentleman's while, with Pierre Sonnerat, for example, leaving in 1772 as a collector for the Jardin du Roi at the Cape and in France's Indian Ocean colonies, at a salary of 300 livres annually.[173]

In 1772, Louis XV ordered the remaking of the Jardin Royal des Plantes, approving 52,000 livres of expenditure.[174] Buffon sought new beds, hothouses, and orangeries, but the special feature of the project was the new École de Botanique. Between 1774 and 1787, Antoine Laurent de Jussieu elucidated and displayed in this ground his 'natural system' of the families of plants.[175] This search for the 'Natural Order' within the Jardin's collections responded to the anti-Linnaean agenda of Adanson and Buffon. But clearly, as Spary argues, it was also animated by the faith that nature's order might be applied to man's government of the world.[176] The contemporary Physiocratic enthusiasms, it thus might be argued, achieved more in renovating the science of plants than in reforming France. The classification and cultivation of plants acquired new resources, and clearly some inspiration, from its association, via agriculture, with Enlightened government. The secrets of the Plant Kingdom failed to rescue the Bourbon monarchy, but the science of the monarchical state launched the modern science of botany.

France's collapse into Revolution, and the defeat of Napoleon, obscured the remarkable successes of late *ancien régime* science. France between perhaps 1770 and 1820, Cardwell has suggested, 'produced a galaxy of scientific genius that, *ceteris paribus*, outshines all others from the beginnings of science to the present day'.[177] Lavoisier and Jussieu, Buffon and Lamarck, Lagrange and Laplace, Guy-Lussac and Ampère flourished in a society in which science was prized by the state. The Committee of Public Safety, the Directory, and Napoleon only extended a tradition of state patronage inaugurated by the Bourbon monarchy. This support did yield practical fruit. After 1763, it is worth noting, the French Navy was unmatched at a technical level, and was able to hold its own in the War of the American Revolution. The Admiralty paid close attention to French naval architecture, and even after the Battle of Trafalgar, carefully studied captured vessels. The application of science by the French monarchy to the improvement of agriculture won equal attention on the other side of the Channel.

Conclusion: A Prospect on Banks at Kew, 1772–1820

In 1772, Louis XV approved Buffon's plan for the augmentation and scientific reorganization of the Jardin du Roi, and dispatched Sonnerat to the Indian Ocean. George III, in 1772 also, enclosed Love Lane, an ancient public thoroughfare which had linked Richmond to the Saxon quay at Kew, making the demesnes of Caroline and Augusta one royal garden.[178] In that year too, George III invited Banks to become, informally, master of his garden at Kew, and sent Francis Masson to the Cape 'for the discovery of new Plants, towards the improvement of the Royal Botanical Gardens at Kew'. The activity of the French Crown would later provide much other inspiration for the English *jardin du roi*.

That the Hanoverians might quietly imitate the style of the Bourbon court may surprise less than the suggestion that they took from it an enthusiasm for agriculture. English agriculture, after all, was the model which others sought to emulate. It was through travel in that island, and through authors such as Evelyn and Tull, that Dufay, Buffon, and Duhamel began their agricultural experiments.[179] They envied the efficiency of English agriculture, and in particular its intensive use of horses, cattle, machinery, and crop rotations.[180] The Physiocrats, one might argue, wished the Crown to assume the Providential responsibilities with which the English agrarians had invested the private entrepreneur. What had Britain, particularly after its remarkable victories in the Seven Years' War, to learn from Europe?

The English agrarians, however, found much to admire in the French commitment to making agriculture scientific. Arthur Young in *A Course of Experimental Agriculture* (1770) argued indeed that Jethro Tull's work would probably have been forgotten, 'had not some very spirited writers in France, ... gone into the practice of it with so much ardour, as to draw the attention of all Europe'.[181] He praised, in particular, Duhamel de Monceau's treatises on agriculture: 'I heartily wish we had as large a collection of equal authority made in England.' Equally Young drew English attention to the articles in the *Encyclopédie* on 'fermier', 'froment', 'culture', and 'graines', and to Patullo's *Essai sur L'Amélioration des Terres* (1758). If Young and others admired the intellectual seriousness with which the French approached agriculture, they clearly also approved of Quesnay's or Mirabeau's assertion that land stood at the economic and political foundation of society. The advocates of the expansion of the French Crown's powers were speaking the language of the English Whigs.

The successful colonial alliance of botany and French seapower also won attention. Melville in St. Vincent, with his botanic garden and laboratory in the grounds of the Governor's house, clearly followed the example of such Enlightened proconsuls as de la Rivière in Martinique. Johann Reinhold Forster, in his preface of 1772 to the translation of Bougainville's *Voyage au Tour du Monde*, pointed contemporaries' attention to the initiatives of the Compagnie des Indies, and their consolidation under Choiseul:

> We have reason to believe the French to be in a fair way of getting the spices in their plantations, as Mr. de Poivre has actually planted at Isle de France some hundreds of cloves and nutmeg trees. Every true patriot will join in the wish, that our East India Company, prompted by a noble zeal for the improvement of natural history, and every other useful branch of knowledge, might send a set of men properly acquainted with mathematics, natural history, physic, and other branches of literature, to their vast possessions in the Indies ... to gather fossils, plants, seeds and animals, peculiar to those regions.[182]

Forster reminded his readers that such surveys would inevitably yield new 'branches of trade and commerce' to the power which prosecuted them. West Indian planters, who began in the 1770s to respond to the bounties set by Society of Arts, came to similar conclusions. John Ellis, Fellow of the Royal Society and agent for both West Florida and Dominica, urged the introduction of Asian plants, and advised on the means of transporting them.[183] Early in 1772 Valentine Morris, Governor of St. Vincent, urged Banks that the introduction of the breadfruit tree would be 'a great blessing and benefit' to the West Indies.[184] Finally in 1775 the planters of Jamaica, on a motion proposed by Hinton East, Matthew Wallen, and John Hope, voted in their legislature to create two extensive botanic gardens and to place the cost of a full-time botanist on the charge of the colony.[185] The members of the Assembly sought Banks's help in introducing Indian plants.[186] But the first significant cargo of plants from the East Indies only arrived in Jamaica in 1782, when a French ship, originally bound from Mauritius to St. Domingue, was captured by one of Lord Rodney's West Indies squadron.[187] When its French crew perceived that there was no escape they set about destroying the nutmeg, clove, and black pepper trees which they had brought from the East Indies.[188] The private initiatives of the gentlemen of the British Empire had been no match for the co-ordinated activity of the French Marine and Jardin du Roi.

The South Sea voyages represented the one clear example of an alliance of British science and seapower. Here too, of course, France had offered some inspiration. If the *Endeavour* in 1768 was the first Royal Navy vessel to carry an élite party of civilian naturalists, we may note that Bougainville on the *Boudeuse* in 1766 had carried an *équipe* led by the astronomer Véron and the botanist Commerson. But the achievements of Cook's voyages both in geography and natural history set new precedents, and illustrated to contemporaries what might be accomplished if government made science its business.

The British political classes had long distrusted the expansion of the Crown's powers. But the many kinds of crisis which followed American independence, culminating in the draining succession of wars with Revolutionary France, made new kinds of initiative seem necessary. The cruel burden of public debt, the fear of civil strife, worries about the adequacy of the food supply and of public morality gave impetus to strategies for reform. Only wise and powerful government, embodied in the Crown, joined to the patriotic activity of gentlemen, many argued, could rescue Britain from its predicament.

It is in the context of the 1780s and 1790s that Sir Joseph Banks made the Royal Gardens into something more than a pleasure ground. He connected Kew, as we shall see, to projects for the 'improvement' of agriculture in England, Scotland, the West Indies, India, and Africa. George III lent his support, recognizing that the usefulness of the King's garden might demonstrate the utility of a King. Pitt and Dundas lent theirs, hoping that the exploitation of Nature might supply food, raw materials, new 'branches of trade and commerce'. Its practical contributions were, in the end, meagre. Moral sustenance, rather than breadfruit, flax, or dyes, became Kew's principal contribution to British power.

The makers of the first British Empire had found in Christianity, and their cultivation of land, a licence for intrusion in Ireland and the New World. A later sacred theory of agriculture comforted those who imposed themselves on India, Australasia, and Africa. The rational use of Nature replaced piety as the foundation of imperial Providence, government became the Demiurge, and universal progress, measured by material abundance, its promised land.

Edward Gibbon was not alone in imagining that one could find in his nation's 'pure and generous love of science', and its diffusion of agriculture to the islands of the South Sea, an exception to the rule that empire was the handmaid of avarice and cruelty, and evidence for the increase of 'the real wealth, the happiness, and perhaps the virtue of the human race'.[189]

PART II
Nature and Empire

CHAPTER 4
'Improving' the British Empire: Sir Joseph Banks and Kew, 1783–1820

What 'improvement' meant for Georgian Britain, Thomas Weaver made vivid in *Ram Letting from Robert Bakewell's Breed at Dishley, near Loughborough, Leicester* (1810) (Plate 9).[1] Initially the painting seems, like its prosaic title, to offer a flat report of detail: the foreground is dominated by Mr. Bakewell's rams. But then the eye wrestles with the epic bulk of the animals, whose luminous bodies are pink and ample as swine.[2] Two stockmen, in implausibly immaculate white coats, achieve an almost hieratic poise over their miraculous charges. Upright in tails are the gentlemen: a bustling crowd pressing at the entrance for a view of beasts and mechanics, while inside a chosen few survey the scene with expressions of utmost *gravitas*. The hub connecting these three dense presences is Bakewell, his gaze greeting that of a portly figure, fourth from the door frame: Sir Joseph Banks, President of the Royal Society. The viewer, like the gentlemen, has clearly been invited to participate in something more august than the rutting of sheep.

Bakewell had begun his experiments with sheep and cattle in 1745.[3] Larger breeds were welcomed in an age when hunger was clearly the enemy of public order.[4] Across the Channel, famine had preceded revolution, and Pitt had seen the consequences of his refusing British flour to the French government in June 1789.[5] Livestock had a special place in English attempts to increase the product of the land, and in particular in the Norfolk four-course rotation, which 'Turnip' Townshend and Coke of Holkham had devised and advertised. Sheep were 'the golden hoof', for they gave wool, mutton, and manure, while eating the sainfoin, clover, and turnips planted on newly drained land. They allowed the farmer, therefore, to make money at the same time as he prepared the soil to yield bumper crops of wheat. As marginal land became more profitable, landowners discovered a new appetite for the enclosure of the commons. Banks's uncle rejoiced on hearing of his nephew's plan to convert a neighbouring marsh into his pasture:

> I am extremely glad to find the drainage is likely to answer so well ... for in this Age of improvement tis not impossible that fen may become the finest richest country in green Britain.[6]

Drainage and the extensive grazing of livestock accompanied the enclosure, between 1760 and 1820, of half of Bakewell's Leicestershire and a third of Banks's Lincolnshire, and of some six million acres nationally, a quarter of all cultivated acreage.[7] Animal breeding, with its promise of 'improved' animals, had as much symbolic value for the enclosers as practical importance. A vast breed such as Bakewell's 'New Leicester', for example, despite the fact its flesh was notoriously unpalatable, was hoofed evidence that private profit implied public benefit. The advocates of agrarian improvement worked with passion to spread new beasts and techniques first to large farmers, and thus to their tenants. The 'Sheep Shearings' which Coke began in 1778, and which were the model for the occasion captured on Weaver's canvas, were as much concerned with the spectacle of 'improvement' as its reality. We may discover, then, in *Ram Letting*, a moral drama of which Bakewell, Banks and the other top-hats are the heroes. Its subject is, literally, the dissemination of progress, through the alliance of science and property.

In 1810, also, Banks played a role in a colonial version of Weaver's theatre of improvement.[8] In that year Sir Thomas Maitland, Commander-in-Chief in Ceylon, which the British had seized from the Dutch during the 1790s, created a botanic garden. Maitland had long argued that the future of Ceylon, and the only hope of augmenting colonial revenue, lay in the cultivation of crops which might be sold on the world market. He believed, however, that only 'the example of two or three Individuals cultivating here either Corn, Coffee, or Cotton to their Individual Benefit', would persuade the Ceylonese to honour their responsibilities to the rich soil of their island.[9] The natural potential of the island demanded European farming, which had been prohibited in 1801. Maitland persuaded Whitehall in 1810 to rescind this rule, and intended the botanic garden to lead the conversion of Ceylon to export crop production. Banks charged William Kerr, the gardener he sent from Kew, to work 'for the benefit of the commercial interests of the island, and for the advancement of the Science of Botany'. The success of coffee in Ceylon, in the end, resulted from the quite independent activity of European planters, who by 1812 formed a local agricultural society.[10] But the new garden stood as an emblem of Britain's enlightened regime in Ceylon, and as one of the achievements which preceded Maitland's rapid promotion to Major-General in 1811, Governor of Malta in 1813, and Commander-in-Chief in the Mediterranean in 1815. 'I believe it to be unquestionable', wrote Liverpool in 1811, 'that the best administered of all the King's colonies in any quarter of the globe is the island of Ceylon.'[11]

Bakewell's rams and Maitland's garden shared more, we may argue, than the blessing of Sir Joseph Banks. Both were part of a hypothesis about the morality of an individual or a nation taking command of resources once under others' control. In the seventeenth century, as I discussed earlier, the tangling of religious and economic thought had helped justify both enclosure at home and conquest in Ireland and New England. Christian assumptions continued to govern in the age of Banks, when vessels with names like the

Bounty and *Providence* were charged with moving plants between the hemispheres. But these missions, like the 'improvement' of Leicestershire or Ceylon, took encouragement from a later negotiation of *Genesis*: the idea of cosmopolitan progress. Through the most advanced knowledge and techniques, 'improvers' would organize the best possible future, both for those they expropriated and subordinated, as for themselves. That secular utopia depended on the market: the idea of 'improvement' had at its heart the theory that Nature was best used to yield commodities which might be traded widely, rather than to support local subsistence. As Arthur Young phrased the gentlemanly consensus: 'the best use the land can be put to, is to cultivate THAT crop, whatever it be, which produces the greatest profit VALUED IN MONEY.'[12] The most useful goods, such as sheep or coffee, would be most highly valued by the market, and their production was evidence of economic virtue. Political economy thus, itself under the influence of religious and scientific assumptions, provided a new prism through which both enclosure and colonial expansion appeared moral and necessary.[13] Animal breeding and botanic gardens, as means through which nature was made to yield commodities, stood, in turn, as tokens of the righteousness of property and empire. They shared one other attribute: both had secured the patronage of the British Crown in the era after the American War.

Kew was at the centre of royal efforts to furnish useful animals and plants for the empire's farmers. In 1787, George III decided, as he wrote Banks, that improving the wool of this country was 'a most national object'.[14] He imported merino sheep, then the object of a Spanish royal monopoly, through Banks's secret help.[15] 'His Majesty's Spanish Flock', which roamed the grounds of the royal gardens of Kew and Windsor, provided stock for English breeding, and seven rams and three ewes which left for New South Wales in 1804.[16] George III took a personal interest in the enterprise, writing, for example, to Banks in 1787 complaining that he was 'much hurt' that Banks had not advised him of his recent visit to Kew, as he would have liked to see him, and that while he was pleased that two rams and two ewes had been sent for he 'would wish for 20 ewes and 10 rams'.[17] The King refused to allow the first shearing of the merinos in 1788 until Banks was able to attend.[18] By this time, George III had extended his patronage to economic botany, and had resuscitated the botanic garden of St. Vincent in 1785.[19] By 1787, it was planned that this garden would be the entrepôt through which Asian and Pacific plants, brought by Bligh on the *Bounty*, would be introduced to the West Indies, and through which New World plants would return to Kew. Ceylon in 1810, like St. Vincent in the 178
was one of a new kind of dependency, in which the Governor wiel
executive powers of his sovereign unrestrained by a legi
the 'Crown Colony'. Where Maitland founded a botan
brought it into communication with Kew, he merely the
dition of state patronage which the King had personally

George III's involvement with agriculture and 'imp

explanation. Agriculture in Britain had traditionally found ideological life in 'Country' politics, that is among those such as Whigs after 1688, or Walpole's opponents in the 1730s, who distrusted the power of the court or Crown. It was true that George I and Caroline had made identification with Whig agricultural enthusiasm, taking Jethro Tull, for example, into their patronage. But agriculture, as a practice which connected Englishmen to the territory of the nation, had more to offer to those who argued that liberty and sovereignty rose upwards from landowners to the monarch, than to those who wished to assert the prerogatives of the Crown. The symbolic significance of Coke of Holkham having worn the clothes of a Norfolk yeoman to visit George III, when he bore the news that Parliament had voted to end the American War, was clear to contemporaries.

After 1783, however, both George III and Pitt the Younger attempted to appropriate 'improvement' as a cause, respectively, of the Crown and of Tories. They responded to those whom Bayly has styled 'agrarian patriots', who had come to see agriculture as the solution to the moral and material crises which a defeated Britain faced. Agrarian activists, such as Arthur Young and Sir John Sinclair, argued that 'improvement' required the efficient agency of the state, and indeed Young reasoned, the leadership of the King.[20] As Young argued, on his return from his travels in France: 'There is but one all-powerful cause which instigates mankind, and that is GOVERNMENT.'[21] The sense of national emergency, particularly after the French Revolution, stimulated a new tide of loyalist sentiment, and a belief that English liberty could only be secured by government assuming new powers for both coercion and 'improvement'. The drift of Rockingham Whigs towards Pitt, culminating in the defection of the Portland Whigs in 1794, created a new weight of support for an expansion of the Crown's efficiency.[22] On this tide, Pitt founded the Board of Agriculture in 1793, making farming an official concern, and bringing Whig grandees such as the 5th Duke of Bedford, and figures such as Sinclair, Young, and Banks, under an official umbrella.[23] George III, similarly, agreed in 1799 to become the patron of the Royal Institution, which sought, on the model of France's Conservatoire des Arts et Métiers, to apply science to the needs of the nation, and especially to agriculture.[24] The Board and the Royal Institution symbolized the new alliance between English agrarian enthusiasm and the Crown, and Bakewell's experiments benefited directly from their patronage.

George III made deliberate and public gestures of solidarity with the 'agrarian patriots', contributing articles (under the pseudonym 'Ralph Robinson') to the *Annals of Agriculture*, the campaigning journal Young had founded in 1784, including one in 1786 on Mr. Ducket, a ploughing innovator.[25] By 1789, he erected a farm yard and farm offices adjacent to the Richmond gardens. In 1792, he assumed personally the post of Ranger of Surrey, with its responsibility for woods and farming in that county, and proceeded to drain a lake at Kew, in order to have more arable land.[26] The King, we may argue, sought to show his usefulness to the British people, taking such a personal interest in the arts and manufactures of his kingdom that he came to be called 'Farmer George' and 'The Buttonmaker'.[27] From the 1780s onwards, George III sought to win his subjects' loyalty, and his right to intervene in domestic and foreign policy, by making himself the empire's first gentleman, the paradigm of an 'improver'.[28]

The gardens at Kew became a theatre for the exhibition of royal virtue. But the King's sheep rearing, his interest in economic botany, indeed his wider concern with agriculture, were as much responses to contemporary ideas of Enlightened monarchy as to the gentlemanly enthusiasm of his subjects. Agriculture had won royal patronage across Europe in the 1760s, while Bourbon princes, and in particular Louis XVI, had made ploughing, animal husbandry, and artisan crafts into royal hobbies. The Jardin du Roi had seen Daubenton's experiments with the royal flock and Buffon's collaboration with the botanical projects of the Ministry of the Marine long before George III and Banks conspired to make Kew useful. Lest we concede too much to the theory that George III sought to remake the monarchy in the image of the middle classes, we might take note of the grandiose architectural plans for a new palace at Kew. Some £500,000 were squandered, between 1794 and 1811, on a project which owed more to the example of absolutist princes than to the ordinary Englishman.[29] George III intended this new palace to crown a royal estate which he had continually sought to expand and improve after the death of his mother in 1772. Augusta's Kew and George II and Caroline's Richmond were amalgamated, and the freehold to the Capel lands and adjacent estates purchased, and public land annexed.[30] He commissioned from the architect James Wyatt plans for a Gothic castle, and by 1806, at the cost of some £100,000 a vast crenellated system of soaring towers, turrets, gates, and keep arose on the Thames across from Brentford (see Plate 11). Any hope of completion ended with the King's relapse into insanity in 1811. It was abandoned, and by 1827 George IV ordered the 'Castellated Palace' dynamited. But while the dream of a Hanoverian Trianon passed, the idea of the Crown leading 'improvement' proved more enduring. The ornamental programme of European absolutism was put aside, but its administrative ambitions continued to win attention.

'Improvement', once a slogan for the local activity of the gentry, became a new criterion for responsible authority, and a mission towards which government might legitimately expand its powers. Under the continual pressure of war with France, English agrarians began to see the state as a necessary instrument of their reform programme, while the Crown's ministers, and such proconsuls as Maitland, found a justification for their extraordinary powers in the cornucopian promise of agriculture. Despotism needed the idea of Enlightenment, as much as progress appeared to need wise government. Both the varieties of the human conscience and the expanse of Creation were estates which those at the vanguard of reason had both a duty and a right to 'improve'. These new ideological currents sustained both new state initiatives at home and that remarkable wave of imperial expansion, which between 1790 and 1815 led to the acquisition of territories in India, Africa, the West Indies, the Mediterranean, the Indian Ocean, and the Pacific.[31]

It may seem perverse, indeed an oxymoron, to conjecture an imperialism of the Enlightenment. Yet benevolent and emancipatory hopes, as we have seen, easily lent their sanction to coercive projects. British 'improvers' moved, at home and abroad, in the faith that they ultimately knew better than those on the ground. Their confidence depended, in part, on the assumption that they possessed a more profound understanding of how Nature worked. Already at the beginning of the eighteenth century, as we examined earlier, political arithmetic had supported the logic of colonization in Ireland and the Mercantile system. The Scientific Revolution, by which we mean the rise of an increasingly mathematical and mechanistic approach to the world, appeared to offer Europeans new and special modes of reason. The emergence of 'Physico-Theology', deliberate reconciliations of Christian and scientific approaches to the cosmos, around eighteenth-century Europe, testified to the authority of the new modes of knowledge.[32] Ephraim Chambers in his *Cyclopaedia* (1728) thus proclaimed to George I that the Arts and Sciences 'make the difference between your Majesty's Subjects and the Savages of Canada, or the Cape of Good Hope'.[33] The French missions to Lapland and Ecuador in the 1740s, as they confirmed Newton's predictions about the shape of the earth, demonstrated the power of the new sciences. They suggested, moreover, the possibility of a new system of measurement, based, unlike cubits or feet, on the proportions of the Earth itself, rather than those of the human body. The mechanical philosophy, at the same time, found application across the natural world. There is a direct connection between Stephen Hales's *Statickal Essays*, with its explanation of the circulation of sap in plants and blood in animals, Quesnay's theory of the heart, and his later model of the flow of wealth through an economy. Adam Smith, and later David Ricardo, similarly found in Newtonian gravitation and Montesquieu's theories of climate, new 'natural' ways of addressing the origins of wealth. The idea of government ordered by laws derived from the nature of Man and the universe found many kinds of political expression, conservative as well as revolutionary. By the second half of the century, statesmen around Europe became enthusiastic users of information, and patrons of surveys and censuses. The 'spirit of quantification' found application to government for practical reasons: people had to be counted, if taxation and conscription were to be planned rationally, and land had to be mapped and measured, and its natural resources inventoried, to allow its best defence and exploitation.[34] But the urgency with which the Jacobins, for example, set about the reforms which led to the metric system had an ideological basis: progress depended on the application of the Order of Nature to human society. The desire to make society and economy 'natural' also moved scientists and politicians in Georgian Britain. From 1814, for example, the Royal Society, under Banks, and the Admiralty, organized missions to the Arctic in search of 'natural principles' with which they might regulate the inflated 'artificial' war economy; high-latitude pendulum experiments, they hoped might be the basis of a reform of British weights and measures.[35] Even Tories were persuaded that Britain needed to be measured against the nature of the world. The late eighteenth-century inflection of the idea of 'improvement', the new scientific and political–economic language of agrarian enthusiasm, is a clear product of this era.

The faith that information was necessary for efficient government created new opportunities for men of science. We may argue that the 1780s and 1790s in Britain represent a classic example of what Bayly has called 'knowledge panics': moments when statesmen, moved by fear more than by the rational needs of the state, anxiously sought expert advice and organized public investigations.[36] For the concern of gentlemen like Banks or Young to expand the Crown's efficiency was answered by the desire of statesmen and civil servants to become (or appear to be) agents of progress. Pitt, described by some admiring contemporaries as 'the minister of progress and enlightenment', and his lieutenants, including Charles Jenkinson (created Baron Hawkesbury in 1786, and Earl of Liverpool in 1796) at the Board of Trade, Henry Dundas at the Home Office and the Board of Control, William Fawkener and George Chalmers at the Privy Council, Sir Charles Middleton at the Navy Board, Sir Evan Nepean and Lord Mulgrave at the Admiralty, George Rose and William Lowndes at the Treasury, John Palmer at the Post Office, brought new ambition and energy into British government.[37] A desire for informed policy led to a deliberate recruitment of technical and scientific expertise—Jeremy Bentham for advice on prison reform, Richard Price for calculation of the sinking fund, and Joseph Banks for guidance on colonial administration, agriculture, African and Arctic exploration, whaling, commercial policy, weights and measures, the adulteration of flour, bullion and coinage, naval stores, and the work of the Board of Trade, the Privy Council, the East India Company, and the Admiralty.

European policy, and in particular the post-1763 Bourbon reform programme, stimulated many British initiatives. Indeed, historians of British imperialism should note the direct influence of French precedents on Pitt's remaking of the administrative apparatus of British imperialism in and after 1784. In that year, the Crown assumed direct supervision over Britain's overseas affairs. Pitt made the Privy Council the master of the affairs of the East India Company under its Board of Control for India, and of colonial policy under its Committee for Trade and Plantations.[38] Harlow is, of course, correct to identify in Henry Dundas (later Melville) for India, or Charles Jenkinson (later Hawkesbury and Liverpool) for the colonies, and in the 'Second British Empire' they helped to make, extensions of an imperial programme already in train before the American War. The usual anglocentric interpretations invoke the intellectual influence of Adam Smith's attack in Book IV of the *Wealth of Nations* on the pernicious consequences of the 'government of an exclusive company of merchants' usurping the political and cultural responsibilities of a sovereign. Or, as in the case of Harlow, they point to the free ports in Dominica and Jamaica in 1768, or to Jenkinson's recommendations on the powers of Governors-General in Bengal in 1778. But the characteristic imperial reforms of Pitt's ministry: the imposition on the East India Company of the control of the Crown, the experiments with free ports in the West and East Indies to capture the commerce of Spanish America and China, and the reinvention of the colonial governor in the 'Crown Colony' as an enlightened despot, had immediate precedents in the reform of the French empire under Choiseul. Before the British Crown enclosed the East India Company within its sovereignty through the Regulating Act of 1773 and India Bill of 1784, Louis XV had taken command of the Compagnie des Indes, taking direct control of its African and India Ocean outposts (1763–71). He did so with the encouragement of the *économistes* who asserted, in an argument to which Smith added no novelties in 1776, that 'La Souveraineté accordée à une compagnie commerçante a été la cause de notre destruction dans ces contrées éloignées'.[39] The English entrepôts merely imitated the experiment initiated by Choiseul in Careenage in St. Lucia and Mole St. Nicholas in 1767, and by Praslin in France's Indian *comptoirs* in 1769. The executive powers vested by the French ordinance of 1 February 1761 in its Governor-Generals, in concert with Intendants, to preside over budgets and administrating, ordering peace and war, and submitting annually 'projets d'amélioration' for their domains, resemble closely those exercised by Governors of Britain's Crown Colonies. The construction of an 'Improving' British imperialism would draw quietly on these and other Bourbon initiatives.

Central to the new species of British imperialism which emerge at the end of the century is the idea that colonization was an enterprise of amelioration. Antislavery, and the evangelical aims to which it was connected, were only crests on this larger wave. The idea that Britain might 'improve' exotic peoples was a curious amalgam of religious and intellectual modesty and hubris. It is worth noting that the racism at the centre of this Georgian *mission civilisatrice* was tempered by a recognition of the capacities and achievements of darker peoples which would be less common a century later. An insecurity about Britain's advantages was based on the realities of power. Europeans in the early modern period were waterborne parasites: quick to command trade or settle at the coast, or along rivers, but slow to penetrate inland. In Asia, Africa, and in much of the Americas, their real influence was limited by their dependence on local allies. It was only during the next century, when technologies such as steam engines, applied to shipping, railways, migration, and war, changed the balance, that Europeans became able to impose relations of 'collaboration' on their own terms. But Britain had no overall technical superiority circa 1790. As Banks mused to Lord Macartney, in the tenor of Voltaire and Lord Kames:

> The great inventions which actually serve as the basis of our present stage of civilization were all known to the Chinese long before they were rein-

vented or stolen from them by us—printing, paper-making, gunpowder, and the arts of purifying the most refractory metals.[40]

Banks, thus, urged Macartney to steal the techniques which made contemporary China wealthy at the expense of British bullion: the confection of porcelain, and the cultivation and curing of tea.[41] African knowledge was thought no less worth recruiting. Thomas Falconer, when he proposed a mission up the River Senegal to Banks in 1773, reported the 'carving and other works of art which show that civility is far advanced in some of those regions'.[42] Henry de Ponthieu, a decade later , wrote that the French

have long accustom'd to avail themselves in [Caribbean] plants in Physic and surgery being instructed by the new Negroes that arrive from the different parts of the African continent,

and urged that the British also should interrogate their slaves for botanical and geographical information.[43] In these native capacities, of course, lay a reason for British intervention. They suggested that others were fit objects of missionary or commercial enthusiasm, and might benefit from British supervision.

If Christian Providentialism was the ideological taproot of the 'First British Empire', Enlightenment doctrines of cosmopolitan progress, anglicized in the Georgian idea of 'Improvement', sustained its successors. As an 'Ode for His Majesty's Birthday' in the *Gentleman's Magazine* of June 1786 exulted, George III was

O'er the cheer'd nations, far and wide
Diffusing opulence, and the public good.[44]

What distinguishes British imperialism, from the late eighteenth century onwards, is this faith in its capacity and right to increase the happiness of barbarians. The new view was expressed with concision by William Colebrook, the companion of Raffles, in his reflections on the people of Java:

they possess in aggregate as large a share of natural intelligence and acuteness, of patriotism & enthusiasm, as will be found among the lower orders of any country; & it goes for to confirm the universal doctrine that Mankind in the same circumstances is always the same ... Java might in 30 years or less be elevated into a respectable & eminent free state ... [if Java was established] under the protection of England 'till by introduction of Arts and Education the people might be fitted to govern themselves.[45]

Empire was now a process of preparing the rest of the world to become fully human. Britain had the right to rule in Java because it was preparing the Javanese for civilization and political sovereignty. Empire was justified as an instrument of development, or as Raffles put it, of 'the fostering and leading of [new races] of subjects and allies in the career of improvement'.[46] We may hear, almost as a distant echo, Mill's declaration in *On Liberty* that 'Despotism is a legitimate mode of government in dealing with barbarians, provided the end be their improvement'.[47]

This chapter is concerned with how this new imperialism of the Enlightenment hoisted the Royal Botanic Gardens at Kew on to the stage of world history. It is a story coextensive with the rise of Sir Joseph Banks to prominence in the public life of Georgian Britain, to which we now turn.

The Making of Sir Joseph Banks

On 10 August 1771, Mr. Joseph Banks was presented to George III at Kew on his return from his voyage around the world on the *Endeavour*. Banks gave his sovereign a golden coronet, decorated with feathers, a gift from a prince on the coast of Chile. George III offered, in exchange, his friendship, and over the next month Banks and Daniel Solander, the student of Linnaeus, visited many times to discuss the botanical and landscape paintings with which the expedition had returned from the South Seas. In 1772, he invited Banks to help reorganize the botanic garden, and the naturalist became a frequent Saturday visitor of the King.

It was South Sea glory which made Banks a Georgian cultural figure of the first rank.[48] He was elected to the Society of the Dilettanti in 1774, which included men like Henry Dundas and George Yonge who would extend his reach into the East India Company, the War Office, and the very ear of the Prime Minister. In 1778 he became President of the Royal Society, a post he held until his death in 1820. In that same year, he was elected Very High Steward of the Dilettanti, and a member of 'The Club' of Samuel Johnson and Sir Joshua Reynolds.

Banks, contrary to the opinion of some contemporaries and biographers, who perceived him as a statesman of science above the strife of political faction, actively courted both marks of prestige and public responsibilities.[49] In 1781 he quietly used his connections with the King and Lord North's government to secure his creation as a baronet.[50] Pitt and his political circle would elevate Banks, after a little prim hesitation on his part, to become one of the Knights of the Bath in 1795, and to the Privy Council from 1797. His close association first with the King, but also with the increasingly repressive regime of the 1790s, led many contemporaries, including writers of political verse, to describe him as a base fawner towards the powers-that-be, an image framed with brutal eloquence in James Gillray's caricature of 'The Great South Sea Caterpillar, transformed into a Bath Butterfly' (see Plate 10) which showed the President of the Royal Society, wearing the red ribbon of the Knights of the Bath, gazing upwards into the sun of royal patronage.

But the platform on which both his maritime and social successes rested was his private wealth, which derived chiefly from his estates in Lincolnshire, Middlesex, and Derbyshire and from money made by his uncle and maternal grandfather in Jamaican commerce and privateering along the Spanish coast of Central America.[51] Estate rents in Lincolnshire, Middlesex, and Derbyshire, rose through war-time inflation from £7,000 in 1791 to £12,300 in 1807 and, with the encouragement of the Corn Law of 1815, to £16,000 in 1820.[52] He literally bought his way on to the *Endeavour* expedition, through a contribution of several thousand pounds for its expenses. His wealth allowed him to purchase a vast library and collection of plant and animal specimens (see illustration 13), and in particular, to keep a remarkable team of naturalists—Daniel Solander, Jonas Dryander, Robert Brown, and John Lindley among them—as his retainers at his mansion at Soho Square in London. His London house put him within reach of the British Museum, learned societies, and government offices, while from Spring Grove, his Middlesex estate, he visited the King at Kew and Windsor. His social origins connected him to men of influence, including, for example, to Lords of the Admiralty: his education at Harrow, Eton, and Christ Church Oxford, for example, linked him to Constantine Phipps, and recreations, including fishing, and perhaps wenching, to the 4th Earl of Sandwich. His position in the Royal Society depended as much on his wealth and social stature as on his intellectual eminence.

Banks took pride in the fact that the Royal Society, unlike continental academies, was controlled by people like himself, 'a set of Free Englishmen elected by each other'.[53] He never mastered any foreign language. This did not mean, however, that he failed to appreciate the achievements of his European contemporaries. He wrote wistfully to Formey, the great secretary of the Berlin Academy:

> I envy you the pleasure you have enjoyed in the friendship of Voltaire, Maupertuis, D'Alembert etc. & I know not whether I judge [right] but I fear I do when I think that the present sun does not strike upon men of equal abilities ...[54]

In the spirit of Kant's 'Was ist Aufklarung?', Banks added: 'But I envy you most the nature of the Great Frederic whose character is not equalled once in a thousand years.'[55] While cultivating his own 'Frederic' at Kew, he maintained a correspondence with European scientific contemporaries from St. Petersburg to Lisbon, in particular those concerned with botany and agriculture.[56] Through Solander, Dryander, and the Forsters, Banks enjoyed also a direct connection to the Linnaean circle and Baltic Cameralism. He cultivated close ties with France, exchanging compliments, and seeds and herbarium specimens, with Buffon and Thouin in Paris, from 1772 on.[57] He urged friends, in particular Charles Blagden, to supply him with detailed intelligence on French scientific life, and in particular on the collections of the

13. Sir Joseph Banks's passion for natural history collecting satirized in a contemporary print.
Wellcome Institute Library.

Jardin and Cabinet du Roi.[58] While he had begun as a partisan of the artificial Linnaean system of classification, he became converted to the advantages of Jussieu's 'natural system'.[59] Banks purchased European books and periodicals extensively, and had runs of the *Mémoires* of the Academies of Paris, Montpellier, Toulouse, and Dijon, the *Corps d'Observations* of the Society of Agriculture, Commerce, and Arts of Bretagne, the journal of the Museum of Natural History, and the Royal Society of Agriculture of Paris, which had no equal in Britain.[60] He had at his disposal the most advanced Cameralist and Physiocratic treatises on the uses of botany for economic government.[61] When Johan Kønig died, while collecting plants for the East India Company, Banks reminded the Court of Directors of the importance of Cameralist natural history:

> It is important not just for science but for the commerce of the East India Company that a worthy successor be found among the naturalists trained in the universities of Northern Europe.[62]

From the separate mention they receive in that catalogue, we know that periodical articles on the introduction of spices and other useful plants to Guyane, Martinique and St. Domingue had equally received his attention.[63] When Banks plotted a future for Kew, there are good reasons therefore to think that he had before his eyes the examples of Linnaeus and Buffon, and the French Crown's application of botany to colonial agriculture.[64]

Banks perhaps imbibed from his European contemporaries the very ideal of the *Philosophe.* He took pride in the arrangements he concluded with the Admiralty for the return of scientific collections taken from French and American vessels on the high seas.[65] When he was elected the most senior foreign member of the Institut National of France, he declared, to the anger of Cobbett and francophobes, that he considered this mark of their esteem to be 'the highest and most enviable literary distinction which I could possibly attain', and proclaimed that men of learning held in common 'the empire of virtue, of justice, and honour'.[66] However, since Britain usually had as much scientific material on the high seas as any other power, his arrangements with Jussieu and Franklin had good pragmatic foundations. It is also clear, moreover, that Banks's cosmopolitan enthusiasm did not extend to willingness to cede economic or political advantage to what he once described as Britain's 'natural enemies'.[67] He applauded France's defeats, sending fine wine to Lord Wellesley in 1810 to celebrate the enemy's collapse in India, Spain, and Persia.[68] It was thus as much with jealous patriotism, and perhaps anxiety, as with fraternal sympathy, that Banks watched the *Philosophes.*

Banks responded, in many ways, to foreign influence, but he remained driven by the concerns of his environment and social class. Agricultural wealth, as well as allowing him to buy social and scientific entrée, provided him with an identity and world view. What his many distinguished biographers have not usually recognized is that Banks brought to London the concerns of the Georgian countryside.[69] Banks spent a large part of each year in the country, and while in London corresponded more with the stewards of his estates than anyone else.[70] It was not on exploration or natural history, but agriculture, fen drainage, corn diseases, flax, hemp, and wool, that he chose to publish his opinions.[71] We may take with a grain of salt Brougham's recollection that Banks only became interested in farming on the King's prompting: agriculture stood at the centre of his intellectual life.[72] It was as a Lincolnshire magnate, and as a product of that English agrarian tradition which we examined in the last chapter, that Banks intervened in public life. The preoccupations of his generation of large landholders were of global extension—reaching from fenland in East Anglia and farmland in the Scottish lowlands, the digging of canals and improvement of roads, to slave trading in Africa, West Indian plantations and East Indian commerce—

and encompassed natural history and gardening, exploration and political economy.[73]

Banks, like Markham or Hartlib before him, saw the landlord as a Providential agent. The proprietor, through his private activity, and his influence on his tenants, turned the natural potential of the Creation into human riches. He argued, thus, that the nation's landowners should charge higher rents:

> Our land is in many parts too low-let that the nation at large has reason to complain of its landowners, for not applying to their tenants a stimulus of rent, sufficient to compel them to draw out from the ground all that nature has lodged in it . . .[74]

Political economy and theology provided him with an explanation for his social class and its prerogative to advise, lead, and if necessary coerce its subordinates. This rural ideal of 'Improvement' shaped his thinking about Britain's overseas dominions. He saw colonial expansion as enclosure on a grand scale, and indeed he urged the East India Company in 1791 to apply the Inclosure Acts of Lincolnshire to its dominions in order to create the Bengali squires which might make India fruitful.[75] In St. Helena and the West Indies, as we have seen in Ceylon, Banks similarly expected government to organize an environment in which private agriculture would thrive.

Banks saw those who worked the land as the centre of national life. But here he was not merely responding to the indigenous Christian agrarian or Whig traditions. There is instead clear evidence that Banks had come under the influence of the Physiocrats. Where he advised Liverpool in 1815 to tighten agricultural protection, his argument owed much to French economic thinking.[76] Banks asserted the primacy of the land as the natural basis of all other wealth, and provided a theory of rent as the foundation of revenue and the consumption of manufactures with which Quesnay or Turgot would have been comfortable. The national debt, he warned the Prime Minister, was serviced with revenue from land taxes, these taxes depended on rents, and the capacity of tenants to pay rents—settled during war-time inflation—depended on the price of corn. Protection was thus a necessary element of the English Constitution:

> the political state of a nation is like a tree: its roots are the farmers, the lower branches traders, its upper branches manufacturers, and its fruit and flowers the nobility and gentry—if its roots are not manured, the tree will droop.

By purchasing foreign corn, Britain not only faced possible famine by becoming dependent on its 'natural enemies', but the wealth it exchanged for food would allow another nation's nobility and gentry to purchase manufactured luxuries.[77] Banks thus recommended a new Corn Law which would fully protect British farmers from foreign competition. Banks had no doctrinaire commitment to Mercantilism: in the 1780s he had argued, on lines which resemble Physiocratic arguments for the liberation of the grain trade in France, for the end to commercial restrictions on the export of wool.[78] His campaign for allowing export rested on the assertion that Britain's 'wool growers' deserved priority over its textile manufacturers. The Crown had a responsibility, natural and fiscal, as well as patriotic, to favour agriculture.

In his faith in the centrality of agriculture, and the need for government intervention, Banks was representative of a generation which had come into its own in an era of perpetual hot and cold war with France. He was not alone in discovering in European policy examples worth British attention. Developments across the Channel had long been kept under observation through travel and through translations, of the *Journal Économique*, for example, in 1754.[79] His contemporaries recorded their admiration of the statesmen and economic thinkers who made the improvement of agriculture into the business of government, often with a disparaging glance at their own countrymen. Sir John Sinclair praised Frederick the Great for having enabled the doubling of his population by his application of 'public encouragement' to the arts and manufactures of his kingdom.[80] Cornelius Varlo in *The Essence of Agriculture* (1786) similarly alluded to the late King of Prussia whose wise policies presumed that 'agriculture is the foundation of the opulence and prosperity of the state'.[81] Articles in the *Annals of Agriculture* advised British readers of the progress of agriculture under royal patronage across the continent, reporting on the work of the Oeconomical Societies, which usually benefited from state help, and on the 'Encouragement of Agriculture by the Empress of Russia'.[82] Young praised French sheep breeding, and in particular Daubenton's *Instruction pour les Bergers et pour les Propriétaires des Troupeaux* (1782), and noted Turgot's encouragement of experiments on wool. Sinclair praised Turgot, also, as inspiring his reflections on British finance, while he praised the 'humane and beneficent principles of a Necker'.[83] Young argued that French exertions, 'the noble efforts of our enlightened and industrious neighbours', represented a perfect contrast to the inertia of the British government on the principal question of the day: agriculture.[84] We must clearly take Young's reference to 'Physiocratical rubbish' in his travels of 1792 more as patriotic horror at the French Revolution than genuine rejection of the policies framed in Britain's still enlightened, but now revolutionary, rival.[85] Young, like Banks, should have instead acknowledged that he had chosen to forge a British Physiocracy: a patriotic political economy, with the union of the Crown and the landowning classes at its centre.

We have much still to learn about how the European Enlightenment shaped the evolution of British policy in the 1780s and 1790s. Much of its impact was hidden by contemporaries' desire to hide, as in the example to Young, how the enemy had influenced them. The construction of the history of the twentieth century already conceals, in the same way, how 'the

West' and 'the East' borrowed quietly from each other. What is clear, however, is that agricultural improvement provided a patriotic vocabulary for the domestication of European thought and policy. One crucial medium for this was the *Annals of Agriculture*, the journal published by Arthur Young from 1784 onwards, which came to attract contributions from a remarkable range of figures including, as we have seen, George III and Banks, but also statesmen such as William Eden and Lord Townshend, and intellectuals such as Jeremy Bentham and Thomas Malthus. It provided a meeting place for the views of 'improvers' of all kinds, and included articles on political economy, techniques of manufacture, imperial policy, scientific discoveries, reports on European affairs, and voyages of exploration, as well as the news on harvests, weather, and advice on crops and culture which one might have expected. Evangelicals contributed to its pages, and the parish clergy of the Church of Scotland and England contributed most of the statistics for Sinclair's survey of Scottish agriculture, and for the Board of Agriculture's 'General View of the Agriculture of Great Britain'.[86] The *Annals* offered a space in which a political generation, products of the eighteenth-century renaissance in the public schools and in the study of classical literature, could inflect the analyses of Scotch and Continental philosophy into the accents of Cicero, Cato, Varro, and Columella. It provided, in particular, an important medium for the anglicization of Cameralist and Physiocratic thought. The sophisticated political–economic arguments which we have seen Banks deploying in the 1790s and in 1815 clearly reflect this influence, as indeed do the reflections on agriculture and population of Thomas Malthus.

But it was a sense of national emergency, as much as ideology, which animated that party which Bayly has called the 'agrarian patriots'. While public debt had mushroomed from £136 million in 1776 to £257 million in 1783, Britain's naval supremacy appeared no longer inevitable.[87] A new conflict with France was always possible, as Arthur Young warned, 'we must in the very enjoyments of peace be preparing for war'.[88] The American war, he argued, had shaken British power 'to its foundations', and 'the prospects of this country at present are complicated and doubtful'. In the crisis of the 1780s, Young and others demanded a patriotic coalition of 'all the wisdom and talents in the nation'.[89] Against the Jacobin threat, he urged: 'We ought all to be animated with one soul, to imitate the activity of the foe, to call new principles of energy into action.'[90] This, in part, was the significance of the Crown for contemporaries: it provided a focus for the coming together of the nation, which negated the divisions of the country by political allegiance and private interest. The agrarian crusade of the 1780s, one may argue, contained the embryo of loyalist responses to the Revolution in the 1790s and to Napoleon in the 1800s. 'Leave the politicians of party to themselves,' Young thundered, 'he only is the true politician who multiplies resources; and that is only to be done in this Kingdom effectually, by *Improvements in Agriculture*.'[91]

We may see Banks himself as motivated by a similar desire for an efficient national policy, above the call of party. His combination of a Whig faith in the landowner and yeoman as the foundation of the Constitution, with fierce loyalty to the Crown, is fully representative of prevailing sentiments.[92] While, as we shall see, Banks rose to political influence with Pitt and his circle, he remained a political independent. He originally hesitated in 1793 about joining the Board of Agriculture, arguing that the Board was 'not likely to benefit the landed interest', and would instead become a honeycomb of patronage to which Pitt would appoint without consulting commissioners.[93] He was a friend of the Duke of Bedford, and maintained a polite connection with Fox, who thanked him in 1802 for the gift of a double white camellia, 'the pride of our greenhouse'.[94] But he feared that the opposition lacked the backbone to respond efficiently to the enemy, as he wrote in 1797, 'Pit [*sic*] rules, Fox grumbles, the French beat all whom they attack'.[95] He distrusted, moreover, Holland House's democratic pretensions: he wrote Liverpool in 1800 that since the Whig Cabinet came into office the Privy Council had been 'wantonly trampled upon'.[96] He found the willingness of Pitt, Dundas, and Liverpool to draw on the advice and expertise of men like himself more congenial.

Banks and his contemporaries saw in agriculture a variety of tonics for British institutions and poultices for its sores. While they shared the contemporary faith that the land provided a moral and civic education, it was agriculture's practical advantages which won their attention. They argued to Pitt and Hawkesbury that national security required British self-sufficiency in food.[97] Unlike manufacture and commerce, moreover, which rose and fell with fashion, farming provided a permanent basis for population, prosperity, and all other kinds of economic activity.[98] They did not deny the importance of cities or exchange, concurring with Paolo Balsamo, the physiocratic Professor of Agriculture at the University of Palermo, that urban luxury and the market gave 'the strongest impulse to circulation'.[99] Nor were they anti-industrial: agriculture, for their purposes, included the mining of coal and lead, the tanning of leather, watermills for timber and cereals, canals, and turnpikes.[100] They merely shared the contemporary opinion, which Gibbon expressed in the *Decline and Fall* that, 'Agriculture is the foundation of manufactures; since the productions of nature are the materials of art.'[101]

The improvement of agriculture, moreover, appeared to many as the key to meeting the challenge of the national debt. Sinclair, quite deliberately, chose in the 1780s to make the history of Britain's finances his subject, and prepared his influential *History of the Public Revenue of the British Empire* (1784) with a clear rhetorical purpose.[102] It was as a parliamentary expert on debt that Sinclair was able to secure for Pitt that £5 million in commercial credit which persuaded the Prime Minister to found the Board of Agriculture in 1793. While Pitt's other advisers, such as Richard Price, projected a sinking fund, British agrarians urged that government should invest capital in 'the encouragement of industry, in promoting the cultivation of the soil, and in extending commerce and navigation'.[103] Young attacked those who spent their time dreaming up visionary schemes for paying the national debt: 'they would have been better employed in teaching the nation the easiest way to bear it. The true secret is to increase your income.'[104] The development of the productive resources of the kingdom was the true compound interest which would make debt tolerable.[105]

Agricultural 'improvement', as the business of inspiring landowners to lead their tenants into the path of progress, could also contribute to national security. Local loyalties would stiffen resistance to any riot or invasion, and the relations of agricultural production—of magnate to large tenant to yeoman—could be converted into a military chain of command. Arthur Young had proposed in 1792 that Britain should match the patriotic enthusiasm of Jacobin France and awaken that feeling 'in the minds of a nation ... that *rising in a mass* ... this generous sentiment, the nobly infectious flame of which catches from soul to soul'.[106] His patriotic crowd (in the innocent years before the great mutinies) was the British Jack-Tar fighting under its officers, but he argued also for a potential rural levée en masse. Banks enlarged Young's suggestion.[107] In *Outlines of a Plan of Defence against a French Invasion* (1794), Banks argued that the traditional ties of country life would provide an immediate militia: 'gentlemen, yeomen, and subaltern graziers' would be the officer corps, while 'lesser farmers, their sons and servants would serve as non-commissioned officers and privates under pay'.[108] These agrarianist defence schemes, communicated to Pitt and Dundas, formed the basis of British organization against the threat of rural disorder and French invasion.[109] Banks himself undertook to serve in a military capacity, receiving the thanks of the Duke of Portland for quelling riots in Lincolnshire, and in 1797 serving as Lieutenant-Colonel of the Supplemental Militia of that county. He participated in patriotic societies in London, becoming President in 1792 of 'The Society for the Preservation of the Public Peace, the Constitution of the Country, and the Liberty and Property of the Subject'.

So central was agriculture to the destiny of the nation, that it deserved the assistance of the state. The British agrarianists of the 1780s and 1790s argued that only the Crown could ensure that, across the nation, private virtue turned Nature into public abundance. The collection and dissemination of information was one basis of improvement, and the Board of Agriculture came to organize a remarkable system of 'Statistical Reports' on the Scottish, English, and Irish counties. These offered evidence for the importance of enclosure and of protection. The Board of Agriculture thus pressed, although without Pitt's support, for a General Enclosure Bill, to allow enclosers more cheaply to assert their right over land.[110] They were more successful with Protection, arguing that a tightening of the Corn Laws would encourage investments and increased production.[111] Banks suggested to the Jenkinsons, for example, in 1800, that if encouraged with tariffs, British farmers could supply all the wants of the country.[112] Such a justification formed the basis of the Corn Laws of 1791, for their redesign in 1795 and 1804, and, as we have seen, for the Corn Law of 1815.[113]

Banks and his contemporaries had grave reservations about Adam Smith. They viewed tariffs as the heat which the Crown could turn up or down, as needed, to force the flowering of prosperity and political cohesion. Young attacked *The Wealth of Nations* 'as intended rather as stigma on the profits of that first of arts, than designed to animate any further exertions in it'.[114] Sinclair followed the other line of argument and noted that the country had flourished under 'mercantilism', with its revenue increasing from £2 million to £36 million sterling,

> it is difficult to assign any other reason for all this prosperity ... but the commercial encouragements which have been enacted by the legislature, and the attention which has been shown to promote the industry and exertions of the people.[115]

Banks in 1800 similarly protested that 'Smith's Principles, like those of Revolutionary France, are based on unqualified liberty but are not founded on reason or experience'.[116] Banks, as we have noted, had no fixed commitment to commercial restrictions, having campaigned for the export of wool. Protection was, however, too valuable an instrument, through which government might encourage one or another direction of 'improvement', to be discarded.

The agrarian view of empire was equally complex. In part, agrarian patriots shared some of Smith's suspicions that overseas possessions had often drained, rather than added, to the kingdom's wealth. Young and Sinclair, alluding to America, warned that 'the future dependence of the State may settle more on the basis of internal resources' than colonies.[117] Young argued, along lines framed by the young Jeremy Bentham,

> all transmarine, or distant dominions, are sources of weakness: and that to renounce them would be wisdom. Apply this in France to St. Domingo, in Spain to Peru, or in England to Bengal.[118]

The East India Company was a particular target, since its commerce required the export of bullion to the East, with Sinclair arguing that the £24 million it had swallowed 'would have rendered every acre in the Kingdom productive of some valuable article'.[119] But whatever their anxieties about territory, they remained strong supporters of British naval power and commerce.[120] Colonies, moreover, as consumers could also encourage British farmers. Young, Lord Sheffield, and the political economist Chalmers thus attacked the West Indian planters who sought the relaxation of protection in 1783 to allow them to import the food and timber they needed from the United States.[121] Young had no quarrel with Britain's West Indian outposts since they served as 'a vivifying support of our husbandry and fisheries'.[122]

Sugar planters were farmers too, moreover. By the same token, the East India Company, as we shall see, could be redeemed by making India an agricultural colony, and a consumer of its exports, instead of merely depending on its trade in luxuries. Banks in 1788 thus prepared an extensive memorandum for the East India Company in which he urged its agrarian future:

> A colony such as this, blessed with the advantages of Soil, Climate, & Population so eminently above its Mother Country, seems by nature intended for the purpose of supplying her fabrics with raw materials; & it must be allowed that a Colony yielding that kind of tribute binds itself to the "Mother Country" by the strongest and most indissoluble of human ties, that of common interest & mutual advantage.[123]

Instead of taking out Britain's silver dollars, and imposing its calicoes on the home market, it might cultivate raw materials.

One of the lessons of the American Revolution, which contemporaries saw through the prism of Montesquieu's *Spirit of the Laws*, was that government and economy had a relationship to climate. As the *Annals of Agriculture* advised: 'planting colonies in climates that produced similar commodities with the "Mother Country" could lead only to rivalry and independence'.[124] Tropical colonies would not produce products, or political elites, which would challenge Britain's. There were some hesitations about New South Wales, and many, other than Banks, initially preferred West Africa as a site for a convict colony.[125] When Banks launched his African Association in 1788, he was joined by representatives of the agrarian movement including Sinclair, Baron Rawdon (later, as Marquis of Hastings, military hero of the East India Company and Governor-General of Bengal), and Lord Sheffield.[126] As worries about the food supply grew, particularly after Malthus's essay, many of these hesitations about temperate agriculture eventually disappeared. But apart from Australia, for which Banks retained a paternal *faiblesse*, he and his generation distinctly preferred land which might yield tropical commodities, in particular raw cotton, for which British manufacturers were developing an insatiable appetite.[127] The British West Indies were, to this extent, model colonies.

'Improvement', for the agrarians, implied a commitment to the reform of the world as a whole, 'the real prosperity and happiness of the human race', and not merely the countryside.[128] Promoting 'the internal Improvement ... of a Powerful Empire' concerned 'the improvement of the people in regard to their health, industry, and morals', and not merely agriculture, mining, and fisheries.[129] Sinclair indeed included the reform of the private body in the task of renovating the body politic, publishing *A Collection of Papers on the Subject of Athletic Exercises* (1806). Banks and his contemporaries paid equal attention to the inner man, and admired the Evangelical movement for promoting the 'spirit of improvement' through education.[130] Banks himself lent his patronage to missionaries, while he complemented his charity and repression in Lincolnshire with becoming 'Patron' of the National School at Horncastle intended to diffuse 'those principles which may render Knowledge, not merely harmless but beneficial to the Possession of the Community at large'.[131] The people of Africa, India, and the West Indies would also be elevated and civilized by the improvement of agriculture, as farming and commerce made them fit for Christianity and education.[132]

Banks was well aware that people had often chosen to resist their 'improvement'. The English peasants made unemployed or landless by enclosure had long made this clear. His own steward wrote regularly of such disturbances:

> As expected there was a mob on Monday on Holland Fen.... They went to Boston and broke Mr. Barton's windows he being a person who was chiefly concerned in getting the Act for Inclosing Holland Fen.[133]

Only the protection of troops saved him when in 1815 a mob arrived at Soho Square in London, ripping down lamp posts, and attacking his door in response to his support for the Corn Law.[134] The African Association learned also that the inhabitants of Africa did not meet their 'improvers' with much enthusiasm:

> They express on all occasions a conviction that the soil and country is their own, saying this is not white man's country, this belong to black man, who will not suffer white man to be master here.... They have no intention of embracing Christianity, saying they are too old for that.[135]

This resistance however had no legitimacy, and at home or abroad it could be crushed. Indeed African and Indian resistance might be dealt with even more ruthlessly since, as George III advised Pitt on India, the government of barbarians could not be carried out 'with the same moderation that is suitable to a European civilized Nation'.[136] Gentleman 'Improvers', armed with insight into the potential of Nature and the destiny of Man, might justly coerce those who would not see the light. The natural sciences, joined to the Pelagian optimism of political economy, lent new sanction to enclosure at home and colonization abroad.

It is in this era after 1783 that Sir Joseph Banks, newly a baronet, came to enjoy real political influence. Pitt and his circle sought his advice on a bewildering variety of questions. He advised, for example, on appointments of naval officers and colonial officials, on British policy towards Australia, Iceland, and Haiti, on the application of steam to coining, his word leading directly to an embargo on the export of potash to France.[137] His world view is easily discerned in advice he gave to Hawkesbury, resembling uncannily the opinion offered by John Dee to Elizabeth I in the *General and Rare Memorials* of two centuries before, that the unification of Great Britain,

Ireland, the Orkneys, Shetlands, and Iceland would furnish an empire which, by its maritime prowess, might 'keep the whole world in awe and if necessary in subjection'.[138] Banks wished to place his knowledge and connections at the service of his nation's power. To this end he contributed, as we have seen, advice on defence against civil disorder and invasion. He assisted, equally, with European policy, providing intelligence, and discreetly conveying foreign visitors into conversations, for example, with Pitt.[139] Baron Vay de Vaja of Hungary, who wished to avoid the attention of the ambassadors of Austria and Prussia, was able to meet Pitt quietly at Banks's home, the President of the Royal Society having smuggled the Prime Minister through a back door from St. Anne's Church into the Soho Square mansion.[140] But it was on imperial matters that Banks gave, with equal discretion, his most wide-ranging and influential advice. With his guidance, Pitt, Dundas, and the Jenkinsons found in botany, and in the Royal Garden at Kew, many answers to the crises of the day. In the mirror of science and political economy, the British Empire would rediscover itself as efficient and moral.

Borrowing from the French: Science and the Second British Empire

The end of the American War in 1783 left the British Empire facing many kinds of difficulties.

Britain's strategic position was less comfortable than it had been for most of the century. From the Nine Years War, the containment of France, Britain's only real 'Blue Water' competitor, had depended on the success of the Royal Navy, and the ease with which coalitions had arisen against Bourbon pretensions. But France in the American War had forged a successful alliance with Spain and Protestant Holland, as well as expatriate English, and had held its own in naval conflict. Its East and West Indian outposts, in particular St. Domingue, were the most valuable colonies in the world, with immensely profitable plantations, and harbours from which a lucrative trade was conducted with Spanish America, Asia, and the Mozambique coast, and out of which the French Navy and privateers could directly threaten Britain's Atlantic and India commerce, already complicated by the Dutch control of the Cape. The American secessionist example had also attracted admirers in Ireland and, to a lesser extent, the West Indies.

Economic problems pressed even more directly. If the West Indies had been the most valuable part of the First British Empire, 'the principal source of the national opulence and maritime power', they had depended on the northern colonies for 'their bread and drink and all the necessaryes of humane life, their cattle and horses for cultivating their plantations, lumber and staves … the very houses in frames, together with shingles which cover them.'[141] Now the United States was independent, the Navigation Acts

Plate 9. Ram Letting from Robert Bakewell's Breed at Dishley, near Loughborough, Leicester *(1810). Sir Joseph Banks stands forth from the door-frame staring over to Bakewell (see p. 85).* Tate Gallery.

Plate 10. The Great South Sea Caterpillar, Transformed into a Bath Butterfly *(1796). This Gillray caricature shows Sir Joseph Banks, newly adorned with the red ribbon of the Order of the Bath, staring upwards at the sun of royal patronage (see p. 94).* British Museum.

Plate 11. George III's crenellated castle at Kew, with an elegant company of promenaders. This grandiose, never completed palace was dynamited in 1828 (see p. 89). Royal Botanic Gardens, Kew.

Plate 12. The Company Garden in Cape Town (1840s) was more an urban playground than a scientific centre (see p. 181). South African Library.

Plate 13. The Great Palm House at Kew, designed by Decimus Burton and Richard Turner, with recreating Victorians (see p. 185). Royal Botanic Gardens, Kew.

Plate 14. The Decimus Burton gates which connected the gardens to Kew Green from 1845 (see p. 186). Royal Botanic Gardens, Kew.

restricted the Sugar Islands access to these vital supplies. At the same time, American raw cotton, needed by the expanding textile industry of Lancashire, was now as much outside of the mercantile system as Brazilian and East Indian. American timber, crucial in particular for the masts of British vessels, and Baltic hemp, flax, and tar could now potentially be withheld from the Royal Navy by foreign powers. The war had placed, moreover, an immense new burden of debt on Britain. This had ultramarine implications, given that the East India Company depended on bullion 'investments' for its trade in India and China.

These economic and strategic problems were connected to issues of morale. In the aftermath of 1783, and even more during the Wars of the French Revolution, British power had a new need to present itself as legitimate and necessary. The Whig attack on the Crown's corrupting influence, and on the power of the state, meant George III and Pitt had themselves to demonstrate their virtue. As this critique also extended to the East India Company, which by the India Act of 1784 was now under the discipline of the Crown, both the Honourable Company and the new India Board needed to prove themselves wise governors. The emergence of an antislavery movement represented a similar public relations challenge for the West Indian and slaving interests, which included the most prosperous merchants of Bristol and Liverpool. But it was not only a home audience which needed persuading. Britain needed, also, to demonstrate its fidelity to creole élites, such as in the West Indies.

But what the French had also shown in the Seven Years' and American Wars, where they had skilfully recruited Amerindians and Indians as their proxies, was the importance of winning the loyalty of 'indigenous' peoples. Britain's ongoing struggle with France was moral as well as military, and affected every area of British interest. In the high days of the 1790s, for example, when Toussaint L'Ouverture's Black Jacobins (with some help from General Yellow Fever) had destroyed 100,000 British troops in St. Domingue, when United Irishmen plotted rebellion with Paris, while at home the great naval mutinies exploded, Tipu Sultan of Mysore wrote to the Representatives of the People in Mauritius and Réunion:

> You have the power and the means of effecting [Indian liberty], by your free negroes. With these new citizens, much dreaded by the English, joined to the troops of the line, we will purge India of these villains.[142]

Against this kind of challenge, Britain depended on winning hearts and minds, as well as on Nelson or Wellington. Empire, more than ever, was a matter of providing economic plenty, order, justice, and opportunity, as much as of coercion. The benevolence of Britain's dominion had to be demonstrated at home and abroad.

The natural sciences in general, and botany in particular, provided solutions to these three kinds of crisis. They provided information on geography and population which had military and strategic significance. As savants plotted the oceans, and discovered the use and culture of new plants and animals, knowledge also found economic application. Equally, the sciences might help to show British government as efficient and wise.

The Royal Gardens at Kew acquired new functions in this era. Before it had been only a recipient of empire's bounty, receiving gifts from America, but little from official sources, not even from Cook's three voyages. From the 1780s onwards, however, it became a *de facto* national collection, to which seeds and bulbs were sent from every part of the world. More strikingly, Kew became a source of plants, and of gardeners, sent outwards to Britain's overseas dominions. Linnaeus, as we examined earlier, had projected a mercantilist natural history which would discover new plants and animals for commerce, while acclimatizing, within the territory of the nation, valuable exotic plants and animals. In the *Hortus Cliffortianus* (1737) he had compared this movement of living things, indigenous to particular places, to new homes, to the world-wide commerce in goods, while in the 'Hortus Uppsaliensis' (1745) he expressed the hope that his botanic garden might organize a global trade in living things to the benefit of the Swedish kingdom. With a similar economic metaphor, Banks urged Dundas in 1787 that Kew might become 'a great botanical exchange house for the empire'.[143] Banks, more aware than Linnaeus of climate as a limit to acclimatization, never thought of seducing tropical plants to grow in English fields. His aim instead was the translation of economic crops between the East to West Indies, and horticultural exotics, as in the case of the Cape flora, from South to North. But the successful search for useful or beautiful plants, and the introduction of exotics into local agriculture, depended on colonial botanic gardens and on sending out men with expertise in collecting and culture. In this France had provided the model to be imitated. A letter accompanying a nutmeg tree sent to Kew from Java referred directly to the role of the Jardin du Roi earlier in the century, expressing the hope it might be 'spread to our colonies in the hot climates, as the coffee tree was first spread to the French West Indies, from a plant taken from the Botanic Garden in Paris.'[144] The later achievements of Buffon, Thouin, and Céré were equally before the eyes of contemporaries. The quiet imitation which always accompanies rivalry would shape the patterns of both Britain's scientific exploration, and its projection of botany into the imperial sphere in the 1780s and 1790s.

The political and economic implications of exploration were obvious to contemporaries. Alexander Dalrymple, who had framed the imperial motive for the *Endeavour* expedition, had promised that the South Seas offered vital opportunities for multiplying the commerce of Britain, and the wealth of the East India Company.[145] It was not merely for nostalgic reasons that the vessels bound on Cook's second voyage to the Pacific were initially named in 1771 the *Drake* and the *Raleigh.*[146] La Pérouse's expedition of 1785, the Spanish expedition under Malaspina (1789–94), and Vancouver's (1791–5), all had the possibility of a North-West Passage, an Arctic sea route between

Europe and the East, in their sights.[147] The East India Company similarly sought to master the waters of India and the Eastern Seas which led to China. In 1779, before the British government even had an organized hydrology department, the East India Company appointed Dalrymple its 'hydrographer', while in 1801 it offered £1,200 in *batta* or table money to the officers of the *Investigator* voyage, in order, as Banks put it to Flinders, 'to Encourage the men of Science to discover such things as will be useful to the Commerce of India & to find new passages'.[148] In 1795 the Admiralty created its hydrological department, importing Dalrymple from the East India Company, and beginning the systematic programme of hydrological surveys which would convey British naturalists, over the next decades, to more of the world than any of their European competitors.[149]

If, as Harlow suggests, British expansion in the eighteenth century extended Tudor imperialists' aim of depriving Spain of an American or Pacific monopoly, the practical example of France proved a more direct inspiration.[150] Far more than is usually acknowledged, for example, the great scientific missions of the Royal Navy in the age of Cook were driven by competition with France, and responded to French precedents. Mackay at the opening of *In the Wake of Cook* cited the *Investigator* of 1801—which carried Robert Brown as botanist, the finest surveying and astronomical equipment, an astronomer, a landscape painter, and a geologist—to show how Cook and Banks had introduced a scientific approach to Royal Navy exploration.[151] But there were clear precedents *outre-Manche* for this kind of scientific team, much, as earlier, Cook's Transit of Venus expedition followed the path of the French scientific embassies of the 1740s to Lapland and Peru, Le Caille's observation of the Transit of Mercury (1750) at the Cape of Good Hope, and Bougainville's *Boudeuse*. La Pérouse's *Astrolabe* and *Boussole*, for example, carried a party of leading scientists handpicked by Buffon: two astonomers, two botanists, an engineer, a geographer, a meteorologist.[152] French *esprit de système* had provided a clear blueprint for organized scientific survey. Indeed, it is worth noting that almost every major British voyage of exploration was immediately preceded by a French mission: La Pérouse left 1 August 1785, 30 days before the *King George* and *Queen Charlotte* left also to the North Pacific, similarly Matthew Flinders sailed with his team of scientists in the *Investigator* in July 1801 behind Nicholas Baudin who had left in October 1800 with the *Géographe* and *Naturaliste* and a scientific *équipe* of twenty-two botanists, zoologists, mineralogist, painters, draughtsmen, and gardeners. Even after the Napoleonic Wars, the voyage of King, which carried the Kew collector Cunningham, came to the north-west coast of Australia in the wake of the French *Uranie*.[153] The intellectual initiatives of an imperial rival were well worth imitating.

Fear of France gave similar momentum to British enterprise in Africa, and added further tribute to Kew. From 1773 Banks had considered a voyage of exploration in the Mediterranean and North Africa. In particular he wished that Britain might follow up the efforts of Adanson in Senegambia.[154] Sailing up the Senegal, his friend Falconer believed, would lead to the Niger river which would 'furnish ample material for natural history'.[155] In 1767, moreover, a joint meeting of the Committees on Colonies and Manufactures of the Society of Arts had looked towards Senegambia as a future source of raw cotton for Lancashire.[156] By 1783 Banks knew from his communications with Thouin of the Jardin du Roi that the French planned extensive African and Levantine exploration, results of which were published in 1787.[157] It seems likely that this was one reason for Banks and colleagues founding the Committee of the Association for Promoting the Discovery of the Inland Districts of Africa, the direct precursor of the Royal Geographical Society of 1830, in June 1788, and their sending out of John Ledyard and Simon Lucas in 1788 to Cairo and Tripoli.[158] In 1791, Banks, who opposed neither the slave trade nor chattel slavery, allied the African Association with their evangelical opponents in the Sierra Leone Company, to enlarge the purposes of African exploration.[159] In order to fulfil its charter's intention that it might prove 'highly beneficial to the Manufacturers and other Trading Interests of these Kingdoms', the Company appointed, on Banks's advice, a botanist, the Swede Adam Afzelius, and a mineralogist 'to explore the Company's district and its vicinity'.[160] The African Association in 1793 then persuaded Pitt and Dundas that a British Consul should be posted to Senegambia.[161] Following this, the African Association sent Mungo Park on his first expedition, up the Gambia river.[162]

The imperial significance of the African Association's activities was clear, and Hornemann reported the opinion in Cairo was that it was merely a cover for commercial interests.[163] The French also recognized the danger the philanthropic colony of Sierra Leone represented, and sent a squadron in 1794 to raid and devastate the colony at Freetown.[164] In 1799, when Park's account was published, Banks pressed the government to make Sierra Leone a full-fledged British possession, urging Liverpool to secure to the British throne 'either by Conquest or by Treaty the whole of the Coast of Africa from Arguin to Sierra Leone; or at least to procure the cession of the River Senegal'.[165] He wrote Lord Chatham on the same day to assure him that these new colonies would prove both a source of gold and a market for manufactured goods.[166] Securing this gold was to be the task of a chartered company, while missionaries were to be sent to convince the natives that it was better to be in the control of George III than under their present tyranny.[167] The African Association's report can perhaps be held directly responsible for the British seizure of Goree at the mouth of the Senegal in 1800. In 1802, Banks received a letter from Lallemant, Napoleon's Secretary of the Navy, requesting an account of Mungo Park's and Hornemann's expeditions. Banks sent the latter, but was only willing to forward Mungo Park's account minus its geographical section.[168] He quickly brought Sylvester de Golbery's *Fragments d'un Voyage en Afrique* of that year to the attention of John Sullivan, Under-Secretary of State for the Colonies, warning the government that the French intended to seize the territory of West Africa for plantation colonies.

He hinted at the risks for British interests of arriving late to the scramble to explore Africa:

> I am clear that His Majesty's ministers should be aware of the contents, and hold in mind what will happen, which is that whoever colonizes in that part of Africa with spirit will clearly be able to see Colonial products of all kinds in the European market at a cheaper price than any part of the West Indies can afford it...[169]

The Admiralty shared his concern, and lent its support to Mungo Park's second expedition. Over the next few decades only the Arctic would rival Africa as the target of British naval expeditions. Banks in fact in 1815 made the recommendation to Barrow that steam power be applied to exploring African rivers.[170] Steam riverboats would, in time, show their importance in other imperial theatres, notably against China in the Opium Wars.[171]

Geographical, political or military information could easily also be collected along with trees, shrubs, and flowers. It is likely that the decision of the Crown to dispatch Masson at its expense to collect plants in the Cape had some strategic significance. Sonnerat and de St. Pierre were travelling in the Indian Ocean at this time on behalf of France, while Spaarman and others under Dutch protection were destined for the southern African hinterland.[172] The Cape and the French islands of Mauritius and Réunion were threats to Britain's commerce and settlements in India and the Pacific.[173] The botanical exploration of the Cape by Masson provided information useful to its seizure by Britain, first contemplated during the American War and completed during the later struggles with France.[174]

Botany might indeed provide a cover for espionage. French collectors, using Cayenne, such as Le Blond, had long offered intelligence on the Atlantic coast of South America. In the 1790s, in turn, Alexander Anderson, keeper of the St. Vincent Botanic Garden, offered careful political and strategic reports on the southern Caribbean, and in particular on the Dutch colonies of Demerara and Essequibo.[175] Anderson wrote Sir George Yonge, Secretary of War:

> I well know many insinuations have been made since the last war that it would be a valuable acquisition to Great Britain. . . . I have been particular in mentioning the navigation of the coast of the rivers, as they may be of use at some later period. It is a country open to an enemy and would make no resistance if attacked.[176]

Demerara was 'the most flourishing colony the Dutch have in this part of the world', with sugar, coffee, and especially cotton, under cultivation. It was feared, at this time, that France, from Cayenne, or by invading Portugal, might take control of Brazilian cotton, 'and then farewell

Manchester'.[177] Anderson's advice on Demerara's suitability for cotton had thus the same strategic importance as his news on Dutch defences. As Harlow noted, cotton would be one key reason for the seizure of Dutch Guiana in 1803. As Anderson predicted, under careful cultivation, it provided twice the cotton of the rest of the British West Indies combined by 1812.[178]

With respect to colonial botanic gardens, as to exploration, France had gone before. The Society of Arts in 1762, in parallel with its renewed premium for the founder of a British West Indian botanic garden, offered £100 to the first to plant on a British island, 'the true cinnamon tree which now grows in the Island of Guadeloupe'.[179] But, as we have noted, neither the Society's bounties, nor the projects of West Indian planters, bore much fruit in the two decades after the Seven Years' War. As the keeper of the jail in Antigua wrote to Banks in 1785:

> The French have certainly supply'd all the plants which grow in the English islands.... I do not despair of the right species being brought to these islands from the river Amazon by the French, where I hear it can be begat. I know they have several Plants of the Clove tree and black pepper from Cayenne at Guadeloupe ... they have got two Cinnamon plants from India. The Intendant is a man of letters & a great promoter of every branch of science....[180]

On the other side of the world, Robert Kyd, superintendent of the newly founded Calcutta Botanic Garden, alluded in 1788 to 'the shame of being 20 years behind our neighbours in everything of this kind', and proposed that, since Britain and France now enjoyed a brief peace, five British men-of-war be equipped to raid the Moluccas for clove and nutmeg plants, on the model of Poivre and Cossigny a generation before:

> In pointing out and claiming the assistance of his Majesty's Marine on this occasion, I have not presumed to exercise my own judgement on its propriety ... but [have] given way to ... treading on the paths of custom and former precedent, from its appearing that the French (and very successfully) employed the same means on the same occasion of obtaining the Clove and Nutmeg from the eastern Islands during the interval of the former peace.[181]

France's post-1763 reform programme directly stimulated Britain's post-1783 initiatives in economic botany, as well, as I suggested earlier, its reform of colonial administration.

The application of botany to British colonial government began in the crisis of the old Atlantic heart of the empire. As we noted earlier, British West Indian planters now were nominally cut off from the American supplies on which they depended. They demanded that the Navigation Laws be suspended to allow them to import flour and fish with which to feed their slaves.[182] The British government refused, and had to confront the charge that the 'mother country' sought only to exploit its West Indian colonies. The planters, also, faced a crisis of demand as well as supply, as the French island of St. Domingue was producing sugar and coffee far more cheaply than the British West Indies could manage.[183] It appeared to many that the Sugar Islands might need a new staple. Pitt and Dundas's flirtation with opponents of the slave trade—while in part an anti-French manoeuvre, given that the expanding cultivation of their colonies made them far more dependent than Barbados and Jamaica on new slaves—caused more planter disquiet.

Hawkesbury, with Banks's help, found in economic botany a mode of response to this mixture of practical and ideological problems. He did so in response to pressures from West Indian planters: 'Improvement' was a concern shaping activity at the empire's periphery as well as its centre. In 1775, as we noted earlier, the Jamaican planters had agreed to bear the cost of two botanic gardens out of the colony's revenue. Hinton East, who ran one of these, described its functions in 1784 as the introduction of both useful and ornamental plants, and reported his success with mangoes, mangosteen, and cinnamon.[184] He reminded Banks that 'the acquisition of the best kind of Breadfruit would be of infinite importance in the West Indies'. In the same year, 'several gentlemen of property & liberal education' in Barbados formed the Society for the Encouragement of Natural History and of Useful Arts, with a committee on 'agriculture and botany'.[185] De Ponthieu in 1785 argued that it was a great pity that

> Government has had no botanical survey of the vast woods in the interior of Dominica. I am convinced many kinds of wood & barks might be found there applicable to the purpose of dyeing or to medicinal uses.[186]

The Grenadan planters formed a Physico-Medical Society in 1791 with its own botanic garden.[187] These peripheral agrarians pointed directly to the French Crown's efforts in providing its colonists with Asian plants. As a Jamaican planter wrote to Banks in 1784:

> Had our good People the Attention of the French to their Colonies we should not be long without [breadfruit, spices, and other 'India' plants]. The only Consideration of our Masters is how they can tax our Staple high enough.[188]

By collecting Asian plants and acclimatizing them in the West Indies, Britain could feed its plantation colonies, add to their wealth, and demonstrate its care for its creoles. By 1785 the War Office took the decision to resuscitate its botanic garden in St. Vincent, which had degenerated into a ground for raising cabbages and grazing cows and goats, and appointed Alexander Anderson. Situated at a natural landfall after the Atlantic crossing, and at a point from which a vessel might tack northwards towards Jamaica or the Leewards, or southward to Tobago or Grenada, it was the ideal botanic entrepôt for the West Indies.[189]

The voyages of Bligh on the *Bounty* in 1787 and on the *Providence* and *Assistant* of 1791–3 aimed at bringing new food and economic crops to the botanic gardens of St. Vincent and Jamaica.[190] According to Banks, this project had been planned by Pitt himself.[191] Its particular target, breadfruit, long the object of planters' requests and Society of Arts premiums, was meant to provide food for the slaves, supplementing plantains and cassava, and replacing the flour which American independence now made foreign. With the support of Hawkesbury and Mulgrave, who co-ordinated the support of the Board of Trade and the Admiralty, and on Banks's advice, the *Bounty* left in 1787.[192] Despite its famous end in mutiny, this ambitious mission would be the model for a variety of future British endeavours in economic botany. Its significance may be seen in the fact that when the First Fleet sailed for New South Wales with Governor Phillip in early 1787 it carried no one skilled with plants, but the *Guardian* of 1789 carried a deck loaded with crops, and two gardeners trained at Kew.

It is interesting to note that many feared the French would succeed first with breadfruit. In February 1787 Yonge, Secretary of War, wrote Banks:

> it seems past a doubt the Rima or Breadfruit tree is arrived in the French West Indies. Indeed the cargo of South Sea & Oriental plants must be very considerable.... It must therefore be acknowledged the French are beforehand with us, Monsieur Céré seems to have been the immediate active Instrument on this occasion, having I presume authority from the French government to use his discretion ...[193]

Yonge was, however, wrong. A cargo of exotics had arrived from the East Indies, but it did not include the true breadfruit.[194] Bligh's mission, in reverse of the usual pattern, stung the French Ministry of the Marine and Jardin du Roi into renewed activity.[195] A Jamaican planter had written to a friend in St. Domingue in 1787, mentioning that breadfruit was expected in nine months. La Luzerne, Minister of the Marine and Colonies, who received a copy of the letter formed plans with Thouin at the Jardin du Roi, framed in the best Physiocratic language, for 'Une Correspondance d'Économie Rurale et de Botanique entre Les Colonies Françaises et Le Jardin du Roi'.[196] By the early 1790s, in the midst of political turmoil, this mission, launched on Luzerne's faith that the progress of agriculture meant 'le bonheur de l'humanité', yielded a cargo of breadfruit, cinnamon, cloves, pepper, coffee, Pacific and Indonesian sugar-canes, vanilla, and vetiver to the planters of Cayenne.[197] But by then it was clear that Britain had taken a lead.

In 1787 another scheme directed at the West Indies was secretly underway. Hawkesbury, from 1784 onwards, had been concerned about Britain's cotton supply. Its West Indian planters, whose produce was considered inferior to Dutch, Brazilian, and Asian cotton, were agitating for better varieties. The Board of Trade, with Banks, thus plotted to send Anton Hove, a Polish gardener, into Maratha territories in northern India.[198] Banks prepared for Hove two documents: 'Public instructions' and 'Private'.[199] In the former Hove was instructed to collect plants and seeds for His Majesty's garden at Kew throughout his journey. His private instructions charged him with collecting the finest strains of cotton and detailed information on its cultivation, how soil and climate affected their quality, and how Indians manufactured cotton cloth. For each parcel of seeds returned to Kew, a secret report written in Polish was to be sent separately. By this means, the cotton manufacturers of Britain might be supplied with quality raw materials from within the empire, and with the best Indian techniques, and the West Indian planters might have a new staple.[200]

In these West Indian schemes, we may discern the political uses of the idea of 'Improvement'. Bligh's missions of 1787 and 1791, and the botanic gardens to which they were connected, were, first, very public gestures of solidarity with the West India interest. Economic botany had become a means of showing the benevolent interest of the 'mother country'. At the same time, of course, it added lustre to the careers of politicians like Yonge or Hawkesbury, or Banks himself. Hawkesbury's meetings with planters and merchants over economic matters, and his defence of the slave trade led to the city of Liverpool conferring its freedom upon him, while Banks was feted in London by 'West Indians' who sought to 'testify to the obligations of Jamaica' towards him.[201] At the same time, Bryan Edwards turned the botanic initiatives of his fellow planters into an emblem for the enlightened cast of their administration in his *History Civil and Commercial of the British Colonies in the West Indies*.[202] This treatise was a deliberate response to the economic critique offered in *The Wealth of Nations*, and to the moral indictment made by the Abbé Raynal and the opponents of the slave trade.[203] In his brilliant apology for the West India interest, Williams celebrated the patriotism of the planters of Jamaica in founding a botanic garden, and concluded his first volume with a lengthy appendix based on the *Hortus Eastensis* (1792) which listed the plants in the public garden of that island.[204] Botany had become a symbol of an 'improving' plantocracy.[205] Kew itself also basked in reflected glory, as the origin of the skilled gardeners and collectors who made these enterprises possible, while its hothouses received cargoes of East and West Indian plants.

In the territories of the East India Company, economic botany also found new patronage in the 1780s. In India, as in the West Indies, there had been prior 'peripheral' agrarian interest in botany: Warren Hastings, like the Mughals, had fostered collections of useful and beautiful plants, while private merchants, as in the Bengal Commercial Society, had planned the introduction of exotic crops.[206] But officers of the British East India Company had not usually shared the cultivated interests of their Dutch and French equivalents. As late as 1772, their contributions to the Royal Society had been considered inferior to those of the Hudson's Bay Company.[207] By the early nineteenth century, however, the East India Company was a greater patron of the sciences than the government (or indeed any other body) in the 'mother country'. It established observatories at Madras, Calcutta, Bombay, and St. Helena, initiated an Ordnance Survey, founded botanic gardens in Calcutta and Madras, while resuscitating older Mughal collections, as at Sahranpore.[208]

Political and economic circumstances made necessary this marriage of science and British imperial power, to which botany was to be central. By Pitt's India Bill of 1784, the Crown had assumed a power (and a responsibility) for reform. It was a theatre in which it could have full efficiency: unlike in the West Indies, where Bryan Edwards, Hinton East, and Joshua Steele were exceptions, where planters could avoid taxing themselves to pay for enlightened government, and tended to resist new crops, once the price of sugar improved, as it did with the Haitian Revolution. The East India Company needed to be seen as co-operative by Pitt and George III, who had rescued it from the Whig attack, and efficient and virtuous by a public which, as the Warren Hastings trial showed, was not convinced it deserved its privileges. East Indian trade, which depended on Britain exporting precious metals to Asia and importing luxury goods such as textiles, porcelain, tea, scented woods, spices, and gems, had long been a subject of public disquiet. Gibbon made a coded attack on the East India Company, whose meaning would have been clear and reasonable to contemporaries, where he commented on Rome's Asian commerce that

> The objects of Oriental traffic were splendid and trifling: silk, a pound of which was esteemed not inferior in value to a pound of gold, precious stones ... and a variety of aromatics. ... The labour and risk of the voyage was rewarded with almost incredible profit; but the profit was made upon Roman subjects, and *a few individuals were enriched at the expense of the Public.* As the natives of Arabia and India were contented with the productions and manufactures of their own country, silver, on the side of the Romans, was the principle, if not the only instrument of commerce. It was a complaint worthy of the gravity of the senate, that in the purchase of female ornaments, *the wealth of the state was irrecoverably given away to foreign and hostile nations.*[209]

Crown and Company had good reason to seek to change the nature of Britain's eastern commerce. The Company's need for bullion was a real problem, as well as an issue among its enemies. The East India Company's hope that territorial revenues would fund the China trade had proved vain, and, as Dundas complained to Cornwallis in 1789, Bengal could not 'without ruin, continue the exportation of ... specie'.[210] Debt also created a pressure for reform, in India as in Britain.[211] By 1786 the Company's debt in Britain amounted to almost £12 million, while its Indian debt was almost £10 million.[212] The solution to the Company's predicament lay possibly in more ruthless taxation, or the growth in the tax base, perhaps by the cultivation of commodities, valuable in China and Europe, which might improve the trade balance. But here the Company had to move cautiously, for it faced, in competition with France, ongoing struggle to secure Indian support or acceptance of its supremacy. It could neither tax freely nor easily persuade Indians to try new crops. It had, on the other hand, an interest in establishing a reign of order and plenty. Its regime would inevitably be judged against Indian rulers, their Mughal predecessors, and French contemporaries in the 1780s and 1790s. The battle for Indian collaborators was central to the whole global struggle against France, in an age in which *Citoyen Tipu* might well have reinforced Napoleon if the First Consul had succeeded in Egypt and the Levant.

Crown and Company, needing to govern (and to be seen to govern) well, appointed a new breed of governors, administrators, and judges. The Crown appointed men like Cornwallis and Sir William Jones, who carried a range of intellectual interests, not least in natural history, from Britain to India.[213] They brought contemporary fashions in policy with them, combining older Whig notions of the basis of politics in land, to a newer Physiocratic faith that public patronage of agriculture might lead to a new 'natural' balance in the politics and economics of a territory.[214] We may understand what P.J. Marshall has styled 'the Moral Swing to the East' as in part a consequence of the East India Company, rather than the slave-holding West Indies, being the scene of experiments in enlightened government attractive to the political classes in Britain.[215] It was in India that Jeremy Bentham, who had called 'Emancipate your Colonies!' in the 1780s, and his acolyte James Mill, found reasons to love empire.

The East India Company made agriculture the focus of its new efforts. It sought vigorously to attach itself to the cause of 'Improvement', even in 1789 presenting Banks with a Kashmir sheep it had returned home 'in order to improve the breed of English wool'.[216] Within India, the centrepiece of British initiatives was the Permanent Settlement of Bengal in 1793, which recognized the *zemindars* as the permanent proprietors of the land, fixing taxes in perpetuity, and creating a strong independent judiciary to guard the right to property and its consequences in the Common Law.[217] Its purpose was to create an Indian 'landed interest' which, on good Whig principles, would have a permanent interest in the peace and prosperity of its polity. These Bengali squires, while 'collaborating' with their British suzerains, would bring more of the land into cultivation and irrigation, producing food for Indians and commodities for export, while they, and in time their tenants, would turn to 'the conveniencies of British furniture and ways of living' and become customers for British commodities.[218] By making 'improving' landlords among its subjects, the East India Company would achieve ends which met the needs of Britain, Indians, and the Company itself. As collectors under the Presidency of Fort St. George were later informed in 1799:

> We find it convincingly argued, that a permanent assessment, upon the scale of the present ability of the country, must contain in its nature a productive principle; that the possession of property, and the sure enjoyment of benefits derivable from it, will awaken and stimulate industry, promote agriculture, extend improvement . . . .
>
> . . . we look to the great resources which [India] yet has, in its uncultivated but excellent lands; but these lands must be opened.[219]

As in the fens or the Scottish Highlands, enlightened private property, unencumbered by excessive taxes, would be the basis of progress.

Crown and Company came to recognize in the 1780s that economic botany might answer many of their needs. By 1783, the East India Company came to support Johan Kønig, a Danish botanist, while in 1782, Patrick Russell, one of its surgeons, had encouraged its publishing a list of plants within its territories.[220] But it was in 1786 that Robert Kyd made the moral and political case for a new kind of initiative, urging the Court of Directors to import the sago palm from the Malay Peninsula, and date palms from Persia, as a means of preventing Indian famine.[221] Kyd argued that in any comparison of the riches Britain had accumulated in India to those it had conferred on Indians, 'I am afraid the balance will stand greatly against us'. He pointed also to the example of French botanical endeavour, and to how la Bourdonnaye, by introducing manioc to Mauritius and Réunion, rid those islands of 'the scourge of famine'. By June he had written to Banks, and by September to Cornwallis (the new Governor-General), suggesting that a botanic garden be established in Calcutta to provide a nursery for the introduction of new economic crops, especially spices, as well as sago.[222] Cornwallis sailed in 1786 to assume his appointment as Governor-General with instructions from the Secretary of War to provide a Botanical Dispatch, separate from the normal Political, Civil, and Military Dispatches:

> The Attentions of Government in India, being once awakened to this object, the most extensive and salutary consequences may be hoped for, and every wish of our mind accomplished.[223]

When Cornwallis advised that the Calcutta Botanic Garden had begun, Banks promised Yonge at the War Office that the Calcutta Botanic Garden would help to banish famine in India and win the love of the Asiatics for their British conquerors:

> the latest Posterity who will wonder how their ancestors were able to exist without them & revere the names of their British conquerors to whom they will be indebted for the Abolition of Famine. . . .[224]

The descendants of the rebellious conquered would glance backwards with gratitude at their ancestors' oppressors. Rarely were the ambitions of modern imperialism framed so concisely.

Cornwallis and Kyd in Bengal, Dundas, Hawkesbury, and Banks in London wished the botanic garden to serve also more traditional mercantilist objectives. Banks proposed that the East India Company, through Calcutta, might introduce to India the useful plants of the Dutch East Indies, Cochin China or the Near East, on the model of French success with nutmegs and cloves in the Mascarenes.[225] Banks and Hawkesbury speculated, for example, whether tea, purchased from China at ruinous expense, might be cultivated 'in some Part of the British Dominions in the East and West Indies'.[226] Calcutta was also looked towards to promote opium, since this, as had been suggested for many years, was the one commodity which would allow the Company to trade in China 'with the produce of this country instead of bullion exported from England and Bengal'.[227] Kyd proposed that the garden be the means through which England's existing trade flows with India might be reversed, through promoting the cultivation of raw cotton:

> If it has been remarked 'that the present is pregnant with the future' it humbly appears to me high time for government to lay the foundation of the means of remitting the revenues of the Company to the Mother Country through other channels than those now in use; I mean the fine cotton cloths of India, as what, from the concurrence of the european manufacturers, and the propriety of their claim on Government for being supplied with the crude materials, from which under the efforts of their superior ingenuity freedom and due encouragement, they may outstrip in a short period of time, the more artless and tedious process in use among the natives of India, and annihilate the present means of remittance.[228]

Botanic science, in alliance with Company power, would transform India from a drainer of British bullion, and a competitor with its manufacturers, into a supplier of raw materials.

Banks involved Calcutta in securing Britain's safety as well as its wealth. With American independence, the traditional suppliers of the tall trees necessary for masts had become potential enemies, and Britain turned to the forests of Canada and India.[229] Pitt feared also that a European war might deprive Britain of access to Baltic hemp and flax, the raw materials for sailcloth and rigging.[230] This need for timber and fibre, it has been argued, played a role in the decision taken in 1786 to settle Botany Bay as a convict colony, instead of West Africa.[231] Sir Charles Middleton warned Pitt in 1786:

> It is for hemp only that we depend on Russia, masts can be provided from Nova Scotia. . . . It is materially necessary to promote the growth of [hemp] in this country and Ireland.[232]

Banks, advising Hawkesbury, urged Ireland and India as sources.[233] By 1798 the Navy Board agreed to subscribe to the cost of the passage of six artisans to India and for hemp seed.[234] Calcutta was also involved in promoting the cultivation of timber for the Navy in India, and to this end, barrels of mahogany seed travelled to it from the West Indies, to complement the indigenous teak.[235]

It was Bligh's mission which led the Crown and Company to found a botanic garden in St. Helena in 1787.[236] The garden served Britain in the South Atlantic as Mauritius served France in the Indian Ocean: a resting place for breadfruit, mangoes, and spices between oceans, and perhaps for ornamental plants, from the temperate south, on their way to Kew.[237] But here too the Crown intended botany to render service to an enlightened landowning class. Governor Brooke in 1788 promised the new Planters' Society that the island might 'become a nursery for supplying either hemisphere with the productions of the other'.[238] In addition, along the lines of Pierre Poivre's work in Mauritius, the botanic garden was intended to rescue the island from drought, by introducing and conserving plants which might prevent dessication.[239]

St. Helena's garden—child of Kew, St. Vincent, and Calcutta botanic gardens—contributed to the founding of another East India Company collection. Banks, in imitation of the French initiative of the 1770s, proposed that cochineal, then a Mexican and Brazilian monopoly, could be produced in the East Indies.[240] Banks arranged for slips of nopal cactus, the food of the cochineal insect, to be planted at Kew in preparation for their transportation through St. Helena to India.[241] The Committee of Secrecy of the East India Company voted £2,000 to procure the insects, and detailed notes had been made by Banks and placed in a sealed packet with instructions that it was not to be opened if the ships did not land in Brazil on their way to India. But the President of Madras broke the seal and gave the contents to Dr. James Anderson, Physician-General in Madras, who to the enormous embarrassment of Banks promptly published these documents concerning this project to attack the commercial interests of a nation with which Britain was at peace.[242] 'If the Spaniards take special measures to prevent the insect from being exported from their American dominions', Banks wrote, 'it will be due to Anderson's incredible folly.'[243] But Anderson's 'folly' was to prove the foundation of the Madras botanic garden, for its importance persuaded the Presidency to fund the 'Hon. Company's Nopalry' in 1789.[244]

The prestige of botanic gardens in the British Empire was crowned by Bligh's *Providence* expedition (1791–3). The chain of British botanic gardens established in the preceding decade contributed significantly to the arrival of a healthy cargo of Pacific and Indian plants in the Americas. After Bligh the botanic garden appeared not simply as a place of fashionable retreat but instead virtually a necessary part of modern colonial government. In preparation for his trip to the Cape, Sir John Barrow, the future secretary of the Admiralty, reported having visited Kew Gardens three times a week during 1796, often in the company of Lord Macartney, 'to botanize with Aiton's

Hortus Kewensis in our hands'.[245] When Macartney seized the Cape in the late 1790s, one of his first acts was to assign a portion of the garden of the Governor-General's residence

> for the reception not only of scarce and curious native plants, but also for the trial of such Asiatic or European products as might seem likely to be cultivated with benefit to the colony.[246]

In part he was merely following the example set by his Dutch predecessors who had maintained a formidable collection at the Cape, but he was clearly also moved by contemporary fashion. After the example of Cornwallis, the new model colonial governor was charged with setting in motion the 'improvement' of his territory, within which the encouragement of agriculture had, both for constitutional and economic reasons, central role. Thus in 1801, when the ill-fated Sir George Yonge was appointed the successor of Macartney, he imported Ralph Ducket, with whom George III had been so enamoured, to reside at the garden while practising his ploughing magic under African skies.[247]

By the beginning of the nineteenth century, botanic gardens were a normal part of the consolidation of new conquests, in particular in the Crown Colonies. In 1802, Governor Picton planned a botanic garden for the newly conquered island of Trinidad, and placed a vessel at the disposal of Alexander Anderson, the keeper of the St. Vincent garden, to assist his collection of plants in the Gulf of Paria. In Ceylon in 1810, as we have seen, 'King Tom' Maitland ordered a scientific collection as an instrument of his administration. In that year too, when Mauritius fell, the prized French collections came into communication with the Calcutta–Cape–St. Helena–Kew–St. Vincent system.[248] In 1814, during the brief period of British control of Java, Raffles established the botanic garden at Buitenzorg which would be the pride of the Dutch East Indies and the most important centre for tropical botany and agriculture in the world by the end of the century.[249] In 1818 the War Office realized Picton's plan, and founded the botanic garden of Trinidad, the oldest in continuous existence in the Americas, in its new colony.[250] In Asia, the Caribbean, the Southern Indian and Atlantic Oceans, and the Pacific world, a cluster of botanic gardens arose in correspondence, via Sir Joseph Banks, with the Royal Garden at Kew.

It is not difficult to discern, in these botanic gardens, a complicated theatre of virtue. The Crown Colony Governors who founded many of them were anxious, like Maitland, to demonstrate their enlightened administration. Picton, who came under attack in 1801 for his allowing torture, had particular reason to demonstrate his imperial virtue. The Crown, the East India Company, and perhaps the British nation, sought equally to offer living testimony of their 'improving' administration. The gardener assigned to them, such as Anderson in St. Vincent or Kyd in Calcutta, wished lastly to show their expertise had made a material difference, and thus deserved its salaried reward. We may see an extension of this complicated drama in the series of systematic surveys of colonies, of which the collection of plants and herbal knowledge would be a crucial part.

The harvesting of specimens and information was in part directly connected to the work of botanic gardens. Anderson, as we have seen, used St. Vincent as a base for the exploration of the entire southern Caribbean.[251] In India, Banks similarly intended that the Calcutta garden would be the focus for the wider scientific study of the continent and its resources, and it might become a repository for every Indian plant. Botanical collectors travelled with instructions, framed by Banks, to return to it anything of value: 'Take every opportunity of sending to the Company's Botanical Garden useful or rare or curious plants and seeds, with such observations as may be necessary for their culture.'[252] Connected to this work of regional survey was the task of reporting, with specimens and observations returned to the East India Company and to him. This led to the publication of descriptions and figures of the Indian flora.[253] In Roxburgh's *Plants of the Coast of Coromandel*, both Crown and Company had a symbol of the difference their garden made in India.

But by the 1790s, more grandiose projects essayed the comprehensive collection of information of all kinds.[254] The surveying of natural history followed naturally from efforts to number and describe the people and chart the territory and resources of conquered lands. The precedents for these were complex. Surveying, for strategic purposes, had of course been part of the business of ruling subject peoples for much longer. From the middle of the century the British government, anticipating military needs, had mapped Scotland (1745–61), Quebec (1760–1), eastern North America (1764–70), Ireland (1778–90), and came in the 1790s, with the Ordnance Survey, to map England itself. In making the surveyor the collector of an universal knowledge, Banks and his contemporaries responded also to the old idea of the man of science as 'virtuoso', the student of all natural and artificial phenomena.[255] Banks thus instructed Archibald Menzies, in a language which Boyle had used a century before, to form a complete collection of 'animals, vegetables, and minerals ... as well as arms, implement, and manufactures'.[256] But they were moved equally by newer 'improving' concerns. Surveying was part of agricultural improvement: side by side with each parliamentary enclosure came the chain and the theodolite. Before territory could be consecrated as private property, or taxed, it had to be bounded, and its advantages assessed. Good maps allowed the planning of roads or canals, and accurate surveys were therefore, Roy wrote in 1782, as the Royal Society undertook to initiate an English equivalent to Cassini's, 'the surest foundation for almost every kind of internal improvement in time of peace'.[257] The Board of Agriculture, by the 1790s, had enlarged on this political meaning of 'Survey', with Sinclair arguing that 'Agricultural Surveys'—public enquiries into the surface, soil, and riverine riches of a province, and on the numbers, health, and manners of its inhabitants—would be 'the means of promoting the internal

Improvement ... of a Powerful Empire'.[258] Both Roy and Sinclair found some inspiration in the Cameralist and Physiocratic surveys, such as those conducted by the Habsburgs and by Cassini in France after the War of the Austrian Succession.[259] There, as in Scandinavia, the state had organized the mapping of natural resources, the assessment of soils, discovery of minerals, and counting of population. What is certain is that when Robert Kyd in 1791 collected information in Bengal on soils, rents, wages, population, as well as indigenous plants, he argued for

> the propriety of collecting the necessary data to form a political survey of this part of the Company's possessions, so as to enable government to form a more minute estimate of their actual as well as possible further value,

with a reference to the *Descouvertes Russes*, the survey organized by Catherine the Great's administration.[260] In a quite direct way, Enlightened Despotism influenced innovation in British imperial government at the end of the century.

The application of botanical gardens for economic survey and the improvement of agriculture was visible in Ireland in 1800. In the year of the Act of Union, the Protestant gentlemen in the Dublin Society for Promoting Husbandry and Other Useful Arts showed how their botanic garden was extending the work of the Board of Agriculture in their newly launched *Transactions*. The Glasnevin Botanic Garden was to be

> a complete repository, for practical knowledge, in every thing which respects vegetation, agriculture, trees, farming and all the uses of the surface of the land and its produce; to be the deposit of all the knowledge which statistical views, surveys, and inspections into the state of the country, can furnish, and to be a school for instructing all persons concerned in the produce of land, as to the most efficacious and economical modes of raising, distributing, and using that produce.

In lectures at the garden, a Professor would point out fodder plants both nutritious and poisonous, and which would be useful as dyestuffs or in manufacture. Modern machines 'for shortening labour in agriculture, arts, and manufactures' would be demonstrated to 'country gentlemen and farmers' among whom the Society would 'cultivate the spirit of improving the breed of all sorts of cattle'.[261] The Dublin Society had no difficulty securing aid from the House of Commons to 'enable it to proceed in [its] great objects'.[262] The application of science to agriculture, as we saw in the era of Cromwell, was a powerful justification for an Ireland ruled from London.

India became the stage for a programme of surveys which would only be rivalled by Napoleon's *Description de L'Egypte*. Chartings of the coast of

Coromandel led eventually to Lambton's Great Trigonometrical Survey of India after 1800.[263] Naturalists came to travel on behalf of the East India Company collecting encyclopaedic knowledge on its territory. Buchanan-Hamilton, for example, conducted sustained research on the topography, history, antiquities, religion, fine arts, commerce, and agriculture between 1806 and 1818.[264] Jonville did similar work in Ceylon, and Nathaniel Wallich, from Calcutta, in Nepal, the Himalayas, Singapore, and Penang.[265]

India pioneered this kind of comprehensive survey of the plants, animals, land, and people, but on a smaller scale, and similar research took place in many other British outposts, such as Sierra Leone and New South Wales.[266] The value of these surveys for British proconsuls, as in the case of botanic gardens, was political as well as economic. The great patron of the survey in India was Richard Wellesley, whom Pitt added to the Board of Control for India in the same year as the Board of Agriculture was founded. As Governor-General from 1797, Wellesley lent his support to Lambton, Buchanan, and Mackenzie, explicitly extending the 'Statistical' initiatives of Sir John Sinclair and Young, with his order that his survey 'should not be confined to mere military or geographical information, but that his inquiries should be extended to a statistical account of the whole country'.[267] Like the agrarians at home, he offered the Cameralist argument that knowing a territory was a responsibility for those who controlled it. Indeed Wellesley suggested his nation's 'exalted situation' in India imposed on the British government a duty 'to enlarge the boundaries of general science'. Implicitly, if others accepted such an argument, they had also to concede that Wellesley's support for natural history, and in particular his sponsorship of Buchanan's surveys, represented blessings bestowed by a wise governor on India and Britain.[268] In response to his patron's command to 'investigate the state of agriculture, arts, and commerce ... for the purposes of obtaining such an insight into the state of the country as may be productive of future improvement and advantage', Buchanan reported that Mysore farming was backward and wasteful, while its soils were fertile.[269] This kind of knowledge had obvious uses. Britain, having liberated a people from the tyranny of Tipu Sultan, might now make them fruitful and content: here was an answer to those who criticized his conquest of Mysore. The assimilation of an universal knowledge on a territory was, above all, an ornament to British power: evidence of that enlightened sort of authority which deserved its station.

Conclusion: Kew, Empire, and the 'Sons of Science'

At the climax of Erasmus Darwin's *The Botanic Garden*, an extended lyrical passage described 'Imperial Kew' to which obedient sails from 'realms unfurrow'd' brought plants to be named and ordered. Kew in 1791 presented, to his gaze, a world in a garden:

> Delighted Thames through tropic umbrage glides
> And flowers antarctic bending o'er its tides;
> Drinks the new tints, the sweets unknown inhales,
> And calls the sons of Science to his vales...[270]

The collections of the Royal Garden had vastly expanded under Banks's informal direction. A comparison of the 1789 and 1813 editions of Aiton's *Hortus Kewensis* with John Hill's edition of 1769 illustrates his achievement: there had been 600 species in cultivation at Kew when the *Endeavour* sailed, but 5,500 in 1789, and 11,000 in 1813.[271] Aiton offered Banks in 1814 'his deep sense of his cordial friendship, and ... gratitude for his innumerable donations of the most rare exotics to the Royal Collection of Kew'.[272] He, more fairly, should have given thanks for the generation of hot and cold war with France, which had conspired to extend the reach of British plant collection up African rivers, into the Guianas, the plains of India, and a thousand Pacific harbours. Banks understood the connections between these initiatives: in 1787, the great year of the *Bounty* and of new colonial botanic gardens, Banks wrote excitedly to Sir James Edward Smith, the President of the Linnean Society:

> Botany flourishes most abundantly, the Queen studies diligently under Aiton, the ship which we are sending to Otaheite to bring home the bread-fruit to the West Indies will be bringing plants from thence, the Garden at St Vincent flourishes a new one is established at Bengall & an intervening proposed ... & probably another will soon be starting at Madras.[273]

An imperial crisis made possible, and in some ways necessary, the world-embracing reach of the Royal Botanic Garden.

Very little money was spent directly by George III on the flood of new plants. Masson or Bowie as collectors sent out at the expense of the royal household were exceptions. The most important sources of 'tropic' and 'antarctic' plants were the gardeners trained at Kew who came to be attached to Admiralty vessels, to the botanic gardens of the War Office, to the East India Company, or to the missions of the Board of Trade or the Home Office. Among these, for example, were Christopher Smith, who sailed with Captain Bligh and was after employed at the Company's Calcutta Botanic Garden, Peter Good sent to Calcutta to be trained by Smith in 1796 then in 1801 joining the Admiralty's *Investigator* mission to Australia, or William Kerr foreman at Kew, then gardener to the East India Company to Canton, then worked with Raffles in Java, finally ending as Maitland's first superintendant of the Ceylon Botanic Garden in 1810. Every application of botany to the imperial problems yielded Kew a free ornamental reward: the *Providence* expedition, for example, funded by the Admiralty, the Board of Trade, and colonial legislatures resulted in the introduction of 702 new plants from the Pacific, Asia, and the Caribbean to His Majesty's collection. The St. Vincent,

Calcutta, St. Helena, and Madras gardens all sent plants to Kew, and dried herbarium specimens to Banks and the East India Company.

To this official tribute was added a tide of gifts of plants from explorers, soldiers, administrators, colonists, or missionaries who had (or wished to have) the patronage or friendship of Banks. In 1786, before St. Helena had its botanic garden, Governor Corneille thanked Banks for

> The honour of ... adding any plant from this island to that curious collection which I remembered to have seen some years ago in my much Honoured and Royal Master's Gardens at Kew.[274]

Archibald Menzies scoured the Bahamas similarly for 'that Noble Collection of Plants already at Kew'.[275] West African plants came in the 1790s from Afzelius and Governor Clarkson in Sierra Leone, and from Mungo Park.[276] In the 1800s Governors such as Macartney and Yonge, and missionaries such as Van der Kamp, sent Cape novelties.

That George III and Charlotte were personally identified with Kew made it easy for Banks to solicit presents, and even to twist the arms of those in a position to offer help. Corneille thus framed his willingness to supply Banks with whatever he wanted from St. Helena for Kew by expressing his desire to gratify 'my Royal Sovereign's wishes by adding any thing to his Royal Botanic Gardens'.[277] Writing to Governor Hunter in New South Wales, Banks reminded him that 'Kew Garden is the first in Europe, and that its Royal Master and Mistress never fail to receive personal satisfaction from every plant introduced there from foreign parts'.[278] In an era in which royal favour was a valuable political commodity for the East India Company, Banks similarly advised it that he would inform the King of 'the handsome manner in which the Directors have promoted the science of Botany'.[279] In 1803 Banks pressed the Company to mount a mission to China to collect useful and ornamental plants, urging that the Court should 'doubtless bear the expenses of the gardener as a compliment to the King'.[280]

More enduring however than this was the commitment to patronage of the natural sciences which Banks helped to foster in Admiralty circles.[281] The Royal Navy's enthusiasm for savants, it is true, was never unalloyed, and its hydrography department, only begun in 1795, a petty affair. Yet, viewed as a whole, the programme of hydrological surveys initiated in the 1790s is one of the great monuments of British science. What is important to note is that Banks persuaded the Admiralty to continue to pay naturalists when they returned from expeditions, to arrange and publish their collections. In 1796 he successfully petitioned the Duke of Portland to arrange that the salary of Archibald Menzies the naturalist would be continued so that both his collections and his journal of the expedition might be completed.[282] Similarly in 1805 Banks negotiated with his friend William Marsden, Secretary of the Admiralty, that Robert Brown might enjoy full pay while he arranged and described some of the 3,600 plant species which he had obtained on the voyage of the *Investigator*.[283] By this means a tradition of the Admiralty subsidizing British taxonomy and natural history began. Many Victorian biologists of the first rank, Thomas Henry Huxley, Charles Darwin, and Joseph Hooker among them, would, like Kew, be direct and indirect beneficiaries of this subsidy.

Where Banks and his contemporaries made botany part of the work of imperial 'Improvement', they laid the basis for Britain becoming, by the middle of the next century, the most important centre for comparative biological thinking, and in particular for phytogeography.[284] Her collection of herbarium and living specimens of the world's plants would be unrivalled anywhere but in France. Equally important was the emergence of a system of salaried positions for men with scientific interests, which had hitherto not existed. In 1795, when a young man seeking a post wrote to him, Banks replied 'I do not know there is any trade by which less money has been got than by that of botany, except Mr Masson who travels for the King.'[285] But twenty years later an historian friendly to the East India Company could remind his countrymen that empire had opened 'a field in which every talent might be tried and every generous species of ambition'.[286]

At the peripheries of British power, the age of Banks generated professional opportunities for men of science which did not exist at home. The medical service and surveys of the East India Company, the hydrography of the Admiralty, collecting and botanic gardens offered unmoneyed young men the chance to make natural history their trade. The movement of men like Good or Kerr from posts at Kew, to others in the service of the Admiralty or East India Company, then on to a colonial botanic garden, represented a kind of career mobility which had not existed before. Living and working in strange places was, of course, hard and often dangerous, and unattractive to gentlemen. As Banks wrote to Wilberforce, concerning a botanist for Sierra Leone, 'I know of no regularly bred botanist in England who is likely to be tempted'.[287] But this meant that volunteers had to be compensated—both with some salaries and with promises of further elevation. In 1814, Banks promised Cunningham and Bowie that after braving Brazil, the Cape, and New South Wales, they could expect 'to return to their Native Country before the afternoon of life has closed with a fair prospect of enjoying the Evening in ease, comfort & respectability'.[288] He made real efforts to ensure that his clients did receive some public reward. In 1809, for example, he secured from the War Office a gratuity and pension for Anderson, who 'had brought the St. Vincent garden to such a state of perfection as to surpass any other in the tropics'.[289] A Royal Bounty of £100, similarly, went to the widow of David Lockhart, a survivor from Captain Tuckey's 1816 mission to the Congo, and Superintendent of the Botanic Garden, Trinidad, from 1818.[290]

The gentlemen of science, who sat at such centres of comparison as Kew, Banks's home in Soho Square, the Linnean Society, and the British Museum, similarly benefited from imperial opportunities. This was not limited to the flowers in their gardens or the specimens in their herbaria. In serving as naturalist on an expedition, someone like Robert Brown, respectable but without real means, might have work both stimulating and remunerative. He might moreover add lustre to his reputation and career, and ready himself for high office, perhaps succeeding, like Captain Bligh, in being chosen as a colonial governor. As Banks wrote William Jackson Hooker, when urging him to accompany Raffles to Java, had he himself not joined Cook he would 'probably have attained no higher rank in life than that of a country Justice of the Peace'.[291] The career of Banks himself, from Lincolnshire squire to a confidante of the King and Prime Ministers, showed what might be achieved abroad.

The new Kew, like the whole informal cosmos of imperial science which found its centre in Banks, arose on the basis of the late Georgian idea of 'Improvement'. It prospered as part of an intricate theatre of virtue. Kew, and the botanic gardens and surveys to which it was connected, were evidence for the merit of George III, his ministers, proconsuls, chartered companies, and savants, and their right to their prerogatives. But the success of this drama of enlightened authority depended on the efficient and symbolic competence of men of science as masters of nature's secrets. They, in turn, had both an intellectual and career interest in the new world of British power. The future of Kew after 1820 would be determined by the unfolding of such ties of mutual interest between the 'sons of Science' and reforming politicians and conquerors.

CHAPTER 5

From Royal to Public: The 'Reform' of Kew, 1820–41

In 1820, when both George III and Banks died, the 'King's Garden' at Kew was royal property managed by a gardener, William Aiton. By 1841, Kew was formally under the discipline of parliament, and administered by Sir William Hooker, a distinguished botanist. The Crown personal yielded to the Crown bureaucratic, and the amateur to professional expertise. The unusual pressures which made this necessary—appeals to the public interest, letters to the press, Treasury 'cheese-paring', speeches from Radicals and Tories in parliament, and the more discreet intrigues of different camps of Whig aristocrats and savants—deserve examination. For the story of how Kew became public provides a parable of the politics of reform in nineteenth-century Britain.

As we have observed, Banks and George III had never considered Kew a public garden. Kew was part of the dignity of the monarchy. If Banks gave it some public functions—presiding over a system of exchanges of plants between the hemispheres, training men who might discover new raw materials or persuade foreign crops to grow in India or the colonies—these represented extensions of the personal efficiency of George III. Its vast collection was meant, like those at Schönbrunn or Malmaison, to add lustre to the court. The science of botany, itself, one may argue, found employment at Kew principally in an ornamental capacity: the display of knowledge was itself part of the spectacle. If we recognize Banks as its supremo, his influence there, as at the Home Office, War Office, and the East India Company, did not depend on his official capacity but rather on his reputation and his personal relations with George III, Pitt, and the Jenkinsons. We may recognize in his role at Kew, and the enormous informality of his power, the sunnier side of what Radicals attacked as 'Old Corruption'. Like Trotter, the Paymaster of the Navy, who kept money voted by parliament accruing interest happily in a personal account at Coutts, Banks, who spent his own wealth on Kew, saw no clear boundary between private efficiency and public function. The individual's person and property were separated from the corporate prerogatives of the Crown by a porous membrane.

Kew had prospered therefore on what we may fairly describe as *ancien régime* custom and assumptions, as a theatre of royal power and legitimacy. The death of George III carried therefore significant consequences. The life of the court, even during the Regency, and especially after 1820, moved away from Kew. Before,

> when their Majesties resided at Kew, a Terrace near the river was frequented ... with a concourse of nobility and gentry! Stars and ribbons and garters glistened on the eye in uninterrupted succession,

now, a contemporary complained, a 'sombrous garb' had fallen over the area.[1] George IV did continue his father's consolidation of a royal estate, enclosing more land, and erecting large iron gates and fences. William IV later consecrated a 'Temple of Military Fame' to honour the progress of British arms from 1760 through to 1815. But both of George III's successors were as indifferent to botany as they were to books. The expenditure on Kew declined from £1,900 in the early 1820s, to about £1,500 around 1830, to about £1,300 in the latter part of the decade. In 1823 and 1830, respectively, James Bowie and Allan Cunningham, whom Banks had sent to collect for Kew at the Cape and New South Wales in 1815, were recalled and dismissed. George IV, whose pleasures were urban, preferred to spend on Buckingham House in London, which was intended to contain its own ornamental garden, with four grand conservatories designed by Nash. The project, originally intended to cost £200,000, swallowed the revenues of the Crown lands, consuming some £10,000 a week, until reduced in 1829, on the orders of the Duke of Wellington, to the same each month. At its completion, Buckingham Palace cost £720,000, while both Brighton Pavilion and Windsor Castle had been expensively refurbished. In royal expenditure, gardens ranked well below horses or furniture: out of £174,048 spent in 1836, for example, £10,569 went to all the royal parks, significantly less than went on carriages and livery or upholsterers and joiners. In 1827, William Aiton, once solely charged with Kew, became 'Director General' of all the royal parks and gardens, and in 1828, George III's castle was demolished with dynamite. The Hanoverian Schönbrunn was to be constructed instead in Westminster.

After 1820, in much the same way, the whole Banksian cosmos of imperial science lost its centre. Banks, with his excellent connections, had argued for science's usefulness with politicians, the Admiralty, and chartered companies. Sir Humphry Davy, his successor as President of the Royal Society, lacked both his vision and influence. Without a powerful defender, science was an easy target for those officers of the War Office, Admiralty, or East India Company who wished to prune budgets. In 1821, just months after Banks's death, the Crown retreated from the first botanic garden to have received its sponsorship, at the same time as it stopped funding the Board of Agriculture. The War Office decided to stop paying for the garden in St. Vincent.[2] In 1828, to the shock of astronomers, the Admiralty abolished the Board of Longitude.[3] While Sir John Barrow and the masters of the Royal Navy remained enthusiastic about Arctic and African exploration, Herschel and his allies had to battle in the 1820s to prevent the shutting down of Southern Hemisphere observatories, and again in the mid-1830s to secure support for the mission to the Antarctic which Ross eventually led between 1839 and1843.[4] Similarly, the East India Company complained in the 1830s about the official time which members of its medical service devoted to natural history.[5] It sent around a circular demanding to know the real practical value of botanic gardens and suggested some might be closed.[6] John Forbes Royle, writing from the East India Company garden at Sahranpur, complained of

> the arrival of the Governor-General with the one intention of abandoning the Sahranpore garden. I was obliged therefore to lay aside everything for a while to make out reports, plans, & catalogues of the Gardens so as to exhibit its objects both in a scientific & useful point of view to save it from destruction.[7]

Nathaniel Wallich, Director of Calcutta Botanic Garden, in 1835 waited a year to respond to such official pressure, drily apologizing that he had been too busy supervising the planting of tea in Assam to write earlier.[8]

These episodes, in which administrators attacked the patronage of science, were symptoms of a larger phenomenon. The activist state forged by Pitt was in retreat under the pressure for reduced government expenditure. Paradoxically, as we have argued, the expansion of government's efficiency in the 1780s had been a response to the original call for 'Economical Reform'. The application of science to the 'Improvement' of India and the Crown Colonies, like economic botany and sheep breeding at Kew, and indeed, around these, the whole Pittite concern for policy sanctioned by expertise may be understood as responses to the Whig critique of the Crown, and the wider public disquiet which found expression in the Commissioners for Examining the Public Accounts of 1780. Good government, incarnated in useful and efficient sovereigns, ministers, proconsuls, and chartered companies, was an answer to those who attacked private enrichment and power undisciplined by democracy. 'Virtual representation'—the idea that the manifestly unrepresentative Houses of Commons and Lords effectively prosecuted the interests of the nation as a whole—could only be sustained against the proponents of parliamentary reform if government could be shown wise and benevolent. But the bloating of the British state by the wars against the Revolution and Napoleon, and the private enrichment of such Tory statesmen as the Dundases, or Whig grandees as the Grenvilles, stimulated new middle-class and plebeian critics in the first decades of the nineteenth century.[9] After Waterloo, where Liverpool sought to build a broad conservative alliance of the propertied classes of the nation against the threat of revolution, he had to answer to this tide of opinion. Repression was not an adequate response to the popular attacks of Cobbett's *Political Register* and John Wade's *The Black Book, or Corruption Unmasked!* (1820), or to the philosophical salvos of the Utilitarians, and least of all to the growing evangelical pressure for retrenchment.[10] Tories might dismiss public opinion privately as 'that great compound of folly, weakness, prejudice ...and newspaper paragraphs', but they recognized its power.[11] By 1816, when parliament ended income tax, Liverpool urged Palmerston that he aim at abolishing every office 'which could not be defended as essential to the public service'.[12] Over the next thirteen years, Frederick Robinson and Henry Goulburn applied stringent economies to every area of government expenditure. It was, in a way, a renewal of the Pittite initiatives of the 1780s: this effort at 'cheap government' was matched by the 'Liberal Tory' programme of legal and administrative improvements, and the parliamentary concessions to dissenting Protestants and Catholics of the post-1822 period. Contemporaries however perceived these gestures as too tentative, and in the economic downturn of the end of that decade, new pressures for economical and parliamentary reform emerged.[13] In 1830, the Tories, who had been in power for almost the entire half-century since the American War, lost to Whigs who marched under the banner of 'Peace, Retrenchment, and Reform'. The Great Reform Bill of 1832, which brought Cobbett himself into the House of Commons, created a parliamentary arena in which Radicals such as Joseph Hume could even more effectively press their demand for 'Retrenchment'.

Kew, a most ostentatious product of Crown patronage, and colonial botanic gardens, so obviously consequences of the hypertrophy of government during the war years, were easy targets. It is in this context that Kew's collectors in 1823 and 1830 were recalled, and the scientific establishment which had emerged at many peripheries of the British Empire was pruned by philistine administrators. The change in the tide is visible in the declaration of Russell to Earl Grey in 1848 that: 'Under Pitt and Dundas ... The Tory love of despotism prevailed, and all our colonies were made Russias and Austrias.'[14] Russell was there concerned with the despotic power which the executive exercised in the new Crown Colonies, but his remark applied equally to that imperial *dirigisme*, sustained by Cameralist and Physiocratic ideologies, which had created a network of colonial scientific establishments. We can in an explicit way, long before the age of Cobden, connect the domestic campaign against 'Corruption' and for 'Retrenchment' with Gallagher and Robinson's 'imperialism of free trade'.[15] The campaign to slim the state at home produced, from Palmerston's initiatives in 1816, an overseas military and colonial policy which prized economy. The trim design of Britain's naval and commercial imperialism, its surgical incursions into Singapore, Hong Kong, or Lagos, was only the foreign policy counterpart of the tradition of fiscal conservatism and retrenchment which leads from Goulburn and Peel through to Robert Lowe and Gladstone.

The British political classes had always believed that learning, like charity, should be left to the Church or the volunteer. The direct consequence of the retreat of Crown patronage during the 1820s and 1830s was that science became dependent on the private support of local gentlemen. The planters of St. Vincent, with some assistance from the Governor, kept open their garden (see illustration 14). The Sydney Botanic Garden, founded in 1818, mean-

14. St. Vincent Botanic Garden in 1824, when it was almost exclusively a recreational extension of the Governor's house.

dered along similarly through a mixture of voluntary and official assistance. Elsewhere, private collections quickly eclipsed public initiative. In Cape Town, Baron Ludwig, an apothecary who had married a snuff and beer heiress, and whom the King of Württemberg had ennobled in 1826 in reward for many gifts of South African plants, insects, birds, and mammals, kept a botanic garden which was considered superior to all others.[16] In 1828, the founders of the South African Literary and Scientific Institution pressed, via the Governor, for a properly funded colonial botanic garden, but this won no support in London. In June 1833, they formed a Cape of Good Hope Association for Exploring Central Africa which, through William Harvey, the Colonial Treasurer, sent 'spoils brought from the Interior' to Britain.[17] Within Britain itself, where horticulture was popular among all classes of English society, a similar pattern prevailed. The Horticultural Society, which Banks had helped to found in 1804, planted a 33-acre garden in Chiswick in the 1820s, at a time when Kew appeared less vigorous. While the Treasury forced the recall of Bowie and Cunningham, the Horticultural Society sent out many collectors, at the expense of its members, to China, East and West Africa, Brazil, Mexico, and Central America. In the 1820s, Joseph Sabine, its Secretary, advised Bowie that the Crown could not afford to send out anyone, and 'Kew gardens will soon pass away from its present management'.[18]

Clearly Sabine envisioned his own society perhaps assuming control of the royal garden. Outside London, the botanic garden founded in 1800 by subscriptions of the citizens of Liverpool provided another example of what might be done with Kew.[19] Hothouse stoves, conservatories, ponds, and a long rockery, were open there for the pleasure and improvement of the public. Liverpool, so central to the slave and plantation trades, received 'numerous and valuable presents of seeds' as gifts from its merchants and seamen.[20] This civic ornamental species of the botanic garden was an example of what Kew might become for the nation.

Even during the Regency, Kew came under attack. In 1811, John Claudius Loudon, the 28-year-old landscape gardener, presented his 'Hints for a National Garden' to the Linnean Society.[21] Loudon charged that there was no garden near London suited to its dignity:

> Our royal or national gardens are inferior not only to what might be expected from the wealth and spirit of the nation, or the splendour of Royalty; but even to some of the provincial gardens ... the collection of plants at Cambridge, and the plan and general arrangement of Liverpool Garden, are much superior to anything at Kew or Chelsea.[22]

The collection of a true national garden would be organized to educate and delight the citizen with beautiful and useful plants. He proposed a demotic version of the aristocratic pleasure ground which Repton projected for Woburn Abbey: his public garden should contain specimens of Grecian, Roman, Tuscan, Indian, Turkish, French, Dutch, Old and Modern English gardens. There would be a school for practical gardeners, with a library and course of lectures. Its climax would be a hothouse with a path large enough for carriages to be admitted with 'perpetual verdure, bloom and fruit, jets of water, singing birds and a mild fragrant atmosphere'.[23]

It is easy to defend Kew from the specific attacks contained in this extravagant vision. For example, Loudon's special praise for the botanical collection at Cambridge probably rested on James Donn's *Hortus Cantabrigiensis*, which included very many plants not actually grown in the Walkerian garden.[24] Donn, who was a former student of William Aiton, imported most of the glories of Cambridge from Kew. Kew, unlike Liverpool, had not emerged from a single plan, and lacked the ornamental unity and pretensions of the provincial collection. But Loudon's general charge was unanswerable: England lacked any equivalent to Rumford's 'English Garden' in Munich.

The threat which this ideal of the botanic garden as a democratic pleasure ground might pose to Kew was already clear by 1812, when William Salisbury, with the support of Nash, proposed founding a 6½-acre botanic garden in the Regent's Park.[25] Within months a prospectus was circulated by entrepreneurs which proposed to establish 'a National Botanic Garden, Library, & Reading Rooms in the Regent's Park'.[26] A dinner was held in the

Freemasons' Tavern, with the Duke of Sussex in the chair, as provisional President of an Association to whose superintendence the institution was to be committed. It was a grand project: £20,000 were to be raised for grounds, buildings, library, and hothouses by a variety of categories of subscriptions, and its proposers offered to remove the entire botanic garden of Kew and replant it within their domain. But the matter got nowhere, due at least in part to Banks, who saw no reason for either the destruction of Kew or for the surrender of the King's garden to *hoi polloi*:

> It does not appear to me that any advantage to science would be the consequence of removing the Botanic Garden at Kew to the Regent's Park. . . . The Science of Botany is best improved at a situation remote enough from the crowded populations of the metropolis to prevent the commerce of persons induced by idle curiosity alone to visit it.[27]

The Regent's Park project was blocked on this occasion. But the prospect of some voluntary body undertaking the management of Kew, or perhaps absorbing its collections, remained on the horizon until as late as 1840. It is likely that when Aiton, in the 1820s, began to open the gardens on a regular basis from Midsummer to Michaelmas, he was attempting a defensive act of democratization.[28] Even so, he did not placate the public, who resented the two large and forbidding wooden doors, and the wait for an escort, which separated them from George IV's garden. They complained that while Aiton shared Kew's collections with the royal gardeners of European courts, he denied them to Englishmen.

The lack of royal interest in botany, pressures for economy, and the desire of private gardeners for access to the King's garden, almost led to the destruction of Kew, as we shall see, at the accession of Victoria. But there were two other sets of actors which prevented this outcome: the slender community of professional botanists which Banksian patronage had done much to protect, and the young Whigs who had come to power in the 1830s. It is to these that we now turn. The men of science succeeded in framing an idea of the public interest useful to these political aristocrats.

The 'Decline' of Kew and the Profession of Botany

Every historian of Kew, from 1820 to the present, has described the span from 1820 to 1840 as a period in which Kew 'retrograded' or 'declined'.[29] But did it really? It was true that this was not a time of expansion: the Crown's expenditure on the garden certainly declined, while Aiton's attention was diverted by his new responsibilities, particularly at Buckingham Palace. It seems likely that things pottered on, and presents did continue to arrive from the East and West Indies, naval survey vessels, and foreign botanists. We have little hard evidence on the matter, since William Aiton and his brother removed from Kew, and later burned, most of the official papers of his regime.[30] The earliest provenance of this judgement is the grim report of J.A. Schultes, an Austrian professor of botany, who criticized in 1824 the inaccurate naming of plants and the loss of many prize specimens at Kew:

> with regard to its plan, or its nine or ten stoves, it will not bear comparison with those of Malmaison, the late Duke of Weimar, or Prince Esterhazy of Eisenstadt or the Imperial Gardens at Schönbrunn.[31]

One is unsure how far to credit Professor Schultes's estimate, which in spirit resembles so much the deprecating tenor of other European travellers to Kew.[32] What is certain is that the great publicist for Schultes's view was an ambitious English botanist, William Jackson Hooker, who in 1830 chose to republish *in extenso* the Professor's 'Botanical Visit to England' in the first volume of his *Botanical Miscellany.*[33] Our confidence in the deficiencies of Aiton's stewardship might perhaps be tempered by the insight that British men of science had in that year begun to use 'decline' as political slogan.

In 1827, Sir Humphry Davy had proclaimed to the Royal Society: 'Let it not be said that at a period when our empire was at the highest pitch of greatness, the sciences began to decline.'[34] His junior colleagues responded that this had indeed come to pass. 'Decline' became a favourite trope in the jeremiads of scientists, who complained, during and after the 1830 campaign of Herschel against the Duke of Sussex for the Presidency of the Royal Society, that Britain's political élite had failed to encourage British science, and had corrupted its institutions with the values of the amateur.[35] Charles Babbage, for example, in the opening salvo of his *Reflections on the Decline of Science in England and on Some of its Causes* (1830) charged 'the party which governs' the Royal Society with responsibility for the lag which had emerged between British chemistry and physics and practitioners of 'the more difficult and abstract sciences' on the continent of Europe.[36] Babbage attacked the whole system of Banksian patronage, bitterly noting that the late President of the Royal Society had bluntly told him that he would never be a commissioner of the Board of Longitude because he, with other professionals, had diminished the dignity of the Royal Society by forming the Astronomical Society in 1820.[37] While Whigs campaigned in 1830 on the promise to make parliament more representative of the British people, so scientific reformers demanded that they control their professions and institutions.[38] The salvo which Hooker discreetly discharged against Aiton's management of Kew should be recognized as a shot in a larger war.

That a botanist had attacked a gardener deserves attention. The tiny community of professional botanists had, in some ways, more severe problems with amateurs than their peers in other disciplines. Both the comparative methods of botany, and the history of its emergence as a field of study, left precarious foundations for the professional dignity of botanists. The botanic garden, in particular, had a confused public identity: the botanist had never achieved the identification with his instrument which the astronomer had won over the telescope. Too many distinct purposes and interests, over 300 years of European history, had laid claim to the same space. From 1500 onwards, apothecaries and physicians had made it a repository for medicinal plants. During the next two centuries, monarchs and aristocrats increasingly turned to such collections for ornamental exotics. Religious naturalism treated the *hortus conclusus*, which contained the entire sphere of Creation, as a space for experience and comprehension of God. By 1700 the botanic garden was the focus of work for philosophers who wished to name and classify the diversity of the world's plants. Connected with the new sciences of classification, by 1750 the 'physic garden' was an emblem of civilization: means of, and evidence for, a rational knowledge of nature, and a worthy recipient of the patronage of kings, cities, and universities. Towards the end of the eighteenth century the botanic garden was also seen as a means of improving agriculture, a key instrument of physiocratic projects of turning the state to national renovation. But new functions had supplemented rather than replaced older uses. The purposes of the botanic garden had never been clearly resolved: in what measure should it be useful or ornamental? To whom among apothecaries, gardeners, botanists, agrarian improvers, or its various types of patron, did it really belong? This confusion in the public identity of the botanic garden, and the informality of *ancien régime* patronage, represented a serious obstacle to botanists' ambitions for personal remuneration and status, and for continuity in their research institutions. To pursue these interests, and to secure the scientific dignity of their calling, botanists had to ensure that their discipline achieved mastery in the garden.

Across the Channel there was an example of what they might achieve. The Jardin des Plantes, with its attached Muséum d'Histoire Naturelle, provided a vision of the botanic garden as a scientific paradise, under the direction of salaried natural historians. In the 1820s and '30s, this strange product of Enlightened absolutism, Republican ideals, and Napoleonic patronage, caught the attention of British men of science and their allies. In 1825, Raffles and the Duke of Somerset had sought Cuvier's advice in their endeavour to establish in England 'a Museum of Natural History that may be worthy of the Nation'.[39] They founded the Zoological Society's menagerie in the Regent's Park after 1825 directly on French precedents. But Britain, as the Duchess of Somerset noted, still lacked any real scientific or popular equivalent to the Jardin des Plantes:

> ... a beautiful establishment of the kind might be made in Regent's Park or in the Kensington Gardens – Government already keep 12 men for Kew Gardens & for little purpose – At the Jardin des Plantes they have a variety of lectures *gratis* & the establishment does not cost more than our British Museum & yet what do we have to compare to the Jardin des Plantes?[40]

Not only did Kew fail to render service to the public, it had never sheltered botanical research of any importance. In comparison, the Jardin des Plantes had allowed Jussieu to constitute his 'natural system' of classification, which had begun to attract the most able botanists.[41] With the success of the Zoological Gardens, Hooker in 1830 had good reason to hope for a botanical equivalent.

But British botanists were in a more compromised position than their mathematical and astronomical colleagues. For even as they began to assert their professional identity, they remained dependent on the world of amateurs. It is striking that among those most prominent in the movement for scientific reform—such as Brewster, Whewell, Babbage, or other members of Cannon's 'Cambridge network'—none had anything to do with plants. At the same time, it was clear that the scope of the Lucasian Professor's outrage about 'the decline of science' scarcely included botany or natural history. Indeed among those involved in shaping the idea of science in Britain, botany did not receive the respect as a profound and serious discipline which it had enjoyed one hundred years before. Where the touchstone for scientific pride remained Newton's physics and Herschel's astronomy, taxonomy seemed a lesser discipline. William Whewell, in his sketch of botany in the third volume of the *History of the Inductive Sciences*, for example, delicately underlined the fragility of the categories of botanical classification relative to those of astronomy, and suggested that the study of plants lagged behind that of animals in philosophical rigour.[42] Distinguished botanists such as Robert Brown, John Lindley, George Bentham, and Nathaniel Wallich, certainly conspired with Roderick Murchison and Whewell for the reform of the Royal Society, but none committed himself to the vocal front line of the battle.[43]

The truth was that with the possible exception of physicians and surgeons, no community of scientists had profited more from gentlemanly amateurs than the botanists.[44] It was conspicuous that while Banks had resisted the founding of the Geological Society (1807) or the Astronomical Society (1820), on the grounds that these specialized societies rivalled the pre-eminence of the Royal Society, he had actively assisted at the birth of both the Linnean Society (1788) and the Horticultural Society (1804). The fashionable London scientific societies and the country houses of aristocratic amateurs, while less hospitable to abstract mathematics or astronomy, fed and cushioned the science of plants in an era in which there was little remunerative employment for botanists. A handful enjoyed university appointments, but most among these, such as the lectureships in the Scottish universities or in London, were part of programmes of medical instruction.[45] Their science was thus reduced to the tool of apothecaries, who were not altogether gentlemen by contemporary standards. No university post, in any event, relieved botanists from the need to seek supplementary sources of income. They could not depend on any body of botanical students to pay fees, for as Bentham noted, Professor Sibthorp at Oxford never could muster fourteen scholars, the number he said would induce him to read his lectures, the present professor is Dr. Williams, but he cannot get a single pupil. The Oxonians attend to nothing but classics and a little of divinity.[46]

Horticultural expertise, which equipped the botanist to cater to the whims of amateur gardeners, was a more certain way of augmenting income, and indeed often a means by which a man of science might secure a wealthy or influential patron. It was scarcely surprising that botanists, while willing to join with their colleagues in the physical sciences, were notably muted in their criticism of the patronage of Banks and the grandees who dominated the Royal Society: no community of British savants had been so umbilically tied to the political and scientific old regime.

During the reigns of George IV and William IV, horticultural amateurs, who initiated and funded missions in collaboration with public bodies, became the principal sponsors of scientific exploration. In 1829 Douglas travelled to the Pacific North West with the combined support of the Hudson Bay Company, the Horticultural and Zoological Societies, and the Colonial Office. The Admiralty assisted the Duke of Northumberland and the Earl of Derby when they shared costs for Burke to forage in temperate America, and for Purdie in tropical Central America, and the Hudson Bay Company assisted the Duke of Devonshire when he sent two collectors to search in the North West for plants suitable for temperate England.[47] Great private nurseries—Veitch of Exeter, Lee and Kennedy of Hammersmith, Malcolm, and Loddiges of London—supplied the appetites of private gardeners, and provided employment for collectors, cultivators, illustrators, and taxonomists.[48] Such aristocratic gardeners and horticultural entrepreneurs often invested far more than the Crown could or would afford. Bentham commented that while the hothouses at Kew were very extensive, they were 'not near so handsome as Loddiges, which must still bear the palm in the green and hothouse way'.[49] The ornamental concerns of privately organized and funded botany thus provided a vast and lucrative field of employment. It is difficult to untangle botany from the influence of this world of amateurs and horticultural enthusiasts: every echelon, and any prospect of career mobility, depended on it.

At the bottom of the botanical world was the ordinary collector, usually recruited when he had shown unusual ability as a labourer in royal or aristocratic gardens. For such men, Banks urged Harrison at the Treasury, £30 per annum for expenses in the field should be considered enough 'to render them respectable among their equals'.[50] Banks gave emphasis to what was implicit in this proposal:

> the collectors must be directed by their instructions not to take upon themselves the character of gentlemen, but to establish themselves, in point of board and lodging, as servants ought to do.

The rest of the proposed salary, some £150, would be saved on behalf of the men either to be conferred as a large cash gift if they returned alive, or passed on to their dependants if they perished. For this 'undergardener' type of collector, his dangerous work could be a stepping-stone to appointment as head of a garden, either in the colonies or with luck at home. James Wiles, for example, was rewarded for his part in the success of Bligh's *Providence* expedition with appointment to the position of Superintendent of the Bath nursery in Jamaica, while Peter Good, formerly a Kew foreman, had been rewarded after a trip to Calcutta by appointment as gardener to Banks's friend Lord Seaforth.[51] Collectors might also collect for themselves, on the side, making a fortune on their return to Europe from selling rare specimens to wealthy amateurs. Thus Archibald Menzies, naturalist for Vancouver's mission to the Pacific, was advised 'never to bring more than half a dozen of any rare shell he might find, as that number would always bring him more than any greater quantity'.[52] The dismissal of Bowie in 1823 had as much to do with his private trading in Cape plants as with Treasury parsimony.

For a lucky few apprentice gardeners, the right patron could altogether transform their social position. William Aiton (1731–94), student of Miller at Chelsea Physic Garden, became the client of Bute and then George III, went from manager of Princess Augusta's 'Physic Garden' at Kew, to master of all the Royal 'forcing houses' and pleasure gardens at Richmond after 1783. His son William Aiton (1766–1849) inherited his father's post at Kew, with the help of Banks, and became, as we have seen, George IV's Director-General of all the Royal Gardens.[53] Even more striking was the case of Joseph Paxton, who turned his employer, the Duke of Devonshire, into his close friend, and rose from the muddy-booted foreman of the arboretum of the Horticultural Society in 1826 to the knighted Member of Parliament, architect and railway director of the 1850s.[54]

At the top of the ladder, gentlemen with unusual botanical competence had access to the most dignified positions. In the East India Company or with the Admiralty, a physician with inclinations as a naturalist (and a suitable patron) might be paid to follow their vocation either as superintendent of a botanical garden or as part of a mission of exploration. Such appointments, made through the support of individuals like Banks or Aylmer Bourke Lambert, often decided which of those with botanical gifts had the opportunity to develop their powers. While the undergardener could only hope for some petty compensation or preferment, the 'philosophical traveller' might win fame and social stature on his return from the imperial frontier to the centre of civilization. Robert Brown, for example, began as a minor Army officer in Ireland, but changed the course of his life by catching the attention of Banks and agreeing to sail as botanist on the *Investigator* expedition to the South Pacific and Australia. Banks arranged Admiralty pay, employment as private librarian, finally by a codicil of his will conferring on Brown both an annuity and that stewardship over his collections which Brown parleyed into a permanent position at the British Museum. It is difficult to agree with

Mabberley's heroic portrait of Brown as 'breaking away from the dilettante tradition and personal patronage'.[55] That Brown deserved all that he got as a botanist of remarkable gifts did not mean that he was not also the model of the successful client: the course of his life was essentially decided by the patronage of Banks. Brown, in turn, went on to preside over the fate of other botanists who aspired to careers: William Hooker, for example, needed to make a suitably deferential application to him in order that John Lindley, his friend, might read a paper before the Linnean Society and be introduced to Sir Joseph Banks.[56]

During the two decades after the death of Banks, six figures can be taken as representative of the highest estate of British botany: Sir James Edward Smith, Aylmer Bourke Lambert, Dawson Turner, Brown, Sir William Jackson Hooker, and John Lindley. It is worth pursuing a small prosopographical excursus in order to illustrate, through the path of these six careers, the structure of the botanical profession and the forces which would later wrestle over the destiny of Kew. They show that even at the apex of scientific expertise, botany depended on either private wealth or patronage. Such dependence threatened the scientific identity of the discipline in concrete ways.

Sir James Edward Smith (1759–1828) had literally bought his way into European scientific fame through his purchase in 1784 of the private herbarium of Linnaeus which contained the most valuable early-modern collection of type specimens.[57] His father was an East Anglian silk merchant, and left him a substantial income to support his natural history passions.[58] Smith founded the Linnean Society in 1788 around this collection. His office in the Society, and his important herbarium, made him the focus of correspondence with every serious botanist in the world. But Smith behaved as the proprietor of the learned society he had founded, happily bartering away shells and other specimens, selling the minerals, and taking portions with him as he moved back and forth between London and Norwich.[59] While he took an interest in microscopy and plant physiology, the classificatory concerns which surrounded his herbarium formed the centre of his botanical work.[60] Smith, as editor of *English Botany*, directed an enormous publishing enterprise with the help of G. Shaw and the botanical artist James Sowerby (1757–1822), which yielded thirty-six volumes from 1790 to 1814.[61] He also edited at the same time the *Exotic Botany: Consisting of Coloured Figures, and Scientific Descriptions of such new, beautiful, or rare plants as are worthy of cultivation in the Gardens of Britain*, the cost of which meant that it enjoyed a small and wealthy readership. He became an important patron of taxonomists and draughtsmen, a clearing house for herbarium duplicates, and the colleague of James Sibthorp, Professor of Botany at Oxford, in the *Flora Graeca* (1806–40).

By 1814 Smith was knighted. In botanical circles, Sir James was not a figure to be trifled with. But what was revealed in his unsuccessful campaign for election to the Professorship of Botany at Cambridge was that his scientific work was not universally respected.[62] His election was chiefly blocked because he was a Unitarian. But the controversy did not just reveal the operation of religious prejudice: it illustrated instead that botany did not enjoy a high intellectual reputation. James Monk, Regius Professor of Greek and a Fellow of Trinity, poured scorn on the claims of Smith (and botany itself) to intellectual seriousness. Monk charged that natural history 'was a pursuit which demanded little exertion of the highest powers of intellect'; instead of 'the sublime speculations of Newton, Leibniz, Euler, and La Place', it purveyed a vulgar science of grand names, 'floetz, and trop, and schistus, ... Banksias and Dryandias, and all the *andrias* and *gynias* of the *Systema Naturae*'.[63] He mocked the Linnean Society's pretensions, arguing that it should have fielded

> its auxiliary forces, the Horticultural and Gooseberry Societies, with their irregular troops, the tulip fanciers and prize auricula men: and what with their scientific arrangements, classifications, and pruning-hooks, they no doubt would have formed a very imposing body and might have taken the Botanical Chair by storm.[64]

Botany's connection to horticulture was clearly costing it its intellectual dignity.

Aylmer Bourke Lambert (1761–1842) was another gentlemanly specialist who had inherited a large fortune: from his mother, the only daughter of Viscount Mayo, he received Irish estates and Jamaican plantations, while from his father he inherited both land in Wiltshire and connections to the East India Company and the trade in Bengal muslin.[65] Having discovered the pleasures of botany while playing in hothouses at Boyton, his father's estate in Wiltshire, he made the accumulation of a massive herbarium both his life's work and the ruin of his fortune. This herbarium, which had grown side-by-side with that of Joseph Banks, brought Lambert into intercourse with all the greatest botanists of the age, including de Candolle, von Martius, and Brown, and was frequently referred to in botanical publications.[66] Martius, Botanist to the King of Bavaria, justified his visit to Britain by noting that 'the renowned names of Lambert, Brown, Smith, Hooker, and Turner, and others are strong attractives!'[67] Friend of Banks and Smith, Lambert presided as one of the Vice-Presidents of the Linnean Society from 1796 through to 1842, and was honoured by Smith in the genus *Lambertia* (1798) and by von Martius in *Aylmeria* (1826). It was through being introduced to Lambert at one of Sir Humphry Davy's soirées that George Bentham was introduced into the botanical world, the mere name being enough to open herbaria and the gates of countryhouses to Bentham.[68] While his private herbarium was one of the largest ever assembled, he was content to let others work on his specimens, preparing only a few items for publication.[69] Lambert's spirit as a collector is best revealed by remarks of George Bentham concerning an occasion on which Cuming's Peru and Chile plants were being divided:

> [Brown] in his careful, quiet manner, scrutinising the whole series before he had fixed upon the instructive specimen, whilst Lambert, who at once cast his eyes on the most showy specimen, with large leaves and numerous well-dried flowers, watched with the most keen and anxious countenance their being handled by Brown, in fear his fine specimen should be taken from him.[70]

Similar remarks concerning Lambert came in the *Mémoires et Souvenirs* of de Candolle, in which the Swiss botanist recalled one occasion when he was working in Lambert's herbarium:

> Lambert, qui parlait peu notre langue, venait se mettre à côté de moi quand je travaillais, et dès qu'il me voyait donner quelque attention à une plante, il me demandait d'un air jubilant: 'New?'[71]

For Lambert, and in some measure for Smith too, possession of a new species was the chief mark of the distinction of a botanical collection. In this era, such a connoisseur of plants was the inevitable companion of those with more philosophical interests in botany but slimmer resources.

Dawson Turner (1775–1858), antiquarian and natural historian, was a Yarmouth banker with ties to the Gurney and Barclay banking families, and to the East India trade.[72] While botanical amateurs often preferred to collect the more flamboyant angiosperms, Turner made the cryptogams his forte, conducting pioneering studies of algae, mosses, and their symbionts.[73] Like Lambert and Smith, Turner enjoyed a connection to Banks which meant that he was continually supplied with specimens from the far reaches of the world, including the algae and mosses collected on the Vancouver and Flinders expeditions. His four tomes on *Fucus* stand as a monument to the assistance which the Admiralty gave to natural history from the late 1780s onwards. He was a figure of enormous dynamism, maintaining a vast scientific correspondence while remaining active in business.[74] He also, as we shall see, connected botany to the world of politics.

Robert Brown (1773–1858) is the first botanist who might accurately be described as a scientific professional.[75] He distinguished himself in every theatre of the discipline: collector on the *Investigator*, subtle and meticulous taxonomist of the *Prodromus florae Novae Hollandiae*, pioneering microscopist and discoverer of the cell nucleus and the kinetic phenomenon now known as Brownian motion, Secretary and later Vice-President of the Linnean Society, Brown could comfortably wear the extravagant mantle Humboldt penned for him—*facile princeps botanicorum*, glory and ornament of Britain.[76] Yet the whole career of Brown depended on the patronage of Banks, from the original posting with Flinders, to his succession of Jonas Dryander as the master's librarian and herbarium keeper, to final control over the property at Soho Square, which while partly leased as premises for the Linnean Society, also served from the Dean Street entrance as his residence. His influence on the learned societies and control of the Banksian collections made him a figure influential in the success of the careers of aspiring botanists, securing, for example, Aldridge's dispatch to collect in Trinidad in 1831–3, and Barclay's attachment to the voyage of H.M.S. *Sulphur* to the Pacific.[77] Yet even Brown's admirers among his botanical contemporaries sometimes found him selfish. In 1824, for example, William Jackson Hooker wrote Sir John Richardson, the Arctic explorer and naturalist, concerning some territorial dispute in cryptogamic taxonomy:

> Brown you seem to look upon as offering some obstacle, but if you know Brown as I have known him you will find out more. I grieve to say that there is something about Brown so like a monopolizing disposition as to have injured him in my esteem very considerably.[78]

Brown was apt to interfere when he had not been sufficiently deferred to on the question of an appointment, as in the case of Robert Schomburgk, a German traveller in the mould of Humboldt, who was recruited by the Royal Geographical Society to explore the interior of British Guiana between 1831 and 1835.[79] By all accounts he was, except to his patrons, an exceedingly difficult person, as de Candolle noted in an otherwise glowing tribute to the Scotsman:

> Froid, ironique, réservé sur tous les sujets qu'il n'avait déjà publiés, il m'inspirait d'autres sentiments que l'estime de son talent, qui est très remarquable.[80]

Bauer, the great botanical painter and former client of Banks, expressed positive distrust of Brown, demanding that none of his botanical drawings be passed to the 'prince of botany' before they were published.[81] It was not surprising that enduring animosity would develop between Brown and many of his juniors, most particularly with John Lindley, who dared to work also on the Orchidaceae, and had to struggle with Brown to have any access to the relevant fossil plants in the Banksian herbarium.[82]

After Brown, William Jackson Hooker (1785–1865) provides the second example of a professional botanist. Like Brown, he also came to prominence as part of the Banks/Smith/Lambert/Turner nexus of professional activity and patronage.[83] Coming from Norwich, his discovery of a new species *Buxbaumia aphylla* led him first to Sir James Smith and through him to an introduction to Dawson Turner who became his chief patron, introducing him eventually to Sir Joseph Banks. Hooker sought to marry Turner's daughter (see illustration 15), and submitted to years of arduous work preparing the illustrations for Turner's magnum opus on *Fucus*, producing 234 out of the 238 drawings. But in exchange Hooker inherited a wealth of contacts to British botanists, election to the Linnean Society at the age of 21 in 1806, and appointment on the recommendation of Banks to a mission to explore Iceland in 1809.[84] Hooker made his professional mark among the

15. Lady Maria, daughter of Dawson Turner, wife of Sir William, and a natural historian in her own right. Royal Botanic Gardens, Kew.

plants favoured by his father-in-law, distinguishing himself with his *British Jungermanniae* (1816), which led ultimately to an invitation by Humboldt to write the cryptogamic section of the explorer's projected flora of New Spain.[85]

Established by Turner with a one-quarter share in a brewery, Hooker became a country gentleman at Halesworth, with a garden complete with a private hothouse.[86] During the post-war depression, Hooker explained to Banks that he was finding himself unable to purchase expensive botanical books and to support four children at the same time. Banks replied that the Regius Professorship of Botany was vacant in the University of Glasgow and that the influence of the President of the Royal Society would support his candidacy.[87] In a short time Hooker was off to the west of Scotland.

Unlike Graham, his predecessor at Glasgow, Hooker had no medical training. But he was fully a botanist, and through his own effort turned the university into one of the centres of European botany. This was partly due to his work in developing the botanic garden, in attracting a large lecture audience, and in publishing a *flora* of the Glasgow collection.[88] More important, however, Hooker began to assemble what by the 1830s was recognized by Asa Gray and others as the foremost herbarium in the world. To specimens drawn from the Banks, Smith, and Lambert herbaria, Hooker added the results of his own energetic collecting, purchase, and exchange of duplicates. Gray noted in 1841:

> The herbarium of Sir William J. Hooker at Glasgow, is not only the largest and most valuable collection in the world, in possession of a private individual, but it also comprises the richest collection of North American plants in Europe.[89]

Hooker's hoard of Polar and North Atlantic plants was unrivalled, since he became the recipient of all the plants collected on the many British missions in search of the North-West Passage which followed 1815.[90] With a uniquely rich herbarium and a friendly intelligence, Hooker easily established contact with European contemporaries of the stature of de Candolle, Humboldt, and Lamarck. So well embedded was Hooker in the structures of contemporary botanical life, that it is difficult to evaluate the truth of the bitter remark of an American botanist that

> As to Hooker he is an excellent plodding botanist, with great advantages in help, friends, materials, & means to publish. But he is not a good critic, nor nomenclature, nor Genera-maker!![91]

The cruel consequence of gentlemanly science was that the lustre of an individual's talents was difficult to distinguish from the brilliance of his connections.

John Lindley (1799–1865) was the son of a nurseryman who lived near Norwich in East Anglia.[92] He had wanted to seek a military career, but his father could not afford to buy him a commission. Instead, he travelled to Belgium in 1815 as the agent of Wrench, a Camberwell seed merchant. By 1817 he had befriended Hooker, and indeed de Candolle considered him then as Hooker's 'jeune élève'.[93] Hooker introduced Lindley to Lyell and Brown, through whom Lindley met Sir Joseph Banks.[94] Banks promised Lindley that he would arrange for him to be sent overseas as a naturalist, initially suggesting Sumatra or Madagascar. Instead he brought Lindley in 1819 into his domestic circle, making him assistant to Brown in his library and herbarium. After Banks's death, he became, from 1821, associated with the Horticultural Society, and in particular with its Chiswick garden. When Hooker in 1828 rejected the offer of first occupancy of the botanical chair at the new University College of London, it came into Lindley's hands.[95] From his base at University College and the Horticultural Society, Lindley offered scientific advice to government offices in the manner of Banks: for example entering into an extensive correspondence in 1832 with the Board of Ordnance and the Royal Engineers Office about the suitability of willows for making charcoal which could be used for gunpowder.[96] He also corresponded with powerful horticultural enthusiasts abroad, such as Lord Auckland, Governor General of India.[97] He maintained close relations with European botanists, and was elected to the Imperial Academy of Natural History in Bonn in 1821, and in 1832, through the agency of Martius, whom he had favoured with gifts from Chiswick, the University of Munich conferred on him an honorary D.Phil.[98] Together with Joseph Paxton, Lindley planned the botanical aspects of Hudson Bay Company exploration in North America.[99] Lindley was also a pioneering student of fossil plants, and was in regular communication with geologists including Hutton, Lyell, and Darwin.[100]

Hooker and Lindley, both of whom were gentlemen without independent means, committed a great deal of their energies to serving the appetites of horticultural amateurs. They supplemented their meagre professorial incomes with incessant writing for a popular audience. At the same time, they augmented their personal influence, by forming friendships with aristocratic gardeners, who wanted new exotics for their collections and the approval of experts. Hooker established a connection with the Duke of Bedford, collector of orchids and pine trees, who arranged for him to be knighted on 20 April 1836 at His Majesty's levée. Lindley became the foremost British expert on orchids, and formed close ties with the Duke of Devonshire, naming a genus of plants after the man who fêted him at Chatsworth.[101] Both men spent a considerable part of their professional lives publishing botanical illustrations in small and costly engraved editions.[102]

Lindley, in particular, understood that the way in which he and his colleagues earned their bread was damaging the scientific reputation of botany. In his Inaugural Lecture as Professor of Botany at University College London in 1829, he began by defining botany in distinction from *materia medica* or horticulture.[103] He protested, almost too much, that botany should be regarded as intellectually serious:

> It has been very much the fashion of late years, in this country, to undervalue the importance of this science, and to consider it an amusement for ladies rather than an occupation for the serious thoughts of man.

In what was really a demand that botany become less accessible to amateurs (which, not wholly coincidentally, included all women), he advanced the claims of Jussieu's system against both 'the mischief' of Linnaean classification, which had rendered botany a science of names, while mocking the German *Naturphilosophen* for their 'Botanical Cabala'.[104] What Lindley was forced tacitly to admit was that the amateur world on which his profession depended had distracted botanists from much serious scientific work which their colleagues in zoology had completed: as he concluded, there was a throne waiting for a botanist beside that of Cuvier, botany had ground to cover before it met the zoologists. Similarly in his report to the first meeting of the British Association for the Advancement of Science of 1833, Lindley suggested along *Cuvieriste* lines (although alluding directly to Goethe) that there was a unity of design in the vegetable world, and that plants probably excreted in the manner of animals.[105] Like many British botanists in the 1830s, he tacitly agreed with the censures of the *Edinburgh Review* and Whewell that his colleagues had neglected comparative study of the structure and function of plants.[106]

But if we are to exclude the unofficial Banksian chair in botanical research which had been conferred on Robert Brown, there were no endowments for such philosophical botany in Britain. Instead, in the university positions which represented the pinnacle of the profession, the pressure was for botanists to serve medicine, horticulture, or agriculture. The amateur world remained crucial to both personal subsistence and the survival of the profession: even Lindley, advocate of masculine 'seriousness', would go on to publish to his profit his two-volumed *Lady's Botany* of 1837. If Hooker wished to assert the botanist's right to reform Kew, he needed the help of the amateurs.

Whiggery and Botany

It was Whig aristocrats who came to the rescue of botany in the early nineteenth century. The Russells, Spencers, and Cavendishes, in particular, formed partnerships with Hooker and Lindley. In this we may discover another consequence of the age of Banks. These oligarchs wished also to cultivate a connection to science, progress, and 'improvement'.

Their enthusiasm for the land was quickened by the basis of their own wealth in farming and husbandry. But their interest was ideological as much as it was economic. Agriculture, for Whigs, had always been politics by other means. The improvement of the land, as we saw earlier, was originally prized by those who opposed the power of the Crown and court. The idea of the 'Ancient Constitution', that is the belief that the basis of English liberty lay in the independence of its landowners, who connected parliament to the soil of the kingdom, took encouragement from the Providential theory of the 'improver' as the realizer of the soil's sacred (or natural) potential. Whigs were naturally drawn to the Roman myth of the virtuous politician, when out of power, turning to the plough. The Marquis of Rockingham, as we noted earlier, made farming his special concern after 1768, while he languished in the political wilderness. In much the same way, Coke of Holkham (1752–1842) chose in 1778 to organize his first 'Sheep Shearing', the great agricultural fairs where he mixed with gentlemen and lesser farmers, in parallel with his opposition to the American War. His example was taken up by his friend Francis Russell (1765–1802), the 6th Duke of Bedford, who organized his own annual 'Shearing', and joined Pittites on the Board of Agriculture, while becoming President of the Smithfield Club. But many of their contemporaries—the Cavendishes, Howards, Grosvenors, and in particular Charles James Fox—had then prized literary and oratorical gifts, and urban pleasures, more than the land.[107] For Fox, liberty was to be won in the city, and he found farming, like political economy, to be a distraction from politics. But the next Whig generation, born and raised in a era of almost complete Tory dominance, found the example of Coke and Bedford attractive. In the rational and benevolent cause of 'improvement' they discovered a theatre for the exhibition of their own virtue, and a means of investing new savour into the rhetoric of parliamentary reform which had grown stale in the mouths of such 'aged vestal virgins' as Holland or Grey.[108]

Whigs such as Althorp, Milton, and John Russell (the 6th Duke of Bedford, 1766–1839) found compensations for their exclusion from government in drainage, animal breeding, model farms, 'Sheep Shearings', and the Smithfield Club.[109] They were of a generation which took Malthus seriously. Many of them had attended the lectures at the Royal Institution in which Sir Humphry Davy had suggested how landowners might exhibit their powers of leadership:

> It is from the higher classes of the community, from the proprietors of land; those who are fitted by their education to form enlightened plans, and by their fortunes to carry such plans into execution; it is from these that the principles of improvement must flow to the labouring classes of the community; and in all cases the benefit must be mutual; for the interests of the tenantry must always likewise be the interest of the proprietors of the soil.[110]

His vision of progress through paternalism suited the senatorial ambitions of the Whig élite. In farming, as in politics, it was uncertain how far the people would follow their 'natural leaders'. Indeed, the *Woburn Abbey Georgics,* a satyrical poem of 1813, lamented on the behalf of the Duke of Bedford:

> Patterns we set – they do not heed;
> stock we improve – they do not breed;
> Books we send forth – they cannot read.
> Prizes I offer still in vain;
> None irrigate, or under-drain.[111]

The land remained, all the same, one of the few places in which an aristocracy, out of power, might show its virtue.

The gambling and whoring of Fox's generation lost some of its appeal. Instead, the Duke of Bedford wrote to Hooker in 1836, 'I rejoice at the extension of science in whatever direction it may be found', while Althorp gave the English (later Royal) Agricultural Society of England in 1838 the motto of 'Science with Practice'.[112] The publishing list of James Ridgway of Piccadilly, the main house for Whig pamphlets, illustrates how Whig politics were intertwined with enthusiasm for botany, horticulture, and agriculture. In between the speeches of Lord Erskine on the liberty of the press, of the Duke of Bedford and Earl Grey on parliamentary reform, and Lord John Russell's *Letter to Lord Holland*, Ridgway published John Lindley's *Rosarum Monographia*, Robert Sweet's *Geraniaceae; or, Natural Order of the Beautiful Family of Geraniums* and *The Botanical Cultivator*, Sydenham Edwards's *Botanical Register*, C.C. Western's *Practical Remarks on the Improvement of Grassland*, Greg's *System for Managing Heavy and Wet Lands*; and a *Practical Treatise on Breeding, Rearing, and Fattening Poultry*. Similarly, John Limbird of the Strand, which published the speeches of both Lord Brougham and Grey on the second reading of the Reform Bill in 1831, also printed the *Arcana of Science and Art for 1831: The Annual Register of Useful Inventions and Improvements* and the *Cabinet of Curiosities And Wonders of the World Displayed*.

In the Young Whigs' concern with science, both pure and applied, we may identify something more than a mere return to the roots of Whiggery. It represented yet another example of that urge, so characteristic of the nervous early decades of the nineteenth century, to find principles in Nature which might order human social arrangements.[113] The desire to make politics and economics 'natural' arose in the anxieties of a nation, and a social class, made newly rich and newly vulnerable, as David Cannadine has shown, by the turmoil of the 1790s and 1800s.[114] 'Natural theology', the idea that it was possible to approach the Creator through studying his creation, sustained a number of initiatives. Central to all was the notion that there was a Natural Order, encompassing human society, governed by laws; and the assumption that in human affairs, as in the physical world, there were principles of equilibrium. This vision reached its most explicit expression in the doctrines of Physiocratic economics. Under their influence, Liverpool and Huskisson sought, through the Corn Law of 1815 and the return to the gold standard, to restore order in an economy made 'artificial' by the pressure of public debt and inflation. Althorp's enthusiasm for applying science to agriculture during the 1820s had similarly to do with his concern to bring the Constitution into balance, by allowing the landed interest, made more efficient, to secure its dominant place versus commerce and manufacture.[115] Gardening and natural history, as complements to Evangelism, might also restore the balance in a society distorted by industry and the growth of cities, making peaceful and pious people who might otherwise have become Jacobins. The multitude, through an encounter with the diversity of God's natural creations, might be made moral and content.[116] Whigs preferred to respond to the threat of revolution with education, allotments, public gardens, rather than with mere Tory coercion. Their private enthusiasm for agricultural science, horticulture, and botany was connected organically to their politics.

At Woburn Abbey, the 6th Duke of Bedford constructed a temple to enlightened Whiggery. Woburn as the family home of the Russells was, of course, identified with the politics of reform. But it was also a centre for agricultural experiments: Bedford bred livestock, and instituted complex experiments on the nutritive value of grasses and cereals. He arranged for Ridgway to publish the results in the *Hortus Gramineus Woburnensis* of 1816 and 1824, and later printed other agrarian pamphlets at Woburn itself.[117] What Bedford considered himself to be attempting is made clear where the *Hortus Gramineus* praised Coke of Holkham for his having converted 'an immense tract of barren waste into a highly productive and ornamented country ... and above all, peopled with an intelligent, scientific, and grateful tenantry'.[118] Coke had shown that diffusing efficient farming technique, matched to investments in housing and welfare, could yield a political harvest: the happy deference of social subordinates was the true reward for 'improvement'. Similar political motives also encouraged the vast ornamental gardens, within which plants were ordered and named with scrupulous care, and which Devonshire at Chatsworth and Northumberland at Syon House later imitated.[119] The *Hortus Woburnensis* (1833), which presented Bedford's collection, explained how aristocratic luxury might lead to other social classes turning to the peaceful pleasures of gardening. While 'the peer and peeress' introduced exotics into their stoves and greenhouses, and spent many times the lifetime earnings of their tenants on ornamental buildings, 'the humble cottager' and the manufacturer learned to devote his leisure hours 'to the cultivation of flowers and vegetables'.[120]

Both Whig aristocrats' idolization of scientific husbandry, and their competition with each other as ornamental gardeners, led them to patronize men with botanical expertise. We have, of course, observed this pattern earlier, in the relationships formed between the Duke of Somerset and William Turner, Ralegh and Gerard, and Buckingham and Tradescant, more than two hundred years before. The difference of course lay in the fact that by the early nineteenth century, there were new professional criteria: publications, offices, and the membership of learned societies. At Woburn, Bedford's experiments with fodder crops depended on George Sinclair, and his gardening on John Forbes, both Fellows of the Linnean Society, while the Marquis of Tavistock turned to John Wilson at Hardwick House, and Devonshire to Paxton at Chatsworth. Bedford boasted of the scientific importance of his collection through having Sinclair and Forbes publish botanical studies of his collection: the *Hortus Ericaeus Woburnensis* (1825) which listed the heathers flourishing in a new 'Heath House' designed by the architect Jeffry Wyatt (later Wyatville) who also planned the massive extensions of Chatsworth and Windsor Castle; *Salictum Woburnense* (1829) which recorded Woburn's British and foreign willows; a catalogue of Bedford's Cacti (1837); and the *Pinetum Woburnense* (1839).[121] Bedford and his peers invited other, more distinguished, botanists to praise their collections. Coke and the 5th and 6th Dukes of Bedford thus invited Sir James Smith, Dawson Turner, Lambert, and Hooker to approve their estates.[122] Bedford and Devonshire were Fellows of the Royal Society and the Linnean Society in their own right.

Botanists, always hungry for recognition and patronage, returned the compliment. Smith chose to distinguish one species of willow, *Salix russelliana*, from the *Salix fragilis* of Linnaeus, a feat of botanical heraldry from which Bedford said he derived 'much gratification', while Turner distributed engraved portraits of the Russells, Lord William Bentinck, and other prominent East Anglian agrarian figures.[123] Joseph Paxton, in the dedications of succeeding volumes of his *Magazine of Botany and Register of Flowering Plants,* gratefully groomed the plumage of several wealthy and influential amateurs: the Duke of Devonshire (1834), Duchess of Sutherland (1836), Duchess of Northumberland (1837), Duke of Bedford (1838), Marchioness of Normandy (1838), Duchess of Cambridge (1839), and Earl Fitzwilliam (1840).

The Whigs also recruited botanists to assist in their projects for the 'improvement' of the people. They looked to popular education, like Brougham in his *Practical Observations upon the Education of the People* (1825), to ensure that the multitude would not be seduced by demagogues. Scientific education, of the right kind, seemed particularly important, in order to prevent the poor teaching each other that materialism which might lead them to question the Providential basis of their subordination. In parallel with their support for the University of London, Whigs created the Society for the Diffusion of Useful Knowledge in 1829 to be an instrument for popular education.[124] Apart from a variety of magazines and 'Cyclopaedias', books of portraits of the famous, and the *Working Man's Companion [for persons of humble life]*, there were two great series of books, each available for sixpence: the Library of Entertaining Knowledge and the Library of Useful Knowledge which included science, history, biography, and geography. For the last series, just as the Society for the Diffusion of Useful Knowledge asked T.B. Macaulay to write the history, and Roderick Murchison the geology, they asked John Lindley, then Professor at University College London, to become their botanical expert.[125] Lindley prepared hundreds of articles for the *Penny Cyclopedia,* and was recruited to write *Vegetable Substances, Vegetable Physiology, Botany, The Life of Ray,* and *The History of Botany.*

As the Duke of Somerset had found in Paris his inspiration for the London Zoological Gardens, so Bedford discovered in the Jardin des Plantes an example of a national botanical institution.[126] When William Hooker republished Professor Schultes's damning attack on Kew in 1830, he was probably aware that his patron had already begun looking, with Whig disapproval, at George IV's royal garden. Bedford later proved Hooker's most important political ally. In 1833, when Lord John Russell, Bedford's son, was sitting victoriously in the House of Commons, Hooker reached towards his dream of being a botanical Cuvier. Hooker, who had heard that Aiton was retiring, asked the Duke of Bedford to lobby in his interest. Bedford wrote instantly to the Duke of Argyll, strongly recommending him to succeed Aiton 'should death or resignation cause a vacancy in that Establishment'.[127] With Bedford also writing to Althorp and Grey, the machinery of the 'cousinhood' was in motion and Hooker happily wrote to Dawson Turner, his father-in-law, that if the superintendency of the Kew Garden should fall vacant, 'I am faithfully promised that appointment (but this we must keep to ourselves)'.[128] But Aiton clung on, and then to blunt all hope the Melbourne ministry collapsed in December 1834 and Sir Robert Peel came to power. Hooker wrote bitterly to William Harvey, his botanical friend, that he doubted whether 'the present ministers are ... calculated to serve their country'.[129]

Melbourne was however back at the Treasury by April 1835, and Hooker thought it probable that he might soon have Kew Gardens either as a separate institution, or attached to one of London's medical schools. But there was no movement on the question, the Russells had 'upset the coach', and their influence was, temporarily, on the wane. At the end of the next year Bedford commiserated with Hooker and promised him support in the future:

> I can scarcely believe that you hear of the Botanic Gardens at Liverpool, Birmingham, Manchester, Sheffield etc. without being disturbed by the 'slightest feeling of envy' ... I confess it would afford me much pleasure to see you at the head of such an establishment as the Royal Gardens at Kew, which would open to you so large a field for Botanic & Scientific pursuits.[130]

It was a promise which Hooker would use with skill when Bedford was on the other side of the grave.

The Royal Gardens Committee of 1838

Had Aiton died in 1836, Hooker might have become director of a Kew still attached, in all probability, to the British Crown. But Kew in 1838 became a matter of open controversy, for reasons beyond the concerns of Whig patrons or botanical professionals. On the one hand, horticultural entrepreneurs began to push for access to the collections of Kew, and for the creation of a national ornamental garden. On the other, the latter-day advocates of 'economical reform', in exchange for voting a Civil List, sought rigid economies in royal expenditure. Botanists were forced, for the first time, to fight in public for control of the botanic garden. John Lindley rose to this challenge, and projected that a future Kew, governed by a man of science, might assist the economies of colonies, and serve the instruction and pleasure of the British public. But his plan was not uncontested.

That Kew, as a royal garden, attempted to hoard novelties for itself, had never pleased commercial nurserymen and private collectors. Aiton had jealously kept from the English public both many Cape, Australian, and Indian plants collected in the era of Banks, and other newer acquisitions, such as the the orchids with which Aldridge returned from Trinidad and the Orinoco delta in 1833. In the late 1830s, the gardeners thunderingly demanded access to Kew, in the name of the public interest. In 1837, Rev. William Herbert attacked 'the illiberal system established at Kew Gardens by Sir Joseph

Banks' which sought 'to render the King's collection superior to all others by monopolizing its contents'.[131] Commercial gardeners, and their friends in the horticultural press, were less subtle. Glenny at the *Gardener's Gazette* launched a comprehensive attack on Aiton's administration of Kew:

> The plan for keeping up these gardens, and refusing the public the benefit of the collections under any circumstances, is both foolish and unnational. The state of the place is slovenly and discreditable, and that of the plants disgracefully dirty. . . . A new set of men, or a new master ... has become indispensible, and we give Mr. Acton [*sic*] notice to reform or quit.[132]

In its next week's issue, Glenny renewed the attack, borrowing Herbert's fire, attacked the 'illiberal and unnational' management of Kew, and its 'discreditable monopoly': 'it is so disgusting to see the bad arrangements, the ignorant attendants, the slovenly state of the place, and the abominable state of the plants'.[133] Along the same lines Loudon in the *Gardener's Magazine* castigated 'the miserable and disgraceful system introduced in these gardens by the late Sir Joseph Banks', while demanding the end of the prerogative of the sovereign to dispose of plants as gifts, since, as he noted with irony, 'the exercise of this discretion by the late truly excellent and patriotic king, whose knowledge of plants was on a par with that he possessed of horses, was a serious evil'.[134] An article on 'The Garden' published anonymously by Lindley in the Society for the Diffusion of Useful Knowledge's *Penny Cyclopaedia* also slammed Aiton's selfishness with duplicates and his poor management of Kew.[135] The botanists, horticultural journalists, and the nurserymen entrepreneurs who were their colleagues had laid siege to the royal gardens.

This attack on Kew coincided with wider public disquiet about the 'illiberal' mismanagement of royal estates at the accession of Victoria in 1837.[136] In the face of the fiscal profligacy of her predecessors, parliament sought to enforce economies in the Civil List. The Treasury created a 'Royal Gardens Committee' to enquire into how the management of royal parks and gardens could be reorganized, and how the £13,000 spent on them might be reduced. The Board of Green Cloth, of which the 6th Duke of Argyll, Hooker's friend, was Lord Steward, nominated Edward Ellice, M.P., while the recently amalgamated Surveyor General of Works and the Commisioners of Woods, Forests, and Land Revenues appointed Robert Gordon, M.P.[137] Bedford, mistakenly, thought the Committee might undertake the reform of Kew, and wrote Ellice in January 1838 that government could do no better than to place the whole matter in the hands of Hooker and Lindley.[138]

William Hooker in Glasgow swung between moments of optimism and fear. In February 1838 he was cheered when he heard that Lindley and Joseph Paxton had been co-opted by the Committee to advise on the Royal Garden at Kew, but less so when Lindley, his former protégé, wrote that he wished to become director of a reformed Kew.[139] With the prospect of success seemingly so close, Hooker attempted to muster all possible influence.

With Bedford away botanizing in the south of France, he approached the Duke's younger son, Lord John Russell, a member of Melbourne's cabinet.[140] He wished to offer his own bold vision for Kew's future before Lindley could build a position around himself. He attempted to dissuade Lindley from planning the future of Kew as a scientific institution: 'The whole investigation has reference rather to the management of the Royal Gardens as a source of expense to the public than to their scientific treatment.'[141] John Lindley, however, had his own agenda, and had already almost finished his 'Report on the Present Condition of the Botanic Gardens at Kew with Recommendations for its future Administration'.[142]

Both botanists should however have smelt trouble in the fact that relative to Windsor at 27 acres, Kensington and Hampton Court at 15 each, and Cumberland Lodge with 12, Kew at 10 acres was small beer. A preliminary outline of the mission of the Royal Gardens Committee in fact mentioned nothing about botany, urging instead that the 'Inquiry should break into heads – Flowers, Fruits, Vegetables'.[143] Loudon reported to his readers the intelligence he had gleaned that the Royal Gardens Committee was intended

> to arrange some plan whereby all royal gardeners may act in concert, in such a manner as to produce a regular and sufficient supply [of fruits, flowers, and vegetables]. . . .[144]

Indeed the original draft of the letter of 8 February 1838 which appointed Dr. Lindley to report on the 'Botanical Gardens at Kew' urged him,

> with regard to [Kew] ... you will bear in mind this Garden should be maintained for two distinct purposes, the one her Majesty's use, the other the public service. It is most important that the Royal Residence should be continually and abundantly provided from this place with the most rare and valuable flowers that art can procure at all seasons.[145]

Keeping Kew as simply a source of rare flowers or fruit did not require any significant change of its mission, and indeed might be entrusted to a skilled gardener. What precisely constituted 'the public service' remained open to interpretation.

John Lindley, however, refused bravely not to be limited by the terms of his appointment. After only slightly more than two weeks' work, he made an articulate case in February 1838 for Kew to be made into a national botanic garden. He began with a sustained attack on its administration: on the overcrowded and confused houses, the badly named and ordered plants, and Aiton's refusal to share duplicates.[146] He argued that the public had as much claim to it as the Queen, asserting that while 'undoubtedly it has been in one sense a private garden of the Crown', the large expenses borne by the Treasury and the Admiralty for its collection made it 'a Public Garden also'.[147] Lindley indeed argued that with Buckingham House refurbished at enormous expense, Kew could no longer be reserved for 'Her Majesty's service'. Kew should either be 'taken for public purposes, gradually made worthy of the country, and converted into a powerful means of promoting national science' or abandoned.[148]

A national botanic garden, Lindley argued, was 'one of the first proofs of wealth and civilization'. While France, Prussia, Austria, Bavaria, Russia, Hanover, Holland, and Sweden all possessed such gardens 'liberally maintained with public funds', 'the most wealthy and most civilized kingdom in Europe' had none. Appealing to the gardening public, he promised that a reformed Kew would be 'a powerful means of augmenting the pleasure of those who possess gardens', and that 'such a garden would be the great source of new and valuable plants to be introduced and dispersed through this country'. He reminded the Whig and Radical politicians who had created the institution of which he was Professor, that London, now home of their university, must be the site of such a British national garden. The botanical author for the Society for the Diffusion of Useful Knowledge happily appealed to Broughamites and Benthamites, urging that Kew might serve as an instrument for the education and *adoucissement* of the working classes:

> [Kew] would undoubtedly become an efficient instrument in refining the taste, increasing the knowledge, and augmenting the amount of rational pleasures of that important class of society, to provide for the instruction of which has become so great and wise an object with the present enlightened administration.

A great public botanic garden, Lindley suggested to the politicians, would add to London's peace and civility, as well as to its scientific distinction.

More striking than Lindley's allusion to the civilizing power of the botanic garden, a mere sop to Liberal Anglican opinion, was his projection of Kew's possible contribution to the imperial economy. His argument never received parliamentary sanction, nor was it endorsed later by a Treasury letter, nor by a minute of the Board of Woods and Forests. But I quote it here almost entirely because it formed the most substantial element of that part of the Lindley Report printed for parliament in 1840, and because it was repeatedly referred to by the directors of Kew over the next sixty years. It amounted to a mission statement for Kew as a public institution:

> There are many gardens in British Colonies and dependencies: such establishments exist in Calcutta, Bombay, Sahranpur, in the Isle of France, at Sydney, and in Trinidad, costing many thousands a year: their utility is very much diminished by the want of some system under which they can all be regulated and controlled ... there is no unity of purpose among them ... their powers wasted ... [they afford], it is to be feared, but little to the countries in which they are established; and yet they are capable

of conferring very important benefits upon commerce, and of conducing essentially to colonial prosperity.

A National Botanic Garden would be the centre around which all those minor establishments should be arranged; they should be all under the control of the chief of that garden, ... explaining their wants, receiving their supplies, and aiding the mother country in every thing that is useful in the vegetable kingdom. Medicine, commerce, agriculture, horticulture, and many valuable branches of manufacture, would derive considerable advantages from ... such a system.

From a garden of this kind, Government would always be able to obtain authentic and official information upon points connected with the establishment of new colonies; it would afford the plants required on such occasions ...[149]

It was a remarkable appeal to the centralizing enthusiasms of his contemporaries, and, at the same time, to the older developmental assumptions of the age of Banks. His argument amounted to the proposal that the informal empire of economic botany which Banks had created around Kew might be made into a formal bureaucratic instrument for efficient Utilitarian colonial government. Through a 'National Botanic Garden', and it is in this context that Lindley uses this phrase, imperial agriculture might be brought into harmony with domestic trade and manufacture. Most arresting was Lindley's design of the function of 'the chief of that garden', the man who would sit at the centre of the panopticon of imperial nature. Lindley argued that this 'chief' must be 'a man of high scientific attainments'.[150] It should only slightly surprise that Lindley, with the Duke of Devonshire's support, shortly advanced himself as a candidate.[151]

The Royal Gardens Committee fully endorsed Lindley's proposals for Kew. It agreed that the botanic garden should annex many acres from the 'Pleasure Grounds' of the adjoining Kew Palace, and implicitly approved his proposal that £20,000 be spent on turning Kew into a scientific garden, with £4,000 for each succeeding year. In its resolution of 2 March 1838, it recommended the creation of a board to trustees nominated by the Crown, the Linnean and Horticultural Societies, and the medical academies, to govern Kew in the manner of the British Museum: 'The Institution might at once become an establishment worthy of the Nation, and calculated to promote throughout every part of the Empire the Interests of Science.'[152] The idea of a public institution to serve both 'the nation' and 'the empire' had received its first official sanction.

Hooker fretted in Glasgow, far from the action. Bedford, in early March, advised him of the the disquieting (and, it proved, accurate) opinion of Lord Duncannon that from the perspective of the Treasury,

There is likely to be no vacancy [in the superintendence of Kew] & that the Committee which is now sitting upon the subject – refers rather to the

> management of the Royal Gardens as a source of expense to the public than to the scientific treatment of them under the Lord Steward & that there is no intention in making the changes alluded to by Sir William.[153]

Four days later, however, George Bentham advised him of the contents of Lindley's report and that the Royal Gardens Committee intended to advance his proposals to the Treasury.[154] With Bedford again in France, Hooker wrote frantically to Lord John Russell, and directly urged his claims to Melbourne, the Prime Minister:

> Were my noble friend and patron, the Duke of Bedford, in England at the present time, I would not have ventured to have addressed your Lordship myself ... it is the earnest wish of every lover of Botany and Horticulture that these gardens be rendered worthy of this nation.
>
> Unknown as I must be ... to your lordship, I would beg to observe that I am not to the most distinguished Botanists and Horticulturalists of this and other countries. I may particularly mention among those who would be disposed to speak favourably of my qualifications for such an appointment, His Grace the Duke of Bedford, the Duke of Devonshire, Lord Fitzwilliam, Mr. Campbell of Islay.[155]

Hooker himself wrote the Duke of Argyll, Campbell of Islay, Mrs. Brook (formerly Julia Campbell, a niece of the Duke of Argyll), Robert Brown, and others, seeking their intervention with Duncannon, Lord Lansdowne, and Melbourne, but, as he wrote Dawson Turner, 'I am not at all sanguine of success'.[156] He was relieved that Bedford returned from Nice and urged Lord John Russell to explain to Queen Victoria, 'the vast importance ... of converting the Kew Gardens into a Royal Botanic Garden similar to the Jardin des Plantes in Paris'.[157] But he knew that even if the Treasury did lend its support to the reform of Kew, Devonshire had already gone to Melbourne to recommend Lindley.

But Hooker had taken the pulse of events more accurately than the Professor of University College. Lindley, in his grand scheme 'to make the garden a really scientific establishment worthy of the nation', had mistakenly taken inspiration, perhaps, from the more than £200,000 spent on the University of London, or the huge sums being spent by the aristocratic members of the Horticultural Society, such as the almost £40,000 spent on hothouses by the Duke of Northumberland at Syon House.[158] He would have done better to examine his own experience with the Society for the Diffusion of Useful Knowledge, with which he had struggled over both the level and rate of his remuneration.[159] Liberal schemes for public improvement were not always supported by solid Whig cash. Like Bentham and Chadwick's vision of the future of English government, Lindley's ambitious plans for Kew were doomed by the fundamental contradiction of the Liberals and Radicals: their simultaneous desire for an active 'improving' state and for retrenchment.[160]

The cost of implementing all of Lindley's proposals for the Royal Parks and Gardens amounted to over £78,000. It was unthinkable in the political climate of the late 1830s, when Radicals had just spent years attacking the level of expenditure on Buckingham Palace, that tens of thousands of pounds would be calmly spent on royal gardens. Melbourne commented dryly to Victoria, 'It does not seem a very Prudent Committee', and Victoria in turn wrote in her journal:

> a Dr. Somebody of the Horticultural Gardens, and the gardener of the Duke of Devonshire's at Chatsworth, who never thought of what was economy, were on the Committee, and that he [Melbourne] never quite approved of it from the beginning ...[161]

The financial rigour of the Prime Minister, and his philistinism towards science, gave Sir William room for manoeuvre.

Botany versus Horticulture

Unaware that Melbourne had no interest in the Royal Gardens Committee's suggestions, Hooker continued to lobby. He heard, incorrectly, that Aiton planned to resign, and that the Treasury would support Hooker's right to succeed him.[162] Neither he nor Bedford understood the undertone in Victoria's response to Lord John Russell that she was 'in favour of the plan but ... that the Chancellor of the Exchequer had told her the Treasury was poor'.[163] Bedford considered that all that remained was to persuade Spring-Rice that, 'with all the advantages we possess in every part of the globe', Kew might easily surpass the 'Jardin des Plantes (now Jardin du Roi) at Paris [and] might with propriety be called the Queen's Botanic Garden'.[164] He continued to encourage Hooker that he would use all his influence to ensure that 'the Royal Gardens at Kew ... [might be] formed into a useful, scientific, national establishment with you at the head of it'.[165]

At the same time, 'out of doors' pressure for the reform of Kew rose. John Loudon put the civic case for a national public garden, professionally administered, and 'adapted to the purposes of utility and scientific research', with lecture rooms built, and professors appointed, in the *Gardener's Magazine*.[166] Against the argument that reforming Kew would cost too much, Loudon responded caustically:

> A twentieth, or even fiftieth part of the money wasted by one of the follies of George IV at Brighton, Windsor Castle, or Buckingham House, would suffice to raise a monument worthy of a sovereign and a liberal government.[167]

But Loudon, unlike Lindley, did not assume that the master of such a garden would be a scientific botanist.

Indeed in 1838, the project of making a national botanic garden in the Inner Circle of the Regent's Park returned suddenly to the surface. It had arisen first during the Regency, when Banks helped to quash it, and briefly again in 1827.[168] In 1836, James de Carle Sowerby and Philip Barnes formed the Royal Botanical Society of London with the aim, with the support of subscribers, of planting a botanic garden next door to the successful new Zoological Gardens. It was actually a club of horticultural enthusiasts rather than an academy of botanical savants, but few apart from the botanists and their more astute patrons would have noticed the difference, or cared about it. Sowerby and his colleagues proposed that if Dublin, Edinburgh, and Liverpool enjoyed a public garden, then so should 'the Capital of this great Empire'. They quietly offered in 1838 to relieve the Treasury of the expense of Kew.[169] This proposal of a voluntary solution to the Royal Gardens question had obvious appeal for ministers whose priority was 'retrenchment', rather than botany. As early as June 1838, when the proposal had just barely entered the public eye, Bedford warned Hooker that the Regent's Park 'speculators' had got hold of Lord Melbourne and urged him to interest the Queen in favour of the plan.[170] By November Hooker heard other rumours that the Queen (whose first banana was a gift from the Royal Botanical Society of London), Lord Duncannon (Commissioner of Woods and Forests), and Lord Lansdowne had given their patronage to the garden in Regent's Park, which received its Royal Charter in the next year.[171]

The Royal Botanical Society of London's scheme revealed the dangers of botanists depending on the civic ornamental ideal of the botanic garden. 'Out of doors' pressure for a collection, accessible to the public, and worthy of the nation, might easily lead to Regent's Park annexing Kew, and the gardeners eclipsing the botanists. The popular horticultural press stood ready to squelch the pretensions of botanists, warning the Treasury, with direct reference to John Lindley, to 'beware how you take advice from any body connected with the Horticultural Society or Gardens'.[172] With Lindley, Professor of Botany at University College London, and William Jackson Hooker, Regius Professor of Botany at Glasgow, lobbying vigorously for the prospective position of director of Kew, John Loudon calmly advanced the claims of John Smith, Aiton's foreman at Kew: 'If Mr. Aiton resigns . . . Mr. Smith is, we think, the fittest man in England for the Kew Botanic Garden.'[173] The interests of botanists and gardeners were clearly not the same.

The Duke of Bedford, loyal to what had become his project as much as the botanists', remained Hooker's sheet anchor. He encouraged Hooker to refuse the attractive offer of a Professorship at Regent's Park, and to continue to hope he would have his turn at Kew. Indeed, it might be argued that Bedford remained faithful to the idea of a British Jardin des Plantes, under a professional botanist, while Hooker wavered:

I am sorry to hear that you think of embarking in the speculation about to take place in Regent's Park. I have been repeatedly solicited to become one of the patrons of the project, but have uniformly refused thinking that it would interfere with the more important plan of establishing a great national garden at Kew.[174]

Bedford attacked 'that miserable speculation – a Royal Botanic Garden of 18 acres in the Regent's Park' which would be subject to all the 'antivegetating influence of the metropolis'.[175] Illustrating, with wonderful clarity, the Whigs' deep ambivalence about the urban crowd, Bedford objected to Regent's Park as a site for a botanic garden because it was 'liable moreover to the perpetual cockney intrusion from the City of London who do not care one thing about Botany or any other science'.[176] In October, Bedford advised him in confidence that the Chancellor of the Exchequer had been won over, and that the Royal Botanical Society of London would be left to its own devices.[177] Hooker wrote Bentham joyfully, 'I hear daily from the Duke who I feel confident has succeeded in making Ministers favourable to the substantial improvement of Kew.'[178] Hooker continued to put his trust in the long arm of Whig patronage.

But the problem of Lindley remained. Bedford had suggested that the hope of saving Kew would best be realized by all botanists forming a united front. But Lindley refused to prepare a joint memoir with Hooker: he had said all that he had to say in his report, and saw no reason to give up his priority as author of the only plan for a reformed Kew. Hooker realized that his old friend was not about to give in, and wrote him in November, both appealing for Lindley's sympathy as a man growing old far from his friends, and warning that he could afford to accept a less remunerative position.[179] Lindley continued to believe, however, that he held all the aces. While Devonshire advanced his case in private, petitions came from his friends in London, with Lord Brougham presenting that of University College London to the House of Lords on 24 July.[180] Lindley assumed, with some justification, that he had established himself as the logical candidate for appointment as director of a Kew turned over to science.

In January 1839, Bedford briefly despaired, 'It is obvious to me that the whole is now in the hands of Dr. Lindley. . . .'[181] But things were not as bad as they appeared. Bedford had long urged Hooker to speak directly with the Chancellor of the Exchequer, as Hooker, somewhat dolefully, told Asa Gray: 'he still seems to wish me to see Spring-Rice. And I, that nothing may be wanting on my part, that may by possibility contribute to the furthering of so good a course, have agreed to go.'[182] What Spring-Rice however explained to him, as Hooker immediately wrote Dawson Turner, was that Lindley had hoisted himself by his own petard, 'Lindley's scheme ... for the extension of the Royal Gardens, which he wished to superintend will not be listened to and the appointment which he had carved out for himself will come to nothing'.[183] Whatever Kew's fate, Lindley had made himself, with his grandiose plans, into an unpopular choice for director.

By the beginning of the year Hooker also began to secure Tory support. Hooker had long worried that he had no friends on the other side of the House, as he fretted to Turner in late 1838, 'if there is a change in the Ministry it will be all up with me'.[184] But in late January 1839, Bedford organized a long party at Woburn Abbey to which he invited Lord Aberdeen. Hooker happily reported to Dawson Turner and Asa Gray that Aberdeen had shown great interest in talking about Kew, and has assured him that 'if the Gardens are made over to the country no one will grudge the sum necessary to support them, in the way that is done now that they are the Queen's establishment'.[185] By February, Bedford could assure Hooker, 'I trust you have secured powerful advocates in Lord Aberdeen and Sir Robert Peel.'[186]

Hooker had less to fear from the Tories than from many in Lord John Russell's own party. In April 1839, after a year of prevaricating, the Commissioners of Woods and Forests at last commented on the problem of Kew. They urged the Treasury that far more needed to be spent on the garden, and perhaps more territory added to it, if it was to serve as 'a National Institution for the Encouragement and extension of Botanical science'. The Board endorsed the proposals of the original Royal Gardens Committee that an independent board of trustees should govern Kew, as in the case of the British Museum.[187] Melbourne, however, would have nothing to do with it. He advised Queen Victoria, when he resigned in May 1839, that Kew should cease to be a botanic garden maintained at Crown expense.[188] It is worth bearing in mind that it was Melbourne who urged Her Majesty to grant the charter of the Royal Botanical Society of London. What the First Lord of the Treasury really believed was that if a voluntary civic association was willing to shoulder the expense of a national botanic garden, they could have the Crown collections. This would become clear within the year.

As the spring of 1839 moved into the summer, the fate of Kew slipped out of the public eye. Bedford and Hooker waited patiently, believing that the minute of the Board of Woods and Forests already guaranteed the future of Kew as a botanical institution. Everything appeared to Hooker to be in place: Spring-Rice had communicated support for his candidacy, and Hooker in turn had intimated that while Lindley, with his father's debts to pay, needed a large income, he would take whatever the Treasury offered.[189] Bedford consoled Hooker in July 1839, telling him that just for the moment 'botany will stand a poor chance against finance in the mind of the Chancellor of the Exchequer'.[190] Around this time Lord John Russell had Charles Gore, his former private secretary, appointed a Commissioner of Woods and Forests: Bedford assured Hooker that while Gore was no botanist or horticulturalist he 'will do anything to oblige me'.[191] On 16 October, Bedford urged Hooker to write directly to Melbourne putting his claims, and to promise him that 'I have written today to Lord John Russell to urge him strongly not to slacken efforts in pursuit of the great object'.[192] But, just two mornings later, he collapsed at Woburn and was dead within forty-eight hours.

Hooker was now without his most important patron. Lord John Russell was preoccupied with Jamaica, Canada, and his government's feeble grip in the legislature. At the same time, with Melbourne already in sympathy, the Royal Botanical Society of London continued to strengthen its influence. Lord Surrey, Treasurer of the Household and thus manager of all royal expenditure, was elected to the Council of the Society, while his father, the 12th Duke of Norfolk, was a founder Vice-President and one of the five Fellows named in its Royal Charter of 6 September 1839.[193] If Gore strengthened the hand of Hooker's camp in the Board of Woods and Forests, Lord Duncannon, Melbourne's brother-in-law, remained its other Commissioner, while through Surrey, the Board of Green Cloth, which presided over Kew, was wholly on the side of the Royal Botanical Society of London.

The argument quickly appeared that Crown expenditure on a botanic garden could be replaced with private sponsorship. On 11 February 1840, Robert Gordon invited Lindley to speak with him at the Treasury. According to Lindley's minute of the conversation, the Lords of the Treasury proposed that they wished 'to pull down the houses at Kew and dispose of the plants', possibly as early as 25 March, and wished to know if the Horticultural Society agreed to take part or all of them.[194] Lindley promptly refused, writing two days later a strong condemnation of the proposed destruction of Kew as a botanic garden.[195] But of course the Treasury must have expected such a forthright response from him. It is likely that their offer to Lindley, in his capacity as Secretary of the Horticultural Society, was only a tactic to allow them later, with apparently clean hands, to give everything to the Royal Botanical Society of London's garden at the Regent's Park. Aylmer Bourke Lambert, who moved in Court circles, informed John Smith, Aiton's deputy at Kew, that this was the Treasury's intention:

> I have just been with Sir Charles Lemon and am sorry to say that I found that Kew Gardens are to be broken up and the plants to be sent to the Horticultural [Society] that is if they will accept them – if not they are to be offered to persons belonging to the Regent's Park.[196]

Shortly after, in a Memorial to the Lord Commissioners of the Treasury, the Royal Botanical Society of London happily offered to take responsibility for Kew.[197] Horticulture, with the Treasury's support, seemed about to swallow botany.

But 'out of doors' pressure, orchestrated by Lindley, Lambert, Bentham, and John Smith at Kew, saved the day. Letters in *The Times* blasted the government and its plan to destroy Kew:

> The miscalled Liberal administration are at their shabby tricks again, and if an exposure of their proceedings is not made public, they will probably accomplish a most disreputable & detrimental affair ... the Garden is now on the point of demolition.

... the Lord Steward's Department want the greenhouses and hot-houses of the Botanic Garden to grow grapes and pineapples.[198]

At the same time, Lindley skilfully pulled every political thread he could reach. He wrote directly to Robert Peel and raised the matter with him.[199] He shrewdly lobbied Joseph Hume, acknowledged leader of the Radicals in parliament, and thus a man to whom Melbourne, with his flimsy majority in the House of Commons, had to listen:

I voted for you as a Middlesex freeholder at your unlucky contest for Middlesex – I helped you to many votes on that – for which I never asked nor expected thanks. . . . This however authorises me to ask of you, in return, a half-hour's interview.[200]

With the usual scourge of government profligacy on the side of Kew, the government could not depend on an appeal to retrenchment to carry the day. By 25 February, the government had begun to beat a partial retreat, with Gordon advising the Horticultural Society that the Treasury had only intended to sound out opinion and had not made a formal proposal.[201] But the worry continued: the government had hinted its intentions, only for the moment had popular protest stayed its hand.

It was here that Tory support for Kew, which Bedford had deliberately courted a year before, proved its importance. Aberdeen rose in the House of Lords on 3 March 1840 to denounce the plan to destroy Kew and to insist that the Botanic Gardens at Kew constituted 'part of the State and the dignity of the Crown, which ought by no means to be alienated from it'.[202] Duncannon, who responded on behalf of the government, hotly denied that any such destruction had ever been intended.[203] Aberdeen wrote Lindley to assure him that he did not despair of Kew being 'placed on a footing of national utility and importance'.[204] There was less room for the government to slip out of the obligations made by the Commissioners of Woods and Forests almost a year before. But it was possible to see through the half-truth Duncannon had offered parliament: he had never denied that the Treasury had contemplated transferring the control of Kew to the Royal Botanical Society of London or another private body, all he had said was that, 'to break up these gardens would have been next to impossible; for a great many of the plants could not be removed without insuring their destruction'.[205] He made no commitment to preserving Kew from private management. Many realized that the campaign had not yet been won.

Kew and Its Gardens was published in 1840, on behalf of the botanical friends of Kew, in order to package the whole affair to the nation.[206] It clarified and amplified the claims of Lindley's report, pointing out again the crucial place of a botanic garden in the civic dignity of a modern nation, and directly warning about the motives of those then vying to unburden the Crown of the expense of keeping Kew:

> Among private individuals ... parties less scrupulous may be found; and foreign governments would of a surety become eager competitors for the abstraction of botanical treasures, still of immense value, and connected with events of which Great Britain may be justly proud.

In Europe, they would consider the destruction of the collection at Kew as 'a retrograde movement, a step backwards into barbarism'. It appealed directly to royal sentiment: 'The cradle of the Georges and the Williams we trust should be scrupulously preserved by Victoria!'[207]

This public call for the attention of the Queen was only the sequel to a number of private efforts to persuade Victoria to ignore Melbourne's counsel and support the project of a reformed Kew. Lambert communicated to Victoria and Albert, through a Lady-in-Waiting, that Princess Augusta, a Saxe-Gotha, had been the original founder of the botanical garden.[208] The *Literary Gazette* put this new reason for Kew's survival into wider circulation: 'This far-famed garden was founded by a princess of the house of Saxe-Gotha, the illustrious predecessor of His Royal Highness Prince Albert.'[209] This shameless pandering to the royal vanity was, it appears, not without effect. Lambert informed John Smith on 9 March:

> You will not be a little surprised and I think not less gratified, when I tell you your letter ... giving the particulars of the origins of Kew Gardens and the interest taken in them by the Princess of Saxe-Gotha ... went to the throne and were read by her Majesty and Prince Albert, they were much interested with it – there is no doubt that was the reason Lord Ilchester came to Kew as he is one of her Majesty's household.[210]

By 11 March, the Lord Steward formally consented to the separation of the botanic garden from the Royal Household and its attachment to the Board of Woods and Forests.[211]

But this arrangement still required the sanction of the Treasury. It was left to Joseph Hume, whom Lindley had won over, to prod the government into action: he rose on 4 May during the debate on the Estimates for the Royal Palaces to demand that the Lindley report be published for the House of Commons, and that 'they should be made as useful as possible to the public'.[212] With no public announcement, the Treasury on 25 June 1840 accepted the transfer of the Royal Botanic Gardens at Kew from the monarch to Her Majesty's government.

Conclusion: The Strange Victory of Sir William Hooker

The friends of botany had scored a victory in saving Kew. They had prevailed over horticultural entrepreneurs, who wished to subordinate botany to ornamental gardening. But only by themselves asserting that Kew might itself provide recreation for London. The Russells, who wished government to intervene, had also won over Melbourne, whose priority was retrenchment, and who preferred philanthropy to be a private affair. But the battle had been close. Joseph Hume, whom Lindley cajoled into support of Kew, could easily have gone with Melbourne on the issue of economy: in the same day in which Hume rose to demand the publication of the Lindley report, he also attacked the decision to spend £2,824 for the new Museum of Economic Geology in Craig's Court.[213]

But Hooker was no closer to Kew than he had been in 1834. The government had undertaken to maintain the garden, but it had neither ratified the Lindley report, nor was it seeking a scientist to direct it. Only in November 1840 did Aiton inform the government that he would go.[214] There was still no public agenda for the future of Kew. At the same time, Hooker was desperate for an appointment which would bring him home to England. As the February controversy exploded, he decided to defend Kew, and to advance his own candidacy, by summoning the ghost of dead Bedford.[215]

Hooker sought to mobilize the Russell family to make Kew into a monument to their patriarch, with himself on its plinth. He published what purported to be a letter to his father-in-law, which presented all of the correspondence between Bedford and himself over more than six years: *A Copy of a Letter Addressed to Dawson Turner, Esq., F.R.S., & L.S.; & & on the occasion of the death of the Late Duke of Bedford: Particularly in Reference to the Services Rendered by his grace to Botany and Horticulture.*[216] In this most unabashedly sycophantic and self-promoting document, Hooker managed in a handful of pages to repeat several times how much Bedford wished both a British Jardin des Plantes at Kew and for Hooker's appointment:

> He entirely felt with many others as well as myself, that [the Royal Gardens, Kew] are capable of being converted into a national establishment, of the highest importance to science, and altogether consonant with the majesty of the British name;
>
> ... and while he sought the accomplishment of this object on the purest public grounds, he believed he was acting conformably with the same spirit, in striving to second my wishes that the management of them be confided to my superintendence.[217]

While leaving out Bedford's aside on the threat of 'cockney intrusion', Hooker used his remarks on the Regent's Park botanic garden to bludgeon the Royal Botanical Society of London.[218] Aware of the depth of Lord John Russell's ancestor worship, Hooker appealed to family vanity, noting that Bedford had been proud to have first thought of the idea of the British Institution and would have been 'equally proud to have been the founder of a National Botanic Garden'.[219] At the beginning of April 1840, copies of the book were sent to the Queen, Melbourne, Lord John Russell, Duncannon, Gore, and the 7th Duke of Bedford.[220]

16. Sir William Hooker in his prime. Royal Botanic Gardens, Kew.

That Hooker had adroitly placed this knob of butter would emerge within the next few months. For even with formal transfer of Kew to the government in June 1840, and despite the sweet words of Spring-Rice (now Lord Monteagle), the Treasury continued to quibble about funding. Gore, the Russells' protégé, was given the task of informing Hooker that the Board of Woods and Forests had no means of providing even a petty salary for a scientific director of Kew.[221] On 29 June Melbourne and Duncannon finally approved his appointment at Kew, but plans to fund the meagre salary of £300 per annum (with a £200 housing allowance) through the contingency fund fell through.[222] Hooker complained to Bentham, 'There seems to be an unwillingness to do anything in the gardens which will cost an extra penny.'[223] In the end it was another weekend party at Woburn Abbey which settled the matter. The 7th Duke of Bedford wrote Hooker that he had discussed the matter with Melbourne, Lord John Russell, and Duncannon after breakfast, and that his brother 'who is in truth your best friend, has desired Lord Duncannon to give him in writing a statement of the expenses … he will himself prepare the matter to go to the House of Commons. *I beg you to consider this as confidential.*'[224] A meeting in 'Johnny''s office in Downing Street settled the deal, and on the 25 March 1841, Aiton passed Hooker the keys to all of the Royal Gardens at Kew.[225] Russell patronage had carried the day.

The long march of Sir William Hooker had ended. But his appointment to Kew had been won only on the most unhappy terms. He agreed to take next to nothing for his salary, £500 pounds inclusive of his housing allowance, less than half what Lindley wanted, and was entrusted only with 18 acres of the royal estate.[226]

Kew was now a public institution, but no plan for its future had been voted by the House of Commons or minuted by the Treasury. Unlike the British Museum or the Zoological Society Gardens it had no board of learned and independent governors to defend its interests. The Royal Botanic Gardens had simply been attached to the Board of Woods and Forests. Hooker, and his successors, would be at the mercy of its officers. Since the government had made no explicit statement of its commitment to the science of botany, all Kew's directors could draw on was the Lindley report of February 1838. But while this document clearly defined the public mission of Kew—it was to be 'a powerful means of promoting national science', committed to 'science and instruction' at home, and to quickening colonial agriculture and metropolitan trade and manufacture—it had never received official sanction.[227]

Hooker, whose scientific career, and new appointment, owed so much to old-fashioned patronage, responded to his predicament with a campaign to win new patrons. Hooker encouraged Lord John Russell to secure for Kew (and himself) the help of Prince Albert, so that it might 'stand as high in public esteem as it did in the time of George III and Sir Joseph Banks'.[228] Hooker also used his friendship with the Russells, and his welcome at Woburn Abbey, to form relations with Melbourne, Minto, and other Whigs.[229]

In an age of 'aristocratic government', these personal relationships continued to be useful to Hooker. But already, in the 1840s, the tide was going out on the English *ancien régime*, and the friendship of earls and dukes was no longer a guarantee of safety. Kew remained vulnerable, as Radical pressure for 'retrenchment' became the fiscal orthodoxy of Peel, Goulburn, and Gladstone. The advancement of science, for its own sake, had a small natural constituency: one man's patronage was another's 'corruption'. The dominance of the Whigs in the politics of reform had itself depended on their presenting themselves as servants of a broader public interest. Hooker and his heirs in the future would need, similarly, to present their personal and professional objectives as the needs of the nation. In the process, the directors of Kew learned the uses of empire.

Dundas and the Jenkinsons, the Governors of Crown Colonies, and the servants of the East India Company had found both practical and ideological use for the natural sciences. Botany, as it served agriculture, was both an instrument, and a fetish, of an enlightened imperialism. The patronage of

Hooker and Lindley by Whig dukes was only, as we have seen, a domestic application of this idea that Nature might give efficiency and dignity to political authority. The myth that the scientific use of resources led inexorably to cosmopolitan benefit remained alive in the age of Palmerston. As for Banks and his contemporaries, it comforted those who intruded into exotic territories and attempted to subordinate their inhabitants. But the idea of governing men on principles derived from Nature was also useful to the botanists. The directors of Kew found in their imperial role a means of justifying public support for professional botany. As Sir William discovered, imperial science could sustain the expansion of a scientific empire.

CHAPTER 6
The Professionals and the Empire: The Hookers at Kew, 1841–73

In a mere three decades after 1841, Sir William Hooker and his son turned the small royal garden into a major institution: popular, enlarged, and ornamented, a centre for scientific research, and in communication with planters and administrators on every continent. Their success depended on their response to the opportunites of the early Victorian era, and in particular to that expansion of British influence which was a consistent fact of the age of Palmerston. An appetite for islands and strong points, from which British vessels might command continental trade and navigation, the private enthusiasms of frontier soldiers and settlers, evangelical and free trade optimism led to the annexations of Aden (1838), New Zealand (1840), Hong Kong (1841), Sind (1843), Natal (1844), Labuan (1846), Punjab (1849), Lower Burma (1852), Oudh (1856), Lagos (1861), and Basutoland (1868). The era from 1840 to 1870 also saw the effective penetration of the interiors of Australia, Canada, Bengal, Madras, the Cape, and British Guiana quickened by gold, agrarian, commercial and fiscal ambitions, and the threat of European and local rivals. The Crown's assumption of responsibility for India in 1858 only made formal older arrangements. The consolidation of Kew and this vast and complex process which produced the Pax Britannica were, in peculiar ways, connected. To see why, we need first to re-examine how we understand British imperialism in this era.

It ought to be a commonplace that the expansion of the British Empire in the nineteenth century was often driven by groups which may be assimilated to the idea of the 'professional'. Soldiers and churchmen, diplomats and bankers, found inspiration and career opportunities in the colonial enterprise. The interests of particular vocational parties were frequently better represented in the projection of British influence than colder economic or strategic calculations of the national interest. We have valuable empirical studies of evangelicals or 'gentlemanly capitalists' as mediators of imperial concerns in British public life, but we have not distilled the principle at work in all these cases. Shared assumptions and 'craft' traditions, networks of allies and competitors, internal and external struggles—in short, a variety of kinds of investment in cultural capital—guided action and response in spheres into which mere greed, national and racial passions, and the 'official mind' failed to penetrate. This Weberian theme may allow us to reconcile, eventually,

Schumpeter's warlords, Cain and Hopkins's financiers, and Andrew Porter's missionaries.

Imperial history, it is true, has already given some conceptual attention to the role of individuals and interest groups. Categories such as 'men on the spot' or 'subimperialism' have suggested the importance of these local or regional actors in shaping the fabric of expansion at the periphery. Their agency at home has also found some theoretical expression. Darwin, in particular, has gestured towards the importance of the 'domestic bridgehead'—the 'enclaves of empire-minded or imperial-oriented interests in the metropole' which supported the frontier adventures of Wellesley in one era, or Milner in another.[1] But his concern with lobbies and pressure groups seems limited by the same assumptions which have tended to focus the research of imperial historians on the periphery. One legacy of the imperial experience, only now perhaps in the process of decay, is the presumption that empire was something which happened abroad. The experience of expansion, from this world view, left the main strand of British history untouched. A different landscape opens up once we begin to recognize that the world, from the sixteenth century, colonized Britain. We can take a large step forward when we begin to recognize imperialism to be as impeded and unnatural at the centre as at peripheries. We may fruitfully apply Ronald Robinson's thesis on 'collaboration' to the metropole, and seek to ask, with as much rigour as we would at the periphery, how and why did concrete individuals and groups attach themselves to extraterritorial agents or interests?[2] A variety of professionals—churchmen, bankers, and many kinds of intellectuals—often stood at that European frontier of globalization, importing extra-European concerns into the texture of metropolitan life.

Natural scientists formed one important such category of professional 'collaborators': an interest group central to the weaving of Africa, Asia, and the Americas into the fabric of national life. As Stafford has argued, like merchants and missionaries, they often led, rather than followed, the flag in Africa or the Pacific.[3] At home, as I have suggested in previous chapters, botanists discovered in a wider world the materials for their research and, from the era of Banks onwards, some justification for why they deserved the patronage of the state. It is the purpose of this chapter to bridge this story of the professional uses of empire to the domestic history of British expansion. For this we must begin to explain why and how our 'collaborators'—botanists in general, and the Hookers at Kew, in particular—pinned their colours to the imperial mast.

Historians of Kew, in particular Brockway and Desmond, have tended to see Sir William Hooker as arriving at Kew in 1840 with a clear vision of Kew as the conductor of an orchestra of imperial botanic gardens. Hooker, in fact, was much less clear about his direction: neither his nor Kew's destiny had been decided. At its birth in 1840, Kew's mission as a public institution was essentially to be a recreational garden. It was, if anything, the younger and poorer relation of colonial botanic gardens. That it became, by the late 1870s, the world's premier botanical institution and the centre of a system of botanical and agricultural exchanges across the British empire, needs to be explained in terms of the intervening thirty years. It was out of its weakness, rather than its strength, that Kew became imperial.

The Hookers were not, of course, acting in a vacuum. 'Public science'—the effort to justify scientists' right to resources and respect in terms of their utility—had always complemented private research.[4] By the Hookers' era, men of science also responded to similar campaigns waged by physicians, lawyers, engineers, and civil servants.[5] The shape and success of these initiatives depended on the unprecedented degree to which Victorian politicians and administrators were beginning to seek the help of specialists. The Benthamite vision of the state's responsibility to foster and recruit expertise only represented the most articulate statement of more prevailing assumptions.[6] Professions are imagined communities, but, as in the case of nations, both the ordering images, and their appeal, are constrained by local experience. They do not depend merely on the whims of their protagonists: some must desire, and others must concede, their boundaries. The scale of the evangelical ambitions of English churchmen, for example, and the support they enjoyed from a lay public, depended, in part, on Georgian Britain's exalted circumstances, and on a new hunger for consolation and social pacification awakened by the violent pace of social and economic change. In the same way, the Hookers' turn to the empire responded to the expanding sphere of British power, and to the appeals made by colonial administrators and entrepreneurs faced suddenly with the challenge of vast new territories.

Science and technology had transformed the terms on which Britain encountered the world in the second half of the nineteenth century. They had forged new 'tools of empire', which shrank the world, and made new environments penetrable and profitable.[7] But, as Michael Adas has shown, knowledge and technique mattered far beyond the new insight or powers they allowed Man to exert over Nature.[8] They had a charismatic force: endowing Europeans with a moral and practical right to intervene in exotic places. The idea of the scientist's professional expertise thus became a commodity as useful to those confronting the colonial frontier as it was to scientists themselves. The science of plants found new allies in the age of the Pax Britannica as it garlanded imperial power with a natural legitimacy.

The Predicament of Science in an Age of Reform

In 1840, the Queen had agreed that a portion of the royal estates at Richmond might become a public botanic garden, and on Lady Day 1841 the Board of Woods and Forests, with the delegated authority of parliament, appointed Sir William Hooker, a distinguished botanist, as its first Director. But we would be wrong to deduce that either Victorian administrators or the public had decided that Kew was primarily a scientific institution, or that

Hooker, by virtue of his expertise, deserved special support and encouragement. As we examined earlier, Hooker prevailed not through appealing to the idea that science, because of its usefulness, deserved the patronage of government, and the professional a fair reward, but rather through securing the help of the Russells, a great aristocratic political family. That Hooker was in post instead of Lindley had much to do with the fact that he was willing to accept less than half what his friend desired. His position as a public servant lacked any clear definition. The compromises made at the origin of a public Kew would return to haunt its directors over the next decades.

Parliament from 1840 was Kew's master, but neither House had divided over its destiny. The vision offered in Lindley's report of 1838, of Kew as a 'National Botanic Garden', under a professional botanist, assisting government in everything to do with vegetable nature, had received no official sanction. Indeed Hooker's appointment was under attack from the beginning: Loudon, tribune of popular horticulture, suggested that John Smith, the principal gardener at Kew, should in fact have been placed at the head of the establishment, and that Hooker, although a very good man and a good botanist, was now 'robbing the country of a salary'.[9] The salary in question, Loudon would not have known, was pitiful. At £300 per annum, with £200 for housing, Hooker's annual income was less than one-third of the overdraft which he had accumulated in removing his family, and vast herbarium and library, to Kew.[10] Hooker needed his private scientific collections with him to perform his public functions, for in 1841 all he had inherited at Kew were ten stoves and greenhouses in varying states of disrepair. But while he had little government help for his scientific work, he was free to profit from his privileged access to new plants, and indeed made some £250 per annum as editor of the *Botanical Magazine*, which presented horticultural novelties to its wealthy subscribers.[11] He was, in reality, the underpaid manager of a slightly shabby park, distinguished only by its collection of rare plants. His domain was smaller than the private territory of the Royal Botanical Society of London in Regent's Park, while the East India Company's Director of the Calcutta Botanic Garden presided over 300 acres at more than twice Hooker's salary. The 'Pleasure Grounds' of Richmond Palace remained separate under the continued authority of Aiton, while the royal family retained stretches for hunting and recreation. Duncannon had insisted that no land be annexed from these adjoining domains, to which Hooker had meekly replied: 'there are eighteen acres ... let us see what can be done with them'.[12]

Kew in 1840 had been consigned to the Board of Woods and Forests and Land Revenues. This arm of the state was a bizarre hybrid typical of an era in which, as Rubenstein has commented, older informal *mores* went hand-in-hand with new bureaucratic structures and ideologies.[13] The 'Woods and Works' had become the favoured shelter for a variety of institutions and charities which had moved from private or royal control to the support of the nation, including, in stages after 1835, the King's private roads, Sir Henry de la Beche's Museum of Practical Geology and the Geological Survey of the

United Kingdom. It had been formed in 1832 by the Whigs, by the amalgamation of the Office of Works with the Commission of Woods, Forests, and Land Revenues. On the one hand, it was a product of the desire to complete the reform of public works, an area of the state clotted with sinecures and official peculation, first begun by Whigs in 1782 and Tories in 1815.[14] On the other, this department, which married income generation with public expenditure, gave its three commissioners wholly undemocratic powers of patronage, as they could spend the land revenues of the Crown within their department without the consent of parliament. Much of this was to Hooker's benefit, as the record of expenditure on Kew between 1841 and 1844 shows: in 1841 only £2,078 were voted as a parliamentary grant but an additional £2,500 were assigned from the land revenues of the Board of Woods and Forests, and while the formal parliamentary grant rose only gradually, the land revenues of the Crown supplied £3,700 the next year, and over £4,000 thereafter, making Kew in 1843, the recipient of the largest subsidy from the Board after Windsor Castle.[15]

Radical politicians rose in the Commons to challenge the aristocratic politicians who applied the public revenue of the 'Woods and Works' to patronize favourite causes. In June 1843, Mr. William Williams, one of Hume's closest lieutenants, attacked the vote of income for Princess Augusta, threatening the Tories that their spendthrift indulgence of royal luxury might become an election issue in the future as it had in 1830:

> in nine years they had added by their votes 42 million pounds to the permanent debt of the country, within three years they had added 8 million sterling to the taxation of this country. . . . If they fancied they were not some day or other to answer for this they were mistaken.[16]

Williams then called on the government to publish for the House a full account of all the public money expended on each of the Royal Palaces, Gardens and Parks.[17] The influence of this pressure can be seen in the Treasury minute delivered to Hooker in 1844 which warned him that government could only support literary and scientific institutions if their usefulness was 'rendered as extensive and as public as possible', where as many private sources as possible were drawn upon, and when the strictest economy was observed in salaries and expenses.[18] Both Henry Goulburn, the Chancellor of the Exchequer, and his young protégé William Gladstone, whose values would mark the Treasury for the rest of the century, looked with coolness at any expensive schemes for the 'improvement' of the public.[19] Similarly when the ministry changed in 1845, Lord Morpeth, the new First Commissioner, warned Hooker to bridle his expectations as too much had already been expended on the gardens.[20]

In 1850–1, the 'Woods and Works' was split into two, with Kew and other revenue-expending departments placed under the Board of Works and Public Buildings, while the income-generating part of the department was absorbed into the Treasury. With the reform of the civil service after 1854, the directors of Kew faced increasingly demanding negotiations with their political masters. It was difficult for those who conceived themselves as 'reformers' to distinguish the benevolent patronage of the Old Regime, so important for botany in general and Kew in particular, from rank corruption. The knife which aimed to pare away the fat of the state could easily slip and wound the scientific community. The history of Kew from 1840 to 1872 is centrally the story of how the Hookers sought to secure their personal and professional ends through identifying themselves with the public interest.

The season was not wholly unfavourable to the Hookers. While Victorian politicians shared no consensus that science deserved public support, they increasingly recognized its value. When Lyell met Peel after the 1839 British Association for the Advancement of Science meeting in Birmingham, he commented that Peel

> is without a tincture of science, and interested in it only so far as knowing its importance in the arts and as a subject with which a large body of persons with talent are occupied.[21]

Peel himself joked with Haddington in 1842 that he should not hastily conclude that 'everything which a man of science recommends must be advantageous to the public interest'.[22] But the schoolboy who received the gospel of Sir John Sinclair from Drury at Harrow had a healthy respect for the power of science and technology to transform 'the arts' and thus economic life. *Chemistry in Its Application to Agriculture and Physiology* had been published by Liebig in 1840 and Peel came to look towards science to save British agriculture in the new age of free trade. Botanists responded to these concerns and in June 1841 the Horticultural Society formed a chemical committee to follow up on Liebig, while Lindley communicated with Peel and Aberdeen about the potato famine of 1845 in Ireland.[23] Chemistry and geology, as Peel noted in his address to the agriculturalists at Tamworth, offered important assistance to agriculture. Peelite encouragement secured the futures of the Geological Survey and Museum of Practical or Economic Geology, which Henry de la Beche had founded a decade before, and the Royal College of Chemistry, from 1845, under the direction of Hofman.[24] Under their stimulus wheat yields in Britain rose from an average of 34 bushels per acre between 1830 and 1839 to one of about 52 per acre between 1840 and 1849.[25] The geologists and chemists cemented their position when they turned to mapping coal, and to cracking its tar into dyes and other useful derivatives.[26] The apparent gift of Sir Roderick Murchison for predicting gold in Russia and Australia led to the foundation of public geological surveys in every British colonial outpost.[27] In 1851, the government founded the Royal College of Mines, which shortly absorbed chemical and geological research, and became, with the appointment of Thomas Henry Huxley, a centre of biological research. Under the pressure of the Royal Commission on the

Universities, Cambridge (1851) and Oxford (1853) created honours schools in natural science.

The Queen's Speech of 1853 urged that 'the time had come when the nation should systematize scientific instruction having a bearing upon industry'. To further this, Aberdeen took £186,000 from the profits of the Great Exhibition and £150,000 from parliament to found the Science and Arts Department in South Kensington.[28] With grants from the Privy Council to voluntary schools having increased from £30,000 in 1840 to £541,233 per year in 1855, a Department of Education emerged in 1856 which grew in its influence with the enquiries of the Newcastle Commission into elementary education (1858–64), and the Clarendon and Taunton Commissions of 1861 and 1864 into 'public' and endowed secondary schools. Scientists looked with excitement at the possibility of science becoming part of the curriculum in all schools, as Huxley put it, while urging Joseph Hooker to assist the Department of Science and Arts:

> The English nation will not take science from above so they must take it from below. We the Drs. who know what is good for it, if we cannot get it to take pills we must administer our remedies *par derrière.*[29]

The alliance formed between scientists and those who supported broad popular education resulted in the appointment to the Royal Commission on Scientific Instruction and the Advancement of Science (1870–5) of the Duke of Devonshire, the Marquis of Lansdowne, Sir John Lubbock (archaeologist and anthropologist), Sir James Kay-Shuttleworth (Secretary to the Privy Council Committee on Education, 1839–49), Bernard Samuelson, William Sharpey (Professor of Anatomy and Physiology, University College, London), T.H. Huxley (Professor of Natural History at the Royal School of Mines), William Miller (Professor of Chemistry at King's College, London), and G.G. Stokes (Lucasian Professor of Mathematics, Cambridge). Both the existence of such a Commission, and the fact that it was dominated by scientific teachers and researchers, suggested the much larger place enjoyed by science in public life by the 1870s, compared with the era of Babbage and Herschel. And yet scientists looked at the cold blade of Gladstone's Treasury with distrust. As professionals they now had broad public ambitions, but how far was the nation ready to extend influence to them?

The word 'scientist' was invented by William Whewell in 1834.[30] Over the next decades a community emerged gradually which defined themselves by it. Where I have spoken of the botanical 'professional' for the period from 1820 to 1840, it was more to mark a tendency within the discipline, a nascent 'party' in the Weberian sense, rather than to describe a clearly demarcated class or status group. In the Linnaean Society during the 1820s and 1830s, for example, the members divided themselves between the 'bees', among whom numbered figures like Lindley and Sabine, and the 'drones', captained by Lambert and including the many titled amateurs such as the Duke of

Bedford.[31] But few outside the Linnaean recognized this distinction between productive specialist expertise and amateur connoisseurship, and like geology, botany remained both socially and intellectually a 'gentlemanly science', with the threshold of expertise which allowed participation remaining low enough to admit a sizeable proportion of the educated public.[32] But from the 1850s onwards, 'bee' botanists, represented by Joseph Hooker, chose to push both for more public support for science and for stripping the 'drones' of any power over their disciplines. The two initiatives were connected, as Huxley put it to Joseph Hooker:

> the word 'Naturalist' unfortunately includes a far lower order of men than Chemist, Physicist, or Mathematician. You don't call a man a Mathematician, deserving of his country's reward, because he has spent his life getting as far as quadratics; but every fool who can make bad species and worse genera is a 'Naturalist'.[33]

Putting the professionals in command of learned societies was a necessary preliminary to demanding help from the state and respect from the public.

The scientists' sense of themselves as a party, with interests to defend, was sharpened by the opposition they met in many quarters. In 1818, as we examined earlier, the Regius Professor of Greek at Cambridge had launched a fierce attack on the scientific claims of natural history in general, and the President of the Linnaean Society in particular. Many classicists and churchmen recognized that any gains made by natural scientists in public life might come at the expense of their own pre-eminence. They challenged the scientists' demand for an enlarged place in the eduational curriculum and the cultural life of the nation. B.H. Kennedy, headmaster of Shrewsbury and author of the famous *Latin Primer*, commented to the Clarendon Commission that he opposed any significant introduction of the natural sciences because they did not 'furnish a basis for education'.[34] Benjamin Jowett, Master of Balliol College at Oxford, similarly declared to the Devonshire Commission that he thought that 'A cabinet which consisted of persons who only knew Latin and Greek would probably be a better cabinet [than one] consisting entirely of chemists'.[35] The mandarins saw no reason why their influence over the nation's statesmen should be diminished. Even if Oxford and Cambridge created honours schools in science as acts of defensive modernization in the 1850s, the clerics, classicists, and mathematicians largely excluded scientists from access to endowed positions. Marmaduke Lawson, Sherardian Professor of Botany at Oxford, noted in 1872 that there was not a single scholarship or exhibition in the university granted for botanical proficiency.[36] Henry Latham at Trinity Hall, Cambridge, reported also to the Devonshire Commission that when he had recommended to a parent that his son read natural science because he had shown a taste for geology or botany, the parent always responded '"How, Sir, is my son to get his bread by knowing geology?" and I have no answer to make him.'[37] The mandarins enjoyed this grip they held on the rise of the sciences, and while Jowett conceded that scientists should be free to compete for the scholarships, he still argued that the fellowships should not be opened. The friends of natural sciences, on the other hand, knew their enemy, and Henry Acland, Regius Professor of Medicine at Oxford, spoke for many when he confided to the Devonshire Commissioners that

> there is no doubt that the origin of those institutions in this country from the learning of the ecclesiastics is at this moment in some respects a disadvantage. But that is a question to be handled with extreme delicacy.[38]

While individual scientists rose to positions of public influence, a variety of forces in the schools and universities stood ready to put barriers in the way of their profession. In the aftermath of the publication of *On the Origin of Species*, elements of England's classical and clerical intelligentsia indeed sought, on occasions, to put the men of science in their place.

Politicians and civil servants were often indifferent, if not hostile, to the demand made by scientists for satisfactory remuneration and for public support for their research. Many considered scientific learning more as an enlightened hobby than as work which deserved a reward, and felt its cost should, in a large part, be borne by its happy amateurs. These assumptions help us to explain the risible salary which Sir William Hooker received in 1841, and the official expectation that he would supply the herbarium and library he needed for his public work at his own expense. Those who chose a scientific career and who, unlike the elder Hooker, lacked independent means, assumed the risk of poverty.

The career of Joseph Hooker exemplified the predicament of the professional scientist in this era. Having graduated from Edinburgh in medicine in 1839—almost all of his peers similarly were educated outside of Oxbridge—Hooker accepted a commission as assistant surgeon arranged through his father's friend, James Ross, to travel as naturalist for the expedition to Antarctica (1839–43). But while Joseph Hooker was charged with collecting for the nation, the public had supplied none of his scientific needs:

> Except for some drying paper for plants, I had not a single instrument or book supplied to me as a naturalist – all were given to me by my father ... not a single glass bottle was supplied for collecting purposes, empty pickle bottles were all we had, and rum as a preservative from the ship's stores.[39]

Without much assistance from the Crown, Hooker proved himself on this voyage to be a naturalist of the first rank, and provided the basis for reflections on the geography of plants which later supported the argument in the twelfth and thirteenth chapters of Darwin's *Origin of Species.*[40] On his return, he had been fêted on a minor scale, presented to Victoria and Albert, allowed two years on Admiralty pay to work up his collections, and awarded £1,000 by Sir Robert Peel to publish the plates of new plants. But he fell rapidly from the limelight. He survived simply by sharing his father's shelter, salt, and scientific equipment. As Joseph Hooker later wrote to Henry Bates, 'It was sixteen years before I had an average income of £100 clear from my science ... & it was not until 1855 that I was independent of my father!'[41] While Charles Darwin could retire to Kent on his inherited income, the Hookers had the struggle to find paying work. The support or opposition of political and scientific patrons continued to decide who found such positions throughout this period: while Hooker had the constant and valuable help of his father, T.H. Huxley, after returning from his voyage as assistant surgeon on the *Rattlesnake,* found that the once-friendly Richard Owen could not bear to see his protégé outshine him.[42]

Huxley and the younger Hooker were thus part of a generation more aware than its predecessors of the constraints within which it operated, but also more ambitious, and more willing to fight to secure their ends.[43] They took up the cudgels laid down by Babbage's generation and worked to reform the Royal and other professional societies and to promote the status and influence of science. With John Tyndall (the physicist), Herbert Spencer, Edward Frankland (the chemist) and four others they formed the 'X Club', and in alliance with the education movement and younger scientists like Norman Lockyer (Editor of *Nature,* and Secretary to the Devonshire Commission) and Francis Galton, represented science to the British nation.[44] When Joseph Hooker came into conflict with the First Commissioner of Works after 1870, he had therefore beside him an aggressive and confident group of allies willing to fight his battles through polemical articles in the press and pointed memorials to the government.[45]

But professional scientists struggled as much among themselves as with the state. The scientific controversy which had most impact on Kew in this era was that which surrounded Charles Darwin. It was to Joseph Hooker that Darwin first confided his 'sketch' on the species question of 1842, and his conclusion that species were not immutable—'it is like confessing a murder'.[46] When in 1858, Alfred Russel Wallace sent in his essay on the same problem, it was Hooker who arranged with Charles Lyell that their friend should not be pre-empted, and that Darwin's and Wallace's papers were presented together to the Linnaean Society. While Darwin himself shied away from public controversy, T.H. Huxley became 'Darwin's bulldog', battling opponents from Bishop Wilberforce of Oxford to Richard Owen, the anatomist. It was only a matter of time before those who opposed Darwin decided that Joseph Hooker was also their enemy. Such intellectual strife became connected to less elevated conflict over resources for institutions. For Richard Owen, as Keeper of Natural History at the British Museum, began after 1860 to push without rest for the unification of all national botanical, zoological, and geological collections into a new Museum of Natural History. Struggles over ideas then easily merged into rivalry between professional collections.

The two Hookers thus faced a complex, and shifting, set of challenges. They needed both to make Kew as publicly useful as possible at minimum cost, and to say they were doing so. Their own objectives, as men of science, meshed imperfectly with the concerns of their political masters. They sought a library, herbarium, and museums which would make Kew a serious centre for botanical science. Sir William was constantly concerned with the career of his son, and active winning friends among those who could provide Joseph with opportunities of exploration abroad, and a salary at home while he researched and wrote. Even after the appointment of Joseph as Assistant Director of Kew in 1855, the Hookers continued to need to please those who might allow his eventual succession to the directorship. Throughout this period, the Hookers and the different managers of the botanical department of the British Museum exchanged frankly acquisitive glances at each other's collections. In order to secure this mixture of ends, the Hookers had to translate private and professional desiderata into questions of the public interest.

The haggling of men of science with bureaucrats may not seem, initially, to deserve too much attention. But once we realize that these negotiations depended on an appeal to contemporary experience and assumptions, we may come, through them, to new terms with the Victorian experience.

The Uses of Public Gardens: Recreating the Empire

In 1841, Kew was first and foremost a public garden. Indeed, most of Hooker's political masters prized Kew, in its first decades, principally as a recreational space. We return here in part to a theme we visited earlier: the botanic garden, from the sixteenth century, had always had a political meaning as spectacle. As it summoned the variety of nature to one climax, and ordered and named the pleasures of colour, form, and smell, the garden served to make power appear beautiful and perhaps natural. Popes, princes, aristocrats, or rich merchants, sought to adorn themselves with flowers and fountains. Some among them came to open these grounds to the crowd, for nothing would be lost by impressing the public with the majesty and generosity of their founders or proprietors. With such pleasure grounds, the rulers of cities similarly showed their cities as gentle and prosperous. It is important to realize that many of Hooker's allies in 1841, and most of his enemies, saw Kew's future in these terms: as a place for the amusement and edification of the nation.

The Victorian era was the great age of the public garden. Hyde, Green, St. James, Vauxhall, and Battersea Parks, like their equivalents at the centre of New York and at the eastern and western flanks of Paris, all found their modern form in the middle decades of the nineteenth century. This urban gardening clearly reflected a response to the consequences of rapid growth. Between 1821 and 1851 the population of London had doubled to almost seven million.[47] Through the influence of Chadwick and others, many recognized that this rapid increase in urban population led directly to epidemic disease.[48] In dense cities, flooded with cinders and smoke, poorly drained of garbage and sewage, and afflicted with cholera epidemics and endemic tuberculosis, parks had a sanitary importance.[49] But moral and political health were equally desirable to urban planners. Serpentine lakes and avenues of trees might divert the crowd away from many kinds of evil. They could lead the masses away from alcohol and gambling towards safer pleasures, if not towards religion. The energy which the Victorian English spent on greening cities should be seen as connected to their mania for the building of churches: both revealed piety mixed with anxieties about the impact of industry and democracy. Public gardens similarly attracted the support of those who feared revolution more than vice. Napoleon III's boulevardes and his parks at the Bois de Vincennes and de Boulogne, for example, were part of the same half-political and half-aesthetic goal: grandeur which might tame the crowd.[50]

In Britain, where parliamentary reform in 1832 had only made the unrepresentative character of its democracy more apparent, parks had an additional meaning. Public spaces and institutions were evidence for that 'good government' which the enfranchised élite provided. Many hoped that green nature might yield a political *adoucissement.* We should not forget that the 'age of equipoise' was equally one of significant social protest. In 1848, indeed, Sir William, and sixty of the men then at the end of a massive programme of construction and landscaping, were sworn in as special constables to meet the threat of a Chartist 'mob' on Kew Green.[51] The younger sons of dukes who, as we shall see, helped Sir William Hooker to enlarge and embellish Kew into the finest botanic garden in the world, were animated as much by political apprehensions as by aesthetic ambition.

The provision of recreation and public ornament was also the principal function of the botanic gardens in Britain's overseas dependencies. As the Governor of New South Wales noted in 1846, the botanic garden there depended on the support of its citizens, and was 'scarcely more than a very agreeable promenade for the inhabitants of and sojourners in Sydney'.[52] Both Cape Town's decaying Company garden and Baron Ludwig's collection depended equally on local subscribers who sought a public park, not a research institute (plate 12). In the gardens of Port of Spain, Kingstown, Grahamstown, Calcutta, Peredinaya, and Singapore, lakes and alleys of cabbage palms opened vistas for the pleasure of Europeans and the colonized (see illustration 17). Hooker indeed complained to Herschel that mere gardeners were sent out to the colonies, 'who drink porter and rum and do nothing for science'.[53] But 'mere gardeners' were perhaps engaged in one of the most irreversible and unnoticed effects of imperialism: the protected

17. Lake in Calcutta Botanic Garden, late nineteenth century. Royal Botanic Gardens, Kew.

propagation of European plants, animals, and ideas of landscape, in new conditions.[54] It would be wrong to see any conspiracy here: the British simply took their horticultural passions, and the flowers and fruits they loved, wherever they took up residence, founding horticultural societies in Bengal, the Punjab, Sydney, and elsewhere.[55] These voluntary initiatives led to many new botanical gardens, which, as in Singapore, where an 'Agri-Horticultural' society in 1859 resuscitated Raffles's 1822 'Botanical and Experimental Garden', undertook labours beyond the compass of colonial governments' resources.[56]

India provides a powerful instance of this colonization by gardening. Calcutta, Madras, and Bombay owed their gardens to the agrarian enthusiasms of Banks's era. Mughal gardens were anglicized in Sahranpore and elsewhere. All were strikingly landscaped; and popular among locals. Wherever British soldiers and administrators travelled in the subcontinent, during the early days of the century, they came to plant new grounds, and to introduce familiar plants. In the north, there were public gardens at Agra, Cawnpore, Lucknow, Delhi, Meerut, Umbala and Simla, while in the North-West Provinces, gardens were attached to garrisons 'as a source of recreation and benefit' at Kussowlie, Dugshai, and Lahore.[57] To the east, the soldiers of the

East India Company formed gardens in the 1850s in Pegu, during their invasion of Burma. In the south, one of the first initiatives of the Marquis of Tweeddale in the Madras Presidency was to plant horticultural gardens at Ootacamund complete with 'flower gardens', 'bowers', and 'rustic arches', in the Nilgiri Hills where temperate flora could prosper.[58] Apples, pears, plums, peaches, and favoured varieties of grain were propagated for distribution among Europeans and 'native cultivators'.[59] The report for 1854–5 of McIvor, its superintendent, boasted of having distributed the seeds for radishes, brussel sprouts, and cauliflower for planting in the garrisons of Pondicherry and Ahmednagar, and included an extensive list of fruit trees and shrubs on sale. Already such sales provided more than 40% of the cost of running the garden. There, as in the Cape, hardy Australian and American plants were planted in the drier places.

In these colonial gardens we may discern a complex agenda. They were, of course, at the simplest level, places through which desirable foods and flowers might be disseminated. They were, like public gardens at home, symbols of wise government. But we may also see in them spaces to which Europeans might retreat from the strangeness of alien environments. They often encompassed areas of wilderness, making islands of the same forest plants which encircled the boundaries of civility. They were theatres in which exotic nature was, literally, put in its place in a European system. This spectacle of the inclusion of the strange within the familiar comforted the expatriates and impressed the locals. It was as irresistible an argument for the imperial prerogatives of British civilization as that offered many afternoons in colonial cities, when policemen or soldiers unpacked their shiny instruments on the iron bandstand and unfurled, as they perspired, the swaggering rhythms of 'Rule Britannia'. Indigenous nature, and aesthetic sense, were enclosed in an imported style, much as the power and movement of local bodies were disciplined within the new music of British sports. Beside the lily-covered lakes, the British, and the people they lived among, discovered their roles in the drama of colonizers and colonized. No one who misses this will ever understand how sweet it is to the once-colonized to make the cricket and rugby pitch, the lecture hall, and the English language, into territories where they stand dominant, free to change the game.

At home, the British laboured instead to domesticate the world's plants. As public garden to the nation, Kew received hundreds of unsolicited donations of foreign plants in the early 1840s.[60] In 1845, Aberdeen, then Peel's Foreign Secretary, sent out circulars to British ministers and consuls in all parts of the world urging them to send Kew specimens, while the Admiralty and the Colonial Office were officially asked by Lord Lincoln to assist similarly.[61] From the early 1840s, Sir William Burnett, Physician of the Navy, directed to Kew all seeds collected by naval surgeons. In 1847, the Admiralty made this arrangement formal, asking Hooker to write the botanical section for its *Manual of Scientific Inquiry*.[62]

Each advancing edge of British power resulted in new acquisitions. From

China came seeds and cuttings collected by Fortune whom the Horticultural Society had dispatched in 1842 to forage secretly in the territories opened by the Opium War.[63] Hooker formed ties with the African Civilization Society which supported the 1841 Niger Expedition, and thus the flora of West Africa, with the support of Prince Albert, came into the hands of the Hookers and George Bentham.[64] Robert Schomburgk returned from his expedition to British Guiana, having marked the boundaries of the British colony against Brazil and Colombia, with a particularly important collection of rare tropical plants, including the *Victoria regia*.[65] From New Zealand, where Britain struggled both to war with the Maori and to convert them to Christianity, Sir William Symonds, Surveyor of the Navy, and the Rev. Mr. Colenso of the Church Missionary Society shipped to Hooker 'many cases of the rarer vegetable productions'.[66] From Mexico and Peru, where entrepreneurs were busily fulfilling Canning's prophecy that Spanish America once free would be English, Mr. Staines of San Luis Potosí and John Taylor of the Real del Monte Company supplied cactuses and flowering plants.[67] Shipments of plants from both the Americas travelled courtesy of the Royal Mail West Indian Steam Packets, while the Oriental Steam Navigation Company 'handsomely refused payment for packages going by way of Alexandria ... to and from India'.[68] By 1850, Hooker felt able to write to the Office of Works that in future there would be no need to send out special collectors, since the 'great number of intelligent and scientific men now resident abroad' meant it was possible simply to await, or to solicit, gifts.[69]

English gardeners spent vast sums in efforts to collect and cultivate hardy Ericaceae from the Cape and Australasia, cactuses, orchids, and water lilies from the tropics, and rhododendrons and camellias from India and China. The development of Kew in the 1840s merely represented a heroic public extension of these amateur passions. It was a Chatsworth for the nation, a spectacle of universal nature made British. The priorities set for Kew by the Earl of Lincoln, the Earl of Aberdeen, the Earl of Carlisle, and Lord John Russell, and indeed the royal family, reflected these enthusiasms.

Lord Lincoln, whom Peel appointed as First Commissioner of Woods and Forests in 1841, granted an extra 4 acres to Kew from the still separate Royal Pleasure Grounds, and opened the boundaries between the two.[70] A year later 17 more acres came with the promise that, on Aiton's final retirement, at least 40 acres of the adjoining grounds would be added. Hooker wrote Dawson Turner in 1843, Kew 'will be the finest thing of its kind in Europe'.[71] In 1846 Lord John Russell, an even longer standing patron, became Prime Minister, and the next year the Commissioners of Woods and Forests increased Hooker's salary to £800 per annum, and agreed to bear the substantial cost of purchasing botanical books for Hooker and the garden.[72] Finally the entire Royal Pleasure Grounds were ceded, along with the former royal kitchen gardens, the 'preserve for feathered game' of the King of Hanover and the fishing ground of the Duchess of Cambridge. By 1850 Sir William Hooker had access to several hundred acres of land, running for two miles from Kew Green to the banks of the Thames at Richmond.[73]

Politicians could not have conceded these grounds to Kew without the approval of the royal family. Hooker had however courted Victoria and Albert with skill. In 1841, he ordered that the letter 'A' be emblazoned on the Orangery to honour Augusta, the mother of George III who had started the formal 'Physic Garden' in 1759, and who was, like Albert, of the House of Saxe-Gotha. By October 1842, Victoria had conveyed her sanction for the expansion of the garden, as Hooker wrote happily:

> as far as Her Majesty is concerned I believe I can have every reasonable thing my own way. Prince Albert sent me a rare Japan plant that the King of the French had just sent to Windsor.[74]

Albert begged Hooker to send him any accounts he might receive from his son, Joseph, who was then travelling as the botanist to Ross's Antarctic expedition. Royal favour was to prove important in Hooker's plans for Kew. Hooker wrote delightedly to his father-in-law:

> [Victoria and Albert] have been through the whole ground and every hot-house and greenhouse and through the Old Palace. . . . They were delighted with the model of the New Stove, which I had brought into the Garden for them, so much so that they asked if so handsome a structure could be seen from the palace. This was the very thing I had wished for: for my orders had been to find a site where it could not be seen. . . . [Now] the House [can be] brought from under the trees.[75]

The 'New Stove' in question was the magnificent Great Palm House, the centrepiece of Hooker's remaking of Kew.

The construction of vast conservatories for tropical plants was then at the pinnacle of horticultural fashion, with the Duke of Northumberland spending some £40,000 to construct his stove on the far side of the Thames from Kew. Loudon in 1840 had indeed urged the Crown to build for the 'fine old palms of Kew', just as the Duke of Devonshire was doing for his own.[76] Lord Lincoln, eldest son of the Duke of Newcastle, turned directly to such precedents, and recruited the most fashionable and ambitious architects and landscape gardeners.[77] Decimus Burton, who had designed for the Great Stove at Chatsworth and the Royal Botanical Society of London in Regent's Park, was hired by the government for Kew, as was William Nesfield of Eton.[78] From the beginning, the Commissioners agreed with Hooker that the Palm House (see Plate 13) should be a remarkable building: an uninterrupted area of over 300 feet in length, with a suspended gallery carrying visitors above the palms, all supported by a novel system of arching iron beams, with an underground railway to carry coal to the furnaces, from which the smoke was channelled discreetly to a Venetian campanile a hundred yards away. But the

Palm House was not the only use at Kew of the kind of grand edifice which marked the most sumptuous private gardens of the age. In the same way, Burton was asked in 1845 to design swaggering gates to separate the gardens, like an aristocratic park, from Kew's common (see Plate 14), and to renovate the Pagoda, its most prominent folly, with ornament copied from the contemporary exhibition of the 'Panorama of Nanking' in Leicester Square.[79] Nesfield, with a taste for geometry and prospect which would have pleased Le Nôtre, then turned the Palm House into the climax of the garden, faced with a formal parterre, the Stove joined two magnificent avenues: Pagoda Vista, which led to the crimson Chinese temple, and Syon Vista which led to the Thames, on the other bank of which was Syon House of the Duke of Northumberland.

But the style of the *ancien régime* garden was projected onto more than the topography of Kew. Hooker also turned the gardens to the diplomatic and heraldic uses of an earlier age. A selection of plants left Kew, through Lord Aberdeen, for the garden of Monsieur Guizot at Lisière in Normandy, so perfuming Britain's relations with France.[80] Osborne House, Prince Albert's private retreat on the Isle of Wight, received an even larger collection. Similarly the *Victoria regia*—the giant water lily, which Schomburgk collected in Guiana—was named after the Queen, much as Banks in the 1770s had honoured Charlotte with *Strelizia regina*.[81] Hooker was bitter when Paxton, at Chatsworth, succeeded in the race to bring the lily into flower.[82] Sir William, however, made that into his own *coup*, producing in 1851 a beautiful and costly book: *Victoria Regia, Or an Illustration of the Royal Water Lily.* During his first decade, the royal family loomed large in Hooker's pleasure, and their enthusiasm, as he wrote in 1848, was one of the best signs of his success. Hooker exulted:

> the Queen has been here 3 times in less than six weeks & I was required by her to ask if the palace could not be put into repair for her & the children & the Duchess of Gloucester commanded my attendance twice last week (I have to dine with her today) & the Queen Dowager came with a large suite and remained 3 hours in the Gardens & Museum on Friday. The Estimates are all granted to the full & I have full permission [. . .] to carry a stream of water through the Pleasure Grounds from Richmond into the Botanic Garden. The Palm House now it is filled is the admiration of everybody and the view of the palms from the gallery is most striking. The Queen was enchanted with it.[83]

In 1850, in the same year he proposed to parliament that £27,000 be given to Nesfield for the reformation of St. James's Park, Lord Seymour allowed Hooker to build a special 'Victoria House' where the lily and its flower would be sustained by clouds of Amazonian steam (see illustration 18).[84]

This grandeur came at a price. More than £35,000 went on the Palm House, and £2,000 for the Victoria House.[85] How Hooker justified this

18. Victoria regia *in flower in the Water Lily House (1850).* Royal Botanic Gardens, Kew.

expenditure deserves attention. His 'Report on the Royal Botanic Gardens, and the Proposed New Palm House at Kew' for 1844 drew heavily on Lindley's 1838 report. Hooker sought to argue for what a national botanic garden should be, and to show what his prudent management—replacing plumbing and rebuilding houses—had already achieved.[86] He presented the Palm House, 'this noble structure which will be second to none in Europe', as planned in accordance with 'the strictest economy'. Where Peel in his 1844 minute had asked that private philanthropy be solicited to supplement public expenditure, Hooker showed that he had persuaded the Earl of Derby, the Duke of Northumberland, and the Hudson Bay Company, to supply most of the costs of the expeditions of William Purdie to New Granada and the Caribbean, and of Joseph Burke to North-West America and California.[87] Hooker pointed, in his reports, to the rapid increase in the numbers of visitors to the garden, from 9,174 in 1841, to 46,573 in 1846, to 179,627 in 1850, when he noted that, 'perhaps the benefit the public has derived from these gardens is best shown in the gradual increase of visitors since they were opened to the public'.[88]

Sir William, like Lindley in his report, was not above appealing to what we might call a Whig theory of landscape. He presented his garden as an agent of improvement, and perhaps of political cohesion:

> the minds of the middling and lower ranks are enlarged and enlightened by a display of all that is most beautiful and lovely in vegetable creation; and thus a gradual improvement must ensue in the habits and morals of the people.[89]

We may take this enthusiasm for plebeian visitors with a grain of salt. Hooker confided to his father-in-law in 1845 how much he disliked the throng which the gardens now attracted, although 'it is better for them than going to the public house'.[90] This private view is invisible, however, in Hooker's publications; he boasted instead that one of his first acts had been to open Kew every weekday, from the hours of 1 to 6 p.m, in order to widen the scope for the 'instruction and gratification' of the public.[91] The turnstyle was now the most important gauge of his success. Hooker noted enthusiastically how rapidly numbers increased, from 329,000 in 1851, prominent among them visitors to the Great Exhibition, rising gradually to about 400,000 per annum at the end of that decade.[92]

From 1851 to 1859, William worked under five different Ministries and four First Commissioners of Works. Lord Seymour, whom Russell appointed, was himself an amateur scientist, and was an indulgent First Commissioner.[93] From February to December 1852, during Derby's first cabinet, and from February 1858 to June 1859, under Derby's second, Hooker was then governed by Lord John Manners. Manners—like Lincoln and Seymour, son of a Duke—had however stuck with Derby's Tory rump. He believed his class had a responsibility to join with the 'lower orders' against the urban mammon of manufacturers and Radicals. Had Manners had Hooker in his keep in 1848, he would probably have told the botanist to let the Chartist 'mob' into the garden: his solution to the problems of industrial Britain was later described as 'a curious mixture of public baths, public open spaces, and Church festivals'.[94] The two other First Commissioners—Sir William Molesworth and Sir Benjamin Hall—appointed by Aberdeen and Palmerston respectively, were Radicals of a different cast. As Radicals they were determined that Hooker should serve the instruction and pleasure of the public. Hall, in particular, was a municipal reformer and former President of the Board of Health, and took a civic and sanitary view of gardens.

Seymour in 1852 had gently urged Hooker to accommodate the public earlier in the day, suggesting that at least part of the museum should be accessible before 1 p.m.[95] Sir William Molesworth demanded that Hooker do far more. Hooker complained to Bentham in 1853:

> Molesworth is a queer beast & takes so little interest in the gardens that he has never once paid us a visit since he has been in office! ... But he likes notoriety and in short thinks the gardens & grounds should be made avail-

able to all classes of Her Majesty's subjects & to scientific purposes likewise. . . . He has resolved upon having lectures here next summer.[96]

Molesworth had once been a leading Philosophical Radical, a founder of the *London Review* in 1835 and ally of Joseph Hume in the 1840s, but had broken with Cobden in order to snatch at Aberdeen's offer of a seat in the cabinet. He wanted Hooker to make concrete his old claim that the gardens contributed to the education and improvement of the public and persuaded him to extend the hours of the garden.[97]

There was a new factor at work, however. The Public Health Act of 1848 created a temporary General Board of Health under the direction of the Board of Woods and Forests, which after 1851 passed, like Kew, to the new Board of Works. The arrival of cholera in 1854, for the second time in five years, meant that Sir William Molesworth was more concerned with public health than gardens. His principal lieutenant was Sir Benjamin Hall, who became first President of the new Board of Health in 1854. Hall was converted by the recent epidemic to a Chadwickian belief in the need for a central municipal initiative. In March 1855, he proposed his bill 'for the better local management of the metropolis' which led to the foundation of the Metropolitan Board of Works. 'I was determined', he declared to the Commons, 'on the merciful abatement of the epidemic that ravaged the Metropolis, to turn my attention to the state of this vast city.'[98] Hall so distinguished himself with his proposals that when in July 1855 Molesworth succeeded Russell as Secretary of State for the Colonies, a plum passed to the old Radical by Palmerston in reward for his *volte face* in supporting the Crimean War, Hall was made the new First Commissioner of Works.

Sir Benjamin Hall looked at Kew principally as a tool for the reform of London. He required Hooker to supply geraniums, ornamental trees, and half-hardy shrubs for Kensington and St. James Park, and by the end of 1856, 5,000 seedlings had gone from Kew to the new suburban park of Battersea.[99] In October 1856, he attacked Hooker for failing to decorate the lawns and borders of the paths with abundant 'carpet-beds' of flowers.[100] Hooker regarded this kind of ornamental display as vulgar and, while suitable for an urban park, an inappropriate use of resources for the botanic garden.[101] But he gritted his teeth, and noted in his report for 1856 that 'our flower beds have been greatly increased', while boasting in that for 1857 about his new shrubberies and 'Flower Banks'.[102] He wrote Hall in 1856:

> I have a double interest in maintaining the garden gay and ornamental; I admire the effect, and I believe that our thus gratifying the public is the surest way of making the estimates palatable.[103]

Hooker did succeed in securing approval for a new Temperate House, to accommodate the plants of Australia and New Zealand, the Cape and South America, in the manner that the 'noble Palm House' now protected tropical plants.[104]

Hooker took advantage of the ornamental priorities of his political masters in other ways. Between 1848 and 1851, Joseph Hooker travelled on a survey mission which took him into Sikkim as far as the snows of the Himalayas.[105] It is worth noting that the Treasury and the Admiralty only met half the cost of this expedition, more than £1,000 more had come from Sir William.[106] But after Joseph's disappointment over the Edinburgh chair, Sir William thought this a worthwhile investment. As it turned out, Joseph discovered real horticultural treasures in the foothills of the Himalayas, virtually doubling the number of known rhododendron varieties (see illustration 19). Linnaeus had known only nine species, in 1848 there were perhaps thirty-three in circulation, but Joseph Hooker dispatched from India what today are considered to be twenty-eight entirely new species of rhododendron.

While Joseph was still in Asia, Sir William Hooker presented his son's successes to the nation in three sumptuously illustrated instalments of *The Rhododendrons of Sikkim Himalaya*, for which the Dukes of Devonshire and Northumberland and wealthy horticultural enthusiasts throughout Britain subscribed.[107] These were masterpieces of the art of clientage, elegantly

19. Cartoon allegory of Sir Joseph Hooker being presented with flowers by Himalayan spirits.
Royal Botanic Gardens, Kew.

promoting both father and son, which deserve to stand beside William's earlier effort during his campaign to become director of a reformed Kew—his *Letter to Dawson Turner on the Occasion of the Death of the Duke of Bedford.* Not only was the series dedicated to the member of the royal family who was the immediate neighbour of Kew—'H.R.H. Princess Mary of Cambridge, whose taste for the pleasures of a garden, The First and Purest Pleasures of our race, has made her feel peculiar interest in the Great National Establishment at Kew'—but individual species received the names of Lord Auckland, Lady Dalhousie, and the East India Company Resident at the Court of Nepal, among others. Collected together, the book served as a calling card for the Hookers, which Sir William in 1851 offered to the Prime Minister, urging him that he might look at 'the work entitled "Rhododendrons of the Himalaya Mountains" which I have the honour to send to Lady John'.[108] The new plants themselves were all collected together and planted by 1853 in a grotto near the Thames, the Rhododendron Dell, which remains today, honouring each spring the memory of Joseph Hooker's voyage (see illustration 20). In official reports and publications, Sir William Hooker would refer with regularity to 'the number of new and extraordinarily beautiful Rhododendrons' collected by Dr. Hooker while on a government mission to India.[109]

These rhododendrons, and many other novelties harvested from the fringes of British power, went from Kew to private English gardeners. Hooker in 1850 argued that this was another measure of his public service:

> There is not a respectable nurseryman in the Kingdom who has not profited from the riches of Kew. . . . [The collection] cannot fail to be of great service to nurserymen, to arboriculturalists, and to all gentlemen and landed proprietors interested in planting the best kind of trees and shrubs.[110]

Indeed, despite Hooker's occasional appeals to Lindley's vision of Kew diffusing 'economical, useful, medicinal, and agricultural plants' to the colonies, Kew in the 1840s was almost exclusively an entrepôt, through which exotics were naturalized.[111] Between 1847 and 1849, out of 22,635 plants distributed, 17,166 plants went to nurserymen and private gardeners at home, a further 2,280 to botanic gardens in Britain and Europe, while only slightly more than 10% went out to India or the colonies.[112]

This association of Kew with public recreation and private ornamental gardening had brought clear benefits. But these came at a price. If Kew was, as Hooker wrote in his report for 1856, primarily 'a place for healthful recreation and instruction', and only secondarily, a centre for 'the science of Botany', his requests for funding for scientific research had to take lower priority than his projects for new lakes or plant houses.[113] For men like Molesworth, Hall, and even Manners, the herbaria, libraries, and scientific posts, which Hooker came to demand, ranked below the needs of the parks of London. At a time when they quibbled over estimates with Hooker, and when the vote for Kew was less than £10,000 per year, some £300,000 was spent in the mid-1850s on

20. Victorians strolling through the Rhododendron Dell, where Sir William Hooker planted the many new species with which his son had returned from the Himalays.
Royal Botanic Gardens, Kew.

acquiring the land for Battersea Park alone.[114] The Hookers would have to restrain their ambitions for Kew if it was merely a public garden.

The Uses of Economic Botany: Industry and Empire, Collections and Careers

By the late 1840s, however, Hooker began to give Kew a use beyond beauty. He knew that an appeal for the support for scientific research for its own sake would fail. He reached instead for an economic purpose for the gardens. Lindley in his 1838 report had projected that Kew might be the conductor of an imperial orchestra of botanic gardens. But these gardens remained wholly autonomous. Hooker did nominate the men appointed as superintendents for the colonial botanic gardens in Ceylon, Trinidad, and New South Wales in the 1840s.[115] But his influence depended on the Colonial Secretary seeking his opinion. He decided to strengthen his position at home, and created at

Kew an archive of plant raw materials for the use of the nation's merchants and manufacturers.

One morning in 1846 he arranged on trestles and planks, before the Commissioners of Woods and Forests, his own collection of the 'economic products of the vegetable kingdom'. He proceeded to lecture them on how such a collection might, besides interesting and instructing the public, 'prove of great service to the scientific botanist, the physician, the merchant, the manufacturer, the chemist and druggist, the dyer, and to artisans of every description'.[116] The Commissioners were persuaded, and by 1847 Decimus Burton had converted a former royal fruit store into Hooker's first Museum.[117] In the same year, Hooker instructed British naval officers in the Admiralty's *Manual*, that they should collect and send to the Museum of Economic Botany at Kew:

> Living plants, pressed or dried botanical specimens, fruits, seeds, also of vegetable products. By that term we mean such objects of medicinal substances (barks, roots, gums, resins . . .), dye stuffs, useful fibres, interesting woods, oil seeds, with the oil prepared from them, farinaceous substances, – in *fine*, whatever of vegetable origin deserves attention on account of its utility to man. . . .[118]

They were also to record the techniques through which local people cultivated and used these plants. His Museum of Economic Botany was intended, from the outset, to recruit materials and skills discovered by communities around the world for the use of Britain's industrial civilization. By the 1850s, the Museum was arranged according both to 'natural affinities' and 'qualities and uses', with one apartment devoted to textile fabrics and substances, one case for dye-stuffs, others for gutta-percha, caoutchouc, and products of the coconut, and in the next year separate displays presented the fibres and new materials used in paper manufacture, and 'numerous samples of vegetable oils, waxes, and tallow, all now so eagerly sought by the mercantile world'.[119]

Hooker clearly sought to respond to the dramatic changes taking place around him in the British economy. During the 1840s, coal production increased by 50%, pig iron production doubled, as did the tonnage of steamships carrying long-distance trade.[120] The number of patents sealed in Britain, which had averaged about 270 per year during the 1830s, jumped to about 470 per year in the 1840s, climbing towards 2,000 patents annually by the 1850s.[121] Hooker may well have been encouraged in his idea of a Museum by Prince Albert, who from his election as President of the Society of Arts in 1843 had urged its members to commit themselves to the application of science and art to industrial purposes. In May 1845, in the wake of the successes on the continent of the French Exposition and the German Zollverein Exhibition of 1844, the Society proposed that a periodical 'Exhibition of Works of Industry' take place. The first of the British national expositions was held in 1847, and from that experiment came the idea of 'a Great

Exhibition ... not merely national in its scope and benefits, but comprehensive of the whole world', which came to fruition at the Crystal Palace in 1851.[122]

We may be tempted to underestimate the importance of Hooker's Museum. This is because we continue to have a false idea of the 'Industrial Revolution', and to recognize its meaning only in coal, pig iron, factories, and in the remade landscapes and demography of northern England and France, southern Belgium, the eastern United States, and western Germany. Our poor understanding of the wealth and poverty of nations depends in large part on the arbitrary way in which national histories, or that of 'Europe', have been separated from that of the world as a whole. But the rise of cities and the 'Industrial Revolution' in the West was inseparably connected to plantation farming, ranching, and forestry economies in every other human community. Machines did not merely run on coal, they consumed cotton, wool, dyes, and vegetable oils, and the strength of the peripheral populations which provided these. Wheat, beef, tea, and sugar allowed operatives to meet the brutal pace of work. Shiploads of timber and rubber went to absorb shocks, and indeed electricity, which steel would not have contained. Without plant fibres twined into rope, woven into sacking, and crushed into paper, no administration or commerce could take place, and a whole civilization which depended on commodities being moved and recorded would have collapsed. Only within the lifetime of our parents did the synthetic magic of organic chemists limit industry's utter dependence on plants and on agricultural labour. There were periodic panics about the supply of all these commodities, and projected shortages of fibres or rubber haunted rich men in Victorian cities, much as the spectre of oil crises would worry their grandchildren.[123]

We need to connect the rapid increase in the production of British coal and iron in the 1840s, which we discussed above, to other statistics, such as the importation of gutta-percha from Singapore which went from 230 pounds in 1844, to 1.2 million pounds by 1847, and almost 2 million, by the time Hooker's Museum was open to the public.[124] Strong, light, resistant to acids and electricity, gutta-percha was a miracle material, which lined the floors and printing rollers of textile mills; channelled nitric acid for gold refiners, alkalis for soap makers, and sound in the 'speaking tubes' of coal mines in Monmouthshire. Sir William Hooker had himself first described and illustrated *Isonandra gutta* in 1847.[125] In Prussia, Werner von Siemens, an artillery officer, perfected its use as an insulator for telegraph cables.[126] Several hundred miles of gutta-percha-covered wire were laid along the tracks of the London and North Western and other railways, and underneath the Irish Sea from Holyhead to Howth. Gutta tapping throughout the Malay Peninsula was directly linked to delving for anthracite in Wales, the laying of sleepers at Euston and King's Cross, and the communication networks which made modern capitalist civilization possible. Contemporaries saw the connection, writing in 1852: 'the indigenous population gave themselves up to the search [for gutta] with an unanimity and zeal only to be equalled by that which the railway world animated England about the same time'.[127]

The liaison between economic botany and industrial development may also be seen in India in mid century. The botanic garden at Sahranpur supplied 'large quantities of timber seeds' in order to allow the officers extending the Grand Trunk Road to Peshawar to ensure the future of construction and railway-building.[128] In Burma, Dietrich Brandes, a forester, urged, similarly, the protection of British India's sources of wood and water through the enclosure of teak plantations.[129] The author of the *Flora Andhrica* (1859) urged the importance of the names of plants to 'the officers of the Department of Public Works and the Railway'.[130] Hugh Cleghorn, the Superintendent of the Madras Botanic Garden, indeed argued in 1860 that 'until the system of railways and canals is completed we will not derive the full benefit of the gardens': the transit of plants through the subcontinent depended on its new communication network. As he predicted, the epic engineering works of the Raj—the Holkhar State, Bhopal Ghat, Nagpur and Chattesghur railways; Warrorah Colliery; Narbudda, Ravi, and Empress bridges—were accompanied by the spread of new trees, flowers, and weeds.

In other colonies, introduced plants had made British settlers rich, and their administrations solvent. Ceylon, as we discussed in an earlier chapter, was a typical success story: by 1850, its coffee exports were already worth well over £500,000 annually, by 1860 they were almost three times as valuable, and by the end of that decade, 50% more again.[131] Ceylon's revenues amply exceeded its expenditure: the Colonial Office's ideal situation. Cocoa showered similar prosperity on Trinidad.[132] In the sugar economies of the rest of the Caribbean, many colonists looked to science, and more directly to Liebig's fertilizers, to save them from their depression.[133] Hooker's display would thus have won the attention of anyone with an interest in the colonies.

There was, in short, a concern with economic botany across the British Empire. Some historians of Kew have tended to exaggerate Hooker's place in this movement.[134] Hooker, it is true, believed in the importance of his Museum. His displays, he hoped, would 'suggest new channels for our industry'.[135] British investors might discover foreign plants which 'might be grown in our own colonies possessing a similar climate'.[136] Hooker boasted that in 1854, not a day passed without applicants coming to the Museum of Practical or Economic Botany 'for information about the useful woods, oils, fibres, gums, resins, drugs, and dye-stuffs'. The Museum, Hooker argued in 1855, was 'essential to a great commercial country', and he noted that Napoleon III had established an equivalent on Kew's model. But, as in the era of Banks, private initiative was vastly more important than official action. Britain's merchants, manufacturers, and colonists enjoyed numbers, resources, and urgency of purpose, well beyond that of its botanists. The commodity brokers in Mincing Lane, and administrators and planters abroad, it is true, did write frequently to Hooker. But they sought his personal expertise, much as they consulted Lindley at University College and

Royle at the India Office on other botanical questions, or Murchison on geology. It would be more accurate to see Hooker as having trimmed his sail to catch a prevailing wind, rather than as a *supremo*, organizing the economic botany of the empire. That kind of influence would only be enjoyed by later directors of Kew.

We need also to reinsert Hooker's Museum into its cultural context. The early Victorians saw economic botany as more than the dry subject it appears to be today. It was encompassed instead within the religious assumptions of 'natural theology': the idea that plants, animals, and everything in nature, had been placed there by God for the use or instruction of human beings. J. H. Balfour's *Phytotheology* (1851) sought to illustrate the works of God in the structure and functions of plants, while T.W. Archer began his *Popular Economic Botany* (1853) with the expulsion of Adam from Eden and noted that the Creator had left earth 'clothed with every necessary for men's wants', while *Caoutchouc and Gutta Percha* (1852), published by the Society for the Propagation of the Gospel, derived God's special fondness for mankind from the remarkable utility of rubber. A Museum of Economic Botany, as it presented the uses of the world's plants, thus offered a portrait of Providence. In 1847, Hooker could appeal to many of the eschatological assumptions which animated the Renaissance origins of all botanic gardens. The logic which linked theology and the Victorian enthusiasm for free trade, elucidated with such power by Boyd Hilton, also joined science and colonial expansion. Knowing the world, and including it in the circuit of commerce, was a Christian responsibility. Hooker's Museum presented a spectacle equivalent to that offered by the stoves and beds of Kew. It was a theatre in which visitors might discover their nation's place and purpose, at the centre of the world. The Great Exhibition of 1851 was only a grander expression of the same ambitions.

Yet while Kew represented Britain's position at the crossroads of Providence, it presented also a portrait of its own role. The Museum clearly served Hooker's interest more directly than the empire's colonists and manufacturers. As Hooker put it frankly, his exhibition of the uses of plants 'could not fail to answer the "*cui bono?*" so often propounded'.[137] This tableau showed the utility of Kew and its director to the nation that now stood as arbiter of universal nature. Sir William also knew that his 'Museum of Practical and Economic Botany' might serve many professional ends: his inspiration probably came from Henry de la Beche and his 'Museum of Practical and Economic Geology'. De la Beche had built a professional satrapy on top of his mountain of rock samples: the Treasury not only gave him £3,150 to disburse to local directors of his Geological Survey of the United Kingdom, but provided £2,227 from which he hired assistants and specialist advisers for the Museums in London and Dublin.[138] The geologist had shown how a 'useful' collection could lay claim to public support, and create salaried employment for naturalists. In late 1845, Sir William Hooker had personal reasons to find this precedent attractive.

In the spring of that year, Joseph Hooker, his Admiralty salary finished, had taken up a small position at Edinburgh, filling in for Graham, the Professor of Botany. When Graham died, Joseph advanced himself as a candidate. Sir William Hooker worked with energy, soliciting a vast array of testimonials from scientific friends and colleagues—among whom numbered Humboldt, Lyell, and Darwin—while lobbying Sir Robert Peel.[139] But while Joseph Hooker could count on the support of the Crown, it was quickly apparent that the Edinburgh Town Council, which shared the prerogative of electing the Professor of Botany, had a local candidate, John Hutton Balfour, in mind. Darwin wrote to Sir William in anger, 'What a disgrace it is to our Institutions, that a Professor should be appointed by a set of men, who have never heard of Humboldt and Brown'.[140] In early October Peel wrote Hooker commending 'the very valuable and interesting work for which science is indebted to your son's labours' but also warning that the Town Council was against him.[141] Peel advised Hooker on 9 October that the aldermen had decided by a majority of eleven in favour of Dr. Balfour.[142] It was then, in November 1845, that Sir William Hooker gave 108 of his best botanical drawings to Kew, frankly admitting to his father-in-law:

> My object is to induce Lord Lincoln to form a Museum in which such things may be deposited & then I think a Herbarium will be required and once begun it will not be on a trifling scale ... [Bentham] appointed Joseph one of his Executors and had left his fine Herbarium to the Royal Gardens ... if there would be the necessary accommodation for it. I beg you to consider this as confidential. Unless something of the kind is done here I can see no chance of any opening for Joseph nor indeed, then, any *lucrative* appointment.[143]

The Museum was thus originally intended, as Hooker planned it, to make necessary the appointment of Joseph: 'I had hoped in a short time to form such a collection as to have afforded an opening for an assistant.'[144] Sir William knew that if the government made Joseph his assistant, it might be persuaded later to make him his successor.

Early in 1846, de la Beche appointed Joseph Hooker as Botanist to the Geological Survey of Great Britain.[145] But Sir William recognized that this could not be a permanent appointment, and wanted instead to make the way for him at Kew. Sir William then showed his hand: he took the blunt step of offering his own herbarium and library, the finest then in private hands, to the Crown, in exchange for a commitment that his son would be appointed his assistant and successor. In the autumn of 1846 he approached the Commissioners of Woods and Forests. Lord Morpeth, on receiving Hooker's letter, 'stepped back and smiled and asked a few questions about Joseph', but made no commitments.[146] Sir Joseph Banks, by such a gift, had created a permanent position for Robert Brown at the British Museum a generation before, but such deals were less possible in 1846. While awaiting the Crown's response, Hooker invited the Commissioners to the lecture which marked the beginning of the Museum.

Hooker saw forming an Economic Museum as the preliminary to having the government build and pay for a public Herbarium at Kew. It is worth noting that in 1847, a commission met to consider the future of the British Museum, which in practice, after the death of Banks, had kept the nation's herbarium collection. Robert Brown and his department had received all specimens collected on government missions. While the living plants from Ross's expedition, for example, went to Kew, all the other botanical materials from the *Erebus* and the *Terror* had gone directly to the British Museum.[147] Hooker knew that as the Museum of Economic Botany prospered, Kew would attract herbarium material which would previously have gone to Bloomsbury.

The first clear sign of that rivalry between Kew and the British Museum, which grew through the century, came in 1847. In his testimony to the Royal Commission enquiring into the British Museum, Brown described Kew as 'too distant for the convenience of botanists'.[148] However, ironically as it would later prove, on that occasion the zoologist Richard Owen proposed that with respect to botany, Kew was 'the most appropriate place for a national museum'.[149] When Brown was pressed on the subject by the Commission in March 1849, and asked if he did not think that a botanical collection should be close to a garden, Brown replied pointedly that 'Consulting an Herbarium and visiting a garden are two things so entirely different that they are seldom thought of together.'[150] Hooker thought otherwise, and his Museum of Economic Botany indeed came to act as a magnet drawing public and private collections into his hands. As Hooker happily wrote his father-in-law in 1846, 'It is curious how rapidly vegetable productions are coming into the garden now it is known we are to have a Museum.'[151] As these gifts mounted up, the government would be forced to build and care for them. Sir William urged Dawson Turner to will his herbarium not to himself but to the Royal Botanic Gardens, for this 'would better tell of the esteem in which you hold the Garden & Museum as a great public scientific establishment & in setting a powerful example to others'.[152] Such gifts, added one to another, would force the government to provide for Kew as a scientific establishment, and to make it into the centre of British botany.

In 1850, George Bentham forced the government to act. He offered his great herbarium to the Crown on the condition that suitable conditions be created for its permanent maintenance at Kew. To put this offer into context, one should however note that when he first made it, Bentham was not even fifty years of age: if his uncle Jeremy's longevity was any guide, the nation had about forty years to wait before the matter should have needed any concrete attention. Hooker wrote him, 'Your line in the Herbarium affair has done good & your continued line of conduct will do much greater good, depend on it.'[153] By 1851 Seymour had agreed to build a fine herbarium at Kew: two floors, an internal gallery, with side-lights below and a sky-light above.[154] Molesworth, who replaced Seymour as First Commissioner of Works, saw Kew principally as a recreational paradise, and hesitated about the costs. Despite the terms of the Queen's Speech of 1853—with its championing of the cause of science—the Treasury had not, by any means, opened the coffers of the state to Athena: behind Peelite rhetoric stood Gladstone. The Chancellor of the Exchequer held Economy as 'the first and great article ... in my financial creed'.[155] T.W. Philipps, senior civil servant at the Board of Works, wrote Hooker confidentially that 'I really doubt whether the Treasury, under present circumstances, will allow us money for such objects'.[156] To the anger of Philipps, Hooker passed on his letter to Bentham who proceeded to announce that he would rescind his offer, keeping his own library, while assigning part of his herbarium to the University of Cambridge and giving the rest to Hooker.[157] By March 1854, Philipps and the government formally accepted Bentham's terms, and began to build facilities for research at Kew.[158]

The completion of the herbarium after 1855 meant a genuine change in Hooker's position. Before any scientific work he did was essentially a supplement to the ornamental and economic aspects of his job, now he had the means to form Kew into a centre for botanical research. Here lay the beginning of a divergence of interests between the directors of Kew and their political masters, who in the end were usually concerned with managing roads, bridges, sewers, and parks, not arcane research. In 1857 Hooker began to show the value of his garden by listing the number of scientists who have 'taken up their abode at Kew, for weeks together', including Weddell working on Urticaceae, Howard on the cinchonas, Lindley on orchids, Henslow for the diagrams required by the President of the Board of Trade for the use of national schools, and Seeman on the South Pacific flora.[159] In his omnibus report of 1859, Hooker boasted that Kew had 'the most extensive and practically useful Herbarium and Library ever formed', and noted the important botanical work 'more or less completely carried out by means of the ready access granted to these collections' during the preceding six years including Joseph Hooker's floras of New Zealand and Tasmania, Weddell of Paris's work on Urticaceae, Sonder of Hamburg's study of the Cape flora, Schott of Schönbrunn's review of the Aroideae, Asa Gray's botany of the exploring expeditions of the United States, and Grisebach of Göttingen's *Flora of the British West Indies.*[160] In his estimates for 1861, Sir William Hooker claimed that there was scarcely a botanical work of any repute published 'on the continent of Europe, in America, or in England, that is not largely indebted to Kew for much of its value'.[161] Hooker, in effect, was offering an entirely new criterion for the public value of Kew, one which did not depend either on the physical terrain of the gardens or an appreciative public. In little more than a decade it would be clear that not all First Commissioners of Works would allow the Hookers to pay their dues in this new coin.

The new herbarium and library inevitably increased the scope for rivalry between the British Museum and Kew. The botanical department of the British Museum was clearly in decline in this period: the truth was that Brown was now over seventy years of age, and the 'place' created for him by

Banks at the Museum was now, quite likely, less a privilege than a burden. Many contemporary botanists complained that the mills of British Museum botany ground fine but exceedingly slow. Lord Seymour, according to Hooker, considered Brown 'as a useless drone in the British Museum'.[162] Joseph Hooker later described to Thiselton-Dyer the state of the apartments in Soho Square from which the Linnean Society was run: 'the largest of which was occupied by Brown's huge collections; the great proportion of which consisted of Bundles that had never been opened and were never dusted'.[163] John Ball testified twenty years later to the Devonshire Commission that he had seen parcels of botanical materials in the British Museum which had been unopened since the time of Sir Joseph Banks, asserting that 'he lacked that combination of qualities which makes a good administrator of a national collection'.[164] As de Candolle noted in his *Mémoires et Souvenirs*, Brown was a shy and reclusive man, or as Ball put it in 1872, 'fully engaged in his own studies, he had no desire to encourage the visits of strangers'.[165] The British Museum was for all these reasons not popular among contemporary botanists, and from the Hookers' perspective, its collections should go to Kew.

The death of Brown on 10 June 1858, brought the matter into open discussion. Panizzi, who undoubtedly wished to annex 4,000 square feet for his books, wrote the Lords Commissioners of the Treasury on 14 June, to ask 'whether it may be expedient or otherwise to remove the botanical collection from the Museum'.[166] A subcommittee of British Museum trustees, including Sir Roderick Murchison and Sir Philip Egerton, took evidence two days later. Beforehand Murchison urged Lindley, who had been at war with Brown for almost thirty years, to support the British Museum's right to keep its botanical collections, 'I know you are heartily against the *Delenda est Carthago*'.[167] But the Hookers and Lindley had decided otherwise. Sir William Hooker gave a resounding 'yes' to the question, put by Murchison, as to whether transferring the herbarium of the British Museum to Kew would be of advantage to science, urging that 'it would be expedient for the safety of the collection that it should be removed to a better atmosphere ... [away from] the smoke and dirt of London'. His statement was corroborated by his son, and by Lindley who said that the transfer would be of 'the greatest advantage'. Richard Owen, who had become Superintendent of the Natural History Collections in 1856, agreed, arguing that the nation should support only one museum for any branch of natural history, and that Kew was already *de facto* Britain's national herbarium.[168] Owen in 1858 clearly thought like Panizzi, that less botany would mean more space for his concerns, zoology and palaeontology. In his Presidential Address to the British Association for the Advancement of Science in Leeds in 1858, in which he called for a Natural History Museum to represent the animals and plants of the British Empire, Owen took care to pay due respect to 'the National Botanical Establishment at Kew'.[169] Bentham was more guarded, suggesting only that the Banksian collections should go to Kew. A memorial of 21 June 1858, signed by Huxley,

Lindley, and Darwin endorsed this proposal, suggesting further that the fossil plants should also move to Kew. In October, William Hooker dined with Lord John Russell, and thought he had secured support for the transfer.[170] The move was never, however, approved or implemented: Richard Owen had changed his mind, and had made Murchison of his party.[171]

From the late 1850s on, therefore, Hooker was concerned to strengthen Kew's identity as a scientific institution. Plant houses and lakes could not help much here. Economic botany, on the other hand, could easily be used to justify his need for the best possible scientific resources. In 1859, Hooker made this link explicit, arguing that the Herbarium and Library of a 'National Botanic Garden' were essential to its provision of technical advice to 'Manufacturers, Travellers, and men engaged in the Arts, Sciences, or Horticulture'.[172] It was as a useful garden that Kew, as a centre for research, deserved the support of the nation.

The Synergy of Science and Empire: Surveys and the Colonial Floras

The success of Hooker's Museum of Economic Botany may be gauged from the fact that, to the detriment of the British Museum, all botanical collections made at government expense went after 1854 first to Kew.[173] Merchants, soldiers, diplomats, and missionaries followed this official example, with Baring Brothers and Admiral Sir Michael Seymour sending Japan products for the Museum, 'Rajah' Sir James Brooke collecting fungi and other productions of Borneo, William Munro foraging for botanical curiosities below the guns of Sebastopol, W.D. Christie (Minister Plenipotentiary to the Argentine) sending grass seeds, and the Revs. William Ellis, David Livingstone, and E. Johnson supplying ornamental and economic plants from Madagascar, central Africa, and Indochina respectively.[174] Its collections grew in harmony with the steady expansion of British interests in the middle of the century, which had themselves propelled a new wave of missions of exploration, naval and land surveys.

Joseph Hooker had himself sailed, through the patronage of Lord John Russell and Lord Auckland (First Lord of the Admiralty), with a salary of £400 per annum, to survey Borneo. He was charged with reporting on the capabilities of Labuan, and its suitability for the production of 'cotton, tobacco, sugar, indigo, spices, gutta-percha etc'.[175] After Auckland's death, the younger Hooker concentrated instead on a survey of Sikkim as far as the snows of the Himalayas. Other surveys left for the Fiji Islands, the estuaries of the Old and New Calabar Rivers in the Bight of Guinea, and the interiors of Australia, Canada, and British Guiana. These many missions extended the Admiralty and East India Company initiatives of the era of Banks. The old Cameralist and Physiocratic notion of the scientific inventory of the natural resources of territories for the use of government found new relevance.[176] Britain's new enthusiasms for antislavery and free trade also gave impetus to surveying, as they linked geographical and botanical knowledge to the progress of 'legitimate' trade, on which depended the African future of Christianity and Civilization.

Adam Smith in chapter vii of Book IV of the *Wealth of Nations* (1776) had asserted that 'The mutual communication of knowledge, and all sorts of improvements [follows necessarily from] an extensive commerce, from all countries, to all countries.' The Evangelical churchman Richard Raikes proceeded in 1806 to give theological purchase to Smith's materialist optimism, arguing in 'Considerations on the Alliance Between Christianity and Commerce', that 'our gifts of knowledge and religion ... might, by the aid of our commerce, be spread to every nation of the globe. ... By commerce only shall we supply these previous steps to religious information. The merchant must pave the way for the missionary.'[177]

John Campbell in his *Maritime Discovery and Christian Missions* (1840), and most famously, David Livingstone, similarly contended that before commerce came exploration, and only when 'the last abode of savage man shall be discovered' would the real age of Evangelism begin.[178] Rear-Admiral Richards, Hydrographer of the Admiralty, echoed the prevailing assumptions:

> We have first to gain a general knowledge of the coasts of a country, then as commerce and intercourse increases, more minute surveys are necessary ... the survey of a country prepares the way for commerce and civilization.[179]

Humanitarian and Evangelical enthusiasm for exploration were supplemented by the desire for soldiers on the spot, colonial administrators, and the newly professionalized civil service at home, to be seen to be agents of progress.

The opportunities for salaried employment for botanists began to increase significantly. The Admiralty paid for Kirk to travel with Livingstone in east–central Africa, Milner with Denham on the *Herald* expedition to Fiji and the South Pacific; the Colonial Office funded Borgeau to accompany Palliser to North America, Lyell to collect with the survey of the boundary between the United States and British North America, and Seeman to explore and report on the economic prospects of Fiji; the Admiralty in 1857 shared the costs with Kew for Charles Wilford to collect in Hong Kong, Japan, and North China, as part of the survey of the coast of Manchuria; while the Foreign Office supported Barter to collect as part of Baikie's second Niger Expedition, and the ill-fated Motley who with his family was 'massacred by natives' in Banjermassing, Borneo.[180] Successful missions spawned other excursions to the imperial frontier. In the case of the two surveys of the Fiji Islands, science, in Stafford's phrase, both led and followed the flag. The influence of botanical surveys was clear both in the 1859 resolution of the Assembly of New South Wales on 'accepting the sovereignty of the Fiji Islands', which noted their suitability for 'the growth of the cotton of commerce', and in the dispatch of Seeman to confirm the fact.[181]

If the cotton famine stimulated economic botany in the Pacific, railways and public works in India, the antislavery movement carried waves of botanists to West and East Africa. Just as the Sierra Leone Company had employed Afzelius in the 1790s, on Banks's nomination, the 1841 Niger Expedition had carried Theodore Vogel as 'Chief Botanist', and Baikie's *Pleiad* had carried Charles Barter, a former Kew gardener. The rôle of Kew in the whole programme of imperial surveys can be seen in the selection and supervision of Gustave Mann, whom Hooker nominated in September 1859 as 'one of the most scientific and energetic of the Gardeners in the Royal Gardens of Kew', to replace Barter as botanist to the Niger Expedition.[182] The Foreign Office responded within days advising Hooker that Lord John Russell 'will avail himself of your recommendation, and will appoint Mr. Mann accordingly'.[183] Hooker drew up the terms of Mann's appointment for the Foreign Office, asking him to report in detail on

> ... economical plants, fibres, gums, resins, dye-stuffs, drugs, agricultural plants, raw materials, ... [and] the various articles of household and domestic economy that they furnish, utensils, implements, arms, poisoned arrows, clothing etc. . . .[184]

He also charged Mann to prepare a complete and accurate account of the territory he passed through and of its potential for agriculture. Such advice was needed if Britain was to find a 'legitimate' commodity to replace the slaves which it was no longer willing to buy. Kew was similarly turned to by Evangelicals in Africa, as in 1862, when the Colonial Chaplain and the Wesleyan General Superintendent at Cape Coast Castle on the Gold Coast sought Sir William's help with specimens of cinchona, vanilla, sassafras, and cocoa, which they might 'propagate ... in this settlement, as articles of Horticultural and Agricultural produce and commerce'.[185]

Through botany, philanthropy might be joined to profit. What we might consider today as economic intelligence was processed with system at Kew. When Mann sent thirty-one types of wood to Kew, Hooker immediately invited the Admiralty's Timber Inspector from Woolwich Yard to assess their potential value for naval construction.[186] Lt.-Col. J.A. Grant, similarly, reported on 'the Vegetable Products of Central Africa' to the meeting of the British Association for the Advancement of Science in 1870 from studying collections which Speke had 'made over to the Royal Herbarium, Kew'.[187]

The programme of surveys, however, met the scientific needs of the Hookers even better, perhaps, than it did the objectives of missionaries and merchants. That priority which the Foreign Office granted Kew, in the choice of botanical specimens collected at public expense, over the British Museum, was due to Lord Russell's hope that botany would 'legitimate intercourse and *thereby indirectly affect the slave trade*'.[188] But mere accumulation of specimens was not the Hookers' only reward for their services to cosmopolitan morality. The project of systematic survey ideally served the research needs of a central concern in contemporary botany: phytogeography. Tournefort, while exploring the mountains of Armenia for Louis XIV in 1700, had discovered that in ascending mountains, vegetations characteristic of successively higher latitudes appear.[189] The concern he inaugurated in the territorial distribution of plant families had become central to the intellectual interests of Joeph Hooker. The younger Hooker, who was Darwin's confidante, recognized that this was the fundamental puzzle of botany, and his work from the 1850s established the importance of the subject.[190] The new wave of surveys was needed, from a botanical perspective, to fill in the many large holes in their map. The antislavery agenda thus allowed Hooker to dispatch Gustave Mann, a latter-day Tournefort, to the Cameroon mountains, which, at the equator, represented a crucial region for 'botanical geography'.[191] By the late 1850s, then, there were many convenient overlaps between the 'internal' technical ambitions of scientists, and those of the commercial and religious allies of imperial expansion.

Sir William Hooker began to argue that the benevolent effects of botanical surveys depended on scientists being paid to report and publish on their collections. At a stroke, he transformed a scientific desideratum into an imperial necessity. This was the origins of the 'Colonial Floras' scheme. The Admiralty, from Banks's era, had agreed to pay its best naturalists while they monographed collections made on its survey missions. In the 1850s, Hooker appealed to this principle, and sought to persuade the government to support a scheme for publication at public expense of a series of floras of the British West Indies, Hong Kong, British India, the Cape, West and South Africa, New Zealand, Ceylon, Mauritius, British Guiana, Honduras, and Australia, which would comprehensively survey the plants of particular territories under British rule.

His first successful effort came in 1851 when Sir William appealed to Lord John Russell, then the Prime Minister, that Joseph be given a grant 'to render available to the public good the truly important and valuable collections he has made, at the cost of our government, in Sikkim Himalaya & other parts of the East Indies'. With the collections made by Thomas Thomson in the Western Himalayas, his hoard 'would be the foundation of a perfect *Flora Indica* ... [a] Flora of the British Possessions in India'.[192] Neither the India Board nor Company however was willing to fund more than one volume.[193] By 1857, however, Hooker persuaded Labouchère at the Colonial Office to sponsor the publication of a *Flora of the West Indies*, which would be 'intelligible to any men of ordinary intelligence'.[194] If other floras could be as cheaply produced, Hooker felt the government might be persuaded to support the publication of studies of all the surveys they had commissioned.

The specific impetus for a comprehensive guide to the plants of the empire came from the grandiose initiative of a proconsul on the periphery. Sir William Denison, Governor of New South Wales, in 1859 proposed to the government 'a National work on the Astronomical Features, the terrestrial physics, Botany, Zoology, and Geology of the Colonial Possessions of the British Empire'.[195] Sir Roderick Murchison in an address to the Royal Geographical Society praised Denison's project as tending to 'unite by closer bonds all parts of the empire'.[196] The Colonial Office, and in particular Gladstone's Treasury, was rather more sceptical about the matter. When Downing Street consulted Hooker, the botanist shrewdly endorsed only a distinct scheme for the empire's plants.

In his report for 1859, Sir William Hooker urged that the Colonial Floras scheme be fully supported, for

> it will be productive, at comparatively little cost, of immense benefit to the Colonies and the Mother Country, and raise this establishment to a position pre-eminent for practical utility in all that concerns Scientific and Economic Botany, as well as Horticulture.[197]

By May 1860, Elliott wrote from the Colonial Office, on behalf of Newcastle, to assure Hooker of its support.[198] In an extensive memorandum of 1861, Sir William formally outlined his proposals. Such floras, he argued, were a natural extension of the work of the Museum of Economic Botany. Indeed, it was argued, the immediate classification of botanical specimens was vital to any future colonial economic progress. Hooker claimed that these floras had long been in demand by entrepreneurs and officials at home and in the colonies:

> The publication by government of a series of inexpensive 8vo. works, illustrative of the vegetable products of the British possessions, has long been contemplated by the Director of the Royal Gardens of Kew. To him, in his official capacity, incessant applications for information on the vegetable products of our colonies are made, by the home and colonial governments, and by private individuals, especially merchants and manufacturers, and he is habitually applied to by travellers and emigrants … the want of them is a great obstacle to the development of the productive resources of the colonies.[199]

The needs of 'colonists, manufacturers and travellers, as well as … scientific botanists, horticulturalists, and amateurs' justified the expenditure. The Treasury harrumphed that the colonies would have to pay for such work themselves. But while the gold-rich Australian governments were compelled to do so, the Colonial and Foreign Offices agreed to honour botany in their own estimates.[200]

From 1859 until his death in 1865, Hooker had the comfort of having three allies in high Cabinet positions: Russell was at the Foreign Office, the Duke of Newcastle (who, as Lord Lincoln, had presided over the rapid expansion of Kew from 1841 to 1846) was Secretary of State for the Colonies, while the Duke of Somerset (who as Lord Seymour had agreed that Kew should have its Herbarium) was First Lord of the Admiralty. It was with confidence that

Hooker could write to his superiors in the Board of Works in 1863 that the Colonial Floras scheme had the backing of the Foreign Office, the Colonial Office, and the Admiralty:

> I know it to be the feeling of the Duke of Somerset, and I believe it is equally that of the Duke of Newcastle and of Earl Russell that such an application as is needed to the Treasury should emanate from the Chief of the Department to which I have the honour to belong and I cannot for a moment doubt that it would be successful.[201]

The core of Hooker's 1859 plan thus became reality.[202]

The Colonial Floras scheme fulfilled several scientific objectives. It contributed to the accumulation of systematic knowledge of plant distribution. It undoubtedly assisted Joseph Hooker and George Bentham in their work on the *Genera Plantarum*, the herculean effort at reorganizing all plant taxonomy which they undertook from 1858 onwards.[203] It also provided income for individual botanists: the Colonial governments of Australia authorized the payment of £1,200 to Bentham, those of South Africa promised £1,500 for Harvey and Sonder, New Zealand offered Joseph Hooker £150 for a single volume, the Colonial Office similarly giving Bentham £150 for one on the Hong Kong flora.[204] The two volumes projected for West Africa at the beginning would spring to the seven tomes of the *Flora of Tropical Africa* by the end of the century, with four others still then projected, as the formalization of Britain's *imperium* swept new territory into the reach of its collectors.

How far did the Colonial Floras add to imperial prosperity? It is difficult to say, for there is no clear evidence on the question. By the end of the century, however, the Librarian of the Colonial Office would write the Deputy Director of Kew to seek his advice as to the disposal of the many unused volumes of Colonial Floras.[205] It is likely that the great publishing enterprise mattered more for the evolution of contemporary botany than for the growth of the imperial economy.

Kew Steps into the Limelight: The Cinchona Initiative

As late as 1859, Sir William Hooker presented the ornamental and horticultural dimension of Kew as the first of 'the chief objects of the Government in establishing and supporting' the garden.[206] Hooker also boasted about the new crowds, ushered to Kew by omnibus and rail. By the 1860s about half a million visitors a year came to the gardens.[207] The Hookers also courted the royal family in the old way, as Sir William wrote in 1860:

> At this very moment Professor Henslow & Dr. Hooker have left my house to give a Botanical lecture (the first of four) at Buckingham Palace. Science is now fostered by Royalty.[208]

Joseph Hooker in 1861 received 'the little princes Alfred & Leopold' for botany lessons.[209] The return of Lord John Manners to the Office of Works in 1866 led to predictable instructions to Joseph Hooker to provide flowers for the moral improvement of the masses. He required the Director of Kew

> to allot at proper season the surplus Bedding plants and flowering annuals in Kew Gardens to the Clergy, School Committees & Others who may apply on behalf of the poorer inhabitants of London.[210]

Similarly in 1867, when the Army wanted saplings with which to replant the camp at Aldershot, they turned to Kew.[211] But such services by the Hookers to public instruction, royal amusement, and horticultural supply merely disguised the change then underway in the public responsibilities and identity of Kew.

A better symbol of mid-Victorian Kew was a 159-foot spar from a Douglas fir which a timber merchant from the new colony of British Columbia sent to Kew in 1861. With the help of a party from the Royal Dockyards in Woolwich it was planted as a flag pole, which supported the Union Jack at nearly twice the height of the surrounding trees, on the site of the Temple of Victory built by Sir William Chambers almost one hundred years before.[212] Sir William Hooker pronounced it admirably calculated to impress on the public the 'size and bulk of the timber trees of one of our own colonies, British Columbia'.[213] It equally represented the conquest of Kew by imperial concerns, and in particular by economic botany. Central to this shift was the scheme to collect seeds of cinchona for plantation in East and West Indian British colonies after 1860.

Malaria and other fevers had long represented the most powerful barrier to the projection of European influence in the tropics.[214] General Yellow Fever had lent decisive help to the maroons in the wars against the British in Jamaica, and to the armies of Toussaint L'Ouverture in St. Domingue. Mungo Park's 1805 Niger Expedition was virtually decimated by disease, as its surgeon reported:

> Thunder, death, and lightning: – the devil to pay: lost by disease Mr. Scott, two sailors, four carpenters, and thirty-one members of the Royal African Corps, which reduces our numbers to seven.[215]

Half a century later, Gustave Mann, botanist to the Niger Expedition, told a similar story, reporting the deaths of Dutch and French naturalists and of the Consul of Lagos, 'the third consul appointed to that place in two years'.[216] Elsewhere in Africa, parts of the Mediterranean, South and East Asia, disease limited the penetration of soldiers, merchants, missionaries, or naturalists, and lent advantages to those who resisted European power.

Europeans found a valuable weapon against these fevers in the scientific knowledge of Andean peoples. For centuries before Pizarro, mountain communities had discovered that the bark from local trees operated as a powerful febrifuge. By the seventeenth century, very wealthy Europeans began to use what they called 'Jesuits' bark' as a treatment for malarial fevers.[217] Spain, which controlled the Andes, kept the bark's price high, and never succeeded in extracting significant quantities. One reason for this faliure was that European botany knew little about *Cinchona*, the genus of plants which was the source of the drug. In the era of Buffon and Banks, both the French and the British searched for species of cinchona, the source of the bark, in their West Indian and the Guianese possessions. But they failed to find equivalents, while the supply of cinchona began to dwindle as a result of over-extraction, as Humboldt observed in his voyage to New Spain.

The importance of cinchona increased as the new engines of free trade and antislavery intensified British interest in the tropics. At the same time, Dr. T.R.H. Thomson, physician for the Niger Expedition of 1841, had shown to his own satisfaction that quinine, the alkaloid extracted from the bark, prevented fever.[218] On the Niger Expedition of 1854, Dr. William Baikie proved on the steamer *Pleiad* that quinine both treated and often prevented malarial and other fevers.[219] The drug made possible the safe passage of Gustave Mann through Cameroon.

The idea of quinine's efficacy itself awakened new imperial enthusiasms. In 1858, the share announcement for the Central African Company explained that the sacrifice of European life which attended European assaults on the Niger had deterred private individuals from risking life and property in opening a trade with Central Africa. Quinine, it proposed, meant that a public company could now seek, with confidence, to expand African commerce, to afford scientific and missionary societies a wider field for their operations, and thus eventually to improve 'the moral and material condition of the people'.[220] By the middle of the century therefore, quinine was not simply a 'tool of empire', in Headrick's terms, it was also a European fetish, a symbol of the power of science to put nature on the side of imperialism. A short river of quinine links Baikie's 1854 Niger Expedition to Palmerston's decision to annex Lagos in 1861, and ultimately to the Berlin Conference of 1884–5, at which Africa was partitioned among the powers of Europe.

The idea of naturalizing cinchona in other European colonies had arisen in the eighteenth century. Spain, and later the independent Andean republics, were naturally opposed, of course, to any attempt to break their monopoly. But no European colonial power acknowledged this attempt by weak nations to control the plant. In 1835 John Forbes Royle suggested that mountainous parts of India, and in particular Khasia and the Nilgiris, might be suitable for cinchona. But the Dutch in Java stole the march: during 1853–4, Justus Charles Hasskarl, Superintendent of the Buitenzorg garden, travelled to South America in disguise to collect seeds. A race thus began, in which Britain, Holland, and France all sought to secure the best varieties of cinchona for plantation in Asia.

In early 1858, British businessmen in Ecuador, and Walter Cape, the chargé d'affaires in Quito, prodded the government on the matter. In lieu of over £1 million sterling in overdue debt and interest payments, the government of Ecuador had granted to English bondholders 4½ million acres of land, so constituting the Ecuador Land Company. In a memorial to the Board of Trade they urged that 'the transportation of the cinchona tree to India and some other British colonies ... forms part of our contemplated undertaking'.[221] The new India Office, constituted in the wake of the Crown's assumption of control over India after the popular revolt against British rule of 1857, enthusiastically offered its support. We may note that Royle had been the East India Company's adviser on botanical affairs in the 1850s, and that Lindley had replaced him, through the Hookers' lobbying of John Stuart Mill and Lord Stanley, in the India Office.[222]

Kew had a central role in the execution of the cinchona scheme. It was the administrative focus of all stages of the project: the systematic collection of the best varieties of cinchona in South America, the germination of seed in British greenhouses, their transport to botanic gardens in British Asia, and introduction into plantations. Markham, Weir, Cross, and Spruce were prepared at Kew to hunt for cinchona.[223] In 1860 the Treasury made a grant to Kew to fund the construction of a double forcing house to germinate the seeds 'and if necessary nurse the sickly plants *en route* to India'.[224] The scheme, extended into Sikkim, Ceylon, Madras, Jamaica, and Trinidad, brought Sir William into communication with a wider range of colonial officials, planters, and merchants than ever before. Joseph Hooker swept up his friend Charles Darwin in the excitement, and Darwin wrote to the Superintendent of the Ceylon Botanic Garden to suggest a technique of artificial fertilization, noting that, 'the growth of Cinchona is so important for mankind, that I am sure you will excuse me making this suggestion'.[225] In short, the cinchona scheme was an enormous imperial botanical and agronomic project for which the only real precedent were the Bligh missions for breadfruit almost a century earlier. The spirit of Banks was walking again at Kew.

Cinchona assumed an heroic aura. Bidie, a soldier in the Indian Army, wrote in 1879:

> To England with her numerous and extensive colonial possessions, it is simply priceless; and it is not too much to say, that if portions of her tropical empire are upheld by the bayonet, the arm that wields the weapon would be nerveless, but for Cinchona bark and its active principles.[226]

The increase in the supply of quinine febrifuge, from a variety of sources, led to its application to civil servants and soldiers in India and the colonies, and ultimately to the workers on tropical plantations and forests in British Guiana, Burma, Malaya, Fiji, and elsewhere. By the same token, the cinchona scheme established the reputations of individuals and institutions. Clement

Markham, once a minor clerk in the India Office, became a lion of London society. Reference to the cinchona scheme similarly became an established part of any appeal by Kew's directors to the usefulness of their institution.

But it is worth noting, parenthetically, that the great British cinchona scheme was a failure. As Anderson, the Director of Calcutta Botanic Gardens, wrote confidentially to John Lindley, almost all the plants died, cuttings and all. 'What a shameful job the expedition of Markham seems to have been,' he wrote.[227] Herman Crüger, the Superintendent of the Trinidad Botanic Garden, was entirely unable to germinate the seed he received.[228] Despite the tide of hoopla which would carry Markham to a secure position in the India Office, and lend his voice great authority in the councils of the Royal Geographical Society, he had collected little cinchona of quality. The cinchonas introduced by Spruce, Cross and others, at significant public expense, were similarly poor. British India had received chiefly the inferior red bark varieties (*C. succirubra* etc.). But because of the personal and institutional reputations at stake, in particular those of the India Office and Kew, the low quinine content of British bark was never publicly admitted.

In 1865 Charles Ledger, the adventurer who in 1858 had secretly carried Alpacas from Peru to Australia, arrived in India bearing seed he had collected in Bolivia.[229] No British authority would take them.[230] He took his seed to the Dutch who promptly bought 20,000 of them for introduction into Java where they quickly established themselves as far superior to all others. In 1879 George King toured the Dutch East Indies and reported that

> I have no hesitation in saying that all the species of cinchona are to be found in greater perfection in Java than in Sikkim or the Nilghiris, and ... I believe I may also say than in Ceylon.
>
> The cinchona trees of which the bark has yielded the Dutch such a high percentage of quinine [in some cases as high as 13.7%] have all been raised from a parcel of seed purchased in 1866 by the Dutch government from an English collector named Ledger after our own India Office had declined to buy them ... [*C. ledgeriana* is] much richer in that alkaloid than any other known variety or species of cinchona.[231]

In 1880 Thiselton-Dyer at Kew had to advise the Colonial Office that it should set about introducing *C. ledgeriana* to Ceylon from Java, warning that 'it is obvious that if capable of being produced in quantity it must drive all other kinds from the market'.[232] Langden, the Governor of Ceylon, complained to the Colonial Secretary in response that it had been known as early as 1872 that Ledger's yellow bark was in a class of its own, but it was only through private initiative that it had been brought over from Java in the late 1870s.[233] It was too late: except in the 1880s, when Ceylonese cinchona was rapidly uprooted to make room for tea, and was dumped at a loss on the world market, all the Queen's technocrats could never make British plantations compete with Dutch suppliers of the bark.

But the failure of the botanists to do better than a private entrepreneur would only be known retrospectively. In its immediate aftermath, the cinchona scheme appeared a great success, and would be the model for many other later interventions into colonial agriculture. It re-established the importance of the connection between Kew and satellite colonial botanic gardens, and reminded the public that the botanical expert in London could transform the success of the imperial enterprise. During the next decades other projects would move ipecacuanha, rubber, and sisal, again from Britain's 'informal empire' in Latin America, to the plantations of the East and West Indies. The ultimate result of the cinchona scheme was Kew's control over a new network of colonial gardens of 1880s and the 1890s.

When Joseph Hooker succeeded his father as Director in 1865, the scale of Kew's imperial work was growing rapidly. Over 8,000 plants were sent annually from Kew to various colonies between 1863 and 1872, double what had prevailed during Sir William Hooker's regime. Indian and colonial officials consulted Joseph Hooker on an increasing variety of colonial questions. Joseph Hooker began to acquire powers of patronage which his father had only dreamed of. In 1869 he wrote Sir Austen Henry Layard, the excavator of Nineveh, then the Chief Commissioner of Works, regarding a youth whom Layard wished to help:

> I would have given him a capital place in India; with £150, rising by £50 to £450, outfit of £40 , & passage out and home! But he declines going to India. I have given away 7 such appointments in 2 years! and all successfully.[234]

The cinchona scheme established a precedent for the recruitment from Kew of botanical advice concerning both policies and personnel. By 1870, Hooker reported that 'The demands on this establishment, especially from India and the Colonies ... and from planters, forest and garden superintendents ... increase annually'.[235] Kew began, gradually, to regain that rôle as a centre of imperial economic botany which it had not enjoyed since the ministry of Pitt the Younger.

The Ayrton–Hooker Controversy: A New Identity Crystallizes

Why had Joseph Hooker attached himself to imperial work with such vigour? In part, with the cinchona and Colonial Floras schemes, he was inheriting an agenda set by his father. Clearly, in India as well as Jamaica, he responded to contemporary needs. There were also scientific reasons: Hooker's special expertise in the botany of South Asia, Australia, and New Zealand, and his concern with botanical geography, made the whole world his province. It is clear also that Hooker enjoyed the influence and prestige such work gave him. He certainly wished to secure the position of Kew. But there were other reasons why in the 1860s he might have sought to attach himself to conspicuously public responsibilities.

Hooker was acutely conscious of the cultural divide which the publication of Darwin's *Origin of Species* had opened between science and the British public. He lacked Huxley's sheer appetite for polemic, but shared his friend's concern for the cause of science as a profession. He chose his battles carefully: in 1862, for example, when Lubbock proposed a Memorial from scientists in support of the authors of *Essays and Reviews,* Hooker refused because it would be 'prejudicial both to the cause and interests of science *at this particular juncture*'.[236] In 1862, he similarly argued that scientists should eschew standing *en bloc* with Bishop Colenso. He was probably hesitant about rushing into these extradisciplinary religious controversies because he recognized that the friends of Darwinism had to conserve their ammunition for battles specific to their area of expertise. On the other hand, Hooker was clearly not reticent about his scientific views: he had helped Huxley to demolish Bishop 'Soapy Sam' Wilberforce in 1860, and in his 1868 Presidential Address to the British Association for the Advancement of Science in Norwich, he had explained the significance of Darwinism for botany, and had denounced 'natural theology'. He understood the cost of these stands: in 1869, Lyell and Murchison approached the Duke of Argyll at the India Office to nominate Hooker for a Knighthood in the Star of India, but the Duke refused because, as Hooker put it to Darwin, 'The fact is the Duke could do it with a stroke of a pen, but he don't like my Darwinism and my Address and I am right proud of that!'[237] Joseph Hooker must have found the obvious public value of economic botany, particularly where applied on a grand imperial scale, to be useful in his difficult political situation.

The importance of these connections formed between Kew and the wider world became clear between 1870 and 1873. During these years, Hooker became ensnared in an extensive bureaucratic war with Acton Smee Ayrton, the Chief Commissioner of Works.[238] This conflict represented a collision between two strands of what social scientists have given the proleptic name of 'modernization': the technocrat clashing with the bureaucrat. We may see in Hooker, as MacLeod does, a representative of the Victorian scientific professional, the hero of a small but articulate interest group, and in Ayrton, an example of Gladstonian liberalism's concern with making government accountable to democracy. Or we may see both men as appealing, in the names of science or parliamentary sovereignty, to older absolutist powers of direction. The director of Kew inherited an office constituted in the age before the civil service reforms, and claimed adminstrative prerogatives unequalled by his equivalents in other departments. The Minister, like his Cabinet colleagues, ultimately asserted powers which derived from the idea that the Crown had delegated irresistible right to those officers who served the pleasure of parliament. Whatever lens we apply, the Office of Works of 1870 was no longer the cosy Board of Woods and Forests of the 1840s, which had directed public money towards palaces and worthy public institutions.

Ayrton's department had extensive, and expanding, responsibilities for roads, bridges, sewers, parks, and a wide variety of construction. Kew, from his perspective, was only another part of the public service, to be brought under tight and efficient administrative control.

Ayrton was a veteran of the Radical battles of the 1850s and 1860s. Like Joseph Hume, he had made money in India and then returned to enter politics, entering the House as representative of the tough East End constituency of Tower Hamlets. He had risen to prominence within the Liberal Party as a scourge of all public expenditure, and as part of the cohort which supported Sir Benjamin Hall and the movement for municipal reform.[239] He presented his administration as 'marked by zeal for economy in the public interest'.[240] Gladstone had named him Parliamentary Secretary to the Treasury in 1868, and in November 1869 he was made First Commissioner. Ayrton had no vain patrician desire to turn his post into a means of patronizing 'improvement'. In the name of retrenchment, he intended to flex his muscles over the department he had been given.

Ayrton's war with Hooker had begun even while he was still at the Treasury. In March 1869, Hooker had applied to the Treasury for the government to pay his costs to attend a Botanical Congress in Russia. Ayrton refused to sanction the expenditure. Hooker complained, with impolitic anger, that this action demonstrated the failure of government to support British science.[241] He failed to persuade Lowe to overrule Ayrton, succeeding only in making his future master his enemy. We may compare Hooker's protest to the later demand of architects that the Chief Commissioner of Works should 'direct improvements and adornments' rather than merely seeking to repress expenditure.[242] Neither scientists nor architects seemed to realize that the Prime Minister prized retrenchment above all else. Gladstone explained his attitude to public finance in his speech to the Corn Exchange in Edinburgh a decade later: it was, he pronounced, the mark of a 'chicken-hearted Chancellor of the Exchequer' when

> he shrinks from upholding economy in detail, when because it is a question of only £2000 or £3000, he says that is no matter. He is ridiculed no doubt for what is called saving candle-ends and cheese-parings in the cause of the country ... resistance in detail to jobbery and minute waste and extravagance is the first of wholly sound financial rules.[243]

When the Chief Commissioner arrived at his post ready to trim Hooker's haughty wings, he knew that if he did so in the name of frugality, that he could count on the support of the Prime Minister.

From his arrival at the Office of Works in November 1869, Ayrton sought to remind Hooker that he was a subordinate and that he should 'have the goodness to govern [himself] accordingly'.[244] In the name of reform, he began to interfere with Kew, exerting control, in the name of prudent administration, over appointments and physical plant. By appointing

Douglas Galton, R.E., as 'Director of Works', for example, he deprived Hooker of control over his hothouses. Ayrton blocked the appointment of a Hooker nominee as an assistant to the Curator, demanding that the post go to the person who had done best in a relevant civil service test.[245] Finally, in 1870 he attempted to suborn the Curator himself, John Smith.[246] He offered Smith the post of 'Surveyor, or Secretary, of the Parks', and in December called him away to superintend the laying out of the grounds around the Albert Memorial. He instructed Smith 'to make obedience to [Hooker's] orders subservient to his interpretations of the First Commissioner's Instructions'. Ayrton knew that his insistence on ministerial sovereignty would appear quite reasonable. In 1872, the Treasury indeed lent its support, advising Hooker that while he was head of Kew, with full discretionary powers, he was 'of course in subordination to the First Commissioner of Works'.[247]

Hooker first protested directly to Gladstone. But fearing that he and his 'Mammon of a Ministry' might not respond, he also begged the help of Earl Russell. But the Whigs no longer controlled that kind of influence in the party: the reform coach had left Johnny long behind. Gladstone attempted to mollify Hooker, writing him in October from Balmoral that Ayrton had only friendly intentions. Hooker responded angrily, eventually writing Algernon West, the Prime Minister's Private Secretary, accusing Ayrton of 'Evasion, misrepresentation, and misstatements'. Eventually, in April 1872, he warned the Prime Minister that his 'Scientific and Horticultural friends' would soon be forced to turn the matter into a public controversy.[248]

Hooker indeed had potent allies. Men like Huxley and John Tyndall were skilled and aggressive polemicists, with excellent connections with the press and to the world of government. Ayrton's actions, Huxley threatened, were 'an injury and an affront to all the men of science of this country', these were 'persons who have means of making themselves heard'.[249] As Tyndall reassured Hooker: 'They shall know that men of science can use a sledgehammer.'[250] Memoranda in support of Hooker were submitted by the Royal Society and a variety of other associations. They sought the support of the Tories, among whom such amateur scientists as the 14th and 15th Earls of Derby and the Marquis of Salisbury were numbered.[251]

The elder Hooker had enjoyed ties with the Whigs, Joseph like many of his generation turned increasingly to the Tories. Huxley, even in 1858, had cast an admiring glance towards Disraeli, describing his circle as his 'scientific Young England'.[252] Hooker in that year had also praised Lord John Manners's support for the new Temperate House: 'Govt. are going to be liberal to science this year – & we expect £30,000 for our new Kew House but this is private at present ... I do not doubt their ability to get any amount of money for *Public Museums*.'[253] Lord Stanley had proved a friendly Foreign Secretary in Derby's third Cabinet of the 1860s. By 1872, Tyndall advised Derby that men of science felt that 'the sin of this transaction lies at the door of Mr. Gladstone, who backs up this dog in office'.[254] Derby and Lord John

Manners were quick to respond, and to advise him that they were willing to fight the battle in parliament.[255]

In June 1872, a twenty-five-page memorial, chiefly the handiwork of Tyndall and Huxley, went to Gladstone, bearing the signatures of Charles Lyell, Charles Darwin, George Bentham (President of the Linnaean Society), Henry Holland (President of the Royal Institution), George Burrows (President of the Royal College of Physicians), George Busk (President of the Royal College of Surgeons), Henry Rawlinson (President of the Royal Geographical Society), James Paget (Surgeon Extraordinary to Queen Victoria), and William Spottiswoode (mathematician and physicist).[256] It was leaked by early July, and triggered a wave of articles in the press attacking Ayrton.[257] They created the context for Derby to call for the papers in late July 1872.[258]

But in making the Tories their allies, the scientists only caused the Liberal Party to pull tightly in around Ayrton. The white knight of their polemic was easily represented as a bully who refused to submit to the democratic authority of parliament. 'The question of Ministerial authority', a Liberal journalist noted, 'was of far greater importance than Dr. Hooker's rule in Kew Gardens.'[259] The government could also point to the fact that scientists did not stand unanimously with Hooker. George Airy, the Astronomer Royal, stood at a distance from Huxley's camp.[260] In June 1872, in the midst of the controversy, the Prime Minister conspicuously recommended Airy for a knighthood in the coveted Order of the Bath. Ayrton found an important ally in another recipient of Liberal honours, Richard Owen.[261] Owen, who had fought many other scientific battles with Huxley, was easily mobilized against Hooker. His own campaign for the Natural History Museum depended on the support of Gladstone, and he saw, at the same time, that the controversy might allow his botanical colleagues to secure advantages. The Ayrton–Hooker controversy, once merely a battle between the new professionals of science and those of the state, now also became a struggle over the place of Darwinian evolution in the life sciences, and a war between the scientific empires of Kew and the British Museum.

Hooker bore some responsibility for the alacrity with which Owen and his British Museum circle supported Ayrton. In March 1871 he had advised the Royal Commission of Scientific Instruction and the Advancement of Science that the botany department of the British Museum was a disaster, that its collections should come to Kew, and 'the two herbaria should be rearranged under one head, and be brought under one system of management'.[262] John Ball (a former Under-Secretary of State for the Colonies) and Thomas Thomson (Superintendent of Calcutta botanic garden, 1854–61), both known as his friends, later seconded this suggestion, proposing that only duplicates remain at the British Museum.[263]

The Museum organized its defence. William Carruthers, the newly appointed Keeper of the Botanical Department of the British Museum, protested vehemently against Kew's annexing of his collection. With Owen's support, he doubled his staff, and lured away some of Hooker's subordinates.[264] When Sir Henry Holland visited Gladstone in 1871 to urge him to separate Kew from the Board of Works, the Prime Minister enigmatically replied that

> The natural time for considering the question ... will arise when the Natural History collections of the British Museum are transferred to South Kensington, and there will be a question as to the means by which the management can be carried on, & also whether the Kew Gardens ought to be brought in the same circle.[265]

Gladstone, it is likely, had been lobbied by Owen, and had begun to consider that the Museum of Natural History might well be allowed to annex Kew.

Owen had many reasons to wish to damage Hooker and any cause championed by T.H. Huxley. Adrian Desmond has argued that Owen rose to prominence in the 1830s and 1840s as the enemy of radical Lamarckian interpretations of the unity of life.[266] He was a natural enemy of the transformist doctrines shared by Darwin, Hooker, and Huxley. Darwin reported to Lyell the hostile conversation he had with Owen in December 1859, after the publication of the *Origin of Species*:

> Under guard of great civility, he was inclined to be most bitter and sneering against me ... He added another objection to the book ... that it explained everything & that it was improbable in the highest degree that I would succeed in this. I gently agreed with this rather queer objection, & [said if] it comes to this then my book must either be very bad or very good.[267]

Owen had been on the losing end of a number of debates with Huxley during the 1850s and the 1860s on palaeontology, the hippocampus, and a variety of questions related to evolution. He fancied himself the 'British Cuvier', at which Huxley joked with Hooker, 'he stands in the same relation to the French as British brandy to Cognac'.[268] In 1871, also, Darwin had published *The Descent of Man*, in which he deftly turned many of Owen's zoological observations into evidence in support of his own argument. There were therefore personal, scientific, and political reasons for Owen to wish to do Ayrton's dirty work.

In June 1872, Owen provided Ayrton a 'Statement relative to the Botanical Department respectively under the Trustees of the British Museum and the Commissioners of Works' for release to parliament.[269] He cleverly used Sir William Hooker's achievements in making Kew an ornamental park against his son. Owen claimed that while his subordinates sought 'the advancement of botanical science', Kew was merely for horticulture and recreation. Like Regent's Park zoo, its chief application was 'the instructive pleasure of the public'. He argued that Hooker should chiefly be occupied with the 'progressive selection' of new varieties of ornamental and useful plants, that his botanic garden should be 'geographically arranged', and that he particularly concern himself with such 'physiological' studies as experiments aimed at 'turning urban sewage into fodder'. He added that he was not aware of any new flowers or fruit created at Kew since a herbarium had been established, and that if the herbarium collections at Kew were transferred to the British Museum,

> the Director would recover the time for the discharging of his physiological duties at Kew, and the Keeper of botany at the British Museum would be better enabled to fulfil his nomenclative and descriptive functions in London.

Owen thus presented Ayrton with an argument for taking from Hooker the part of Kew most precious to his work.

It was a brilliantly malevolent strike at Hooker, Huxley, and behind them, Darwin. His Swiftian vision of acres of Kew devoted to earnest research with human excrement aptly expressed his intentions. The nub of his proposal, eminently sensible to an outsider, was that the new Natural History Museum at South Kensington should house the principal British collections in natural history, like the Muséum d'Histoire Naturelle in Paris. This would have been a grand turning-of-the-tables against the Hookers and their friends, who in 1847, 1858, and 1871, had plainly expressed a desire to have the Museum's herbarium at Kew. The mention of the 'menagerie' at Regent's Park was a direct jab at Huxley, who in 1858, in a hit at Owen, had suggested that the palaeontological collections of the British Museum be put with the zoo 'where the living beasts are'.[270] Where he urged that progressive selection and geographical arrangement should become Hooker's work at Kew, he aimed another well-placed blow. For Darwin had quoted extensively from the evidence of plant and animal breeders, and had leaned heavily on Hooker's phytogeography. The anti-Darwinist had cudgelled the pro-Darwinists with *topoi* borrowed from the *Origin of Species.*

Owen's intervention allowed Ayrton's allies to rise in parliament in July and August 1872 to dismiss the memorialists. The Duke of St. Albans noted that 'the distinguished name of Professor Owen' was not among its signatories.[271] Baron Stanley of Adderley suggested that Hooker's camp represented only a strident element of the scientific community.[272] Others reminded the Commons that the job of the Commissioner of Works was to curtail expenditure, and this naturally provoked the hostility of subordinates. Owen had muddied the waters. Huxley and Company recognized that scientific voices could not win the battle alone. They were forced instead to recruit support from the wider society, to which end they gave the June Memorial wide circulation.

The Memorial presented the history of Kew from 1840. It celebrated the epic labours of Hooker *père et fils*, and of their personal and financial sacrifices. It appealed also to what I have called the 'Whig theory of landscape', praising their contribution to 'the elevation and refinement of the tastes and conduct of the working classes', noting that 37,795 visitors visited Kew on Whit Monday without 'a single case of drunkenness, riot, theft, or mischief of any kind' being reported.[273] The memorialists reminded Gladstone that since the construction of the Herbarium, Kew had become the undisputed centre of national botanical research. They paid, lastly, special attention to Kew's imperial role. Their centrepiece was the story of the introduction of the cinchona plant, 'the commercial success of which is established', and the more than thirty Kew gardeners employed in India in forestry, cotton, tea, and cinchona plantations. From Kew would emanate, they promised, a 'series of complete Floras of India and the Colonies' vital to industry and government.

Kew's imperial work, once subordinate to its function as a pleasure garden, came increasingly to define its contribution to the public good.[274] Hooker reminded Gladstone that he conducted 'a responsible and onerous correspondence' with the Admiralty, and the Foreign, Colonial, and Indian Offices. He wrote the same month to Edward Cardwell, then Secretary for War, describing Kew as 'an institution that for 30 years has endeavoured to benefit the Colonies'. His case was supported from many sides. The West India Committee warned Gladstone that the threat of Hooker's resignation or removal from Kew caused great anxiety among the planters and merchants of Britain's oldest colonies.[275] Other articles and memoranda described the important role of Hooker and Kew in the planting of cinchona in the East and West Indies.[276] Major-General Richard Strachey of the India Office testified to the Devonshire Commission that Hooker should not be subject to the Board of Works, and that if he was liberated from Ayrton, Kew would be able to render even more service to India.[277] Hooker's contributions to military intelligence also won attention. His *Himalayan Journals* were described as 'the most perfect staff officer's report, containing accurate information on every point that could be useful to the commander of an expedition, regarding hills, valleys, elevation, distances, rocks, soil, trees, vegetation, roads, rivers, bridges', and as the basis of a successful campaign against the Rajah of Sikkim in 1861.[278] While in 1851 magnificent rhododendrons had been the emblem of Hooker's achievements in Sikkim, twenty years later his contribution to the mastery of an alien landscape mattered more.

The imperial theme received further attention in a second memorandum, submitted in January 1873, in favour of Kew retaining its botanical collections. Its author was M.J. Berkeley (Botanical Director of the Royal Horticultural Society) and it was signed by Charles Darwin and virtually every prominent botanist in the United Kingdom—C.C. Babington at Cambridge, Marmaduke Lawson at Oxford, William Thiselton-Dyer at the Royal Agricultural College at Cirencester, George Bentham, J.H. Balfour at Edinburgh, R. Bentley of the Royal Pharmaceutical Society, G. Dickie at Aberdeen, and E. Perceval Wright at Trinity College, Dublin. They opposed the transfer to South Kensington, first, on scientific grounds, arguing that 'a Botanical Garden ... which is confessedly the most important in the world' required as perfect a Herbarium and Library as possible.[279] But this argument was quickly seconded by a powerful reference to Kew being a central institution of modern British empire:

> the records of the Colonial and India Offices will show of what immense importance the establishment at Kew has been to the welfare of the entire British Empire, and that weighty questions ... could not be satisfactorily answered without reference to the library and herbarium.[280]

Imperial economic botany was now the proof of the importance of 'pure' botanical research, and now secured Kew's right to maintain its integrity as an institution.

A variety of victories came to Hooker and his allies. By 23 January, the Treasury had assured Berkeley that Her Majesty's Government had not formed the intention of removing the collection at Kew to South Kensington.[281] A mark of public approval also came quickly when the trustees of the estate of John Stuart Mill presented his herbarium to Hooker.[282] In August 1873, Gladstone relieved Ayrton of the Board of Works, and the next year the electors of Tower Hamlets consigned him to extra-parliamentary oblivion. Finally, in its 'Fourth Report', published in 1874, the Devonshire Commission gave Kew victory over the British Museum of Natural History. It supported existing arrangements by which all collections made at government expense went first to Kew, with only a set of duplicates going to the British Museum. A final twist, which bore all the signs of having come from the wrist of Huxley, was its suggestion that while Kew could arrange its herbarium to support work in taxonomy, 'the collections at the British Museum should be maintained and arranged with special reference to the Geographical Distribution of Plants and Palaeontology'.[283] In short, Owen's botanists at South Kensington were urged to organize their specimens in the way most likely to reveal those relationships of species to environments for which the phytogeography of Joseph Hooker and the *Origin of Species* gave the best explanation. The scientific empire at Kew, tied to a growing world of overseas activity, and to the ambitions of professionals at home, had prevailed for the while.

Unnoticed by contemporaries, in little more than a decade a fundamental shift had taken place in Kew's identity as an institution. In 1859, Sir William Hooker had described Kew as primarily 'a place for healthful recreation and instruction', and only secondarily a centre for science. Joseph Hooker by 1872 presented the gardens as principally committed to pure research and the imperial economy.[284] 'Kew never was regarded as one of the Parks, and never should be', he wrote, 'its primary objects are scientific & utilitarian, not recreational'. The popular aspect of the gardens had only been 'superadded to the scientific and the utilitarian'. Where Hooker proposed that an act of parliament reconstitute Kew outside of the Board of Works, he noted that 'it might be founded on the fact that Kew has enormously developed, that its chief duties are to the Colonies, India, the Admiralty, and that it is the first Botanical Institution in Europe'.[285] Science, subordinated to empire, now constituted Kew's mission.

Conclusion: Science and the 'New Imperialism'

In the years after the Ayrton controversy, Joseph Hooker healed his personal relations with Gladstone, honouring the Leader of the Opposition with invitations to the Royal Society, and exchanging a correspondence with him over the botanical evidence for the age of the Earth.[286] But Hooker could not forget that his status as a former guest at Hawarden had not protected him from persecution at the hands of a Liberal minister. The lesson of the crisis of 1870 to 1873 was that Kew had to be defended in terms of its service to the public, and colonial work offered powerful evidence of such service.

Kew had acquired imperial responsibilities in a somewhat haphazard way. It was for recreation, after all, that the garden had principally been saved in the 1840s. Most British people, at all periods of its history, knew it only as a place where one looked at plants or picnicked. But the Hookers, through persuading the Crown to construct a library and herbarium around the collections formed by Bentham and themselves, had made Kew into an international centre for the science of botany. Years of assiduous correspondence with planters, settlers, and administrators abroad, and with manufacturers and politicians at home, had turned the Royal Botanic Garden also into an agency which advised on the economy and government of the British Empire. The cinchona scheme, whatever its practical faliures, had cemented an alliance of interests between men of science and another emerging professional caste: imperial administrators. If we may see the Hookers as reaching for influence abroad, a variety of overseas agents sought their advice. The contribution of science to late nineteenth-century British imperialism is principally the story of the evolution of these relationships of mutual benefit between savants at home, and modern major-generals and proconsuls at the periphery.

At the heart of this engagement between science and colonial government were the old Christian assumptions about the sacred origins of Man's place in Nature. 'Natural Theology' might have been a declining idol of the educated classes, but the Providential intuitions at its centre had found new incarnation, and not merely in the doctrines of political economy. They were translated, as we shall discuss in the next chapter, into the bureaucratic enthusiasms of mid century. But inner faith always seeks outward evidence of its grace. For the governors and consuls sitting in their tropical manor houses, science became both a tool for government, and a talisman against the unhappy thought that the legitimate power they represented might be wholly counterfeit. Kew and its colonial equivalents, with their scientific plots, ornamental lakes, and museums, prospered as they helped to sustain the fraudulent charisma of modern imperialism.

CHAPTER 7

The Government of Nature: Imperial Science and a Scientific Empire, 1873–1903

It was in the last quarter of the century that Kew reached the zenith of its influence, as both a scientific and an imperial institution. In both respects, its achievement may be accommodated within the narrative of the Victorian climax of the Pax Britannica. But that larger story may itself be subordinated to another theme: the global triumph of the idea of bureaucratic government as the key to social efficiency. If the British Empire was ever more than a fiction, a name which gave identity to a chaotic variety of political and economic relationships, it was in the network of administration ordered from London: dispatches and Blue Books, ambitious men watching Whitehall watching them as they governed. If William Thiselton-Dyer came to consolidate a scientific empire at Kew, he did so through the relations he established with those who undertook, at home and abroad, to realize the imperial idea. Why did they turn to science?

Empire as Government

John Pope-Hennessy, Consul in Borneo in 1868, exemplified the administrator who took pride in both his political and natural historical achievements. On the one hand, his diplomacy had worked 'to foster the commerce of Labuan by causing certain rivers to be opened to British traders'.[1] On the other, he proudly reported to the Royal Society, and his superiors in the Foreign Office, his organization of a scientific mission to observe a solar eclipse:

> We left Labuan Monday at noon, and arrived at Barram Point at five o'clock next morning. . . . A tent was fitted up in an open space between a casuarina plantation, and the following corps of observers landed at ten o'clock: Captain Reed, Lieutenant Ray, Lt Ellis & myself, our four telescopes being securely adjusted on large tripod stands manufactured for the occasion. Four other officers landed with us, Dr O'Connor to note the physiological phenomena, Dr Wright to watch the magnetic needle; & Mr Doyley and Mr Roughton to mark the time – fowl, pidgeons, and cattle taken, and their behaviour observed, during the course of the eclipse. . .[2]

For Pope-Hennessy, and many of his civil and military contemporaries, scientific passions appeared to have accompanied attempts at 'good government'.

They recognized that Nature was the necessary ally of policy. Sir John Kirk, Sir Harry Johnston, and their successors, for example, sought East African commodities, with Kew's help, which might replace slaving in the local economy.[3] Governors everywhere sought to develop new exports and to raise revenue, and after the cinchona scheme, looked to Kew for help. Sir John Grant, former Lieutenant-Governor of Bengal, taking command of Jamaica, newly a Crown Colony after the Morant Bay Rebellion, turned to botany to revive agriculture, and thus to solve the economic crisis which had aggravated the political upheavals of 1865. In St. Helena, as in Jamaica, the Governor also renovated scientific gardens which had last received official support in the age of Banks. By the 1850s and 1860s, a new goal began to acquire influence among administrators: conservation.[4] Major-General Richard Strachey, charged with the organization of the Indian Forest Service, thus sought Joseph Hooker's help in the 1860s.[5] Kew benefited from this association with enlightened administration: as Hooker wrote in 1874, when the colonial government in New Zealand granted £100 to Kew to fund its help in forest conservation, 'I am very glad of all this ... as it will tend to impress government with the practical value of Kew to the State, of which the last Government were absolutely ignorant, and showed no wish to be instructed'.[6] Above all, as the proconsuls raised their telescopes, they found a celestial explanation for the position they (and their nation) now occupied. Such avocations were, moreover, an acknowledged mark of high capacity: Pope-Hennessy's lens was clearly keened as much on the rising star of his career as on the movement of sun spots.

These peripheral bureaucrats gave the scientists at Kew wide influence. We know surprisingly little about them, in comparison with Rhodes, Goldie, Mackinnon, and the other 'men on the spot' of the 1870s, 1880s, and 1890s. The historiography of imperialism has tended to privilege explanation of the circumstances of annexations over the facts of government on the ground. Yet, we may argue, understanding the priorities of administration on the ground may well add significantly to our understanding of the history of expansion. These desiderata included the opening of territory to commerce and exploitation; the creation of a revenue base to offset the expense of government; the preservation of internal order and the security of frontiers; the imposition, via laws, of British modes of labour, property, exchange, and justice; and, in varying degrees, the support of Christianity, education, and sanitation, and the political consultation of 'responsible' local people. It is possible to see this administrative agenda, as Robinson and Gallagher did: as a consequence of conquests which arose from the worried but dispassionate calculations of the 'official mind', as it faced European rivals and African resistance, and from the aggressive adventures of 'men on the spot'.[7] The broad reach of British expansion in the nineteenth century, they argued, can be understood in terms of the maxim 'trade without rule if possible, trade with rule if necessary', and of the political and strategic facts which tipped the balance towards rule in India in one generation, and in Africa in another. This thesis remains generally sound, and yet the willingness of Gladstone, Salisbury, and their contemporaries to contemplate 'rule', on such a spectacular scale, needs to be understood in terms of more than the political contingencies of the 1880s. Territorial acquisitions became significantly more plausible in the second half of the century for reasons beyond the route to India, and troublesome Egyptians, Afrikaners, or Frenchmen.

We need to recognize that 'continuity' in Victorian imperialism encompassed government as well as economy: its credo might be framed as rule in the interest of both Britain and subject peoples, such interest being defined by the British, via their own institutions if possible, via Britain's if necessary. Lugard's description of Britain's 'dual mandate' only made articulate presumptions which had animated the more lively sort of proconsul, certainly by the 1850s and 1860s, and arguably since the 1780s.[8] (Lugard himself, in the earliest stages of his career, took part in the search for East African rubber.)[9] But with 'rule', as with 'trade', the parameters of necessity shifted dramatically over the course of the nineteenth century—and for reasons which were often European rather than Asian or African. We may choose to hesitate about identifying a Victorian 'revolution in government', but what is clear, from the 1830s onwards, under both Whig and Tory leaders, is a vastly expanded number of Royal and other public commissions, regulatory agencies, statutary boards, committees of the Privy Council, and ultimately government ministries. This bureaucratic tide rose slowly but continually throughout the Victorian era, and at its crest it made the burden and risk of 'formal empire' appear necessary in some contexts, and palatable in others. If a rapidly expanding textile industry made Chinese or Argentinian trade barriers, or unexplored markets, unacceptable to the age of Palmerston and Cobden, so a new confidence in the efficiency of government made apparent anarchy, indolence, ignorance, or merely resistance to 'civilized' lifeways, increasingly intolerable. The capacities of colonial administrations to transform local conditions were, by the same token, newly exalted. New competitive criteria for the civil service came to prevail in Indian and colonial appointments, and men appointed to distant responsibilities lived in anxious service to the ideal of competence prized by the machinery of selection and promotion.

New confidence in the power of government had arisen for many reasons. The impact of ideas of Enlightened administration, mediated by Bentham, Mill, and Comte, was clear. The complex problems thrown up by industry and urbanization, in particular cholera and other epidemic disease, encouraged the recruitment of expertise and the expansion of the state. In Britain, moreover, as elsewhere in Europe, the expansion of bureaucracy amounted often to a democratization by other means, as older élites granted new spheres of responsibility to 'responsible' middling elements, while at the same time resisting constitutional concessions. The example of European governments—in particular France under Napoleon III, and Prussia—encouraged the reform of education and the military.

Between 1870 and 1914, British administration encompassed vast new colonies at the same time as, at home, the state significantly expanded its empire over national life. Herbert Spencer's attack on the growth of bureaucratic government in *Social Statics* (1851) eloquently diagnosed the disease, but was powerless to stem its tide. The Tories, once the vigilant opponents of creeping Benthamism, became the patrons of expanded government. That Hooker was pleased by the Tory victory of 1874 can be explained in part by his fight with Ayrton, but also by his belief that they sought to govern well and not, like Gladstone, merely cheaply.[10] We may discover fuel for his optimism in the speech made by Disraeli at the Crystal Palace on 24 June 1872, where the Tory leader proclaimed the union of 'imperialism and social reform'.[11] Both historians and contemporaries, such as Morley, have used this speech to mark the emergence of a 'New Imperialism' from the waters. But, on inspection, Disraeli's plea was for government to assume responsibility for public health, '*sanitas sanitatem omnia sanitas*', the conditions of labour, and social cohesion, not a call to annex the Gold Coast or war with the Transvaal.[12] Disraeli was continuing his campaign of 1867 to yoke the horses of democracy to the Tory chariot: 'imperialism' was for him an inclusive category, an 'imagined community' within which the differences between classes could be reconciled.[13] In the name of the 'national principles' of the Conservative Party, Disraeli advanced an expanded role for the state as the protector and improver of the lives of the people. 'Young England', once hostile to Utilitarian schemes for the extension of the state's power, now found in Enlightened administration an attractive alternative justification for the rule of the Few over the Many. When the Tories stole the mantle of Palmerston from the Liberals, they borrowed, at the same time, elements from the social agenda of the 'Radicals'. By 1886, Joseph Chamberlain had to sacrifice few of his principles to join forces with Salisbury.

Both the overseas and domestic aspects of the 'New Imperialism' were founded on the enormous powers for production, and for the exercise of influence at a distance, which European science and engineering had unleashed. Through steam ships, railways, telegraphs, and the repeating rifle, Europeans became able to establish their dominion over the landmass of India, the African hinterland, and the American West.[14] Once Europeans were merely waterborne parasites, able to command trade only beside rivers or at the coast, now they set the terms of 'collaboration' on every continent. By the same means, Napoleon III or Bismarck could intervene in the local sphere of French or Prussian life with ease undreamed of by Napoleon I or Frederick the Great. But technology not only allowed the state, in the name of a common interest, to interfere with everyday life at home and abroad: it also encouraged statesmen and citizens to desire such responsibility. Differences in technology and culture, between and within societies, appeared to justify the authority of national or racial élites and to invest them with paternalistic responsibilities: the idea of the *mission civilisatrice* embraced both the working classes and the Irish at home, and the Jamaicans and Egyptians abroad.[15] New areas of interest and competition were consequences of new technologies. Without the Suez or Panama Canals, for example, the histories of expansion in both the Old and New World would have been quite different. All in all, 'High Imperialism' deserves to be treated as a phenomenon of the age of steam.

While the power at the disposal of Europeans had changed radically, there was less novelty at the level of ideology. Here we must dissent from the popular hypothesis of a crucial 'hardening' of European attitudes to non-Europeans in the middle of the century.[16] This toughening of imperial will has sometimes been blamed on the rise of scientific racism, premised on misreadings of Darwin. Others have suggested that a 'protonationalism' of mid-century, and the perceived violence of Indians in their Revolt of 1857 and of Jamaicans in the Morant Bay Rebellion in Jamaica of 1865 were the catalysts. Before this watershed, most parties assume, lay a more gentle era, in which Enlightenment universalism sustained a respect towards Indians, Chinese, and others. There is, however, little evidence in the British response to those who resisted them in the eighteenth or early nineteenth centuries to justify such confidence. In 1823, when British humanitarianism is supposed to have been reaching towards its high-water mark, colonists and government responded with a campaign of terror to the Slave Rebellion in Demerara, as indeed they had on every other occasion of West or East Indian insurrection. In the countryside they killed hundreds, often at random, while there is no estimate of the unofficial floggings and torture visited on many times that number, some thirty-three were officially executed, and 'dead bodies in chains and decapitated heads were on poles along the colony's roads'.[17] Those who seek to explain racism in the Second British Empire, as if it was merely a Victorian phenomenon, strangely seem to forget that it was the foundation of the First. Extraordinary violence was at all times part of the colonial repertoire, and no quarter was given to those who got in the way of Britain's interests, and who, at the same time, lacked the power to hold their place. If there was a shift in mid-century, it was a change in 'means' first, and in attitudes after. It was Europe's ability to abuse non-Europeans with relative impunity which underlay the hardening of European racism. As Tacitus noted in another imperial age, *proprium humani ingenii est odisse quem laeseris*, which is to say that it is in the nature of men to hate those whom we hurt. Biology merely provided a new vocabulary with which to express old explanations for dominance, subordination, and violence. We need to explain, then, the circumstances which placed Europeans in a position where they were at risk of becoming violent, and thus of discovering themselves as legitimate tyrants. The answer lies in steam-powered merchants, missionaries, evangelists, warlords and 'improvers', steam-powered ambition and arrogance, steam-powered crises and competition.

The Industrial Revolution had released new and turbulent social forces which campaigns for external national glory appeared uniquely able to appease. As Salisbury proposed in 1869, with respect to the future of the Conservative Party, 'the ruder class of minds would be more sensitive to [the] traditional emotions' associated with pomp and national feeling.[18] British politicians could see how conservative forces had managed nationalism to the benefit of the party of order in Italy, France, and Prussia during the 1860s. With the passage of the Second Reform Bill, the future of Britain's national identity, that Pandora's box which British politicians had conspired to keep shut since the French Revolution, became an open question.[19] That Damascus Road on which the Conservative Party became the pioneer of parliamentary reform, was also the path on which the Disraeli who thought colonies were 'millstones' discovered himself as the imperial populist, and friend of government, of the Crystal Palace.

The rise of government, and its alliance with empire, responded also to external threat. It was Prussian success in the wars of the 1860s which stood directly at the origins of the Devonshire Commission on Scientific Instruction, for example. In education, as in public health, Matthew Arnold and others argued, Britain had much to learn from its Continental neighbours. The migration of the Industrial Revolution to the rest of the world, accompanied as it was, by declining prices, and economic Protection, both damaged British manufacture and awakened the hope for reciprocal action.[20] An imperial *Zollverein*, if not a political federation, seemed increasingly attractive in an era of economic competition from Europe, and in which the United States and Russia threatened British interests in North and South America, Asia, and the Pacific.[21] The cultural manifestations of this late Victorian strategic and economic crisis ranged from rallying essays such as Dilke's *Greater Britain* (1868), Seeley's *Expansion of England* (1883), or Froude's *Oceana* (1886), to societies such as the (Royal) Colonial of 1868, and the Fair Trade and Imperial Federation movements of the 1880s.[22] Its foremost political product was Chamberlain, the veteran of 'gas and water socialism' in Birmingham, who looked to the Crown to advance the health and education of all its citizens, and to lay the infrastructure through which all the resources of Britain and its overseas possessions would be pulled into circulation. Chamberlain and his contemporaries watched with anxiety the commercial and colonial efforts of rivals. Germany, for example, was feared to have applied the best of modern science to its African advantage:

> botanists and experts in forestry have traversed and reported on its forests, geologists on its mineral resources; and the government having obtained the best advice is prepared for an outlay of capital. . . . In Africa little has yet been done by the British Government to take stock of their possessions.[23]

These perceptions awakened activity.

What we see, particularly by the turn of the century, is something which resembles a return of the imperial *dirigisme* of the era of Banks, Pitt, and the Jenkinsons. The pressure of retrenchment and the relative safety and prosperity of Britain after the Napoleonic Wars had led after 1820 to the retreat of the ambitious governmental agenda of the war years. Crises in public health and order did however enable significant initiatives in social and sanitary engineering during and after the 1840s. The scope of bureaucratic government grew partly in response to these pressures, and also as a way of circumventing more significant political concessions to the middle classes. The perception of crisis by the later decades of the century allowed a reopening of the policy agenda. A nervous glance towards European rivals in the aftermath of a blundered imperial war, in the 1900s as in the 1780s, awakened new enthusiasm for professional advice and the expansion of the scope of active government. There were ideological bridges between the two ages: Bentham and Ricardo, themselves products of the Napoleonic War era, also underpinned the political imagination of the age of the Webbs. 'National efficiency', the idea that the material and human resources of the British nation ought to be mobilized and developed, that the state should draw on technical expertise, and that colonies should be more efficiently linked with the 'mother country', was in its outlines a century older.[24] That Enlightenment confidence in the capacities of the Crown to engender progress which had answered to the needs of the 1780s and 1790s was retrieved from the attic of national policy. Continental ideologies played their part in both periods: just as English agrarians borrowed from Cameralists and Physiocrats during the 'imperial meridian', so Utilitarians and T.H. Green and his acolytes took reinforcement from Comte and Hegel.[25]

Yet, at the periphery of British power, active government never depended on this recrudescence of governmental ideology. Enlightened despotism had been built into the administrative structures of British imperialism. If the British state had intervened in Ireland, in both the seventeenth and nineteenth centuries, in ways unparalleled in England, so it had been in India and new colonies that the Crown had acquired an efficiency unlimited by representative government.[26] From Wellesley to Bentinck to Dalhousie, *dirigisme* was entrenched in the traditions of the East India Company, and the death of John Company did not end its influence. The Raj's mark was felt on all the colonial world: it is telling that Governor Grant, with his projects for renovating Jamaica's economy, had come to his post from Bengal. John Stuart Mill, who like his father made his living from governing India, exempted those nations still in 'nonage' from the right to self-determination. This idol of the liberal tradition, with his eye surely on the East, thus felt able to argue, in terms which would have had the sympathy of any contemporary Tsar, that 'Despotism is a legitimate mode of government in dealing with barbarians, provided the end be their improvement.'[27] 'Crown Colony' government, the strange child of racism and humanitarianism, the dominant idiom of empire wherever whites were in a minority, itself allowed almost unlimited power to an enlightened (or tyrannical) executive. It strictly reduced 'native' participation and armed the British imperial administrator with almost total local authority. The colonial governor understood it was his responsibility to engineer social order and economic prosperity within his demesne. It was under this model of despotic paternalism that the British Empire expanded.

In Joseph Chamberlain we may see reconciled the domestic and imperial dimensions of late nineteenth-century *dirigisme.* His political vision was formed by his three years as Mayor of Birmingham in the 1870s, during which he had 'parked, paved, assized, marketed, Gas-and-Watered, and *improved*' the town.[28] His own metal business had, in addition been hurt by foreign competition, and this had made him see both a British *Zollverein,* and the retention of Ireland within the Westminister parliament, as vital to the national interest. But he had also seen Britain's Enlightened Despotism at work in the colonies: in 1889, during his visit to Egypt, he had observed Lord Cromer, planning the improvement of irrigation, agriculture, health, and education of his Mediterranean Raj.[29] By 1895, Chamberlain similarly sought to apply railways, harbours, social and medical reform to pulling the people and resources of West Africa, the West Indies, and all the Crown Colonies into the cycle of capitalist civilization. He would be the most important ally of Thiselton-Dyer and Kew at the end of the century.

Chamberlain's agenda was, of course, somewhat beyond the prevailing orthodoxies of his age. He underestimated the importance of 'invisible' exports to his nation, and ordinary consumers' preference for cheap food over patriotism. But that majority of the decision-makers which held fast to free trade and cheap government, came also to favour forms of intervention. If protective tariffs were unpalatable, the Crown might still assist the 'invisible hand' in the West Indies and West Africa, in particular through applying science and technology. Colonial governments also came to offer social and economic initiatives as a substitute for extending the boundaries of political inclusion. Like the opponents of parliamentary reform in eighteenth- and nineteenth-century Britain, the latter-day proponents of 'virtual representation' in the Crown Colonies offered 'good government' as a substitute for democratic sovereignty.

To recapitulate briefly, in setting the context for the climax of Kew's influence, this chapter has so far offered three theses on 'High Imperialism'. First, that expansion must be understood in terms of the history of bureaucracy, and not merely of economics or strategy or diplomacy. The appetite for, or tolerance of, colonial acquisitions depended on the confidence that new territory and people could successfully be governed. Second, that there was a high tide in bureaucratic confidence in the second half of the nineteenth century, which bore up the domestic and imperial policies of every European nation with it. Thirdly, that the will (or need) to govern, and other social and political causes of 'imperialism' to which it was related, depended on science and technology, and the industrial modes of production, communication, transport, and war they enabled. It was not new European attitudes which propelled empire, rather it was a new capacity for agency beyond Europe which distilled to proof strength older arrogance, prejudice, ambition, and illusion.

But there was continuity between early and late modern imperialism, I am suggesting, at an ideological level. The British Empire of an ageing Victoria depended on an idea of universal 'improvement' constituted proximately in secular terms, in the era of Pitt the Younger and Banks, and ultimately in the sacred and Providential currency of Renaissance Christianity. Earthly power had always discovered itself as necessary relative to Nature and God. What had changed over four centuries were the limits of necessity, and the categories through which it was bounded. But resistant at the centre of all this was the idea that the command of resources was made legitimate by their most efficient use, which I described in earlier chapters as the economics of *Genesis.* Those who best used land.and labour had the right to control both: this argument has endured from the age of Spencer and Ralegh, to those of Locke, Malthus, Mill, Curzon, and ourselves. For the Skinner school, this justification was merely a legacy of Roman Law, part of the cumbersome intellectual inheritance which the moderns, they contend, were calmly willing to inhabit. There may however be more practical and material reasons for the recrudescence of this argument, or at least for why it proved so popular. Taking the view from Olympus, we may see British Imperialism, over the long term, as a campaign to extend an ecological regime: a way of living in Nature. It was premised on the virtues of sedentary agriculture and husbandry, private property, and production for exchange, and ultimately manufacture. There were, of course, eruptions of Romantic doubt, and celebrations of untamed territory and barbarians, throughout its history. But the faith that enclosure was the key to 'improvement', and that cosmopolitan benefit depended on private enrichment, proved more appealing, especially to those favoured enough to sit within the juggernaut. The idea of Adamic prerogative prized the volunteer: the individual who fenced and farmed the wilderness. But the Crown, both incarnated and as fiction, was always a necessary part of the drama, as a mobilizer of collective efforts, force, and legitimacy. The Imperial Prince passed on his baton to proconsuls and bureaucrats, his Providential magic now achieved through scientists and social engineers, men who knew the secrets and destiny of Nature.

Efficient Conquerors and Profligate Natives: Exploitation and Conservation

Science and technology were implicated in many aspects of late nineteenth-century imperialism. The knowledge of nature, applied to navigation and war, enabled conquest. As it enabled mining, forestry, and plantation agriculture, it made such acquisitions profitable. It lent confidence to those who were suddenly thrust into a position of responsibility for vast and strange territories. The promise of future riches, sustained by geology and botany, steam ships and telegraphs, repeating rifles and machine guns, encouraged speculation in regions where diplomacy and capital might once have feared to tread. As such, new imperial means amounted, as in Egypt, to new imperial motives. Science and technology, lastly, provided an identity, they were evidence of the progressive and altruistic virtues of the conquerors.

Scientists derived equal advantages from their participation in the colonial enterprise. Stafford has elegantly shown how Sir Roderick Murchison derived metropolitan advantages from his geological and geographical interventions overseas.[30] Younger and more junior men forged careers as they travelled with the commissions which delimited the political and juridical boundaries of new colonies. Others found colonial appointments as a means of escape from Britain, where, even after the Devonshire Commission and the Endowment for Research Campaign, scientific posts were few, underpaid, and often without prestige.[31] In 1882, for example, to the surprise of Sir Louis Mallet, Kew's nominee for Superintendent of the Government Cinchona Plantations in Madras was Marmaduke Lawson, the Professor of Botany at Oxford.[32] 'I am sick of Oxford,' he explained to Thiselton-Dyer, 'and shall be glad to get away from it.' Lawson complained that after fourteen years, his fight to establish a modern botanical department had got nowhere: 'So far as natural science goes, Oxford has been to me either a hostile or callous stepmother'.[33] Lawson was not alone: his friends Duthie and Trimen had gone to superintend the botanic gardens at Sahranpore in the North-West Provinces and Peredinaya in Ceylon. When technical posts within Britain, as the leader writer in *Nature* complained, were 'scarcely worth a pittance', such a flight to the colonies was understandable.[34] Colonial service also meant often a dramatic change in status: after languishing for eighteen years as an assistant in the Botanical Department of the British Museum, Trimen was catapulted in 1879 to his post in Ceylon, where he was subordinate only to the Governor. If the 'efficiency' of Britain required the scientist, the botanists and chemists had their own reasons to put themselves at the service of empire.

The story of cinchona, the plant which took Lawson from Oxford, is a parable of the relations of mutual benefit struck between science and British empire. As we discussed earlier, the varieties of cinchona brought at great public expense to British colonies were inferior to that acquired by the Dutch in Java from Charles Ledger. As a result, only the Dutch variety sold well on the world market, and while efforts to produce British cinchona continued they were barely commercially viable. By 1890, Jenkin and Phillips, drug brokers on Mincing Lane, advised the Deputy Director of Kew that 'the immediate future for cinchona is not promising'.[35] Thiselton-Dyer admitted to the Colonial Office in 1893 that cinchona cultivation in Jamaica had not been seriously attempted for more than a decade, while in Ceylon, tea had almost entirely replaced 'Peruvian bark'.[36] But if cinchona had failed as an economic crop, it had acquired other political uses.

When the cinchona project was planned in the aftermath of the Indian Mutiny, it was intended solely to produce stocks of quinine for British soldiers, administrators, and merchants in Asia, Africa, and the Caribbean. In 1870 the possibility of producing quinine cheaply and plentifully enough to make it available to the Indian masses was scarcely considered by the government of Bengal.[37] As late as 1875, George King, Superintendent of the Calcutta Botanic Garden, urged his superiors that cinchona's benefits should be extended to reach all the population. At this time in London and Calcutta, the consensus was that too much cinchona was being planted. King reminded his superiors that quinine, because of its high price, was 'almost unobtainable by the mass of the population of India', and that the quantity which the government donated for charitable dispensaries amounted to only a few days' consumption.[38] By 1876, he organized the production of cheap febrifuge in Sikkim, out of crude extracts of cinchona, and its distribution through the Royal Mail's post offices in India in 5-pice packets (about one English farthing). His initiative was quietly appropriated by Clement Markham in his 1880 account, which dared to claim that the health of the Indian people had in fact been the entire reason for the whole expedition.[39] In the 1890s this became a standard India Office position, as the Secretary to the Government of Bengal boasted: 'The Government does not aim at a profit, the sole object in establishing the cinchona plantations being to secure for the people a cheap remedy for fever.'[40] The cinchona scheme, an agronomic failure in any commercial sense, came thus to symbolize the humane mission of British empire. By the same measure, however, it represented the public value of imperial science: 'putting quinine within the reach of the poorest', King promised, was an answer to those who asserted that scientific men were impractical and burdens on government.[41] The truth, unfortunately, was that even that crude and diluted source of quinine was, at 5 pice, too dear for most Indians to use regularly. Forms of quinine were however distributed to plantation workers, soldiers, and administrators throughout Britain's new tropical dominions (see illustration 21). They supported, moreover, Lawson's comfortable billet in Madras.

The complex role of cinchona deserves further analysis in terms of the role of the commodity within the history of imperialism. Commodities, for the political economist, are natural objects exchanged within and between societies. Such objects have a material life: that is they are things with weight, density, colour, smell, flavour, or uses relative to other things. But these things also always have symbolic efficiency: they journey through the world carrying meanings woven around them by the cultures in whose orbit they circulate. For the Christian economic tradition which informed doctrines of free trade, a thing acquired a moral significance once it was available to all of Adam and Eve's heirs. Creation's human and natural riches, scattered to the four corners of the Earth after the Fall, ought to be brought into communication with one another. Or, in a younger idiom, free exchange between the peoples living in every climate might allow cornucopian abundance and

21. The Coolie Dispensary at the Royal Botanic Gardens in Calcutta, with the physician in his white robes, holding up a bottle of quinine, suffering the little children to come unto him.
Royal Botanic Gardens, Kew.

world peace, or at least 'the greatest good to the greatest number'. Commerce, by either the high or the low roads, led surely to cosmopolitan benefit. Modern imperialism, however much it served to prosecute the private interests of elements of powerful nations, always identified itself with this sacred work of expanding the scope of world trade. The natural scientist, as he named the natural riches of new territories, and mapped the uses of the world's things, was allied with this moral project. Botany, by this token, had liberated cinchona from the narrow confines of Andean peoples, and planted it in new soils for the benefit of the whole world. More generally, the Hookers and Thiselton-Dyer, and the naturalists at the frontier whom they directed, came to advise the right uses for plants. The scientists, at many points, mediated how colonized lands and peoples became the commodities of Civilization.

This right to intervene, and to reorder the uses of resources and labour, had long found sanction, as we have noted earlier, in the proposition that knowledge allowed the best use of nature. Reason, premised on the needs of nature and society, had over previous centuries justified the expropriation of the common lands of English, Irish, and Xhosa pastoralists, of Highland crofters, and the aborigines of New England and New South Wales. The idea of scientific agriculture had sustained what we might call a myth of the Profligate Native: that whoever was on the spot was wasting its resources, and that therefore they might legitimately be expelled, or submitted to

European tutelage.[42] In earlier chapters we have examined how this myth recurred in British settlement in seventeenth-century America, and eighteenth-century India.

Its shadow fell too on Victorian Africa, where Gustave Mann, the botanical collector whom Hooker had recommended to Lord John Russell, complained in Fernando Po that 'The island could grow ten times as much palm oil as it does, if the natives would make use of the nuts growing here, but these people have so little necessaries of life.'[43] In Cameroon, in similar vein, he deplored the refusal of Africans to move to European rhythms, and to produce commodities for export:

> Work and the smallpox are two things of which the Africans are especially afraid, and provided with the food and the riches of the soil and mildness of the climate they disregard almost all other requirements which labour might obtain for them and waltz through life as in a dream with their heads wrapped in clouds too deep to receive the instructions given to them. I must say that were it not for the oppressive idleness of the Africans that this place could raise plenty of cacao by cultivation . . . for this place is undoubtedly very suitable for it. . . .[44]

For Mann, the African was morally culpable where she refused to grow plants needed by the world market. (A related note was struck by Mann where he explained depopulation in the Bight of Biafra, to which British slavers had made their own signal contribution, as due to polygamy and the 'promiscuously mixed up' youth.) By the same argument, the propagation of agriculture in Africa was a moral enterprise, as the discipline of labour might uplift Africans from their sloth and depravity. It is for this reason that the *Pall Mall Gazette* argued that 'a competent and capable botanist may do more to open up the country than a dozen mining engineers, for the discovery of a single plant useful to commerce may be of greater value to Africa than many gold mines'.[45] Dusky Adam would redeem Africa when he ploughed its soil for Europe. The British entrepreneur and colonial administrator, advised by botanists, would identify the crop, and teach him how to wield his spade.

No community had the right to deny access to the environment it occupied, if others were better equipped to make use of it. Thus Benjamin Kidd argued in *The Control of the Tropics* (1898), the hot lands 'will never be developed by the natives themselves' and that, as a consequence,

> the right of these races to remain in possession will be recognised; but it will be no part of that recognition that they shall be allowed to prevent the utilization of the immense natural resources which they have in charge.[46]

For Sir Charles Bruce, proconsul *extraordinaire*, Governor, at various times, of British Guiana, the Windward Islands, Mauritius, and Ceylon, 'the very existence of [tropical] colonies as civilised communities required the intervention of capital and science of European origin'.[47] For Kidd, 'our civilisation' was unwilling to tolerate the wasting of the resources of the richest regions of the Earth 'through the lack of the elementary qualities of social efficiency in the races possessing them'. His justification of imperialism was unusual only in its clarity and frankness. It was, in its essence, an old argument, and it endured to the twilight of the colonial order. For J.S. Furnivall in 1948, for example, 'Tropical peoples forfeited their independence because, under the guidance of their native rulers, they were unable to qualify as citizens of the modern world by complying with its requirements.'[48] And we will continue to find versions of this argument recurring so long as temperate peoples need to explain why they interfere with the sovereignty of the middle regions of the world.

The Profligate Native justified the 'conservation' of plants and animals, as well as their exploitation. Concern about the human impact on the environment was, as Richard Grove has shown in *Green Imperialism*, of great antiquity, and was quickened among Europeans in the early modern era by their discovery of their devastating effects on the islands they colonized.[49] By the eighteenth century, fears about how deforestation caused a decline in rainfall and in soil fertility led to the creation of forest preserves in many colonies. For Grove, radical or devout naturalists posted overseas, often with the help of local people, discovered the need to campaign against the mindless destruction of colonial environments. Under the influence of Poivre and Humboldt, he suggests, this brave and enlightened party fought to save the natural order. This argument, particularly its assertion that modern environmentalism stemmed from these peripheral initiatives, is appealing. We must however call into question Grove's opposition of the histories of exploitation and conservation. Conservation, while apparently contradicting the ethic of exploitation, was premised on the same paternalist ideology of command.

Conservation, both within Britain and its colonies, began as Preservation: the claim of an exclusive right of exploitation of a limited natural resource. The Crown claimed game and timber reserves, as aristocrats had long done on their private account.[50] By the seventeenth century, two surveyors had been appointed to adminster His Majesty's woods. From the closing of the Baltic trade with the first Dutch War of 1654, England began to turn to America for naval timber, especially for masts.[51] The 1691 charter of Massachusetts claimed all mast trees for the Royal Navy, and in 1704 royal surveyors marked them with a broad arrow declaring the Crown's right, with a £100 penalty for any felled.[52] Pines, as sources of pitch and turpentine, also found protection in Massachusetts. Conservation was originally just an act of enclosure by the state. It still proceeded on this logic when, from the eighteenth century onwards, it became inflected by faith in a Nature ordered by rational laws, and the idea of cosmopolitan benefit. Whatever contemporary justifications were offered by Physiocrats or Cameralists for forest preserves in the eighteenth century, they appealed ultimately to the Crown's prerogatives and needs, now sanctioned by reason instead of God.

The Crown, as we discussed in earlier chapters, had agreed to become the improving landlord of the nation.

The nineteenth-century claim that resources should be managed, or withdrawn from use, in the interest of everyone, and of Nature itself, only seemed novel. It merely transferred to the state, advised by Science, rights and responsibilities once vested in monarchs. Conservation policies, implemented across the world, particularly from the 1860s onwards, depended on the power and legitimacy which bureaucratic government had acquired by the middle of the century. Imperialism became 'Green' for a reason not examined by Grove: both colonial expansion and environmentalism, in their modern incarnations, depended on the argument that the state might manage nature for both national and cosmopolitan benefit. If the Raj's forest policy marked a signal departure, it depended on the collaboration of scientists like Dietrich Brandes, who argued that teak forests in Burma deserved rational cropping, and officials like Lord Dalhousie, whose memorandum of 1855, at the foundation of the system, asserted the East India Company's right to command all resources.[53] If 'Edenism' and 'Orientalism' explain anything, it is because they provided a language which served contemporary economic and political ends. Exploitation and conservation were the common ends of policy, not alternatives. Sir William Hooker thus wrote that reafforestation in Ascension and St. Helena, perhaps Kew's first direct experiment at environmental intervention, had succeeded because of 'the consequent rapid increase of the fertility, water supply, pasture land, and vegetable produce of the island'. The Victorian friends of Conservation sought to channel the use of colonial environments, and scarcely questioned Europe's right to choose the direction. Wilderness, in the end, was a kind of land use.

Whenever exploitation and conservation came into conflict, the latter usually gave way. If colonial governments began to manage forests in many British colonies, British entrepreneurs, with the support of the state, cleared vast expanses of soil on every continent in order to plant crops valued by the world market. At the same time that 'slash and burn' agriculture was under attack in India, the official pamphlet on cinchona cultivation in the West Indies advised that the plant preferred 'newly cleared forest', that is bush where the trees had been felled and then put to the torch. Even where contemporaries cared about desiccation, as a consequence of deforestation, they usually argued that the new plants introduced would be as good as their predecessors in attracting rain and holding moisture. Clement Markham in 1865 thus noted that while coffee planters in Ceylon cleared everything, with 'No regard whatever ... paid to forest conservancy, belts of verdure are neither left along the water-courses nor on the hill-tops', yet there had been no diminution of the water supply. In a report on cinchona in Madras, also from 1865, Markham struck the same anti-desiccationist note, arguing that a plantation was even better for the water balance than the 'original jungle', as the 'beautiful foliage [of the cinchona trees] will be even more effectual in wringing moisture out of the passing clouds'. This view, that land, if used rather than left as 'waste', might serve the best ends of both Man and Nature, is rarely contradicted in the archives.

By the middle of the century, however, the myth of the Profligate Native now embraced conservation, and seizing natural resources now found justification in the danger of their overuse by exotic peoples. The Dutch, British, and French, for example, explained their collection of cinchona in the Andes, over the objections of South American nations, in terms of how the people on the spot were driving the tree out of existence. The same argument supported the illegal export of Brazilian rubber seeds, via Kew, to British colonies in East Asia. The threat of a world rubber shortage, construed as an environmental problem, made state intervention appear imperative wherever plants yielded latex. India-rubber gatherers in Central America, *The Globe* warned in 1884, were destroying the supply of *Castilloa elastica*, and that 'unless the natives can be prevented from destroying the trees, only one result can attend this Gladstonian activity'.[54] Similar anxieties surfaced about rubber in East Africa that 'through the ignorance and greed of the natives, the source of supply may become annihilated' (see illustration 22).[55] Complaints that 'natives', on another continent, would drive the tree which yielded gutta-percha into extinction, arose too in the 1880s and 1890s. A colonial resident wrote, 'the Malays, who now take out licences in that state to collect gutta-percha obtain it by cutting down immature trees no thicker

22. Burning down 'bush' in the Gold Coast to facilitate the extraction of Funtumia elastica *(1890s).* Royal Commonwealth Society.

23. Kayas collecting gutta-percha in Sarawak (1900). Royal Commonwealth Society.

than a man's wrist'.[56] The solution to these depradations, wrought by those who responded with too much vigour to the itch of the 'invisible hand', was state control, guided by scientists. The Forest Departments of the Raj, for example; acquired sovereign rights to control access to India's forests. This solution was implemented across the British Empire.

Conservation found easy sponsorship wherever the interests of Nature most nakedly coincided with those of the nation. The preservation of naval timber in the age of Evelyn had its immediate equivalent in that of Chamberlain. Gutta-percha had by then become a strategic commodity. Submarine telegraphy was vital to European economic, diplomatic, administrative, and military communication by the end of the nineteenth century.[57] Concern about 'native' depradations in the forests of the Malay Peninsula, Sumatra, and Borneo was inspired by economics and strategy before ecology (see illustration 23). In 1891 merchants had proclaimed a 'gutta-percha famine' and the *India Rubber and Gutta-Percha and Electrical Trades Journal* warned that 'Submarine telegraphy is menaced', noting that the plan to lay cable to Algeria from France had collapsed because of the shortage.[58] In that year, the French government announced that it would create gutta plantations in Indochina, while Thiselton-Dyer urged the Colonial Office to promote more sustainable extraction in South-East Asia.[59] By 1898, after telegraphy had demonstrated its value at Fashoda, Thiselton-Dyer suggested that Britain secure its supplies of gutta through plantations in the Malay Peninsula and New Guinea.[60] But the Resident of Penang advised that since the tree which yielded gutta-percha took thirty years to attain a girth of three feet, it paid 'no company and private individual to cultivate it'.[61] By December 1899, Thiselton-Dyer therefore argued to Chamberlain that the Crown had to assume control of the gutta forests in the Malay Peninsula, reminding him that without the plant London would have no means of communicating with the front in a future South African war.[62] 'The only mode in which this can be arrested is to demand definite areas of forest, & close them to collectors'; this, he advised 'is what would be done under similar circumstances in India'.[63]

The trans-imperial campaign to save resources from overexploitation by indigenous people never directed its fire at the European buyers of tropical commodities. In August 1904, the editor of *The India Rubber and Gutta-Percha and Electrical Trades Journal* complained that 'Islands such as Mindanao and Tavi Tavi cannot stand this for any length of time, and already the gutta-percha trees have entirely disappeared from the vicinity of the coast regions' due to the activity of locals. But where had the gutta-percha extracted gone, except to the subscribers of his journal? Similarly we see Dyer in 1877 demanding forest control in Jamaica to prevent the extinction of *Pimenta acris* while complaining 'The negroes are cutting down all the young Black cinnamon trees, wherever they can get them, to secure the leaves', but suggested no similar sanctions against the Bay Rum manufacturers who demanded the fragrant leaves.[64] Conservation, for many Victorians, clearly was the task of saving environments from those who lived in them. It was, in the end, another justification for expanding the power of the state and the technocrat.

By 1900, the administration of conservation had become a new reason for public support of Kew, as a journalist wrote:

> one melancholy proof of the necessity to our colonies of such a botanical centre as Kew . . . is seen in looking at the once flourishing countries which supported the great nations of antiquity. Persia, Palestine, Asia Minor, Greece, North Africa, Cyprus, have all been changed through man's ignorance and improvidence. . . . Under the guidance of Kew this is impossible in modern days.[65]

Imperial power, advised by science, would decide how nature was exploited, to the benefit, putatively, of everyone. Intertwined with the practical functions of botanic gardens and forest reserves was responsibility for demonstrating that convergence between Europe's special prerogatives and the needs of Nature. The men of science at Kew were uniquely prepared for this task at the end of the nineteenth century.

William Thiselton-Dyer: The 'New Botany' and Colonial Agriculture

The individual most responsible for the 'High Imperial' phase of the history of Kew was William Turner Thiselton-Dyer, Assistant Director from 1875 and Director after 1885. His appointment was itself a product of the era in which imperial service formed the centre of Kew's work. In October 1874, a mere few months into the new Tory administration, Joseph Hooker applied to the Board of Works for the appointment of 'a Secretary', noting that it was Kew's new overseas responsibilities which principally justified the cost of this post:

> the duties which have most increased upon me are the making official and semiofficial reports, called for by the Secretary of State for the Colonies, for India & other departments at home, & by the local governments abroad, upon the introduction, culture, diseases, [of crops] ... I am in constant communication with the aforesaid public officers, [and] with Governors of colonies.[66]

Hooker noted that such duties 'must increase with the extension of our Foreign and Colonial possessions', since Kew had become in all matters relating to the vegetable world, 'the official referee and servant of every department of the British Government at home and abroad'. In other communications he listed his recent work with coffee diseases in Ceylon, the introduction of Liberian coffee to Jamaica, cinchona to St. Helena, and the foundation of a botanical garden for the Straits Settlements. Hooker argued that a person of acquirements similar to his own should be recruited 'so that in the event of death or accident' the country would not be deprived of this botanical and agronomic expertise. He nominated Professor William Thiselton-Dyer of the Horticultural Society as a suitable candidate.[67] While the Board of Works responded without enthusiasm, once the matter reached the Treasury, Sir Stafford Northcote and W.H. Smith quickly gave their assent.[68] Finally, in March 1875, through his Private Secretary, Disraeli took the trouble to consult Hooker over the appointment of Thiselton-Dyer.[69]

Long before Thiselton-Dyer inherited Hooker's throne, he had effectively been Director of Kew. For Hooker had often been an absentee master during the last ten years of his administration, serving as President of the Royal Society between 1873 and 1878, journeying to Europe, North Africa, and in the American West (illustration 24), and concentrating on taxonomy while at home.[70] Hooker had happily delegated his powers and burdens to the young man. As Dyer reflected,

> [Joseph Hooker] was not happy in his life at Kew and as an administrator he was not a success, he had no illusions about it and continually fretted; he took no interest in its work except the Arboretum. He only really enjoyed life at that time in foreign travel.[71]

In 1876, busy in London, Hooker wrote apologetically, 'I hope you do not think that I am never more to appear at Kew.'[72] Thiselton-Dyer, on the other

24. Sir Joseph Hooker on a scientific expedition to the American West (1877).
Royal Botanic Gardens, Kew.

hand, was a brilliant and enthusiastic administrator. As Hooker noted in 1880, when he thanked Dyer for liberating him for the *Genera Plantarum* & *Flora of British India*, 'I cannot too highly appreciate your zeal & the astonishing amount of work you have gone through & the energy you are prepared to throw into it.'[73] At his retirement in 1885, he thanked Thiselton-Dyer as the person most responsible for making Kew into 'the most satisfactory, useful, & popular scientific department of government'.[74] It is to the younger man that we must turn to understand how Kew reached the zenith of its influence.

Born exactly a century after Sir Joseph Banks, Thiselton-Dyer enjoyed a career that was the product of a different age of middle-class opportunity, of sciences in the university, and of Darwinism in biology.[75] Unlike Sir William Hooker or Brown, he never depended on the patronage of amateurs, while unlike Joseph Hooker or Huxley he did not need to go abroad on an Admiralty mission of exploration to establish his reputation. Educated at a grammar school, he went briefly to King's College in London, but left with a scholarship at Christ Church to read mathematics at Oxford, changing to the new natural sciences honours school in which he took 1st class honours in 1867. In 1868 he was appointed Professor of Natural History at the Royal Agricultural College in Cirencester, leaving in 1870 for the Royal College of Science in Dublin, returning to London in 1872 to serve as Professor at the Royal Horticultural Society. While in Dublin, Thiselton-Dyer came into correspondence with Joseph Hooker, and undertook to prepare the *Flora*

Capensis which remained unfinished when Harvey died in 1866.[76] In 1872, also, Joseph Hooker employed him, out of his own pocket, as a personal secretary to help, four mornings each week, with correspondence, cataloguing, and the *Genera Plantarum.*[77] While there he fell in love with Harriet Hooker, Joseph's daughter, whom he married in 1877 (illustration 25). Thiselton-Dyer thus became connected to Kew at the climax of the Ayrton–Hooker *contretemps.* Hooker shared with his son-in-law how he and his father had struggled with their civil service masters, for whom economy was everything:

> I am more accustomed to the delays, disappointments, that attend all Govt. work under indifferent masters than you are. I had plenty of it in the Navy & in the fourteen years of my Directorship. I had the same fights about alterations, & repairs, the same struggles to get new buildings additions & above all to increase staff for the Gardens, Herbarium & Library.[78]

It was not surprising either that Thiselton-Dyer was shrewd and tough in his dealings with politicians, or that he learnt, from the older generation of Huxley and Tyndall, how to engage the sciences with the public interest.

25. William Turner Thiselton-Dyer and Harriet Hooker, daughter of Sir Joseph Hooker.
Royal Botanic Garden, Kew.

It is likely that Thiselton-Dyer, like his professional elders, began to gravitate towards the Tories in the 1870s. What is certain is that he, with Hooker and the 'X Club', was the target of a fierce attack in the Liberal press in 1877. In that year, Joseph Hooker accepted knighthood under the Star of India on the Conservatives' nomination, and Thiselton-Dyer, appointed Assistant Director a year before, married his daughter. This conjunction of events was woven into a diatribe against 'the Royal Society clique' which, with Conservative help, had made bureaucratic government serve their professional ends:

> Since the Conservatives came into power, Whitehall has become a veritable 'Tom Tiddler's Ground' for the needier and greedier class of scientific or pseudoscientific office seekers. . . . No sooner were the Conservatives well seated in power than the Director in Question declared his duties so onerous as to necessitate the services of a sub- or Assistant Director. . . .
>
> Contrary to the recommendation of the Civil Service Commissioners and every principle of common sense and justice, a young and untried man was appointed to the lucrative office. . . . The rationale of this very suitable appointment, was not, however left long in doubt, the Assistant-Director soon after became son-in-law to the Director. . . .
>
> . . . The Universities have poured out a swarm of youths who have made a trade of science, and who must find something to do.
>
> . . . the efforts to sweep all public grants and patronage into one net become more and more shameless. The Physical Laboratory, the Science Commission, the Instruments Exhibition, the Physiography Chair, the worst parts of the *Challenger* Expedition, the 'scientific grant', ... the appointment of an Assistant-Director to assist a Director who was not required. . . . When an office cannot be immediately got by the clique for their protégés or tools, they are sent off on expeditions. . . . Finally , to provide employment for anyone too ignorant to be sent as a naturalist or an astronomer, or whose want of mathematics prevents him being made an Observatory Director, a new examinership or chair is provided. Or if all methods fail, then a well-paid Royal Commission to inquire into something or the other is by much importunity got out of the Government, and the impecunious hanger-on made the salaried secretary of it.[79]

This assault, which probably had been guided from South Kensington by the bitter Richard Owen, illustrated in silhouette what Huxley, Tyndall, and their allies had achieved. While Disraeli, Derby, and Salisbury attempted to realize a Conservative style of wise and efficient administration, the leaders of 'public science' had presented their disciplines as appropriate objects of state patronage. As a result, Thiselton-Dyer's generation indeed enjoyed new professional responsibilities.

The colonies and India were particular objects of attention for Disraeli's administration. The new Assistant Director shrewdly began to use this obsession to secure his and Hooker's ends. Kew's work overseas, in particular, came to justify, as it had during the Ayrton–Hooker crisis, why its grounds had to serve scientific research first, and public recreation only second. In 1877, residents of Richmond and Kew began to pressure Hooker to open the gardens before 1 p.m. His response, which reads as having come from Thiselton-Dyer's pen, was telling: 'This agitation ... appears to me to proceed upon a mistaken apprehension of the scope and objects of the Royal Garden as an imperial and not local institution.'[80] Since Kew was now 'the botanical headquarters of the British Empire and its dependencies ... [and was never intended to be] a local or even metropolitan place of recreation', its Director felt justified in refusing to yield to the popular demand. In a private letter, Hooker gave fuller expression to his motivations: 'If we open the gardens in the forenoon, Kew will attract all the excursionists who now go to Richmond, Bushy, & Hampton Court ... & we shall be swamped with a clutch of visitors who care nothing for the instruction offered by the plants.'[81] Imperial service was thus the means through which the domestic boundaries of the scientific empire of Kew were secured.

In 1881 similar arguments secured salary increases for Kew's administrators. Sir Joseph, in prose redolent of his Assistant Director, argued that the labours of the Director of Kew had been 'indefinitely augmented' since 1875 by a variety of imperial responsibilities:

> 1. The delegation to him of the chief duties of the 'Reporter on Vegetable Products to the Secretary of State for India', together with the vast collection in the India Museum ...
> 2. By the rapid development of India and Colonial Gardens, Experimental Farms, Plantations, Forest Reserves etc. in respect of all of which the Director of Kew is expected to take an active interest. . . . He makes all appointments to them, selecting them chiefly from the élèves of Kew, & he corresponds directly with the Governors of almost every British Colony ... the appointments made within the last ten years under this head, by the Director of Kew & on his sole responsibility represent an expenditure in salaries of probably not less than £50,000 annually.[82]

Kew had become 'the botanical centre of the world, and literally carries on all the Economic and Scientific work of the Empire under the direction of various departments of state'. The Board of Works should therefore increase the salaries of the Director, his Assistant Director, the Keeper of Kew Herbarium, and should provide for more clerical support.[83] Thiselton-Dyer, whether he drafted the original document or not, could still notice that the tight fists of Gladstone's Treasury yielded, and in a few months his own stipend had risen to £1,200 per annum.[84] Two historical essays from Thiselton-Dyer's pen suggest too that the example of Banks and 'the efforts made nearly 100 years ago to improve the circumstances of our Colonial Possessions' had provided their own stimulus.[85]

If the benefits of imperial service were clear to Thiselton-Dyer, it is also true that he had more to offer to empire than the Hookers. Both William and Joseph were brilliant herbarium botanists, but neither had the physiological interests that might have equipped them to assist agriculture. Until the 1860s there was no teaching of laboratory botany to students anywhere in Britain.[86] Even then, as F. O. Bower remembered, 'Collecting, classifying, and recording were the order of the day, while anatomy, physiology, and the study of the complete lifecycle, especially in the lower forms, was wholly neglected.'[87] Sir William Hooker and Dawson Turner were exceptions among their contemporaries as students of fungi, algae, mosses, and ferns, but even their work was confined to describing dried specimens. That the angiosperms received almost all serious attention was in part a consequence of the dependence of botany on those who were primarily interested in showy flowers. As William Hooker had suggested in the *Encyclopaedia of Geography* of 1834, the cryptogams failed to excite 'general interest'.[88] Joseph Hooker was not unsympathetic to their students, and indeed preferred Michael Berkeley, a pioneering student of fungi, over C.C. Babington, for the chair of Botany at Cambridge in 1861.[89] Babington however won the chair, and it was from Germany rather than the fens that the winds of change came. In 1851 Hofmeister made the epochal announcement that there was a life cycle common to all land vegetation involving two phases: one spore-bearing (asexually reproducing) generation alternating with one gamete-bearing (sexually reproducing) generation.[90] Bower in his memoirs referred to the world of difference the English Channel then made: 'While official botany at Cambridge had been splitting analytically the varieties of *Rubus*, the laboratory of Hofmeister ... was glowing with a new synthetic flame and a true comparative morphology had begun.'[91] With Hofmeister, the reproduction and embryology of the lower plants became interesting to all botanists, as through the cryptogams botanists might perhaps discover that habit of reproduction which unified all plants.[92] While with the *Genera Plantarum*, Joseph Hooker led British botany further into the traditional taxonomic work of the discipline, German universities attracted botanists from around the world with their histological microscopy, the study of life cycles, physiology, heredity, and pathology.[93]

Thiselton-Dyer was part of a generation excited by the 'New Botany', which they met through the 1862 translation of Hofmeister's *Higher Cryptogamia*.[94] His first post was moreover at the Royal Agricultural College: in Britain, as in the United States, students of agriculture were those most quick to take an interest in Darwin, laboratory biology, plant pathology, genetics, and breeding.[95] Rothamsted, rather than London or Oxbridge, was the centre of plant physiology in Britain before 1870: John Lawes and Henry Gilbert over their fifty-year partnership issued some 132 papers, making seminal contributions to the study of subjects as diverse as the nitrogen cycle, carbohydrate metabolism, the design and practice of field experiments, and field technique.[96] Thiselton-Dyer's first book, *How Crops Grow*, was an excursion into botanical physiology along the practical lines set by

Rothamsted.[97] When he returned to London in 1872, Thiselton-Dyer became the most important British evangelist for the 'New Botany'. When T.H. Huxley fell sick in 1873, it was Dyer who took charge of the lectures at the newly opened Normal School of Science and initiated a special course in experimental botany, including evolutionary theory, comparative morphology, and extensive practical laboratory study. The remarkable impact of Thiselton-Dyer as a teacher at the Normal School was clear in the case of Marmaduke Lawson, the Professor of Botany at Oxford who came to South Kensington in the summer of 1873: during the previous term, Lawson had lectured only on structural, systematic, and economic botany, but after Thiselton-Dyer he preferred to offer instead the comparative anatomy of cryptogams and plant physiology.[98] In 1875 and 1876, Thiselton-Dyer's demonstrators at South Kensington were Marshall Ward, later considered the father of plant pathology in Britain, and S.H. Vines. Thiselton-Dyer supervised the translation of Julius von Sachs's *Lehrbuch* into English in 1875, presenting to his contemporaries the cutting edge of German research.[99] As Walter J. Farlow, pioneer of the 'New Botany' at Harvard, noted in 1913, no other book had a greater influence in shaping the course of modern botany.[100] Combining new laboratory skills with acumen in herbarium taxonomy, and real gifts as a teacher, lecturer, and administrator, Thiselton-Dyer, by the 1870s, was the pre-eminent botanist of his generation in Britain.[101]

The Devonshire Commission had questioned Hooker in June 1872 about the state of experimental enquiry at Kew. Joseph Hooker responded that there was little of it at Kew, partly because there were no facilities for it, but also because there was little public remuneration to support and encourage researchers.[102] In its Fourth Report, the Royal Commission had urged that 'it is highly desirable that opportunites for the pursuit of investigations in Physiological Botany should be afforded at Kew to those persons who may be inclined to follow that branch of science.'[103] By November 1874, Sir Phillip Jodrell wrote Hooker offering to undertake to support the cost of such a laboratory, but only if the government agreed to build an improved fireproof herbarium and library.[104] Joseph Hooker succeded in persuading the Board of Works that it should accept Jodrell's offer since 'the Jardin des Plantes & the Principal German gardens all had their laboratories'.[105] By October of the next year construction began on the Jodrell Laboratory, the first botanical laboratory in the United Kingdom.

Hooker wrote Darwin in December 1874 advising him, with enthusiasm, of Jodrell's offer, and suggesting the new facilities could house the research of George Romanes.[106] But neither he nor Huxley understood all the implications of the 'New Botany', and despaired of physiology giving Thiselton-Dyer the career he deserved. Instead Huxley felt in early 1875 that Thiselton-Dyer should follow the Hooker path through taxonomy to administration:

> So far as the selection of line of life goes, it is clear to me that he has come to the crossroads; and that he must make up his mind whether he is going to take the turn that leads to Kew (& systematic and distributional Botany) or the other turn that leads to morphology and physiology and God knows where ... I have told him that I think he ought to take the Kew turn ... and go along that road without looking back.[107]

Thiselton-Dyer, after this, began to retreat from the laboratory. But his encouragement of research at the Jodrell meant that already by 1880 if someone had alluded to 'the Kew turn' they might have meant experimental research as much as immersion in the herbarium.[108] The Jodrell provided a home for young British botanists when they returned after study at the feet of Julius von Sachs at Wurzburg or Anton de Bary at Strasbourg.[109]

The 'New Botany' made Kew newly able in the 1870s to affect the imperial economy. Botany which concerned living plants in specific environments had much more to give to agriculture than herbarium work, as would first become clear with plant pathology, and then with genetics. Since plant diseases are often fungal in origin, cryptogamists held the key to fighting some of the main enemies of imperial agriculture. Marshall Ward, for example, a student of de Bary, and protégé of Thiselton-Dyer, identified the fungus, *Hemileia vastatrix*, which had ravaged the coffee crop in Ceylon, and his work was extended by Abbay at the Jodrell.[110] John Harrison, one of the founders of sugar cane breeding, was a former scholar in natural science at Christ's College Cambridge, where his tutor was the 'New Botanist' and South Kensington élève Sydney Vines, and had also studied at Rothamsted.[111] The insights and concerns of the 'New Botany' drove Harrison at his Caribbean post to search for the improvement of yields through fertilizers, and of heredity through breeding.[112] John Willis, a former student of Marshall Ward and Senior Assistant to F.O. Bower at Glasgow, prepared while Superintendent of the Ceylon Botanic Garden the first major study on tropical agriculture.[113] By their training, Thiselton-Dyer, Ward, Harrison, and Willis were better equipped to answer the practical problems of colonial agriculture than any preceding botanical generation. An examination of the publications done based on work at the Jodrell Laboratory at Kew reveals how the new techniques and concerns shed light on many questions of relevance to the imperial economy.[114]

At the same time, many 'New Botanists' were concerned with the adaptation of plants to specific local environments, and had scientific reasons to wish to be posted on the imperial periphery.[115] If herbarium work, by its comparative nature, depended on the large central accumulation of research material, many kinds of physiological questions, on the other hand, could only be examined in the living plant community. If the first German generation of the 1850s and 1860s was content to remain in universities, the 'New Botanists' of the 1870s onwards, in Cittadino's phrase, took 'nature as the laboratory'. In his essay on 'The Needs of Biology', Thiselton-Dyer argued that his science required local research stations at the periphery of European power:

> The various forms of life have been diligently collected and labelled ... [but] the more important and vastly more arduous detailed investigation of the individual forms themselves has to be seriously prosecuted. And this ... requires access to the organisms in a living state. ... At the present moment the needs of this kind of investigation comprise two distinct things. First, persons should be sent, not to collect but to reside and study in foreign countries – such as our colonies. ... Or, what would be a better plan, 'stations' might be maintained at a few suitable positions in foreign countries.[116]

Colonial work now meant an opportunity to reach to the frontier of the discipline. So while 'New Imperialist' politicians and administrators were unusually open to scientific advice, 'New Botanists' had their own 'internal' intellectual and professional reasons to oblige.

This 'local' inclination of the revolution in botany was encouraged by a parallel transformation in agricultural science. The source of that upheaval was the United States: in the midst of the Civil War, Congress in 1862 established the United States Department of Agriculture, and passed the Homestead Act and the Morrill Act which founded the land-grant colleges.[117] Science joined to agriculture was intended to serve political ends: the Homestead Act would create a class of American 'yeomen' which, with the help of the Department of Agriculture and the new universities, and armed with Liebig's fertilizers, would carry liberty and civility to the West.[118] After the War, the new colleges became pioneers in 'agricultural extension'. Through many small outposts at the frontier, the Americans argued, seeds and skills might be diffused, and techniques best suited to local soils and climates implemented. The Hatch Act of 1886 provided a solid basis of Federal support for the expansion of the system. The American example inspired all of Europe, as agricultural scientists began to argue that local 'stations' were needed to complement experimental centres such as Rothamsted.

It was in the Dutch colony of Java that the 'New Botany' and the new agriculture first found a common imperial expression. During the short British conquest of Java at the end of the Napoleonic Wars, Raffles had founded the botanic garden of Buitenzorg. The Dutch Governors of Java had continued his patronage, developing it into a colonial botanic garden as fine as its British equivalent in Calcutta.[119] But it became something quite new after 1870, when R.H.C.C. Scheffer and later Melchior Treub became its Directors. By 1876, Scheffer founded, as annexes to Buitenzorg, the Tijikeumeuh Agricultural Experiment Station with an attached agricultural school to train Javanese in cultivating new crops.[120] After 1880, Treub established small stations for research and 'extension' relative to sugar-cane, coffee, and cinchona.[121] At the same time, Treub made Buitenzorg into a centre of 'pure' 'New Botanical' research into tropical plants, establishing a laboratory which drew scientific visitors, particularly from German laboratories.[122]

After 1880, Thiselton-Dyer clearly wished to imitate the pure research and the extension work conducted around Buitenzorg. What the Dutch were doing in their East Indian colonies—with a large central garden and several smaller local stations—why could the British not also do in South Asia, the West Indies, and West Africa? The concerns of the 'New Botany', the methods of agricultural extension, and the needs of the New Imperialism, together pushed Thiselton-Dyer to reorder the British system of colonial botanic gardens. He presented his vision in a lecture to the Royal Colonial Society in 1880, in which he promised that Kew would serve colonial administrations at every periphery of British power.[123] One can quite understand why Thiselton-Dyer refused in 1883 to stand for the Professorship of Botany at Oxford, even though a letter signed by nineteen senior figures urged him to do so.[124] On the one hand he had just rescued Lawson from the discomfort of a scientific chair in an ancient university, on the other, there was far more important work to do from Kew.

Economic Botany and 'Free-Trade' Empire, 1876–95

'Free trade' remained economic orthodoxy throughout the last decades of the century, despite the murmurs of Chamberlain and others. This should not surprise given Britain's stake, as financial superpower, in the capacity of peripheral economies to maintain their flow of interest payments to the City of London.[125] The Treasury and the Colonial Office were usually allergic towards applying tariffs to benefit colonial economies. It was however entirely acceptable for administrators to apply the Crown's powers to the development of new industries and the better exploitation of resources.

Kew became a crucial clearing-house for scientific advice on such economic questions, and in 1887, Thiselton-Dyer founded the *Bulletin of Miscellaneous Information* (known as the *Kew Bulletin*) primarily to disseminate agricultural and commercial information. In 1876, for example, the Governor of Labuan decided to create a new industry by introducing the oil palm to Borneo from West Africa. Thiselton-Dyer thus placed him in contact with the appropriate Gold Coast officials and Liverpool merchants.[126] In the 1880s, when in the wake of the Report of the Famine Commissioners the search was on for new staples which might be introduced for India, Kew urged the Foreign Office to obtain a staple cereal of Abyssinia, and advised in the *Kew Bulletin* how the seed might be 'advantageously introduced to certain hill stations in India.'[127] Thiselton-Dyer's correspondence connected colonial governors and entrepreneurs in the colonies to manufacturers and commodity brokers at home. The Sierra Leone Coaling Company in 1890, for example, wrote Kew offering a small sample of fibre which it thought might be 'suitable for rope-making' and asking his advice on its commercial value.[128] The West African fibre, like the bowstring hemp received from the Royal Niger Company in the same year, went to the Death Fibre Company of Leadenhall Street, London, who provided a valuation.[129] The African Lakes Corporation of Glasgow similarly turned to Kew to request slips of a variety of rubber the Germans were cultivating in the Cameroon.[130] The reputation of Kew, and the reach of Thiselton-Dyer's influence, were founded on this type of exchange of information. What is worth bearing in mind is that Kew, by virtue of its metropolitan stature, was able to lay claim to any successes achieved in colonies by entrepreneurs or local botanists. Locals were, however, allowed to keep their failures as their own.

How the co-operation of botanists and colonial officials produced prosperity, and professional benefits for each other, became clear with rubber. The demand for rubber, a raw material with hundreds of uses, had rapidly increased in the second half of the nineteenth century: imports into Britain rose from £300,000 in 1854 to £1,300,000 in 1874.[131] All of this rubber came from Amazonian Brazil and Peru, and represented a drain on British foreign reserves. By the mid 1870s, Joseph Hooker and Clement Markham had devised a project on the model of the cinchona scheme to transfer rubber from South America to the East to the profit both of Britain and themselves.[132] With the assistance of Henry Wickham and the British Consul in Brazil, and of the superintendents of colonial botanic gardens—in particular Thwaites in Ceylon and Ridley in Singapore—rubber reached plantations in British Asia. By 1893, Hecht, Levi, & Kahn, rubber brokers in Mincing Lane, London, pronounced a sample of Para rubber produced in Ceylon as 'saleable in large quantities'.[133] But it was not until early in the next century, when almost 100,000 acres of Malayan territory was planted with *Hevea brasiliensis*, that the enormous success of this scheme became obvious.[134] More immediately, however, British colonial governors in Africa discovered indigenous rubber-bearing plants which overnight turned jungle into a source of huge profits. Sir John Kirk, who had travelled with Livingstone while serving as Political Administrator for the Foreign Office in Zanzibar, sent to Kew a valuable Zambezi latex source, *Funtumia elastica*.[135] Sir Alfred Moloney, who had taken a course at Kew, similarly discovered a rubber-bearing species, *Landolphia owariensis*, on the Gold Coast, which by 1893 had already yielded exports worth hundreds of thousands of pounds sterling.[136] In British Guiana, the keeper of the colonial museum helped to uncover a variety of hard and soft rubbers, such as *Forsteronia gracilis*, which the Silverton India Rubber, Gutta-Percha and Telegraph Works pronounced as valuable.[137]

Other economic crops provided similar successes. On the suggestion of Thwaites, the Director of the Botanic Garden, tea was introduced into Ceylon: in 1873, only 23 pounds were exported, but by 1895 Ceylon sent 74 million pounds, representing about 40% of the tea consumed by Britain. In 1883, Thiselton-Dyer urged the India Office to promote kapok as a crop 'of possible interest to Indian commerce'.[138] Kapok (*Eriodendron anfractuosum*) was a tropical tree, which produced seeds (which themselves yielded oil) wrapped in a wool which was water-repellent and insect-proof, and which resisted steam sterilization longer than sheep's hair.[139] By 1896, the cultivation of kapok was said to be 'ousting coffee' in Burma.[140] Kew also stood as entrepôt for the transfer of New World cacao plants from Trinidad to the Gold Coast, where from the 1880s, as I shall discuss below, they became the basis of a new peasant industry and a valuable export.

These transfers of economic crops not only benefited Kew directly, as the botanists received credit for whatever succeeded, but indirectly, because fungi and other plant pathogens were transported with the crops. By 1870 epidemics of plant diseases had begun in the major tropical centres of European economic botany, such as Ceylon, Java, Jamaica, and Trinidad, from which they diffused outwards.[141] Sugar-cane disease hit Queensland, Malaya, and Mauritius by 1877, and again in 1888.[142] In 1879 Pernambuco reported that the 'Sickness of sugar cane which makes awfull [sic] progress in our richest districts'.[143] The *Fiji Times* in 1889 warned 'the coffee disease is spreading far and wide,' while the *Louisiana Planter and Sugar Manufacturer* discussed the ravages of 'Sereh Disease' in East Indian sugar-cane and 'Red Rot' in the West Indies.[144] Many colonial planters privately suspected what the *Ceylon Observer*, with respect to a new pest of tea, said publicly: 'There is no doubt that this pest was introduced into the Botanical Gardens on imported plants – whether from Kew, or some other country remains an open question. . . . All our most serious insect pests are imported ones.'[145] But these diseases spread by eager imperial technocrats simply created more positions for botanists.

In 1877, Thiselton-Dyer nominated Daniel Morris for the post of Assistant-Director of the Botanic Garden of Ceylon. Morris was another protégé of Thiselton-Dyer: a former university gold medallist in the natural sciences course at Trinity College, Dublin, and a star pupil of the botany school at South Kensington. In Ceylon Morris brought his experimental expertise to bear on coffee-leaf disease, and introduced from Kew disease-resistant varieties of Liberian coffee.[146] His departure in 1879 to direct the Botanical Department of Jamaica caused Ceylon planters to comment on the advantages of the 'New Botany' over the old: 'Mr. Morris has been in this country over a year, Dr. Thwaites more than thirty: who has told us most about leaf disease?'[147] The Chamber of Commerce in Colombo demanded the appointment of a mycologist to help them fight the disease.[148] In the same way, from the West Indies to the United Provinces in India, mycologists became employees of every colonial government.[149]

But it was for their positive economic assistance that the botanists became most in demand. The depression which struck the world economy in the 1880s bit with particular force in the primary product export economies of the colonies. In the territories of the Royal Niger Company, for example, the palm oil trade had collapsed in the middle of the decade. Economic botany offered a means of discovering new industries as profitable as rubber had become in the Gold Coast. The report of the Royal Niger Company for 1888 began by thanking Thiselton-Dyer and Kew for their assistance, while explaining that in the context of the 'heavy political burdens thrust upon the Company by "The Scramble for Africa"'and the decline in value of palm oil by almost 50% in four years, the only hope for an improvement in the dividends paid by the company lay 'in the discovery and purchase of new products in their Central African districts'.[150] The Imperial British East Africa Company in 1890 similarly asked for Kew's help in its experiments with 'tea, tobacco, cocoa, rice, jute'.[151] 'From the very first', Sir Harry Johnson wrote from British Central Africa in 1894, 'we have realised the importance of a Botanical Garden and of a scientific staff.'[152] Much as the fiscal crisis of the East India Company, a century before, had galvanized the search by naturalists for new trade goods, so the chartered companies, and the administrators who came in their wake, looked to botany for help in turning their new power into revenue.

Economic botany in the 1880s, again as in the 1780s, found application to the West Indian sugar economy. A century earlier the planters had sought mercantile liberty to buy food from the newly independent United States, now they wanted protection for their sugar. The French, the Austrians, and the Germans were flooding the world market with bounty-supported beet sugar. In the early 1880s alone, Germany's exports of beet sugar doubled.[153] By 1884, the world sugar price had fallen by 30%.[154] At the same time, the United States was pressing the British West Indian colonies to enter into a reciprocal tariff regime. The planters thus began to urge London either to match the German subsidy, or to allow them to establish preferential arrangements with the United States. The Colonial Office responded that such arrangements 'would be at variance with the general commercial policy of Great Britain'.[155] In this context, colonial governments sought help from Kew, both relative to alternative crops, and for assisting sugar. The Board of Trade wrote Hooker, asking him to collect information on cinchona cultivation in Java for the West India Committee: 'As we can do so little for the West Indian people as to sugar bounties we are all the more anxious to get them any information which they think will help them.'[156] Scientific advice was offered since the adjustment of tariffs was politically impossible.

The West Indian crisis led to the creation of a regional system of botanic gardens. The Royal Commission on West Indian Finance of 1882–4 took testimony from Daniel Morris in Jamaica and concluded that the future of the plantation economies lay either in the scientific improvement of sugar cultivation and extraction, or in the introduction of new crops. Sir William Robinson, Governor of Barbados, wrote to Thiselton-Dyer for advice, musing, with more enthusiasm than agronomic nous, that 'since tea and sugar should naturally grow side by side', Ceylon's new crop might also be brought to the Caribbean.[157] More practically, he urged 'a thorough change in our cane plants'. In November 1883 Thiselton-Dyer wrote to Wingfield at the Colonial Office to propose the foundation of a botanic garden in Barbados at which 'maintenance of, propagation, and distribution of all the best varieties of sugar cane might be the first duties assigned'.[158]

He advised the Colonial Office that small agricultural experiment stations in Barbados, and the Leeward and Windward Islands could be managed from Jamaica.[159] The House of Assembly of Barbados, which had never been a Crown Colony, resented any attempt to submerge its sovereignty in a federal arrangement, and independently voted a grant of £100 per annum for 'the Establishment and Maintenance of a Botanical Station and the Development of the Minor Industries of Barbados.'[160] In the Windward and Leeward Islands—all safely, like Jamaica, under Crown Colony control—the British political administrators arranged grants of several hundred pounds for local stations.[161] Botanical gardens thus emerged in Grenada and Barbados in 1886, St. Lucia and Dominica in 1889, and British Honduras in 1894, while the St. Vincent garden was resuscitated, yet again, in 1890.

In these small and cheap botanical stations we may see the influence of agricultural 'extension' in the United States and Java. There was also the example of Sir Alfred Moloney, who in 1883 had ordered a nursery garden at Kokomaiko (in what became Nigeria) 'to make natives know the value of their country'.[162] He wrote Thiselton-Dyer, at the same time as Kew was addressing the West Indian crisis, to ask him to pressure the Colonial Office to agree to a fully fledged botanic garden.[163] Thiselton-Dyer, however, urged Whitehall instead to follow Moloney's example of science on the cheap, proposing that in the West Indies small experimental stations, 'without an expensive establishment and a large expenditure' might promote knowledge of local plants and disseminate imported plants.[164] One interesting common strand linking the application of the Crown's power to economic botany in West Africa, the West Indies, and elsewhere was that it often depended on an extension of government's coercive resources. Kokomaiko was the site of the debtors' prison of Lagos, while Dodds, where Barbados's experimental station opened in 1886, was a reformatory, the superintendent of which simply assumed additional responsibilities for the scientific establishment. Convicts provided the labour needed in both places, and indeed in Fiji were responsible for clearing and planting a stretch of Crown land, on the orders of the Colonial Secretary, for a botanical garden.

In 1885 Thiselton-Dyer assumed the position of Director of Kew on the retirement of Sir Joseph Hooker. Daniel Morris, fresh from his successes in Ceylon and Jamaica, became its new Assistant Director, and undertook to superintend 'the general botanical policy of the West Indies'.[165] With remarkable speed, the botanical stations proved themselves able to make the kind of scientific breakthrough which the 'New Botanists' expected them to: in 1888, at Dodds plantation in Barbados, the discovery was made for the first time in four centuries of European cultivation that sugar-cane could be grown from seed.[166] This was of both scientific and practical significance, for it opened the way for botanists to improve the sugar content of the cane as the Germans and French had done for the beet.[167] The Royal Society noted that since sugar-cane could after all grow from seed, 'By cross-fertilization and a careful selection of seedlings, it will now be possible to raise new and improved varieties of sugar canes.'[168] At the same time, the West Indian botanical stations promoted the use of chemical fertilizers, and by 1890 there were record crops of sugar.[169] In Barbados, these technical interventions, combined with a merciless depression of wage levels, made sugar profitable, in spite of beet competition. The West Indian planters were thus appeased.

Another political use of botanical extension appeared in West Africa. By the late 1880s, it was decided 'to extend the system of botanic stations to the West African colonies.'[170] Sir Alfred Moloney in 1887 got the botanic garden he had long sought for Lagos. It was intended as a means of social engineering, as much as of adding to the Niger territories' prosperity. For it was feared, even at this early stage, that too many young Africans sought to become 'merchants and clerks', and Moloney hoped that they might be diverted 'in the direction of agricultural pursuits'. Daniel Morris appointed a Jamaican, James MacNair, as its superintendent. It is not improbable that Morris imagined that MacNair, who is described as a 'a creole gardener', would, by virtue of his skin colour, be an effective propagator of the gospel of capitalist agriculture. Morris urged that 'three or four sons of important chiefs' be placed under MacNair's tutelage, so that the plants and skills acquired there would be disseminated into the hinterland.[171] 'Agricultural extension' was intended as an instrument of both economic and political colonization. Colonial governors, with the help of Kew, founded similar botanical stations in Fiji in 1889, Aburi in the Gold Coast in 1890, the Niger Coast Protectorate in 1891, the Gambia in 1894, and Sierra Leone in 1895.

By the late 1880s there was a hierarchy of colonial botanic gardens. 'First-class establishments' were under the direction of a scientific officer, inevitably British, who carried the title of Director. These included Calcutta ('The Kew of India'), Ceylon, Mauritius, and Jamaica botanic gardens. Thiselton-Dyer intended these to be analogues of Buitenzorg—fully equipped with a herbarium, library, museum, and laboratory—and managing networks of smaller establishments in a large surrounding region.[172] Perediniya in Ceylon, he wrote the Colonial Office, 'seems destined to play the part of Kew to the Colonies and possessions of the Empire in the East Indies ... [serving] the new seats of British planting enterprise in the Malay Peninsula, North Borneo, and Fiji'.[173] At lower echelons were 'second-class gardens', such as those in British Guiana or Malaya, governed by practical horticulturalists with the title of Superintendent, and 'botanical stations', conducted by a gardener, who might be non-white, although never in the territory of his birth, with the supervision of a local committee.[174]

The system of colonial botanic establishments formed by Thiselton-Dyer represented a mixture of centralized and decentralized administration. This had obvious advantages: Kew enjoyed the benefits of an informal bureaucratic empire without bearing its costs. Since local colonial governments paid the salaries of botanists and supported their gardens, Thiselton-Dyer did not have to squeeze from the Treasury, or ultimately the British taxpayer, much of the cost of scientific work. On the other hand, Kew depended on the collaboration of local officials to extend its influence to new territories, and to continue earlier initiatives. As Thiselton-Dyer lamented in 1889, 'A new Colonial Government regime may regard with apathy and even hostility the work of its predecessor.'[175] Yet this lack of direct control did allow Kew to step back from examples of failure, and to claim any possible botanical or agricultural success as its own achievement. For example, while Morris presented the discovery of sugar-cane seedlings, made in Barbados rather than in London, as the achievement of Kew, he took no responsibility for the sugar-cane diseases spread partly through his advice.[176]

Thiselton-Dyer's system of colonial economic botany attracted imitators among other European powers. In 1882, Don Vidal y Soler examined Kew with a view to the better exploitation of Spain's colonies in the Philippines. Louis Gentil, who had been trained by Kew for colonial work in Africa, was hired away by the Belgians in the early 1890s to preside as 'L'Inspecteur forestier de L'Etat de Congo'.[177] In 1891, Alfred Engler with the support of the Colonial Division of the Foreign Office, founded the *Botanische Zentralstelle für die Kolonien* around the Berlin Botanical Gardens.[178] The German botanical gardens, wrote Professor Strasburger in 1893, 'are now called upon to advance colonial interests, and have as their model the magnificent achievements in which the Botanic Garden at Kew, near London, may justly take pride'.[179] The *Notizblatt des königlischen botanischen Gartens und Museums zu Berlin*, essentially a *Kew Bulletin* for the German Empire, began publication from 1895. Two houses of the Berlin garden were dedicated to colonial affairs, and they corresponded with experimental stations in Africa. By 1904, a British visitor described the new Agricultural Biological Institute at Amani in German East Africa, with its team of botanists, zoologists, and chemists, as the future 'Kew of tropical Africa'.[180]

Similarly in the French Empire, Thiselton-Dyer's work was emulated.[181] In 1897, Jean Dybowski, agricultural proconsul for the Third Republic in Tunisia, began to advocate the foundation of several colonial *jardins d'essai* and a metropolitan institution to co-ordinate their work. He and others pointed to the almost one hundred establishments under Kew's direct or informal management. Albert Milhe-Poutingon, a senior officer of the Union Coloniale Française, described the garden at Kew as the real intermediary between Britain's diverse dependencies, and as the largest and best informed centre of information on tropical plants in the world.[182] The French Ministry of the Colonies dispatched him, and the Jardin des Plantes sent M. Poisson, on official visits to Kew.[183] In his report, Milhe-Poutingon described Kew as 'un des principaux facteurs de la prospérité des possessions britanniques'.[184] In 1900 the Chamber of Commerce of Lyon sent Allemand to Kew to study 'ces diverses collections se rapportant à la colonisation', while its equivalent in Nantes proposed a colonial agricultural institute.[185] Economic botany appeared to offer answers to the problem of exploiting the vast chunks of territory which the colonial powers in 1884 had annexed out of greed, and fear of each other, in Berlin.

The Green Edge of 'Constructive Imperialism', 1895–1903

Economic development, and in particular that penetration of territory which agriculture alone enabled, acquired a strategic importance in this period. No one then was certain that the diplomatic arrangements arrived at in the 1880s and 1890s represented permanent political reality. Indeed, most assumed that colonial boundaries would be redrawn in future conflicts. As British planters in Borneo declared in 1889, reopening a question sealed since the Congress of Vienna, 'In the tremendous European and Asiatic War now rapidly approaching, it is absurd to expect that so weak a nation as Holland ... will escape' and that when the last rifle was fired, and 'the last battered iron-clad towed into dock', the Dutch flag would no longer fly from Sumatra to Papua.[186] While some historians believe that the 'official mind' at Whitehall was not exercised by these passions for revising the map, the documents of the 1890s suggest that functionaries thought the global jostling for advantages was still on. In 1895, for example, the Colonial Office calmly speculated about swapping Dominica, British for a century, with France, in exchange perhaps for Dahomey and its hinterland, which in turn might go to the Germans who would then yield Togo and control of the Volta to Britain.[187] From Berlin to Washington, strategists calculated that the colonial world might well be ripe for repartition.[188] This meant that the practical occupation of new territories, and their settlement and employment by the occupying power, acquired a political importance. As Rosebery argued in 1893, practical efforts at the 'development' of territory needed to match the prevailing efforts at at 'pegging out claims for the future'.[189] If powers were to keep the colonies they had enclosed, they had to 'improve' them. The developmental initiatives implemented in tropical spaces by Britain, France, Germany, and the United States at the beginning of the twentieth century were responses to this imperative. Infrastructure like railways and ports, and scientists like geologists and botanists were instruments of both profit and power. The imperial botanical network ordered by Thiselton-Dyer had new reasons to be in fashion.

In 1895, Joseph Chamberlain turned down Salisbury's offer of the Exchequer, asking instead for the Colonial Office. He had declared his interest in this post in a speech before the general election, in which he had explained to Birmingham the importance of colonial policy. Britain could not continue to occupy the great spaces of the Earth, Chamberlain argued, if it was unwilling 'to develop them' using British capital and British credit. His case, both in its premises, and in the agrarian metaphor on which it depended, demonstrated his debt to those assumptions about 'improvement' which we have seen active in many earlier moments of British imperialism.

'We are landlords of a great estate', he announced, and ' it is the duty of the landlord to develop his estate.'[190] Indirectly or directly, Britain would reap a reward for such initiative. The 'undeveloped estates' possessed overseas by the British Crown, he noted in another address, must be developed 'for the benefit of their populations and for the benefit of the greater population which is outside'.[191] His priority was to introduce the infrastructure of railways, harbours, roads, and irrigation, through which territories might be fully integrated into the world economy.[192] But the task of discovering those exports which might allow colonies to import from Britain remained. The intermesh of economic and strategic imperatives led Chamberlain to Thiselton-Dyer and Morris in 1895.

Both the Director and his deputy were already, for other reasons, acquainted with Chamberlain. The politician was an orchid enthusiast, always seen with one in his buttonhole, and maintained a busy horticultural correspondence with Kew.[193] The Royal Society had in 1882 elected him to its fellowship.[194] His sons, Austen and Neville, had sought Morris's advice on their investments in sisal in the Bahamas since 1892. Thiselton-Dyer cultivated their father with gifts and exchanges of rare plants, and just as Banks and Hooker had flattered princes and aristocrats in the names of species, so a later generation honoured this politician through *Anthurium chamberlainii*. Chamberlain, in turn, was Kew's best friend in the House of Commons, even while he was in opposition. It was he who ensured that parliament voted funds for the completion of the Temperate House (illustration 26).[195] But it was for economic advice, rather than ornament, that he looked to the botanists when he came to power.

The agrarian dimension of late nineteenth-century European expansion deserves attention. Agriculture, wrote Bruce in 1910, echoing Kidd, was the ultimate purpose of 'the struggle of the nations of the northern temperate zone for the control of the tropics'.[196] It was, Milhe-Poutingon told the International Colonial Congress in Brussels in 1897, 'le premier facteur du développement économique des colonies'. He reported in 1898, having visited Kew, that Thiselton-Dyer had agreed, and had argued, in terms which would have roused a smile of assent from Quesnay or Banks, that 'L'agriculture est la base du commerce et ... le commerce coloniale est la source principale du traffic du Royaume-Uni.'[197] The agricultural passions of Chamberlain (and, one might add, Cecil Rhodes) deserve to be placed into the context of persistent assumptions about the economic and political importance of the land. In his 'Unauthorized Programme' of 1885, Chamberlain had proclaimed that England's agricultural workers should each have 'three acres and a cow'. The making of citizens, that is people capable of civic participation, still was associated with the acquisition of property, and especially, with farming. His demand chimed, not coincidentally, with the unfulfilled American promise to its slaves of 'forty acres and a mule'. Even in the midst of the 'Second Industrial Revolution', agriculture continued to inform projects for political and economic enclosure and inclusion. Agriculture had a

26. The Temperate House, the largest single glasshouse, only finished with the help of Joseph Chamberlain, who ensured that parliament voted funds for its completion.
Royal Botanic Gardens, Kew.

practical and ideological importance to the 'New Imperialism' which deserves attention. Chamberlain had not chosen the metaphor of 'undeveloped estates' by chance: agriculture was central to his vision.

The science of plants had much to contribute to the profitability of colonies. One priority was the discovery of indigenous plants, such as the rubber trees which had yielded tens of thousands of pounds sterling in Gold Coast exports annually since the 1880s. The other was the introduction of new cultivars, the importance of which had also been demonstrated in the Gold Coast. Only in 1890 had Sir Arthur Griffith established a botanic station at Aburi, but even in 1894 it was credited with having stimulated 'the recultivation of coffee on the part of the natives'.[198] Cocoa, which came to West Africa from the Trinidad Botanic Garden, via Kew, proved even more important. In 1895 the harvest was already worth £2,275, in 1900 it amounted to £27,280, and by 1904 the colony produced some 11 million tons, worth some £200,025.[199] The success of cocoa in West Africa was due mainly to the private initiative of peasants who had migrated into the region, but Kew and the Colonial Office claimed the victory as their own. An exhibit on Gold Coast cocoa, Chamberlain wrote Thiselton-Dyer, would show the Paris Exposition of 1900, 'what has been done under your guidance'.[200] The Director modestly acknowledged his praise, and noted that this crop alone represented 'a powerful argument for the utility of the Botanic Station system'.[201]

It was in the West Indies, however, that 'Constructive Imperialism' most fully united the activity of the Colonial Office and Kew.[202] The crisis in the West Indian sugar economy had assumed a strategic significance in the 1890s. European bounties on beet sugar, from the 1880s on, had forced the

West Indies to depend on the United States for the sale of its staple. The consequences of this became clear in late 1890, when the United States attempted to wrest preferential tariffs from the British West Indies, using the stick of the McKinley Act. The Governors of Jamaica and British Guiana advised that the Americans took more than half of their exports, while in Barbados the figure was closer to 90%.[203] The Governor of the Leeward Islands warned that in the event of a conflict between Britain and the United States, the planters would quickly side with the Americans.[204]

This news packed a punch circa 1890. For the strategic destinies of Canada and the British West Indies were, for contemporaries, intertwined. The crisis in the West Indian economy thus had broader imperial implications. Sir John Seeley, in one of Chamberlain's favourite books, had predicted the Antilles and the Northern Dominion would fall inevitably into the gravitational field of the United States.[205] The possible loss of the white population, territorial expanse, and resources of Canada was intolerable to Conservative and Liberal Unionist policy. Such a loss could not be prevented unless the strategic naval bases of Bermuda, Antigua, St. Lucia, and Port Royal in Jamaica remained in British hands. In 1896, with the British Guiana–Venezuela border dispute, the threat of war between Britain and the United States appeared, and the Colonial Defence Committee warned that if the United States were to take Bermuda, 'a great step would be gained towards what would be her undoubted aim to deprive Great Britain of her American possessions and the West Indies'.[206] Canada apart, imperial élites sought to keep the West Indies and other Crown Colonies under the Union Jack, for they were, a contemporary argued, 'as essential to the solidarity of the empire as the self-governing colonies'.[207] Crown intervention in the West Indies, as with 'constructive imperialism' as a whole, had a strategic as well as economic motive.

In the autumn of 1896, Chamberlain had launched the Royal Commission to Enquire into the Condition and Prospects of the West India Sugar-Growing Colonies. There were three principal commissioners—Sir Henry Norman, Sir Edward Grey, and Sir David Barbour—but Sidney Olivier, the future luminary of the Fabian Colonial Bureau, accompanied as Secretary, and Daniel Morris, the Assistant Director of Kew, as 'Expert Adviser in Botanical and Agricultural Questions'.[208] The Kew man was no mere afterthought: Morris had lobbied Chamberlain, months before, about 'a scheme for his employment as a sort of travelling director of tropical cultivation'.[209] The Commission made a startling declaration of responsibility for the West Indies, the first instance of an argument which later would justify the Colonial Development and Welfare Programmes of the 1940s, and by later translation, 'development' aid after decolonization: 'We have placed the labouring population where it is, and created the conditions, moral and material, under which it exists, and we cannot divert from ourselves responsibility for its future.'[210] The drift of the West Indies into the informal empire of the United States was a prominent feature of its report, which offered a table which showed graphically how in 1882 Britain had commanded 50.7% of West Indian exports, to 22% for the United States, while in 1896, the 'mother country' only took 5.8%, to the Americans' 70.8%.[211] Most of the Commission's proposals met heavy weather at the Treasury. To many in London, £120,000 for central sugar factories in Barbados and £460,000 to improve ports, railways, roads, telegraph and wireless communication, seemed an unfair burden to place on the British taxpayer. But its other suggestion, that 'improvement of methods of cultivation' become an end of Crown policy, found support. Daniel Morris, in a subsidiary report, proposed the establishment of a 'Department of Economic Botany and for Agricultural Instruction in the West Indies.'[212]

In 1898, Chamberlain argued at Westminster that 'these grants are the necessary expenses of empires'.[213] He reminded the House of Commons that the West Indies, even in its depressed condition, took £2,750,000 to £3,000,000 in British and Irish produce, which represented employment for 40,000 families.[214] The Secretary of State positioned his case for investment by noting that aid to French colonies amounted to almost £3 million, while the Germans, with only a handful of possessions overseas, spent almost as much.[215] Britain, in its own interest, should help the West Indies to rescue itself. The strategic argument for such a rescue was put forward by the Member for Stratford-on-Avon:

> As a matter of self-preservation ... if for no other reason, we should retain control over the West Indies. We know that in a very short time there will be a canal made through the Isthmus of Panama, and that will be one of the strategical points of the world. In the West Indies we have harbours that dominate the canal. . . .[216]

Economic assistance was needed to secure those places from which Britain might, in some future contest, put pressure on the United States. Given that tariffs to protect British West Indian sugar were politically impossible, other means of help had to be offered.

These debates on grants-in-aid to the West Indies, held on 14 March, and 2 August 1898, were remarkable for many reasons. When Chamberlain suggested that a countervailing duty on continental sugar 'would only restore free trade and secure the natural condition of ordinary competition', he unfurled the banner of tariff reform which he and the Tories would follow to ruin in the next decade. Of more enduring importance, Chamberlain's speeches provided, in Amery's phrase, 'the first examples of Imperial planning in the modern sense'.[217] His vision of the future of the dependent world integrated steam ships, telegraphs, agriculture, and urban development. He urged, moreover, that abandoned estates should be acquired by the Crown, and then broken up for the creation of 'an extended peasant cultivating class'. We may easily find Indian and Irish precedents for this project of agrarian reform, and as in these regions, agriculture was intended to serve political as well as economic ends. By encouraging the equivalent to the *ryotwar* caste in the West Indies, Britain might reap a harvest of local plenty and loyalty, as well as enlarged tax revenues and commerce. Chamberlain, lastly, presented the help of the Royal Botanic Gardens at Kew as necessary for the success of any of these endeavours:

> I do not think it is too much to say at the present time that there are several of our important Colonies which owe whatever prosperity they possess to the knowledge and experience of, and the assistance given by, the authorities of Kew Gardens.[218]

From the proposals of the Royal Commission, Chamberlain created the Imperial Department of Agriculture for the West Indies, and recruited Daniel Morris away from Kew to become the Imperial Commissioner of Agriculture.

Run mostly by Morris in Barbados, and partly from Kew, the Imperial Department quickly won fame as a success of colonial policy.[219] With modest imperial funds, Morris established numerous local stations for special research on soil types and for agricultural education. The Imperial Department's uniting of chemists, geneticists, mycologists, and practical farmers provided a portable model to be applied to other regions. It helped too that West Indian agriculture by the eve of the First World War was enjoying a renaissance. But this rebirth, one should note, was owed to many factors over which Morris exercised no agency: the prices of bananas and sugar rose, particularly since the Spanish–American War destroyed Cuban sugar production, and Central European powers ended bounties on beet sugar. Morris was fortunate also to preside over the new sugar-cane varieties produced by breeding becoming established. By 1908, it was estimated that the profit derived in any single colony from the new seedling canes bred by the Imperial Department more than covered the entire cost of the Department from its foundation, and that of all agricultural research in the West Indies for the past quarter of a century.[220] In a letter to the Colonial Office in which he negotiated his pension rights, Morris argued that the introduction of such canes was the most prominent result for which the Department could claim credit.[221] The resulting marginalia in the Colonial Office file read, 'It is hardly too much to say that Sir Daniel Morris has saved the West Indies by bringing old industries up to date and reviving extinct industries.'[222]

The success of the Imperial Department of Agriculture for the West Indies suggested to contemporaries that science might be more formally integrated into colonial government. The usefulness of Kew, and Thiselton-Dyer and Morris, was equally illustrated. Just before Christmas 1898, Chamberlain informed Thiselton-Dyer confidentially that in the New Year's Honours he would be appointed a Knight Commander of the Order of St. Michael and St. George (see illustration 27). The Directors of Kew had come

27. Sir William Thiselton-Dyer, wearing the court dress of the Order of St. Michael and St. George. Royal Botanic Gardens, Kew.

up in the world: while William Hooker had only received a Hanoverian knighthood, and Joseph, the new regalia of the Star of India, Morris received his KCMG in 1900. Elsewhere in the British Empire, admininistrators organized scientific assistance for agriculture on the West Indian model.

In 1900, Thiselton-Dyer persuaded the India Office to respond to 'the continual growth of the population and the chronic recurrence of famines' by expanding its support of science.[223] Crown intervention against famine, a motive for investment in botany in the age of Banks, clearly remained a project in that of Curzon. The India Office assured him that 'the Government here will attach great importance to your weighty remarks', and by June 1901 the India Office advertised for an 'Economic Botanist for the Government of the United Provinces'.[224] With the arrival of Curzon as Viceroy, such turning of the state to agricultural improvement became the order of the day.[225] The Viceroy transformed the Department of Agriculture and Revenue of India along the scientific lines of the West Indian department.[226] In 1902, Henry Phipps donated £20,000 for the foundation of the Agricultural Research Institute in Pusa. Curzon created a Board of Scientific Advice for India in 1903. The Viceroy borrowed Chamberlain's agrarian rhetoric in framing his own vision of 'Constructive Imperialism':

> in view of the fact that the Indian government own the largest landed estate in the world, that the prosperity of the country is at present mainly dependent upon agriculture, that its economic and industrial resources have been very imperfectly explored ... the importance of practical research is preeminent.[227]

Scientific agriculture would again serve a mixture of ends.

By 1905, local adminstrators and the Colonial Office created an Imperial Department of Agriculture for the British West African Colonies and Protectorates, and the Federated Malay States. Every Crown Colony, from the Edwardian period on, was equipped with its own local Department of Agriculture. As Thiselton-Dyer wrote Morris on his retirement in 1911, 'You are perfectly justified in seeing in the work that is going on in India the influence of your department. It has in fact been an object lesson for the whole civilised world.'[228] The alliance of science and government in the 1890s had forged an enduring bureaucratic instrument. Chamberlain and his scientific allies shortly received the sincere compliment of direct imitation in the Development Commission, and the domestic policies of Liberal 'social imperialism'.[229]

The Climax of a Scientific Empire

In 1902 Chamberlain made official what had prevailed *de facto* for a quarter of a century, and named Thiselton-Dyer 'Botanical Adviser to the Secretary of State for the Colonies', at the same time as he named Sir Patrick Manson his Medical Adviser. 'The Colonial Office', a contemporary wrote, 'is a system including five bodies, each revolving, in a sense, on its own axis round the central force of the Secretary of State': the Establishment, the Crown Agents, the Medical Adviser, the Royal Botanic Gardens at Kew, and the Imperial Institute.[230] Kew, in the Edwardian empire, had become the Colonial Office's economic development bureau.

Thiselton-Dyer shouldered immense responsibilities. A weary titan, he apologized to Foster that he could not think of undertaking the Foreign Secretaryship of the Royal Society because he already faced 'as much as I can stand without breaking down'.[231] To understand his achievement, it is worth bearing in mind that around 1880 almost all of the 28 botanical establishments within the British Empire had originally been founded before 1820. In the last two decades of the century, however, more than twice that number emerged *de novo*, while others were resuscitated.[232] The practical influence of Kew now penetrated the interior of every continent. By 1910, Bruce noted that Kew had studded the whole of Africa with its alumni: 'it has at the moment a complete chain of men on the line of the Cape to Cairo railway'.[233] Thiselton-Dyer's close relations with two key civil servants, Sir Robert Herbert and Sir Robert Meade, and later with Chamberlain, meant that his nominees filled almost a hundred appointments. 'I know of no department of government', Thiselton-Dyer wrote Chamberlain in 1898, 'which receives representations made to it by Kew with more absolute confidence than the Colonial Office.'[234] Neither Hooker had enjoyed his direct access to power.

Thiselton-Dyer was able to set the terms on which he collaborated with others, in ways his predecessors would have envied. He dealt coolly, for example, with Sir George Goldie's complaint that Woodruffe, who ran the Abutshi Experimental Botanical Plantations, in the territories of the Royal Niger Company, conducted an official correspondence with Kew independent of the Company.[235] At this time, Clause X of the contract signed by Woodruffe and every agent of the Royal Niger Company prohibited them, during or until ten years after employment by the Company, 'from communicating to the newspapers of Great Britain, or any other countries or to any outside person, official or private, any facts whether commercial, industrial, scientific or political, in connection with the business of the company or the districts occupied by the company'.[236] Kew, of course, paid no portion of Woodruffe's salary. Thiselton-Dyer, however, responded indignantly:

> Our men when they leave Kew always count upon keeping up their connection with us by correspondence. I cannot imagine for a moment that Woodruffe had any idea he was signing away his liberty to write us on technical matters.[237]

Goldie tried politely to insist that his employee might at least send his reports open, so that the Niger government could have the benefit of them.[238] To which Thiselton-Dyer responded by closing Kew's relations with the Company, asserting that 'I can honestly say that while we have spared no pains and labour to assist the work of the Company, I am not aware of any advantage which this establishment has received on its side.'[239] This was a disingenuous profession, since it was through the co-operation of entities such as the Company that Thiselton-Dyer was able to maintain a scientific empire within the empire. Goldie, with his own small reputation as a martinet, shortly entreated Kew to reopen relations on its own terms.

This world of connections deepened Kew's importance as a scientific institution, in particular as a centre for herbarium taxonomy. As Thiselton-Dyer explained in 1892, while inaugurating the *Decades Kewensis*, which reported Kew's taxonomical discoveries, 'The energy and curiosity of the British race . . . traverses and explores every part of the World, and pours into Kew a continuous stream of botanical information and specimens.'[240] Surveyors were busy mapping turbulent colonial frontiers on every continent, and returned a flood of plants.[241] The 'Colonial Floras' scheme, proposed by Sir William Hooker almost half a century before, developed and expanded under Thiselton-Dyer's tenure.[242] In 1891 the Foreign Office pressed Thiselton-Dyer for the 'completion' of the *Flora of Tropical Africa*, as an aid to 'the development of the territories over which this country has recently acquired an influence'.[243] Thiselton-Dyer, in response, argued that the original plan for a comprehensive treatise on Africa's plants had resulted from the elder Hooker's ignorance of the epic scope of such a task, only revealed by 'the recent delimitation of the spheres of influence of the various European powers'.[244] He persuaded Salisbury to agree to four new volumes, and in 1900 to five more, at a rate of £300 per volume.[245] 'I cannot control the expansion of Kew Herbarium', Thiselton-Dyer wrote in 1899, ' because I cannot control the expansion of the Empire. . . . The expansion in the two fields is necessarily correlated.'[246]

The centrality of the Kew herbarium for the science of botany depended on these remarkable new collections, which were added to the riches already assembled by the Hookers and George Bentham. It was an unparalleled facility for comparative work. Its importance depended too on its rôle as the basis for the influential *Genera Plantarum* and the *Index Kewensis*.[247] The writ of the so-called 'Kew Rule', by which only epithets already associated with a generic name are considered from the point of view of priority when the genus is revised, ran far beyond Surrey to the herbaria of Adolf Engler in Berlin, Tedero Caruel in Florence, and Asa Gray at Harvard.[248] On a more banal level, the size of the herbarium sheets used by William Hooker (16½ by 10½ inches), became the standard for most herbaria in the British Commonwealth.[249]

Kew's commitment to imperial taxonomy had, in an earlier generation, hindered the British response to Germany's 'New Botany'.[250] But the prestige and influence which Kew acquired, principally through its contribution to the imperial economy, meant that in the 1880s and 1890s, it was instead the most important agent in the dissemination of physiology, pathology, and comparative anatomy in Britain. There was a domestic and intellectual dimension to Kew's scientific empire: Thiselton-Dyer placed his nominees in senior botanical appointments around the country. In April 1885, for example, Frederick Bower, then in his twenties, newly back from Europe, was working at the Jodrell Laboratory when Thiselton-Dyer, Hooker, and two others walked in. Hooker wasted no time, asking Bower whether he knew that the Crown chair in Botany in Glasgow was vacant. Hooker informed Bower 'that he considered it [his] duty to apply, and that if he consented the four of them would support [him]'.[251] In a matter of days Bower was the new Regius Professor of Botany at Glasgow.[252] Alumni of the Jodrell and the Normal School at South Kensington, including Vines, Lawson, Ward, Lawes, and Wright, and Bower, rapidly filled the botanical lectureships and chairs in Oxford, Cambridge, Dublin, Glasgow, and London. Others, such as Trimen, Morris, and Duthie, found security and power in colonial posts. Both Cambridge and Oxford reorganized teaching and research in botany under Kew's influence.[253] As a founder of the *Annals of Botany*, and first President of Section K (Botany) of the British Association for the Advancement of Science, Thiselton-Dyer was at the hub of the profession.

Kew certainly retained its traditional horticultural and ornamental functions. In 1886, it was still distributing surplus bedding plants for the improvement of the London poor.[254] But under Joseph Hooker and Thiselton-Dyer their importance diminished. Hooker, in particular, had wished to change the perception of Kew as a pleasure garden, arguing in 1881 that in the first quarter century of the public administration of Kew, all of the economic and scientific aspects of Kew had been kept in the background, 'whilst the merely attractive features of the ground were developed.'[255] Perhaps because he felt this popular aspect no longer threatened the scientific identity of Kew, Thiselton-Dyer was less hostile to the ornamental, and is credited with much sensitive landscaping of the garden, with the completion of the Temperate House, and the rebuilding of the Succulent House.[256] Millions of visitors came to Kew each year during Thiselton-Dyer's regime. It is a mark of the confidence of Thiselton-Dyer in his position that, while Sir William Hooker had flattered the Duchess of Cambridge in *The Rhododendrons of Sikkim Himalaya* (1851), Thiselton-Dyer in 1889 suspended the custom of supplying a later holder of this title with flowers.[257] Since Kew proved itself in the spheres of botanical science and the imperial economy, and catered to the pleasure of the democratic crowd, it no longer needed to solicit the sympathy of princesses.

An incident from 1892 showed how much had changed in 50 years. In that summer, Princess Mary Adelaide of Teck—H.R.H the Duchess of Cambridge—gave her patronage to a bazaar in the grounds of the Queen's Cottage at Kew. Thiselton-Dyer, to the consternation of his superiors at the Board of Works, refused to permit royal carriages to cross his grass.[258] Rule No. 1 of Kew's 'Rules of the Park', he noted, forbade riding or driving in the Royal Gardens. Thiselton-Dyer reminded Primrose, the First Commissioner of Works, that in a memorandum sent 18 June 1887 the Board of Works had refused to allow an exception to the Park Regulations Act of 1872 which banned fireworks on Kew Green. He primly noted that he had therefore always assumed that the Board had deliberately denuded itself of any liberty of action in order to free itself from the possibility of undue pressure. Not only did two million commoners a year agree to visit the gardens on foot, but so had the Emperors of France and Brazil, the Kings of Belgium and Saxony, and the Queens of Sweden and Spain. Since 'the multitude' respected the grass, there was 'something indecorous in persons of high rank traversing in a carriage indiscriminately what is not intended for such usage'. The Board and the Duke of Cambridge claimed 'a dispensing power over an act of parliament', and that this was a constitutional question 'which was fought out ... in the time of James II with well known consequences for that sovereign'. This appeal to rules, precedent, democratic sensibilities, and constitutional principle would never have come from the pen of Sir William Hooker. It reflected the confidence of a later generation in the prerogatives of public servants. 'The Crown', he wrote, 'has entrusted me with a national institution.'[259] Against royal pretensions he opposed the sovereignty now delegated to the bureaucracy.

The last serious official crisis came at the end of the century, when the cold war with the Botanical Department of the British Museum of Natural History, smouldering on since the Ayrton affair, burst into flame. From 1874 onwards, the Museum challenged the principle which had assigned all plants collected on government expeditions since 1854 to Kew, and demanded part of the valuable collections of which it had been deprived.[260] Thiselton-Dyer, it was true, treated the Museum with blatant disrespect. In the distribution of duplicates of plants collected in Afghanistan in 1880, for example, Thiselton-Dyer ensured that the Museum was ranked in priority behind Sahranpore, St. Petersburg, Harvard, Calcutta, and a gentleman in Geneva.[261] The Botanical Department of the Museum refused, in turn, to share with Kew any collections, such as Forbes's New Guinea plants, which came its way.[262] James Britten, at its centre, used the *Journal of Botany* to hit at Thiselton-Dyer, particularly with respect to the slow progress of the *Flora of Tropical Africa*.[263] The Museum's trustees then persuaded the Treasury in 1899 to constitute a 'Committee on Botanical Work' to enquire into the question of 'duplication of work and collections' at the two establishments.[264] Thiselton-Dyer feared that South Kensington was scheming again to annex Kew's herbarium. He ordered his defence on the argument that Kew's important colonial work could not be conducted without its herbarium. The Treasury committee concurred, arguing that this collection was 'an instrument of economic and commercial work of Imperial moment'.[265] In 1901, as in 1873, the imperial work of Kew proved the best defence of its institutional integrity.

Thiselton-Dyer took the opportunity of the favourable political climate of 1902 to secure from the Treasury that transfer from the Board of Works which he and the Hookers had longed for. It was the Secretary of the new Board of Agriculture who made the request, but Thiselton-Dyer had certainly prepared the way behind the scenes, and probably supplied the argument that had such a body existed in 1841, the Crown would have consigned Kew to it rather than to the Commissioners of Works.[266] When consulted by the Board of Works and the Colonial Office, he offered no objection, a sure sign, with a wrangler like Thiselton-Dyer, that it was his desire.[267] His manoeuvre was partly motivated by concern that the British Museum might still prevail by *force majeure*: an article in the press hinted in the summer of 1901 that 'the transfer of the control of Kew Gardens to the Trustees of the British Museum is not beyond the range of possibilities'.[268] Thiselton-Dyer clearly felt that he wanted to determine who his own political master should be, and probably did not wish to exchange a position of parity with the Director of the British Museum of Natural History, or consultancy with the Colonial Secretary, for one of subordination. It was true too that the 'New Botanists' also looked enthusiastically at the Board of Agriculture, which took great interest in mycology, plant physiology, and plant breeding. In 1900, Thiselton-Dyer had worked closely with the Board on its Committee on Agricultural Seed.[269] Austen Chamberlain gave the consent of the

Treasury in July 1902, and with effect from 31 March 1903, Kew came under the management of the the Board of Agriculture.[270]

Thiselton-Dyer retired in December 1905 happy in his achievement, noting proudly to the Board of Agriculture that 'I think I am justified in saying that Kew never stood higher in public esteem or received higher recognition throughout the empire and, I may add, the civilised world.'[271] He had been an administrator of brilliance, fortunate enough to operate in a period of history in which his science was appreciated. Neither the institution itself nor any subsequent director would enjoy the breadth of influence which Thiselton-Dyer had exercised from Kew at the dawn of the twentieth century.

Yet this too can partly be seen as a measure of his success: for Kew, during his tenure, had encouraged the rise of institutions which ultimately eroded its importance as a scientific and an imperial institution. As botany came to flourish in the laboratories of the universities, the importance of the Jodrell and of colonial appointments declined. Taxonomy itself developed under the influence of the 'New Botany' to have more interest in local ecological relationships than in the grand intercontinental comparisons from which large centralized herbaria like Kew derived their importance.[272] The Imperial Departments of Agriculture, much as they added to the glory and reach of Kew in the short term, displaced the Director of Kew from a position of direct intervention in many colonies. At home, special bureaux usurped its functions as broker and distributor of economic intelligence. The most important of these was the Imperial Institute, which was wholly renovated after it was attached to the Board of Trade in 1903. Wyndham Dunstan, who directed it between 1903 and 1924, described the Institute in 1907 as a 'Kew of Chemistry', and effectively took over much of the work formerly done by the Museum of Economic Botany.[273] Even in 1905, Dunstan arranged that the British headquarters of the International Association for Colonial Agronomy was his institute, and not Kew. By 1922 Lugard described the Imperial Institute as 'the natural Commercial Department of the Colonial Office'.[274] The scientific empire of Kew reached its zenith under Thiselton-Dyer: he was the last Director to hold in his own hands so many threads of scientific life and imperial policy.

Conclusion: Empire and Development

Kew remained, throughout the twentieth century, a world centre for its science and an important British cultural institution. Its economic initiatives, under Thiselton-Dyer, found many other continuations, in particular in the remarkable co-ordination of imperial science in the interwar era.[275] There was then a proliferation of agencies: the Imperial Institute, the Empire Cotton Growing Association, and the Imperial Bureaus of Entomology and Mycology, were joined by the Imperial Forestry Institute (a product of the

Empire Forestry Conferences of 1920, 1925, and 1928). The Imperial Economic Conference of 1925, and the Colonial Conference of 1927, both urged the importance of scientific research to administration. Out of the Imperial Department of Agriculture for the West Indies, Milner created an Imperial College for Tropical Agriculture in Trinidad and Tobago. A new agronomic élite might then, after Part II of the Natural Sciences Tripos and the one-year diploma in agriculture at Cambridge, become equipped in Trinidad to guide farming in Malaya or Kenya. In 1928, the Colonial Office appointed Sir Frank Stockdale, whose first post had been with the West Indian department under Sir Daniel Morris, as its Adviser for Tropical Agriculture. With Leo Amery, disciple of Chamberlain and Milner, in the saddle at the Colonial Office, Whitehall lent significant encouragement to regional scientific establishments in the West Indies, India, and Africa. In the Colonial Development and Welfare policies of the period after 1945, and in particular in the Ground Nuts fiasco of 1948–9, we may see the apotheosis of the alliance of science and imperialism.

In that era, from perhaps 1918 to 1960, the imperial sun, even as it began to slip under the sea, seemed at its grandest. It was perhaps the real climax of the British Empire, in terms of the scope of territory, policy, institutional co-ordination—whatever the 'relative decline' of economic and military power. The Crown then wrestled with welfare and development, both at home and abroad, and attempted the integration of a world economy with unprecedented concentration. The ghost of Joseph Chamberlain stalked Westminster. Unfortunately neither the cocoa farmers of Ghana nor the rubber tappers of Malaya ultimately agreed to sustain a declining sterling. But the legacies of that era continue in the independent nations of the British Commonwealth, and in the activity of such international agencies as the International Monetary Fund and the World Bank.

In the last quarter of the nineteenth century, bureaucratic government had expanded its empire within the territory of the nation, and into the wider world. Men of science, in particular botanists, became important partners in administration, and beneficiaries of its growth. They should not have been surprised when the process left them behind in its wake. The idea of governing Nature for cosmopolitan benefit found new vehicles. In time, even the pupal shell of empire would be discarded, and politicians, economists, civil servants, and scientists of all races and nations would claim the faith as their own. New flags now wave, and black and brown presidents now dream of opening territory to trade under roofs which once sheltered white governors. The theatre of development continues. Sitting in its harder and more risky seats are many who wish the drama would improve, or merely end.

EPILOGUE

At the Crossroads

In 'The Royal Exchange' (1711), Joseph Addison described how he felt as he walked into the commercial heart of London.[1] That this city was 'an Emporium for the whole earth' awakened 'secret Satisfaction', and gratified his vanity as an Englishman. What pleased him most was that London had become a cosmopolitan centre, a space open to every nation, in which he could rediscover himself:

> Sometimes I am lost in a Crowd of Jews; and sometimes make one in a Groupe of Dutch-men. I am a Dane, Swede, or French-man at different times, or rather fancy myself like the old Philosopher, who upon being asked what Country-man he was, replied, That he was a Citizen of the World.

Which modern reader, wherever the soil of her birth, could fail to feel a shiver of identification?

It was in Rome, Addison implied, with an epigraph from *The Georgics*, that Britain's role as arbiter of the world's exchange found its precedent. The imperial city, in Virgil's verse, presided over the ivory of India, iron sent by the nude Chalbes, the pungent beaver-oil of the Pontus. It was master, by virtue of its power, over 'the laws and eternal covenants' which Nature had imposed on each place. The Royal Exchange, for Addison, has a similar significance. It was more than a crossroads where mankind, in meeting, discovered its universality. It was instead a place in which the products of all climates and soils met and were reconciled. 'Nature', he writes, 'seems to have taken a particular Care to disseminate her Blessings among the different Regions of the World' in order to stimulate that trade which united humanity in a 'common Interest': 'The Fruits of Portugal are corrected by the Products of Barbadoes: The Infusion of a China Plant is sweetened with the pith of an Indian Cane.' The poverty of England's flora, Addison argued, had been remedied through centuries of introductions of plants. London brought the world into communion:

> We repair our Bodies by the Drugs of *America*, and repose ourselves under *Indian* Canopies ... the vineyards of *France* [are] our Gardens; the Spice

> Islands our Hot-Beds; the *Persians* our Silk-Weavers, and the *Chinese* our potters ... our Eyes are refreshed with the green fields of Britain, at the same time that our Palates are feasted with Fruits that rise between the Tropicks.

Britain's greatness lay, in part, in its government of this climax of Nature and nations.

It is easy to see in this spectacle the outline of the Garden of Eden, with the merchant, instead of the farmer, turned into the agent of Creation's redemption. It offered a Providential theory of commerce, in which free exchange between nations, and 'Men thriving at their own private Fortunes, and at the same time promoting the Publick Stock', created prosperity and cosmopolitan harmony. All the secular utopians of classical political economy, from Adam Smith and David Ricardo to their more modern imitators, are clearly in tune with Addison. W.S. Jevons, in *The Coal Question* (1865), quite directly borrowed Augustan cadences where he exulted that

> The plains of North America and Russia are our corn fields; Chicago and Odessa our granaries; Canada and the Baltic are our timber forests; Australasia contains our sheep farms, and in Argentina and the western prairies are our herds of oxen; Peru sends her silver, and the gold of Australia, and South Africa flows to London; the Hindus and Chinese grow tea for us, and our coffee, sugar, and spice plantations are in all the Indies.[2]

There is grandeur in this view of life and labour serving the pleasure and comfort of Britain, and the improvement of the world.

Sir Joseph Banks's suggestion in 1787 that Kew should become 'a great botanical exchange house for the empire', the entrepôt through which plants moved east to west, and south to north, offers another echo of 'The Royal Exchange'. This agrarian *philosophe* clearly saw the collection and movement of plants across the world as an extension of the sacred and secular mission of commerce. Kew, and its colonial partners, would make that province of Nature under British government as fruitful and ornamented as possible. Here, as with Addison, we feel the influence of that Christian Providentialism which was the ideological taproot of European imperialism. Exchanging living things between the corners of Creation was both a moral and an efficient enterprise. For the wealth and order which followed the sheep of enclosers at home, and the rubber of colonizers abroad, benefited the subordinate as well as their new masters. The integration of every part of the Earth into the larger scientific and commercial sphere of Christendom was, manifestly, a need of Nature. This idea, as we have seen, was useful both to those who wished to acquire support for their study of Nature, and to those who sought to explain or justify their government of territory or people. As they ordered the world's plants in space, and organized solutions to human needs, these gardens expressed the purpose and power of monarchy in one era, and bureaucracy in another.

We have pursued the origins and consequences of the assumptions of the age of Addison, Adam Smith, and Joseph Banks, with particular care, from the late sixteenth century to the beginning of the twentieth. We have traced, through the evolution of doctrines of the public interest, how government evolved in the British Isles over the modern period, conceived as a whole. We have explored the interactions of religious, economic, and scientific ideas and policy across the domestic and overseas histories of Britain. At the heart of it all was a tangle of ancient and modern beliefs about how Nature's secrets might be discovered and applied to both private and national profit, and cosmopolitan benefit. We are still in their grip.

Who could fail to share the optimism? At a glance, the modern world might suggest that the practical utopians of the Enlightenment were on the mark. Our physics and chemistry explain with great elegance the processes of Nature, and our biology and agriculture have transformed the scope of human health and pleasure. More people now live longer and richer lives, freer from hunger and disease, than our ancestors would have imagined possible. In the aftermath of the European empires, every part of the world is part of one system of exchange of goods, services, ideas, embodied in the inexorable progress of the English language. Will we not, in time, reach that era of cosmopolitan abundance, harmony, and peace towards which Defoe, Mandeville and Addison, Smith and Ricardo looked?

Perhaps we will reach this promised land. We may hope so, since the world appears set on this career we call 'development' with momentum which Green complaint, lentils and incense will do nothing to reduce. Yet the present signs are not comforting. The market economy seems to quicken conflicts more often than it orders peace. There are wars on every continent today fuelled directly by the roles which local things—oil, diamonds, gold, copper, timber—play as international commodities. Archipelagos of poverty, squalor, fear, and disease imprison millions in the rich countries in circumstances only slightly more pleasant than the billions of the poorer parts of the planet. The downtown steel and glass of Kuala Lumpur, Mexico City, St. Petersburg, Port of Spain, Abidjan, and Johannesburg, or indeed Detroit, Baltimore, Birmingham, and Newcastle, are surrounded by a sea of unhappiness from which few can escape. The brave new world of the internet is the fetish of a tiny minority, a few percent of the world's population. We depend on a dwindling variety of food crops, on soils which are in decay, and aquifiers which are running dry. Some merely smile weakly, and argue that there are 'natural' levels of unemployment or inequality or misery which no policy can alter. While others, like Drs. Pangloss and Fukuyama, respond, 'Give it time'. And it is true that we cannot be sure if these problems are really structural, the necessary consequences of the system.

But there are warnings buried in the background of 'The Royal Exchange'. The promise that universal exchange might lead to cosmopolitan utopia was flawed in its earliest age. Not every citizen of the world was welcome in the marketplace. The products of Nature united mankind, then, in a common despotism. 'The Products of Barbadoes' were wrested from the earth by slaves. From the coffee shops of London ran a trail of misery, torture, and death which penetrated the heart of Africa and the Americas. The prosperity of the 'Sugar Islands' was built on the wreck of amerindian civilizations which had supported a population which the Caribbean would only match again in its latest age. To produce sugar there, or indeed wine in Madeira, an enormously diverse flora and fauna were destroyed. Commercial society, all in all, led to a hollowing out of the world—the extinction of languages and skills, the amputation of part of human experience. Mutual benefit did not necessarily follow free exchange: the market's 'insiders', men like Addison's 'Sir Andrew Freeport' who controlled the terms of trade, languages, currencies, and in whose cities the profits were counted and invested, were the winners. 'Cosmopolitanism' was so often a compliment paid to these arrangements by that relatively homogeneous minority which presided over them. 'Free trade', often amounted in practice to the mercantilism of the dominant players in the world economy. Underneath the purple robe of universalism was a less attractive body of interests. The gentlemen of the Royal Exchange, while they cherished the power of their democratic institutions, did not shrink from consigning distant peoples to tyranny and war. We may ask Addison, as Jasper Griffin asked an American classicist who found in Athens an argument for his republic's empire: 'Was the great democratic society also on offer for the cities which paid tribute, or only for the imperial city?'

Behind the spectacle of the botanic garden can be found other less happy phenomena. Within its own space, and in the infinitely larger territories affected by its work, the ordering of Nature depended upon shantytowns of labour, as a photograph of the living conditions of those who manicured the Calcutta Botanic Garden reminds us (see illustration 28). The introduction of new plants often meant the extinction of many others. While Thiselton-Dyer with his left hand introduced economic crops, with his right he sought to preserve the economy of Nature. The fraud so often at the heart of 'exchange' was most palpable in the world of plants. The botanic garden, as market place, failed to make adequate sense of the local value or meaning of the things in which it transacted. The communities and environments destroyed in the midst of European expansion, according to the wisdom of science and the needs of commerce, are lost forever, and we cannot be sure that any larger universal good has compensated us for this loss. In our own day, conservation has become one of the principal responsibilities of the botanic garden: in a tragic sense, we have achieved the Renaissance ambition that the *hortus conclusus* might enclose the limits of vegetable creation.[3]

But should we care? Were the pyramids, and so much human grandeur not built on slavery and despotism? Is it not enough to cultivate our gardens, and to preserve Arnold's 'sweetness and light' in the charmed circles of our cities and universities? Is the thinned variety of nature and culture not the price

28. A 'Coolie Line' where the workers of the Calcutta Botanic Garden lived with their families (circa 1900). Royal Botanic Gardens, Kew.

we have paid for an infinitely happier and more closely integrated human tribe? These are the unspoken questions at the heart of our modern arrangements. And they are all badly posed, because of the false premise of a separation between subject and object, man and Nature, local and universal, acts and consquences on which they depend. Can we any longer sustain the barbarous belief that a city's happiness is unaffected by the violence and plunder it projects beyond its walls? The interactions between environments and populations have proven more complex than we could have predicted.

In time, all tyrannies end. And as Babylon falls, its walls drag under all the bright flowers which once adorned them. The very real retreat of 'high culture' in the late twentieth-century West is a consequence of it having been, for too long, a status good, denied to the majority. The crisis of 'Civil Society', in so many former Crown Colonies, usually accompanied by the neglect of their botanic gardens, is only one consequence of these polities' origins in arrangements in which the participation of the governed was not a priority. Simone Weil in *The Need for Roots* provided the most penetrating diagnosis of a disease which affects the regions where people once lived at the mercy of the 'vanguard party', as much as those, at the centres and peripheries, of the Western empires:

> Those who keep masses of men in subjection by exercising force and cruelty deprive them of two vital foods, liberty and obedience. . . . Those

> who encourage a state of things in which hope of gain is the principal motive take away their obedience, for consent which is its essence is not something which can be sold.[4]

Our world is still in shock from the great 'modernizing' projects of capital, government, science, and imperialism, all the connected attempts to forge universal systems, usually without the consent of their future beneficiaries. The enormous irresponsibility of the 'Royal Exchange' for the consequences of the transactions settled in its courts deserves our attention. For its impact is felt both a mile from its counting houses, and at the most distant mines and plantations. Even the most comfortable inhabitant of a limestone tower should worry about poverty, disease, illiteracy, and the deaths of music and forests at lower latitudes. For their consequences will find him, and the things he holds most dear.

The story I have followed through five centuries tells of your origins. These systems of ideas and policies, and their consequences, are still with us. What will we do with them? The optimist may look at the century just finished, despite its horrors, as the beginning of a new age in human history. It was only within the lifetime of my parents that it became accepted that women and the poor had as much right to vote as propertied men, that light skins should signal no more dignity or worth than dark ones, and that the colonial subordination of most of the world stood in direct contradiction to the ideals of the West. Few intelligent people now question these assumptions, even if the realities lag behind liberal ideals. Economic and cultural democracy may yet arise on the basis of political inclusion. Our government of Nature is even now responding to changes in the nature of human government.

But cosmopolitanism on what terms? If the limits of any universal system are now clear, where will the centre stand? Perhaps we may begin by rescuing from the 'Royal Exchange' that gracious idea of encounter and reconciliation on which it depended. The charisma of the marketplace is based on the potential for satisfaction of needs which the meeting of people, plants, goods, or ideas inaugurates. To worship the market itself is to miss the point. What matters is the drama of confrontation and collaboration, the answering of hunger, the freedom to come and go at pleasure, the door open to the stranger. In the Caribbean religion of *vodun*, the crossroads can play this rôle as a space in which people secure the needs of the present and the future through negotiation with each other, and with their memories of the dead. It is in homage to this ritual, and for the newly liberated nations of England and India, Ireland and South Africa, Barbados and Scotland, that I offer this history of Nature's government.

Notes

Abbreviations used in the notes

Add. Mss	British Library: Additional Manuscripts
AN	Archives Nationales de France
APS	American Philosophical Society Library and Archives
DC	Darwin Correspondence
Sutro	Microfilm of the papers of Sir Joseph Banks at the Sutro Library, San Francisco, California
BCMHN	Bibliothèque Centrale du Muséum National d'Histoire Naturelle
CBW	*Report to the Lord Commissioners of H.M. Treasury of a Departmental Committee on Botanical Work and Collections at the British Museum and Kew*, London, 1901
CSP	*Calendar of State Papers*
C.U.L.	Cambridge University Library
DAR	*Darwin Papers*
DNB	*Dictionary of National Biography*
DSB	*Dictionary of Scientific Biography*
D.T.C.	British Museum (Natural History), Botany Library: Dawson Turner copies of the Sir Joseph Banks correspondence
E.H.R.	*English Historical Review*
IOL	India Office Library
J.I.C.H.	*Journal of Imperial and Commonwealth History*
K.B.	*Bulletin of Miscellaneous Information, Kew*
Kew	Archives of the Royal Botanic Gardens, Kew
B.C.	Sir Joseph Banks correspondence
C.F.	*Colonial Floras* correspondence
GB Auto. Mss	George Bentham, autobiographical manuscript
Mss LDB	Manuscript bound with *Letter to the Duke of Bedford* (1840)
LS	Linnean Society of London, Library and Archives
Parl. Deb.	*Parliamentary Debates*
P.P.	*Parliamentary Papers*
P.R.O.	Public Record Office, Kew and Chancery Lane
R.C.S.I.	*Royal Commission of Scientific Instruction and the Advancement of Science Minutes of Evidence*, 8 vols. 1872–5
Royal Society	Library and Archives of the Royal Society of London
SAL	South African Library
Sutro	Papers of Sir Joseph Banks at the Sutro Library, San Francisco, California
UCL	Library and Archives of the University College London
SDUK	*Society for the Diffusion of Useful Knowledge Papers*
Yale: Sterling	Yale University Library: microfilm of Sir Joseph Banks Correspondence

Preface

1 See *inter alia* C.A. Bayly, *Imperial Meridian: The British Empire and the World, 1780–1830* (London, 1989); R. Brenner, *Merchants and Revolution: Commercial Change, Political Conflict, and London's Overseas Traders, 1550–1653* (Cambridge, 1992); J. Brewer, *The Sinews of Power: War, Money and the English State, 1688–1783* (London, 1989); P.J. Cain and A.G. Hopkins, *British Imperialism* (London, 1993), 2 vols.; L. Colley, *Britons: Forging the Nation, 1707–1820* (London, 1992); D. Hancock, *Citizens of the World: London Merchants and the Integration of the British Atlantic Community* (Cambridge, 1995); J.M. MacKenzie, *Propaganda and Empire: The Manipulation of British Public Opinion 1880–1960* (Manchester, 1984) and *The Empire of Nature: Hunting, Conservation, and British Imperialism* (Manchester, 1988); P.J. Marshall, 'Imperial Britain', *J.I.C.H.*, 1995, *23*: 380–93; J.G.A. Pocock, 'British History: A Plea for a New Subject', *Journal of Modern History*, 1975, *47*: 601–21; *idem*, 'The Limits and Divisions of British History: In Search of a New Subject', *American Historical Review*, 1982, *87*: 311–36; K. Wilson, *The Sense of the People: Politics, Culture, and Imperialism in England, 1715–1785* (Cambridge, 1995).

2 J. Seeley, *The Expansion of England* (Cambridge, 1883); D.A. Low, *The Contraction of England* (Cambridge, 1983).

3 The incomprehension and hostility with which British historians greeted E. Williams's *Capitalism and Slavery* (Chapel Hill, 1944) and C.L.R. James's *The Black Jacobins: Toussaint L'Ouverture and the San Domingo Revolution* (London, 1938) derived, in no small part, from the challenges these posed to the heroic narratives of the nation cherished by both 'Left' and 'Right'. Edward Said has, more recently, been received with a similar discomfort.

4 I respond here to the pioneering work on science and empire of, *inter alia*, M.H. Edney, *Mapping an Empire: The Geographical Construction of British India, 1765–1843* (Chicago, 1997); R.H. Grove, *Green Imperialism: Colonial Expansion, Tropical Island Edens, and the Origins of Environmentalism, 1600–1860* (Cambridge, 1995); J. MacKenzie, ed., *Imperialism and the Natural World* (Manchester, 1990); J.E. McClellan, *Colonialism and Science: Saint Domingue in the Old Regime* (Baltimore, 1992); M. Osborne, *Nature, the Exotic, and the Science of French Colonialism* (Bloomington, 1994); L. Pyenson, *Cultural Imperialism and the Exact Sciences: German Expansion Overseas, 1900–1930* (New York, 1985), *idem, Empire of Reason: Exact Sciences in Indonesia, 1840–1940* (Leiden, 1989), and *idem, Civilizing Mission: Exact Sciences and French Overseas Expansion, 1830–1940* (Baltimore, 1993); R. Stafford, *Scientist of Empire: Sir Roderick Murchison, Scientific Exploration and Victorian Imperialism* (Cambridge, 1989). I offer discussions of this literature in R. Drayton, 'Science, Medicine, and the British Empire', in R.Winks, ed., *Oxford History of the British Empire, V: Historiography* (Oxford, 1999) and 'Science and the European Empires', *J.I.C.H.*, 1995, *23*: 503–10.

5 I follow the suggestions of F.M. Turner, 'Public Science in Britain, 1880–1919,' *Isis*, 1980, *71*: 589–608; M.J. Rudwick, 'Charles Darwin in London: The Integration of Public and Private Science,' *Isis*, 1982, *73*: 186–266; L. Steward, *The Rise of Public Science: Rhetoric, Technology and Natural Philosophy in Newtonian Britain* (Cambridge, 1993).

6 L. Brockway, *Science and Colonial Expansion: The Role of the British Botanic Gardens* (New York, 1979); R. Desmond, *Kew: The History Of The Royal Botanic Gardens* (London, 1995); D.R. Headrick, *Tentacles of Progress: Technology Transfer in the Age of Imperialism, 1850–1940* (London, 1988), pp. 209–58; D.P. McCracken, *Gardens of Empire: Botanical Institutions of the Victorian British Empire* (Leicester, 1997). I owe a particular debt to Mr. Desmond for rescuing me from writing the more parochial history of Kew which would have followed from the publication of my doctoral dissertation ('Imperial Science and a Scientific Empire: Kew Gardens and the Uses of Nature, 1772–1903', Yale, 1993). He read and commented on it in 1994, but failed to cite it since, he later advised me, he had 'put it aside' before writing. I take encouragement from the fact that Desmond was able so often to agree with the patterns and periods I had described for Kew's history.

7 A. Pagden in *Lords of All the World: Ideologies of Empire in Spain, Britain, and France c.1500–c.1800* (New Haven, 1995) places weight on Roman Law heritage. I prefer to emphasize the Christian and practical economic dimensions.

8 My approach to the issues above has been shaped by my encounter with those Environmental historians sensitive to political economy, in particular W. Cronon (*Changes in the Land: Indians, Colonists, and the Ecology of New England* (New York, 1983) and *Nature's Metropolis: Chicago and the Great West* (New York, 1991)), Donald Worster (*Nature's Economy: A History of Ecological Ideas* (Cambridge, 1985) and R. White (*The Middle Ground: Indians, Empires, and Republics in the Great Lakes Region, 1650–1815* (Cambridge, 1991)). Cronon's stories of the negotiations between settlers and indigenes in New England, and of related rise of Chicago and the West, have much to teach British and Imperial historians.

9 Here I turn inside out the argument of Ronald Robinson, 'Non-European Foundations of European Imperialism: Sketch for a Theory of Collaboration', in R. Owen and R. Sutcliffe, *Studies in the Theory of Imperialism* (London, 1972), pp. 117–42

1 The World in a Garden

1 J. Prest, *The Garden of Eden. The Botanic Garden and the Recreation of Paradise* (London, 1981), p. 17 and *passim.*

2 *Posterior Analytics I*, ch. 4; *Politics I*, ch. 8.

3 *The Parts of Animals, I*, ch. 5.

4 D'Arcy Thompson, *On Aristotle as a Biologist* (Oxford, 1913), p. 12.

5 G.E.R. Lloyd, *Science, Folklore, Ideology. Studies in the Life Sciences in Ancient Greece* (Cambridge, 1983), pp. 119–35.

6 J. Vernet, *De Abd al-Rahman I a Isabel II* (Barcelona, 1989); R. Southern, The *Making of the Middle Ages* (New Haven, 1953), pp. 65–7.

7 *The boke of secretes of Albertus Magnus, of the vertues of Herbes, stones and certaine beastes* (1560?).

8 R. Bacon, *Epistolla de Secrets*, T.M., trans., *Frier Bacon his Discovery of the Miracles of Arts, Nature, and Magick* (London, 1659), p. 249.

9 O. Cockayne, *Leechdoms, Wortcunning, and Starcraft in Early England* (London, 1864–6), 3 vols.

10 A. della Torre, *Storia dell'Accademia Platonica di Firenze* (Florence, 1902).

11 P. Zambelli, 'Platone, Ficino e la magia', *Studia humanitatis; Festschrift für Ernesto Grassi* (Munich, 1973), pp. 126–34.

12 M. Ficino, *Opuscula* (Venice, 1503); G.B. della Porta, *Magia naturalis sive De miraculous rerum naturalium* (Antwerp, 1564); *idem, Phytognomonica* (Rouen, 1650). For the doctrine of signatures see R.W. Crausius, *Dissertatio inauguralis medica de signaturis vegetabilium* (Jena, 1697).

13 G. Fracastoro, *Syphilis sive morbus Gallicus* (Verona, 1530), (Paris, 1531), and (Basel, 1536).

14 K.M. Reeds, 'Renaissance Humanism and Botany', *Annals of Science*, 1976, 33: 519–42; M. Odo, *De virtutibus herbarum et qualitatibus speciebus noviter inventus ac impressus* (Venice, 1508); N. Leoniceno, *De Plinii, & plurium aliorum medicorum erroribus* (Ferrara, 1509).

15 Turner's militant Calvinism (and subversive sense of humour) brought him trouble throughout his life. Henry VIII condemned all his works in 1546—together with those of Wycliff, Tyndal, and Coverdale—as did Mary in 1555, while in 1564 the Bishop of Bath and Wells suspended Turner, ostensibly for 'Nonconformity', but more probably in revenge for Turner having trained his dog to pluck the Bishop's cap from his head.

16 There is a rich trajectory of scholarship in the history of science which addresses the rôle of Protestantism in the Scientific Revolution; for a guide see I.B. Cohen, ed., *Puritanism and the Rise of Modern Science: The Merton Thesis* (London, 1990).

17 Konrad von Megenberg, *Hye Nach Volget Das Puch der Natur* (Augsburg, 1475); G.A. Pritzel, *Thesaurus litteraturae botanicae omnium gentium* (Milan, [1872–7] 1950), 6051; A.R. Arber, *Herbals, their Origin and Evolution: A Chapter in the History of Botany, 1470–1670* (Cambridge, 1912).

18 O. Brunfels, *Herbarium vivae icones* (Strasbourg, 1530), p. 22; L. Fuchs, *De historia stirpium* (Basel, 1542). See also O. Brunfels, *Almanach ewig werend Deutsche und Christich Practick* (Strasbourg, 1526).

19 W. Turner, *The Old Learning and the New* (London, [1537] 1548), sig. A2v; *idem, The Hunting and Fynding Out of the Romyshe Foxe, which more than seven yeares hath bene hyd among the bishoppes of England, after the Kynges Highness had commanded them to be Dryven out of Hys Realme* (Basel, 1543).

20 G. F. de Oviedo, *Historia general y natural de las Indias* (Madrid, 1535) and (Salamanca, 1547); see also B. de Las Casas, *Brevissima relación de la destruycion de las Indias* (Seville, 1552, with a French translation—Paris, 1579); R. Eden, *The Decades of the newe world of West India, conteyning the navigations and conquests of the Spanyardes*

(London, 1555); *Cosmographia Petri Apiani, per Gemmam Frisium apud Lovaniensis medicum ac mathematicum insignem, restituta* (Paris, 1553).

21 N. Monardes, *Joyfull Newes out of the newe founde worlde, wherein is declared the rare and singular vertues of diverse and sundrie hearbes, trees, oyles, plants, and stones*, J. Frampton, trans. (London, 1577).

22 A. Everardus, *De herba panacea, quam alii tabacum, alli petum, aut nicotianam vocant* (Antwerp, 1587); J. Wittich, *Von dem Ligno Guayaco, Wunderbaum, Res nova genandt, von der China, ex occidentali India, von der Sarssa Parilla, von dem Frantzosenholtz Sassafras, und vom dem Grieszholtz* (Leipzig, 1592); Z. Puteo, *Historia de gumma indica anteasthmatica, antehydropica, et antepodagrica* (Venice, 1628).

23 *Lansdowne Mss 107*, f. 155.

24 O. Mattirolo, 'Una sguardo alla Storia della Botanica in Italia', *L'Italia e la Scienza*, G. Petrucci, ed. (Florence, 1932), p. 220; G. Porro, *L'Horto de i semplici de Padova* (Venice, 1591); G. Manetti, 'Historical Notice of the Botanic Garden of Padua', *Gardener's Magazine*, 1839, *15*: 316.

25 Pisa makes some claim to having been planted in 1543, but as an act of policy Padua is clearly older. See K. Reeds, 'Renaissance Humanism and Botany', p. 535; E. Chiovenda, 'Note sulla fondazione degli orti medici di Padova e di Pisa', *Atti del VII Congresse International di Storia della Medicine* (Pisa, 1931), pp. 488–509.

26 'La Vita d'Ulisse Aldrovandi', in *Intorno alla vita e alle opera di Ulisse Aldrovandi* (Bologna, 1902); Reeds, 'Renaissance Humanism and Botany'.

27 A. Wood, *History and Antiquities of the University of Oxford* (London, 1796), *II* (2), p. 896; S.H. Vines and G.C. Druce, *An Account of the Morisonian Herbarium in the Possession of the University of Oxford* (Oxford, 1914), pp. x–xi.

28 G. de la Brosse, *Dessein d'un Jardin Royal Pour La Culture des Plantes Medicinales à Paris* (Paris, 1628) and *Description du Jardin Royale des Plantes Medicinales* (Paris, 1636). For the context see R. Howard, 'Medical Politics and the Founding of Jardin des Plantes in Paris', *Journal for the Society for the Study of Natural History*, 1980, *9*: 395–402 and 'Guy de la Brosse and the Jardin des Plantes de Paris', in H. Woolf, ed., *The Analytic Spirit. Essays in the History of Science in Honor of Henry Guerlać* (Ithaca, 1981), pp. 195–224; A. Debus, *The French Paracelsians: The Chemical Challenge to Medical and Scientific Doctrine in Early Modern France* (Cambridge, 1991).

29 P. Stephens and W. Brown, *Catalogus Horti Botanici Oxoniensis* (Oxford, 1658), 'Praefatio ad lectorem'.

30 See F. Yates, *The Art of Memory* (London, 1966) for discussion of such theatres. Porro, *L'Horto de i semplici di Padova* indeed concludes his book on the botanic garden of Padua with sixty-four pages which examined the students' ability to remember where which family was cultivated.

31 Francis Bacon, for example, compared the rhetorical task of Disposition to the work of 'an apothecary ranging his boxes', while the *Viridarium Chemicum* (1624) offered its readers a journey through 'the pleasure garden of chemistry'. See J. Spedding, R.L. Ellis, and D. Heath, eds., *The Works of Francis Bacon, Baron of Verulam, Viscount St. Alban, and Lord High Chancellor of England* (London, 1857–74), 7 vols., *I*, p. 275; Yates, *The Art of Memory*, p. 371; *idem*, *The Rosicrucian Enlightenment* (London, 1972), p. 89.

32 See F. Yates, *Giordano Bruno and the Hermetic Tradition* (New York, 1964); K. Thomas, *Religion and the Decline of Magic* (New York, 1971); B. Vickers, ed., *Occult and Scientific Mentalities in the Renaissance*; D.C. Lindberg and R.S. Westman, eds., *Reappraisals of the Scientific Revolution* (Cambridge, 1990), esp. B. Copenhaver, 'Natural Magic, Hermeticism and Occultism', pp. 280–1; W. Eamon, 'Technology as Magic in the Late Middle Ages and the Renaissance', *Janus*, 1983, *70*: 171–212.

33 R. Turner, *Botanologia, The British Physician* (London, 1664), sig. A5.

34 G. Baker, *The Newe Jewell of Health* (London, 1576).

35 K. Sudhoff, *Paracelsus: Sämtliche Werke* (Berlin, 1922–33), *II*.

36 C. Webster, *The Great Instauration* (London, 1975), p. 246.

37 N. Culpeper, *Astronomicall Judgement of Diseases* (London, 1651); and *The English Physitian, or an Astrologo-Physical Discourse of the Vulgar Herbs of This Nation* (London, 1652). Gascoigne draws attention to the fact that medicine had enjoyed long-standing ties to the astral sciences; John Gostlin, Regius Professor of Medicine at Cambridge (mourned by generations of Caians as the 'silly goose who gave the Bull to Cats'), was also an author of a treatise on comets, while John Bainbridge (1619–1643) was both Savilian Professor of Astronomy at Oxford and a member of

the Royal College of Physicians. See J. Gascoigne, 'A Reappraisal of the Role of the University in the Scientific Revolution', in Lindberg and Westman, eds., *Reappraisals.*

38 *Les Oeuvres Poétiques et Chrestiennes de Guillaume de Saluste du Bartas* (Geneva, 1615), p. 14; J. Dauphiné, *Guillaume de Saluste du Bartas: Poète Scientifique* (Paris, 1983), *passim.*

39 Prest, *The Garden of Eden*, pp. 1–6 and 54–5.

40 R. Austen, *The Spirituall Use of an Orchard*, ff. 3–4, published with R. Austen, *A Treatise of Fruit Trees* (1653); *NB* 1665 edition of *A Treatise*, published after the Restoration, conspicuously excludes this booklet.

41 See E. Cordus *Botanologicon* (Cologne, 1534); C. Gesner, *Historia plantarum* (Basel, 1541); J. Dantz, *Tabula simplicium medicamentorum* (Basel, 1543); L. Fuchs, *In Dioscoridis historiam herbarum certissima adaptatio* (Strasbourg, 1543); P. Belon, *De admirabili operum antiquorum* . . . (Paris, 1553), 2 vols.; V. Cordus, *Annotationes in Pedacii Dioscoridis Anazarbei de medica materia* (Strasbourg, 1561).

42 A.M. Brasavola, *Examen omnium simplicium quorum usus in publicis est officinis* (Venice, 1545); P.A. Mattioli, *Commentarii, in libros sex Pedacii Dioscoridis ... de medica materia* (Venice, 1554); M. Guilandinus, *De stirpibus aliquot* (Padua, 1558); L. Anguillara, *Semplici* (Venice, 1561); F.T. Sansovino, *Della materia medicinale* (Venice, 1562); A. Ceccarelli, *Opusculum de tuberibus* (Padua, 1564).

43 C.C. Raven, *John Ray* (Cambridge, 1950), pp. 339–40.

44 *Samuel Hartlib His Legacie* (London, 1651), p. 94.

45 A. Coles, *Adam in Eden: Or Nature's Paradise* (London, 1657), 'Dedication'.

46 W. Turner, *The Names of Herbs* (London, 1548), p. 2. It was this old Protestant initiative which impelled the Puritan Nicholas Culpeper to publish his Englishing of the *Pharmacopoeia Londiniensis* in 1649, to the anger of the Society of Apothecaries which preferred to guard its guild secrets behind a Latin veil.

47 R. Dodoens, *Cruydt Boek* (Antwerp, 1554); H. Junius, *Phalli, ex fungorum genere in Hollandia sabuletis passim crescentis descriptio* (Delft, 1564); C. Clusius, *Histoire des Plantes* (Antwerp, 1577); *idem, Rariorum aliquot stirpium per Pannoniam, Austriam, & vicinas quasdam provincias observatarum historia* (Antwerp, 1583); L. Jungermann, *Catalogus plantarum qua circa Altorfium Noricum, et vicinis quibusdam locis* (Altdorf, 1615).

48 Turner, *The Names of Herbs.*

49 N. Monardes, *Dos Libros, el uno quetrat a de todoas las cosas que traen de nuestras Indias Occidentales ... y el otro que trata de la piedra Bezaar* (Seville, 1565 and 1569).

50 G. da Orta, *Coloquios dos simples, e drogas he cosas mediçinais da India* (Goa, 1563); C. Acosta, *Tractado de las drogas y medicinas de las Indias Orientales con sus Plantas* (Burgos, 1578).

51 G. da Orta, *Colloquies on the Simples & Drugs of India*, C. Markham, trans. (London, 1913), pp. 60, 436.

52 Although see also the study of his fellow Huguenots: M. L' Obel and P. Pena, *Nova Stirpium Adversaria* (Antwerp, 1571).

53 C. U. L.: Adv.d.3.21, carries Clusius's signature with the date 6 January 1564.

54 Clusius, all published by Plantin in Antwerp: *Aromentum et simplicium aliquot medicamentorum apud Indios nascentium historia* (1567); *De Simpliciis Medicamentis Ex Occidentali India Delatis* (1574); *Rariorum aliquot stirpium per Hispanias observatarum historia* (1576); *Simplicium medicamentorum ex Novo orbe delatorum ... historia, a N. Monardis* (1579); *Aromatum & medicamentorum in Orientalis India nascentium* (1593).

55 M. Cerementati, 'Ulisse Aldrovandi e L'America', *Annali de Botanica*, 1906, 4: 313–66; J.H. Elliott, *The Old World and the New 1492–1650* (Cambridge, 1970), p. 38.

56 *America*, T. De Bry, publisher and engraver: Part I, *Admiranda narrata ... de commodis et incolarum vitibus Virginiae* (Frankfurt, 1590), pp. 7–12; see also Part II, *Brevis narratio eorum quae in Floridae Americae provincia Gallia acciderunt* (Frankfurt, 1591).

57 Coles, *Adam in Eden*, sig. A3v.

58 *Timaeus*, 30c.

59 *On the Generation of Animals*; *De Anima*, 414a–415a. The most fruitful exploration of the *scala naturae* remains A. Lovejoy, *The Great Chain of Being* (Cambridge, MA, 1936).

60 A. Cæsalpinus, *De plantis libri XVI* (Florence, 1583); for the philosophical foundations of his work see also *idem, Dæmonum investigatio peripatetica* (Florence, 1580).

61 Cæsalpinus, *De plantis*, pp. 1–30.

62 G. Bauhin, *De plantis* (Basel, 1591); *Animadversiones in historiam generalem plantarum Lugduni editam* (Frankfurt, 1601); *Prodromus. Theatri Botanici* (Frankfurt, 1620).

63 G. Bauhin, *Pinax. Theatri Botanici* (Basel, 1623).

64 *Hartlib His Legacie*, pp. 80–1.

65 F. Hernandez, *Rerum medicarum Novae Hispaniae thesaurus, seu plantarum, animalium, mineralium Mexicanorum Historia* (Rome, 1651); U. Chauveton, *Bref Discours .. des Français en la Floride* (Paris, 1579); G. Linocier, *Histoire des Plantes Nouvellement Trouvées en L'Isle Virginie et Autres Lieux ..* (Paris, 1620); J.P. Cornuti, *Canadensium Plantarum, Aliarumque Nondum Editarium Historia* (Paris, 1635); C. de Rochefort, *Histoire Naturelle et Morale des Îles Antilles de l'Amérique* (Rotterdam, 1658).

66 M.C. Karsten, *The Old Company's Garden at the Cape and Its Superintendents* (Cape Town, 1951); W.T. Stearn, *The Influence of Leyden on Botany in the Seventeenth and Eighteenth Centuries* (Leyden, 1961); D.O. Wijnands, *The Botany of the Commelins, 1682–1710* (Rotterdam, 1983); R. Grove, *Green Imperialism: Colonial Expansion, Tropical Island Edens, and the Origins of Environmentalism, 1600–1860* (Cambridge, 1995).

67 K.S. Manild, ed., *Botany and History of Hortus Malabaricus* (Rotterdam, 1980); W.D. Hackmann, 'The Growth of Science in the Netherlands', in M. Crosland, ed., *The Emergence of Science in Western Europe* (London, 1975).

68 R. Grove, 'The Transfer of Botanical Knowledge between Asia and Europe, 1498–1800', *Journal of the Japan-Netherlands Institute*, 1991, *3*: 160–76.

69 A. Stroup, *A Company of Scientists. Botany, Patronage, and Community at the Seventeenth-Century Parisian Academy of Sciences* (Berkeley, 1990), p. 25; N. Broc, *La Géographie des Philosophes: Géographes et Voyageurs Français au XVIIIe Siècle* (Strasbourg, 1974), pp. 20–1; M. Duval, *La Planète des Fleurs* (Paris, 1977), pp. 57–97; D. Jonquet, *Hortus Regius* (Paris, 1665).

70 Sieur de Flacourt, *Histoire de la Grande Isle de Madagascar* (Paris, 1661).

71 R. Boyle, 'General Heads for the Natural History of a Country, Great or Small; Drawn out for the Uses of Travellers and Navigators', *Transactions of the Royal Society*, 1666, *1* (11): 186–9; (18): 315–16; (19): 330–43. These were reprinted in his *General Heads for the Natural History of a Country* (London, 1692). J. Woodward, *Brief Instructions for Making Observations in All Parts of the World* (London, 1696).

72 *Royal Society*, Cl. P. X(i): 3, 4, 13, 20 and 28.

73 *Royal Society*, Cl. P. X(i): 31.

74 *Sloane Mss 1968*: 166.

75 Among these R. Ligon, *A True and Exact History of the Island of Barbados* (London, 1657); J. Josselyn, *New-England's Rarities Discovered: in Birds, Beasts, Fishes, Serpents and Plants of that Country* (London, 1672); *A Voyage to the Islands Madera, Barbados, Nieves, S. Christophers and Jamaica* (London, 1707–25), 2 vols.; J. Lawson, *A New Voyage to Carolina, containing the Exact Description and Natural History of that Country* (London, 1709).

76 'Papers and Draughts of the Reverend Mr. Banister in Virginia', *Sloane Mss 4002*.

77 Ray to Petiver, [1702], *Sloane Mss 4063*: f. 18. See also R.B. Stearns, 'J. Petiver Promoter of Natural Science', *Proceedings of the American Antiquarian Society*, 1953, 62: 243–365.

78 Sutherland to Petiver, 25 March 1700, *Sloane Mss 4063*: ff. 9–10. On Edinburgh see J. Sutherland, *Hortus Medicus Edinburgensis* (Edinburgh, 1683); H.R. Fletcher and W.H. Brown, *The Royal Botanic Garden Edinburgh, 1670–1920* (Edinburgh, 1920).

79 *Ibid.*

80 *Correspondence of John Ray* (London, 1848), p. 159.

81 J. Ray, *Methodus Plantarum Nova* (Amsterdam, 1682) and *Historia Plantarum* (1686–1704); J. Pitton de Tournefort, *Elementes de Botanique ou Méthode pour Connaître les Plantes* (Paris, 1683) and *De optima methodo instituenda in re herbaria* (Paris, 1697).

82 J. Ray, 'Of the Seeds of Plants' and 'Of the Specific Difference of Plants', *Royal Society*, Cl. P. X(i): 16.

83 We may note in passing the importance of the gifts from Alexander Brown and Edward Bulkely in the East Indies, and Mr. Willis from Virginia, and William Vernon from Maryland for the 'artificial' system of Robert Morison, Prefect of the Oxford Botanic Garden; see Vines and Druce, *An Account of the Morisonian Herbarium*, pp. lxvi–lxvii; R. Morison and J. Bobart, *Plantarum Historia Universalis Oxoniensis* (Oxford, 1680 and 1699).

84 See J. Ray, *Historia Plantarum Generalis, I* (London, 1686), sig. A3.

85 J. Ray, *Historia Plantarum Generalis, II* (London, 1688), sig. A3v ('Quis crederet in una provincia Malabara ... inveniri').

86 J. Ray, *The Wisdom of God Manifested in the Works of the Creation* (London, 1691), pp. 7–8.

87 R. Camerarius, *De sexu plantarum* (Tübingen, 1694) and *De convenientia plan-*

tarum in fructificatione et viribus (Tübingen, 1699).

88 See M. Gunn and L.E. Codd, *The Botanical Exploration of Southern Africa* (Cape Town, 1981) and R. Desmond, *The European Discovery of the Indian Flora* (Oxford, 1992), pp. 18–38.

89 M. Adanson, *Histoire Naturelle de Sénégal* (Paris, 1757), pp. x–xxii.

90 M. Adanson, *Les Familles des Plantes* (Paris, 1763), *I*, p. clv.

91 Here Adanson merely enlarged on the critique of the artificial method begun by Buffon in *Histoire Naturelle, I* (Paris, 1749), pp. 1–62.

92 The Linnaeus of the *Classes Plantarum* had of course implicitly advocated such an endeavour.

93 A.-L. de Jussieu, 'Exposition d'un Nouvel Ordre de Plantes Adopté dans les Démonstrations du Jardin Royal', *Mémoires de L'Academie des Sciences* (1774) and *Genera Plantarum* (Paris, 1789). For the context and subsequent implications see P.F. Stevens, *The Development of Biological Systematics: Antoine-Laurent de Jussieu, Nature, and the Natural System* (New York, 1994).

94 *Musaeum Tradescantium: or A Collection of Rarities* (London, 1656), see 'Hortus Tradescantium', pp. 73–178; N. Grew, *Musaeum Regalis Societatis, or A Catalogue & Description of the Natural and Artificial Rarities Belonging to the Royal Society* (London, 1681).

95 *Royal Society*, Cl. P.X(i): 43.

96 See Ray, *The Wisdom of God*, pp. 85–6.

97 'A History of Vegetables', *Royal Society*, Cl. P. X(i): 8.

98 Although alchemy retained an influence over Newton, as is well known, and it is likely over Linnaeus; see B.J.T. Dobbs, *The Foundations of Newton's Alchemy or 'The Hunting of the Greene Lyon'* (Cambridge, 1975); C. Webster, *From Paracelsus to Newton: Magic and the Making of Modern Science* (Cambridge, 1982); W.T. Stearn, 'Signs Used by Linnaeus', in C. Linnaeus, *Species Plantarum*, W.T. Stearn, ed., *I* (London, 1957), pp. 162–3.

99 *Royal Society*, Cl. P. X(i): 12, 14, 32.

100 Thomas, *Religion and the Decline of Magic*, p. 639.

101 S. Shapin and S. Schaffer, *Leviathan and the Air Pump. Hobbes, Boyle, and the Experimental Life* (Princeton, 1985), pp. 283–344; A. Guerrini, 'The Tory Newtonians: Gregory, Pitcairne and their Circle', *Journal of British Studies*, 1986, *25*: 288–311; M.C. Jacob, *The Newtonians and the English Revolution, 1688–1720* (Ithaca, 1976), M.C. Jacob and J.R. Jacob, 'The Anglican Origins of Modern Science: The Metaphysical Foundations of the Whig Constitution', *Isis*, 1980, *71*: 251–67; J.R. Jacob, *Robert Boyle and the English Revolution* (New York, 1977).

102 For reference to Compton as gardener see P. Miller, *The Gardener's and Florists Dictionary, or a Complete System of Horticulture* (London, 1724), *I*; A.M. Coats, 'The Hon. and Rev. Henry Compton, Lord Bishop of London', *Garden History*, 1976, *3*.

103 The list of Samuel Smith, the London publisher of *The Wisdom*, itself offered a representative slice of the new ideology: beside products of the cutting edge of science as Newton's *Principia*, Boyle's *Hydrostaticks*, and Ray's *Historia Plantarum*, were studies in natural theology or Protestant history such as Grew's *Cosmologia Sacra, The State of Rome, when the Reformation Began*, and *The History of the Persecution of the Protestants by the French King*.

104 S. Hales, *Vegetable Staticks: or, an Account of Some Statical Experiments on the Sap in Vegetables* (London, [1727] 1961), p. xxxi.

105 Ray, *The Wisdom of God*, pp. 126 and 8.

106 Raven, *John Ray*, p. 452.

107 Stearn, 'Introduction', p. 153.

108 *Species Plantarum*, 'Dedication'. I prefer this translation of '*deputerade från hela vida verlden*' to Stearn, 'Introduction', p. 152 [my emphasis].

109 *Natural History*, xxvii, 3, W.H.S. Jones, trans. (London, 1992)

2 Plants and Power

1 See C. Linnaeus, *Hortus Cliffortianus* (Amsterdam, 1737); J.G. Volckamer, *Flora Norimbergensis* (Nuremberg, 1700).

2 *Cal Treasury Books*, 1715, vol. XXX, 2: 509.

3 See F. Yates, *Astraea. The Imperial Theme in the Sixteenth Century* (London, [1975] 1993), pp. 48–50; see also N.H. Clulee, *John Dee's Natural Philosophy: Between Science and Religion* (London, 1988) and P. French, *John Dee: The World of an Elizabethan Magus* (London, 1972).

4 J. Speed, *The Most Happy Unions Contracted Betwixt the Princes of the Blood Royall of Theis Towe Famous Kingdoms of England & Scotland* (London, 1603).

5 On the 'Commonwealth tradition' see G.R. Elton, *Reform and Renewal: Thomas Cromwell and the Commonweal Tradition* (Cambridge, 1973); 'The Political Creed of

Thomas Cromwell', *Studies in Tudor and Stuart Politics and Government: Papers and Reviews, 1946–1972* (Cambridge, 1974), *II*, pp. 215–35; 'Thomas Cromwell Redivivus', *Studies in Tudor and Stuart Politics and Government: Papers and Reviews, 1973–1981* (Cambridge, 1983), pp. 215–35; J. Martin, *Francis Bacon, the State, and the Reform of National Philosophy* (Cambridge, 1992), ch. 1.

6 See H. Lyte, *The Light of Britayne* (1588), Dedication: 'Most dread souveraigne Ladie Elizabeth ... the Phoenix of the World: The Angell of England: The Bright Britona of Britayne: even Britomartis President of Britaine; The Chast Diana of Calydonia ... The most noble Lyonesse Atalanta: that keepeth Britannia from Romish Wolves and Foxes . . . I doubt not but our Meleaguer (even Iesus Christe the righteous) when he hath cut off the head of that monstrous Wilde Boare, shall at last take you to his spouse . . . O Diva Potens Elizabetha: my deare and dreade souveraigne.'

7 J. Spedding, ed., *The Life and Letters of Francis Bacon, including All his Occasional Works, Namely Letters, Speeches, Tracts, State Papers, Memorials, Devices, and All Authentic Writings not Already Printed among his Philosophical, Literary, or Professional Works* (London, 1861–74), 7 vols., *I*, pp. 332–42; see discussion by Martin, *Francis Bacon*, pp. 69–71.

8 Spedding, *The Life and Letters of Francis Bacon, I*, pp. 332–42.

9 *Ibid., III*, pp. 90–1.

10 Martin, *Francis Bacon*, pp. 3–5; B.H.G. Wormald, *Francis Bacon: History, Politics and Science, 1561–1626* (Cambridge, 1993).

11 W. Ralegh, *The History of the World* (London, 1614), chs. IX–XI.

12 Ralegh, *History*, p. 200.

13 Yates, *The Rosicrucian Enlightenment*, p. 123. James I and VI alternated between curiosity about, and repulsion towards esoteric doctrines. In 1597 he had attacked 'Geomantie' and 'Arithmantie' as the 'devils schole', and concluded that magic, despite its pedigree, could never be more than 'necromancie'. All the same he allowed that part of 'Astrologia' might be legitimate, such as that star cunning which assisted herbalists 'in knowing thereby the powers of simples'. See James VI & I, *Daemonologie* (Edinburgh, [1597] 1966), pp. 8–14.

14 RH. Jeffers, *The Friends of John Gerard (1545–1612)* (Falls Village, 1967).

15 *The Anonymous Life of William Cecil, Lord Burghley* (New York, [1600] 1990), pp. 126–8; C. Read, 'Lord Burghley's Household Accounts', *Economic History Review*, 2nd series, 1956, 9: 343–8.; see also the dedication of T. Diggs, *Alae seu scalae mathematicae* (London, 1573).

16 L. Digges, *A Geometrical Practise, named Pantometria* (London, 1571), sig. A1v.

17 J. Gerard, *Catalogus Arborum, Fruticum ac Plantarum Tam Indigenarum, Quam Exoticarum, in horto Johannis Gerardi* (London, 1599); for Ralegh as patron of the arts and sciences see V. Harlow, 'Introduction' to W. Ralegh, *The Discoverie of the Large, rich and bewtiful Empire of Guiana* (London, [1596] 1928).

18 C.C. Raven, *English Naturalists from Neckham to Ray: A Study of the Making of the Modern World* (Cambridge, 1947), p. 236.

19 See T. Clayton, testimonial, in J. Parkinson, *Theatrum Botanicum: The Theater of Plants* (London, 1640).

20 D. R. Coffin, *The Villa in the Life of Renaissance Rome* (Princeton, 1979); J.D. Hunt, *Garden and Grove: The Italian Renaissance Garden in the English Imagination: 1600–1750* (Princeton, 1986).

21 J. Summerson, 'The King's Houses', in H.M. Colvin, ed., *The King's Works, IV, 1485–1660, Part II* (London, 1982), p. 3; see pp. 22–4 for the exchange of style between the Valois and Tudor courts.

22 *Holinshed's Chronicle* (London, 1587), *I*, p. 196.

23 F. Bacon, 'Of Gardens', *The Essayes*, M. Kiernan, ed. (Oxford, 1985) pp. 139–40.

24 *Holinshed's Chronicle, I*, p. 209; reprinting of W. Harrison, *The Description and History of England* (London, 1577).

25 See R. Dudley to J. Hotman, 23 January [1588?], Folger Library *Add. Mss* 377 and Parkinson, *Theatrum Botanicum*, p. 1618. In the first instance, I do not entirely exclude the possibility that horticulture merely provided a code for the discussion of military and political matters.

26 Summerson, 'The King's Houses', pp. 272–3.

27 Bacon, *The Essayes*, see Kiernan's note on p. 285; E. Cecil, *A History of Gardening in England* (London, 1910), p. 139; J. Summerson, 'The Building of Theobalds, 1564–1585', *Archaeologia*, 1956, *97*; I. Dunlop, *Palaces and Progresses of Elizabeth I* (London, 1962).

28 Yates, *The Rosicrucian Enlightenment*, pp. 8ff. and R. Strong, *Henry, Prince of Wales and England's Lost Renaissance* (London, 1986).

29 Sir John Norden (1591) quoted by E.S.

Hartshorne, *Memorials of Holdenbury* (London, 1868), p. xxxiii.

30 See C. Clusius, *Exoticorum* (Antwerp, 1605); M. de L'Obel, *In G. Rondelletii . . . animadversiones* (London, 1605); C. Clusius, *Curae posteriores aethiopicum* (Antwerp, 1611).

31 For this, and subsequent references to the Tradescants in this paragraph, unless noted otherwise, see M. Allan, *The Tradescants: Their Plants, Gardens, and Museums, 1570–1662* (London, 1964), pp. 26–113, and P. Leith-Ross, *The John Tradescants* (London, 1984).

32 *A Letter from Dr Ducarel, F.R.S and F.S.A. to William Watson, M.D., F.R.S. Upon the Early Cultivation of Botany in England* (London, 1773), pp. 8–9.

33 Tradescant to E. Nicholas, 31 July 1625, quoted in Allan, *The Tradescants*, pp. 45, 115.

34 See H. Trevor-Roper, *Princes and Artists: Patronage and Ideology at Four Habsburg Courts 1517–1633* (London, 1975).

35 For Mollet's role as a carrier of French and Dutch geometrical fashion see F. Hopper, 'The Dutch Classical Garden and Andre Mollet', *Journal of Garden History*, 1982, *2*; and A. Mollet, *Le Jardin des Plaisirs* (1651); M. Batey, *Oxford Gardens: The University's Influence on Garden History* (Amersham, 1982), pp. 52–3.

36 *Catalogus plantarum horti medici oxoniensis* (Oxford, 1648), sig. B1v.

37 See R. Drayton, 'Henri IV et la Fondation de l'*Hortus regius monspeliensis*', in J.-A. Rioux, ed., *Le Jardin des Plantes de Montpellier. Quatre Siècles d'Histoire* (Montpellier, 1994); M. Deleuze, *Histoire et Description du Muséum Royal D'Histoire Naturelle* (Paris, 1823), vol. I, pp. 7–25; Duval, *La Planète des Fleurs*, p. 52; G. de la Brosse, *De la Nature, Vertu et Utilité des Plantes* (Paris, 1628); *idem, Description du Jardin Royal des Plantes Médicinales Estably par le Roi Louis le Juste à Paris* (Paris, 1636); R. Howard, 'Guy de la Brosse: Botanique et Chimie au debut de la révolution scientifique', *Revue d'Histoire des Sciences*, 1978, *31*: 325–6.

38 A. Stroup, *A Company of Scientists: Botany, Patronage, and Community at the Seventeenth-Century Academy of Sciences* (Berkeley, 1990); Y. Laissus and A.-M. Mouseigny, '*Les Plantes du Roi*: Note sur un Grand Ouvrage de Botanique Préparé au XVII Siècle par L'Académie Royale des Sciences', *Revue d'Histoire des Sciences*, 1969, *22*: 193–236.

39 R. Morison, *Hortus regius Blesensis* (London, 1669).

40 *CSP*, 1660, pp. 6 and 281; 1677, p. 751.

41 Vines and Druce, *An Account of the Morisonian Herbarium*, p. xxvii.

42 F.R. Cowell, *The Garden as Fine Art* (London, 1978), p. 162.

43 For a reflection on how the poverty of Charles II constrained his ambitions as a patron, see N. Smuts, 'The Political Failure of Stuart Cultural Patronage', in G. Lytle and S. Orgel, eds., *Patronage in the Renaissance* (Princeton, 1981), pp. 165–87.

44 Vines and Druce, *An Account of the Morisonian Herbarium*, p. xxvii.

45 See D. Jacques and A.J. van der Holt, *The Gardens of William and Mary* (London, 1988); W.T. Stearn, 'Horticulture and Botany', in R.P. Maccubbin and M. Hamilton-Phillips, eds., *The Age of William III & Mary II: Power, Politics and Patronage, 1688–1702* (New York, 1989), pp. 179–85; H.M. Colvin, ed., *The History of the King's Works* (London, 1963–73), *V*, pp. 170–4, 457–8.

46 M. Colvin, ed., *The King's Works, V*, pp. 170–1; P.R.O.: WORK 5/ 51-52.

47 Colvin, ed., *The King's Works, V*, p. 332; N. Japikse, ed., *Correspondentie van William III en van Hans Willem Bentinck* (Gravenhage, 1927), *I*, p. 246: 'M. Le Nôtre me fera un plan pour les jardins projectez à Windsor.'

48 H. Wise and G. London, *The Retir'd Gard'ner* (London, 1706), *I*, p. 295.

49 *Sloane Mss 2928* and *3343*, ff. 1–3, 4–6.

50 *Sloane Mss 3343*; Duke and Duchess of Beaufort to J. Petiver and W. Sherard to J. Petiver, [January] 1700 and 21 September 1700, *Sloane Mss 4063*, ff. 1 and 44; G. Rowley, 'The Duchess of Beaufort's Succulent Plants', *Bradleya*, 1987, *5*: 1–16; A.M. Coats, 'The Hon. and Rev. Henry Compton, Lord Bishop of London', *Garden History*, 1976, *3*; J. Evelyn, *The Diary of John Evelyn* (London, 1952), 27 August 1678 and 30 October 1683.

51 W.E. Houghton, 'The English Virtuoso in the Seventeenth Century', *Journal of the History of Ideas*, 1942, 3:51–73 and 190–219.

52 J.A. Bennett, 'The Mechanics Philosophy and the Mechanical Philosophy', *History of Science*, 1986, *24*: 1–28.

53 C. Webster, *The Great Instauration* (London, 1975), *passim*.

54 J. Ward, *The Lives of the Professors of Gresham College* (London, 1740), p. xi.

55 T. Sprat, *The History of the Royal Society* (London, 1667), p. 113.

56 J. Ray, *Wisdom of God Manifested in the*

Creation (London, 1691); W. Derham, *Physico Theology* (London, 1713) and *Astro Theology* (London, 1715).

57 See R. Drayton, 'Knowledge and Empire', chapter for P.J. Marshall, ed., *Oxford History of the British Empire, II: The Eighteenth Century* (Oxford, 1998), pp. 231–52 and G. Hudson, 'A Polite and Literary Pursuit: Natural History in the Augustan Age', unpublished essay ms.

58 See I. Rand, 'Company of Apothecaries Physick Garden', *Royal Society*, Cl. P. X (i): 48.

59 On Sloane see A. Macgregor, ed., *Sir Hans Sloane: Collector, Scientist, Antiquary, Founding Father of the British Museum* (London, 1994); E. St. John Brooks, *Sir Hans Sloane: The Great Collector and His Circle* (London, 1954).

60 *The Diary of John Evelyn, V*, p. 48.

61 Summerson, 'The King's Houses', pp. 1ff.

62 G. Kipling, 'Henry VII and the Origins of Tudor Patronage', in Lytle and Orgel, eds., *Patronage in the Renaissance*, pp. 118–19.

63 Summerson, 'The King's Houses', pp. 222–34.

64 Colvin, ed., *The King's Works, III*, p. 124.

65 Colvin, ed., *The King's Works, V*, p. 217; P. Reutersward, 'A French Project for a Castle at Richmond', *Burlington Magazine*, 1962, *104*: 533–5.

66 Colvin, ed., *The King's Works, V*, p. 218.

67 J. Macky, *A Tour Through England* (London, 1724), *I*, p. 66.

68 D. Defoe, *A Tour Through the Whole Island of Great Britain* (New Haven, [1724] 1991), pp. 64–5.

69 R. Desmond, *Kew: The History of the Royal Botanic Gardens* (London, 1995), p. 5.

70 *DNB, III*, pp. 1048–54; her Victorian biographer advises us here that apart from 'conniving in her husband's amours' she 'was more German than English to the last in her conceptions'.

71 Caroline's political gardening has received much attention in the last two decades; see J. Colton, 'Merlin's Cave and Queen Caroline, Garden Art as Political Propaganda', *18th Century Studies*, 1976, *10*: 1–20; *idem*, 'Kent's Hermitage for Queen Caroline at Richmond', *Architectura*, 1974, *2*: 181–9; and, most exhaustively, K. Stempel, *Geschichtsbilder im frühen englischen Garten* (Munster, 1982), 2 vols. I am particularly indebted to Stempel, *Geschichtsbilder, I*: pp. 43–181.

72 *A Description of the Royal Gardens at Richmond in Surry* (London, n.d. [1735]), p. 19.

73 See M.C. Jacob, *The Newtonians and the English Revolution, 1688-1720* (Ithaca, 1976); M.C. Jacob and J.R. Jacob, 'The Anglican Origins of Modern Science: The Metaphysical Foundations of the Whig Constitution', *Isis*, 1980, *71*: 251–67; J.R. Jacob, *Robert Boyle and the English Revolution* (New York, 1977).

74 *Craftsman*, no. 499, 24 January 1736.

75 *Craftsman*, no. 503, 21 February 1736.

76 *A Tour Thro' the Whole Island of Great Britain Divided into Circuits or Journeys* (London, 1724), pp. 281–3.

77 G. West, *Stowe, the Gardens of the Right Honourable Richard Lord Viscount Cobham* (London, 1732), pp. 10–11.

78 H.St.J. Bolingbroke, *Letters on the Spirit of Patriotism and on the Idea of a Patriot King* (Oxford, 1917), p. 48.

79 Bolingbroke, *Letters*, pp. 52–4 (original emphasis).

80 Capel's sister, the Duchess of Beaufort, was also a famous contemporary collector—see Rowley, 'The Duchess of Beaufort's Succulent Plants'.

81 *Craftsman*, no. 478, 6 September 1735.

82 R. Mabey, *The Flowering of Kew* (London, 1988), p. 15. For the significance of this reference to China see J. Addison, *The Spectator*, no. 414, 25 June 1712; P. Wittkower, 'English Neo-Palladianism, the Landscape Garden, China and the Enlightenment', *L'Arte*, 1969, *2*: 30; H. Honour, *Chinoiserie: The Vision of Cathay* (New York, 1961); O. Siren, *China and the Gardens of Europe* (New York, 1950).

83 *Gentleman's Magazine*, 1748, *18*: 301–2.

84 G. Eriksson, 'The Botanical Success of Linnaeus: The Aspect of Organization and Publicity', *Yearbook of the Swedish Linnaeus Society*, 1978, pp. 57–66.

85 J.R. Seeley, 'The House of Bourbon', *E. H. R.*, 1886, *1*: 104.

86 J. Amman, *Stirpium variorum in imperio Rutheno sponte provenientium* (St. Petersburg, 1739); J. E. McClellan III, *Science Reorganized: Scientific Societies in the Eighteenth Century* (New York, 1985), p. 77.

87 See R.S. Calinger, 'Frederick the Great and the Berlin Academy of Sciences', *Annals of Science*, 1968, *24*: 239–49.

88 N. Broc, *La Géographie des Philosophes: Géographes et Voyageurs Français au XVIIIe Siècle* (Strasbourg, 1974), pp. 24–5; Duval, *La Planète des Fleurs*, pp. 117–22.

89 N. Jacquin, *Plantarum rariorum horti Caesarei Schoenbrunnensis* (Vienna, 1797).

90 For an attempt to rescue 'Bute's scientific activities from the "enormous condesention" of political historians and historians

of science' see D. Miller, '"My favourite studdys": Lord Bute as naturalist', in K.W. Schweizer, ed., *Lord Bute: Essays in Reinterpretation* (Leicester, 1988), pp. 213–39.

91 Peter Collinson to Linnaeus, 10 April 1755, in J.E. Smith, ed., *A Selection from the Correspondence of Linnaeus and Other Naturalists* (London, 1821), *I*, p. 32; Miller, 'My favourite studdys', p. 217.

92 J. Hill, *The Idea of A Botanical Garden in England* (London, 1758), p. 13.

93 P. Toynbee, *Satirical Poems of William Mason* (London, 1926), p. 49.

94 See W. Chambers, *Plans, Elevations, Sections, and Perspective Views of the Gardens and Buildings at Kew in Surrey* (London, 1763), pp. 3–20.

95 See Chambers, *Plans, Elevations*, plates 20–1. His designs did not always reflect the oriental knowledge to which he aspired: the ceiling of the Alhambra was covered with French decorative motifs of the period while there are Gothic elements to its exterior.

96 Chambers, *Plans, Elevations*, p. 3.

97 Ellis to Hillsborough, [1763], LS: *Ellis Corr.*

98 R. Drayton, 'Collection and Comparison in the Sciences: A Seminar Manifesto', *Sphaera*, Occasional Paper No. 1 (Oxford, 1996).

99 BCMHN *Mss* 307.

100 W.T. Aiton to Banks, 2 April 1800; *Add. Mss 33980*, f. 230; Banks to Sir James Burgess, Under-Secretary, Foreign Office, 4 July 1795; *D.T.C. 9*: 221–6; H.B. Carter, 'Sir Joseph Banks and the Plant Collection From Kew Sent to The Empress Catherine II of Russia 1795', *Bulletin of British Museum (Natural History)*, 1974, *4*(5): 281–385.

101 George Annesley to Banks, 13 December 1802; *D.T.C*: *13*: 324–8.

102 Banks to Blandford, 4 December 1797, *D.T.C. 10*: 214–16; Banks to Blandford, 17 July 1805, *Add. Mss 33981*, f. 216.

103 James Bruce to Banks, 11 January 1774, *D.T.C. 1*: 67–8, Charles Blagden to Banks, 7 July 1776 and 28 October 1777, *D.T.C.*: *1*: 120–2, 148–51; John Christopher to Banks, 20 June 1783, *Add. Mss 33977*, ff. 201–3; Sir John Murray to Banks, 23 December 1788, 16 August 1789, 9 December 1792, *Add. Mss 33978*, ff. 282–3, 256–7, *33979*: f. 139; John Greg, 21 December 1776, *Add. Mss 33977*, ff. 61–2; William U. Buee to Banks, 3 May 1797, *Add. Mss 8098*, f. 439.

104 W. A'Court to Banks, 25 August 1802, *Add. Mss 33981*, f. 44.

105 Sir Thomas Stamford Raffles to Banks, 18 September 1814 and 22 March 1820, *D.T.C. 19*: 68–74 and *Add. Mss 33982*, ff. 211–12; Philip King to Banks, 31 July 1795, *D.T.C. 9*: 244–5; H. de Ponthieu to Banks, 23 January 1778 and 19 January 1785, *Kew: B.C. I*: 70 and 190.

106 F. Masson, 'An Account of Three Journeys from the Cape Town into the Southern Parts of Africa; Undertaken for the Discovery of New Plants, Towards the Improvement of the Royal Botanical Gardens at Kew', *Philosophical Transactions*, 1776, *66*: 268–317.

107 See *Kew: Kew Collectors–Papers Relating to 1791–1865*, and Banks to James Smith and George Austin, 31 July 1789, *D.T.C. 6*: 196–203; Banks to G. Caley, 16 November 1798, *D.T.C. 11*: 116–17; Banks to W. Kerr, 18 April 1803, *D.T.C. 14*: 61–8; Banks to A. Cunningham and J. Bowie, 1 June 1816, *Kew: B.C. II*: 340.

108 Banks to Sir George Harrison, Assistant Secretary to the Treasury, 1 September 1814, *D.T.C. 19*: 56–63; 'Cape of Good Hope: Botanical Collectors', *P. P.*, 1821, *21*: 37–8.

109 Banks to Harrison, 1 September 1814, f. 63; 'Cape of Good Hope: Botanical Collectors', p. 39. For Anton Hove see *idem* to Banks, 31 January 1786, *Kew: B.C. I*: 223.

110 See the appreciative mention of the King and his Observatory at Kew in the preface to N. Maskelyne, *Astronomical Observations* (London, 1776).

111 William Herschel to Banks, August 1785, *D.T.C. 4*: 163–8.

112 For Charlotte and her course of instruction see Banks to Sir James Smith, 15 August 1787, LS: *Smith Mss I*, ff. 87–8; and R. Thornton, *The Temple of Flora* (London, 1799–1807).

113 W.T. Aiton, 'Introduction' to F. Bauer, *Delineations of Exotick Plants Cultivated in the Royal Gardens at Kew* (London, 1796), p. i.

114 E. Darwin, *The Botanic Garden*, Canto IV, ll. 554–86 (my emphasis). This quote which alludes to Charlotte as well as George's botanical expertise might serve in a small way as a rebuttal to J. Brown, 'Botany for Gentlemen. Erasmus Darwin and *The Loves of Plants*', *Isis*, 1989, *80*: 593–621.

115 Banks to Cunningham, 20 February 1817, *D.T.C. 20*: 17–19.

116 A. Stroup, *A Company of Scientists: Botany, Patronage, and Community at the Seventeenth-Century Parisian Academy of*

Sciences (Berkeley, 1990); E. Spary, 'Making the Natural Order: The Paris Jardin du Roi, 1750–1795', PhD dissertation, University of Cambridge, 1993; M. Deleuze, *Histoire et Description du Muséum Royal d'Histoire Naturelle* (Paris, 1823) *I*, pp. 115–17, 140–1, and 193–245.

117 A. Young, *Travels during the Years 1787, 1788, and 1789 Undertaken more Particularly with a View to Ascertaining the Cultivation, Wealth, Resources, and National Prosperity, of the Kingdom of France* (London, 1792), p. 69.

118 Quoted in A.R. Steele, *Flowers for the King: the Expedition of Ruiz and Pavon and the Flora of Peru* (Durham, NC, 1964), pp. 57–8. For Spain's efforts at the scientific exploration of their colonies during its *Illustrada* see also J.C. Divito, *Las Expediciones Científicos Españolas durante el Siglo XVIII: Expeditión Botanica de Nueva Espana* (Madrid, 1968); F.J.P. Sarmiento, *La Ilusion Quebrada: Botanica, Sanidad y Politica científica en la España Ilustrada* (Barcelona, 1988), pp. 31–42, 73–134; I.H.W. Engstrand, *Spanish Scientists in the New World: The Eighteenth Century Expeditions* (London, 1981); see H. Ruiz and J. Pavon, *Flora peruviana et chilensis* (Madrid, 1798–1802), 3 vols.

119 *Breves Instruccoens aos correspondentes da Academia das Sciencias de Lisboa sobre as remessas dos productos e noticias pertencentes a historia da Natureza para formar hum Museo Nacional* (Lisbon, 1781); W.J. Simon, *Scientific Expeditions in the Portuguese Colonies Overseas (1783–1808)* (Lisbon, 1983).

3 The Useful Garden

1 Robert Cotton, 'How the Kings of England have Supported and Repaired Their Estates', in J. H[owell], ed. *Cottoni Posthuma* (London, 1651), pp. 182–4.

2 E. Kerridge, *The Agricultural Revolution* (London, 1967), p. 342; *Samuel Hartlib His Legacie* (London, 1651), p. 74.

3 G. Markham, *The Inrichment of the Weale of Kent* (London, 1631), p. 24.

4 H. Plat, *The New and Admirable Art of Setting Corne* (London, 1600), sig. A2v.

5 C. Hill, *The English Bible and the Seventeenth Century Revolution* (London, 1993), pp. 126–53.

6 J. Appleby, *Economic Thought and Ideology in Seventeenth-Century England* (London, 1976).

7 B. Supple, *Commercial Crisis and Change in England, 1600–1642* (Cambridge, 1959), p. 235; R.H. Tawney, eds., *Tudor Economic Documents* (London, 1984), 3 vols. *II*, p. 45.

8 Bacon, *The Essayes*, Kiernan, ed., p. 93, where he quotes Virgil: 'Terra potens armis atque ubere glebae.'

9 See *The Oxford English Dictionary* on CD-ROM, and R. Williams, *Keywords*, (New York, [1976] 1983), pp. 160–1.

10 J. Dee, *General and Rare Memorials Pertayning to the Perfect Arte of Navigation* (London, 1577), p. 33.

11 *A Compendious or Briefe Examination of Certayne Ordinary Complaints* (London, 1581), ff. 3r and 18r.

12 J. Lee, *Considerations Concerning Common Fields and Inclosures* (London, 1654), p. 3.

13 Lee, *Considerations*, p. 39.

14 Kerridge, *Agricultural Revolution*, p. 328 and *passim*.

15 C. Webster, *The Great Instauration* (London, 1975).

16 C. Dymock, *An Essay for Advancement of Husbandry-Learning: or Propositions for the Erecting of a Colledge of Husbandry*. (London, 1651), Preface; and S. Hartlib, *The Reformed Spiritual Husbandman with An Humble Memorandum Concerning Chelsy College* (London, 1652).

17 Dymock, *An Essay for Advancement of Husbandry-Learning*.

18 W. Blith, *The English Improover, or, A New Survey of Husbandry* (London, 1649), p. 3.

19 I am indebted to Simon Schaffer for having guided me to sources used below; see S. Schaffer, 'The Earth's Fertility as a Social Fact in Early Modern Britain', in R. Porter and M. Teich, eds., *Nature and Society in Historical Context* (Cambridge, 1997), pp. 124–47.

20 'Enquiries concerning Agriculture', *Philosophical Transactions*, 1665, *1*: 91–4; M. Hunter, *Establishing the New Science: The Experience of the Early Royal Society* (Woodbridge, 1989).

21 R.G. Albion, *Forests and Seapower: The Timber Problem of the Royal Navy, 1652–1862* (Cambridge, 1926).

22 See Schaffer, 'The Earth's Fertility'; J. Houghton, *A Collection of Letters for the Improvement of Husbandry and Trade* (London, 1681–1703) and *idem*, *England's Interest, or the Gentleman and Farmer's Friend* (London, 1703).

23 S. Hartlib, *A Discours of Husbandrie Used in Brabant and Flanders*, sig. A2r–4v; Webster, *The Great Instauration*, p. 476.

24 *Hartlib His Legacie*, sig. A2v.

25 Blith, *The English Improover*, p. 6; Moore,

Bread for the Poore, p. 39, quoted by Hill, *The English Bible*, p. 131.

26 G. Plattes, *England's Wants* (London, 1667), pp. 11–12.

27 A. Yarranton, *England's Improvement By Land and Sea* (London, 1673), pp. 45–7.

28 N.P. Canny, *Kingdom and Colony: Ireland in the Atlantic World, 1560–1800* (Baltimore, 1988), p. 13. For the relation of the 'agriculturalist' argument to the Roman law distinction between 'natural' and 'civil' possession, see A. Pagden, *Lords of All the World: Ideologies of Empire in Spain, Britain and France c. 1500–c. 1800* (London, 1995), p. 79.

29 J. Spedding, ed., *The Life and Letters of Francis Bacon* ... (London 1861–74), 7 vols., *III*, p. 69.

30 G. Boate, *Ireland's Naturall History* (London, 1652), pp. 112–17.

31 *Ibid.*, p. 113.

32 *Ibid.*, p. 122.

33 T.C. Barnard, *Cromwellian Ireland: English Government and Reform in Ireland* (Oxford, 1975); Canny, *Kingdom and Colony*, p. 80.

34 S. Innes, *Creating the Commonwealth: The Economic Culture of Puritan New England* (New York, 1995); K.O. Kupperman, *Settling with the Indians: The Meeting of English and Indian Cultures in America, 1580–1640* (Totowa, 1980).

35 R. Johnson, *Nova Britannia: Offering Most Excellent Fruits by Planting in Virginia* (London, 1609), sig. B1r.

36 Here and below I quote William Cronon, *Changes in the Land: Indians, Colonists, and the Ecology of New England* (New York, 1983), pp. 56–7.

37 S.M. Kingsbury, *Records of the Virginia Company in London, III, 1607–1622* (London, 1906), p. 400.

38 Johnson, *Nova Britannia*, sig. B4v–C1.

39 J. Worlidge, *Systema Agriculturae, Part II* (London, 1689), p. i.

40 L. Roberts, *The Treasure of Traffic, Or a Discourse of Foreign Trade* (London, 1641).

41 See D. Armitage, 'The British Empire and the Civic Tradition', PhD dissertation, University of Cambridge, 1992, p. 34.

42 *A Description of the State of the Colony and Affaires of Virginia* (London, 1620), sig. A4.

43 Bacon, *The Essayes*, p. 107.

44 J. Brewer, *The Sinews of Power: War, Money and the English State, 1688–1783* (London, 1989), p. 168.

45 On British 'mercantilism' see D. Baugh, 'Great Britain's "Blue Water" Policy, 1689–1815', *International History Review*, 1988, *10*: 33–58; Brewer, *Sinews of Power*, pp. 168–9.

46 See the venerable but still valuable argument of E.F. Heckscher, *Mercantilism* (London, 1955).

47 T. Mun, *England's Treasure by Forraign Trade* (Oxford, [1667] 1967), p. 5; J. Viner, 'Power versus Plenty as Objectives of Foreign Policy in the Seventeenth and Eighteenth Centuries', *World Politics*, 1948, *1*: 1–29.

48 Webster, *The Great Instauration*, p. 458 and Appendix V.

49 H. Robinson, *Certain Proposalls In Order to the Peoples Freedome and Accommodation in some Particulars. With the Advancement of Trade and Navigation of this Commonwealth in Generall* (London, 1652), p. 11; Webster, *The Great Instauration*, p. 457.

50 G. Plattes, *A Description of the Famous Kingdome of Macaria* (London, 1641); reprinted in Webster, ed., *Samuel Hartlib*, pp. 79–90; subsequent citation will refer to the latter edition.

51 Plattes, *Macaria*, p. 82.

52 W. Goffe, *How to Advance Trade of the Nation and Employ the Poor* in *Harleian Miscellany*, 1808–13, *IV*; Webster, *The Great Instauration*, p. 455.

53 Robinson, *Certain Proposalls*, p. 11; Webster, *The Great Instauration*, p. 457.

54 Yarranton, *England's Improvement*, p. 11.

55 *Ibid.*, pp. 127ff.

56 See R. Drayton, 'Knowledge and Empire', in P.J. Marshall, ed., *Oxford History of the British Empire* (Oxford, 1998), *II*, pp. 231–52 and Webster, *The Great Instauration*, pp. 34–47.

57 S. Hartlib, 'Epistle Dedicatory', in Boate, *Ireland's Naturall History*, sig. A4v and r.

58 R.S. Wilkinson, 'The Alchemical Library of John Winthrop and his Descendants', *Ambix*, 1963, *11*: 33–51, *13*: 139–86; Webster, *The Great Instauration*, p. 46.

59 Webster, *The Great Instauration*, p. 402.

60 *Ibid.*, pp. 462–3.

61 W. Petty, *The Political Anatomy of Ireland* (London, 1691), p. 21.

62 *Ibid.*, p. 21, my emphasis.

63 See I.B. Cohen, *Interactions: Some Contacts Between the Natural Sciences and the Social Sciences* (London, 1994).

64 P.H. Buck, 'People who Counted: Political Arithmetic in the Eighteenth Century', *Isis*, 1982, *73*: 28–45; L.G. Sharp, 'Sir William Petty and Some Aspects of Seventeenth Century Natural Philosophy', DPhil dissertation, University of Oxford, 1977; K. Thomas, 'Numeracy in Early Modern England', *Transactions of the Royal Historical Society*, 1987, *37*: 103–32.

65 *Sir William Petty's Political Arithmetick* (Glasgow, 1751), pp. 23–4.

66 J. Locke, *Two Treatises of Government*, P. Laslett, ed. (Cambridge, 1988), p. 291.
67 J. Smith, *England's Improvement Reviv'd in a Treatise of All Manner of Husbandry and Trade by Land and Sea* (London, 1673), pp. 10–13.
68 Smith, *England's Improvement*, pp. 179–248.
69 G. Markham, *A Way to Get Wealth* (London, 1631), part II.
70 G. Markham, *The English Horseman* (London, 1607); *The Famous Whore* (London, [1609] 1868); *The Pleasure of Princes* (London, 1614); *Hunger's Prevention: or the Whole Art of Fowling* (London, 1621).
71 On the 'virtuoso tradition' see J. Gascoigne, *Joseph Banks and the English Enlightenment* (Cambridge, 1994), pp. 57–118.
72 Quoted in N. Wood, *John Locke and Agrarian Capitalism* (London, 1984), p. 57.
73 J.G.A. Pocock, *The Ancient Constitution and the Feudal Law* (Cambridge, 1987).
74 A.J. Sambrook, 'The English Lord and the Happy Husbandman', *Studies in Voltaire and the Eighteenth Century*, 1967, *55*: 1357–75; R. Feingold, *Nature and Society: Later Eighteenth-Century Uses of the Pastoral and the Georgic* (Hassocks, 1978).
75 Lord Ernle, *English Farming Past and Present* (London, [1911] 1961), p. 173.
76 *The Hyp Doctor*, no. 32, 20 July 1731; Ernle, *English Farming*, p. 173.
77 For an exploration of the connection between landed wealth and the new financial interests of Hanoverian Britain, see P.J. Cain and A.G. Hopkins, 'Gentlemanly Capitalism and British Expansion Overseas. *I*. The Old Colonial System, 1688–1850', *Economic History Review*, 2nd series, 1986, *39*: 501–25.
78 R. Davis, *The Industrial Revolution and British Trade* (Leicester, 1979), p. 45.
79 P. Richardson, *Empire and Slavery* (London, 1968), p. 43.
80 E. Burke, *Observations on the Late State of the Nation* (London, 1769).
81 K. Wilson, 'Empire, Trade, and Popular Politics, The Admiral Vernon Agitation,' *Past and Present*, pp. 96–109; R. Pares, 'American versus Continental Warfare, 1739–1763,' *E.H.R.*, 1936, *51*: 429–65.
82 Bolingbroke, *Works, II*, p. 249.
83 J. Kramnick, *Bolingbroke and his Circle: The Politics of Nostalgia in the Age of Walpole* (Ithaca, 1968), p. 35.
84 L. Colley, *Britons: Forging the Nation, 1707–1837* (London, 1994).
85 See P.K. O'Brien and S.L. Engerman, 'Exports and the Growth of the British Economy from the Glorious Revolution to the Peace of Amiens', in B.L. Solow, ed., *Slavery and the Rise of the Atlantic System* (Cambridge, 1991), pp. 177–209.
86 E. Williams, *Capitalism and Slavery* (London, 1964). After two generations of denial, British historians are gradually coming to terms with Williams's vision of the eighteenth-century economy.
87 E.B. Schumpeter, *English Overseas Trade Statistics, 1697–1800* (London, 1960); from tables V and VI which neither include Scotland nor indeed the East India cargoes smuggled in.
88 Cain and Hopkins, 'Gentlemanly Capitalism, *I*', 519; T.J. Halton and J.S. Lyons, 'Eighteenth Century Trade: Home Spun or Empire Made?' *Explorations in Economic History*, 1983, *20*: 163–82.
89 See D. Richardson, 'The Slave Trade, Sugar, and British Economic Growth, 1748–1776', *Journal of Interdisciplinary History*, 1987, *17*: 759–63; R.G. Wilson, *Gentleman Merchants* (Manchester, 1971), pp. 41–2.
90 R.A. Austen and W.D. Smith, 'Private Tooth Decay as Public Economic Virtue: The Slave–Sugar Triangle, Consumerism, and European Industrialization,' in J. Inikori and S. Engerman, eds., *The Atlantic Slave Trade: Effects on Economies, Societies, and Peoples in Africa, the Americas, and Europe* (London, 1992).
91 M. Postlethwayt, *The African Trade, the Great Pillar and Support of the British Plantation Trade in North America* (London, 1745), p. 6; this argument of course is drawn directly from Williams.
92 See chapter 1, and R.P. Stearns, 'Colonial Fellows of the Royal Society of London, 1661–1788', *William and Mary Quarterly*, 1946, *3*: 208–68; D.J. Struik, *Yankee Science in the Making* (New York, 1962); 'Papers and Draughts of the Reverend Mr. Banister in Virginia', *Sloane Mss 4002*.
93 See Drayton, 'Knowledge and Empire'.
94 For the British Isles see D.G.C. Allan, *William Shipley, Founder of the Royal Society of Arts: A Biography with Documents* (London, 1979); D. Spadafora, *The Idea of Progress in Eighteenth-Century Britain* (New Haven, 1990), pp. 76–78; D.D. McElroy, *Scotland's Age of Improvement: A Survey of Eighteenth-Century Literary Clubs and Societies* (Washington, 1969); for North America see B. Hindle, *The Pursuit of Science in Revolutionary America, 1735–1789* (Chapel Hill, 1956); for

Barbados and Grenada see Joshua Steele to Joseph Banks, 14 July 1781, *Add. Mss 33977*: f. 135; J. Steele to the Society of Arts, 14 July 1784, *Society of Arts Archives*, A11/45; and [ ] to Sir Joseph Banks, 9 March 1791, *Sutro*, Sir Joseph Banks Correspondence: Reel 20.

95 See *Musaeum Rusticum et Commerciale* (London, 1764–6); *De Re Rustica* (London, 1771); *Memoirs of Agriculture and other Oeconomical Arts* (London, 1768, 1771, and 1782); *A Register of the Premiums and Bounties given by the Society of Arts, Manufactures, and Commerce* (London, 1778).

96 G. Jacob, *The Country Gentleman's Vade Mecum* (London, 1717); J. Laurence, *A New System of Agriculture, Being a Complete Body of Husbandry and Gardening* (London, 1726); R. Bradley, *A Collection for the Improvement of Husbandry* (London, 1727); *idem*, *A Complete Book of Husbandry* (London, 1727); J. Evelyn, *Terra* (London, 1729); J. Tull, *The New Horse-hoeing Husbandry* (London, 1731); W. Ellis, *The Practical Farmer* (London, 1731); *idem*, *A Complete System of Improvements* (London, 1749).

97 D. Hudson and K.W. Luckhurst, *The Royal Society of Arts, 1754–1954* (London, 1954), p. 87.

98 *Society of Arts Archives: Minutes of Committee*, 1758–60, 1760–2, 1762–3, 1763–4; *Premiums Offered by the Society Instituted at London for the Encouragement of Arts, Manufactures, and Commerce* (London, 1765–70).

99 *Society of Arts Archives Minutes of Committee*, 1758–60 (3), ff. 103–6 and 1766–7 (6), ff. 8–9.

100 'Provincial Gardens in America', *Society of Arts Archives: Minutes of Committee* 1758–60 (3), f. 166; and R.A. Howard, 'Botanical Gardens in West Indies History', *Garden Journal*, July–August 1953: 118.

101 L. Guilding, *An Account of the Botanic Garden in the Island of St. Vincent, From its First Establishment to the Present Time* (Glasgow, 1825), p. 5.

102 *Society of Arts Archives: Manuscript Transactions, 1772–3*, ff. 55–141.

103 H. Home, *The Gentleman Farmer, being an Attempt to Improve Agriculture, by Submitting it to the Test of Rational Principles* (Edinburgh, 1776), esp. pp. 300–409.

104 S. Hartlib, *A Further Discoverie of the Office of Publick Address* (London, 1648), *Samuel Hartlib His Legacie* (London, 1651), pp. 83–9.

105 I. Ross, *Lord Kames and the Scotland of his Day* (Oxford, 1972); A.V. Chitnis, 'Agricultural Improvement, Political Management and Civic Virtue in Enlightened Scotland', *Studies on Voltaire and the Eighteenth Century*, 1986, *245*: 475–88; J.V. Golinski, *Science as Public Culture* (Cambridge, 1989); C. Withers, 'Cullen's Agricultural Lectures', *Agricultural History Review*, 1989, *37*: 144–56.

106 Brewer, *Sinews of Power*, *passim*.

107 'Plan for Reducing the Carib Landholders in St. Vincent', *Add. Mss 338343*, f. 267.

108 See, in the conclusion of this chapter, my discussion of the French precedent for this.

109 Renault [1785], AN: Mar D[3] 35, f. 162.

110 G.L.C. Cuvier, 'Éloge Historique de Sir Joseph Banks. Lu le 2 Avril 1821', *Recueil des Éloges Historiques*, 1827, *III*.

111 C. de Brosses, *Histoire des Navigation aux Terres Australes* (Paris, 1756), 2 vols., *I*, pp. 4–5.

112 J. Martin, *Francis Bacon, The State and the Reform of Natural Philosophy* (Cambridge, 1992), pp. 2–5, 175.

113 R. Hahn, *The Anatomy of a Scientific Institution: The Paris Academy of Sciences, 1666–1803* (London, 1971) and A. Stroup, *A Company of Scientists: Botany, Patronage and Community at the Seventeenth-Century Academy of Sciences* (Berkeley, 1990).

114 V. L. Seckendorff, *Teutscher Fürsten Stat* (Frankfurt, 1656); J.J. Becher, *Politische Discurs* (Frankfurt, 1668); P. W von Hörnigk, *Österreich über Alles wenn Es Nur Will* (Frankfurt, 1684); W. von Schröder, *Fürstliche Schatz und Rentkammer* (Leipzig, 1686). On Cameralism see A.W. Small, *The Cameralists* (Chicago, 1909); K. Tribe, *Governing Economy: The Reformation of German Economic Discourse 1750–1840* (Cambridge, 1988), pp. 19–21; P. H. Smith, *The Business of Alchemy: Science and Culture in the Holy Roman Empire* (Princeton, 1994).

115 M. Raeff, *The Well-Ordered Police State* (New Haven, 1988).

116 J. Plumb, *The Growth of Political Stability in England* (London, 1967), pp. 11–12.

117 R. Vierhaus, *Germany in the Age of Absolutism*, J. B. Knudsen, trans. (Cambridge, 1988), pp. 12–30; Tribe, *Governing Economy*, pp. 19–90.

118 F. Szabo, *Kaunitz and Enlightened Absolutism, 1753–1780* (Cambridge, 1994), pp. 158–9.

119 J.J. Spengler, *Économie et Population, Les Doctrines Françaises avant 1800* (Paris, 1954); S.C. Kaplan, *Bread, Politics, and Political Economy in the Reign of Louis XV* (Amsterdam, 1976), 2 vols.; J. Komlos, *Nutrition and Economic Development in the*

Eighteenth-Century Habsburg Monarchy (Princeton, 1989).

120 See H.M. Scott, ed., *Enlightened Absolutism: Reform and Reformers in Later Eighteenth Century Europe* (London, 1990); F. Bluché, *Le Despotisme Éclairé* (Paris, 1968); F. Venturi, *Settecento Riformatore* (Milan, 1969–87), 5 vols.

121 Here and below, my argument is much in the debt of Tribe's seminal work, *Governing Economy.*

122 Sir Robert Filmer's *Patriarcha*, against which Locke framed his ideal of Adam the *zoon oekonomikon*, amounts to precisely such an appeal to the Edenic origins of monarchical sovereignty.

123 Tribe, *Governing Economy*, p. 19.

124 Tribe, *Governing Economy*, pp. 32–3; F. Felsing, *Die Statistik als Methode der politischen Ökonomie im 17 und 18 Jahrhundert* (Leipzig, 1930).

125 P.G.M. Dickson, *Finance and Government under Maria Theresa, 1740–1780* (Oxford, 1987), *II*; Szabo, *Kaunitz and Enlightened Despotism*, pp. 113–17.

126 On physiocracy see G. Weulersse, *Le Mouvement Physiocratique en France de 1756 à 1770* (Paris, 1910), 2 vols.; R.L. Meek, *The Economics of Physiocracy* (London, 1962); E. Fox-Genovese, *The Origins of Physiocracy* (Ithaca, 1976); G. Vaggi, *The Economics of François Quesnay* (London, 1987).

127 Buffon to Montbeillard, 20 January 1768, H.N. de Buffon, ed., *Correspondance Générale Recueillie et Annotée* (Geneva, 1971), 2 vols., *I*, no. 121; quoted in E.C. Spary, 'Making the Natural Order: The Paris Jardin du Roi, 1750–95', PhD dissertation, University of Cambridge, 1993, chapter 1. The medical origins of the *Tableau Économique*, in particular the connections between Quesnay's theories of the circulation of the blood in the body and of wealth in an economy, have been provocatively suggested by V. Foley, 'An Origin of the Tableau Économique', *History of Political Economy*, 1973, *5*: 121–50.

128 J. Cartelier, ed., *Physiocratie* (Paris, 1991), p. 237.

129 AN: Col F[3] 161, f. 1.

130 See the Colbertian manual: *Introduction Générale pour la Teinture des Laines de Toute Couleur et pour la Culture des Drogues ou Ingrédients qu'On y Emploie* (Toulouse, 1671).

131 See J.H. Furstenau, *Gründliche Anhaltung zu der Haushaltungskunst* (Lemgo, 1736), and particularly D. Heister, *Oratorio de hortorum academicorum utilitate* (Helmstadt, 1739).

132 On Linnaeus in his context see F. Stafleu, *Linnaeus and the Linnaeans: The Spreading of Their Ideas in Systematic Botany, 1735–1789* (Utrecht, 1971); T. Frängsmyr, 'Linnaeus in his Swedish Context', in J. Weinstock, *Contemporary Perspectives on Linnaeus* (London, 1985), pp. 183–6; L. Koerner, 'Purposes of Linnaean Travel', in D.P. Miller and P.H. Reill, eds., *Visions of Empire: Voyages, Botany, and Representations of Nature* (Cambridge, 1996), pp. 117–52, and 'Carl Linnaeus in His Time and Place', in N. Jardine, J.A. Secord, and E.C. Spary, eds., *Cultures of Natural History* (Cambridge, 1996), pp. 145–62. The two Koerner essays are particularly important.

133 See S. Mulle-Wille's remarkable dissertation: 'Varietäten auf ihre arten Zurückführen: Zur Begründung eines natürlichen Systems der Pflanzen durch Carl von Linné (1797–1778)', PhD dissertation, University of Bielefeld, 1997.

134 M. Roberts, *The Age of Liberty, Sweden 1719–1772* (Cambridge, 1986); D. Kirby, *Northern Europe in the Early Modern Period* (London, 1990), pp. 370–1.

135 Koerner, 'Purposes', p. 127; T. Lempiäinen, 'Botanical Exploration by the Academy of Turku', *Botanical Journal of Scotland*, 1994, *46*: 581–8.

136 C. Linnaeus, *Dissertatio: Flora oeconomica* (Uppsala, 1748); *Oeconomia naturae* (Uppsala, 1750); *Quaestio historico naturalis, cui bono? breviter soluta* (Uppsala, 1752).

137 See as contemporary examples of this Hippocratic influence, which inspired botanists to collect plants indigenous to particular environments: H. Rupp, *Flora Jenensis sive enumeratio plantarum, tam sponte circa Jenam, & in locis vicinis nascentium* (Frankfurt, 1726); C. Erndtel, *Warsavia physice illustrata sive de aere, aquis, locis et incolis Warsaviae eorundemque moribus et morbis tractatus, cui annexum est viridarium vel catalogus plantarum circa Warsaviam nascentium* (Dresden, 1730).

138 K. Hagberg, *Carl Linnaeus* (London, 1957), p. 124.

139 Koerner, 'Purposes', pp. 145–6 and 'Carl Linnaeus', p. 151.

140 Frängsmyr, 'Linnaeus in his Swedish Context' and Koerner, 'Purposes'. Linnaeus's faith in the botanist's powers clearly parallels the hopes of baroque chemistry, and indeed his use of alchemical symbols in manuscripts would probably reward closer examination.

141 P. Wagner, 'The Royal Botanical Institution at Amalienborg. Sources and Inspiration', *Botanical Journal of Scotland*, 1994, *46*: 599–604.

142 C. Linnaeus, *Miscellaneous Tracts Relating to Natural History, Husbandry, and Physick*, B. Stillingfleet, trans. (London, 1759).
143 Szabo, *Kaunitz*, pp. 160–1; H.M. Scott, 'Reform in the Hapsburg Monarchy, 1740–90', pp. 151–2 in Scott, *Enlightened Absolutism*..
144 See G.A. Suckow, *Öekonomische Botanik* (Mannheim, 1777); J. Meyer, 'Okonomische-botanische Beobachtungen', *Bemerkungen der Kuhrpfalz physikalische ökonomische Gesellschaft*, 1779, 346–52; F.J. Marter, *Vorstellung eines ökonomischen Gartens nach den Grundsatzen der angewandten Botanik* (Vienna, 1782).
145 See the *Mémoires* of the Accademia di Agricoltura of Turin and the Accademia Economico-Agraria of Florence.
146 D. Vandelli, *Memoria sobre a utilidade das jardinys botanicos a respeito da Agricultura* (Lisbon, 1770).
147 'Biographie de Dr Domingo Vandelli, 1728–1816', BCMNH: *Mss* 2445 (3).
148 See Plumier's report on the timber of Martinique and St. Domingue from 1685, and the 'Mémoires sur les Simples de Cayenne' (1721), in AN: Col F^3 92, ff. 14–29.
149 G. de Milhau, 'Histoire de l'Isle de Cayenne et Province de Guianne' (1732), p. 63 and map on pp. 58–9, BCMNH: M2129.
150 Desportes to Maurepas, 10 July 1736, AN: Col F^3 92, f. 38.
151 See also his *Sur l'Exploitation des Bois* (Paris, 1764).
152 See in particular 'Rapport de Duhamel de Monceau au Petit Ecole de la Marine qu'il dirige a Paris' [1749], AN: Mar G 89, and his *Éléments de l'Architecture Navale* (Paris, 1758). We may note the coincident foundation of the École des Ponts et Chaussées in 1747.
153 AN: Mar B^2 301, 307, 314, 321.
154 See 'L'Oeuvre de Buffon au Jardin du Roi', BCMNH: *Mss* 1934, XXI, f. 1r and 8–9; Spary, 'Making the Natural Order', *passim*; Y. François, 'Buffon au Jardin du Roi,' in Muséum d'Histoire Naturelle, *Buffon* (Paris, 1952); Y. Laissus, *Buffon: Côté Jardin* (Paris, 1987); L. Roule, *Daubenton et l'Exploitation de la Nature* (Paris, 1925); Y. Letouzey, *Le Jardin des Plantes à Croisée des Chemins* (Paris, 1989).
155 AN: O^1 107, f. 280.
156 'Sommaire des Arrangements Convenus avec M de Poivre', AN: Col C^1 2, f. 216.
157 AN: Col C^1 3, f. 103r.
158 Cossigny to Lacépedé, 21 Nivoise An 7, AN: Col F^3 162, f. 32. See, in general, M. Ly-Tio-Fane, 'Pierre Poivre et l'Expansion Française dans L'Indo-Pacifique', *Bulletin de L'École Française d'Extrème-Orient*, 1967, *53*: 453–511 and *The Odyssey of Pierre Poivre* (St. Louis, 1959).
159 'Le Troupeau du Roi', AN: O^1 2125.
160 H. Froidveux, 'Un Projet de Voyage du Botaniste Adanson en Guyane en 1763', *Bulletin de Géographie Historique* (1893); E. Daubigny, *Choiseul et la France Outre-Mer* (Paris, 1892).
161 See 'Arbres et Arbustes à l'Épicerie', BCMNH: *Mss* 308, II 'Essais sur l'Art de l'Indigotier', AN: Mar G 101, f. 183.
162 On the Mascarene initiative see M. Ly-Tio-Fane, *The Triumph of Jean Nicholas Céré and his Isle Bourbon Collaborators* (The Hague, 1970).
163 AN: Col F3 92, ff. 64 and 92–4; *Instructions sur la Manière de Planter et Cultiver avec Succès les Plantes et Grains de Gérofliers et Muscadiers* (1772).
164 'Mémoires sur L'Extension des Cultures Coloniales aux Antilles Françaises', AN: Col F^3 92, ff. 110–6.
165 'Voyage à Oaxaca par Thierry de Menonville', AN: Col F^3 131; T. de Menonville, *Traité de la Culture du Nopal et de l'Éducation de la Cochinelle* (Paris, 1787).
166 See the fruit of this collecting referred to in Buffon to Castres, 22 March 1785, AN: Col F^3 92, f. 134.
167 La Luzerne to Thouin, 5 January 1788, BCMNH: *Mss* 308, ff. 1–3.
168 See the Forest Law of Mauritius, 'Ordonnance pour la Conservation des Bois de l'Île de France', 30 March 1778, AN: Col A20, f. 173. See R. Grove, *Green Imperialism: Colonial Expansion, Tropical Island Edens, and the Origins of Environmentalism, 1600–1860* (Cambridge, 1995), *passim*.
169 Tribe, *Governing Economy*, p. 122.
170 *Physiocratie* (Yverdon, 1768), p. viii.
171 In Spain and Portugal, economic ideology had a similar impact on royal support for natural history. This was often due to the direct influence of French courtly science. See, for example, the case of Felix de Avellar Brotero (1744–1828), student of Daubenton and Jussieu, who carried French agro-botanical concerns to Portugal, where he was Professor of Botany at Coimbra (1791–1810) and the Museo Real d'Ajuda. See BCMNH: *Mss* 2440–1.
172 See invoices submitted by Buffon in AN: O^1 2124, 2125 and 2126 which show the dramatic scale of expenditure, involving hundreds of thousands of livres, in the 1770s.

173 See liasse 6, in AN: O[1] 2124; and the minute of 15 December 1781 in AN: O[1] 2125.

174 Buffon, 'Mémoire', 22 June 1777, AN: O[1] 2125. 36,000 livres were spent in 1773, 16,000 in 1774, with a further 24,000 in 1775.

175 Jussieu's initiative stands at the origins of all subsequent attempts at a 'natural system' of botanical classification; see P.F. Stevens, *Nature and the 'Natural System': Antoine Laurent de Jussieu and the Foundations of Botanical Systematics* (Chicago, 1994).

176 Spary, 'Making the Natural Order'; Y. Laissus, 'Le Jardin du Roi', in R. Taton, ed., *Enseignement et Diffusion des Sciences en France au XVIIIe Siècle* (Paris, 1964), pp. 287–341.

177 D.S.L. Cardwell, *The Organization of Science in England* (London, 1972), p. 27.

178 Great Britain, 12 George III Cap. XXXV.

179 A. Bourde, *The Influence of England on the French Agronomes, 1750–1789* (Cambridge, 1953), and his remarkable *Agronomie et Agronomes en France au XVIIIe Siècle* (Paris, 1967), 3 vols.

180 See, for the interest taken in horses by H. L. Bertin, the Physiocratic Minister of Agriculture, Mining, and Manufactures (1763–80), G. Ferry and J. Mulliez, *L'État et la Rénovation de L'Agriculture au XVIIe Siècle* (Paris, 1970), pp. 111–50.

181 A. Young, *A Course of Experimental Agriculture* (London, 1770), 2 vols., *I*, pp. 10–16.

182 R. Forster, Translator's Preface to L. de Bougainville, *A Voyage Round the World Performed by Order of His Most Christian Majesty, in the Years 1766, 1767, 1768, and 1769* (London, 1772), pp. xvii–xix.

183 J. Ellis, *Directions for Bringing over Seeds and Plants, from the East Indies and Other Distant Countries, in a State of Vegetation* (London, 1770); *idem, Some Additional Observations on the Method of Preserving Seeds from Foreign Parts, for the Benefit of our American Colonies* (London, 1773); *idem, A Description of the Mangosteen and Breadfruit; the First Esteemed one of the Most Delicious; the Other the Most Useful of All the Fruits of the East Indies. To Which are Added Directions to Voyagers for Bringing over Vegetable Productions, Which Would be Extremely Beneficial to the Inhabitants of the West Indian Islands* (London, 1775); translated and printed in French as *Description du Mangosteen et du Fruit à Pain* (Paris, 1779).

184 Valentine Morris to Banks, 17 April 1772, *Add. Mss 33977*, f. 18. See also Hinton East to Banks, 19 July 1784, *Kew: B.C. I(2)*: 168.

185 J. Hope to Banks, 4 September 1775, *Kew: B.C. I*: 52.

186 R. Poore to Banks, 18 November 1778, *Kew: B.C. I*: 78.

187 B. Edwards, *The History Civil and Commercial of the British Colonies in the West Indies* (London, 1794), *I*, p. 477.

188 M. Wallen to Banks, 23 September 1784, *Add. Mss 33977*, f. 267.

189 See the concluding paragraph and footnote to the 'General Observations on the Fall of the Roman Empire in the West', published after ch. XXVIII, *The Decline and Fall of the Roman Empire, II* (London, 1781)

4 'Improving' the British Empire

1 Thomas Weaver, *Ram Letting from Robert Bakewell's Breed at Dishley, near Loughborough, Leicester* (1810). Tate Gallery (T. 03438). It hangs on the left after the main entrance.

2 Harriet Ritvo notes that breeders encouraged artists to emphasize the size of cattle, much the same is clearly going on with Weaver's heroic rams; see H. Ritvo, *The Animal Estate* (London, 1987), pp. 58–9.

3 H.C. Pawson, *Robert Bakewell: Pioneer Livestock Breeder* (London, 1957); N. Russell, *Like Engend'ring Like: Heredity and Animal Breeding in Early Modern England* (Cambridge, 1986).

4 See Dundas to Pitt, 12 and 22 November 1792, P.R.O.: PRO 30/8/157/1, ff. 144–53 and 154–61.

5 See Marquis de Luzerne to Pitt, 25 June 1789, P.R.O.: PRO 30/8/163/1, ff. 34–7 and Pitt to Luzerne, 3 July 1789, P.R.O.: PRO 30/8/102/2, ff. 180–1. For Pitt's long interest in the French supply of grain see N.H. Gouldhawke to Pitt, 18 March 1789, P.R.O.: PRO 30/8/139/1, ff. 140–1.

6 Hodgkinson to Banks, 15 July 1767, *Yale*: Sterling Reel 1.

7 R. Williams, *The Country and the City* (London, [1973] 1985), p. 96; K. Thomas, *Man and the Natural World* (New York, 1983), p. 262; W.G. Hoskins, *The Making of the English Landscape* (London, 1955), pp. 177–86; E. Hobsbawm, *Industry and Empire* (London, 1969), p. 101.

8 'Establishment of a Botanic Garden', 5 May 1810 and 22 August 1812, P.R.O.: C.O. 54/38 and 44; Banks to Kerr, 30 June 1810, *D.T.C. 18*: 45–6; Sec. of State for the Colonies to Maitland, 5 June 1810, P.R.O.:

C.O. 54/22, ff. 43–8. See for Banks's continued involvement, Banks to Sir A. Johnstone, 25 June 1816, *D.T.C. 19*: 294–6.

9 Maitland to Castlereagh, 21 May 1806, P.R.O.: C.O. 54/22, ff. 40–1. See also 'Memorandum on the Encouragement of Agriculture', 1 December 1807, P.R.O.: C.O. 54/26.

10 Maitland to Sec. of State for the Colonies, 12 June 1812, P.R.O.: C.O. 54/43.

11 Liverpool to Eldon, 4 September 1811, *Add. Mss 38328*, f. 163.

12 A. Young, *Farmer's Letters to the People of England: Containing the Sentiments of a Practical Husbandman, on Various Subjects of the Utmost Importance* (London, 1767), p. 84.

13 B. Hilton's *The Age of Atonement: The Influence of Evangelicalism on Social and Economic Thought, 1785–1865* (Oxford, 1988) provides a remarkable guide to the commerce between religious and economic thought in this era.

14 George III to Banks, 29 November 1787, *D.T.C. 5*: 283.

15 See H. Carter, *His Majesty's Spanish Flock: Sir Joseph Banks and the Merinos of George III of England* (London, 1964); Joseph Banks, *Some Circumstances Relating to Merino Sheep* (London, 1809).

16 George III and Banks kept a quite regular correspondence on the matter. See Banks to George III, 10 August 1787, *D.T.C. 5*: 205–6; George III to Banks, 10 August 1787, *D.T.C. 5*: 207; George III to Banks, 29 November 1789, *D.T.C. 5*: 283.

17 George III to Banks, 10 August 1787, *D.T.C. 5*: 207.

18 *Kew: B.C. I(3)*: 301.

19 D. Mackay, *In the Wake of Cook: Exploration, Science and Empire, 1780–1801* (London, 1985), p. 129.

20 See *Annals of Agriculture*, 1784, *1*: 60–4.

21 A. Young, *Travels during the Years 1787, 1788, and 1789 Undertaken More Particularly with a View to Ascertaining the Cultivation, Wealth, Resources and National Prosperity, of the Kingdom of France* (London, 1792), p. 29.

22 See Arthur Young's dedication of *A Course of Experimental Agriculture* (London, 1770) to Rockingham 'as a testimony of my veneration for so good and great a patron of agriculture'.

23 See R. Mitchison, 'The Old Board of Agriculture, 1793–1822', *E.H.R.*, *74*, 41–69; *idem*, *Agricultural Sir John: the Life of Sir John Sinclair of Ulbster, 1754–1835* (London, 1962); for Pitt's hesitations see J. Ehrman, *The Younger Pitt: The Reluctant Transition* (London, 1983), *II*, p. 468.

24 M. Berman, *Social Change and Scientific Organization: The Royal Institution, 1799–84* (Ithaca, 1978).

25 See 'Ralph Robinson', 'Mr. Ducket's Mode of Cultivation', *Annals of Agriculture*, 1786, 7: 65–71.

26 W. Jones and J. Malcolm, *Survey of the Agriculture of Surrey* (London, 1794), p. 8; R. Desmond, *Kew: The History of the Royal Botanic Gardens* (London, 1995), p. 95.

27 See 'The Button Maker' from *Oxford Magazine*, quoted in L. Melville, *Farmer George* (London, 1907), p. 75:

Then shall my lofty numbers tell
Who taught the royal babes to spell
And sovereign art pursue
To mend a watch or set a clock
New pattern shape for Hervey's frock
or buttons made at Kew.

28 L. Colley, 'The Apotheosis of George III: Loyalty, Royalty and the British Nation, 1760–1820', *Past and Present*, 1984, *102*: 94–129. J. Brooke, *King George III* (London, 1974), *passim*; H.M Scott, *British Foreign Policy in the Age of the American Revolution* (Oxford, 1990), pp. 1–28.

29 H. Colvin, ed., *The History of the King's Works* (London, 1963–73), *V*, p. 355.

30 T. Richardson, 'The Royal Gardens of Richmond and Kew with the Hamlet of Kew', British Library Map Room: p. 52/4460. On the urging of Lady Essex the Capel property was later bought by the Crown in the 1790s; see Lady Essex to Pitt, 8 December 1790, P.R.O.: PRO 30/8/133/1, ff. 96–7.

31 The best guide on this is C.A. Bayly, *Imperial Meridian: The British Empire and the World, 1780–1830* (London, 1989).

32 W. Derham, *Physico Theology* (London, 1713) and *Astro Theology* (London, 1715); B. Nieuweutyt, *Het Vegt Gebruik der Werelt Beschwingen* (Amsterdam, 1717); S. Klingenstierna, *Dissertatio de perfectionibus divinis ex contemplatione rerum naturalium illustratis* (Uppsala, 1740), F.C. Lesser, *Die Offenborung Gottes in der Natur* (Nordhausen, 1750).

33 E. Chambers, *Cyclopaedia, or an Universal Dictionary of Arts and Sciences* (London, 1728), 2 vols., *I*, 'Preface'.

34 T. Frängsmyr, J.L. Heilbron, and R.E. Rider, eds., *The Quantifying Spirit in the Eighteenth Century* (Oxford, 1990).

35 M. Bravo, 'Science and Discovery in the Admiralty Voyages to the Arctic Regions in Search of a North-West Passage', PhD

dissertation, University of Cambridge, 1992; B. Hilton, *Corn, Cash, and Commerce: The Economic Policies of the Tory Governments, 1815–30* (Oxford, 1977). I await Dr. Bravo's forthcoming book with keen anticipation.

36 C.A. Bayly, 'Knowing the Country: Empire and Information in India', *Modern Asian Studies*, 1993, *27*: 38.

37 P. Mandler, *Aristocratic Government in the Age of Reform: Whigs and Liberals, 1830–52* (Oxford, 1990), p. 25. On the other hand, *The Reign of the British Robespierre* (1795) compared domestic repression and the Prime Minister's expansion of debt to Jacobin 'public safety' measures. For the reform movement see V. Harlow, *The Founding of the Second British Empire, 1763–1793* (London, 1952–64), 2 vols., II, pp. 225–53; Ehrman, *The Younger Pitt, I*, pp. 303–26; J. Torrance, 'Social Class and Bureaucratic Innovation: The Commissioners for Examining the Public Accounts, 1780–1787,' *Past and Present*, 1978, *78*: 56–81; *II*, pp. 225–53; Mackay, *In the Wake of Cook*, pp. 22–3.

38 Harlow, *The Founding of the Second British Empire, II*, pp. 233–45.

39 *La Politique Indien ou Considérations sur Les Colonies des Indes Orientales* (Paris, 1768).

40 Banks to Lord Macartney, 22 January 1792, *Yale*: Sterling Reel 6.

41 Banks to Macartney, 22 January 1792, *Yale*: Sterling Reel 6.

42 T. Falconer to Banks, 8 December 1773, *Kew*: *B.C. I(1)*: 90.

43 H. de Ponthieu to Banks, 23 January 1778 and 29 April 1783, *Kew*: *B.C. I(1)*: 70 and *I(2)*: 131.

44 I owe this reference to Mr. Jeremy Osborn, my doctoral student, who is writing a dissertation on India's place in Georgian public opinion.

45 W. Colebrooke to [ ], 4 August 1815, *Yale*: Sterling Reel 6.

46 Lady Raffles, ed., *Memoir of the Life and Public Service of Sir Thomas Stamford Raffles* (London, 1835), pp. 108–9; P.J. Marshall, 'British Assessments of the Dutch in Asia in the Age of Raffles', in P.J. Marshall, ed., *India and Indonesia during the Ancien Regime* (Leiden, 1989), p. 2.

47 J.S. Mill, *On Liberty* (London, [1859] 1982), p. 69.

48 Banks had, of course, also first distinguished himself as a naturalist at sea, when he accompanied the H.M.S. *Niger* to Newfoundland and Labrador; see A. Lysaght, *Sir Joseph Banks in Newfoundland and Labrador, 1766* (London, 1971).

49 See for example, *The Correspondence of Sir John Sinclair Bart.* (London, 1831), 2 vols., *I*, p. 404; and H. Dupree, *Sir Joseph Banks and the Origins of Science Policy* (Minneapolis, 1983), pp. 14–15.

50 See J. Robinson to Banks, 23 March 1781, *Yale*: Sterling Reel 1; H. Carter, *Sir Joseph Banks, 1743–1820* (London, 1988), p. 176.

51 *Yale*: Sterling Reel 1; Carter, *Banks*, pp. 18–20.

52 This and following data on Banks's income is from Appendix XXII, XXIII, and XIV of Carter, *Banks*, pp. 580–3.

53 Banks to Windischgrätz, June 2 [undated], *Kew*: *B.C. III(1)*: 3.

54 Banks to Formey [undated–1780s?], *Kew*: *B.C. III(1)*: 12.

55 *Ibid.*

56 See *inter alia* the more than 100 pieces of communication between Banks and P.M. Broussonet between 1782 and 1803 in *Add. Mss 8095, 8096, 8097, 8098, 8099, 8100.*

57 Buffon to Banks, 10 June 1772 and 23 June 1783, *Add. Mss 8094*, ff. 15–16 and 153–4; Thouin to Banks, 2 March 1781, 1 July 1781, 3 December 1781, 8 October 1782, 22 June 1783, *Add. Mss 8095*, ff. 52, 53, 54, 114, and 233–4.

58 Blagden to Banks, 11 June and 10 July 1783, *D.T.C. 3*: 46–8 and 67–91.

59 See Banks to J.E. Smith, 25 December 1817, LS: *Smith Mss 20*, ff. 80–1; see A.G. Morton, *John Hope, 1725–1786, Scottish Botanist* (Edinburgh, 1986) , pp. 24–35; A.L. de Jussieu, 'Exposition d'un Nouvel Ordre de Plantes Adapté dans les demonstrations du Jardin Royal', *Memoires de l'Académie des Sciences de Paris*, 1774; 175–97.

60 J. Dryander, *Catalogus bibliothecae historico-naturalis Josephi Banks* (London, 1796–1800), 5 vols.; see *I, Scriptores generales* (1798).

61 D. Vandelli, *Memoria sobre a utilidade das jardinys botanicos a respeito da Agricultura* (Lisbon, 1770); G.A. Suckow, *Öekonomische Botanik* (Mannheim, 1777); J. Meyer, 'Okonomische-botanische Beobachtungen', *Bemerkungen der Kuhrpfalz physikalische okonomische Gesellschaft*, 1779, 346–52; R. Willemet, *Phytographie Économique de la Lorraine* (Nancy, 1780); F.J. Marter, *Vorstellung eines ökonomischen Gartens nach den Grundsatzen der angewandten Botanik* (Vienna, 1782); M. Delarbre, *Discours sur l'Utilité et Nécessité d'un Jardin Botanique à Clermont Ferrand* (Clermont Ferrand, 1782).

62 Banks to Thomas Morton, Secretary of

the East India Company, 22 February 1787, *D.T.C. 5*: 133–7.

63 D. Lescallier, 'Mémoires sur les Épiceries de l'Inde naturalisées dans la Guiane', *Mémoires de la Société Royale d'Agriculture*, 1788, 28–36; see Dryander, *Catalogus bibliothecae historico-naturalis, III, Botanici* (1797).

64 It has been more conventional to see Banks as responding to the domestic example of the Chelsea Physic Garden and the Society of Arts. See H.C. Cameron, *Joseph Banks: The Autocrat of the Philosophers* (London, 1952), pp. 63–4; Carter, *Banks*, pp. 25–32; Mackay, *In the Wake of Cook, passim.*

65 A. de Jussieu to Banks, 25 August 1779, *Add. Mss 8094*, ff. 221–2; Banks to Benjamin Franklin, 9 August 1782, *Add. Mss 8095*, f. 81; Banks to Jussieu, Banks to [Jussieu?], 24 June 1796, *Kew: B.C. II*: 226, 10 August 1796, *D.T.C. 10*: 63–4; Banks to L. Deschamps, 28 July 1803, *D.T.C. 20*: 100; For the history of such arrangements see G. de Beer, *The Sciences Were Never at War* (London, 1960); A.H. Dupree, 'Nationalism and Science—Sir Joseph Banks and the War with France', in D.H. Pickney and T. Ropp, eds., *A Festshrift for Frederick B. Artz* (New York, 1964).

66 For Misogallus's attacks see 'A Letter to the Right Honourable Joseph Banks, KB', *Cobbett's Annual Register*, 1802, *1*: 327–33, and *2*: 743–5; Cameron, *Banks*, pp. 216–17.

67 Banks to Liverpool, 10 February 1815, *D.T.C. 19*: 144.

68 Banks to Wellesley, 11 January 1810, *Add. Mss 37309*, f. 329.

69 The principal studies of Banks are Cameron, *Banks*; Carter, *Banks*; J. Gascoigne, *Joseph Banks and the English Enlightenment: Useful Knowledge and Polite Culture* (Cambridge, 1994); and Mackay, *In the Wake of Cook*. Professor Gascoigne's *Science in the Service of Empire: Joseph Banks, the British State and the Uses of Science in the Age of Revolution* (Cambridge, 1998) was not available when this chapter was written. He uses Weaver's *Ram Letting* (p. 73) to support an agrarian interpretation of Banks's 'neomercantilism' in ways which encouragingly echo my 1993 dissertation.

70 See especially the 3,500 pieces in the collection of Yale University Library, and large swathes of the 10,000 pieces of Banks material held in the Sutro Library in San Francisco.

71 Banks's publications on agriculture include: 'Two Letters on Wool Prices and Spinning', *Annals of Agriculture*, 1788, *9*: 288–91; 'Instructions Given to the Counsel against the Wool Bill', *Annals of Agriculture*, 1788, *9*: 479–506; 'Notes on Spinning', *Annals of Agriculture*, 1788, *10*: 217; 'On the Hastings Turnip: Extract from a Letter from Soho Square, 16 December 1790', *Annals of Agriculture*, 1791, *15*: 77–8; 'On the Oeconomy of a Park', *Annals of Agriculture*, 1804, *39*: 550–8.

72 'I have heard him say that he took to farming by the King's desire ... in 1811, I well remember him saying, he had ceased since then being a farmer, having only "taken up the trade by his Majesty's command"', in H. Brougham, *Lives of the Philosophers of the Time of George III* (London, 1855), p. 368.

73 See D. Hancock, *Citizens of the World* (Cambridge, 1996) for an illuminating example of the connections between these spheres of British endeavour.

74 *Annals of Agriculture*, 1793, *19*: 190. See also the instructions sent by Banks to James Roberts, under-steward of his estates in Lincolnshire, concerning poor relief: having sent several barrels of herrings, and a ton and a half of rice (together with recipe for cooking rice), to be distributed among the poor of Mareham and Revesby in December 1800 and February 1801, he instructed Roberts in April that families of labourers who could work were to lose half the ration of rice.

75 Banks to Thomas Morton, Secretary of the East India Company, 7 January 1791, IOL: *Mss* E/1/1/86, f. 21b.

76 Banks to Liverpool, 10 February 1815, *D.T.C. 19*: 139–44.

77 *Ibid.*, 144.

78 A healthy dose of self-interest could here, as on the issue of rents, be discerned. His steward, Benjamin Stephenson, had advised him that his tenants were unable to pay their rents because of the precipitous decline of wool prices with the American War. See Stephenson to Banks, 7 April 1781 and 3 September 1781, *Yale*: Sterling Reel 1. See H.B. Carter, ed., *The Sheep and Wool Correspondence of Sir Joseph Banks, 1781–1820* (Sydney, 1979), pp. 43-77; and [J. Banks], *The Propriety of Allowing a Qualified Exportation of Wool, Discussed Historically* (London, 1782).

79 *Select Essays in Commerce, Mines, Agriculture, Fisheries and Other Useful Arts* (London, 1754).

80 J. Sinclair, *The History of the Public Revenue*

of the British Empire (London, 1784, 1785, and 1803), 3 vols., *I*, pp. 524–5.

81 C. Varlo, *The Essence of Agriculture. Being a System of Husbandry, Through All its Branches Suited to the Climate and Lands of Ireland* (London, 1786), p. 3.

82 *Annals of Agriculture*, 1784, *2*: 233–7; *Annals of Agriculture*, 1786, *6*: 67–91.

83 Sinclair, *The History of the Public Revenue of the British Empire*, *I*, p. v; *II*, p. 117; *III*, p. 315.

84 *Annals of Agriculture*, 1784, *1*: 448.

85 Young, *Travels*, p. 141.

86 Sinclair, *General View of the Agriculture of the Northern Counties and Islands of Scotland ... with Observations on the Means of Their Improvement* (London, 1795), pp. 280–1. The model here may well have been Linnaeus's use of the Lutheran Church to collect information and to introduce new plants.

87 Sinclair, *The History of the Public Revenue of the British Empire*, *I*, p. 475; see also *II*, appendix 4.

88 *Annals of Agriculture*, 1784, *1*: 10.

89 *Ibid.*

90 A. Young, *National Danger & the Means of Safety* (London, 1792), pp. 38 and 55.

91 'A Coup d'Oeil on the Present State of the Nation', *Annals of Agriculture*, 1784, *1*: 119–23.

92 He wrote grimly in 1792, to censor the illustrator of Hume's *History of England*, that an image of Roundhead yokels beating an officer of the King in the 1640s was not 'a happy one in times like the present'. Banks to R. Bowyer, [November 1792], *Kew: B.C. II*: 87.

93 Banks to R. Shepherd, 31 July 1793, *D.T.C. 8*: 239.

94 Fox to Banks, 7 May 1802, *D.T.C. 13*: 99–100.

95 Banks to J. Hunter, 30 March 1797, *D.T.C. 9*: 93–5.

96 Banks to Liverpool, 6 July 1800, *Add. Mss 38234*, ff. 97–8.

97 Sinclair to Pitt, 5 January 1795, P.R.O.: PRO 30/8/178/1, ff. 150–1; Sinclair to Pitt, [December 1797], P.R.O.: PRO 30/8/135, ff. 241–2, 143–5; H. Johns, 'Farming in Wartime, 1793–1815', in E.L. Jones and G.E. Mingay, eds., *Land, Labour and Population in the Industrial Revolution* (London, 1967); W.E. Mitchinton, 'Agricultural Returns and the Government during the Napoleonic Wars', *Agricultural History Review*, 1953, *1*: 29–43.

98 Banks to Richard Shepherd, Archdeacon of Bedford, 1 August 1793, *D.T.C. 8*: 239.

99 *Annals of Agriculture*, 1790, *13*: 466. Young argued in these terms for the importance of towns to the 'National Husbandry'; see 'Importance of London to the National Husbandry', *Annals of Agriculture*, 1795, *23*.

100 G.E. Mingay, *The English Landed Society in the Eighteenth Century* (London, 1963), pp. 190–201; J.R. Ward, *The Finance of Canal Building in Eighteenth-Century England* (London, 1974).

101 E. Gibbon, *The Decline and Fall of the Roman Empire* (London, [1776] 1993), *I*, p. 62.

102 Sinclair, *The History of the Public Revenue of the British Empire*; see also J. Sinclair, *Hints Addressed to the Public on the State of Our Finances* (London, 1783); *idem*, 'Amount and Collection of the Public Revenue', *Annals of Agriculture*, 1791, *16*: 113–21.

103 Sinclair, *The History of the Public Revenue of the British Empire*, *I*, p. 521.

104 *Annals of Agriculture*, 1784, *1*: 60.

105 This argument would have been reasonably persuasive given that sugar, beer, and other products of agriculture provided the bulk of those excise taxes which were the backbone of revenue; see J. Brewer, *The Sinews of Power: War, Money and the English State, 1688–1783* (London, 1989), p. 189.

106 Young, *National Danger & the Means of Safety*, p. 71 [my emphasis].

107 *Sutro*: CR 1: 1–17.

108 *Outlines of a Plan of Defence against French Invasion: Intended for the County of Lincolnshire But Applicable to all Other Countries Whose Inhabitants are Sensible of the Danger of the Present Crisis*, 4 April 1794, f.1, *Sutro*: CR 1: 35.

109 For the communication of Young's proposals to the highest circles of policy see A.S. Matthew to Pitt, [November 1792], P.R.O.: PRO 30/8/156/2, ff. 182–5.

110 Sinclair to Pitt, [December 1797], P.R.O.: PRO 30/8/135, ff. 241–5; Ehrman, *The Younger Pitt*, pp. 468–9.

111 Banks to Hawkesbury, 16 September 1800, *Add. Mss 38234*, ff. 152–3.

112 Banks to Liverpool, 27 February 1800, *D.T.C. 12*: 38–9.

113 Sir John Sinclair to Banks, [1791], *Add. Mss 33979*, f. 106; Ehrman, *The Younger Pitt*, pp. 444–5; Hilton, *Corn, Cash and Commerce*; D.G. Barnes, *A History of the English Corn Laws from 1660–1846* (London, 1930), chapter IV. For 1795 see also the comments of Sir John Sinclair *vis-à-vis* oats in Sinclair, *General View of the Agriculture of ... Scotland*, p. 277.

114 *Annals of Agriculture*, 1784, *1*: 380.

115 Sinclair, *The History of the Public Revenue of the British Empire, I*, p. 522.
116 See Banks to Liverpool, 28 September [1800], *Add. Mss 38234*, ff. 164–5.
117 *Annals of Agriculture*, 1784, *1*: 7.
118 Young, *Travels*, p. 180.
119 Sinclair, *The History of the Public Revenue of the British Empire, I*, p. 524; see also *II*, pp. 101–3; see also his argument for investment in Scotland in his *General View of the Agriculture of … Scotland*, appendix VI, pp. 38–9; appendix VIII, p. 45.
120 J. Sinclair, *Thoughts on the Naval Strength of Great Britain* (London, 1782).
121 *Annals of Agriculture*, 1784, *1*: 384; John Lord Sheffield, *Observations on the Commerce of the American States* (London, 1784); G. Chalmers, *Opinions on Interesting Subjects of Public Law and Commercial Policy Arising From American Independence* (London, 1784).
122 *Annals of Agriculture*, 1784, *2*: 341–2.
123 J. Banks to W. Devaynes (Chairman, Court of Directors of East India Company), 27 December 1788, *D.T.C.* 6: 103–11.
124 *Annals of Agriculture*, 1784, *1*: 23.
125 Banks was, of course, the most important advocate of Australia's claim to British settlement. See his testimony to the Bunbury and Beauchamp Committees in 1779 and 1785 in *Journal of the House of Commons*, *37*, col. 311 and *40*, col. 1161.
126 *Sutro:* A 1: 38, ff. 1–3; *Annals of Agriculture*, 1789, *11*: 13–20.
127 On the cotton question see Harlow, *The Founding of the Second British Empire, II*, pp. 280–93.
128 Sinclair, *General View of the Agriculture … of Scotland*, pp. 280–1.
129 J. Sinclair, 'Plan for .. the Agricultural Surveys', in W. Pitt, *General View of the County of Stafford* (London, 1796), p. v.
130 See, for example, Sinclair's praise of the Society for the Promotion of Christian Knowledge in *General View of the Agriculture of … Scotland*, pp. 69–70.
131 C. Madley, '4th Report on National School at Horncastle', mss of 1818, *Yale*: Sterling Reel 6. See also his role in providing teachers for Haiti for which Henri Christophe would describe him, unaware of Banks's views on slavery, and his friendship with Pitt and Dundas who had unleashed war against the infant revolution from 1794 to1798, as 'one of the best friends of Haiti'; see *Add. Mss 39301*, f. 85 and *8100*, f. 219.
132 'Sierra Leone', *Sutro*: A 1–2; G. Maxwell to W. Keir, 20 July 1804, *Add. Mss 37232*, f. 53; R. Raikes, *Two Essays* (London, 1825), pp. 40–73.
133 Stephenson to Banks, 8 June 1768, *Yale*: Sterling Reel 1.
134 Carter, *Banks*, p. 515.
135 [   ] to Banks, 30 March 1794, *Sutro* A 2: 76, f. 3.
136 George III to Pitt, 14 June 1786, P.R.O.: PRO 30/8/103/1, ff. 197–8.
137 George Rose to Banks, 1 February 1789, *Add. Mss 33978*, f. 225; Banks to Hawkesbury 30 December 1807, Banks to Hawkesbury, 13 February 1794, *D.T.C. 9*: 5–6.
138 Banks to Hawkesbury, 30 December 1807, *D.T.C. 17*: 78.
139 Banks to Pitt, 23 and 29 March, and 28 June 1790, P.R.O.: PRO 30/8/136, ff. 47–8 and 'Minute of 20 March 1790', Pitt to Banks, 29 March 1790, Pitt to Banks, 8 May 1790, in *Sutro*: Reel 21.
140 Banks to Pitt, 29 March 1790, *Sutro:* Reel 21.
141 Samuel Vetch (1708), quoted in C.M. Andrews, *The Colonial Period in American History* (New Haven, 1934–8), *IV*, p. 347.
142 Tipu Sultan to Representatives of the People in Mauritius and Réunion, 2 April 1797, *The Dispatches, Minutes and Correspondence of the Marquis Wellesley*, M. Martin, ed., (London, 1837), *V*, p. 3.
143 Banks to Dundas, 15 June 1787, *D.T.C. 5*: 184–91.
144 G. Staunton to Banks, 30 March 1793, *Sutro*: Reel 20.
145 See A. Dalrymple, *An Account of the Discoveries Made in the South Pacifick Ocean Previous to 1764* (London, 1767); and *idem*, *A Plan for Extending the Commerce of this Kingdom and the East India Company* (London, 1769).
146 *Gentleman's Magazine*, 1771, *41*: 565.
147 For Spain see W.L. Cook, *Flood Tide of Empire: Spain and the Pacific Northwest, 1543–1819* (New Haven, 1973), D.C. Cutter, 'Spanish Exploration along the Pacific Coast', in R.G. Ferris, ed., *The American West: An Appraisal* (Santa Fe, 1963).
148 Quoted in Mackay, *In the Wake of Cook*, p. 5.
149 See H. Fry, *Alexander Dalrymple and the Expansion of British Trade* (London, 1970); C. Lloyd, *Mr. Barrow of the Admiralty: A Life of Sir John Barrow, 1764–1848* (London, 1970); G.S. Ritchie, *The Admiralty Chart: British Naval Hydrography in the Nineteenth Century* (London, 1967).
150 Harlow, *The Founding of the Second British Empire, I*, pp. 12–61.
151 Mackay, *In the Wake of Cook*, p. 4.
152 J.J.H. Labillardière, *Relation du Voyage à la*

Recherche de la Pérouse, pendant les Années 1791–1792 (Paris, 1799), 2 vols.; J. Dunmore, *Pacific Explorer: the Life of Jean-François de la Pérouse, 1741–1788* (Sydney, 1985).

153 Carter, *Banks*, pp. 368–70; M.F. Péron, *Voyage de Découverte aux Terres Australes* (Paris, 1807), 2 vols.; M. Flinders, *A Voyage to Terra Australis* (London, 1814), 2 vols.

154 The catalogue of Banks's library suggests he was aware of the French study of Africa, as it includes, besides Adanson's *Relations Abrégées d'un Voyage Fait en Sénégal pendant les Années 1749–53, Imprimé avec son Histoire Naturelle de Sénégal* (Paris, 1757), J. Demonet, *Nouvelle Histoire de L'Afrique Française* (Paris, 1762), 2 vols.; F. Proyart, *Histoire de Congo, Kakongo et autres Royaumes d'Afrique* (Paris, 1776). See Dryander, *Catalogus Bibliothecae Historico-Naturalis Josephi Banks* (1798), *I*, pp. 129–30.

155 T. Falconer to Banks, 19 May 1773 and 8 December 1773, *Kew: B.C. I*: 35 and 42.

156 Meeting of 28 January 1767, *Society of Arts Archives: Minutes of Committees*, 1766–7 (6), ff. 8–9.

157 Thouin to Banks, 22 June 1783, *Add. Mss 8095*, ff. 233–4; A. Volney, *Voyage en Syrie et en Égypte* (Paris, 1787).

158 See *Annals of Agriculture*, 1789, *11*: 13–20; Cameron, *Banks*, pp. 88, 241.

159 He wrote to one correspondent that he abhorred those who asserted that it was sinful to employ slaves since slavery had existed from the beginning of Providence, and that if the trade was ended many Africans would die of starvation; see Banks to [ ], [ ], *Rhodes House Library*: British Empire Mss r. 2. But Banks's African society was publicly identified with these evangelicals, so much so that Bryan Edwards, the Jamaican planter who was a member of the African Association, complained to Banks: 'Hitherto the motives and labours of the African Association have been considered by the merchants and masters of ships trading from Liverpool to Africa, *as hostile to the slave trade* ... Surely it is not necessary to make these men our enemies!'; see Edwards to Banks, 14 June 1796, *Kew: B.C. II*: 140.

160 31 GIII Cap LV; Wilberforce to Banks, 21 December 1791, *D.T.C.* 7: 293–4; [Court of Directors of Sierra Leone Company] to Banks, 28 December 1791, *Kew: B.C. II*: 58; *Substance of the Report of the Court of Directors of the Sierra Leone Company* (London, 1792).

161 H. Beaufoy to Banks, 27 June 1793, *Sutro*: A 2: 49.

162 M. Park, *Travels in the Interior Districts of Africa, Performed under the Direction and Patronage of the African Association, In the Years 1795–1797* (London, 1799).

163 F. Hornemann to Banks, 18 October 1797, *Kew: B.C. II*: 184. See A.A. Boahen, *Britain, The Sahara, and the Western Sudan, 1788–1861* (Oxford, 1964).

164 Afzelius to Banks, 13 November 1794, *Add. Mss 33979*, ff. 282–5; Banks to Afzelius, 17 February 1795, *D.T.C.* 9: 197–8.

165 Banks to Liverpool, 8 June 1799, *Add. Mss 38233*, ff. 94–5.

166 Banks to the 2nd Earl of Chatham, 8 June 1799, *D.T.C. 11*: 233–5. William Brass, a collector dispatched at Banks's and two others' personal expense to West Africa, had forwarded somewhat febrile intelligence concerning the abundance of gold: 'Gold Dust is all over the whole country the blacks have verry little knowlidge whear to reach the most profitable place, only taking it whear there is water to wash it. . . . I packed a Handkerchieful of Earth and sand and I gave it to a Negro Slave, who washed it and found half a guinea worth of gold dust in so small a parcel of Earth.' See W. Brass to Fothergill, 10 October 1780, *Kew: B.C. I*: 96–7.

167 Banks to Liverpool, 8 June 1799, *Add. Mss 38233*, ff. 94–5.

168 Lallemant to Banks, 14 June, 9 July 1802 and 9 April [1803], *Add. Mss 8099*, ff. 180 and 181; *8098*, p. 457.

169 Quoted in Carter, *Banks*, p. 424.

170 Banks to Barrow, 6 August 1815, *D.T.C. 19*: 170.

171 D.R. Headrick, *The Tools of Empire: Technology and European Imperialism in the Nineteenth Century* (New York, 1979).

172 See B. de St. Pierre, *Voyage de L'Île de France, à L'Île de Bourbon, au Cap de Bonne Espérance* (Amsterdam, 1776); C.P. Thunberg, *Resa uti Europe, Africa, Asia, forrattad aven 1770–1779* (Uppsala, 1788–93); A. Spaarman, *A Voyage to the Cape of Good Hope, towards the Antarctic Pole* (London, 1785), a translation of *Resa till Goda Hopps-Udden*.

173 See Dundas to Pitt, [1786]; P.R.O.: PRO 30/8, ff. 333–6; Pitt to Cornwallis, 28 August 1787, P.R.O.: PRO 30/8/102/1, ff. 77–8.

174 Indeed it appears that the Dutch East India Company also perceived this as possible and was very unwilling to permit Masson to enter the hinterland on his

second expedition; see F. Masson to Banks, 21 January 1786, *D.T.C. 5*: 10–11. See also Ehrman, *Pitt The Younger* Pitt, *I*, pp. 50 and 388.

175 For the range of Anderson's expeditions see LS: *Mss*, ff. 610–7.

176 A. Anderson to Yonge, 1 July 1791, *Kew*: *The Botanical Gardens. St. Helena & St. Vincent.*

177 *Sutro*: Po 1: 1.

178 Harlow, *The Founding of the Second British Empire*, II, p. 292.

179 *Society of Arts Archives*: *Minutes of Committee*, 1762–3 (6), f. 16.

180 H. de Ponthieu to Banks, 27 September 1785, *Kew*: *B.C. I(2)*: 205.

181 Kew: R. Kyd, *Remarks on the President of the Royal Society's Propositions for the Introduction of the Tea Plant into the Company's Provinces* (1788).

182 See *Reflections on the Proclamation of the Second of July 1783 Relative to the Trade between the USA and the West-Indian Islands* (London, 1783); *Considerations on the Present State ... between the Sugar Colonies and the United States* (London, 1784); B. Edwards, *Thoughts on the Late Proceedings of Government, respecting the trade of the West India islands with the United States of North America* (London, 1784).

183 Planters testified to the Privy Council in 1788 that the yield of sugar per acre in St. Domingue, where rich volcanic soils were being exploited for the first time, was five times that in Jamaica, thus profit margins in St. Domingue were two to three times those of the British West Indian planter, thus British West Indian sugar could not 'retain in the European market that ascendancy' which it previously enjoyed. See *Report of the Privy Council, 1788*, Part V; E. Williams, *Capitalism and Slavery* (London, 1964), pp. 122–3.

184 H. East to Banks, 19 July 1784, *Kew*: *B.C. I(2)*: 168.

185 J. Steele to Banks, 14 July 1781, *Add. Mss 33977*, f. 135; J. Steele to the Society of Arts, 14 July 1784, *Society of Arts Archive*: A11/45.

186 De Ponthieu to Banks, 18 January 1785, *Kew*: *B.C. I(2)*: 189.

187 [ ] to Sir Joseph Banks, 9 March 1791, *Sutro*: Reel 20.

188 M. Wallen to Banks, 23 September 1784, *Add. Mss 33977*, f. 267.

189 De Ponthieu to Banks, 27 September 1785, *Kew*: *B.C. I*: 205.

190 'Certain Particulars Respecting the Breadfruit Tree', (1787), P.R.O.: HO 42/11.

191 Banks to Barrow, 12 August 1815, *D.T.C. 19*: 174–8.

192 See Banks to Hawkesbury, 30 March 1787, *D.T.C. 5*: 143–6.

193 Yonge to Banks, 3 February 1787, *Kew*: *B.C. I(3)*: 258. See also Yonge to Banks, 18 September 1788, *Kew*: *B.C. I(3)*: 321.

194 *Affiches Americaines*, 24 April 1788.

195 This and following from 'Pièces relative au Projet d'une Correspondance Agriculto-Botanique entre les Différentes Colonies Françaises et le Jardin du Roi', BCMHN: *Mss* 308.

196 Luzerne to Thouin, 5 January 1788, BCMNH: *Mss* 308, ff. 1–3.

197 See AN Mar G 101, ff. 214–7; 'La Mission de Joseph Martin à l'Isle de France', BCMHN: *Mss* 48.

198 W. Fawkener to Banks, 2 April 1787, *D.T.C. 5*: 148.

199 Hawkesbury to Hove, 30 March 1787, P.R.O.: B.T. 6/246; see also *D.T.C. 4*: 122–7.

200 Banks to Hawkesbury, 29 September 1788, *Add. Mss 38223*, f. 202.

201 Bryan Edwards to Banks, 9 May [1799], *Kew*: *B.C. II*: 220.

202 B. Edwards, *The History Civil and Commercial of the British Colonies in the West Indies*, 2nd edn (London, 1794), 2 vols.

203 See 'Dedication', Edwards, *History of the West Indies, I*.

204 Edwards, *History of the West Indies, I*, pp. xxxiv–vvx, appendix; *II*, ch. 1.

205 A. Broughton, *Hortus Eastensis, or a Catalogue of Exotic Plants in the Garden of Hinton East, Esq.* (Kingston, 1792), and T. Dancer, *A Catalogue of Plants, Exotic and Indigenous in the Botanic Garden, Jamaica* (Kingston, 1792).

206 See P.J. Marshall, 'The Bengal Commercial Society of 1775: Private Business Trade in the Warren Hastings Period', *Bulletin of the Institute of Historical Research*, 1969, *42*: 173–87.

207 Royal Society, *Journal Book Copy*, *27*: 199.

208 See M. Archer, 'India and Natural History: The Role of the East India Company', *History Today*, 1959, *11*; D. Kumar, ed., *Science and Empire: Essays in Indian Context, 1700–1947* (Delhi, 1991); S. Sangwan, *Science, Technology and Colonisation: An Indian Experience, 1757–1857* (Delhi, 1991); M. Edney, *Mapping an Empire: The Geographical Construction of British India, 1765–1843* (Chicago, 1997), *passim*.

209 Gibbon, *Decline and Fall, I*, p. 64 (my emphases). Gibbon in a footnote dangling

from the paragraph makes clear the possibility of comparing 'ancient with modern' circumstances.

210 Quoted in A. Aspinall, *Cornwallis in Bengal* (Manchester, 1931), p. 185.

211 On the significance of the issue of debt in 1772, and in the period after 1784, see A. Tripathi, *Trade and Finance in the Bengal Presidency, 1793–1833* (Calcutta, 1979), pp. 2–7; P. Griffiths, *A Licence to Trade: The History of the English Chartered Companies* (London, 1974), pp. 108–9; M.E. Yapp, 'The Brightest Jewel', in K. Ballhatchet and J. Harrison, eds., *East India Company Studies* (Hong Kong, 1986), pp. 43–51.

212 Tripathi, *Trade and Finance in the Bengal Presidency*, p. 2.; Aspinall, *Cornwallis in Bengal*, p. 5.

213 For the record of Jones not just as a founder of comparative linguistics but as a supplier of plants and information to Kew, see Banks to Sir William Jones, 6 January 1788 and 17 September 1789, *D.T.C.* 6: 1, 228–30; see also Sir W. Jones, 'The Design of a Treatise on the Plants of India', *Transactions of the Asiatick Society of Bengal*, 1788, 2: 345–52. For the seriousness with which Cornwallis, Wellesley, and many of their successors patronized natural history, see Archer, 'India and Natural History' and R. Desmond, *The European Discovery of the Indian Flora* (Oxford, 1992).

214 See R. Guha, *A Rule of Property for Bengal: An Essay on the Idea of Permanent Settlement* (New Delhi, [1963] 1981); E. Stokes, *The English Utilitarians and India* (Oxford, 1963), pp. 3–8.

215 P.J. Marshall, 'The Moral Swing to the East: British Humanitarianism, India, and the West Indies', in Ballhatchet and Harrison, *East India Company Studies*, pp. 69–96.

216 Devaynes to Banks, 21 June 1789, *Kew: B.C. I(3)*: 352

217 Stokes, *The English Utilitarians and India*, pp. 3–5; Guha, *A Rule of Property*; J. Mill, *The History of British India* (London, [1818] 1820), *I*, pp. 247–81.

218 Guha, *A Rule of Property*, p. 49.

219 *Fifth Report on the Affairs of the East India Company* (London, [1812] 1866), *II*, pp. 320–1; see also pp. 324–5.

220 J. Kønig to Banks, 12 August 1783, *Add. Mss 8095*, f. 194; I.H. Burkill, *Chapters in the History of Botany in India* (Calcutta, 1965), pp. 12–15; P. Russell to Banks, 26 December 1784, *Add. Mss 33977*, ff. 279–80.

221 R. Kyd to Court of Directors of East India Company, 13 April 1786, *D.T.C. 5*: 29–32.; and Kyd to Banks, 26 April 1786, *Sutro*: Reel 18.

222 Kyd to Banks, 1 June 1786, *D.T.C.* 7: 36–9; Kyd to Court of Directors of the East India Company, 30 August 1786, *D.T.C.* 7: 40; Kyd to Cornwallis, Sept 1786, *D.T.C. 5*: 63–70.

223 G. Yonge to Banks, 8 April 1787, *Kew: B.C. I(2)*: 263.

224 Banks to Yonge, 15 June 1787, *D.T.C. 5*: 184–91; Kyd to Cornwallis, September 1786, *D.T.C. 5*: 63–70. See also Roxburgh to Banks, 1 December 1793 and 14 January 1794, *Add. Mss 33979*, ff. 224 and 240.

225 Banks to Yonge, 15 June 1787, *D.T.C. 5*: 184–91. Both Kyd and his successor, William Roxburgh, sought to introduce the best sorts of black pepper, cinnamon, clove, nutmeg, and other spices from the Dutch East Indies colonies in the Malaccas; see Kyd to Nathaniel Smith, Director of the East India Company, 10 November 1789, *D.T.C.* 7: 70–1; Roxburgh to Banks, 10 December 1784, 30 December 1794, 19 January 1795 and 13 July 1797, *Add. Mss 33977*, ff. 274–5, *33979*, ff. 292–3, *33980*, ff. 41–2 and 101–4.

226 'Memorandum', *Sutro*: Te 1: 3; Banks to Hawkesbury, 29 September 1788, *Add. Mss 38223*, ff. 201–6; Banks to W. Devaynes, 27 December 1788, *D.T.C. 6*: 103–9; M. Hoh-Cheung, *The Management of Monopoly: A Study of the English East India Company's Conduct of its Tea Trade, 1784–1833* (Vancouver, 1984).

227 J. Kerr to Banks, 9 November 1773, *Sutro*: O 1: 1.

228 Kyd, *Introduction of the Tea Plant.*

229 See G. Wentworth (Surveyor of Woods) to Lord Commissioners of H.M. Treasury, 21 October 1783, P.R.O.: T 1/ 594, ff. 306–9.

230 On the political importance of supplies of hemp and naval timber see John Call to Pitt, 19 March and 2 April 1788, P.R.O.: PRO 30/8/119/1, ff. 29–61; T. Bryant to Pitt, 5 September 1790, P.R.O.: PRO 30/8/116/2, ff. 352–5; John Call to Pitt, 25 September 1793, P.R.O.: PRO 30/8/119/1, ff. 76–9. Pitt even had a spy to report on the market for hemp in Europe, see W. Miles to Pitt, 14 March 1788, P.R.O.: PRO 30/8/159, ff. 182–3.

231 A. Frost, *Convicts and Empire: A Naval Question, 1776–1811* (Melbourne, 1980); but see M. Gillen, 'The Botany Bay Decision, 1786: Convicts not Empire', *E.H.R.*, 1982, *97*: 740–66.

232 Middleton to Pitt, 26 August, 5 and 10 September 1786, P.R.O.: PRO 30/8/111, ff. 154–6.

233 Abbé Brules, *On the Mode of Culture and Dressing of Hemp* (London, 1790), *Kew: Banks, Hemp 1764–1810.*

234 G. Sinclair to Banks, 25 November 1798, *Kew: B.C. II*: 209; Banks to Roxburgh, 7 January 1799, *Add. Mss 33980*, f. 170; H. Inglis to Banks, 6 January 1801, *Add. Mss 33980*, f. 260; Banks to [ ], August 1802, *Kew: Banks, Hemp 1764–1810*, f. 56; Banks to Court of Directors of the East India Company, [ ] January 1803, *Kew: B.C. III*: 58–60; Banks to [ ], 15 May 1801, *Kew: Banks, Hemp 1764–1810*, ff. 51–2.

235 See D. Kumar, 'Patterns of Colonial Science in India', *Indian Journal of the History of Science*, 1980, *15*: 107; R.G. Albion, *Forests and Sea Power: The Timber Problem of the Royal Navy, 1652–1862* (Cambridge, 1926).

236 R. Brooke to Banks, 17 June 1787, *Kew: B.C. I*: 275; Patrick Russell to Banks, 10 October 1788, *Add. Mss 33978*, f. 206; Patton to Banks, 7 September 1802, *Add. Mss 33981*, f. 62.

237 See R. Brooke to Banks, 17 July 1787, 2 February 1789, and 25 May 1789, *Kew: B.C. I*: 275, 336 and 349.

238 'Address to the Planters, 5 November 1788', *Sutro*: SH 1: 3.

239 R. Grove, *Green Imperialism: Colonial Expansion, Tropical Island Edens, and the Origins of Environmentalism, 1600–1860* (Cambridge, 1995), *passim*; Mackay, *In the Wake of Cook*, pp. 179–80; Brooke, 'Address to the Planters, 8 June 1789'.

240 Here again we may see the influence of French precedent: Thierry de Menonville had in 1777 with the support of the Ministry of the Marine stolen cochineal insects and their nopal cactus host from Mexico and introduced them to St. Domingue; see T. de Menonville, *Traité de la Culture du Nopal et de l'Éducation de la Cochinelle* (Paris, 1787).

241 Banks to Thomas Morton (Secretary of the East India Company), 17 November 1791, *D.T.C. 7*: 283–7, *Kew: B.C. I*: 55.

242 J. Anderson, *Letters to Sir Joseph Banks* (Madras, 1788); *Letters on Cochineal* (Madras, 1788); *Letters on Cochineal Continued* (Madras, 1789), *Correspondence on the Introduction of the Cochineal Insects from America, the Varnish and Tallow Trees From China* (Madras, 1791). See also J. Anderson to R. Brooke, 12 January 1790 and 15 September 1790, *Kew: The Botanical Gardens. St. Helena & St. Vincent.*

243 Banks to Thomas Morton (Secretary of the East India Company), 17 November 1791, *D.T.C. 7*: 283–7, *Kew: B.C. I*: 55.

244 By 1797 the project was relaunched, and in 1802 the Company offered a premium of £500 for the collector who brought living nopal cactus to London, £1,000 if the insect was also brought, and a further £1,000 if the insect with cactus were to be successfully transported and introduced in Bengal. See H. Inglis (Chairman of the East India Company) to Banks, 27 March [1797], *Kew: B.C. III*: 44; Banks to Court of Directors of the East India Company, [ ] June 1802, *D.T.C. 13*: 152–6; Banks to R. Sproat, 27 August 1802, *Add. Mss 33981* ff. 53–4.

245 *An Autobiographical Memoir of Sir John Barrow, Bart.*, (London, 1847), *I*, p. 138.

246 *An Autobiographical Memoir of Sir John Barrow*, *I*, p. 216.

247 See the opinion of Cornwallis on Yonge in *The Correspondence of Charles, First Marquis Cornwallis* (London, 1859), *I*, p. 162.

248 See *A Catalogue of the Exotic Plants Cultivated in the Mauritius, at the botanic garden Monplaisir, Reduit and other Places* (Mauritius, 1816).

249 Raffles to Banks, 18 September 1814, *D.T.C. 19*: 68–74.

250 For the creation of the Trinidad botanic garden see Palmerston to Banks, 9 December 1818, *D.T.C. 20*: 149–50.

251 L. Guilding, *An Account of the Botanic Garden in the Island of St. Vincent* (Glasgow, 1825), p. 6.

252 Banks to Dundas, 15 June 1787, *D.T.C. 5*: 184.

253 See W. Roxburgh, *Plants of the Coast of Coromandel, Selected from Drawings Presented to the Hon. Court of Directors of the East India Company, Published under the Direction of Sir Joseph Banks* (London, 1795); Hunt Institute for Botanical Documentation, *A Selection of Late 18th and Early 19th Century Indian Botanical Paintings* (Pittsburgh, 1980).

254 Although we may see precedents in the kind of data supplied to Banks by Helenus Scott, physician and founder of the East India Company's garden at Bombay, on Indian cotton, metallurgy (including iron ore, copper, and steel production), alkali and soap manufacture, drugs and dyestuffs, and Hindu antiquities see Banks, 'List of Articles sent by Dr. Scot of Bombay to Sir Jos. Banks', *Add. Mss 33979*, f. 274; and respectively, Scott to Banks, 7 January 1790, *Add. Mss 333979*, ff. 1–13; Scott to Banks, 12 January 1800 and 1 August 1801, *Add. Mss 33980*, ff. 213–14; Scott to

Banks, 19 January 1792, *Add. Mss 33979*, ff. 127–30; Scott to Banks, 7 February 1792, *Add. Mss 33979*, 135–8; and Scott to Banks, 19 January 1796, *Add. Mss 35262*, ff. 14–15.

255 This interpretation of Banksian science is central to Gascoigne's *Sir Joseph Banks and the English Enlightenment.*

256 Banks to Menzies, 22 February 1791, *Kew: Kew Collectors—Papers Relating to 1791–1865*, ff. 279–84.

257 W. Roy, *An Account of the Measures of a Base on Hounslow Heath* (London, 1781).

258 Sinclair, 'Plan for the Agricultural Surveys'.

259 B.H. Vaysieul, 'À Propos d'une Nouvelle Économie Politique sous l'Ancien Régime: Formation du Territoire National et Travaux de la Carte de France', *Bulletin de l'Association des Géographes Français*, 1979, *462–3*: 249–56; Edney, *Mapping an Empire*, pp. 42–80.

260 Kyd to Banks, 7 September 1791, *Sutro*: Reel 21.

261 *Transactions of the Dublin Society*, 1800, *1*: xi.

262 *Ibid.*, x.

263 Edney, *Mapping an Empire*; A. Dalrymple, *Memoir Concerning a Survey of the Coast of Choromandel* (London, 1784).

264 See F. Buchanan, *A Journey From Madras Through the Countries of Mysore, Canowa and Malabar* (London, 1807), 3 vols.

265 See N. Wallich to Banks, 24 July 1817. *Kew: B.C. II(3)*: 524–5.

266 *An Account of the Natural Products of Sierra Leone Being the Substance of Two Reports Made to the Directors of the Sierra Leone Company* (London, 1794); Park, *Travels in the Interior Districts of Africa*; J. Oxley, *Journals of Two Expeditions into the Interior of New South Wales Undertaken by Order of the British Government, 1817–1818* (London, 1820).

267 Minute, 4 September 1799, IOL: P/254/41.

268 M. Vicziany, 'Imperialism, Botany and Statistics in Early Nineteenth Century India: The Surveys of Francis Buchanan (1762–1829)', *Modern Asian Studies*, 1986, *20*: 625–61.

269 Edney, *Mapping an Empire*; Buchanan, *A Journey from Madras, I*, pp. 125–6.

270 Darwin, *The Botanic Garden*, Canto IV, ll. 564–86.

271 W. Aiton, *Hortus Kewensis* (London, 1810–13), 5 vols.; J. Hill, *Hortus Kewensis. Sistens herbas exoticas, indigenasque rariores, in area botanica, Hortorum Aug. Pr. Cambriae Dotissae, apud Kew, in comitatu Surreiano, cultas* (London, 1769); J. Britten, 'The History of Aiton's *Hortus Kewensis*', *Journal of Botany*, 1912, *50*: 1–16.

272 W. Aiton, *An Epitome of the Second Edition of Hortus Kewensis* (London, 1814).

273 Banks to Smith, 15 August 1787, LS: *Smith Mss I*, ff. 87–8.

274 Don Corneille to Banks, 23 February 1786, *Kew: B.C. I(2)*: 226.

275 A. Menzies to Banks, 8 June 1786, *Kew: B.C. I(3)*: 234.

276 Banks to Wilberforce, 8 April 1793, *D.T.C. 8*: 196–7; Park to Banks, 16 November 1805, *Add. Mss 37232*, f. 64.

277 Corneille to Banks, 30 June 1786, *Kew: B.C. I(3)*: 279.

278 Banks to Hunter, March 1797, quoted in Desmond, *Kew*, p. 99.

279 Banks to W. Ramsay, 22 October 1795, IOL: *Mss* E/1/1/88.

280 Banks to J. Bosanquet, 8 April 1803, *Add. Mss 33981*, f. 91; Banks to J. Roberts, Director of the East India Company, 28 April 1803, *Add. Mss 33981*, f. 104.

281 See for example Barrow (Secretary of the Admiralty) to Banks, 29 July 1815, *D.T.C. 19*: 167–8; Banks to Barrow, 6 August 1815 and [1 December] 1815, *D.T.C. 19*: 170, 221–2.

282 Banks to Duke of Portland, 3 February 1796, *D.T.C. 10*: 15–16.

283 Banks to Marsden, 19 October 1805, *D.T.C. 16*: 149–50; Banks to Barrow, 19 October 1805, [ ] January 1807, *Add. Mss 32439*, ff. 185 and 237–45; R. Brown, 'General Remarks, Geographical and Systematical on the Botany of Terra Australis', appendix III of Flinders, *Voyage to Terra Australis*; and, on its model, A. Cunningham, 'A Few General Remarks on the Vegetation of Certain Coasts of Terra Australis and More Especially of its Northern Shores', appendix to P.P. King, *Narrative of a Survey of the Inter-tropical and Western Coasts of Australia, Performed Between the Years 1818 and 1822* (London, 1827), *II*.

284 J. Brown, 'A Science of Empire: British Biogeography before Darwin', *Revue d'Histoire des Sciences*, 1992, *44*: 451–75.

285 Banks to G. Caley, 7 March 1795, *D.T.C. 9*: 199–200.

286 R. Grant, *A Sketch of the History of the East India Company* (London, 1813), pp. 380–1.

287 Banks to Wilberforce, 21 December 1791, *D.T.C. 7: 294*.

288 Banks to J. Bowie and A. Cunningham, 18 September 1814, *Kew: Kew Collectors. J. Bowie and A. Cunningham, 1814–18, I.*

289 Banks to Lord Palmerston, 26 November 1809, *D.T.C. 17: 285–8.*

290 Palmerston to Banks, 17 August 1815, *Sutro*: Reel 20.

291 Banks to W.J. Hooker, 19 June 1813, *Kew: Letters to W.J. Hooker I*: 39.

5 From Royal to Public

1 J. Evans, *Richmond & Its Vicinity*, (Richmond, 1825), pp. 130–1.

2 L. Guilding, *An Account of the Botanic Garden in the Island of St. Vincent from Its Establishment to the Present Time* (Glasgow, 1825), p. 23. I am indebted to Professor R. Howard of Harvard University for a gift in 1985 of a facsimile of Guilding's *Account.*

3 A. Thackray and J. Morrell, *Gentlemen of Science: Early Years of the British Association for the Advancement of Science* (Oxford, 1991), pp. 42–3; J.L.E. Dreyer and H.H. Turner, *History of the Royal Astronomical Society* (London, 1920), pp. 55–60.

4 J.F.W. Herschel, F. Beaufort, P.M. Roget to J. Barrow, 20 November 1828 and 3 February 1831, P.R.O.: ADM 1/ 4282.

5 IOL: E/4/752, ff. 408–9.

6 See Court of Directors of the East India Company to Governor of Bengal, 29 September 1830. *Kew: India: Calcutta Botanic Gardens, 1830–1928*, f. 5.

7 J.F. Royle to Lindley, [11 January 1832]. *Kew: Lindley Letters*, f. 778.

8 N. Wallich to H.J. Princep, Secretary to the Governor of Bengal, 18 May 1836. *Kew: India: Calcutta Botanic Gardens, 1830–1928*, f. 14.

9 J. Dinwiddy, *From Luddism to the First Reform Bill in England, 1810–1832* (Oxford, 1986); P. Harling, *The Waning of 'Old Corruption': The Politics of Economical Reform in Britain, 1779–1846* (Oxford, 1996).

10 B. Hilton, *The Age of Atonement: The Influence of Evangelicalism on Economic and Social Thought, 1785–1865* (Oxford, 1988), pp. 204–8.

11 Peel to Croker, 23 March 1820, quoted by Harling, *The Waning of 'Old Corruption'*, p. 154; J. Parry, *The Rise and Fall of Liberal Government in Victorian Britain* (London, 1993), pp. 27–49.

12 Liverpool to Palmerston, 30 December 1816, *Add. Mss* 38264, f. 72.

13 *An Address to the Electors of Great Britain* (London, 1826).

14 Russell to Grey, 21 November 1848, quoted in W.P. Morrell, *The Colonial Policy of Peel and Russell* (Oxford, 1930), p. 208.

15 J. Gallagher and R. Robinson, 'The Imperialism of Free Trade', *Economic History Review*, 2nd series, 6: 1–15.

16 J. Burnet to W.J. Hooker, 20 June 1842, *Kew: Africa Letters, 1830–44*, f. 18; 'Ludwigsberg Garden', SAL: *Mss* MSB64.

17 E. J. Burrow to John Barrow, 20 July 1833 and W. Harvey to W. J. Hooker, 1 July 1835, *Kew: Africa Letters, 1830–44*, ff. 20 and 49.

18 Bowie to John Smith, 5 July 1850, *Kew: Kew Collectors. J. Bowie and A. Cunningham, 1814–18, I.*

19 *A Catalogue of the Plants in the Botanic Garden at Liverpool* (Liverpool, 1808).

20 *Ibid.* p. v.

21 J.C. Loudon, 'Hints for a National Garden', 10 December 1811; LS: *Mss* SP 716.

22 *Ibid.*, ff. 1–2.

23 *Ibid.*, f. 9r.

24 See J. Donn, 'Preface', *Hortus Cantabrigiensis* (Cambridge, 1796); S.M. Walters, *The Shaping of Cambridge Botany: A Short History of Whole-Plant Botany in Cambridge from the time of Ray into the Present Century* (Cambridge, 1981), p. 45.

25 *P.P.*, 1812 (357), *12*: 433; P.R.O.: CRES 2/754; G. Meynell, 'The Royal Botanic Society's Garden, Regent's Park', *London Journal*, 1980, *6*: 135–46.

26 See 'Circular' (London, n.d. [1813?]), *Sutro*: Reel 18.

27 Banks, remarks on 'Prospectus for a Plan for Establishing a National Botanic Garden, Library, & Reading Rooms in the Regents Park', (London, n.d. [1813?]), *Sutro*: Reel 18.

28 Evans, *Richmond and Its Vicinity*, p. 122.

29 *Kew Gardens with the Pleasure Grounds and Park* (London, 1850), p. 6; W.T. Thiselton-Dyer, 'Historical Account of Kew to 1841', *K.B.* 1891, pp. 279–327, pp. 314–22; M. Allan, *The Hookers of Kew, 1785–1911* (London, 1967); R. Desmond, *Kew: The History of the Royal Botanic Gardens* (London, 1995), pp. 127–49.

30 See Hooker to Turner, 26 March 1841, *Kew: Letters to Dawson Turner.*

31 *Philosophical Magazine*, 1824, *4*: 365–6.

32 See APS: *Mss* of Malesherbes, 'Voyage en Angleterre', ff. 77–9; see also the visit to Richmond of F. Guizot in *An Embassy to the Court of St. James in 1840* (London, 1862), p. 169.

33 W.J. Hooker, *Botanical Miscellany*, 1830, *1*: 48–78, see p. 65.

34 H. Davy, *On the Progress and Objects of Science* (London, 1827).

35 Thackray and Morrell, *Gentlemen of Science*, pp. 47–57; F.M. Turner, 'Public Science in Britain, 1880–1919', *Isis*, 1980, *71*: 589–608.

36 C. Babbage, *Reflections on the Decline of Science in England and Some of its Causes* (London, 1830), pp. v–x, pp. 1–2; see Babbage's remarks on Lyell's *éloge* of Cuvier, *Life, Letters, and Journals of Sir Charles Lyell, Bart.* (London, 1881), 2 vols., *I*, p. 385.

37 Babbage, *Reflections*, p. 78.

38 See for example the remarks of J. Herschel, *Preliminary Discourse on the Study of Natural Philosophy* (London, 1831), p. 7; 'Mr. Babbage's Observations on the National Encouragement of Science', *Edinburgh Journal of Science*, 1830, *3*: 58–76; W.H. Fitton, *A Statement of Circumstances Connected with the Late Election for the President of the Royal Society* (London, 1831); Thackray and Morrell, *Gentlemen of Science*, p. 36.

39 Seymour to Raffles, 2 March 1825, IOL: *Ms. Eur. D.* 742/24, ff. 39–40.

40 Duchess of Somerset to Raffles, 7 April 1825, IOL: *Ms. Eur. D.* 742/27, ff. 6–7.

41 See J. Lindley, F.R.S., *An Introductory Lecture Delivered in the University of London on Thursday April 30, 1829* (London, 1829), pp. 4–5; P.F. Stevens, *Nature and the 'Natural' System': Antoine Laurent de Jussieu and the Foundations of Botanical Systematics* (Chicago, 1994); I am indebted to Dr. Stevens of the Gray Herbarium at Harvard for communication on Jussieu, de Candolle, Bentham, and the history of botany in this era.

42 W. Whewell, *History of the Inductive Sciences* (London, 1837), *III*, pp. 253–4, 366–74 and 444–8.

43 Thackray and Morrell, *Gentlemen of Science*, p. 56; D.J. Mabberley, *Jupiter Botanicus: Robert Brown and the British Museum* (London, 1985), p. 279.

44 For a discussion of courtly medicine see A. Desmond, *The Politics of Evolution: Morphology, Medicine, and Reform in Radical London* (Chicago, 1989), pp. 101–16.

45 J. Hooker, *A Sketch of the Life and Labours of Sir William Jackson Hooker* (Oxford, 1903), p. lxi.

46 *Kew: GB Auto. Mss*, f. 188.

47 W. Hooker to A. Gray, 11 July 1839, *Harvard University: Asa Gray Correspondence*, ff. 2–3.

48 Hooker to Gray, 5 November 1840, *Harvard University: Asa Gray Correspondence*; a variety of studies describe the vibrant horticultural industry of the age: J. Harvey, *Early Nurserymen* (London, 1974), pp. 107–34; M. Hadfield, *A History of British Gardening* (London, 1960), pp. 282–96; E.J. Willson, *West London Nursery Gardens: The Nursery Gardens of Chelsea, Fulham, Hammersmith, Kensington, and a Part of Westminster, Founded before 1900* (London, 1982); J.H. Veitch, *Hortus Veitchii: A History of the Rise and Progress of the Nurseries of Messrs. James Veitch and Sons, Together with an Account of the Botanical Collectors and Hybridists Employed by them and a List of the Most Remarkable of their Introductions* (London, 1906).

49 *Kew: GB Auto. Mss*, f. 179.

50 Banks to Harrison, 1 September 1814, *D.T.C. 19*: 56–7; 'Cape of Good Hope: Botanical Collectors', *P.P.*, 1821, *21*: 37–8.

51 J. Wiles to Banks, 16 October 1793, *Kew: B.C. II*: 103.

52 *Kew: GB Auto. Mss*, f. 171.

53 J.L. Gilbert, 'The Life and Times of William Townsend Aiton', *Journal of the Kew Guild*, *8*: 688–93; *K.B.*, 1910: 306–8.

54 D. Cannadine, 'The Landowner as Millionaire: the Finances of the Duke of Devonshire c. 1800–1926', *Agricultural History Review*, 1977, *25*: 77–91; M. Hadfield, *A History of British Gardening*, pp. 304–6; V. Markham, *Paxton and the Bachelor Duke* (London, 1935).

55 Mabberley, *Jupiter Botanicus*, p. 397.

56 W.J. Hooker to Brown, 8 November 1818, *Add. Mss 32440*, f. 203.

57 Whewell, *History of the Inductive Sciences*, *III*, pp. 330–1.

58 M. Walker, *Sir James Edward Smith, M.D., F.R.S., 1759–1828* (London, 1988), p. 3; W.T. Stearn, 'The Smith Herbarium', *Taxon*, 1967, *16*: 168–78.

59 See W.T. Stearn, 'An Introduction to the *Species Plantarum* and Cognate Botanical Works of Carl Linnaeus', in C. Linnaeus, *Species Plantarum* (London, 1957), *I*, pp. 1–176.

60 For evidence of the first point see J.E. Smith, 'An Introductory Discourse on the Rise and Progress of Natural History', *Transactions of the Linnean Society*, 1791, *1*: 1–55; *idem*, *A Syllabus of a Course of Lectures on Botany* (London, 1795); *idem*, *An Introduction to Physiological and Structural Botany* (London, 1807).

61 *English Botany; or Coloured Figures of British Plants, with their Essential Characters, Synonyms, and Places of Growth* (London, 1790–1814), 36 vol.; see also J.E. Smith, *Icones plantarum rariorum descriptionibus et observationibus illustratae* (London, 1790–3).

62 See J.E. Smith, *Considerations Respecting Cambridge, More Particularly Relating to its Botanical Professorship* (London, 1818).

63 J. Monk, *Quarterly Review*, 1818, *19*: 438.

64 *Ibid.*, 434–46; J. Monk, *A Vindication of the University of Cambridge from the Reflections of Sir James Edward Smith, Contained in a Pamphlet Entitled, Considerations Respecting Cambridge* (London, 1818); J.E. Smith, *A Defence of the Church, and Universities of England, Against such Injurious Advocates as Professor Monk* (London, 1819); Walker, *Smith*, p. 48.

65 H.S. Miller, 'The Herbarium of Aylmer Bourke Lambert, Notes on its Acquisition, Dispersal, and Present Whereabouts', *Taxon*, 1971, *19*: 489–553; see p. 493.

66 See e.g. J. Lindley, *Collectanea Botanica* (London, 1821), Tab. 1 of *Bromelia fästuosa.*

67 Martius to Lambert, 21 January 1825, *Kew: Lambert Letters*, f. 85.

68 *Kew: GB Auto. Mss*, f. 168.

69 A.B. Lambert, *A Description of the Genus* Cinchona, *Comprehending the Various Species of Vegetables from Which the Peruvian and Other Barks Are Taken* (London, 1797); *idem*, *A Description of the Genus* Pinus (London, 1803–24), 2 vols.; *idem*, 'A Description of a New Species of *Psidium*', *Transactions of the Linnean Society*, 1815, *11*: 231–2; *idem*, 'A Description of the Mustard Plant of the Scriptures', *Transactions of the Linnean Society*, 1837, *17*: 445–6. See also H.W. Renvena, 'Aylmer Bourke Lambert and his Description of the Genus *Pinus*', *Journal of the Linnean Society*, 1930, *48*, 439–66.

70 O.B.D. Jackson, *George Bentham* (London, 1906), p. 78.

71 A.P. de Candolle, *Mémoires et Souvenirs d'Augustin-Pyramus de Candolle* (Geneva, 1862), p. 269.

72 The Dawson Turner Papers at Trinity College, Cambridge remain still a largely unexploited resource. Biographical details are provided by W.R. Dawson, 'Dawson Turner, F.R.S. (1775–1858)', *Journal of the Society for the Bibliography of Natural History*, 1958, *3*: 303–10 and W.H. Bidwell, *Annals of an East Anglian Bank* (Norwich, 1900). For the range of his interests see his publications: *Sepulchral Reminiscences of Old Yarmouth* (Yarmouth, 1838), *Outlines in Lithography From a Small Collection of Prints* (Yarmouth, 1840), *Guide to the Historian, the Biographer, the Antiquary, the Man of Literary Curiosity, and the Collector of Autographs: Towards the Verification of Manuscripts, by Reference to Engraved Facsimiles of Handwriting* (Yarmouth, 1848).

73 *A Synopsis of the British Fuci* (Yarmouth, 1802), 2 vols.; 'Descriptions of Four New Species of *Fucus*', *Transactions of the Linnean Society*, 1802, *6*: 125–36; *Muscologiae hibernicae spicilegium* (Yarmouth, 1804); 'Descriptions of Four British Lichens', *Transactions of the Linnean Society*, 1804, *7*: 86–95; *Fucus, sive plantarum fucorum generi a botanicis ascriptarum icones, descriptiones et historia* (London, 1807–19), 4 vols.

74 Lyell, *Life, Letters, Journals, I*, p. 41.

75 Nothing on Brown is anywhere as complete as Mabberley, *Jupiter Botanicus*, a remarkable biography despite its sometimes hagiographic tenor; see also: J.J. Bennett, 'Robert Brown, D.C.L.', *Proceedings of the Royal Society of London*, 1858, *9*: 527–32; W.T. Stearn, 'Robert Brown', *DSB, II*, pp. 516–23; *idem*, 'Robert Brown', *Brunonia*, 1977, *1*: 1–7; J.C. Stephenson, 'Robert Brown's discovery of the nucleus in relation to the history of cell theory', *Proceedings of the Linnean Society of London*, 1932, *144*: 45–54.

76 R. Brown, *Prodromus florae Novae Hollandiae et Insulae van-Diemen, exhibens characteres plantarum quas annis 1802–1805 per oras utiusque insulae collegit et descripsit Robertus Brown* (London, 1810).

77 *Gardener's Magazine*, 1835: 5.

78 W. Hooker to Sir J. Richardson, 14 August 1824, *Kew: Letters to Sir John Richardson, 1819–43.*

79 See W. Hooker to G. Bentham, 23 January 1833, *Kew: Sir William Hooker's Letters to Mr. Bentham, 1823–41:* f. 78. For a discussion of Schomburgk see D.G. Burnett, 'El Dorado on Paper: Traverse Surveys and the Geographical Construction of British Guiana, 1803–1844', PhD dissertation, University of Cambridge, 1997.

80 De Candolle, *Mémoires et Souvenirs*, p. 267.

81 See F. Bauer to Lindley, 17 February 1832, *Kew: Lindley Letters, A–K*, f. 46.

82 Brown to Lindley, 31 January 1831 and 11 August 1831, *Kew: Lindley Letters, A–K*, ff. 131 and 133.

83 J.D.H. Hooker, 'A Sketch of the Life and Labours of Sir William Jackson Hooker', *Annals of Botany*, 1902, *16*: 9–221; F.O. Bower, 'Sir William Hooker, 1785–1865', in F.W. Oliver, ed., *Makers of British Botany* (Cambridge, 1913), pp. 126–50; Allan, *The Hookers of Kew*; *idem*, 'William Jackson Hooker', *DSB, IV*, 492–95.

84 W.J. Hooker, *Journal of a Tour in Iceland in the Summer of 1809* (Yarmouth, 1811 and 1813), 2 vols.

85 See W.J. Hooker, *British Jungermanniae* (London, 1816).

86 See comment on *Catasetum hookeri* in Lindley, *Collectanea Botanica*, Tab. 40.

87 See letter quoted in J. Hooker, *A Sketch of the Life and Labours of Sir. William Jackson Hooker* (Oxford, 1903), p. xxvii.

88 W.J. Hooker, *Catalogue of Plants in the Royal Botanic Garden of Glasgow* (Glasgow, 1825); F.O. Bower, 'Notes on Botany in the University of Glasgow in the Eighteenth Century', *Transactions of the Natural History Society of Glasgow*, 1903, 7: 121–36; J.B. Hay, *A Historical Sketch of the University of Glasgow* (Glasgow, 1839); A.D. Boney, *The Lost Gardens of Glasgow University* (London, 1988), pp. 260–2.

89 A. Gray, *American Journal of the Sciences and Arts*, 1841, *40*(i).

90 See W.J. Hooker, 'Botanical Appendix', to W.E. Parry, *Journal of a Second Voyage of Discovery of a North West Passage from the Atlantic and the Pacific* (London, 1821, 1822–3); *idem*, *The Botany of Captain Beachey's Voyage* (London, 1828); *idem*, *Flora Boreali-Americanae or the Botany of the Northern Parts of British America* (London, 1829–40), 2 vols.

91 C.C. Rafinesque to J. Torrey, 21 December 1836, *New York Botanical Garden—Letters to John Torrey, 1819–40* (read from microfilm held by the archives of the Academy of Natural Sciences Philadelphia, on deposit with the American Philosophical Society); see also remarks on Hooker in Rafinesque to Torrey, 11 February 1833.

92 See G. Lindley, *A Guide to the Orchard and Kitchen Garden* (London, 1831); G. Lindley to D. Turner, 10 April 1830, *Trinity College, Cambridge: Dawson Turner Papers.*

93 De Candolle, *Mémoires et Souvenirs*, p. 272.

94 W.J. Hooker to C. Lyell, 2 November 1818, f. 1, APS: *Darwin–Lyell Papers*; R. Brown, 8 November 1818, *Add. Mss 32440*, f. 203.

95 *Kew: GB Auto. Mss*, ff. 448–9.

96 *Kew: Dr. Lindley's Official Correspondence, 1832–54*, ff. 1–14.

97 Auckland to Lindley, 18 March 1838, 12 August 1838, *Kew: Lindley Letters, A–K*, ff. 30–3.

98 Martius to Lindley, November 1831, *Kew: Lindley Letters, L–Z*, f. 587r.

99 See Paxton to Lindley, 18 January 1838, *Kew: Lindley Letters, L–Z*, ff. 700–6.

100 J. Lindley, *The Fossil Flora of Great Britain* (London, 1831–2), 3 vols. See Lindley correspondence with Hutton in the Hancock Museum, Newcastle upon Tyne; Lyell, *Life, Letters, Journals, 1*, p. 178; C. Darwin to Lindley, 8 April [1840], *Kew: Lindley Letters, A–K*, f. 189.

101 See Devonshire to Lindley, 14 August 1837 and [1840], *Kew: Lindley Letters, A–K*, ff. 277 and 281.

102 Hooker edited *Curtis's Botanical Magazine, Botanical Illustrations; Being a Series of Figures* (Edinburgh, 1822), *Exotic Flora, Containing Figures and Descriptions of New, Rare or Otherwise Interesting Exotic Plants* (London, 1823–7), *Hooker's Botanical Miscellany Containing Figures and Descriptions of Such Plants as Recommend Themselves by their Novelty, Rarity, or History, or by the Uses to which They are Applied in the Arts* (London, 1830–3); while Lindley, whose first book was *Rosarum Monographia; or A Botanical History of Roses* (London, 1820), later published *Collectanea Botanica, or Figures and Botanical Illustrations of Rare and Curious Exotic Plants* (London, 1821), *The Botanic Register* (London, 1829–47), *The Genera and Species of Orchidaceous Plants* (London, 1830–40), *Sertum Orchidaceum* (London, 1838), *Pomologia Brittanica* (London, 1841), and *Orchidaceae Lindenianae, or Notes upon a Collection of Orchids Found in Colombia and Cuba* (London, 1846), while editing the *Flower Garden* with Sir Joseph Paxton.

103 J. Lindley, F.R.S., *An Introductory Lecture Delivered in the University of London on Thursday April 30, 1829* (London, 1829), pp. 4–5.

104 I made this point about Lindley's assertion of the need to give botany a masculine seriousness in my thesis, from which, via Jim Secord, it has been developed in A. Shteir, *Cultivating Women, Cultivating Science: Flora's Daughters—Botany in England, 1760–1860* (Baltimore, 1996).

105 J. Lindley, *On the Principal Questions at Present Debated in the Philosophy of Botany* (London, 1833), pp. 27 and 56–7.

106 *Edinburgh Review*, 1833, *57*: 68–9; see also E. Chadwick, 'Animal Physiology', *Westminster Review*, 1832, *16*: 192–203.

107 P. Mandler, *Aristocratic Government in the Age of Reform: Whigs and Liberals, 1830–1852* (Oxford, 1990), pp. 13–70; R. Adair, *A Sketch of the Character of the Late Duke of Devonshire* (London, 1811), esp. W.R. Spencer, 'The Late Duke of Devonshire', pp. 19–28; F.M.L.Thompson, *English Landed Society in the Nineteenth Century* (London, 1963), pp. 25–43.

108 E.A. Wasson, *Whig Renaissance: Lord Althorp and the Whig Party, 1782–1845*

(London, 1990), p. 72; Mandler, *Aristocratic Government*, pp. 85–95; A. Mitchell, *The Whigs in Opposition, 1815–1830* (Oxford, 1967), pp. 138–48.

109 E.A. Wasson, 'The Third Earl Spencer and Agriculture, 1818–1845', *Agricultural History Review*, 1978: 89–99; Ritvo, *The Animal Estate* (London, 1987).

110 H. Davy, *Elements of Agricultural Chemistry* (Hartford, 1819), p. 21; see G. Foote, 'Sir Humphry Davy and His Audience at the Royal Institution', *Isis*, 1952, 43: 6–12.

111 *Woburn Abbey Georgics or, the Last Gathering* (London, 1813), Canto III, pp. 42–3.

112 Bedford to Hooker, 3 December 1836, *Kew: Mss LDB*; N. Goddard, *Harvests of Change: The Royal Agricultural Society of England, 1838–1988* (London, 1988).

113 B. Hilton, *Corn, Cash, Commerce: The Economic Policies of the Tory Governments, 1815–1830* (Oxford, 1977), pp. 308–10; Hilton, *The Age of Atonement*, pp. 21–6, 298–314, and *passim*; M. Bravo, 'Science and Discovery in the Admiralty Voyages to the Arctic Regions in Search of a North-West Passage', PhD dissertation, University of Cambridge, 1992.

114 D. Cannadine, 'The Making of the British Upper Classes', in *Aspects of Aristocracy* (London, 1995), pp. 9–36.

115 Wasson, *Whig Renaissance, passim.*

116 P. Beauchamp [G. Grote], *Analysis of the Influence of Natural Religion, on the Temporal Happiness of Mankind* (London, 1822); H. Brougham, *A Discourse of Natural Theology: Showing the Nature of the Evidence and the Advantages of the Study* (London, 1833); P. Corsi, *Science and Religion: Baden Powell and the Anglican Debate, 1800–1860* (Cambridge, 1988).

117 G. Sinclair, F.L.S., F.R.S., *Hortus Gramineus Woburnensis: Or, an Account of the Results of Experiments on the Produce and Nutritive Qualities of Different Grasses and other Plants used as the Food of the More Valuable Domestic Animal, Instituted by John, Duke of Bedford* (London, 1824); W. Yarrell, F.L.S., *Some Observations on the Economy of an Insect Destructive to Turnips* (Woburn, 1837).

118 Sinclair, *Hortus Gramineus Woburnensis*, pp. v–vi.

119 See P.F. Robinson, *History of Woburn Abbey* (London, 1833); J.D. Parry, *History and Description of Woburn and Its Abbey* (London, 1831); G. Blakiston, *Woburn and the Russells* (London, 1980). On Devonshire see A.W.J. Clifford, *A Sketch of the Life of the Duke of Devonshire* (London, 1870); J. Lees-Milne, *The Bachelor Duke: A Life of William Spencer Cavendish, 6th Duke of Devonshire, 1790–1858* (London, 1991).

120 J. Forbes, *Hortus Woburnensis: A Descriptive Catalogue of upwards of Six Thousand Ornamental Plants Cultivated at Woburn Abbey* (London, 1833), p. v.

121 [G. Sinclair], *Hortus Ericaeus Woburnensis: Or a Collection of Heaths in the Collection of the Duke of Bedford at Woburn Abbey* (London, 1825); [J. Forbes], *Salictum Woburnense: Or, a Catalogue of Willows, Indigenous or Foreign, in the Collection of the Duke of Bedford at Woburn Abbey* (London, 1829); J. Forbes, *A Catalogue of the Different Species of Cactae in the Gardens at Woburn Abbey* (London, 1837); J. Forbes, *Pinetum Woburnense or a Catalogue of Coniferous Plants in the Collection of the Duke of Bedford, at Woburn Abbey* (London, 1839).

122 See J.E. Smith to D. Turner, 20 December 1811; Coke to Turner, 4 January 1812; Bedford to Turner, 3 February 1837; Bentinck to Turner, 7 June 1837; P. Hunt to Turner, 26 October 1837; *Trinity College, Cambridge: Dawson Turner Papers*; Bedford to A.B. Lambert, 12 October 1839, *Kew: Lambert Letters*, f. 36.

123 Bedford to Smith, 11 November 1804, *Kew: Mss LDB*, p. 6.

124 The best account of the Society remains M. Grobel, 'The Society for the Diffusion of Useful Knowledge, 1826–1846', PhD dissertation, University of London, 1932, pp. 142 and 180 (available at Manuscript Room of University College Library). Its General Committee united 'Young Whigs' such as Lord John Russell and Althorp with Radicals, Evangelicals, and Utilitarians such as Joseph Hume, Zachary Macaulay, Brougham, and James Mill.

125 See J. Lindley to T. Coates, 24 August 1829, 4 February 1831, 17 May 1832, 16 September 1834, 24 July 1836, and fifteen other pieces to 1843; UCL: *SDUK Archives*.

126 Bedford to Hooker, 29 September 1839, *Kew: Mss LDB.*

127 Bedford to Hooker, 29 March 1834, *Kew: Mss LDB.*

128 Hooker to Turner, 23 April 1834, *Kew: Extracts from Letters to Dawson Turner.*

129 Hooker to W.H. Harvey, 19 December 1834, *Kew: Letters to Dr. W.H. Harvey, 1832–60.*

130 Bedford to Hooker, 3 December 1836, *Kew: Mss LDB.*

131 W. Herbert, *Amaryllidaceae* (London, 1837), pp. 247–8.

132 *Gardener's Gazette*, 7 October 1837.

133 *Gardener's Gazette*, 14 October 1837; see also Aiton's reply in *Morning Chronicle*, 16 October 1837 and the return shot in *Gardener's Gazette*, 21 October 1837.
134 *Gardener's Magazine*, 1838, *14*: 70.
135 *Penny Cyclopaedia*, 1838, *11*: 74.
136 P.R.O.: T 29/397, T 90/190; G. Meynell, 'Kew and the Royal Gardens Committee of 1838', *Archives of Natural History*, 1982, *10*: 469–77, pp. 469–70, the latter article remains an excellent guide to the controversy.
137 P.R.O.: T 29/397; *P.P.*, 1831–2 (9), *4*: 751; 1833 (530), *2*: 531.
138 Bedford to Hooker, 4 January 1838, *Kew: Mss LDB.*
139 Hooker to Lindley, 20 February 1838, *Kew: Lindley Letters, A–K*, f. 470.
140 W.J. Hooker to Lord John Russell, 12 February 1838, P.R.O.: PRO 30/22/3A.
141 Hooker to Lindley, 22 February 1838, *Kew: Lindley Letters, A–K*, f. 3a.
142 Memorandum no. 4 of the Royal Gardens Committee, P.R.O.: T 90/190.
143 Red Bound Notebook, P.R.O.: T 90/190, f. 1r.
144 *Gardener's Magazine*, March 1838, *14*: 194.
145 'Draft of Letter of Appointment of Lindley', 8 February 1838; in P.R.O.: T. 90/190, ff. 3–4.
146 J. Lindley, 'Report on the Present Condition of the Botanical Gardens at Kew with Recommendations for its Future Administration', No. 4 of 'Royal Gardens Committee. 1838', P.R.O.: T. 90/190, ff. 3–11.
147 *Ibid.*, f. 12.
148 *Ibid.*, f. 17.
149 *Ibid.*, ff. 21–2; *P.P.*, 1840 (292), *29*: 259–66, p. 5.
150 *Ibid.*, p. 2.
151 W. Hooker to D. Turner, 13 March 1838, *Kew: Extracts from Letters to Dawson Turner.*
152 Royal Gardens Committee, 'Minutes ... and Resolutions', P.R.O.: T 90/190, no. 5, f. 10.
153 Bedford to Hooker, 2 March 1838, which quotes from Gore to Adam, 19 February 1838; *Kew: Mss LDB.*
154 W. Hooker to G. Bentham, 6 March 1838, *Kew: Sir William Hooker's Letters to Mr. Bentham, 1823–41*, f. 148r.
155 W. Hooker to Lord John Russell, Hooker to Melbourne, Hooker to Melbourne, 7 March 1838, 6 March 1838, 26 March 1838, *Royal Archives, Windsor: Melbourne Papers* 49/143; 49/144; 49/145.
156 Hooker to Turner, 13 March 1838, *Kew: Extracts from Letters to Dawson Turner.*
157 Bedford to Lord John Russell, 21 March 1838, P.R.O.: 30/22/3A.
158 *Kew: GB Auto. Mss*, ff. 448–9 and 485.
159 J. Lindley to T. Coates, 14 August and 12 September 1837, UCL: *SDUK Archives.*
160 A. Brundage, *England's 'Prussian Minister': Edwin Chadwick and the Politics of Government Growth, 1832–1854* (London, 1988).
161 *Royal Archives (Windsor)*: Queen Victoria's Journal, 30 April 1838; Meynell, 'Kew and the Royal Gardens Committee', p. 471.
162 W. Hooker to Sir J. Richardson, 17 April 1838, *Kew: Letters to Sir John Richardson, 1819–43.*
163 Bedford to Hooker, 2 June 1838, *Kew: Mss LDB.*
164 Bedford to Hooker, 9 June 1838, *Kew: Mss LDB.*
165 Bedford to Hooker, 16 June 1838, *Kew: Mss LDB.*
166 *Gardener's Magazine*, 1838, *14*: 69.
167 *Ibid.*
168 P.R.O.: CRES 2/754; Meynell, 'The Royal Botanic Society's Garden, Regent's Park'.
169 *Memorial to the Commissioners of Woods and Forests of the Royal Botanical Society of London*, 4 September 1838, P.R.O.: T90/189.
170 Bedford to Hooker, 30 June 1840, *Kew: Mss LDB.*
171 Hooker to Turner, 4 August 1838, *Kew: Extracts from Letters to Dawson Turner.*
172 *Gardener's Gazette*, February 1838.
173 *Gardener's Magazine*, March 1838, *14*: 194.
174 Bedford to Hooker, 30 June 1838, *Kew: Mss LDB*; Hooker to Turner, 4 August 1838, *Kew: Extracts from Letters to Dawson Turner.*
175 Bedford to Hooker, 6 June and 9 October 1838, *Kew: Mss LDB.*
176 Bedford to W. Hooker, 30 June, 1838. *Kew: Mss LDB*; note that when Hooker quotes the letter, in the 1840 collection of his correspondence with Bedford which in the midst of the controversy he unabashedly forwards to the Prime Minister, the Queen, and every possible influential member of the Russell family, he tactfully edits out this potentially embarrassing passage; see *Kew: LDB*, p. 19.
177 Bedford to Hooker, 9 and 15 October 1838, *Kew: Mss LDB.*
178 Hooker to Bentham, 24 and 26 October 1838, *Kew: Sir William Hooker's Letters to Mr. Bentham*, ff. 171 and 173.
179 W. Hooker to Lindley, 3 November 1838, *Kew: Lindley Letters, A–K*, f. 373.
180 *Journal of the House of Lords*, 1837–8, *70*: 613.

181 Bedford to Hooker, 16 January 1839, *Kew: Mss. LDB.*
182 Hooker to A. Gray, 3 January 1839, *Harvard University: Asa Gray Correspondence.*
183 Hooker to Turner, 18 January 1839, *Kew: Extracts from Letters to Dawson Turner.*
184 Hooker to Turner, 15 November 1838, *Kew: Extracts from Letters to Dawson Turner.*
185 W. Hooker to A. Gray, 7 February 1839, *Harvard University: Asa Gray Correspondence*; Hooker to Turner, 29 January 1839, *Kew: Extracts from Letters to Dawson Turner.*
186 Bedford to Hooker, 22 February 1839, *Kew: Mss LDB*; see also Hooker to Turner, 15 April 1839, *Kew: Extracts from Letters to Dawson Turner.*
187 Lord Duncannon, B.C. Stephenson, A. Milne, Commisioners of Woods and Forests to the Rt. Hon. Lord Commissioners of H.M. Treasury, 24 April 1839, *Kew: Royal Gardens Kew. Reports and Documents, 1784–1884.*
188 Melbourne to Queen Victoria, 7 May 1839 quoted by Meynell, 'Kew and the Royal Gardens Committee of 1838', p. 472.
189 Hooker to Harvey, 14 June 1839, *Kew: Sir William Hooker—Letters to Dr. W.H. Harvey, 1832–60.*
190 Bedford to Hooker, [ ] July 1839, *Kew: Mss LDB*; Hooker to Turner, 27 July 1839, *Kew: Extracts from Letters to Dawson Turner.*
191 R. Russell, ed., *Early Correspondence of Lord John Russell, 1805–1840* (London, 1913), *I*, p. 90; Bedford to Hooker, 14 September 1839, *Kew: Mss LDB.*
192 Bedford to Hooker, 16 October 1839, *Kew: Mss LDB.*
193 P.R.O.: WORK 16/181; Meynell, 'Kew and the Royal Gardens Committee of 1838', p. 474.
194 'Minutes of Conversation at the Treasury with Robert Gordon', 11 February 1840, *Kew: Creation of the Royal Gardens in 1840.*
195 Lindley to R. Gordon, 12 February 1840, *ibid.*
196 Lambert to Smith, 13 February 1840, *Kew: Lambert Letters*, f. 239.
197 *Memorial*, 24 February 1840, P.R.O.: T 90/189.
198 *The Times*, 21 and 24 February 1840; Loudon, *Gardener's Magazine*, 1840, *16*: 232.
199 Lindley to Sir Robert Peel, 12 February 1840, *Kew: Creation of the Royal Gardens in 1840.*
200 Lindley to Hume [February 1840], *ibid.* For Loudon see Lambert to Smith, 25 February 1840, *Kew: Lambert Letters*, f. 240.
201 Meynell, 'Kew and the Royal Gardens Committee', p. 473; *The Times*, 24 and 25 February 1840.
202 *The Times*, 4 March 1840; *Hansard*, 1840, 3rd series, *52*: 846–7.
203 *Ibid.*
204 Aberdeen to Lindley, 5 March 1840, *Kew: Creation of the Royal Gardens in 1840.*
205 *Hansard*, 1840, 3rd series, *52*: 847.
206 F. Scheer, *Kew and Its Gardens* (Richmond, 1840).
207 *Ibid.*, pp. 1–5, 9, and 48.
208 Lambert to Smith, 25 February 1840, *Kew: Lambert Letters*, f. 240r.
209 *Literary Gazette*, 22 February 1840.
210 Lambert to Smith, 9 March 1840, *Kew: Lambert Letters*, f. 244.
211 Minute 18811, 13 March 1840, P.R.O.: CRES 8/22.
212 *Hansard*, 1840, 3rd series, *53*: 1184; *P.P.*, 1840 (292), *29*: 259–66.
213 *Hansard*, 1840, 3rd series, *53*: 1189–90.
214 Hooker to Turner, 20 and 23 April 1840, *Kew: Extracts from Letters to Dawson Turner*; W.T. Aiton to Her Majesty's Commissioners for Woods and Forests, 19 November 1840, *Kew: Kew 85: Director of Kew, General.*
215 Hooker to Turner, 3 March 1840, *Kew: Extracts from Letters to Dawson Turner.*
216 Printed only for private distribution: Glasgow, 1840.
217 *Kew: LDB*, p. 2.
218 *Ibid.*, p. 19.
219 *Ibid.*, p. 23.
220 Hooker to Bedford, 3 April 1840, *Kew: Mss LDB.*
221 Hooker to Turner, 25 June 1840, *Kew: Extracts from Letters to Dawson Turner.*
222 Hooker to Turner, 29 June 1840, *ibid.*
223 Hooker to Bentham, *Kew: Sir William Hooker's Letters to Mr. Bentham, 1823–41*, f. 228.
224 7th Duke of Bedford to W. Hooker, 5 December 1840; enclosure in Hooker to Turner, 17 December 1840, *Kew: Extracts from Letters to Dawson Turner.*
225 Hooker to Turner, 24 January and 26 March 1841, *ibid.*
226 W. Hooker to Lindley, 13 August 1840, *Kew: Lindley Letters, A–K*: f. 476; a turn of affairs foreshadowed in W. Hooker to D. Turner, 13 March 1838, *Kew: Sir W.J. Hooker's Letters to Dawson Turner.*
227 *P.P.*, 1840 (292), *29*: 259–66, pp. 2–4.
228 W. Hooker to Lord John Russell, 24 March 1841, P.R.O.: PRO 30/22/4A, ff. 155–6.

229 W. Hooker to G. Bentham, 20 September 1841, *Kew. Sir William Hooker's Letters to Mr. Bentham, 1823–41*, f. 284.

6 The Professionals and the Empire

1 J. Darwin, 'Imperialism and the Victorians: The Dynamics of Territorial Expansion', *E.H.R.*, 1997, *112*: 641.

2 R. Robinson, 'Non-European Foundations of European Imperialism: Sketch for a Theory of Collaboration', in R. Owen and R. Sutcliffe, eds., *Studies in the Theory of Imperialism* (London, 1972), pp. 117–42.

3 R. Stafford, *Scientist of Empire: Sir Roderick Murchison, Scientific Exploration and Victorian Imperialism* (Cambridge, 1989).

4 F.M. Turner, 'Public Science in Britain, 1880–1919', *Isis*, 1980, *71*: 589–608. See the development of the concept in M.J. Rudwick, 'Charles Darwin in London: the Integration of Public and Private Science', *Isis*, 1982, *73*: 186–266, and L. Steward, *The Rise of Public Science: Rhetoric, Technology, and Natural Philosophy in Newtonian Britain* (Cambridge, 1993).

5 W.J. Reader, *Professional Men: The Rise of the Professional Classes in Nineteenth-Century England* (London, 1966); H.J. Perkin, *The Rise of Professional Society: England since 1880* (London, 1989).

6 R. MacLeod, ed., *Government and Expertise: Specialists, Administrators and Professionals, 1860–1919* (Cambridge, 1988).

7 The phrase comes from the title of D.R. Headrick, *The Tools of Empire: Technology and European Imperialism in the Nineteenth Century* (New York, 1979); see also *idem, The Tentacles of Progress: Technology Transfer in the Age of Imperialism, 1850–1914* (Oxford, 1988) and *idem, The Invisible Weapon: Telecommunications and International Politics, 1851–1945* (Oxford, 1991).

8 M. Adas, *Machines as the Measure of Men: Science, Technology, and Ideologies of Western Dominance* (Ithaca, 1989).

9 Hooker to Turner, 26 March 1841, *Kew. Extracts of Letters from Dawson Turner.*

10 J. Hooker to W. Thistelton-Dyer, 7 March 1899, *Kew. Sir Joseph D. Hooker — Letters to Thiselton-Dyer, 1870–1909*, f. 175.

11 M. Allan, *The Hookers of Kew, 1785*–1911 (London, 1967) p. 178.

12 Hooker to Turner, 24 and 27 January 1841, *Kew. Extracts of Letters from Dawson Turner.*

13 W.D. Rubenstein, 'The End of "Old Corruption" in Britain, 1780–1860', *Past and Present*, 1983, *101*: 55–86.

14 See H.M. Colvin, ed., *The King's Works* (London, 1963–73), *VI*, chs 1–4; 'Inquiry into the Board of Works', *P.P.*, 1812–13 (329), *5* 'Second Report of the Select Committee on Windsor Castle and Buckingham Palace', *P.P.*, 1831 (329), 4.

15 P.R.O.: LRRO 24/1–7; *P.P.*, 1843 (343), *30*: 2.

16 *Parl. Deb.*, 1843, *49*: 1327–8.

17 'Account of Public Money Expended on Each of the Royal Palaces, Gardens and Parks', *P.P.*, 1843, (343) *30*; see also an earlier appeal to Peel for tighter control on public works expenditure: *A Letter to the Rt. Hon. Sir Robert Peel, Bart., M.P. on the Expediency of a Better System of Control Over Buildings Erected at Public Expense; and on the Subject of Rebuilding the Houses of Parliament* (London, 1835).

18 See 'Treasury Minute' and Treasury to Board of Woods and Forests, 2 and 4 July 1844, *Kew.* [Kewensia] *Royal Gardens Kew. Reports & Documents, 1784–1884.*

19 See the Chancellor's complaint to the Prime Minister about some of his colleagues willingness to indulge 'extravagant expenditure especially when concerned with the encouragement of fine arts and the improvement of the people by gratuitous exhibition', Goulburn to Peel, [ ] June 1845, *Add. Mss. 40576*, f. 44. Gladstone served at the Exchequer between 1852 and 1858, 1859 and 1866, then as First Lord of the Treasury from 1868 to 1874, and 1880 to 1885.

20 Hooker to Turner, 6 September 1846, *Kew. Extracts of Letters from Dawson Turner.*

21 *Life, Letters, and Journals of Sir Charles Lyell, Bart.* (London, 1881), 2 vols.*II*: p. 47.

22 Peel to Haddington, [1842], *Add. Mss 40456*, f. 98.

23 *Proceedings of the Horticultural Society of London, 1833–1844* (London, 1844); Peel to Lindley, 28 January [1845], *Kew. Lindley Letters, L–Z*, ff. 710–15; Aberdeen to Lindley, [1845], *Kew. Lindley Letters, A–K*, ff. 2–4.

24 See *R.C.S.I.*, *I* (1872), p. 30 and *II* (1874), p. 372.

25 See B.R. Mitchell, *British Historical Statistics* (Cambridge, 1988), p. 195; M.J.R. Healy and E.L. Jones, 'Wheat Yields in England, 1815–1859', *Journal of the Royal Statistical Society*, 1962, ser. A, *75*.

26 For the professional development of British geology see R. Stafford, 'Geological Surveys, Mineral Discoveries,

and British Expansion, 1835–71', *J.I.C.H.*, 1987, *12*(3): 5–32, see pp. 7–8; and *idem*, 'Annexing the Landscapes of the Past: British Imperial Geology in the Nineteenth Century', in J.M. MacKenzie, ed., *Imperialism and the Natural World* (Manchester, 1990), pp. 67–89; M. Rudwick, *The Great Devonian Controversy: The Shaping of Scientific Knowledge among Gentlemanly Specialists* (London, 1985); P.J. McCartney, *Henry de la Beche: Observations on an Observer* (Cardiff, 1977), pp. 34–5.

27 Stafford, *Scientist of Empire*.

28 *Lectures on the Results of the Great Exhibition of 1851* (London, 1851), *I*, p. 197; W.H.G. Armitage, *Four Hundred Years of English Education* (Cambridge, 1964), pp. 119–20.

29 Huxley to J. Hooker, 6 October 1864, *Kew: Letters from T.H. Huxley, 1854–95*, f. 90.

30 S. Ross, '"Scientists": The Story of a Word', *Annals of Science*, 1962, *18*: 65–86.

31 *Kew: GB* Auto. Mss, f. 462.

32 See Thackray and Morrell, *Gentlemen of Science*; Rudwick, *The Great Devonian Controversy*, pp. 17–18.

33 Huxley to Hooker, 29 July 1859, *Kew: Letters from T.H. Huxley, 1854–95*, f. 41.

34 *P.P.*, 1862 (89) *23*: 289.

35 Jowett in response to Sir J. Kay-Shuttleworth, Bart., 10 December 1870. *R.C.S.I.*, *I* (1872), p. 255.

36 *R.C.S.I.*, *II* (1874), p. 363.

37 *R.C.S.I.*, *I* (1872), p. 325.

38 *Ibid.*, p. 175.

39 Quoted in W.B. Turrill, *Joseph Dalton Hooker: Botanist, Explorer, and Administrator* (London, 1963), p. 15.

40 J.D. Hooker, *Flora Novae-Zeelandiae* (London, 1853–5); *idem.*, *Flora Tasmaniae* (London, 1855–60).

41 J. Hooker to H.W. Bates, [n.d.], APS: BH 76.

42 C. Bibby, *T.H. Huxley: Scientist, Humanist and Educator* (London, 1959), p. 72.

43 See Turner's description of 'the second era of Victorian public science', in Turner, 'Public Science in Britain', p. 589.

44 See R. MacLeod, 'The X-Club: A Social Network of Science in Late Victorian England', *Notes and Records of the Royal Society of London*, 1970, *24*: 305–22, and *idem*, 'The Support of Victorian Science: The Endowment of Research Movement in Great Britain, 1868–1900', *Minerva*, 1971, *9*: 197–230.

45 See below, and R. MacLeod, 'The Ayrton Incident: A Commentary on the Relations of Science and Government in England, 1870–1873', in A. Thackray and E. Mendelsohn, eds., *Science and Values* (New York, 1974), pp. 45–78.

46 Darwin to J. Hooker, [11 January 1844], CUL: *DAR* 114: 3.

47 D. Owen, *The Government of Victorian London, 1855–1889* (London, 1982), chs. 1 and 2.

48 *Inquiry into the Sanitary Condition of the Labouring Populations of Great Britain* (London, 1842); *Report of the Royal Commission on the State of Large Towns and Populous Districts* (London, 1844–5).

49 C. Hamlin, 'Providence and Putrefaction: Victorian Sanitarians and the Natural Theology of Health and Disease', *Victorian Studies*, 1985, *28*: 381–411; H.A. Malchow, 'Public Gardens and Social Action in Late Victorian Britain', *Victorian Studies*, 1985, *29*: 97–124.

50 D. Pinkney, *Napoleon III and the Rebuilding of Paris* (Paris, 1972).

51 Hooker to Bentham, 9 April 1848, *Kew: Sir W. Hooker's Letters to Mr. Bentham, 1842–62*, f. 481r; see also Hooker's remarks to Harvey on 6 May 1848: '"La Belle France" is going to the dogs & when they come to cutting one another's throats as they will do bye and bye, it will be a lesson for this country', (*Kew: Sir W. Hooker—Letters to Dr. W.H. Harvey, 1832–60).*

52 *Kew: Sydney Botanic Gardens, 1856–1900*, f. 8.

53 Hooker to Herschel, 22 January 1846, *Royal Society*: HS 9/456.

54 It is beyond my purposes here to offer a full critique of Alfred Crosby's *Ecological Imperialism: The Biological Expansion of Europe, 900–1900* (New York, 1986) except to note that this political dimension to the making of his 'neo-Europes' is wholly understated in his argument.

55 See, for example, the discussion of the foundation of the Australasian Botanic and Horticultural Society in *The Sydney Magazine of Science and Art* (Sydney, 1858).

56 B. Tinsley, *Visions of Delight: The Singapore Botanic Gardens Through the Ages* (Singapore, 1989).

57 W. Jameson, *Report on the Botanical Gardens of the Government, North West Provinces* (Roorkee, 1855), pp. 4–6.

58 H.F. Cleghorn, *The Forests and Gardens of South India* (London, 1861).

59 *Report on the Horticultural Gardens, Ootacamund* (Madras, 1853), pp. 2–3.

60 'Report', *P.P.*, 1845 (280), *45*: 4; and 1846 (345), *25*: 3.

61 Hooker to Turner, 15 December 1845, *Kew: Extracts of Letters from Dawson*

Turner, *P.P.*, 1845 (280) *45*: 4–6.

62 Admiralty to W. Hooker, 29 December 1847; *Kew*: *R.B.G. Kew and the Admiralty*, f. 4; J.F.W. Herschel, ed., *Admiralty Manual of Scientific Enquiry* (London, 1849).

63 See Hooker to Lindley, [24] February 1844, *Kew*: *Lindley Letters, A–K*, f. 480; R. Fortune, 'Sketch of a Visit to China, in Search of New Plants', *Journal of the Horticultural Society of London*, 1846, *1*: 209.

64 See W.J. Hooker, 'Introduction', *Niger Flora* (London, 1849), and J.D. Hooker and G. Bentham, *Flora Nigritiana* (London, 1849); Hooker to Lindley, 3 January 1848, *Kew*: *Lindley Letters, A–K*, f. 481; Hooker to Bentham, 1848, *Kew*: *Sir W. Hooker's Letters to Mr. Bentham, 1842–62*, ff. 48–53; *P.P.*, 1845 (280), *45*: 4.

65 R.H Schomburgk, *A Description of British Guiana, Geographical and Statistical: Exhibiting its Resources and Capabilities, Together with the Present and Future Condition and Prospects of the Colony* (London, 1840).

66 *P.P.*, 1845 (280),*45*: 4–5.

67 *P.P.*, 1846 (345) *25*: 3.

68 *P.P.*, 1845 (280), *15*: 5 and 1846 (345) , *25*: 3.

69 Hooker to Office of Works, 4 December 1850, *Kew*: *Kew Collectors, 1785–1865*, f. 21.

70 *Kew*: Kew 85 *Director of Kew, General*, f. 10; W. Hooker to Turner, 13 November 1841, *Kew*: *Extracts of Letters from Dawson Turner*.

71 Hooker to Turner, 22 May 1843, *ibid.*

72 W. Hooker to Dawson Turner, 2 July 1845 and 3 October 1846, *ibid.* and Commissioners of Woods and Forests to Lords Commissioners of His Majesty's Treasury, 7 May 1847, *Kew*: Kew 85 *Director of Kew, General.*

73 'Kew Gardens', 1 March 1884, *Kew*: *Royal Gardens Kew. Reports and Documents, 1784–1884*, doc. 49; W. Hooker to Turner, 4 October 1842 and 13 July 1843, *Kew*: *Letters to Dawson Turner*; J. Hooker, *A Sketch of the Life and Labours of Sir William Jackson Hooker* (Oxford, 1903), pp. lvi–lxx.

74 W. Hooker to Turner, 7 June 1842, *Kew*: *Letters to Dawson Turner.*

75 W.Hooker to Turner, 4 October 1843, *ibid.*

76 *Gardener's Magazine*, 1840, *16*: 591; the contemporary interest is also made clear by the article of Dr. John Lhotsky, F.H.S., of Bavaria in the same issue: 'On a New Method of introducing Palms of large size into Hot-houses', p. 596ff.

77 W. Hooker to Turner, 9 March 1844, *Kew*: *Letters to Dawson Turner.*

78 P.R.O.: WORK 2/4, ff. 187–90; W. Hooker to Bentham, 7 February 1844, *Kew*: *Sir W. Hooker's Letters to Mr. Bentham, 1842–62*, f. 369; G.F. Chadwick, 'Paxton and the Great Stove', *Architectural History*, 1957, *121*: 127–8.

79 P.R.O.: WORK 1/27, ff. 343 and 428; W. Hooker to Turner, 9 July 1845, *Kew*: *Letters to Dawson Turner.*

80 See W. Hooker's conspicuous footnote to *P.P.*, 1846 (345), *25*: 3.

81 In this era also, to the anger of Americans, John Lindley, Hooker's friend and former rival, named the giant Californian redwood, *Wellingtonia gigantea*. See W. Hooker to Herschel, 1 November 1858, *Royal Society*: HS 9/462

82 W. Hooker to Bentham, 11 December 1849, *Kew*: *Sir W. Hooker's Letters to Mr. Bentham, 1842–62*, f. 569: 'The glorious Victoria, all that one could wish to see ... the fact is Paxton has been giving all his attention of late to certain objects and neglecting others'; Hooker to Bentham, 18 April 1850, *ibid.*, f. 595r: 'What an aristocratic plant [the *Victoria regia*]; no one of lower grade than a Duke can get it to blossom!'

83 W. Hooker to Turner, 21 August 1848, *Kew*: *Extracts of Letters from Dawson Turner*; see also W. Hooker to Bentham, [July 1848], *Kew*: *Sir W. Hooker's Letters to Mr. Bentham, 1842–62*; f. 490r; W. Hooker, *Kew Gardens; or a Popular Guide to the Royal Botanic Gardens of Kew* (London, 1847), pp. 2–5.

84 *P.P.*, 1850 (402) *34*; W. Hooker to Turner, 7 December 1850, *Kew*: *Extracts of Letters from Dawson Turner.*

85 P.R.O.: WORK 2/7, ff. 267–9; H. Colvin, ed., *The History of the King's Works* (London, 1963–73), *V*, p. 446.

86 *P.P.*, 1845 (280), *45*: 1–2.

87 W. Hooker to Bentham, 16 February 1843, *Kew*: *Sir W. Hooker's Letters to Mr. Bentham, 1842–62*; Hooker, 'Report', *P.P.*, 1845 (280) *45*, p. 3. Burke was collecting animals for Derby's menagerie; see R. Desmond, 'From Rhododendrons to Tropical Herbs, 1820–1939', in N. Hepper, ed., *Plant Hunting for Kew* (London, 1989), pp. 12–13.

88 *P.P.*, 1846 (345), *25*: 3; 'Estimates ... 1849' and 'Report of Sir William Hooker ... 1850', in *Kew*: [Kewensia] *Royal Gardens Kew. Reports & Documents, 1784–1884.*

89 Hooker, 'Report', p. 4; *P.P.*, 1845 (280)*45*.

90 W. Hooker to Turner, 24 June 1845; *Kew*: *Extracts from Letters to Dawson Turner.*

91 Hooker, *Kew Gardens* pp. 1–9; see also 'Report from Sir William Hooker on the Royal Botanic Gardens and the New Palm House at Kew for 1846', p. 2; *P.P.*, 1846 (345), 25: 3, 'Estimates ... 1849' and 'Report of Sir William Hooker ... 1850', in *Kew.* [Kewensia] *Royal Gardens Kew. Reports & Documents, 1784–1884.*

92 'Report ... 1851', p. 9; 'Report ... 1852', 'Report ... 1853', 'Report ... 1854', 'Report ... 1855', 'Report ... 1857', 'Report ... 1860', *Kew.* [Kewensia] *Royal Gardens Kew. Reports & Documents, 1784–1884*, docs. 23, 24, 25, 26, 39, and *Kew. Kew Gardens. Annual Reports 1844–1870.*

93 Among Seymour's memoirs is a note of a visit to Kew during which he took water from the cistern in the Victoria House to examine under a microscope; see entry for 3 April 1854, in W.H. Mallock and D. Ramsden, eds. *Letters, Remains, and Memoirs of Edward Adolphus Seymour, Twelfth Duke of Somerset* (London, 1893), pp. 281–3.

94 E.L. Woodward, *The Age of Reform, 1815–1870* (Oxford, 1938), p. 109; C. Whibley, *Lord John Manners and His Friends* (Edinburgh, 1925), 2 vols.

95 W. Hooker to Bentham, 5 January 1852, *Kew. Sir W. Hooker's Letters to Mr. Bentham, 1842–62*, f. 656R.

96 W. Hooker to Bentham, 4 December 1853, *ibid.*, f. 743r.

97 Although the claim of a biographer that 'He has the credit of having opened Kew Gardens to the Public on Sundays', is untrue; see *DNB, XXXVIII* p. 124.

98 3 *Parl. Deb. 137*: 699–722; 18 & 19 V Cap. 120; *The Times*, 14 August 1855.

99 *P.P.*, 1872 (335), *47*: 74–5; 'Report ... 1856', p. 5, *Kew.* [Kewensia] *Royal Gardens Kew. Reports & Documents, 1784–1884*, doc. 32.

100 B. Hall to W. Hooker, 5 October 1856, *P.P.*, 1872 (335), *47*; 3 *Parl. Deb.*, *213*: 17.

101 Hooker, *A Sketch of the Life and Labours of William Jackson Hooker*, p. lxvi.

102 'Report ... 1857', pp. 1–2.

103 W. Hooker to Sir B. Hall, 10 October 1856, *P.P.*, 1872 (335), *47*: 76.

104 'Report ... 1856'.

105 'Memorandum, relating to a Plant Collector in Central Asia', 15 September 1847, *Kew: Kew Collectors—Papers relating to 1791–1865*, ff. 8–11.

106 'Memorandum to the Rt. Hon. W.E. Gladstone', p. 5, *Kew. Papers relating to Kew, 1867–72.*

107 Sir W.J. Hooker, ed., *The Rhododendrons of Sikkim–Himalaya; Being an Account, Botanical & Geographical of the Rhododendrons Recently Discovered in the Mountains of Eastern Himalaya From Drawings and Descriptions Made on the Spot During a Government Botanical Mission to that Country By Joseph Dalton Hooker, R.N., M.D., F.R.S, F.L.S.* (London, 1849); *ibid.*, Part II (London, 1851); *ibid.*, Part III (London, 1851).

108 W. Hooker to Russell, P.R.O.: PRO 30/22/9E, f. 228.

109 'Report ... 1850', p. 1; 'Report ... 1851', p. 1; 'Report ... 1852', p. 10; 'Report ....1857', p. 2; from *Kew.* [Kewensia] *Royal Gardens Kew. Reports & Documents, 1784–1884*; and *Report on The Progress and Condition of the Royal Gardens of Kew from 1853 to 1859* (London, 1859), p. 7.

110 'Report ... 1850', pp. 1–3.

111 'Report ... 1846', p. 2, *Kew.* [Kewensia] *Royal Gardens Kew. Reports & Documents, 1784–1884*, doc. 14; see also Hooker, *Kew Gardens*, p. 8.

112 The top five colonial recipients were: Sydney Botanic Garden (392), Ascension Island (330), Trinidad Botanic Garden (215), Calcutta Botanic Garden (211), and Bombay Botanic Garden (160); see 'Report ... 1850'.

113 'Report ... 1856', p. 3; W. Hooker to Board of Works, 31 December 1856, *Kew.* [Kewensia] *Royal Gardens Kew. Reports & Documents, 1784–1884*: doc. 53.

114 *P.P.*, 1857 (15), *48*.

115 W. Hooker to Bentham, 27 May, 3 and 30 June 1843, *Kew. Sir W. Hooker's Letters to Mr. Bentham, 1842–62*, 352r, 354, and 374; W. Hooker to Russell, 3 September 1847, P.R.O.: PRO 30/22/6F, ff. 24–7.

116 Hooker, *A Sketch of the Life and Labour of Sir William Jackson Hooker*, p. lxxvi.

117 P.R.O.: WORK 1/30, ff. 194, 222–3, and 245; W. Hooker to Bentham, [1846], *Kew. Sir W. Hooker's Letters to Mr. Bentham, 1842–62*, f. 441.

118 'Admiralty Manual of Scientific Inquiry', *Kew. R.B.G. Kew and the Admiralty*, ff. 4–6.

119 'Report ... 1852', and 'Report ... 1853'.

120 S. Pollard, 'A New Estimate of British Coal Production, 1750–1850', *Economic History Review*, 2nd series, 1980, *33*: 2; P. Riden, 'The Output of the British Iron Industry Before 1850', *Economic History Review*, 2nd series, 1977, *30*: 3; Mitchell, *British Historical Statistics*, pp. 247, 280, and 535–6.

121 Mitchell, *British Historical Statistics*, pp. 438–9 quotes *Titles of Patents and Inventions* (London, 1754), 2 vols.; *Report of the Commissioners for Patents and Inventions S.P.* 1876, *XXVII*.

122 D. Hudson and K.W. Luckhurst, *The Royal Society of Arts, 1754–1954* (London, 1954), pp. 187–206.

123 See, for example, *A Few Words on Paper, Flax, Hemp, and Plantain Fibre* (London, 1855); J. F. Royle, *The Fibrous Plants of India Fitted for Cordage, Clothing and Paper* (London, 1855). Cinchona, rubber, and gutta-percha 'crises' will be discussed below.

124 *Caoutchouc and Gutta Percha* (London, 1852), pp. 116–86.

125 *London Journal of Botany*, 1847, *17*: 463; susbsequent names for the plant include *Dichopsis percha*, *Isonandra percha*, and *Isonandra hookerii*; see E.F.A. Obach, *Cantor Lectures on Gutta-Percha* (London, 1898).

126 See letter concerning the commemoration of a half-century of telegraphy, A. Siemens to Thiselton-Dyer, 13 July 1897, *Kew: Malaya. Gutta Percha, 1876–1904*.

127 *Caoutchouc and Gutta Percha*, p. 116.

128 Jameson, *Report on the Botanical Gardens*, p. 4.

129 D. Brandes, *Report on the Teak Forests of Pegu* (London, 1860), p. 37.

130 W. Elliott, *Flora Andhrica* (Madras, 1859), pp. 4–5.

131 W. Sabondière, *The Coffee Planter in Ceylon* (Guernsey, 1866).

132 *Cocoa as Grown in Trinidad* (London, 1879).

133 P. Lovell Phillips, *An Essay on Tropical Agriculture with Some Remarks on Certain Analyses of Barbadian Soils* (Glasgow, 1845), p. iv; *idem, Hints to Young Barbadian Planters* (Bridgetown, 1857).

134 L. Brockway, *Science and Colonial Expansion: The Role of the British Botanic Gardens* (New York, 1979), *passim*.

135 D. Oliver, *The Official Guide to the Kew Museums. A Handbook to the Museums of Economic Botany of the Royal Gardens, Kew* (London, 1861), p. 1.

136 Report ... 1850', p. 3.

137 *Report on ... 1853–9*, p. 9.

138 'First Report of the Select Committee on the Woods, Forests, and Land Revenues of the Crown', *P.P.*, 1849 (513), *20*: appendix L, p. 219.

139 Hooker to Peel, 10 August 1845, *Add. Mss 40572*, ff. 127–9; W. Hooker to Harvey, 26 August 1845, *Kew: Sir W. Hooker—Letters to Dr. Harvey, 1832–60*; Hooker to Bentham, [August 1845], *Kew: Sir W. Hooker's Letters to Mr. Bentham, 1842–62*, f. 429r.

140 C. Darwin to W Hooker, 25 August 1845, *The Correspondence of Charles Darwin, III*, F. Burckhardt, ed. (Cambridge, 1987), 5 vols., p. 240.

141 Peel to W. Hooker, *Add. Mss 40574*, ff. 297, 299, and 303.

142 Peel to W. Hooker, 9 October 1845, *Add. Mss 40774*, f. 306.

143 W. Hooker to Turner, 22 November 1845, *Kew: Extracts of Letters from Dawson Turner*.

144 W. Hooker to Turner, 15 December 1845 *ibid.*

145 Darwin to J.D. Hooker, 25 February 1846, *The Correspondence of Charles Darwin, III, p.* 293; L. Huxley, *ed., The Life and Letters of Sir Joseph Dalton Hooker* (London, 1918), I, p.207.

146 W. Hooker to Turner, 3 and 27 October and 3 December 1846; *Kew: Extracts of Letters from Dawson Turner*.

147 W. Hooker to Gray, 5 November 1840, *Harvard University: Asa Gray Correspondence*; Barrow to Hooker, 26 April 1844, *Kew: R.B.G. Kew and the Admiralty*.

148 *Report of the Commissioners Appointed to Inquire into the Constitution and Government of the British Museum, 1847, with Minutes of Evidence* (London, 1850), p. 179.

149 *Ibid.*, p. 133.

150 *Ibid.*, p. 529.

151 W. Hooker to Turner, 27 October 1846, *Kew: Extracts of Letters from Dawson Turner*.

152 W. Hooker to Turner, 18 October 1848, *Kew: Extracts of Letters from Dawson Turner*.

153 W. Hooker to Bentham, 15 March 1850, *Kew: Sir W. Hooker's Letters to Mr. Bentham, 1842–62*, f. 592

154 W. Hooker to Bentham, 21 December 1851 and 5 January 1852, *ibid.*, 651 and 655.

155 F.W. Hirst, *Gladstone as Financier and Economist* (London, 1931), p. 242.

156 Philipps to W. Hooker, 7 March 1854, in *Kew: Sir W. Hooker's Letters to Mr. Bentham, 1842–62*, ff. 761–2.

157 Philipps to W. Hooker, 17 March 1854, *ibid.*, ff. 763–4.

158 W. Hooker to Bentham, 20 March 1854, *ibid.*, f. 774.

159 'Report ... 1856'.

160 *Report ... 1853 to 1859*, p. 10.

161 'Report ... 1859', *Kew:* [Kewensia] *Royal Gardens Kew. Reports & Documents, 1784–1884*: doc. 38.

162 W. Hooker to Bentham, [ ] July 1851, *Kew: Sir W. Hooker's Letters to Mr. Bentham, 1842–62*, f. 635r.

163 Hooker to Thiselton-Dyer, 19 December 1909, *Kew: J.D. Hooker Letters to Thiselton-Dyer, 1870–1909*, f. 214.

164 *R.C.S.I., I* (1872) p. 471.
165 R.*C.S.I., IV* (1874), p. 29.
166 A. Panizzi to the Treasury, 14 June 1858, *Kew: R.B.G. Kew and the British Museum.*, ff. 54–5.
167 Murchison to Lindley, 25 June [1858], *Kew: Lindley Letters, L–Z*, f. 666.
168 *Kew: R.B.G. Kew and the British Museum, Correspondence 1858–1901*, f. 59; W.T. Stearn, *The Natural History Museum at South Kensington* (London, 1981), p. 34.
169 *Report of the British Association for the Advancement of Science, 1858* (London, 1859), pp. lxxix–lxxxi and xcvii.
170 W. Hooker to Huxley, 28 October 1858, *Kew: Letters from J.D. Hooker to T.H. Huxley*, f. 44.
171 R. Owen, *On the Extent and Aims of a National Museum of Natural History* (London, 1862).
172 *Report... 1853 to 1859*, p. 3.
173 See J. Winter Jones to Rt. Hon. the Lords Commissioners of the Admiralty, 4 July 1874; in *Kew:* [Kewensia]: *R.B.G. Kew and the British Museum, Correspondence, 1858 to 1901*, f. 80.
174 *Report ... 1853 to 1859*, pp. 13–14; W. Munro to Lindley, 24 April 1855, *Kew: Lindley Letters, L–Z*, f. 662.
175 J.D. Hooker, *Himalayan Journals; Or Notes of a Naturalist in Bengal, Sikkim and Nepal Himalayas, the Khasia Mountains* (London, 1854), *I*:, p. viii; for Russell's involvement see Sir William Hooker to Russell, 25 August 1851, P.R.O.: PRO 30/22/9E, ff. 221–2.
176 See Stafford, *Scientest of Empire*, and S. Zeller, *Inventing Canada.: Early Victorian Science and the Idea of a Transcontinental Nation* (Toronto, 1987).
177 R. Raikes, *Two Essays* (London, 1825), pp. 40 and 73.
178 D. Livingstone, *Missionary Travels and Researches in South Africa* (London, 1857), p. 673.
179 *R.C.S.I., II* (1874), p. 182.
180 *Report ... 1853 to 1859* , pp. 11–13; Admiralty to W. Hooker, 14 October 1857, Hammond (Foreign Office) to Hooker, 24 September 1859, and Baikie to Russell, 16 September 1859, in *Kew: West Africa: Niger Expedition*; 'Report... 1857', p. 6.
181 P.R.O.: CO 201/509, ff. 280–4; B. Seeman, 'Remarks on a Government Mission to the Fiji Islands', *Journal of the Royal Geographical Society* 1862, *32*: 51–62.
182 Hammond (Foreign Office) to W. Hooker, 24 September 1859, W. Hooker to Russell, 27 September 1859, *Kew: West Africa: Niger Expedition*.
183 Hammond to W. Hooker, 5 October 1859, *Kew: West Africa: Niger Expedition.*
184 'Memorandum of Instruction to Gustave Mann', *Kew: West Africa: Niger Expedition.*
185 [ ] to Hooker, 13 July 1862, and Newcastle (Sec. of State for the Colonies) to Hooker, 30 August 1862, *Kew: Gold Coast: Botanical Station, 1862–1905*, ff. 1 and 3.
186 Mann to Russell, 26 February 1861, and Admiralty to Hooker, 13 July 1861, *Kew: West Africa: Niger Expedition*; 'Report ... 1861', *Kew:* [Kewensia] *Royal Gardens Kew. Reports & Documents, 1784–1884*, doc. 40.
187 *Report of the British Association for the Advancement of Science*, 1870 (London, 1871), p. 229.
188 Lord John Russell to W. Hooker, 23 April 1861 [my emphasis]; Livingstone to Murchison, 23 April 1863; *Kew: C.F.*, f. 115.
189 J.D. Hooker, 'On Geographical Distribution', *Report of the British Association for the Advancement of Science, 1881* (London, 1882), p. 729; *Nature*, 1881, *24*: 443–8.
190 *Inter alia*: Hooker, *Flora Novae-Zealandiae* ; *idem, Flora Tasmaniae*; *idem* and T. Thomson, *Flora Indica* (London, 1855) I; *idem*, 'Outlines of the Distribution of Arctic Plants', *Trans. Linn. Soc.*, 1862, *23*: 251–348; *idem.*, 'Lecture on Insular Floras', *Journal of Botany*, 1867, *5*: 23–31.
191 Mann to the Secretary of the Admiralty, 20 June 1861, *Kew: West Africa: Niger Expedition*, f. 40.
192 W. Hooker to Lord John Russell, 25 August 1851; P.R.O.: PRO 30/22/9E, ff. 221–2 and 228.
193 Hooker and Thompson, *Flora Indica* .
194 A. Grisebach, *Flora of the British West Indian Islands* (London, 1864). See W. Hooker to Sec. of State for the Colonies, 14 May 1857, *Kew: C.F.*; C. Fortescue to W. Hooker, 12 June 1857, and J. Wilson to H. Merivale, 27 May 1857, *Kew: C.F.* In 1897 the Librarian of the Colonial Office would suggest to the Under-Secretary Edward Wingfield that this proposal was the origin of the Colonial Floras scheme; see [CN?] Librarian of the Colonial Office to E. Wingfield, 22 January 1897; *Kew: C.F*, f. 15.
195 W.F. Elliott (Colonial Office) to W. Hooker, 5 November 1859, *ibid.*; see also Denison's earlier proposal for an 'encyclopedia of the natural history of the entire empire' in Denison to Murchison, 19 April 1859,

quoted in R. Stafford, *Scientist of Empire: Sir Roderick Murchison, Scientific Exploration and Victorian Imperialism* (Cambridge, 1989), p. 53.

196 Stafford, *Scientist of Empire*, p. 53; *Journal of the Royal Geographical Society*, 1859, *29*: *102–224*.

197 'Report ... 1859', p. 18.

198 Elliott to W. Hooker, 12 June 1860, *Kew*: *C.F.*

199 W. Hooker, 'Memorandum', 28 February 1861, *ibid.*

200 See Merivale to W. Hooker, 24 February 1859, and Elliott to W. Hooker, 24 April 1861, *ibid.*

201 W. Hooker to the First Commissioner of Works, 30 November 1863, *ibid.*

202 Livingstone to W. Hooker, 10 August 1863, and E. Hammond to W. Hooker, 17 September 1863, *ibid.*

203 G. Bentham and J. Hooker, *Genera plantarum ad exemplaria imprimis in herbariis kewensibus servata definita* (London, 1862–83), 3 vols.

204 'Memorandum on Colonial Floras', [1863], *Kew*: Kewensia 73.

205 Librarian of Colonial Office to Daniel Morris, 31 October 1892, *Kew*: *C.F.*, f. 37.

206 *Report ... 1853 to 1859*, p. 4.

207 See 'Report' for 1860s through to 1870s in *Kew*: *Kew Gardens. Annual Reports, 1844–70* and *Kew*: [Kewensia] *Royal Gardens Kew. Reports & Documents, 1784–1884.*

208 W. Hooker to Mrs. Buxton, 13 June 1860, APS: *Misc. Mss. Collection.*

209 J. Hooker to Mrs. D. Oliver, 27 June 1861, APS: BH 76.

210 Board of Works to J. Hooker, *Kew*: Kew 245 *Supply, Exchange, of Trees, Plants, Etc. by Kew Gardens.*

211 War Office to Asst. Sec. of Board of Works, 19 October 1867, *ibid.*

212 *Kew*: Kew 18 *Flagstaff, 1859–1919.*

213 'Report ... 1861', p. 19.

214 See K.G. Davies, 'The Living and the Dead: White Mortality in West Africa, 1684–1732', in S. Engerman and E.D. Genovese, eds., *Race and Slavery in the Western Hemisphere: Quantitative Studies* (Princeton, 1975), pp. 83–98; P.D. Curtin, *Death By Migration: Europe's Encounter with the Tropical World in the Nineteenth Century* (Cambridge, 1989).

215 John Martyn to [ ], 1 November 1805, *Letters and Papers of, or relating to, Mungo Park, the Explorer (1804–11), Add. Mss. 37232*, f. 63.

216 Mann to W. Hooker, 25 May 1861, *Kew*: *West Africa: Niger Expedition*, f. 37.

217 For the history of the entry of cinchona into the European pharmacopoeia see F.I. Ortiz Crespo, 'Fragoso, Monardes and pre-Chinchonian knowledge of Cinchona', *Archives of Natural History*, 1995, *22* (2): 169–81; F. Guerra, 'The Introduction of Cinchona in the Treatment of Malaria', *Journal of Tropical Medicine and Hygiene*, 1977, *80*: 112–40.

218 T.R.H Thomson, 'On the Value of Quinine in African Remittent Fever', *The Lancet*, 28 February 1846.

219 W.B. Baikie, *Narrative of an Exploring Voyage up the Rivers Kwóra and Bínue (Commonly Known as the Niger and the Tsadda) in 1854* (London, 1856).

220 Statement of M. Laird, 10 April 1858; in 'Share Announcement: Central Africa Company (Limited)', pp. 6–7; in *Kew*: *Royal Niger Company, 1858–91*, ff. 2–3.

221 *Memorial to the Board of Trade of the Ecuador Land Company*, 13 August 1858; *Kew*: *[Miscellaneous Reports] Ecuador, Peru & Bolivia, 1859–1913*, ff. 102–4. See also *Proceedings of the Royal Geographic Society*, 1859–60, *4*: 33 and Stafford, *Scientist of Empire*, p. 136.

222 See W. Hooker to J. Lindley, 8 November 1858; *Kew*: *Lindley Letters, A–Z*, f. 482.

223 'Report ... 1859', p. 18.

224 'Report ... 1860', p. 18.

225 Darwin to G.H.K. Thwaites, 15 June 1862, APS: *DC* 278.

226 G. Bidie, *Cinchona Cultivation in British India* (Madras, 1879), p. 2.

227 T. Anderson to J. Lindley, 8 May 1861; *Kew*: *Lindley Letters, A–K*, ff. 20–1r.

228 J. Hooker to Darwin, [22 February 1864], CUL: *DAR* 101: 186–7.

229 G. Gramiccia, *The Life of Charles Ledger (1818–1905): Alpacas and Quinine* (London, 1988).

230 See J.E. Howard, 'Origin of the *Calisaya ledgeriana* of Commerce', *Pharmaceutical Journal*, 13 March 1880: 730.

231 'Visit of Dr. King to Java', 22 November 1879, *Kew*: *Dutch East Indies, Cultural Products, 1870–1906*, f. 9.

232 W. I. Thiselton-Dyer to R.H. Meade (Colonial Office), 14 May 1880, *Kew*: *Ceylon, Cinchona, 1859–90*, f. 50.

233 J.R. Langden to Earl of Kimberley, 25 August 1880, *ibid.*, ff. 62–3.

234 J. Hooker to Layard, 11 November 1869, APS: BH 76; see also the case of John Scott in J. Hooker to Darwin and Darwin to J. Hooker, 19 and 22 May 1864, CUL: *DAR* 101: 220–1 and 115: 236.

235 'Report ... 1870', p. 5, *Kew*: Kew 73 *Correspondence relating to Dr. Hooker and the Management of Kew Gardens.*

236 L. Huxley, ed.,*Life and Letters of Sir Joseph Dalton Hooker, II* (London, 1918), p. 55.
237 *Life and Letters of Sir J.D. Hooker, II,* p. 147; Argyll offered perhaps the last articulate defences of 'natural theology' in the British intellectual tradition in *The Reign of Law* (London, 1867) and *The Unity of Nature* (London, 1884).
238 R. MacLeod, 'The Ayrton Incident', *passim.* I offer a fuller treatment of the incident in ch. V of 'Imperial Science and a Scientific Empire: Kew Gardens and the Uses of Nature, 1772–1903', PhD dissertation, Yale University 1993.
239 See 3 *Parl. Deb., 158*: 69–85 and *188*: 1682.
240 *DNB,* 1st supplement, *I,* p. 89.
241 3 *Parl. Deb. 213*: 23.
242 Quoted by MacLeod, 'The Ayrton Incident', 51.
243 Speech to the Corn Exchange, 29 November 1879, in W.E. Gladstone, *Political Speeches in Scotland November and December 1879* (Edinburgh, 1879), p. 148.
244 A.S. Ayrton to J. Hooker, 17 August 1871, *Kew: Papers relating to Kew, 1867–72: Ayrton Controversy, I,* ff. 12–17.
245 *P.P.,* 1872 (335) *47*: 4.
246 This and the following account is from Joseph Hooker to First Commissioner of Works, 31 August 1871, *Kew:* Kew 73 *Correspondence relating to Dr. Hooker and the Management of Kew Gardens.*
247 Stronge to J. Hooker, 25 April 1872, *Kew: Papers Relating to Kew, 1867–72: Ayrton Controversy, I,* f. 164.
248 J. Hooker to Gladstone, 19 August 1871, J. Hooker to Lady Russell, 26 August 1871; Gladstone to Hooker, 4 October 1871, Hooker to West, 30 October 1871, and Hooker to Gladstone, 22 April 1872, *ibid.,* ff. 18, 24, 45, 70, 159.
249 Huxley to R. Lowe, 6 May 1872, *ibid.,* f. 184.
250 Tyndall to J. Hooker, 18 May 1870, *ibid.,* f. 210.
251 See Derby's address of January 1875 as Rector of Edinburgh University in *Nature,* 1875, *11*: 241; T.H. Sanderson and E.S. Roscoe, eds., *Speeches and Addresses of Edward Henry, XVth Duke of Derby* (London, 1894), 2 vols.
252 Huxley to J. Hooker, 5 September 1858, *Kew: Letters from T.H. Huxley, 1854–95,* f. 30.
253 J. Hooker to Huxley, [ ] December 1858, *Kew: Letters from J.D. Hooker to T.H. Huxley, 1851–94,* f. 47.
254 Tyndall to Derby, 2 April 1872, *Kew: Papers Relating to Kew, 1867–72: Ayrton Controversy, I,* f. 139.
255 Derby to Tyndall, 7 May 1872, and Manners to J. Hooker, 24 May 1872, *ibid.,* ff. 185 and 217.
256 J. Lubbock to W.E. Gladstone, 20 June 1872, enclosing 'Memorial to the Rt. Hon. W.E. Gladstone', *P.P.,* 1872 (335), *47*; copy in *Kew: Papers Relating to Kew, 1867–72: Ayrton Controversy, I*; reprinted in *Nature,* 11 July 1872.
257 *The Times,* 8 July 1872; *The Guardian, The Daily News, The Standard* on 10 July 1872; *The Echo, Pall Mall Gazette, Nature,* 11 July 1872; *The Economist, The Civil Service Gazette, Saturday Review,* and *The Athenaeum,* 13 July 1872.
258 3 *Parl. Deb. 213*: 1–23.
259 *The Echo,* 24 July 1872.
260 Tyndall to J. Hooker, 11 June 1872, *Kew: Papers Relating to Kew, 1867–72: Ayrton Controversy, I,* f. 227.
261 On Owen see Nicolaas A. Rupke's masterful *Richard Owen: Victorian Naturalist* (London and New Haven, 1994).
262 *R.C.S.I, I* (1872), pp. 434–6.
263 *Ibid.,* pp. 473ff.
264 J. Hooker to Huxley, 2 August 1871, *Kew: Letters from J.D. Hooker to T.H. Huxley, 1851–94,* f. 108.
265 Gladstone to Holland, 8 November 1871, *Kew: Papers Relating to Kew, 1867–72: Ayrton Controversy, I,* f. 89.
266 A. Desmond, *The Politics of Evolution* (London, 1989), pp. 276–334 especially; *idem, Archetypes and Ancestors: Palaeontology in Victorian London* (London, 1982); and *idem, Huxley: From Devil's Disciple to Evolution's High Priest* (London, 1997).
267 Darwin to Lyell, 12 December 1859, APS: *DC* 184.
268 Huxley to J. Hooker, 18 June and 5 September 1858, *Kew: Letters from T.H. Huxley, 1854 –95,* ff. 27 and 30.
269 *P.P.,* 1872 (335) *47*: appendix III, pp. 169–75; a copy was also submitted as a memorandum to the Devonshire Commission, see *R.C.S.I., IV* (1874):, pp. 174–8.
270 Huxley to J. Hooker, 5 September 1858, *Kew: Letters from T.H. Huxley, 1854–95,* f. 30.
271 3 *Parl. Deb. 213*: 16.
272 *The Times,* 31 July 1972; *Kew: Papers relating to Kew, 1872–3: Ayrton Controversy, II,* f. 383.
273 'Memorial', p. 7.
274 J. Hooker to Gladstone, 31 August 1871, and Hooker to Cardwell, 27 October 1871, *Kew: Papers relating to Kew, 1867–72: Ayrton Controversy, I,* f. 67.
275 West India Committee to Gladstone, 20 July 1872, *ibid.,* f. 313.

276 *Darjeeling News*, 24 and 31 August 1872; Gov. J.P. Grant, Jamaica; J.E. Howard, *Gardener's Chronicle*, 24 August 1872.
277 *R.C.S.I., II* (1874), p. 209.
278 *The Standard*, 13 August 1872; see *Himalayan Journals, II*, p. 239.
279 'Copies of Letters and Memorial Addressed to the Rt. Hon. W.E. Gladstone on the subject of the National Herbaria; with replies from the Lords Commissioners of Her Majesty's Treasury', 3 January 1873, p. 2, copy also as enclosure with Thiselton-Dyer to Primrose, 19 March 1889, *Kew:* Kew 96 *J.A. Britten's Attack in the* Journal of Botany *on the Staff of Kew Re: Preparation of Flora of Tropical Africa*.
280 *Ibid.*, p. 3.
281 W. Law to M.J. Berkeley, 23 January 1873, *ibid.*, p. 7.
282 J. Hooker to Dawson Turner Hooker, 12 November 1873, APS: BH 76.Br.
283 *R.C.S.I., IV* (1874), pp.1–10.
284 J. Hooker to R. Lingen (Treasury), 19 February 1872, and Hooker to A. West (10 Downing St.), 26 February 1872, *Kew: Papers Relating to Kew, 1867–72: Ayrton Controversy, I*, ff. 105 and 114.
285 J. Hooker to Bruce, 21 February 1872, *ibid.*, f. 106.
286 J. Hooker to Gladstone, 15 November 1875 and 9 March 1878, *Add. Mss 44448*, f. 135 and *44456*, f. 135

7 The Government of Nature

1 P.R.O.: FO 12/ 34A.
2 'Governor Hennessy's Observations on the Total Eclipse of the Sun', *Proceedings of the Royal Society*, 1868, *105*.
3 Sir J. Kirk, Sir H. Johnston, and F. Holmwood, to Thiselton-Dyer, *Kew: British East Africa Protectorate, 1874–1906*, ff. 63–95.
4 R. H. Grove, *Green Imperialism: Colonial Expansion, Tropical Island Edens, and the Origins Of Environmentalism, 1600–1860* (Cambridge, 1995) is the best guide to the emergence of this theme in British colonial policy.
5 See J. Hooker to Strachey, 6 June 1863, APS: BH 76.2.
6 J. Hooker to H. Barkly, 6 July 1874, *L.* Huxley, ed., *The Life and Letters of Sir Joseph Dalton Hooker* (London, 1918), *II*, p. 7; NB this correspondence was personal not official, Barkly was Governor in South Africa not New Zealand.
7 R. Robinson and J. Gallagher, *Africa and the Victorians: The Official Mind of Imperialism* (London, 1961).
8 F. Lugard, *The Dual Mandate in British Tropical Africa* (London, 1922).
9 'Captain Lugard's Report on Rubber Plants', *Kew: British East African Protectorate, Rubber and Copal, 1874–1906*, f. 139.
10 For his resentment of the penny-pinching 'd—d Liberals' whose administration was 'characteristically illiberal and illbred', see J. Hooker to Darwin, 19 January 1882, CUL: *DAR* 104: 176–7.
11 T.E. Kebbel, ed., *Selected Speeches of the Late Right Honourable the Earl of Beaconsfield* (London, 1882), *II*, pp. 523–35; B. Semmel, *Imperialism and Social Reform* (London, 1960).
12 P. Smith, *Disraelian Conservatism and Social Reform* (London, 1967), pp. 160–1.
13 See the description of the function of the Primrose League in M. Pugh, *The Tories and the People* (London, 1985).
14 D.R. Headrick, *Tools of Empire: Technology and European Imperialism in the Nineteenth Century* (New York, 1981), and *idem*, *Tentacles of Progress: Technology Transfer in the Age of Imperialism, 1850–1940* (London, 1988).
15 M. Adas, *Machines as the Measure of Men: Science, Technology, and Ideologies of Western Dominance* (Ithaca, 1989), pp. 208–10 and *passim*; B. Semmel, *The Governor Eyre Controversy* (London, 1962); L.P. Curtis, *Anglo-Saxons and Celts: A Study of Anti-Irish Prejudice in Victorian England* (Bridgeport, 1968).
16 R. Hyam, *Britain's Imperial Century, 1815–1914: A Study of Empire and Expansion* (London, 1976), pp. 155–65 offers the most skilled application of this argument.
17 E. Viotti da Costa, *Crowns of Glory, Tears of Blood: The Demerara Slave Rebellion of 1823* (New York, 1994), pp. 207–50.
18 'The Past and Future of the Conservative Party', *Quarterly Review*, October 1869: 541–2.
19 See L. Colley, 'Whose Nation? Class and National Consciousness in Britain, 1750–1830', *Past and Present*, 1986, *113*: 97–113, p. 109.
20 See Paul Kennedy's argument in 'The Theory and Practice of Imperialism', *Historical Journal*, 1977, *20*: 761–9 that the 'new imperialism' was merely the long-range consequence of the spread of industrialization to Europe and the United States.

21 Hyam, *Britain's Imperial Century*, pp. 167–80.

22 American expansion, wrote Bruce, was 'the main factor in concentrating English and colonial opinion on the imperial question,'; C. Bruce, *The Broad Stone of Empire: Problems of Crown Colony Administration* (London, 1910), *I*, 155.

23 C.T. Hapberg Wright, 'German Methods of Development in Africa', *Journal of the African Society*, October 1901: 37–8; 'German Methods of Colonial Development', *The Standard*, 1 January 1902.

24 The best studies of the 'National Efficiency Movement' remain Semmel, *Imperialism and Social Reform*, and G.R. Searle, *The Quest for National Efficiency* (London, [1971] 1990).

25 J. Hamburger, *Intellectuals in Politics: John Stuart Mill and the Philosophic Radicals* (London, 1965); Searle, *The Quest for National Efficiency*.

26 See Stokes, *The English Utilitarians and India*.

27 J.S. Mill, *On Liberty* (London, [1859] 1982), p. 69.

28 J.L. Garvin, *Life of Chamberlain* (London, 1932), *I*, p. 202 (Chamberlain's emphasis).

29 D. Dilks, *Neville Chamberlain: Pioneering and Reform, 1869–1929* (Cambridge, 1984), p. 37.

30 R. Stafford, *Scientist of Empire: Sir Roderick Murchison, Scientific Exploration and Victorian Imperialism* (Cambridge, 1989).

31 F.M. Turner, 'Public Science in Britain, 1880–1919', *Isis*, 1980, *71*: 589–608; R. MacLeod, 'The Resources of Science in Victorian England: The Endowment of Science Movement, 1868–1900', in P. Mathias, ed., *Science and Society, 1600–1900* (Cambridge, 1972), pp. 113–61.

32 Mallet to J. Hooker, 6 May 1882, *Kew: Madras. Cinchona, 1860–97*, f. 143.

33 M. Lawson to W.T. Thiselton-Dyer, 13 May 1882, *ibid.*, f. 153.

34 *Nature*, 1874, *11*: 237.

35 Jenkin and Phillips to Morris, 3 November 1890, *Kew: Ceylon. Cinchona, 1859–90*, f. 202.

36 Thiselton-Dyer to E. Fairfield (Colonial Office), 24 June 1893, *Kew: Ecuador, Peru & Bolivia, 1859–1913*, f. 38.

37 C.B. Clarke to the Secretary of the Government of Bengal, 1 July 1870, p. 3, *Kew: Sikkim. Cinchona, 1862–1900*, f. 8.

38 G. King to the Secretary of the Government of Bengal, p. 2, *ibid.*, f. 22.

39 C. Markham, *Peruvian Bark* (London, 1880).

40 *Kew: Sikkim. Cinchona, 1863–1900*, f. 128.

41 G. King to W.I. Thiselton-Dyer, 24 September 1893, *ibid.*, f. 137r.

42 Here I respond to the argument of Syed Hussein Alatas, *The Myth of the Lazy Native : A Study of the Image of the Malays, Filipinos and Javanese from the 16th to the 20th Century and Its Function in the Ideology of Colonial Capitalism* (London, 1977), which explains the recurrence of the idea that indigenous peoples were slothful, and so needed to be coerced to work by beatings, taxes, or the destruction of food crops.

43 Mann to Russell, 29 May 1860, *Kew: West Africa: Niger Expedition.*

44 Mann to Hooker, 27 February 1862, *ibid.*

45 *Pall Mall Gazette*, 23 March 1891.

46 B. Kidd, *The Control of the Tropics* (New York, 1898), pp. 35–52.

47 Bruce, *The Broad Stone of Empire*, p. 26.

48 J.S. Furnivall, *Colonial Policy and Practice: A Comparative Study of Burma and Netherlands India* (Cambridge, 1948), p. 489.

49 Grove, *Green Imperialism*, *passim*.

50 For the story of game, see J. M. MacKenzie's seminal *The Empire of Nature: Hunting, Conservation, and British Imperialism* (Manchester, 1988).

51 R.G. Albion, *Forests and Sea Power: The Timber Problem of the Royal Navy, 1652–1862* (Cambridge, 1926).

52 W. Cronon, *Changes in the Land: Indians, Colonists, and the Ecology of New England* (New York, 1983).

53 S.R. Rajan, 'Imperial Environmentalism: The Agendas and Ideologies of Natural Resource Management in Colonial Forestry', D.Phil. dissertation, University of Oxford, 1994.

54 *The Globe*, 19 February 1884.

55 *Kew: British East African Protectorate, Rubber and Copal, 1874–1906*, f. 95.

56 C.B.H. Mitchell to Joseph Chamberlain, 27 October 1899, *Kew: Malaya. Gutta Percha, 1876–1904*, f. 36.

57 P.M. Kennedy. 'Imperial Cable Communications and Strategy, 1870–1914,' *E.H.R.*, 1971, *86*: 728–52; M. Gorman, 'Sir William O'Shaughnessy, Lord Dalhousie and the Establishment of the Telegraph System in India,' *Technology and Culture*, 1971, *12*: 581–601; B.S. Finn, *Submarine Telegraphy: The Grand Victorian Technology* (London, 1973); Headrick, *The Tentacles of Progress*, ch. 4.

58 *India Rubber and Gutta-Percha and Electrical Trades Journal*, 9 May 1891.

59 *Ibid.*, 8 April 1891 and Thiselton-Dyer to

Meade (Colonial Office), 24 August 1891, *Kew. Malaya. Gutta Percha, 1876–1904*, f. 76.

60 Thiselton-Dyer to E. Wingfield (Colonial Office) and H.B. Cox to Thiselton-Dyer, 27 December 1898 and 23 January 1899, *ibid.*, *Queensland Agricultural Journal*, March 1898: 198.

61 'Report of the Resident of Penang,' 23 November 1899, *Kew. Malaya. Gutta Percha, 1876–1904*, f. 240.

62 Thiselton-Dyer to C.P. Lucas (Colonial Office), 26 December 1899, *ibid.*, f. 38.

63 Thiselton-Dyer to C.P. Lucas (Colonial Office), 23 January 1900, *ibid.*, ff. 240–60.

64 'Report ... 1877', pp. 26–7, *Kew. [Kewensia] Royal Gardens Kew. Reports & Documents, 1784–1884*, doc. 48.

65 *Daily Chronicle*, 15 July 1901.

66 J. Hooker to Secretary of the Board of Works, 27 October 1874, *Kew. Appointment of Assistant Directors, 1874–98*, ff. 2–3.

67 A.B. Mitford to First Commissioner, 16 November 1874, *ibid.*, ff. 4–5.

68 Northcote to Sir Robert Helps and Smith to Hooker, [ ] and 27 February 1875, *ibid.*, ff. 11 and 12.

69 Daly to J. Hooker, 12 March 1875, *ibid.*, f. 17.

70 J.D. Hooker and J. Ball, *Journal of a Tour in Marocco and the Great Atlas* (London, 1878); J.D. Hooker and A. Gray, 'The Vegetation of the Rocky Mountain Region and a Comparison with that of Other Parts of the World', *Bulletin of the U.S. Survey*, 1882, *6*: 1–62.

71 Thiselton-Dyer to Prain, 24 November 1921, *Kew. J.D. Hooker—Letters to Thiselton Dyer*, f. 1.

72 J. Hooker to Thiselton-Dyer, 21 September 1876 *ibid.*, f. 35.

73 J. Hooker to Thiselton-Dyer, 1 January 1880, *ibid.*, f. 74.

74 J. Hooker to Thiselton-Dyer, 13 October 1885, *ibid.*, f. 105.

75 William Turner Thiselton-Dyer, b. 1843 d. 1928, *DNB* (1922–30), pp. 830–2.

76 J. Hooker to Thiselton-Dyer, 4 April and 12 November 1870 and 25 June 1871, *Kew. J.D. Hooker—Letters to Thiselton-Dyer*, ff. 2–4.

77 J. Hooker to Thiselton-Dyer, 9 September 1872, *ibid.*, f. 7.

78 J. Hooker to Thiselton-Dyer, 1 January 1880, *ibid.*, f. 74.

79 *The Echo*, 19 July 1877.

80 'Report ... 1877', p. 5.

81 Hooker to [ ], 31 May 1878, APS: BH 76.

82 'Memorandum relative to the Requirements of Kew Gardens', 29 November 1881, *Kew. Director of Kew, General*, ff. 1–2.

83 'Memorandum', ff. 3–7.

84 Lord J. Cavendish to First Commissioner of Works, 8 April 1882, *Kew. Director of Kew, General.*

85 Thiselton-Dyer, 'Historical Account of Kew to 1841'; and *idem*, 'Botanical Enterprise in 1796,' *K. B.*, 1893: 80–1.

86 F.O. Bower, 'Seven Decades of Botany', *Nature*, 1926, *118*: 415–16.

87 F.O. Bower, *Sixty Years of Botany in Britain* (London, 1938), p. 20.

88 *An Encyclopaedia of Geography* (London, 1834), p. 290.

89 Hooker wrote Huxley: 'I do hope the University will not make asses of themselves & elect B[abington]', see Hooker to Huxley, 11 April 1861, *Kew. Letters from J.D. Hooker to T.H. Huxley, 1851–94*, f. 71.

90 See J. Reynolds Green, *A History of Botany, 1860–1900* (Oxford, 1909), p. 46.

91 Bower, *Sixty Years*, p. 21.

92 C.W. Wardlow, 'The Unification of Botanical Science', *Nature*, 1944, *153*: 126.

93 E.G. Pringsheim, *Julius Sachs: Der Begründer der neuren Pflanzenphysiologie, 1832–1897* (Jena, 1932); W. Bohm, 'Die Entwicklung der Feldmethoden zum Stadium der Pfalznen wurzeln Seit der Mitte des 19 Jahrhunderts', *Sudhoffs. Arch.*, 1984, *68*: 217–24; S.H. Vines, 'Reminiscences of German Botanical Laboratories in the 'Seventies and 'Eighties of the Last Century', *New Phytologist*, 1925, *24*: 1–8.

94 J. Reynolds Green, *A History of Botany in the United Kingdom* (London: 1914), p. 525.

95 See G.P. Clinton, 'Botany in Relation to Agriculture', *Science*, 1916, *43*: 1–13; R. A. Overfield, 'Charles E. Bessey: The Impact of the "New Botany" on American Agriculture, 1880–1910', *Technology and Culture*, 1975, *16*: 162–81.

96 J. Russell, 'Rothamsted and Agricultural Science', *Nature*, 1923, *111*: 466–70; W.R. Bottomley, 'Sir Joseph Henry Gilbert, 1817–1901', in F.W. Oliver, ed., *Makers of British Botany* (Cambridge, 1913), pp. 233–42.

97 W.I. Thiselton-Dyer and A.H. Church, *How Crops Grow* (London, 1869).Church, Thiselton-Dyer's collaborator, was himself a pioneering 'New Botanist', see D. Mabberley, *Revolutionary Botany: 'Thalassophyta' and other essays of A.H. Church* (Oxford, 1981).

98 See Reynolds Green, *A History of Botany in the United Kingdom*, p. 535.

99 J. von Sachs, *Textbook of Botany*, A.W. Bennett and W.I. Thiselton-Dyer, trans. (London, 1875).

100 W.G. Farlow, 'The Change from the Old to the New Botany in the United States', *Science*, 1913, *37*: 78–86.

101 For more traditional taxonomy, see W.I. Thiselton-Dyer and H. Trimen, *Flora of Middlesex* (London, 1869). Thiselton-Dyer's versatility as a biologist can be seen from his remarkable essay, 'The Needs of Biology', in which he provides a panorama of the future of biology with suggestions about research into enzymes ('ferments'), heredity, and ecology. See W.I. Thiselton-Dyer, 'The Needs of Biology', in *Essays in the Endowment of Research* (London, 1876), pp. 226–43.

102 *R.C.S.I., II* (1874), p. 234.

103 *R.C.S.I., IV* (1874), p. 10.

104 Sir T.P. Jodrell, 11 November [1874], *Kew: Jodrell Laboratory*.

105 J. Hooker to A.B. Mitford, 23 December 1874, *ibid.*

106 J. Hooker to Darwin, 22 December 1874, CUL: *DAR* 103: 239–40; Darwin to George Romanes, 23 December 1874, APS: *DC* 456.

107 Huxley to J. Hooker, 5 March 1875, *Kew: J.D. Hooker—Letters to Thiselton-Dyer*, f. 27.

108 For the more than 120 important papers published between 1876 and 1900, on the basis of work conducted at the Jodrell, see *CBW*, pp. 174–6.

109 See for example, the remarkable work achieved by F.O. Bower at the Jodrell: 'On Plasmolysis and its Bearing upon the Relations between Cell-Wall and Protoplasm', *Quarterly Journal of Microscopical Science*, 1883, *23*: 151–69; 'On the Comparative Morphology of the Leaf in the Vascular Cryptogams and Gymnosperms', *Philosophical Transactions*, 1885, *175*: 565–615; 'On Apospory and Allied Phenomena', *Transactions of the Linnean Society*, 1887, Botany, *2*: 301–26.

110 H. Abbay, 'Observations on *Hemileia vastatrix*, the So-called Coffee-leaf Disease', *Journal of the Linnean Society, Botany*, 1878, *17*: 173–84; T.J. Barron, 'Science and the Nineteenth Century Ceylon Coffee Planters', *J.I.C.H.*, 1987, *16*: 5–21.

111 *Report of the West Indian Royal Commission* (London, 1897), 4 vols., Appendix C, p. 128.

112 See 'Mr. Harrison's Application for Government Analyst and Professor of Chemistry in Demerara or Trinidad,' Governor of Barbados to Secretary of State for the Colonies, September 1889, P.R.O.: C.O. 28/221; John Harrison to Daniel Morris, 25 November 1889, *Kew: Windward Islands Letters 1865–1900*.

113 J.C. Willis, *Agriculture in the Tropics: An Elementary Treatise* (Cambridge, 1909).

114 *Inter alia*: D.H. Scott, 'On the Lactiferous Tissue of *Manihot glaziovii* (The Ceara Rubber)', *Quarterly Journal of Microscopical Science*, new series, 1884, *24*: 193–203; *idem*, 'On the Appearance of Lactiferous Vessels in *Hevea*', *Journal of the Linnean Society, Botany*, 1885, *21*: 568–73; A. Calvert, 'On Lactiferous Tissue in the Pith of *Hevea brasiliensis*', *Annals of Botany*, 1887, *1*: 75–7; G. Massee, 'Vanilla Disease', *Kew Bulletin*, 1892: 111–20; *idem*, 'On *Trichospheraeia sacchari*, Mass.—a Fungus Causing a Disease of the Sugar-cane', *Annals of Botany*, 1893, *7*: 515–32; *idem*, 'Tea Blights,' *K. B.*, 1898: 105–12; *idem*, 'Cocoa Disease in Trinidad', *K.B.*, 1899: 3–5.

115 E. Cittadino, *Nature as the Laboratory: Darwinian Plant Ecology in the German Empire, 1880–1900* (Cambridge, 1990), pp. 65–81.

116 Thiselton-Dyer, 'The Needs of Biology', pp. 236–7 [my emphasis].

117 W.D. Rasmussen, *Readings in the History of American Agriculture* (Urbana, 1960); P.W. Gates, *Agriculture and the Civil War* (New York, 1965).

118 E. Foner, *Free Soil, Free Labour, Free Men: The Ideology of the Republican Party Before the Civil War* (New York, 1970).

119 M. Treub, 'Kurze Geschichte des botanischen Gartens zu Buitenzorg', in *Der botanische Garten ' 's Lands Plantentuin' zu Buitenzorg auf Java. Festschrift zur Feier seines 75 järigen Bestehens (1817–1892)* (Leipzig, 1893), pp. 23–78.

120 Treub, 'Kurze Geschichte' and Headrick, *The Tentacles of Progress*, p. 220.

121 H.H. Zeijlstra, *Melchior Treub: Pioneer of a New Era in the History of the Malay Archipelago* (Amsterdam, 1959).

122 Cittadino, *Nature as the Laboratory*, pp. 78–9; H. Graf zu Solms-Laubach, 'Der botanische Garten zu Buitenzorg auf Java', *Botanische Zeitung*, 1884, *43*.

123 W. Thiselton-Dyer, 'The Botanical Enterprise of the Empire', *Proceedings of the Royal Colonial Institute*, 1879–80, *11*: 273–306.

124 J. Burdon Sanderson, E. Ray Lankester, G. W. Child, C.L. Shadwell *et al.* to Thiselton-Dyer, 5 November 1883, *Kew: Appointment of Assistant Directors, 1874–97*, f. 39.

125 See P.J. Cain and A. G. Hopkins, *British Imperialism* (London, 1993), 2 vols., *I*.

126 *Inter alia* H.J. Ussher to Earl of Carnarvon, J. Irvine (of James Irvine & Co., Liverpool) to Hooker, 14 October and 27 December 1876, *Kew: Oil Palm, 1876–1913*, ff. 3–42; 'Oil Palm in Labuan: a Success and a Failure,' *K.B.*, 1889: 259–67.

127 *Report of the Indian Famine Commission* (London, 1878); Morris to V. Lister (Foreign Office), 23 June 1886, *K.B.*, 1887: 3–6.

128 Sierra Leone Coaling Company to the Curator, Royal Botanic Gardens, 22 March 1891, *Kew: Oil Palm, 1876–1913*, f. 59.

129 'Memorandum on the Experimental Cultivation of Economic Crops in West Africa', *Kew: Royal Niger Company, 1858–91*, f. 68.

130 African Lakes Corporation, *Kew: Central America. Cultural Products, 1856–1909*, f. 71.

131 B.R. Mitchell, *British Historical Statistics* (Cambridge, 1988), pp. 474–8.

132 The best accounts of the transfer of rubber are W. Dean, *Brazil and the Struggle for Rubber: A Study in Environmental History* (Cambridge, 1987), pp. 7–36 and A. Coates, *The Commerce in Rubber: The First 250 Years* (Singapore, 1987); see also *Life and Letters of Sir J. D. Hooker, II*, p. 5–7; C. Markham, 'The Cultivation of Caoutchouc-Yielding Trees in British India', *Journal of the Royal Society of Arts*, 1876, *24*: 475–81.

133 Hecht, Levi, & Kahn to J.R. Jackson, 27 February 1893, *K.B.*, 1893: 159.

134 *Kew: Malaya. Rubber, 1852–1908*; H. Ridley, *The Story of the Rubber Industry* (London, 1912).

135 'The Agricultural Resources of Zanzibar', *K.B.*, 87–92; *Kew: British East Africa. Rubber, 1874–1906*; C. Eliot, 'The Progress and Problems of the East African Protectorate', *Journal of the Royal Colonial Institute*, 1905, *37*.

136 *CBW*, p. 76; *Kew: Gold Coast. India Rubber, 1882–1906*; 'West African Rubber', *K.B.*, 1889: 63–6; A. Maloney, *Sketch of the Forestry of West Africa, with Particular Reference to its Principal Commercial Products* (London, 1887).

137 See E.´im Thurn correspondence in *Kew: Central America and British Guiana Letters, 1865–1900*.

138 Thiselton-Dyer to Mallet (India Office), 20 July 1883, *Kew: Dutch East Indies: Cultural Products, 1870–1906*, f. 26.

139 'Kapok and its Uses', *U.S. Consular Reports*, August 1904.

140 *British North Borneo Herald*, 1 August 1896.

141 See T.J. Baron, 'Science and the Nineteenth Century Ceylon Coffee Planters', *J.I.C.H.*, 1987, *16*: 5–21.

142 'Report ... 1877', pp. 37–8 and 'Report ... 1878', *Kew:* [Kewensia] *Royal Gardens Kew. Reports & Documents, 1784–1884*, pp. 48–9.

143 *Kew: Brazil, Cultural Products etc., 1852–1908*, f. 309.

144 *Fiji Times*, 12 October 1889 and the *Louisiana Planter and Sugar Manufacturer*, 20 February 1892.

145 *Ceylon Observer*, 17 June 1898; see also 24 November 1881 for the suggestion the tea and cinchona funguses were introduced with Australian eucalyptus trees.

146 *Ceylon Observer*, 23 March 1879.

147 *Ceylon Observer*, 26 May and 10 July 1879.

148 *Ceylon Observer*, 29 August and 10 September 1879.

149 Thiselton-Dyer to Under-Secretary of State for India, 20 November 1900, *Kew: India. United Provinces, 1839–1928*, f. 67.

150 'Report of the Council for 1888', p. 2, *Kew: Royal Niger Company, 1858–91*, f. 113.

151 Thistelton-Dyer, 28 July 1890, *Kew: Zanzibar, Cultural Products etc., 1868–1918*, f. 10

152 Sir Harry Johnson to the Earl of Kimberley, 13 October 1894, *Kew: Nyasaland. Botanic Station, etc., 1878–1905*, f. 47.

153 R.W. Beachey, *The British West Indies Sugar Industry in the Late 19th Century* (Oxford, 1957), p. 58.

154 B. Albert and A. Graves, eds., *Crisis and Change in the International Sugar Economy, 1860–1914* (Edinburgh, 1984), p. 1.

155 See 'Memorandum on the Negotiations with the United States on Behalf of the British West Indies', 6 January 1885, P.R.O.: C.O. 884/4.

156 C. Waterman (Board of Trade) to Thiselton-Dyer, 1 June 1886, *Kew: Dutch East Indies: Cultural Products, 1870–1906*, f. 17.

157 W. Robinson to Thiselton-Dyer, 28 October 1883 and 22 January 1884, *Kew: Barbados Agriculture. Agricultural Products, 1884–1905* and *Kew: Barbados. Sugar Cane Experiments, 1883–1900*.

158 Thiselton-Dyer to Wingfield, 19 November 1883, *Kew: ibid.*

159 *Ibid.*, and Derby to Governors of Barbados, Leeward Islands, Bahamas, and British Honduras, 14 February 1885, *K.B.*, 1887: 2–3.

160 Robinson to Secretary of State for the Colonies, 12 November 1885, P.R.O.: C.O. 318/83/216; on the anti-federal attitudes of the Barbadian plantocracy see B.

Hamilton, *Barbados and the Confederation Question* (London, 1956).
161 *K. B.*, 1887.
162 *Lagos Times*, 14 February 1883.
163 Maloney to Thiselton-Dyer, 29 November 1883, *Kew: Lagos Botanical Station, 1883–90*, f. 4.
164 Thiselton-Dyer to R. H. Meade, 18 March 1884, *ibid.*, f. 10.
165 Thiselton-Dyer to Morris, 26 December 1885, P.R.O.: C.O. 318/318.
166 For the history of this discovery see R.H. Drayton, 'Sugar Cane Breeding in Barbados: Knowledge and Power in a Colonial Context', BA thesis, Harvard University, 1986. Significantly the discovery was made simultaneously and independently at a 'New Botanical' experiment station in Java; see P.J.S. Cramer, 'Sugar Cane Breeding in Java', *Economic Botany*, 1953, *27*: 143.
167 Discussion of Harrison and Bovell's discovery took place at the Linnean Society and the Royal Society while an article presented the matter in *Nature*; see *Nature*, 1890, *41*: 478 and *42*: 258–9.
168 See *Nature*, 1890, *42*: 91.
169 *Report of the West India Royal Commission*, p. 29.
170 *K.B.*, 1888: 149.
171 *Ibid.*: 153.
172 *CBW*, p. 75.
173 Thiselton-Dyer to Meade, 2 February 1882, Thiselton-Dyer to Meade (Colonial Office), 2 February 1882, *Kew: Ceylon Botanic Gardens, 1847–1900*, f. 434.
174 Thiselton-Dyer to A. Godley (India Office), 29 October 1888, *Kew: Calcutta Botanic Garden, 1830–1928*, f. 216r.
175 *K.B.*, 1889: 259–62.
176 See *K.B.*, 1891: 10–24.
177 L. Gentil, 'Les Jardins Botaniques d'Aburi', *Bulletin de la Société d'Études Coloniales*, 1901; *Kew: Gold Coast, 1861–1905*, f. 66.
178 A. Engler, 'Die botanische Zentralstelle für die deutschen Kolonien an königlische botanische Garten der Universität Berlin und die Entwicklung botanischer Versuchstation in den Kolonien', *Botanische Jahrbücher*, 1893, *15*.
179 Quoted in Cittadino, *Nature as the Laboratory*, p. 137; E. Strasburger, 'The Development of Botany in Germany in the Nineteenth Century', *Botanical Gazette*, 1895, *20*: 257.
180 *Kew: German East Africa Miscellaneous, 1896–1928*, f. 28.
181 For a magisterial examination of the place of botany in the imperialism of the Third Republic, please see C. Bonneuil, 'Mettre en Ordre et Discipliner Les Tropiques: Les Sciences du Végétal dans l'Empire Français, 1870–1940', Thesis, University of Paris VII, 1997, 2 vols. See also J. Dybowski, *Jardins d'Essai Coloniaux* (Paris, 1897); Thiselton-Dyer, 'Memorandum', *Kew: Kew Gardens and the Natural History Museum Departmental Committee, 1901*, f. 67.
182 M. A. Milhe-Poutingon, *Jardin Botanique et Jardins d'Essai: La Manoeuvre Africaine* (Paris, 1898), p. 6.
183 Thiselton-Dyer maintained an active correspondence with scientists and ministerial functionaries in Paris, see *Kew: French Letters, 1865–1900, A–K*, 346ff, and *L–W*, ff. 819ff.
184 *CBW*, p. 17; A. Milhe-Poutingon, 'Rapport Présenté au Ministre des Colonies sur une Mission aux Jardins Royaux de Kew', *Revue des Cultures Coloniales*, 1898, *3* (18).
185 A. Isaac (President of the Chamber of Commerce of Lyon) to Thiselton-Dyer, 24 July 1900, *CBW*, p. 74; see also J. Laffey, 'The Roots of French Imperialism: The Case of Lyon', *French Historical Studies*, 1969, *6*: 78–92.
186 *The British North Borneo Herald*, 1 May 1889.
187 'Anglo-French Deal, 1895', especially R. H. Meade to Chamberlain, 13 December 1895, *Chamberlain Papers*: 9/6/3C/1.
188 F. Fischer, *Germany's Aims in the First World War* (London, 1967); E.R. May, *Imperial Democracy: The Emergence of America as a Great Power* (New York, 1961).
189 W.L. Langer, *The Diplomacy of Imperialism, 1890–1902* (New York, 1950), 2 vols., p. 78.
190 *The Times*, 1 April 1895.
191 4 *Parl. Deb. 36*: 642.
192 S.B. Saul, 'The Economic Significance of "Constructive Imperialism"', *Journal of Economic History*, 1957, *17: 173–92*; R.V. Kubicek, *The Administration of Imperialism: Joseph Chamberlain at the Colonial Office* (Durham, NC, 1969).
193 *Kew: English Letters, Cha–Con, 1866–1900*, ff. 8–52; *Chamberlain Papers*: 4/12.
194 G.G. Stokes to J. Chamberlain, 18 December 1882, and Chamberlain to Stokes, 22 December 1882, *Royal Society*: MC 12/291.
195 J. Chamberlain to Thiselton-Dyer, 20 July 1892 and 24 November 1893, *Kew: English Letters, Cha–Con, 1866–1900*, ff. 14 and 19; and 16 June 1904, *Kew: English Letters, A–C, 1901–5*, f. 272.
196 Bruce, *The Broad Stone of Empire, I*, p. 174.
197 *Rapport sur une Mission aux Jardins Royaux de Kew* (Paris, 1898), p. 14.

198 Gentil, 'Les Jardins Botaniques', 66; F.M. Hodgson to Under-Secretary of State for the Colonies, 23 October 1894, *Kew: Gold Coast: Botanical Station, 1862–1905*: f. 9.
199 'Annual Report ... 1904', *ibid.*, ff. 135–6.
200 R. Antrobus (Colonial Office) to Thiselton-Dyer, 6 February 1899, *ibid.*, f. 277.
201 Thiselton-Dyer to R. Antrobus, 9 September 1902, *ibid.*, ff. 288–300.
202 Chamberlain had his own reasons to worry about that region's agriculture, since his sons at this time struggled with £50,000 of unprofitable investments in fibre production. See Dilks, *Neville Chamberlain*, chs, 3, 4, and 5.
203 Sir H. A. Blake to Lord Knutsford, 15 December 1890; Viscount Gormanston to Lord Knutsford, 14 January 1891; Sir W. Sendall to Lord Knutsford, 2 and 14 January 1891; P.R.O.: C.O. 884/4/68.
204 Sir W. F. Hayes-Smith to Lord Knutsford, 29 December 1890, P.R.O.: C.O. 884/4/68.
205 J. Seeley, *The Expansion of England* (London, [1884] 1902), p. 19.
206 Memorandum of the Colonial Defence Committee, 19 December 1896, from P.R.O.: CAB 11/11.
207 Bruce, *The Broad Stone of Empire, I*, p. 28.
208 'Charter of the West India Royal Commission', P.R.O.: C.O. 380/146.
209 Chamberlain to Thiselton-Dyer, 5 March 1896, *Kew: English Letters, Cha–Con, 1866–1900*, f. 33.
210 *Report of the West Indian Royal Commission*; *P.P.* 1910 *XI*, p. 49.
211 *Ibid.*, p. 34.
212 *Ibid.*, p. 98 and Appendix A.
213 4 *Parl. Deb.*, *54*: 1541.
214 4 *Parl. Deb. 63*: 878.
215 4 *Parl. Deb. 54*:1542.
216 4 *Parl. Deb. 63*:1563.
217 J.L. Garvin and J. Amery, *The Life of Joseph Chamberlain* (London, 1932–67), 6 vols., *III*, p. 243.
218 4 *Parl. Deb*, *63*: 882.
219 Bruce, *The Broad Stone of Empire II*, pp. 129–34; W.T. Thiselton-Dyer, 'What Science Has Done for the West Indies', *West Indian Bulletin*, 1911, *11*; D. Morris, 'The Imperial Department of Agriculture in the West Indies,' *United Empire*, 1911, *2*.
220 D. Morris, 'Address to 8th Agricultural Conference', P.R.O.: C.O. 318/318.
221 Morris to Secretary of State for the Colonies, 6 March 1908, *ibid.*
222 Initial sheets, *ibid.*
223 Thiselton-Dyer to Under-Secretary of State for India, 29 November 1900, *Kew: India. United Provinces, 1839–1928*, ff. 67–8.
224 C.E. Barnard to Thiselton-Dyer, 19 January 1901 and H. Walpole to Thiselton-Dyer, 2 June 1901, *ibid.*, ff. 71–91.
225 R.M. MacLeod, 'Scientific Advice for British India', *Modern Asian Studies*, 1975, *9*: 343–84.
226 *Summary of the Administration of Lord Curzon of Kedlestone in the Department of Agriculture and Revenue* (Simla, 1905).
227 Quoted in MacLeod, 'Scientific Advice', 355; Curzon to Grey, 2 April 1903, IOL: *Mss. Eur.* F111/232; *Nature*, 1903, *67*: 568–9.
228 Thiselton-Dyer to Morris, 16 January 1911, P.R.O.: C.O. 318/325.
229 R. Olby, 'Social Imperialism and State Support for Agricultural Research in Edwardian Britain', *Annals of Science*, 1991, *48*: 509–26; E.J. Russell, *A History of Agricultural Science in Britain, 1629–1954* (London, 1966), p. 268.
230 Bruce, *The Broad Stone of Empire*, II, p. 170.
231 Thiselton-Dyer to Foster, 29 October 1899, *Royal Society*: MC 17/287.
232 A.C. True and D.J. Crosby, *Agricultural Experiment Stations in Foreign Countries* (Washington, 1904); L. Busch and C. Sachs, 'The Agricultural Sciences and the Modern World System', in L. Busch, ed., *Science and Agricultural Development* (Totowa, NJ, 1981), pp. 131–56.
233 Bruce, *The Broad Stone of Empire, II*, p. 116.
234 Thiselton-Dyer to Chamberlain, 28 May 1898, P.R.O.: C.O. 318/293.
235 Goldie to Thiselton-Dyer, 22 March 1890, *Kew: Royal Niger Company*, f. 32.
236 See *Pall Mall Gazette*, 20 April 1896.
237 Thiselton-Dyer to Goldie, 16 June 1890, *Kew: Royal Niger Company*, ff. 34–6.
238 Goldie to Thiselton-Dyer, 25 June 1890, *ibid.*, f. 40.
239 Thistleton-Dyer to Goldie, 25 June 1890 (cited above), f. 41.
240 *K.B.*, 1892: 82–6.
241 See *inter alia* J. Aitchison, 'The Botany of the Afghan Delimitation Commission', *Transactions of the Linnean Society*, 1888, 2nd series, *3*: 1–139; G.F. Scott Elliot, 'The Botanical Results of the Sierra Leone Boundary Commission', *Journal of the Linnean Society*, 1894, *30*: 64–100; 'Botany of the Ashanti Expedition,' *K.B.*, 1898: 75–82.
242 J.D. Hooker, *Flora of British India* (1872–97), 7 vols.; J. Baker, *Flora of*

Mauritius and the Seychelles (London, 1877); see 'Botanical Survey of the Empire', *K. B.*, 1905: 1–44.

243 T.V. Lister to Thiselton-Dyer, 21 March 1891, *Kew: C.F.*, f. 168.

244 See 'Diagnoses Africanae', *K.B.*, 1894: 17–18.

245 H.W. Primrose to Secretary of the Treasury Board, 12 May 1891, and Thiselton-Dyer to R.L. Antrobus (Colonial Office), 26 November 1900, *Kew: C.F.*, ff. 170–2.

246 Thiselton-Dyer to First Secretary of Works, 7 January 1899, *Kew: Kew Gardens and the Natural History Museum Departmental Committee, 1901*, f. 1r.

247 *Index Kewensis plantarum phanerogamarum . . . sumptibus beati C.R. Darwin, ductu et consilio J.D. Hooker, confecit B.D. Jackson* (Oxford, 1893–5), 2 vols.

248 P.F. Stevens, 'George Bentham and the Kew Rule', in D.L. Hawksworth, ed., *Improving the Stability of Names: Needs and Options* (Königstein, 1991), pp. 157–68 (I am indebted to Dr. Stevens for an offprint of this article).

249 W. T. Stearn, *The Natural History Museum at South Kensington* (London, 1981), p. 299.

250 For this view see Bower, *Sixty Years*, p. 20.

251 Bower, *Sixty Years*, p. 35.

252 See F.O. Bower, 'A Century of Botany, 1835–1935', *Nature*, 1935, *136*: 938–41, 976–8; and 'Appointment to a "Crown" Chair of Botany: Glasgow 1885', *The Linnaean*, 1985, *1*(6): 19–26.

253 *K.B.*, 1929: 67–8; W. Gardiner, *The Foundation and Re-Establishment of the Cambridge Botanical Museum* (Cambridge, 1904).

254 Thiselton-Dyer to Secretary of the Board of Woods and Forests, 25 January 1886, *Kew: Supply, Exchange, of Trees, Plants etc. by Kew Gardens.*

255 'Memorandum', f. 3.

256 *K. B.*, 1928: 70 and 1914: 298 and 393.

257 Thiselton-Dyer to H.W. Primrose, 25 April 1889, *Kew: Supply, Exchange, of Trees, Plants etc. by Kew Gardens.*

258 Thiselton-Dyer to H.W. Primrose, 23 and 25 June 1892, *Kew: Royal Carriages Passing Through Kew Gardens Contrary to Rules. Subordination of Director to the First Commissioner of Works Regarding Rules.*

259 Thiselton-Dyer to Primrose, 23 June 1892, *ibid.*

260 These included the plants of the Niger expedition collected by Barter and Mann, plants of East Africa collected by Livingstone, Kirk, and Meller, and those taken on Schomburgk's survey of the Gulf of Carpenteria. See J. Winter Jones to Lords Commissioners of the Admiralty, 4 July 1874, *Kew: R.B.G. Kew and the British Museum. Correspondence, 1858–1901*, ff. 80–1. For the British Museum perspective on this see Stearn, *The Natural History Museum*, pp. 294–301.

261 Thiselton-Dyer to Mallet (India Office), 22 January 1880, *Kew: Afghanistan, Botanical Exploration, 1879–88*, ff. 11–12

262 Thiselton-Dyer to Carruthers, 17 October 1890, *Kew: R.B.G. Kew and the British Museum. Correspondence, 1858–1901*, f. 242.

263 Thiselton-Dyer to Secretary of the Treasury, 4 December 1893, in *Kew: J.Britten's Attack in Journal of Botany on the Staff of Kew, Journal of Botany*, 1893, *31*: 352; D. J. Mabberley, *Jupiter Botanicus: Robert Brown and the British Museum* (London, 1985), p. 386.

264 *Kew: Kew Gardens and the Natural History Museum Departmental Committee, 1901*, ff. 25–30.

265 *Report to the Lords Commissioners of H.M. Treasury of a Departmental Committee on Botanical Work and Collections at the British Museum and Kew* (London, 1901), p. 16; see also *The Scotsman*, 15 November 1901.

266 T.H. Elliott to The Secretary of the Treasury, 10 April 1902, *Kew: Transfer from Office of Works to Board of Agriculture –1903*, ff. 4–7.

267 Thiselton-Dyer minute to Secretary of the Board of Works, 1 May 1802; C.P. Lucas (Colonial Office) to Thiselton-Dyer, 6 June 1902; *Kew: Transfer from Office of Works to Board of Agriculture–1903*, ff. 11 and 15.

268 *The Scotsman*, 15 July 1901.

269 See W. Bateson, 'Toast to the Board of Agriculture, Horticulture and Fisheries', *Report on the Third International Conference on Genetics* (London, 1907), pp. 75–7; *Committee on Agricultural Seed. Cmd. 489 and 493* (London, 1901).

270 A. Chamberlain (Treasury Board) to Secretary of the Board of Agriculture, 25 July 1902, *Kew: Transfer from Office of Works to Board of Agriculture–1903*, f. 17.

271 Thiselton-Dyer to the Secretary of the Board of Agriculture, December 1905, *K. B.*, 1928: 74.

272 Stevens, 'The Kew Rule', 165.

273 M. Warboys, 'The Imperial Institute, the State and the Development of the Natural Resources of the Colonial Empire, 1887–1923', in J.M. MacKenzie, ed., *Imperialism and the Natural World* (Manchester, 1990), pp. 164–86; Warboys, 'Science and British Colonial imperialism',

chs. 2 and 4; W.E. Dunstan, 'Some Imperial Aspects of Applied Chemistry', *Bulletin of the Imperial Institute*, 1906, *4*: 310–19.

274 Lugard, *The Dual Mandate in British Tropical Africa*, p. 188; the Board of Trade by 1918 maintained its own Commercial Intelligence Branch.

275 This great age of imperial science is still to find its historian, but see C.W. Forman, 'Science for Empire', PhD dissertation, University of Wisconsin, 1941.

Epilogue

1 *The Spectator*, no. 69, 19 May 1711.

2 Quoted in Ronald Hyam, *Britain's Imperial Century, 1815–1914: A Study in Empire and Expansion* (London, 1976), p. 87.

3 V.H. Heywood, 'Botanic Gardens and the Conservation of Plant Resources', *Impact of Science on Society*, 1990, *40*: 121.

4 S. Weil, *The Need for Roots: Prelude to a Declaration of Duties Towards Mankind*, A.F. Wills, trans., (London, 1987), p. 14.

Index